LOUISE NICHOLSON'S
INDIA COMPANION

Fully revised and expanded edition of
Louise Nicholson's *India in Luxury*
with a new section on Pakistan

D0294010

Louise Nicholson's INDIA COMPANION

Fully updated and expanded edition of
Louise Nicholson's INDIA IN LUXURY

With a new section on Pakistan

VERMILION

LONDON

For my parents

The author would particularly like to thank Cox & Kings Travel Ltd
for their assistance in preparing this book.

First published in Great Britain in 1991 by Century
Random Century Group Ltd
This edition published in 1993 by Vermilion, an imprint of Ebury Press
Random House, 20 Vauxhall Bridge Road,
London SW1V 2SA

Random House Australia (Pty) Ltd
20 Alfred Street, Milsons Point, Sydney, New South Wales 2061, Australia

Random House New Zealand Ltd
18 Poland Road, Glenfield, Auckland 10, New Zealand

Random House South Africa (Pty) Limited
PO Box 337, Bergvlei 2012, South Africa

British Library Cataloguing in Publication Data

Nicholson, Louise
Louise Nicholson's India
I. Title
915.4

ISBN 0–09–178315–1

Original maps by John Grimwade,
revisions by Leslie Robinson
Dynasty chart by Louise Nicholson
Line illustrations on pp 24–25 by Mohan Lal Soni

Cover: contemporary ikat silk sari
woven in Andhra Pradesh, courtesty the author
Filmset in Palatino by SX Composing Ltd, Rayleigh, Essex
Printed and bound in Great Britain by
Mackays of Chatham PLC, Chatham, Kent

Papers used by Ebury Press are natural, recyclable products made from
wood grown in sustainable forests. In addition the paper in this book is
acid free and recycled.

About the author

After studying History of Art at Edinburgh University, Louise Nicholson began her career campaigning for the conservation of buildings with the Victorian Society. She then crossed the floor into the commercial art world to work in the department of Islamic and Indian manuscripts at Christie's, the auctioneers. Since 1981 she has been a freelance journalist, researcher, writer and lecturer, covering all aspects of India which she frequently visits. She wrote a weekly column for *The Times* throughout the Festival of India in Britain 1982, and more recently was Assistant Producer for the six-part television documentary *The Great Moghuls* screened in 1990. As well as devising and accompanying tours of Moghul India, she is a founder member of The Indian Art Circle and is the UK co-ordinator of a children's charity in Calcutta.

Louise Nicholson's other books include *Delhi, Agra and Jaipur* (1989, revised 1991), *The Red Fort* (1989) and *London: Louise Nicholson's Definitive Guide* (1988, revised 1990), which won the London Tourist Board's award for Commended Guide Book of the Decade. Louise Nicholson, her husband and their two sons live in London.

Also available from Random Century
Princess: The Autobiography of the Dowager Maharani of Gwalior *Vijayaraje Scindia*
A Princess Remembers: The Memoirs of the Maharani of Jaipur *Gayatri Devi and Santha Rama Rau*
Letters from India *Lady Wilson*
The Memsahibs *Pat Barr*
On a Shoestring to Coorg *Dervla Murphy*
The Waiting Land *Dervla Murphy*

Contents

Acknowledgements

I am abashed by the enthusiasm and generosity with which friends in Britain and India have greeted the idea of this book. Their contribution to the following chapters has been invaluable and I am deeply grateful.

In Britain, I would like to thank especially the staff of the Government of India Tourist Office and the High Commission for India for their constant support. British Airways regularly carry home all my extra luggage. I am indebted to many individuals including Robert Alderman, Sarah Anderson, John Bethell, Anthony Blond, Paddy Bowring, Idrone and Roger Brittain, Andrew Brock, Tina Brown, Sandeep Chatterjee, Julia Clarke, Bruce Cleghorn, Shona Crawford Poole, Mitch Crites, Teresa de Chair, Niranjan Desai, Simon Digby, Josceline Dimbleby, Margaret Erskine, Harry Evans, Lillian Fonseca, Jack Franses, Sarah Giles, Christoph Goodhart, Nicholas Grace, Joss Graham, Germaine Greer, Sarah Gristwood, Kenneth Griffiths, Michael and Claire Hamlyn, Derek Healey, Laura and Sarah Hesketh, Niall Hobhouse, Yasmin and Shahid Hosain, Anthony Hutt, Gour Kanjilal, Shashi Kapoor, Peter Kaufeler, M. M. Kaye, Philip Knightley, Bernard Levin, Andrew Logan, Joanna Lumley, Victoria Mather, Gita Mehta, Malcolm and Kitty Muggeridge, Dr and Mrs Seyid Mohammed, Veronica Murphy, Prince Ali Murza and Princess Ara Murshidabad, Christina Noble, Pepita Noble, Amy Osborne, Camellia Panjabi, Indar and Aruna Pasricha, Emma Playfair, Shubita Punja, Frances and Richard Rice, Carol Robertson, Jancis Robinson, Phillis Rogers, Lady Jane Sheldon, Kranti Singh, Robert Skelton, Gavin Stamp, Cob Stenham, Edwin Taylor, Andrew Topsfield, Dr Anthony Turner, Lucia van der Post, Nick van Gruisen, Jay Visva-Deva, John Warrington, Brian Witham, Carol Wood and Mark Zebrowski. My husband, Nick, and my brother-in-law, Tim, have been constant supports.

In India, my thanks go first to the Welcomgroup and the Taj group of hotels and to Cox & Kings Travel Ltd. Throughout India, staff of the Government of India Tourist Offices and state Tourist Offices have been generous with their time and knowledge.

However, it is immediate help from individuals that I would like to acknowledge most of all. I would particularly like to thank my driver Anand, Arun and Rupam Bahl, Baiji, Anil Bajaj, Anoop Banerjee, S. K. Beri, G. D. Brara, D. K. Burman, Sreelata Bhatia, Dr T. K. Biswas, D. S. Chauda, Veena Chawla, Malti Chopra, Sarla Chopra, Dr Das, Sudir and Meena Deshpande, Ravi Dubey, Allan Fernandes, Trevor and Penny Fishlock, Sanjay Ganguli, Feroz Gimi, Harish Gorsia, Mr and Mrs Guhan, B. S. Gupta, Kushru Irani, Jaya Jaitley, Guli and Vihar Juneja, S. K. Kandhari, Kunal Kapoor, Shanjay and Zareen Khan, Prem Kumar, V. Lakshminarayanan, Lakshmi Lal, Zelma Lazarus, Ena Malhotra, Nutan Malhotra, Gulam Mohamad Major, Mr Mangalick, K. M. Mathew, Mario Miranda, Naomi Meadows, S. K. Mukherjee, Umaima Mulla-Feroze, Shanka Sheela Nai, Aman Nath, Mrs Vibha Pandhi, Girish Patel, Naveen Patnaik, Primo Pereira, Dileep Rao, Ratna Sahai, Babla Senapati, Rabindra Seth, Arun Sharma, R. K. Sharma, Dr Maurice Shellim, K. G. Shenoy, Indu Shridhar, Toby Sinclair, Brijendra Singh, I. V. Singh, Malvika and Tajbir Singh, Moyna Singh, Partha Talukdar and Bob and Anne Wright.

* * * * *

Now, for this new and enlarged edition, I am again indebted to many of the above. To them I would like to add special thanks to Cox & Kings Travel Ltd, who hosted me for a final research trip and made available all their resources. K. K. Gurung gave his expertise to the wildlife sections, Yasmin and Shahid Hosain theirs to the Pakistan section. In addition, I thank particularly Arun Acharya, M. J. Akbar, Roy Alderson, Shekhar Bhatia, Dileep Bobb, Robert Borgerhoff Mulder, Caroline Cotton, Pat Cronshaw, Philip Davies, Srienaphie Ellepola, M. Everitt, Sue Garner, Geraldine Gartrell, Andrew Gilmour, Serge Guilbert, Satish Gujral, Salman Haider, Leslie Hunter, Brigid Keenan, Peter Kerker, Hugo Kimber, Dr Lea, Rosie Llewellyn-Jones, Brendon Lynch, Kuldip Nayar, Mani Maan, Philip Magor, Paul McManus, George Michell, Bruce Palling, Steven Pettitt, Rajesh Prasad, Lekha Podder, Gill Pyrah, Raghu Rai, Agha Gul Rez, Victoria Schofield, Diana Shirley, Glenvil Smith, Sybella Stanley and Paul Zisman, Michael Sugich, Christopher Tadgell, Peter Taylor, Jane Thomas, Giles Tillotson, Hashim Tyabji, Steve Webster, Sally Worsley, Zoe Yalland, Shafiq uz-Zaman.

Once again, Margaret Cornell tackled the now even greater challenges of editing, proofreading and indexing, while Leslie Robinson squeezed more information on to the maps.

Most importantly of all I thank you, the travellers, who write to me from all over the world with additions, tips and corrections on what I have included, what I should have included and, just occasionally, what I should omit. India is huge, complex and in places it is changing fast. Your opinions are invaluable. So please keep writing.

Introduction

My husband introduced me to India for our honeymoon a decade ago. He gave me a month in paradise. Our days were entirely free from the disasters faced by many first-time visitors to India. This was largely thanks to the generosity of our friends who know India well and gave us the benefit of their experiences. This book, originally the product of that and a few other visits to India, aimed to give everyone the opportunity to explore and enjoy all that India has to offer unhampered by practical problems.

The aim remains the same. But now, six years and twenty-five more trips to India later, this totally revised, enlarged and reorganised guide will, I hope, do its job better. India is moving fast, especially in its services to visitors. Equally, you the visitor are becoming more intrepid, and even on a short holiday want to experience not merely the wonder of the Taj Mahal but also the magic of quieter, more off-beat places. So, quite apart from the updating on existing material, there are almost 200 new places to seek out, all plotted on the revised maps. Some are for the temple or archaeological keen, others plunge into rural life, still others are journeys through breath-taking landscape. And the section on Pakistan, now an easy place to visit, enables travellers to complement a North India adventure with a few days spent seeing some of the glories of the sub-continent's early history as well as some stunning hill and mountain scenery.

To make sense of India's complex history, there is a new dynasties chart; and to help recognise some of India's distinctive birds and flowering trees, there are drawings of the most common species.

The most energetic and demanding person is rarely, if ever, bored in India. The whole land is ablaze with exotic traditions, crafts, peoples, food, wildlife, buildings and colours. It is a dynamic land, where old and new thrive side by side. It is a land to which the first-time visitor often believes he is going solely to see the great monuments of past empires but, once there, finds himself mesmerised by street life, by the daily political soap opera, by inventive local transport methods, by the thousand ways of cooking lentils, or simply by the giant billboards for adventure films. In India, just when one subject – perhaps Sultanate architecture, perhaps the complex marriage system, perhaps the art of tea cultivation – seems be within grasp of understanding, it becomes all too clear how much more there is to see and learn.

A first visit to India may well be a daring adventure in several ways. For one thing, India is a land where every detail of life is different, fascinating and stimulating, however familiar it might at first appear. For another, you, like so many before you, may get hooked. If you find yourself dreaming of your next visit to India on the plane home, then you, too, have been caught by this extraordinary, awe-inspiring, beautiful, outrageous and often witty land.

Transliteration note

As far as possible, the English transliteration of Indian words follows the common usage in India today. Thus, Pune rather than Poona, Varanasi rather than Banaras, Shimla rather than Simla and sati rather than suttee.

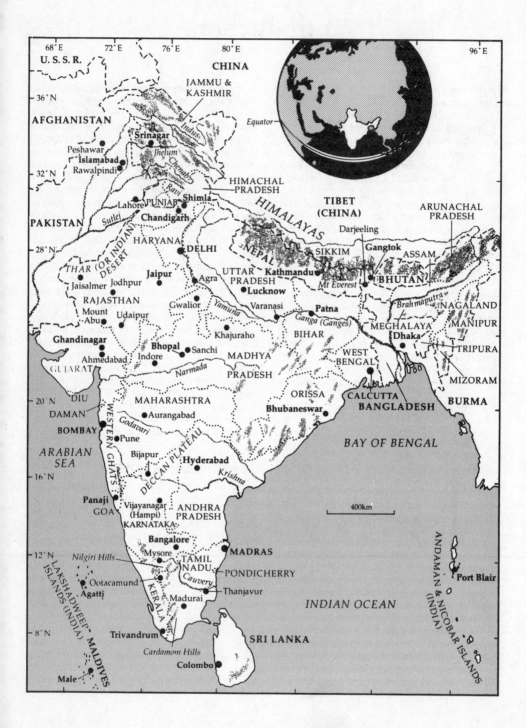

Dreams to departure:
Pre-India preparation

The map

The first step towards realising the dream of going to India is to buy Bartholomew's World Travel Map no. 15: Indian sub-continent, India, Pakistan, Bangladesh, Sri Lanka (see bookshop lists, p. 18). The vastness of India is quickly apparent. The browns and greens of deserts, mountains and fertile areas stretch from 8 to 37 degrees latitude and from 68 to 97 degrees longitude. The size is baffling. Indians living near the southern tip are as far away from their capital, Delhi, as Athens is from London. Hopping from Delhi to Bombay or Calcutta is much the same as going from London to Madrid or Rome.

Clearly, a visit to India must be selective – unless you have a few years on your hands to explore it all. But there really is little point in going to India for less than three weeks. Those who think that two weeks will be enough for the first visit do not understand the complications of travelling inside the country and the mental adjustment needed to make sense of it all. It takes at least three days to throw off jet lag and get used to the climate, pace and rhythms of India – the coda to this is that a well-organised and well-designed package tour removes so much of the worry and organisation that a fulfilling two-week tour is possible for the keen and energetic, but not for the faint-hearted. Conversely, it is unlikely that a first-time visitor will be able to concentrate and absorb the onslaught of visual and mental stimulations which the country provides for more than about four weeks, unless the pace can slow down considerably for a few days now and then.

From the second visit onwards, you will be able to judge how much of India you can take in at a time. Some people, equipped with their first experiences, will be able to tackle a long stay. Similarly, they will be able to go to selected parts of India for short, intensive spells.

After buying the map, the next step is to decide which parts of India to visit. This is the most crucial decision for a successful and happy trip, and depends upon numerous personal likes and dislikes and a few salient truths and tips.

When to go where

CLIMATE It is quite possible to go to India the year round, avoiding blistering heat and monsoons, provided you choose your area. While it is roasting in the South, it can be mild in Delhi and the Himalayan peaks will be covered in snow. Whatever climate suits you, it can be found somewhere in India throughout the year.

The plains of India are at their freshest and best during the winter. The optimum season to travel in northern India, to Rajasthan and around Delhi, is between September and March, although it can be quite chilly in December and January. To the east, the more extreme combination of heat, humidity and monsoon leaves only November to February fairly comfortable. Southern India is hot all the time but again best between November and February. Even then, some people will find the heat disagreeable. The green strip of Kerala down the Malabar Coast is more temperate, with a much gentler climate.

The scorching pre-monsoon heat, the monsoon deluge and the post-monsoon humidity strike almost everywhere some time between May and September. The stultifying pre-monsoon heat is to be avoided throughout India. But when the rains come, they have their own attraction, provided the humidity between showers is bearable. It is a repeated agony-ecstasy cycle: each storm is a crescendo of seering heat and humidity which breaks to give mental and physical relief and the most deliciously sweet and fresh air. Some cities, such as Varanasi in Uttar Pradesh, have gloriously thundering river torrents during monsoon, and an equally pleasant lack of tourists. Others, notably the normally dry Mandu in Central India, are particularly lush and beautiful during and immediately after the rains. Also worth remembering is that the more unfashionable a place is during monsoon, the more likely its hotels will offer a seasonal discount.

Monsoon is the traditional time to go up into the hills. In the lower Himalayas, the choice is wide, from Shimla right across to Darjeeling, even nipping out of India to Nepal, Pakistan or Bhutan. The weather intensifies as the slopes get higher and the air thinner, bringing winter snow, spring and summer blossoms under soft sunshine, and rich autumn colours. Here the rainy months are very localised and should be checked out carefully.

Other cool spots are mostly British-built retreats from boiling Madras and Bombay, such as Ootacamund and Kodaikanal in the Nilgiri and

1

Cardamom hills dividing Tamil Nadu and Kerala states, Mahabaleshwar and Pune in the Western Ghats of Maharashtra, and Mount Abu on the Rajasthan-Gujarat border.

See under When to Go and Hard Facts chapter headings for more guidelines. See also weather chart below.

Weather Chart

T = Temperature (°C)
R = Rainfall (mm.)

City			Jan	Feb	Mar	Apr	May	Jun	Jul	Aug	Sep	Oct	Nov	Dec
Ahmedabad	T	max.	29	31	36	40	41	38	33	32	33	36	33	30
		min.	12	15	19	23	26	27	26	25	24	21	16	13
	R	avg.	4	0	1	2	5	100	316	213	163	13	5	1
Aurangabad	T	max.	29	32	36	38	40	35	29	29	30	31	30	29
		min.	14	16	20	24	25	23	22	21	21	20	16	14
	R	avg.	3	3	4	7	17	141	189	146	179	62	32	9
Bangalore	T	max.	28	31	33	34	33	30	28	29	28	28	27	27
		min.	15	16	19	21	21	20	19	19	19	19	17	15
	R	avg.	4	14	6	37	119	65	93	95	129	195	46	16
Bhopal	T	max.	26	29	34	38	41	37	30	29	30	31	29	26
		min.	10	13	17	21	26	25	23	23	22	18	13	11
	R	avg.	17	5	10	3	11	137	429	308	232	37	15	7
Bombay	T	max.	31	32	33	33	33	32	30	29	30	32	33	32
		min.	16	17	20	24	26	26	25	24	24	23	20	18
	R	avg.	0	1	0	0	20	647	945	660	309	117	7	1
Calcutta	T	max.	26	29	34	36	36	34	32	32	32	31	29	27
		min.	12	15	20	24	26	26	26	26	26	24	18	13
	R	avg.	13	22	30	50	135	263	320	318	253	134	29	4
Cochin	T	max.	31	31	31	31	31	29	28	28	28	29	30	30
		min.	23	24	26	26	26	24	24	24	24	24	24	23
	R	avg.	9	34	50	139	364	756	572	386	235	333	184	37
Coimbatore	T	max.	30	33	35	35	34	31	30	31	32	31	29	29
		min.	19	19	21	23	23	22	22	22	22	22	21	19
	R	avg.	7	4	5	70	76	35	37	18	42	127	127	25
Darjeeling	T	max.	9	11	15	18	19	19	20	20	20	19	15	12
		min.	3	4	8	11	13	15	15	15	15	11	7	4
	R	avg.	22	27	52	109	187	522	713	573	419	116	14	5
Delhi	T	max.	21	24	30	36	41	40	35	34	34	35	29	23
		min.	7	10	15	21	27	29	27	26	25	19	12	8
	R	avg.	25	22	17	7	8	65	211	173	150	31	1	5
Hyderabad	T	max.	29	31	35	37	39	34	30	29	30	30	29	28
		min.	15	17	20	24	26	24	22	22	22	20	16	13
	R	avg.	2	11	13	24	30	107	165	147	163	71	25	5
Jaipur	T	max.	22	25	31	37	41	39	34	32	33	33	29	24
		min.	8	11	15	21	26	27	26	24	23	18	12	9
	R	avg.	14	8	9	4	10	54	193	239	90	19	3	4
Jammu	T	max.	18	21	26	33	39	40	35	33	33	31	26	21
		min.	8	11	15	21	26	28	26	25	24	19	13	9
	R	avg.	71	54	57	25	17	61	321	319	151	29	8	29
Jodhpur	T	max.	25	28	33	38	42	40	36	33	35	36	31	27
		min.	9	12	17	22	27	29	27	25	24	20	14	11
	R	avg.	7	5	2	2	6	31	122	145	47	7	3	1
Lucknow	T	max.	23	26	33	38	41	39	34	33	33	33	29	25
		min.	9	11	16	22	27	28	27	26	25	20	13	9
	R	avg.	24	17	9	6	12	94	299	302	182	40	1	6
Madras	T	max.	29	31	33	35	38	37	35	35	34	32	29	28
		min.	20	21	23	26	28	28	26	26	25	24	23	21
	R	avg.	24	7	15	25	52	53	83	124	118	267	309	139
Madurai	T	max.	30	32	35	36	37	37	36	35	35	33	31	30
		min.	21	22	23	25	26	26	26	25	25	24	23	22
	R	avg.	26	16	21	81	59	31	48	117	123	179	161	43

Weather Chart

T = Temperature (°C)
R = Rainfall (mm.)

City			Jan	Feb	Mar	Apr	May	Jun	Jul	Aug	Sep	Oct	Nov	Dec
Panaji	T	max.	31	32	32	33	33	31	29	29	29	31	33	33
(Goa)		min.	19	20	23	25	27	25	24	24	24	23	22	21
	R	avg.	2	0	4	17	18	580	892	341	277	122	20	37
Port Blair	T	max.	29	30	31	32	31	29	29	29	29	29	29	29
		min.	23	22	23	26	24	24	24	24	24	24	24	23
	R	avg.	29	26	23	71	363	589	435	436	516	329	205	157
Pune	T	max.	31	33	36	38	37	32	28	28	29	32	31	30
		min.	12	13	17	21	23	23	22	21	21	19	15	12
	R	avg.	2	0	3	18	35	103	187	106	127	92	37	5
Puri	T	max.	27	28	30	31	32	31	31	31	31	31	29	27
		min.	18	21	25	27	27	27	27	27	27	25	21	18
	R	avg.	9	20	14	12	63	187	296	256	258	242	75	8
Shimla	T	max.	9	10	14	19	23	24	21	20	20	18	15	11
		min.	2	3	7	11	15	16	16	15	14	10	7	4
	R	avg.	65	48	58	38	54	147	415	385	195	45	7	24
Srinagar	T	max.	4	8	13	19	25	29	31	30	28	23	15	9
		min.	−2	−1	3	7	11	14	18	18	13	6	0	−2
	R	avg.	73	72	104	78	63	36	61	63	32	29	17	36
Trivandrum	T	max.	31	32	33	32	31	29	29	29	30	30	30	31
		min.	22	23	24	25	25	24	23	23	23	23	23	23
	R	avg.	20	20	43	122	249	331	215	164	123	271	207	73
Varanasi	T	max.	23	27	33	39	41	39	33	32	32	32	29	25
		min.	9	11	17	22	27	28	26	26	25	21	13	9
	R	avg.	23	8	14	1	8	102	346	240	261	38	15	2

INDIAN FESTIVALS Bursts of colour, song, drums, trumpets, dance, elephants in fancy dress, banners, fireworks, processions and ecstatic enjoyment punctuate the Indian calendar. Indians are quite blasé about their constant stream of glorious festivals, so much so that one Calcuttan even suggested that tourists might wish to avoid Durga Puja, Calcutta's most spectacular major festival. But, for Westerners, the Indian art of celebration outshines any Easter Parade, Christmas, Bastille Day or Thanksgiving.

There is a festival for everything, from weddings and elections to the all-important harvest and the arrival of the rains – even festivals to honour bullocks and snakes. There are Muslim, Christian, Sikh, Buddhist and Jain festivals. But the vast plethora of Hindu gods and goddesses have the most. Every temple deity has its own special festival, as well as various extras. A deity may visit a fellow deity in another temple, take a bath, change her clothes or collect his wife. It may be the god's wedding anniversary or annual holiday. Or a festival may celebrate the past triumphs of a hero god, as recounted in the great Indian epics. Hindu gods have very worldly emotions and life-styles and are an integral part of Hindu life. Hindu and Muslim festivals, as well as the big markets and fairs, attract the quality performers of classical and folk dance, music and singing. And some festivals attract pilgrims, itinerant entertainers and visitors from all over India, and last for up to ten days.

Although you are bound to bump into small festivals, to coincide with one of the major festivals is a memorable experience. However, it is not very straightforward to find one. Only four festivals have absolute fixed dates, and they are not the best. They are Republic Day (January 26), Independence Day (August 15), Mahatma Gandhi's Birthday (October 2) and Christmas Day (December 25). Hindu religious festivals are calculated according to the lunar calendar, roughly keeping within a four-week span. The final decisions are made annually by the pundits for the following year. Muslim festivals move right around the year. By November, the worldwide Indian tourist offices can supply a list of the following year's major festival dates.

The next trick is to be in the right place for the right festival. For instance, the September-October festival of Dussehra is best seen at Varanasi (Banaras) and Delhi, where it is called Ram Lila; at Calcutta, where it is called Durga Puja; and at Mysore, where it is Dassehra. Holi is best in Rajasthan, Pongal in Tamil Nadu and Muharram at Lucknow. See pp. 283-5, for a list of the bigger festivals and see under When to Go and Hard Facts chapter headings for details about them. One or two travel agents organise package tours specifically to coincide with big

3

festivals and fairs.

Where to go

THE SELECTION PROCESS India has everything. Only you can decide what you want to see and how you want to see it. Your idea of a dream holiday in India may be rushing up mountains, palace-hopping in Rajasthan, drooling over Dravidian temple architecture, making long train journeys, watching the local craftsmen or spotting wildlife from an elephant's back.

The following chapters try to give an idea of the range on offer. But one man's fascination is another's absolute boredom. Recently, one Indophile recommended Bijapur, one of his favourite cities, to a friend. His friend drove through the night from Bombay and arrived to find an unsympathetic atmosphere, no accommodation and buildings not to his taste at all.

There is far more to India than the golden triangle of Delhi, Agra and Jaipur and, although the Taj and Fatehpur Sikri are magical, there is no compulsion to visit them first. They will still be there next time. Many people see the Côte d'Azur before Paris, Tuscan villages before Rome and Disney World before New York or Washington. In addition, the Indian golden triangle is much more enjoyable outside the tourist rush of September-March. There is so much else to see and do that it seems a shame to follow the Western throng.

It is best to select one or two areas of the country and combine visits to monuments with wanders in town bazaars and outings to nearby villages by car and train. This way, you can see how people live, work and celebrate their festivals. This is far more rewarding than taking a plane every other day to a new set of isolated monuments. And a few days in a game park, walking the hills or soaking in the sun always happily tag on to the front or back of two or three weeks of sightseeing and travelling – they even make a good half-way break.

ARCHITECTURE India is full of sublime buildings, despite the ravages of countless marauders. There are Buddhist, Hindu, Muslim, Jain and colonial monuments of the highest quality throughout the country. But some are much easier to get to and better equipped for tourists than others. The more isolated sites suggested in this book will, I hope, repay the longish journeys to get to them and the more modest accommodation.

Old Delhi and Agra – with the nearby palace-city of Fatehpur Sikri – boast the greatest Mughal monuments, and a trip to Lahore completes the triad of great Mughal capitals. Rajasthan is covered in hilltop forts and sumptuous,

wedding-cake palaces, many of which are now converted into hotels. All these are very easy to visit. So are the rock temples of Ajanta and Ellora, outside Aurangabad; the Jain temples outside Udaipur; the eastern Hindu temples of Orissa and Khajuraho; the sacred Hindu city of Varanasi, and the Buddhist structures of Sanchi, near Bhopal. All of these are served with airports and comfortable hotels.

The rewards of the more hardy and intrepid traveller are sensational. In Karnataka, the magnificent ruined city of Hampi and the Hoysala temples are a bit of an effort to reach, as are some of the temple cities of Tamil Nadu such as Chidambaram, Srimushnam and the tongue-twister Gangakondacholapuram. Karnataka's other treasures are beginning to be visited – Bidar, Bijapur and the early Hindu temples in and around Badami – but few make detours to Kakkundi, Ittagi, and Kukkunur. Relatively few reach the central Indian monuments at Mandu, either just two hours' drive from Indore. And fewer still think of connecting a visit to the magnificent Gwalior Fort with Sanchi's splendours via the ruined palace forts of Datia and Orchha, and then the monuments of Chanderi, Udayapur and Udayagiri. Accommodation may not be luxurious in these places – even downright basic – but the quality of the buildings most certainly is.

RELIGIONS India has no state religion. Its 850 million people belong to almost every sect of the world's various religions. And it was in India that two of the world's great religions were born, Hinduism and Buddhism. From these were born Sikhism and Jainism. However, it is Hinduism which dominates and whose daily practice is easy and fascinating, if extremely complex, for the visitor to observe. In essence the principal religions and their breakdown are as follows. The places in brackets refer to fuller explanations in the text.

Hindus 83%, worship in a temple, religious texts the Vedas, Bhagwat Gita, Mahabharata and Ramayana (see Varanasi, Khajuraho, Kanchipuram and Thajevur)

Muslims 11%, worship in a mosque, religious text the Qu'ran (see Delhi)

Christians 2.5%, worship in a church, religious text the Bible (see Cochin)

Sikhs 2%, worship in a gurdwara, religious text the Guru Granth Sahib (see Pakistan)

Buddhists 0.7%, worship in a temple, various scriptures (see Sarnath)

Jains 0.5%, worship in a temple, various scriptures (see Palitana)

Zoroastrians 0.01%, worship in a fire temple, religious text the Zend Avesta (see Bombay)

Jews number just 5,600, their best preserved synagogue at Cochin

WILDLIFE SANCTUARIES The parks of India, Nepal and Pakistan cover thousands of square kilometres and give sanctuary to a wide range of threatened species of mammal, reptile and bird, as well as flowers and trees. India is an important area for animal conservation work (see p. 131 on Project Tiger). Visitors explore the parks by jeep and on elephant. However, few are yet as well run as the African parks and accommodation may be quite simple. Exceptions include Ranthambhore in Rajasthan, whose popularity is such that visitors are now controlled; the three adjoining parks of Nagarhole, Mudumalai and Bandipur south of Mysore; Bandhavgar in Madhya Pradesh and Corbett north-east of Delhi. Up in Nepal, the Royal Chitwan National Park is the nearest thing to Kenya in comfort and style. See Wildlife Sanctuaries section at the end of each chapter.

BEACHES Considering the length and beauty of its coastline, India has few good beach resorts. Goa is best, a world class resort with hotel and beach choice, good facilities and good food. The upmarket choice then extends to Covelong, south of Madras, the escapist islands of the Maldives and, politics permitting, to the smart beaches of Sri Lanka. Off-beat beaches include those in Kerala, south Gujarat, on the Orissa and Andhra Pradesh coast, and on the remote Andaman and Nicobar Islands, although the lack of fellow Westerners may mean that locals do not welcome too much flesh being exposed. All these areas are very beautiful and perfect places for switching off (see Chapter 9).

CLUBS AND SPORTS The network of thriving social clubs with good sports facilities is a legacy of the Raj days, when they were developed to their height. India is sports-crazy. Cricket is not only played on every available patch of green (or brown), but on a bigger pitch several games can be played simultaneously. Some fielders take part in two matches at once. Apparently there is never an accident. Golf and tennis are just as popular.

The clubs are often in the city centre. The better ones have excellent facilities (golf, tennis, swimming, indoor games, libraries, etc.) and charming buildings set in acres of immaculate gardens and lawns. Some are more exclusive than others. Temporary membership is usually granted to foreigners. A few have reciprocal arrangements with Western clubs. A few have rooms to stay in. The relevant Secretary is the person to approach for details. Useful clubs are listed in the chapters below.

BIG CITIES India's big cities are much more difficult to visit than their equivalents in Europe and America. They are huge, sprawling and over-populated. International flights arrive into Delhi, Bombay, Calcutta and Madras, all cities with fine colonial buildings to see, and rare opportunities to see India's great musicians and dancers. Delhi and Bombay have the best restaurants in the country and something almost approaching the Western idea of a night life. Both cities are essential for stocking up on information, bookings and literature on the way into India and have the best shopping on the way out. A full two days in either city at the beginning and end of the trip makes things run much more smoothly in between. See also Information and Reservation sections for Delhi, Bombay, Calcutta and Madras.

MOVING AROUND Just as important and amusing as deciding which places to visit is deciding how best to get to them. For instance, few journeys are as enjoyable as the flight up from Srinagar to Leh, the train from near Coimbatore to Ooty, the ferry from Kottayam to Alleppey or the drive from Jammu to Srinagar. See also Travel Reservations section in Chapter 2, and the Getting There; Getting Away and Hard Facts sections of the following chapters.

Package holidays: the pros and cons

Booking flights and hotels in India from home can be a slog, particularly if you are not sticking to the big hotel chains. And booking trains and planes, hiring cars and generally getting around is quite hard work in India. The overwhelming advantage of a package holiday is that someone else does the hard work and the worrying.

Package holidays have come a long way in recent years, particularly the more unusual holidays for small groups. There are trips which specialise in wildlife, flowers, trekking, Rajasthan palaces, trains and there is even a gourmet tour.

The good firms have been ferrying travellers around for some years and have developed their own character and reputation. They have representatives throughout India who meet and look after clients. They inspect their hotels carefully and switch allegiance if necessary. They have good guides for monuments and expert sherpas for trekking. They apply for all the necessary visas. Furthermore, because they can do good deals with air carriers and hotels, the prices they offer can often be substantially less than arranging the same trip oneself. The most successful example of this is Kuoni's 7-night Taj tour to Delhi, Agra and Jaipur, currently selling for £650 all in. The most dramatic example is Inspirations East's two-week charter beach holidays which start at a knock-down £425.

Tour operators are increasingly sensitive to

5

the tourist who cannot abide group living. They take great care and trouble over planning and booking tailor-made trips for individuals. They run tours where the flight and hotel room are the only fixed items – all meals, sight-seeing and trips are optional. The larger firms offer optional extra weeks for individual tour members to go on a houseboat in Kashmir, to a Goa beach or to visit Nepal. These are hitched on to the front or back of the main sight-seeing tour. Again, they do all the booking and worrying, you just pay a flat fee. And some firms can also offer clients the option of going off on their own after the tour, so long as they fly out of India with one of their tour groups. In high season, there are plenty of flights.

Having avoided most of the old phobias of being part of a travelling circus and of not being able to stay in one place long enough, the only big disadvantage of a package deal is that, even with tailor-made trips, it is not that easy to change the programme. So, if you decide you want to visit Khajuraho instead of Varanasi or to spend extra days in Udaipur and skip Jodhpur, it can be difficult to arrange. And it is maddening to discover that there is a major festival coming up two days after you leave town. This flexibility is crucial to many travellers and is why, for them, it is better to go solo. Outside the high season, getting into the recommended hotels is usually quite easy, except where indicated in the chapters below.

The worldwide Indian Tourist Offices supply an impartial list of tour operators who go to India from any country. Below are a few of the many British operators to give an idea of the range of tours available. All of these firms have a consistently high reputation for quality and service both in Britain and in India and can do tailor-made trips.

BRITISH TOUR OPERATORS
It is best to get several brochures to find what suits you. Here are some of the current best (in alphabetical order). See also Insurance, below.

GENERAL TOUR OPERATORS
(Some run specialist tours, too.)

Abercrombie & Kent, Sloane Square House, Holbein Place, London SW1 (tel: 071 730 9600). Primarily catering for the individual traveller with well-advised, tailor-made itineraries to satisfy every curiosity; occasional specialist tours.

Bales Tours Inc, Bales House, Barrington Road, Dorking, Surrey (tel: 0306 76881). Mrs Bales keeps a close eye on her dozen wide-ranging, good value tours into India, Nepal and Bhutan which range from an introductory 10 days to a 3-week Top Market Tour to India and Nepal; some tours include Sikkim, two fly direct to Madras.

Cox & Kings Travel Ltd, St James Court, Buckingham Gate, London SW1 (tel: 071 931 9106). Knowledgeable experts advise in the UK office and also accompany all tours. Has regained its reputation for both individual travel and tours. Offices in Delhi, Bombay, Madras and Bangalore.

Greaves Travel, 33/34 Marylebone High Street, London W1 (tel: 071 487 5687). The UK arm of a US company which runs upmarket yet competitively priced regular tours, plus a good wildlife/sightseeing combination ending in Nepal.

Hayes & Jarvis (Travel) Ltd, Hayes House, 152 King Street, London W6 (tel: 071 748 5050). The regular tours done comfortably, plus beaches and Maldives, some accompanied.

Jasmin Tours Ltd, High Street, Cookham, Maidenhead, Berkshire (tel: 06285 31121). Wide-ranging prices from extremely good value to a deluxe Club-class one.

Kuoni Travel Ltd, Kuoni House, Dorking, Surrey (tel: 0306 740500). Reliable packages in their Kuoni 3 bargain brochure (including the 7-night introduction) and their Kuoni Worldwide brochure (including Hong Kong, Bangkok and Thailand extensions).

Maya Holidays Ltd, Premier House, 2 Gayton Road, Harrow, Middlesex (tel: 081 863 1835/6744). Tours plus individual travel include a fast-moving, 3-week India introduction, good tours to the East and South, plus extras to the Andamans, etc.

Page & Moy Holidays, 136/140 London Road, Leicester (tel: 0533 552521). Tours range from a double-quick, week-long taste to a heady Goa-Nepal combination.

Pettitts India, 14 Lonsdale Gardens, Tunbridge Wells, Kent (tel: 0892 515966). The classic Eternal India tour has Gwalior and Orchha added in, and other imaginative tours focus on southern caves, Orissan temples and northern hill stations; plus special interest tours. Office in Delhi.

Pleasureseekers, 52 Haymarket, London SW1 (tel: 071 930 3803). Tailor-made travel for individuals, with a fat brochure of imaginative ideas to work on.

Swan Hellenic Art Treasures Tours, 77 New Oxford Street, London WC1 (tel: 071 831 1616). With an emphasis on art and culture, these detailed tours always have a lecturer (often a university historian) and range from a thorough look at Rajasthan palaces to a focus on Buddha, South India, Gujarat and Kashmir.

SPECIALIST TOUR OPERATORS
WILDLIFE:
David Sayers Travel, c/o Andrew Brock Travel Ltd, 10 Barley Mow Passage, London W4 (tel:

071 995 3642). Botanical and garden tours include a splendid one of North India by elephant.

ExplorAsia Ltd, 13 Chapter Street, London SW1 (tel: 071 630 7102). The umbrella for Tiger Tops, Mountain Travel Nepal and Himalayan River Exploration, they run the most experienced and up-market wildlife tours, the best camps in wildlife parks in Nepal (Royal Chitwan and Royal Bardia) and are opening one in India at Corbett NP in 1992. Experts lead safaris, mountain climbs and river-rafting expeditions. Offices in Delhi, Bombay, Kathmandu.

Ornitholidays, 1/3 Victoria Drive, Bognor Regis, West Sussex PO21 2PW (tel: 0243 821230). Simon Boyes, and sometimes Lawrence Holloway, take bird-lovers to Bharatpur, Corbett National Park and Nainital; to Assam, Kasirangar and Manas national parks and Sikkim; and to Kashmir and Ladakh.

Cygnus Wildlife Holidays, 57 Fore Street, Kingsbridge, Devon (tel: 0548 856178). Bird-watching trips with ornithologists have expanded into photography trips to Delhi, Agra, Bharatpurs Kolead Ghana bird sanctuary and Ranthambore Tiger Reserve and to trips to Sikkim, Darjeeling, Assam and South India.

TREKKING, MOUNTAINEERING AND ADVENTURE
The advantage of taking a package is that the tour operator does the considerable quantities of paperwork for permissions to go into more remote or politically sensitive areas. They also produce reams of advice on health, packing, survival, etc.

Exodus Expeditions, 9 Weir Road, Balham, London SW12 0LT (tel: 081 675 5550; brochure orders on 081 673 0859). Good value and fun trekking and adventure holidays. Trekking includes a huge range of Himalayan trails; adventure can be trucking around Rajasthan, using jeep, train and boat up the Brahmaputra River in Assam, or taking six months to do the London-India drive.

ExplorAsia Ltd, see above for details. For adventure as comfortable as it can be.

Himalayan Kingdoms, 20 The Mall, Clifton, Bristol BS8 4DR (tel: 0272 237163). Trails and expeditions for the healthy, keen and energetic into Himachal Pradesh, Sikkim, Bhutan, the Hindu Kush and elsewhere, designed for the walker and/or climber.

Karakoram Experience, 32 Lake Road, Keswick, Cumbria CA12 5DQ (tel: 07687 73966). Trekking and mountaineering for the more adventurous, often at quite high levels; a popular expedition is up to Bagirathi peak in the Gangotri area.

West Himalayan Holidays Ltd, c/o Andrew Brock Travel Ltd, 10 Barley Mow Passsage, London W4 (tel: 081 995 3642). Founded by Kranti Singh and Christina Noble, who lived in the Kullu Valley for 20 years. Whether on easy or challenging walks, groups and individuals benefit from their intimate knowledge.

OTHER SPECIALIST OPERATORS INCLUDE:
Coromandel, Andrew Brock Travel Ltd, 10 Barley Mow Passage, London W4 (tel: 081 995 3642). A wide range of off-beat tours for individuals or groups includes textiles in Rajasthan and Gujarat, Chalukyan and Hoysala temples, an Indian elephant safari, Kashmir, the Andamans and Goa.

The Curry Club, PO Box 7, Haslemere, Surrey (tel: 0428 2452). Adventurous and fun gourmet food tours with Pat Chapman, the club's mentor.

Butterfield's Indian Railway Tour, Burton Fleming, Driffield, North Humberside (tel: 026 287 230). Puff-puff your way around India for 18-32 days of wonderful sights, whacky lifestyle and simple comforts.

Explore Worldwide, 1 Frederick Street, Aldershot, Hampshire (tel: 0252 319448). Probably as near to exploring as a pre-planned group tour can go, including a seriously off-beat, good value camping and walking tour to see tribes in the Orissa hinterland.

Inspirations East, PO Box 990, Windsor, Berkshire (tel: 0753 830883). The first operator to do charter holidays tours to the Goa and Trivandrum beaches. Choice of hotels; optional extra sightseeing weeks. Prices from £425 for two weeks of sun-soaking.

Going solo: Booking up yourself

THE FLIGHT TO INDIA It is much better to take a direct flight. This gives a certain guarantee of arriving on time. Once a plane lands to re-fuel or collect or dump passengers, any amount of delay can begin.

When booking the international flight, seats on internal Indian Airlines flights and Vayudoot flights can also be booked and paid for (see below). There are non-stop direct flights from London to Delhi and Bombay, and direct but stopping flights to Calcutta and Madras. Each connects with the rest of India on the internal flights. See Getting There: Getting Away section for each city.

THE FARE At the time of going to press, the current London-India-London air fares range from the incredibly low £412 bucket shop return fare to a hefty £2,631. Trailfinder and the other agents listed below will find some of the cheapest fares, although there are countless bucket shops to hunt around. Bucket shops advertise in the newspapers and in magazines.

There is even a big price range for the two national carriers, Air India and British Airways. To give an idea, their current rates and multi-tiered fare structures are listed below. Other airlines which have good, regular and reliable services to India include Air France, Lufthansa, Pan Am, SAS, Swissair, Singapore Airlines, Thai Airways and Japan Airlines.

Air India, 17-18 New Bond Street, London W1 (reservations tel: 071 491 7979; flight information at Heathrow tel: 081 897 6311).

British Airways, First, 156 Regent Street, London W1 (reservations 081 897 4000; flight information at Heathrow tel: 081 759 2525).

Both airways offer some non-stop direct flights to Delhi and Bombay; Air India has flights going on to Calcutta and Madras; their New York-India flights stop at London. The ticket structure for both airlines is as follows. Firstly, restricted tickets: one-way Apex £433; return PX – called Visit India by Air India (bought at any time but subject to a 50% cancellation fee; valid for 14-90 day trip) £700 (more in high season July-Aug and Dec-Jan); return Excursion (valid for 10-90 days) £899 (£1,041 high season). Secondly, unrestricted tickets: Economy single £525 return £995; Full economy (can make a stop-over) single £748 return £1,564; Business single £877 return £1,721; First single £1,564 return £2,983.

TRAVEL AGENTS
It is always worth enquiring if there are discount fares available. The following should be able to help.

Trailfinder, 194 Kensington High Street, London W8 (tel: 071 938 3939, economy; 071 938 3444, business and first class) and 46-48 Earls Court Road, London W8 (tel: 071 938 3366, economy). Complete travel centres to serve every pocket, from budget traveller to the big splurge. Their pride is in being able to 'find the best value tickets that prevailing regulations and man's ingenuity allow'. Computer-equipped staff book anything from a single flight to package tours. The Kensington High Street office also has a full immunisation centre (tel: 071 938 3999) and provides travel insurance, hotel discounts, currency and travellers cheques, visas (tel: 071 938 3848), permits, bookshop (tel: 071 938 3999) and information for clients (tel: 071 938 3303). Worth checking out the special India-London flight prices for UK passport holders.

Greaves, 40-41 Marylebone High Street, London W1 (tel: 071 486 6646), especially good for British Airways flights.

Welcome Travel, 55-57 Well Street, London W1 (tel: 071 439 3627), especially good for Air India flights.

BAGGAGE WEIGHT LIMITS Both the above airlines restrict baggage. On some flights it is simply one piece per person; on others it is 20 kilos per person except for club, business and first class who may take 30 kilos. Overweight charges are calculated at one per cent of the first class fare. Cabin baggage is strictly one small piece besides a handbag.

FLIGHTS WITHIN INDIA There are two internal airline networks: Indian Airlines and Vayudoot.

Indian Airlines run an extensive network of internal flights. Their timetable undergoes modest revision once or twice a year. It is wise to book all internal flights when booking the international flight, whichever carrier you use, particularly in the high season. It is important that the seats are 'confirmed' and that you re-confirm each one in India. On arriving at a city where a flight is to be taken, re-confirm your ticket as soon as possible. (Your hotel will do this for a few rupees.) See diagram overleaf.

Vayudoot, the newer airline, serves some of the more remote areas plus some regular ones. It is divided into four regions: North, South, East and West. Despite using small planes and flying most sectors only two or three times a week, it is often possible to get seats on a Vayudoot flight when an Indian Airlines one is full. Their routes do change, but Government of India Tourist offices hold the latest schedules. Flights can be booked through travel agents or at Vayudoot airports. See diagram overleaf, and see Booking In, below.

BOOKING IN AND CHECKING IN Indian Airlines is the world's second largest domestic airline. Using a fleet of Airbuses, Boeing 737s, A320s and turboprops, it makes an average of 250 flights every day to link 61 cities in India and 10 in neighbouring countries. There are, however, various drawbacks. In high season most flights are not merely fully booked; they are over-booked and have depresssingly long waiting lists. Airports are not always close to a city – Udaipur's is 40 minutes' drive away, with a basic cafe to cheer up passengers waiting for the often delayed planes. Since no batteries are permitted in the plane's passenger cabin (they must be packed and go in the hold, together with scissors, nail files and other sharp objects), it is not possible to enliven waiting time with music from a radio or personal stereo. Check-in time has been reduced to 75 minutes (45 minutes for passengers with hold luggage only) but is still ludicrously long.

Then, to the booking system, which is now on computer. In theory, foreigners have a certain priority, since 25% of all seats are reserved for them, but early booking is wise, particularly between October and March. Whether seats are booked outside India (when making the international booking) or inside India, all payment must be made either in foreign currency or, if in rupees, with an encashment certificate as proof that the same or more hard currency was officially converted in India. Finally, if the booking is made outside India, it is important to confirm all flights on arrival 'just in case', as the official explained, 'the international airline failed to make the booking with Indian Airlines when issuing your ticket'. In all, a short distance is usually covered as quickly – and far more interestingly – by car, train or bus. Vayudoot seats, often available when Indian Airlines is fully booked, can be booked outside India or, once there, at the airport or at one of their five city centre offices (see Chapter 2, Travel Reservations section).

DISCOUNT INTERNAL FLIGHTS For those travelling extensively, the three Indian Airlines discount schemes are well worth considering. The Youth Fare, restricted to 12-30 year olds, gives 25% discount off the US dollar fare prices for any internal flights and for the India-Nepal route. The Discover India ticket costs a flat US$400 and is valid for 21 days on the domestic network all over India but no repeats (except in order to get from one destination to another). South India Excursion gives a 30% discount on US dollar fares on more precise conditions: the airports on offer are Madras, Tiruchirapalli, Trivandrum, Coimbatore, Cochin, Bangalore and Madurai, and bookings must include a flight to the Maldives or Sri Lanka from one of the first three. All can be bought outside and inside India.

INTERNAL TRAINS A train journey is as much part of a visit to India as seeing a festival or strolling round a bazaar. Tickets are best bought on arrival, whether single or Indrail Passes (see below); prices can increase when bought abroad. The chapters below give suggestions for some of the more interesting trips (see Getting There: Getting Away sections).

INDRAIL PASSES If you want to take several journeys by train – and it is certainly a good way of seeing the countryside – there are a variety of rover tickets, called Indrail Passes. In Britain, they can be bought at a month's notice from some travel agents, such as Thomas Cook (45 Berkeley Street, London W1, tel: 889 7777); or from the enthusiastic Dr Dandapani who runs SD Enterprises, 21 York House, Empire Way, Middlesex (tel: 081 903 3411), reportedly 'refreshingly efficient'. In India, they are bought at the large stations (see Information and Reservations sections of Delhi, Bombay and Calcutta

chapters).

Indrail Passes must always be paid for in foreign currency. Rates are cheap and it is best to buy the Air-Conditioned First Class ticket. Validity ranges from 7 days (US$110non/ac, US$220ac) up to 90 days (US$400non-ac, US$800ac).

HOTELS There are some exceedingly luxurious hotels in India, both modern and old, whose well-trained, smiling and spoiling staff compete at international level but whose prices are well below their competitors. They often serve the best food in town and offer excellent facilities, such as swimming pools, health clubs, travel desks and extensive room service.

The top hotels divide into two types: modern and efficient but often lacking character; old and slightly less efficient but with bundles of character. There are a few rare exceptions that combine both, such as the Taj, Bombay, the Oberoi Grand, Calcutta, the West End, Bangalore, and one or two of the palace hotels in Rajasthan. Of the new hotels, the Mughal Sheraton at Agra and the Maurya Sheraton in Delhi are very good and have a distinct character. Most British people tend to go for character, but businessmen would need the efficiency.

The palace hotels are unique to India. Rajasthan is littered with palaces. It was at Jaipur that the lucrative trade of turning the Rambagh Palace into a hotel was initiated by the Maharaja. Many saw his success and jumped on the band-wagon. Today, a tourist can live like a maharaja in these wildly extravagent, romantic piles. The better ones are run either by the Taj or Welcomgroup hotel chains. The more relaxed ones are still under the management of the now ex-maharajas, often with their charming old retainers. Palace hotels are not restricted to Rajasthan. There are some in Gujarat and some around Mysore in Karnataka.

Outside the tourist towns, accommodation tends to be simple, as does the food. It is the price you pay for seeing some of the wonders of India that the general tourist has yet to discover.

The places suggested in the following chapters are the best available – or the only ones available. Old Raj hotels are full of atmosphere, such as the seaside Gopalpur-on-Sea in Orissa and the revamped Malabar in Kerala.

The government-run accommodation falls into several categories. There are Guest Houses, Circuit Houses, Rest Houses, Forest Rest Houses, Dak Bungalows, Tourist Bungalows, etc. The best grade is a Circuit House, but Indian government officials take precedence in the allocation of rooms. So if, for instance, a booking is at the Hampi Power Station Guest House, right by Vijayangar in Karnataka, it is wise to have a fallback in mind. The lowest

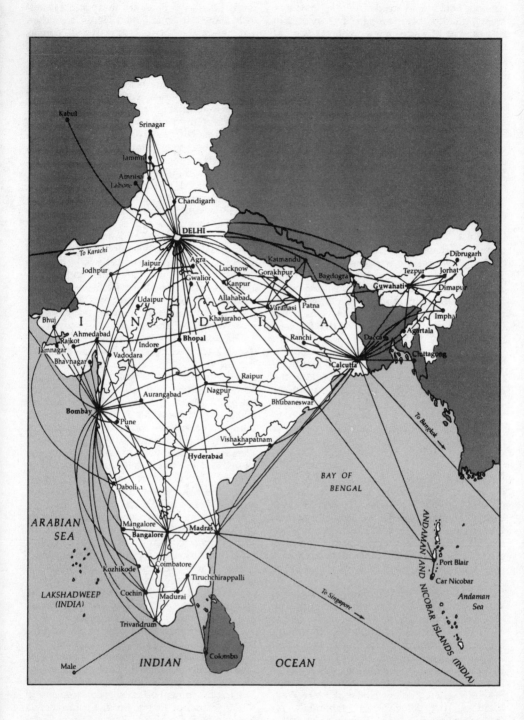

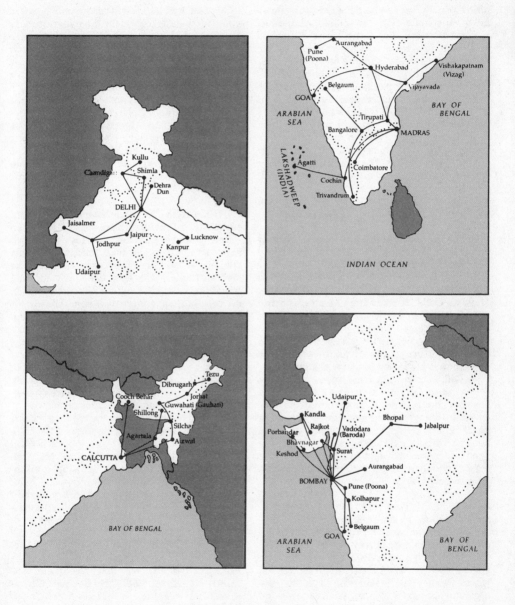

grade is a Dak Bungalow. All grades are usually clean and simple. They often do not provide food unless it is ordered in advance. They may have fans rather than built-in air-conditioning. Many do not accept credit cards. All are very cheap. The local offices of the Indian Automobile Association (q.v.) and the local tourist offices usually know where the Dak Bungalows are on any route. Some of the older buildings have great charm, such as the Tourist Bungalow at Quilon in Kerala which was built as the British Residency, but can be a bit down at heel.

There are also the Indian clubs which, as noted earlier, have excellent facilities, spacious buildings, extensive grounds and are often right in the city centre. If introduction through a member is required, you will find that most businessmen, both Western and Indian, will belong to the good clubs of the city, since they are the social centres. Some Indian clubs have reciprocal membership with overseas clubs. If you are a club member at home, it is worth checking with your secretary for reciprocal membership before setting off. See also section above.

Unlike Europe, where a tiny hotel in Paris or Rome is family run and delightful, most tiny hotels in big Indian cities are pretty awful. Furthermore, there are not enough top hotels to service the ever-itinerant Indian businessmen. Thus, for Delhi, Bombay and Calcutta, as many reliable and central hotels as possible have been listed, together with their prices, which are higher than elsewhere in India but well worth paying. The prices quoted for these and for beach hotels are aimed to serve as a guideline. They will, of course, increase annually.

The Indian system of awarding stars to hotels has very strange criteria, best ignored. As elsewhere in the world, the management team is crucial to a hotel's success. Recently, a dismal hotel in the South was transformed into a very good one by the arrival of a new manager. The recommendations below are almost all based on personal experience.

HOTEL FACILITIES   Of the hotels recommended below, all the large ones have air-conditioning unless otherwise noted. It can be individually controlled by a switch in your room. Understandably, the Indians are very keen on getting cool, so hotel staff turn it up to full whenever they can, making the room like a refrigerator. In modest places, where there is no air-conditioning there are fans. Almost every hotel has room service; some operate it around the clock. Except for the very tiny places, all hotels and clubs have a good laundry service. There is often something called four-channel music in your room. Rarely do four channels work and those that do usually have fuzzy reception and blare out repetitive music, Indian or Western. A few hotels boast televisions. This only has significance if the hotel runs in-house videos and, increasingly in deluxe hotels, Cable News Network's hotel news service. In all but remote places, bills can be settled with credit cards.

Some of your hotels will be very much part of your trip to India, especially the palace ones, so an idea of their character and history is given in the recommendations below. As palace hotels are converted private residences, rooms vary enormously. Sometimes a particular room or view is significant and this is indicated too. In bigger cities, the hotels are social centres for the smart locals, offering places to meet and some of the best restaurants, shops, bookstalls, beauty salons and health clubs – so advance booking for restaurants and health clubs is wise. The clubs are social centres for sports and relaxation, particularly at week-ends. This is especially true of Calcutta.

HOTEL BOOKING   The sooner, the better, especially during the high season (October-February) and even more especially over Christmas when Indians also take holidays. Whether booking by letter, telex, telegram or fax (in the big cities only), it is essential to ask for confirmation of the booking, and in some cases of the precise room or view you would like if it is available, although it can rarely be guaranteed. It is also essential to take the written confirmation (letter, telex or cable) with you. Even the best hotels have been known to deny that their guest has made a reservation. It is also worth asking to be met at the airport or railway station. Room rates may be subject to service charge, government tax and state luxury tax.

To make booking easier, the big hotel chains have a central reservations system:

Oberoi Hotels Hotels at Agra (opens 1992-3), Bangalore, Bhubaneswar, Bombay (2), Calcutta, Darjeeling, Delhi (2), Goa, Gopalpur-on-Sea, Hyderabad, Kathmandu (Nepal), Khajuraho, Shimla (2), Srinagar and in Kathmandu (Nepal) and Colombo (Sri Lanka). Central reservations at Oberoi Maidens, 7 Sham Nath Marg, Delhi, 110054 (tel: 2525464; telex 66303/78163; fax 2929800). UK bookings: LRI, 113-119 High Street, Hampton Hill, Middlesex TW12-1PS (tel: 081 941 7400, freephone 0800 282811, fax 081 941 5168). US bookings: Oberoi Hotels (tel: freephone 800 2230888 PIA or 800 8005 OBEROI).

Taj Group of Hotels Recently bought the Savoy Group and extended into the South. Hotels now at Agra, Bangalore, Bombay (2), Calcutta, Delhi (2), Cochin, Goa (3), Jaipur (4), Khajuraho, Lucknow (opening 1991), Mysore, Ootacamund (Ooty) (2), Madras (3), Maldives (2), Udaipur,

Varanasi (Benares) and in Kathmandu (Nepal), Male (Maldives) and Colombo (Sri Lanka). Their more modest chain, Gateway Hotels & Getaway Resorts, has hotels at Bangalore, Chiplun, Hyderabad and Nasik. Central reservations at Taj Mahal Inter-Continental, Apollo Bunder, Bombay 400039 (tel: 2023366/2022524; telex: 112442/113791; fax: 2872711). UK bookings: St James Court Hotel and Apartments, Buckingham Gate, London SW1 (tel: freephone 0800 282699 or 071 828 5909; telex: 938075; fax: 071 630 7587); or through Utell International House, 2 Kew Bridge Road, Brentford, Middlesex TW8-0JF (tel: 081 995 8211; fax: 081 995 2474). US bookings: Taj Group of Hotels, 230 Park Avenue, Suite 466, New York 10169 (tel: 212 972 6830; telex 229993; fax: 212 687 0743; or freephone 800-i-luv-taj/800 458 8825); or through Utel International, 10605 Burt Circle, Omaha, Nebraska 68114 (tel: freephone 800 44 UTELL). **Welcomgroup Hotels** at Agra, Aurangabad, Bangalore, Baroda, Bhavnagar, Bombay, Delhi, Gwalior, Jodhpur, Khimsar, Madras (2), Mangalore, Patna, Srinagar (houseboats and hotel), Vadodara (Baroda) and Port Blair (Andaman hotels Islands); plus hotels opening soon at Ahmedabad, Bangalore, Bhubaneshwar, Indore, Jaipur, Pune and Vishakapatnam. Central reservations at Maurya-Sheraton, Diplomatic Enclave, New Delhi (tel: 3030101/3014127/3010849/ telex: 652107; cable: WELCOTEL; fax: 3012892). UK bookings for hotels in the Sheraton Group (Agra, Bombay, Delhi, Madras (2)) can be made through Sheraton Reservations System (tel: freephone 0800 353535; fax: 071 731 0532). US bookings: ITC Ltd, 342 Madison Avenue, New York 10173 (tel: 212.986.3724; telex: 426083 ITCL UI); plus reservation for hotels in the Sheraton Group can be made through Sheraton Reservations System (tel: freephone 800 325 3535).

Clarks Group of Hotels Hotels at Agra, Jaipur, Lucknow, Patna and Varanasi. Central reservations: UP Hotels Ltd, 1101/2 Surya Kiran, 19 Kasturba Gandhi Marg, New Delhi (tel: 351467; telex: 2447; cable: UPHOTEL).

The extensive **Ashok Group** of government-run hotels are, on the whole, disappointing, although they might be useful at Bangalore, Bharatpur, Bhubaneswar (an exceptionally good one), Kovalam (sensational building, badly run), Mysore (beautiful palace, badly run), Udaipur and Bijapur. Of their Delhi 8 hotels, the Ashok is splendidly spacious and the Kanishka very central. Central reservations: Ashok Reservation Service, Hotel Samrat, Chanakyapuri, New Delhi 110021 (tel: 603030; telex 031 72333; fax: 6873216). UK bookings: S & D Enterprises Ltd, 21 York House, Empireway, Wembley, Middlesex HA9-0PA (tel: 081 903 3411; telex: 94012027.

Visas and permits

All foreign nationals entering India must hold a valid visa. They are quite easy to obtain. Your nearest Indian mission (embassy, consulate or high commission) supplies the form. The completed form, together with three passport photos and the fee, is then either delivered (with cash or postal order, no cheques) back in person or sent by post (with a crossed British postal order made payable to 'The High Commission of India, London'; no cash to be sent). In London, the fee for British nationals of non-Indian origin is currently £23 single entry, £34.50 double or triple entry; longer visas possible by special referral; British nationals of Indian origin pay £7 for all these categories. Delivery times are Mon-Fri 9.30am-1pm; collection times are 4.30-5.30pm the following working day; applications by post should allow 3 weeks, but up to 3 months if applications are made for restricted areas. Foreign nationals and those with UK passports issued overseas can also expect long delays.

Permits are needed for restricted and protected areas, which require more form-filling. They are much easier to get at home than in India. Again, apply to your Indian mission. It is better to go equipped with all the permits you may need. They often take several weeks to be issued, so it is best to apply for them as soon as dates are fixed and certainly six to eight weeks ahead of departure. If an area is sensitive, such as the north-eastern states, then the permit may not be issued. Permits are currently needed for Darjeeling (but not if flying up for less than 15 days), Jaldapara (West Bengal), Kasiranga and Manas (Assam), Shillong (Meghalaya); Rumtek, Phodang and Dzongri (Sikkim); some of the Andaman and Nicobar Islands. In addition, there may sometimes be temporary restricted areas.

A visa is also necessary for Pakistan, available from the Pakistan High Commission, Bhutan, available from the Royal Bhutan Government or their missions abroad, and for Nepal, available at Kathmandu airport or from the Nepalese missions abroad. A visa is not necessary for the Maldives nor for visits of less than 30 days to Sri Lanka.

If all this seems like an obstacle race, The Visa Shop, Charing Cross Underground Shopping Arcade, London WC2 (tel: 379 0419/0376; fax: 497 2590), open Mon.-Fri. 9.30am-7pm, Sat. 10am-2pm, will speedily obtain any of these visas for £10 each.

PROHIBITION India is officially committed to prohibition. Currently, the only state with total prohibition is Gujarat. Other states have partial prohibition, which can mean anything from one dry day a week to one a month. On dry days, most hotels will serve alcohol on room service. On all other days, hotels serve alcohol. Your hotel and the local tourist office will tell you what the current restrictions are in that particular state.

Health

Having the right injections at the right time is essential. Everyone going to India should have a full course against typhoid, be up to date with polio, tetanus and cholera and have a gamma globulin injection immediately before departure. This last is against hepatitis A, and surveys done on the US Peace Corps and the Voluntary Service Overseas volunteers both concluded that, provided you accept the time limitations, it is very effective. There are two dose types: the smaller for two to three months, the larger for five to six months.

In addition, there are three other jabs that Dr Lea of the British Airways Immunisation Centre in London recommends travellers should consider. People going off the beaten track might consider a course of injections against rabies, understanding that they should be started preferably six weeks before departure and that they offer only part-protection: if bitten, the serum starts to fight disease while the patient is taken to hospital quickly. Meningitis is now found

Finally, Japanese encephalitis, a mosquito-borne disease of a paralytic variety, is found in the paddy fields of the Ganga delta, Kerala and Tamil Nadu. Locals have been diagnosed with it, but few travellers – although some may have suffered and possibly doctors have not known to be on the look-out for it. The vaccine is two shots a week apart, the second one a minimum of three weeks before departure. If time is short, then use a good insect repellant.

There are two good immunisation clinics in London. They are specialists whose sole job is to ensure that everyone sets out with the correct protection for the country to which they are going. The centres are at British Airways, First, 156 Regent Street, London W1 (tel: 071 439 9584), open Mon-Fri 8.30am-12.15pm and 1.15-4.15pm, Sat 10am-noon and 2-4.15pm, with adjoining chemist who stocks mosquito repellant, Mosi-guard bands impregnated with very strong mosquito repellant, the Masta water filter called Travel Well (currently £30, claimed to be 'the only thing which makes water both safe and palatable'), iodine drops for instant sterilisation, syringes and needles, etc. BA also runs a City clinic at Cheapside (tel: 071 606 2977), others at Victoria and Heathrow, and has about two dozen franchised immunisation clinics around Britain; to find out the nearest one to you, phone 071 831 5333. The other recom-mended London clinic is Trailfinder, 194 Kensington High Street, London W8 (tel: 071 938 3999). The Department of Health and Social Security (DHSS) publishes a useful leaflet called *Protect Your Health Abroad* (SA35). For telephone information on malaria, call the Malaria Reference Laboratory on 071 636 8636.

Insurance

It is essential to make a small payment against the possibility of all kinds of disasters. Package holidays often include insurance but it may not be enough for you. A tour operator should be a member of AITO (the Association of Independent Tour Operators), which monitors companies, or ABTA (the Association of British Travel Agents), which is bonded so that if a company goes bust the traveller is protected.

Personal insurance is usually an optional extra and well worth paying since it should cover baggage loss, money loss, health, third party liability, travel delay and a certain percentage of the cancellation fee if made for personal reasons (e.g. a family death). If in doubt, ask for a copy of the company's insurance cover. It is worth first checking the regular household and health insurance, since this might already be enough cover. If not, most banks and insurance companies have their own holiday and business travel insurance schemes. The form can be completed when you pick up your travellers cheques.

For health, the policy should cover all medical costs, hospital benefits, permanent disabilities and the full flight home – all four seats if you are unfortunately lying flat out.

Money

The big hotels, shops, restaurants and Indian Airlines take credit cards. However, although they all accept a wide range, they are not consistent as to precisely which ones they do accept. There are even discrepancies within one hotel chain. It is best therefore to take all those you possess.

Travellers cheques are the safest form of money and can also be used directly to settle bills. The best currencies to take are US dollars and pounds sterling. If you enter India with more than £1,000 (or equivalent) in cash, it must be declared.

It is forbidden to take Indian rupees into or out of India.

What to pack

In principle, the less the better. It is impossible not to buy things in India. The most reluctant and miserly shoppers succumb within the first few days unless they are held back. The trick seems to be to take as little as possible in the first place and even allow for some of that to be used up (creams, shampoo, etc.) or thrown out at the end.

HAND LUGGAGE Best kept to a minimum and in one small case, otherwise the airline may ask for it to be checked into the hold. It is much safer to keep all documents in your hand luggage: passports, tickets, confirmations of bookings, insurance policies, travellers cheques, permits, visas, immunisation certificates, etc. Despite the claims at airports, it is also safer to keep all film and breakable bottles with you. Each airline has its own rules about what is and is not permitted in hand luggage and a list is usually clearly displayed at the check-in counter – penknives, matches, nailfiles, etc. are best packed in hold luggage.

CLOTHES Essentials are a subsistence supply of loose cotton clothes – man-made fibres are extremely uncomfortable and sweaty. Winter travellers from Britain can pick up bargain summer clothes in the January sales. Hotel laundries are fast and good, if a bit brutal. If the supply proves to be inadequate, European designs are substantially cheaper in India than elsewhere and are sold in the hotel shopping arcades. In addition, clothes can be copied and tailored in one day, using fabric bought by the metre – not everything is sold in sari lengths. Apart from the big cities, where suits and silk are rampant, people do not dress up very grandly in the evenings.

Other essential clothes are a pair of socks or oversocks for visiting temples and mosques, otherwise there is frantic scurrying from shadow to shadow to avoid burning the soles of the feet. A jumper is useful for the hills and cool desert evenings, trousers for wildlife parks; a hat for sunny sight-seeing; bathing costume or trunks for hotel pools and beaches (topless and bottomless are not yet the done thing in India). If forgotten, all these are available in India. There is an inexhaustible choice of comfortable, good-looking, cheap sandals in India (see Delhi, Bombay and Madras shopping sections), so two pairs would be enough to be going on with. For temple and mosque visits, it is better if shoes can be slipped on and off easily.

MEDICINES It is tempting to take a medicine trunk with every possible preventive and curative potion. In fact, just a few tubes, pots and pills will save most disasters. Dr Lea, of the British Airways Immunisation Centre in London, gives helpful advice for that hardy perennial of tropical travelling, jippy tummy, also known as Delhi Belly in India. (She also advises on jabs, see p. 14)

To lessen the risk of learning more about Indian lavatories (on the whole, not pretty) than Hindu monuments, Dr Lea does not recommend taking a preventative pill. Rather, she advises that when Delhi Belly strikes you should preferably stop eating solids and take as much safe fluid as possible. The best mix is 1 flat teasp. salt, 4 heaped teasps. sugar to 1 litre mineral/boiled water – an easy way to do this is to pack some Rehydrat or Dioralyte sachets (good for all ages, including babies and the elderly) and dilute them with safe water; also, oral rehydration sachets promoted by the World Health Organisation should be on sale and cheap at any local chemist. If travelling or work demand instant stability, then take Imodium or Lomotil, abiding by the recommended dosage. If problems persist after 3-4 days (sooner for infants), seek professional help or consult your hotel doctor; should you be dehydrated, he may put you on a drip for a few hours.

Since India suffers from the Aids virus, in case of any illnesses or accidents, it is wise to take a supply of sterilised syringes and needles.

As for malaria, drugs for this date very quickly. Currently, the advice is to take two pills: Nivaquine (or Avloclor), 2 pills weekly starting a week before departure; and Paludrine, 2 pills daily starting the day before departure, continuing both sets until at least 4 weeks after your return. For all pills consult an immunisation clinic, see p. 14.

A tube of antiseptic cream and some simple dressings do not take up much room.

Water is always a worry, particularly since it is important to drink plenty to prevent dehydration. Bisleri bottled water, sold in hotels and restaurants, is reliable. To drink the so-called boiled water put in the hotel room with greater confidence, use Steritabs, Puritabs or other water purifying pills in the strengths recommended. For those with delicate stomachs going for an extensive trip, one former foreign correspondent strongly recommends investing about £100 in a Katydin, a Swiss water purifying pump available from mountaineering shops which filters almost everything except the vigorous hepatitis virus; less expensive is the water-purifier called Drink Well; if in doubt about any water, a few drops of iodine left in the water for 10 minutes (30 minutes if it is cold stream water) will sterilise perfectly well.

Be sure to pack a full supply of any regular medicines you take as many drugs will not be available in India.

Lipsalve guards against damage from both the dry heat and the thinner mountain air. A very good anti-mosquito stick or aerosol, such as Autan or Jungle Juice, is essential, as is a soothing cream for when the little horrors get biting before the anti-mosquito potion is on. Mosi-guard bands impregnated with a very strong mosquito repellant reportedly work well on the ankles, 'if you don't mind looking like a champion tennis player while gazing at the Taj'. Mosquitos seem at their hungriest during the early evening and when you are asleep. Indians suffer as much as Westerners. On the BBC radio programme, 'Desert Island Discs', the Maharani of Jaipur chose a never-ending supply of anti-mosquito potions as her single permitted luxury on the island.

Very few Western cosmetics of any quality are available in India, but there are good herbal ranges such as Sharnaz Husain. A regular visitor once said: 'Everything available in Boots is not available in India.' This is no longer true. However, do take a generous supply of pre and post sun lotions (still not imported), razors, razor blades (Wilkinson's local blade is Wiltek) and shaving cream; make-up and perfume. Tampax can be bought in general household stores and hotel chemists. A universal basin plug seems to be essential in even the most deluxe hotel baths.

SIGHT-SEEING PACK For daily travelling about, these are invaluable: a hand towel and a small bar of soap for washing before and after eating or to freshen up in the heat; a roll of soft lavatory paper for its original purpose and also for handkerchiefs – the roll keeps much cleaner than boxes of paper handkerchiefs; and a plastic bottle for drinking water.

SIGHT-SEEING EQUIPMENT The Bartholomew's map of India (not available in India) helps you locate what you are driving through, passing by in a train or flying over. Nelles maps, published in five parts, are also good. State maps give more detail. For guide books, the most exhaustive on monuments is the new two-volume *Penguin Guide to the Monuments of India* and the best on practical, modern travelling in India is Lonely Planet's *India* (see p. 18 below for details and bookshops). Depending on your itinerary, there are other invaluable guides, such as bird books (see bibliographies at the end of the appropriate chapters).

Quality camera film is now much easier to find in India, particularly Fuji film; but it is wisest to stock up before you set off. If you take too much, it makes a perfect thank-you present for the embarrassing kindnesses shown by Indians in museums, hotels and socially. By numbering the films as they are used, and even jotting down subjects in a notebook, the record of the trip stays in order; it is surprising how quickly the memory can muddle up views and monuments. A pair of binoculars helps with looking closer at birds, wildlife and detailed carving on buildings.

READING MATTER Now is your chance to read the great tomes you have been eyeing for years. In general, night life in India is non-existent, airport lounges are grim (planes are prone to delays) and there is a limit to how long watching Indian life from a train carriage remains fascinating on a long journey (the daily Kerala Express takes almost two days to do its 3,000 km Delhi-Trivandrum run). To get in the mood, there is plenty of very good fiction set in India and some superb travel accounts and biographies. Some relate to specific parts of India, such as Paul Scott's *Raj Quartet* (hill stations) and R. K. Narayan's Malgudi novels (based on Mysore); E. M. Forster's *The Hill of Devi* is letters from Central India, and Gayatri Devi's *A Princess Remembers* is the Maharani of Jaipur's memoirs. John Keay's *Into India* and Trevor Fishlock's *India File* are both excellent introductions to India. See pp. 19-21 and the more specific chapter bibliographies for more suggestions.

If you intend to pick up any of the glorious and extremely cheap furnishing fabrics or to order a carpet or dhurrie, it is a good idea to take the necessary measurements and colour matches with you. The brightness of the Indian sunlight befuddles the memory for precise tones.

GADGETS Electricity works most of the time in most parts of India. And that is as firm as it gets. Contrary to popular belief, candles and matches are brought to even the most modest hotel rooms soon after the lights go out. But the big hotels have their own generators. Voltage is 220, with the occasional 230. It is best to take your own transformer.

Perhaps the most useful gadget is an anti-mosquito machine. Chemists stock the small No-Bite machine, which proudly calls itself 'The World's No.1 Mosquito killer' and works by putting an electrical pulse through a blue tablet lasting 10 hours. So take plenty of tablets. When the electricity stops, mosquito coils (available in India) have some effect – including a pungent smoke which makes the eyes smart, and they work best when you are down wind.

A travelling iron is often quicker than sending garments to be ironed; the Sanyo steam travelling iron is very light. A penknife is useful for opening bottles and peeling fruit.

A small, short wave radio rescues you from piped music in hotel rooms. All India Radio has regional stations whose programmes are listed in the local paper. BBC World Service broadcasts on short wave on 13.82m (08.00-13.30hrs), 16.86m (09.00-15.15hrs), 19.91m (09.00-18.30hrs), 24.80m (14.00-18.30hrs), 25.51m (09.00-13.30hrs), 25.53m (11.30-16.15hrs), 30.80m

(13.30-18.30hrs), 31.88m (15.00-21.15hrs), 41.9m (13.30-16.15hrs), and 42.11m (16.00-18.30hrs) – the times given are GMT. There are small chunks throughout the day on medium wave at 212m. A personal stereo and some favourite tapes are a good idea; more serious music addicts have been known to take a slim compact disc player for evenings of Mahler in their hotel room. Batteries for flash, radio, razors, etc. must be packed too.

PRESENTS   Very important. The kindness, generosity and hospitality of Indians know no bounds. If you arrive in India with just one address, or none at all, you are bound to leave with many. Despite deregulation, anything foreign is still fashionable. Half bottles of duty-free Scotch whisky (not malt) go down very well for men (it is extremely expensive in India). Videos are owned by a startling number of seemingly modest households and blank tapes for VHS machines are extremely popular. A recorded tape must be VHS on the PAL system. European table mats, drinks coasters, soap and pretty floral porcelain pots are light in weight but always welcome. Despite independence, most Indians are loyal royal followers and amused by things with a royal connotation or a crest. Children love the latest small toy cars. And all Indians seem to be crazy about gadgets. Unused film makes a good leaving present.

TRAVELLING WITH CHILDREN   India is extremely indulgent, tolerant and loving towards children. No hotel seems to be without children and they can be taken to all tourist monuments and to all restaurants, simple or smart, any time of day. The problems lie elsewhere.

It is vital to ensure that all regular jabs for the home country are up to day, including boosters. Then, most children can have most of the jabs listed on p. 14; it is particularly recommended that toddlers have the rabies course since they are face to face with wandering dogs and just a playful scratch could be dangerous.

It is important to pack enough anti-diarrhoea medicines (see above), plus plenty of high factor sun cream, several hats that cover the nape of the neck, and a spare pair of good-fitting worn-in sandals. Sight-seeing will be more fun with a pair of binoculars to focus in on all the carved detail of strange animals; crayons and paper, or a scrap book and glue, will also be useful for dull moments. India abounds with good bookshops. Packets of wet wipes will be essential, especially for trying to keep hands clean; some brands are antiseptic.

For a baby or toddler still in nappies, it is best to take a full supply – plenty of travellers are spotted at Heathrow with a bag of Pampers. Also, on a short trip take full supplies of the dried milk the baby is used to having, plus some dried food to help him or her acclimatise gently to local ingredients – one businesswoman took her six-month-old daughter on a three-week-long working trip, carried all her milk and food from the UK and didn't have a single hiccup. A nappy sack with attached changing mat is essential, since changing facilities for babies are rarely satisfactory.

On arrival, it is important to allow several days for children's bodies to adjust to the time, humidity, heat, water and food changes. Throughout the trip, all babies and children should be encouraged to drink plenty of extra fluids and to wash their hands as often as possible – this is especially important for the hands-in-the-mouth aged toddlers. And when they do get Delhi Belly, it is vital to treat it immediately with Rehydrat or an equivalent (or to make up mixtures of salt, sugar and water, see medicines, above) to prevent dehydration.

As with travelling with children elsewhere, short journeys with breaks to run around are usually successful and worth planning carefully – the Midway cafe-motels along the Delhi-Agra-Jaipur route make good road stops. Trains are a good way to travel, since there is usually an option for air-conditioning, and there are corridors for stretching legs and spacious lavatories; buses are quite the reverse. It is best to avoid midday travel.

For recreation, more and more hotels have swimming pools but they are usually not attended by qualified lifeguards and some are empty during the winter, so it is worth checking. See also Keeping Fit and Beautiful sections in each chapter for public swimming pools and other sports; and Space and Peace sections for local parks which are at their freshest early morning and late afternoon. Just as elsewhere in the world, children will make friends quickly.

Useful addresses

INDIAN MISSIONS ABROAD
These issue visas and permits.
High Commission for India, India House, Aldwych, London WC2 (tel: 071 836 8484). There is also an Assistant High Commission at 86 New Street, Birmingham (tel: 021 643 0366).
Embassy of India, 2107 Massachusetts Avenue, NW, Washington, DC 20008, USA (tel: 202.939.7000/9806).
Consulate General of India, 3 East 64th Street, New York, NY 10021 USA (tel: 212.879.7800).
High Commission for India, 3-5 Moonah Place, Yarralumla, Canberra, ACT2600, Australia (tel: 062 733999/733774/733875).
High Commission for India, PO Box 4045, 180 Molesworth Street, Princes Towers (10th floor), Wellington, New Zealand (tel: 736390/736391).

**GOVERNMENT OF INDIA TOURIST OFFICES
ABROAD**

Usually extremely helpful and knowledgeable staff. Offices packed with literature on every area and aspect of India. Supply lists of following year's festival dates; Indian Airlines timetable; basic maps; information on trains; and lists of government and state tourist offices and their services and tours.

7 Cork Street, London W1 (tel: 071 437 3677/8). 30 Rockefeller Plaza, Room 15, North Mezzanine, New York, NY 10020 USA (tel: 212.586.4901).

Note: Since there is no office in Australia or New Zealand, potential travellers to India are recommended to write direct to the head office, asking for information on the areas of India they wish to visit. The address is: 88 Janpath, New Delhi (tel: 3320008/3320005).

Find out more

The bulk of books written about India have been published in India or London. They fall into two broad categories: those published before the 1930s and those published since the 1960s, when the renaissance of interest in India's history and culture began and India opened up as a general travel destination. The recent publications range from huge coffee-table tomes with magnificent photographs of rarely seen tribals to very readable general histories, a plethora of Victorian diaries, countless novels by Indians and Westerners, and highly practical guides to the monuments. The few old books mentioned below are well worth seeking out in good libraries – and a good browse in the travel and India sections usually brings splendid rewards.

The following reference libraries and bookshops should help in locating titles mentioned in the bibliographies below and at the end of chapters. All will answer enquires or orders. The bookshops mail worldwide.

London

LIBRARIES

The National Art Library, Victoria and Albert Museum, London SW7 (tel: 071 589 6371). Open Tues.-Sat., 10am-5pm. Open to the public for reference.

Commonwealth Institute, Kensington High Street, London W8 (tel: 071 603 4535). Library open to the public for reference Mon.-Sat., 10am-5.00pm.

India Office Library and Records (British Library Reference Division), 197 Blackfriars Road, London SE1 (tel: 071 928 9531). Open Mon.-Fri., 9.30am-5.45pm; Sat., 9.30am-

12.45pm. Open to the public for reference. Open to members to borrow books that are up to 25 years old. Membership is by recommendation by a sponsor who belongs to a reputable firm or institution. All enquiries should be addressed to The Superintendent of Reading Rooms.

The London Library, 14 St James's Square, London SW1 (tel: 071 930 7705). Open to members only, Mon.-Sat., 9.30am-5.30pm, Thurs. until 7.30pm. Membership costs £75 per annum. Members living in London may borrow 10 books at a time; members living outside London may borrow 15 books. Address enquiries to The Librarian.

School of Oriental and African Studies, Malet Street, London WC1 (tel: 071 637 2388). Open Mon.-Thurs., 9am-8pm; Fri., 9am-6.30pm; Sat., 9.30am-12.30pm (later closings during term time). Day reference ticket available on proof of identity; annual membership for reference and lending £5 for SOAS graduates, £10 for others (and £50 deposit against borrowing books). Application forms from the Issue Desk, SOAS Library.

BOOKSHOPS

Books from India, 45 Museum Street, London WC1 (tel: 071 405 7226). The biggest stock of books and maps printed in and out of India to be found outside India. All subjects; booklists.

Daunt Books for Travellers, 83 Marylebone High Street, London W1 (tel: 071 224 2295). Huge and beautiful ground floor and basement stocked by knowledgeable staff with books published all over the world. Usually open until late.

Hatchards Ltd, 187 Piccadilly, London W1 (tel: 071 437 3924), covers all subjects, with a very helpful travel section on the ground floor.

St George's Gallery Books Ltd, Art Booksellers, 8 Duke Street, London SW1 (tel: 071 930 0935). Adept at obtaining any book in print, not just on art.

Travel Bookshop, 13 Blenheim Crescent, London W11 (tel: 071 229 5260). Stocks guides, maps, history and fiction currently in print, plus out of print titles. Knowledgeable, helpful staff. Supplies an Indian list.

The Travellers' Bookshop, 25 Cecil Court, London WC2 (tel: 071 836 9132). Good wideranging stock, and helpful staff.

Edward Stanford Ltd, 12 Long Acre, London WC2 (tel: 071 836 1321). Stocks maps, guides and travel writing. Booklist available.

Waterstone & Co. Ltd, 121 Charing Cross Road, London WC2 (tel: 071 434 4291). Well-briefed, efficient staff.

Note: In the US, Travelers Bookstore at 22 West 52nd Street, New York (tel: 212 664 0995) is run by knowledgeable staff, takes orders and credit card payments by phone and posts books to customers.

Select background bibliography

For titles on more specific or local topics, see Find Out More section at the end of each chapter.

PRACTICAL HELP

Health is for most people the greatest worry about travelling in the sub-continent. These books should dispell most anxiety.

Dawood, R.: *Travellers' Health*, London, revised ed. 1989

Hatt, J.: *The Tropical Traveller: An Essential Guide to Travel in Hot Climates*, London, 1982

Turner, Dr A. C.: *The Traveller's Health Guide*, London, 1985

GENERAL GUIDE BOOKS

India – a travel survival kit, Lonely Planet, South Yarra, Australia, 1981, 4th edition 1990. Jam-packed with essential factual information – no hotel, restaurant, bus route or train connection is left unturned. The best available for practical help.

Nagel's Guide to India and Nepal, Geneva, Switzerland, 1980. Laboriously comprehensive.

A Handbook for Travellers in India, Pakistan, Nepal, Bangladesh and Sri Lanka (Ceylon), by L. F. Rushbrook Williams, 22nd edition, John Murray, London, 1978. The classic Victorian travel book, originally published in 1859, but still strong on itineraries, architecture and off-beat treats. This will be its last edition.

India, Insight Guide, APA Productions, London, 1985. Introductory essays on aspects of India punctuated by almost-too-good photographs – the Insight trademark.

Guide Bleu, Harrap out of print but stocked in good libraries, available in French and English and not to be confused with the Blue Guide series, this comes with strong recommendations from well-travelled art historians.

The Cadogan Guide: India London, revised edition 1989, good introductory guide by S. Kusy.

SPECIALISED GUIDE BOOKS

An Illustrated Guide to Delhi, Agra and Jaipur by Louise Nicholson, 1989, revised edition 1991. An in-depth look at all aspects of the Golden Triangle.

India by Rail by Royston Ellis, 1989, available from Brandt Publications, 41 Nortoft Road, Chalfont St Peter, Buckinghamshire. The essential manual for train travellers.

Moghul India by Giles Tillotson, London, 1990. Slim but useful book, part of a new series, *Architectural Guides for Travellers*.

The Penguin Guide to the Monuments of India, Vols I & II, London, 1990. Volume I covering Buddhist, Jain and Hindu buildings is by George Michell, volume II covering Islamic, Rajput and European buildings is by Philip Davies. Text and plans indispensable for anyone interested in exploring India's multitude of monuments.

NOVELS, TRAVEL WRITING AND PERSONAL VIEWS

Note: Most public libraries will turn up several published Indian diaries; those listed below are especially interesting and have recently been reprinted.

Ackerley, J.R.: *Hindoo Holiday*, London, 1931, 1983

Allen, C., ed.: *Plain Tales from the Raj*, London, 1975

Brennan, J.: *Curries and Bugles: A cookbook of the British Raj*, London, 1990

Cameron, J.: *An Indian Summer*, London, 1974

Chaudhuri, N. C.: *The Autobiography of an Unknown India*, London, 1951 and 1991; this recounts his early Calcutta life and the complexities of India and the British; its sequal is *Thy Hand, Great Anarch!: India 1921-1952*, London, 1987

Collins, L. and Lapierre, D.: *Freedom at Midnight*, India, 1976

Cowasjee, S, ed: *More Stories from the Raj and After, from Kipling to the Present Day*, London, 1986

Desai, A: *Clear Light of Day*, London, 1980, just one of many novels set in India – this one in Delhi.

Eden, Emily: *Up the Country: Letters form India*, London, 1972

Fay, E.: *Original Letters From India*, edited by E. M. Forster, introduced by M. M. Kaye, London, 1986

Fishlock, T.: *India File: Inside the Subcontinent*, London, 1983

Forster, E. M.: *Passage to India*, London, 1924, 1983

Foster, W. ed.: *Early Travels in India*, London, 1921

Frater, A.: *Chasing the Monsoon*, London, 1990

Galbraith, J. K.: *John Kenneth Galbraith introduces India*, London, 1974

Jhabvala, R. P.: *To Whom She Will*, the first of many novels and volumes of short stories set in India

Kaye, M. M.: *The Far Pavilions*, London, 1978. Part One of her autobiography, *The Sun in the Morning*, was published in London, 1990

Kaye, M. M., ed: *Moon of Other Day, M M Kaye's Kipling, Favourite Verses*, London, 1988

Keay, J.: *Into India*, London, 1973

Kipling, R.: *Kim*, London, 1901: his copious other writing on India, particularly his short stories and verse are found in *Plain Tales from the*

Hills, Barrack-Room Ballads, Just So Stories, Jungle Book and *Wee Willie Winkie*, etc.

Lloyd, S.: *An Indian Attachment*, London, 1984

Longford, E., intro.: *A Viceroy's India: leaves from Lord Curzon's notebook*, London, 1984

Mehta, G.: *Karma Cola*, Glasgow, 1981

Mehta, G.: *Raj*, London, 1989

Mehta, Ved: *Walking the Indian Streets*, London, 1961. His many other books about India include *Portrait of India*, *The New India* and *A Family Affair: India under Three Prime Ministers*

Mohanti, P: *Changing Village, Changing Life*, London, (1991). This and earlier books such as *My Village, My Life* (1973) and *Through Brown Eyes* (1985) are inspired by his Orissa home, Nanpur.

Morris, Jan: *The Pax Britannica Trilogy*, London, 1968-78

Morris, John: *Eating the Indian Air*, London, 1968

Murphy, D.: *Full Tilt*, London, 1965

Naipal, V.S.: *Area of Darkness* (London, 1964), *A Wounded Civilisation* (London, 1977) and *India, A Million Mutinies Now*, (London 1990) are his diverse responses to India

Narayan, R. K.:*Under the Banyan Tree and Other Stories* (1985); his many other novels inspired by his Mysore home include *Swami and Friends* (1935), *The Man-Eater of Malgudi* (1961), *The Painter of Signs* (1977) and *Talkative Man* (1985).

Premchand: *Godan*, Bombay, 1979, just one of his many novels and short stories

Rushdie, S.: *Midnight's Children*, London, 1981

Scindia, V.: *Princess, the Autobiography of the Dowager Maharanai of Gwalior*, London, 1985

Shand, M.: *Travels with my Elephant*, London, 1991

Singh, K.: *I Shall Not Hear the Nightingale*, Bombay, 1983, one of his many books on India

Scott, P.: *The Raj Quartet*, London, 1966-75; he followed this with *Staying On* (1977)

Theroux, P.: *Great Railway Bazaar*, London, 1980

Tytler, H.: *An Englishwoman in India: The Memoirs of Harriet Tytler 1828-1858*, London, 1988

Wilson, Lady: *Letters from India*, introduced by Pat Barr, London, 1984

Wood, M.: *Third Class Ticket*, London, 1983

THE HINDU EPICS

So much of Indian life, religion, festivals, painting and sculpture and art relates to the two long epics, the Mahabharata and the Ramayana (see Glossary), that curiosity might be roused to find out more about them. Of the several translations, those by C. Rajagopalachari are both very readable: *Mahabharata*, Bombay, 1979, and *Ramayana*, Bombay, 1978, both published by Bharatiya Vidya Bhavan. If these are too long and confusing, R. K. Narayan's *The Mahabharata* (London, 1978) and S. R. Rao's illustrated *The Mahabharata* (Hyderabad, 1985) and *The Ramayana* (Hyderabad, 1988) provide clear plot

and personality outlines. Also, there are amusing cartoon comics, each with a short episode from one of the epics, available worldwide wherever there is an Indian community, and on every news-stand in India.

HISTORY, SOCIETY AND RELIGION

The Cambridge History of India, vols I-VI, still provides a good basis – Cambridge's new 30-volume *History of India* is currently emerging, treating subjects thematically rather than chronologically, e.g. C. A. Bayly's *Indian Society and the Making of the British Empire* (1987)

Akbar, M. J.:*Nehru, The Making of India*, London, 1989; his other books include *India: The Siege Within* (London, 1985) and *Riot After Riot* (India, 1988)

Allen, C. and Dwivedi, S.: *Lives of the Indian Princes*, London, 1985

Anand, M.J. and Dance, L.,eds: *Kama Sutra*, New Delhi, 1982

Baker, S.: *Caste: At Home in Hindu India*, London, 1990

Basham, A.L.: *The Wonder that was India*, London 1954, revised 1985

Barr, P.: *The Memsahibs, In Praise of the Women of Victorian India*

Dowson, J.: *A Classical Dictionary of Hindu Mythology and Religion*, Calcutta, 1982. Of the several dictionaries of the gods, this is one of the clearest to follow

Gandhi, M. K.: *An Autobiography or The Story of My Experiments with Truth*, first published 1927-9, London, 1982

Hibbert, C.: *History of the Indian Mutiny*, London, 1978

Huyler, S. P.: *Village India*, New York, 1985

Humphreys, Christmas: *Buddhism*, London, 1951

Kulke, H. and Rothermund, D.: *A History of India*, Delhi, 1987

Macaro J., trans: *The Bhagavad Gita*, London, 1962

Mason, P.: *The Men Who Ruled India*, London 1953-4 and 1986

Mehta, Ved: *Mahatma Gandhi and His Apostles*, London, 1982

Moraes, Dom: *Mrs Gandhi*, London, 1980

Moon, Sir P.: *The British Conquest and Dominion of India*, London, 1989

Moorhouse, G.: *India Britannica*, London, 1983

Nehru, J.: *An Autobiography*, Delhi 1936, paperbacks Delhi 1980 and London 1989; this account of India's freedom struggle is complemented by his *The Discovery of India* and *Glimpses of World History*

Patnaik, N.:*A Second Paradise: Indian Courtly Life 1590-1947*, London, 1985

Pouchepadas, J. and Nou, J.-L.: *The Last Maharajas*, Delhi, 1981

Sen, K. M.: *Hinduism*, London, 1961

Spear, P. and Thapar, R.: *A History of India*, vols. 1 and 2, London, 1978

Tully, M.: *From Raj to Rajiv*, London, 1987

Watson, F.: *A Concise History of India*, London, 1974

Woodford, Peggy: *Rise of the Raj*, London, 1978

Yule, H. and Burnell, A. C.: *Hobson-Jobson: A Glossary of Colloquial Anglo-Indian Words and Phrases . . .* , first published in 1903, new edition edited by W. Crooke, Delhi, 1984

ART, ARCHITECTURE AND PERFORMING ARTS

Bayly, C., ed: *The Raj: India and the British 1600-1947*, London, 1990. An art catalogue with extended historical essays

Binney, E.: *The Mughal and Deccani schools from the collection of Edwin Binney, 3rd*, Portland, Oregon, 1973

Baroda, Maharaja of, and Fass, V.: *The Palaces of India*, London, 1980

Binney, E. and Archer, W. G.: *Rajput Miniatures from the collection of Edwin Binney, 3rd*, Portland, Oregon, 1968

Brown, P.: *Indian Architecture*, vols. I and II, Bombay, 1942, later reprints

Chandra, P.: *The Sculpture of India 3000BC-AD1300*, Washington, 1985

Davies, P.: *Splendours of the Raj:British Architecture in India 1660-1947*, London, 1985

Falk, T. and Archer, M.: *Indian Miniatures in the India Office Library*, London, 1981

Fass, V.: *The Forts of India*, London, 1986

Guy, J. and Swallow, D., eds: *Arts of India 1550-1900*, London, 1990

Hambley, G.: *Cities of Mughal India*, London, 1968

Harle, J. C.: *The Art and Architecture of the Indian Subcontinent*, London, 1986

Huntington, S. L.: *The Art of Ancient India*, New York, 1985

The India Magazine, monthly periodical concerning all aspects of Indian arts and culture, founded in 1980, on sale at news stands

In the Image of Man, Festival of India Exhibition Catalogue, Arts Council of Great Britain, London, 1982

Jayakar, P.: *The Earthen Drum: An Introduction to the Ritual Arts of India*, New Delhi, 1980

Keay, J.: *India Discovered; The Achievement of the British Raj*, London, 1981

Marg: Periodical concentrating on the arts and culture of India, often devoting an issue to a single topic, published in Bombay, back copies often sold in bookshops.

Morris, Jan and Winchester, S.: *Stones of Empire: The Buildings of the Raj*, Oxford and New York, 1983

Tadgell, C.: *The History of Architecture in India*, London, 1990

Tillotson, G.: *The Rajput Palaces: The development of an architectural style 1450-1750*, London, 1987

Tillotson, G.: *The Tradition of Indian Architecture: Continuity, Controversy and Change since 1850*, London, 1989

Welch, S. C.: *India: Art and Culture 1300-1900*, New York, 1985

WILDLIFE AND CONSERVATION

Ali, S.: *The Book of Indian Birds*, Bombay 1979

Pereira, W. and Seabrook, J.: *Asking the Earth: Farms, Forestry and Survival in India*, London, 1990

Sinclair, T.: *Indian Wildlife*, Singapore, 1987, part of the APA/Insight Guide series

Woodcock, M.: *Collins Handguide to the Birds of the Indian Sub- Continent*, London, 1980

GENERAL PHOTOGRAPHIC BOOKS

Gandhi, I. and Nou, J.-L.: *Eternal India*, New Delhi, 1980

Lloyd, B.: *The Colours of India*, London, 1988

Rai, R.: *Dreams of India*, London, 1988

India survival code

Finding your kind of happiness in India

Everyone has their own idea of a good time. If it is pressing buttons, eating green salads, having a clockwork time-table and painting the town red every night, then India is not for you. India's feasts lie elsewhere, among its landscape, colour, peoples, traditions and its extraordinary service. It is a country accustomed to pampering. In Europe, good service has almost disappeared except for a large fee. In the United States, good service is more common – but also at a price. However, India still provides willing service – and often ingenious solutions to practical problems – at a relatively small cost. And it is done with a smile and good grace. But it is important to reward good service with a suitable fee (see Tipping and Bargaining, below).

Indian comforts are sometimes topsy-turvy. For instance, a hired car always comes with a chauffeur, costing roughly Rs600-800 per day (constant petrol increases are reflected in car hire prices) but the roads are often a single track of bumpy, dusty tarmac. You can stay in a four-roomed suite of a palace, but there might not be sufficient electric light to read by.

For visitors used to the way things work in Europe and America, there are a string of potential disasters, but they can be easily averted. For instance, in the West a train ticket is often bought 30 seconds before the train departs. In India, it can take hours of queuing, first for the ticket, then to reserve the berth. The process is best done the day before, preferably using a hotel travel desk to do it for you for a small fee.

Below are some tips to help you find happiness and avoid disaster.

Manners

Indian hospitality is so indulgent to Western habits that it is easy to forget that there is a strong Indian code of politeness.

LANGUAGE Because Indians speak a very colloquial English, with plenty of idioms ('hop in the back', 'just a tick', etc.), it is easy to assume you are understanding one another perfectly. This is not necessarily the case. Misunderstandings are as easy between a Westerner and an Indian as between an American and an Englishman. The most common difficulty for a Westerner is to understand when an Indian means yes and when he means no. A smile and a curious movement of the head as if it is about to drop off means yes. The problem is that it can also mean 'I don't know'. In addition, there is a natural eagerness to please, so if you ask the way in the street you will probably be pointed in one direction whether or not it is the correct one; this is all part of the Indian adventure, and you will eventually find your quest.

GETTING YOUR OWN WAY Almost certainly, there will be a moment when you will no longer find the incomprehensible Indian ways deliciously mysterious but very annoying. At these moments, to repeat your needs slowly and with an enormous smile is likely to get results far more speedily than bursting into a tirade, which will bring incomprehension from the very people you are trying to communicate with. If stronger action is needed to remedy the problem, the best policy is to go straight to the top, be it to the director of a travel firm or to the manager of a hotel. Should you still be dissatisfied, put your complaint in writing as you would all over the world.

SPEED The all-pervading bureaucracy in India covers up a great deal of laziness. With a bit of persuasion, information that you have been assured cannot be discovered will somehow be found out, and jobs that have been declared impossible will be done. The best policy is to persist and never take no for an answer. Conversely, since India is always a surprise, some things will happen lightning fast.

DOING BUSINESS Many Indian businessmen are extremely hard-working and dynamic. An Indian is often happy to make appointments from dawn through until midnight. However, he is also liable to arrive at your hotel at any hour and to ring you from the lobby, expecting to hold a meeting in your room immediately. Alternatively, he will patiently await your return to the hotel for several hours. Since this concept of constant accessibility is part of Indian life, and since the telephones are unreliable, it is quite acceptable for you to arrive at an Indian office and introduce yourself without prior notice.

PESTERING In the cities and at tourist sites,

you will be offered all sorts of services. You may be invited to see a shop or factory, which you may wish to accept. But beware of buying anything until you compare prices in other places. You may be offered a guided tour of a monument. But, unless the guide is hired from the Tourist Office and has taken the full government training, he is unlikely to enlighten you very much; going to the chowkidar (guard) of the monument should restore your peace. A lad offering to find you a hotel (or an airport taxi driver offering a similar service) is likely to be a professional tout who receives payment from the hotel for every guest he brings in. You can be sure that he will not have your interests at heart. To reject any of these offers only requires a very firm 'No, thank you'. Pesterers have a knack of knowing those who mean it.

BEGGING   Begging is part of Indian life, despite being officially illegal. Beggars around the big hotels are not going to starve that night if you fail to empty your purse. These beggars are professionals, working in gangs for a master, each group with its own beat. By giving, you perpetuate a pernicious system. As one Westerner who has travelled much in India with tourists concluded: 'The supreme arrogance of dispensing relatively large amounts of money to the poor in cities or in rural areas is perhaps the single most destructive action of tourists in India'.

The serious poverty of India lies off the regular tourist routes and would be upsetting for most Westerners to encounter. To remedy it requires far more commitment than a few rupees. So, if you wish to give money to a beggar, it is best to give a small amount (well under Rs5). But beware: you will get no more peace from other beggars, so give only shortly before leaving an area. A far better way of helping is to give to a reputable and registered charity when you return home. There is a huge variety, each focusing on India's different problems – cities, rural villages, families, children, schools, the physically handicapped, etc.

BARGAINING   Also part of Indian life. From the moment you arrive at the airport, you begin to bargain, unless you are being met. A taxi fare that might appear very cheap to you may well be four times the going rate. It should be as much a matter of pride for you to play the game of haggling as it is for the taxi driver. He will still end up with a good deal and you will pay less. Both parties will be happy with the outcome. The same principle applies to bargaining for all other human services and to all shopping. You may be absolutely sure an Indian will never under-sell his labour or his wares. If in doubt about a price, ask your hotel reception desk for advice; in the case of taxi charges, ask the driver to wait and check with the hotel before paying him.

TIPPING   Lavish tipping is not as common in India as in the West, although the habit and expectancy is growing. The usual tip for carrying luggage, at the airport or anywhere else, is Rs5 per bag. (Where the airport has a baggage charge per piece, you do not have to tip the porter further.) Hotels will add various taxes and sometimes a service charge to your bill. You may feel that that is enough. But, if you have had a regular room boy or maid, it is customary to give him or her a tip of about Rs5-10 per day handed over personally. Be sure to ignore all those who arrive to witness your departure and claim to have served you. If you hire a car and driver, a good driver should be given a tip, usually about Rs30-50 for a full day. The extent of a guide's service varies greatly but, if you feel pleased, a tip of Rs30-50 for a day's work is appropriate. You are not obliged to tip any form of taxi or rickshaw transport, nor any grade of restaurant.

DRESS   Transparent and low-cut dresses and very short skirts and short shorts do not go down well with the majority of people. And they are absolutely disapproved of in holy places. Leather (belts, shoes, bags, etc.) will also offend in holy places – in some temples, such as the Kali Temple at Amber, visitors will be asked to remove them before entering.

INDIAN HOMES   If invited to dinner at someone's home, it is usual to arrive a little after the time invited, except where it is an official event. A present of flowers, European chocolates or anything brought from abroad goes down well. Otherwise, a box of good Indian sweetmeats is most appropriate. Indian evening timetables follow a regular pattern. Hours of drinking, whether alcoholic or not, end with very late dinner – sometimes around midnight – eaten very fast before everyone goes home. Chatting Westerners quite often miss out entirely. It is certainly a good idea to have a snack before going out. In more traditional homes, the women will probably not appear.

PHOTOGRAPHY   In addition to removing shoes at temples and mosques, many of the faithful will not wish to be photographed. Throughout India, women and all Muslims may well not like the camera. The best thing is to ask if in doubt. It is far safer to take film home to be developed. Quality in India is disappointingly low.

1. Pipal (ashvatha, pipal) 2. Ashok (ashok) 3. Neem (limbe, neem) 4. Tamarind (imli, chinch) 5. Crape jasmine (chandni, tagara) 6. Banyan, Indian fig bar, vata) 7. Mango (amb) 8. Black plum (jaman, jambul) 9. Indian laburnam (amaltas, gurmala, suvarnaka) 10. Areca palm, betel-nut palm (supari) 11. Flame of the forest (butea gum, dhak, palasha) 12. Kapok (sveta salmali, hattian)

1. Hoopoe (hudhud) 2. Roseringed parakeet (lybar tota) 3. Peacock (mor, mayura) 4. Redvented bulbul (bulbul, guldum) 5. Whitebacked or Bengal vulture (gidh) 6. Black drongo, king crow (bujanga, kotwal, kalkalachi) 7. Roller, blue jay (nilkant, sabzak) 8. Cattle egret (surkhia bagla, gai bagla) 9. Common pariah kite (cheel) 10. Indian myna (desi myna) 11. Red-wattled lapwing (tituri, titeeri)

Money

The Indian rupee is divided into 100 paise. A good supply of smaller coins pays for all the things that are constantly being done for you. As in Italy, there is a constant small-change problem.

CHANGING MONEY   There is a choice between your hotel, which is quicker and open all hours, and the bank, which usually has a better rate but is slow and generally open only during the morning. Unless you are counting every paise, the hotel is better. Be sure to keep all certificates of transactions – you will need them for certain purchases in rupees (e.g. train tickets) and if you wish to change spare rupees back into hard currency at the airport when you leave. Ensure that you are not given any torn notes as they may be refused in shops.

COUNTING   India does not count in thousands and millions but in lakhs and crores. A lakh is a hundred thousand and a crore is ten million. Thus, the official population of India at the 1981 census is written 68,51,84,692 or 68.52 crores – incidentally, it is now estimated to be well over 80 crores.

SPENDING YOUR MONEY   Large hotels, shops, restaurants, and Indian Airlines take credit cards. And, mercifully, the bills usually take several weeks to get back home. It is tempting to spend now and pay much later. However, you will need cash at the very small hotels, rest houses, etc., and for transport, for buying in bazaars and for tipping.

Arrival in India

TIME   Standard Time is 5½ hours ahead of Greenwich Mean Time and 9½ hours ahead of US EST. Despite its size, India has a single time zone.

CUSTOMS   It is as well to have your inoculation certificates with your passport. You may also be asked how much money, in cash and travellers cheques, you are bringing into the country (see p. 14). Currently a video camera must be declared and entered in your passport. Also, such gadgets as typewriters, word processors and special camera equipment will sometimes be entered, too. Anything entered in the passport must be taken out of India each time you leave, even if the trip is for 2 days to Nepal; it will be marked in your passport and re-entered on your return into India.

AIRPORT TO HOTEL   Once through customs, you may be faced with a crowd of porters jostling very close to you, all offering to carry your bags or find you a taxi or a hotel. The best policy is to choose one person very firmly. The rest will disappear immediately.

If you are being met by your hotel, someone should make themselves known to you if you just stand around and look as if you are waiting to be met. A few hotels have cars at the airport as a matter of course, so it is worth enquiring at the Tourist Office or Hotels Reservations Desk. Delhi airport has an official taxi booking system and rate card.

If you are not being met, while waiting for your luggage to come up you can go to the bank to buy rupees. You can also go to the Tourist Office desk to find out the going rate for a taxi to your hotel and to pick up maps and local information.

Armed with the knowledge of the going rate, you can bargain with the taxi driver until he comes down to the right price. If you do not come to an agreement, there is always another taxi driver who will. Once the price is agreed, it is important to see your luggage is all safely put in the taxi. Only then should you pay off your porter. If a fellow passenger is travelling your way, it is perfectly acceptable to share a taxi into town and each be delivered to a different address. Alternatively, you can go straight to the taxi rank, ask the driver to pay off your porter and, on arrival at your hotel, ask the driver to wait while you change money (which is far quicker than at the airport).

Throughout India, meters on taxis and auto rickshaws are liable to be broken – or drivers will claim they are broken. Occasionally, there is a meter that works. If so, it is important to ensure that it is started only when you begin your journey.

Hotels

CHECKING IN   Even the plusher hotels give off-season discounts, so it is a good idea to enquire when checking in whether any are available. It is quite common to be told: 'I am very sorry but we can only offer you 25% discount.' Occasionally the Front Manager will look blank when you arrive, denying all knowledge of your booking. Producing the written confirmation helps him find the booking after all.

It is always worth asking for a room overlooking the sea, the hills or the town, whatever is appropriate, and then going to look at your room before the luggage goes up. If you are shown one over the staff quarters, ask to see another until you find one you like. If you requested a particular room when you booked, producing the written confirmation that it would be yours if possible can help – but such rooms can rarely be guaranteed. If you do not ask for one of the best rooms, somebody else certainly will.

SECURITY It is wise to keep a close eye on your luggage to ensure it arrives at your room and not somebody else's. At night, you should always lock your room from the inside. And be wary of balcony windows and ground floor windows, too – in some areas, it is the monkeys who are the thieves. If in doubt, close them and use the air-conditioning. Most hotels have a safe for valuables such as jewellery, tickets, passport and money. It is very unwise to leave any valuables in your room.

USING THE HOTEL All the big hotels are well equipped with what are by world standards and despite India's high inflation rate, reasonably cheap services. Therefore, whether on business or on holiday, you can be free of drudgery. In the first place, no matter whether you arrive in town by train, boat, plane or bus, the hotel can meet you. If you will be leaving town by air, your first and most essential job is to ask the hotel to have your seat re-confirmed, or it may be given to someone else. This should be done as far in advance as possible (the fee is Rs15-30) and then once more 48 hours before departure. If you need train tickets bought and train seats reserved (often two separate operations), the hotel will do that, too. Many hotels have in-house travel agents who will advise and book everything (see Travel Reservations, below).

LAUNDRY SERVICE Usually very quick and efficient (including dry cleaning), although prices are rising. The tariff is often two-tiered: normal and same-day express.

MUSTY SMELLS Some hotel rooms are well-aired; others are not; still others reek of stale spices or the kitchen's dish of the day. Burning some joss sticks bought in the local market cures the lot.

ILLNESS Big hotels have a good doctor on call. He can be summoned very quickly and should always be consulted in cases of bad Delhi Belly, dizziness or a bad cut. There may also be a chemist in the hotel shopping arcade.

ROOM SERVICE Often very extensive, with elaborate six-page menus in your room. It usually operates all day or even, as in many city hotels, around the clock.

The hotel Bell Captain (Head Porter) keeps stamps and wraps and sends parcels. He gets you taxis and, in Delhi, keeps copies of the useful publication, *Delhi Diary*. If you are keen on experiencing Indian post office queues, then

allow several hours. The Bell Captain also orders and delivers newspapers.

HOTEL BOOKSTALLS Stock newspapers, including the *International Herald Tribune*, also magazines, maps, novels, books on India and the best quality postcards. They stock guidebooks and will also quickly obtain almost any book not displayed on the shelves. Guides published by the Archaeological Survey of India are worth seeking out at their headquarters in Delhi, next to the National Museum.

TELEVISION The national television network, Doordarshan, alternates English programmes with ones in Hindi and the regional languages – a good chance to catch a colourful Hindi epic on Sunday morning, the latest Indian answer to *Dynasty* and the main English news programmes at 8.45am and 9.30pm. Some hotels have Western video films; a few in the big cities have the Cable News Network news service.

TELEPHONE AND BUSINESS FACILITIES Some hotels have direct dial telephones for local calls, and a few for international calls as well. Operational success varies but the operator will help. Locally, it is often quicker, and expected, simply to go directly to the destination. Telephone directories are a confusing delight. Subscribers are often listed under their employers (who have supplied the telephone), with both business and 'residence' numbers.

If calling through the operator, long-distance calls within India are graded: top grade is called lightning, the fastest and most expensive; international calls have to be booked and can take time. The hotel mark-up on telephone charges can be very high, so it is wise to check before telephoning. Cables can be urgent or ordinary. Urgent get there; ordinary may not. Hotel secretarial services are usually excellent. Telexes have a variable success rate in reaching their destination. Fax has arrived in big city hotels but it is expensive. The express postal service is good, and couriers such as Federal Express have a large network of reliable local agents.

The hotel will also help with sport, leisure, beauty, fitness, culture and it often has extremely good shops, patronised by locals who know what's what. Where there is any night life, it is usually at the hotel.

CHECKING OUT AND HOTEL TAXES Since most international flights depart early in the morning, it is wise to ask for the bill the night before departure to avoid a rush or a queue on leaving. On checking the bill, it is essential to understand which taxes, both central and local, you are required to pay. Current legislation should be checked with the accounts department and, if necessary, clarified with the duty manager. For instance, the Luxury Tax (also called Expenditure Tax) charged in hotels whose basic room price of more than Rs400 per night is payable by foreigners only if they are settling their bill in Indian currency; if not, although it will have been added to the bill (a government requirement), it should be shown at the end of that same bill to have been subtracted. For a stay at a deluxe hotel, this may amount to quite a sum, and there have been numerous complaints of the tax not being subtracted. The Sales Tax levied in restaurants on food and drink is payable by all.

Information

NEWSPAPERS The Indian newspaper industry flourishes, printing the staggering figure of more than 22,000 newspapers of which 1,802 are dailies. Some 4,000 are in English, the second most popular newspaper language after Hindi, so there is a range of English-language papers in every area. The principal daily English newspapers in India are *The Hindu*, published in Delhi and the South; *The Indian Express*, published in more than a dozen cities all over India to achieve the largest English language circulation, and *The Times of India*, which publishes in Delhi, Bombay, Bangalore and some northern cities.

The newspapers provide all-India and local news, views and gossip as well as an entertainments section listing cultural performances and film and radio broadcasting programmes. (Television is barely worth watching.) Advertisements are a treat to read, particularly the matchmaking marriage columns of Sunday's *The Times of India*. Currently the big press barons include the Birlas, who own *The Hindustan Times*, and the Goenkas of Madras, who own *The Indian Express*.

MAGAZINES Big business, too. General news and a good read are found in *India Today*, *The Week* (published in Kerala), *Sunday* and *The Illustrated Weekly of India*. *Business India* is the best-read business magazine; *The India Magazine*, published monthly, is the best for general culture. There is a deluge of film magazines, full of bitchy gossip and interviews, of which the best-read is *Screen*. For children, delightful strip-cartoon comics recount episodes from the great Hindu epics – a good way of brushing up on who's who in the gods.

TOURIST INFORMATION Found in two separate organisations. There are 21 Government of India Tourist Offices spread over the country. Each has an excellent and well-trained staff; many are bright young sparks with more

than one degree and dreams of going to work in America. They carry information on the area they serve as well as on everywhere else in India. The three best are in Delhi, Bombay and Calcutta where a team of India experts manages to answer almost any question and the shelves of their offices are piled high with informative brochures and city maps. The Government of India Tourist Offices often take bookings for ITDC tours (see below).

The second organisation is the network of State Tourist Offices, again often staffed by very knowledgeable people. However, they only hold information on their own state and are remarkably blinkered about their neighbours, however near. The most extreme example is Agra, in Uttar Pradesh, on the borders of Madhya Pradesh and Rajasthan, where you have to skip between three state tourist offices to get a full idea of the sights in the area.

In cities where there are central and state tourist offices, each usually keeps different information, so both are worth visiting. As they are government-run bodies, their advice may sometimes be biased, such as in giving a blanket recommendation to government emporia for shopping or state-run hotels. But their sightseeing tours are often extremely good value and led by good quality guides. In the main, you get a far better introduction with a morning's tour than you would on your own, even if you hire a car and driver.

ITDC AND STATE TDC Both central and state tourist organisations have long-winded titles. In their literature and in the following pages, they are frequently abbreviated from Government of India Tourism Development Corporation to ITDC and from, say, Kerala Tourism Development Corporation to KTDC.

While the tourist offices carry certain information, the hotel management often know the city's sports, restaurant and shopping facilities better. Where membership is required for, say, golf or tennis, someone on the hotel staff can often introduce a guest. People in the hotel business invariably know where the best haunts are to find good local food, although these may well be simple cafés in bazaars and hotel staff will need some persuasion that you are seeking good food rather than fancy surroundings. The many smart women now working in the hotel trade certainly know the best and cleverest places to shop. Furthermore, the really big hotels have a hospitality desk devoted to helping guests find what they want in town.

BOOKSHOPS The big cities are well equipped. These are the places to get stocked up with information for the rest of the trip. Since shops are usually small and piled high, it is worth asking for the books you want, just in case they need to be fetched from the go-down (warehouse). All too often the guardian of a fantastic site says cheerily: 'Sorry, no guide books here, madam. But you can get one in Delhi.' This is not much use if you are in Karnataka. In addition to its bookshops, Delhi has a tourist office for every state and the central office of the Archaeological Survey, a gold-mine of superb publications.

NAMES, ADDRESSES AND INITIALS Many streets have two names – pre-Independence and post-Independence. Locals usually refer to the former; most town plans are printed using the latter. For instance, the main street of Madras is known to all as Mount Road but is officially Anna Salai. Few people, even taxi-drivers, know precise addresses and some quite important buildings include 'behind' or 'near' or 'opposite' in their official address. Further-more, the Indians have a penchant for bestow-ing very long names on streets and states but re-ferring to them always by initials. For example, Benoy- Badal-Dinesh Bagh in Calcutta is known as BBD Bagh. Almost every town has an MG Road, standing for Mahatma Gandhi. The first question one Indian asks of another when they meet is where he comes from. The answer may well be MP, UP and HP (meaning Madhya, Uttar or Himachal Pradesh). The cult of initials extends even to people. A man may be known by all his friends and work colleagues as VJ or SK without anyone ever asking what the letters stand for.

Directions are often given by the most fami-liar landmarks, cinemas, just as pubs are used in Britain. A building will be 'just by The Majestic' or 'near The Paradise'.

Travel reservations

TRAVEL AGENTS As in all countries, some are better than others. The good Indian travel agents are efficient, reliable and still very cheap. And they save you endless bother. Some have offices inside hotels and keep very long hours. They will meet you from the airport, make hotel reservations, organise transport and car hire, buy tickets, arrange cultural programmes, wild-life safaris and have their own package tours. Their regional offices are spread throughout India. Among the biggest and best are:
Mercury Travels, founded in 1951 by M. S. Oberoi who also began the big hotel chain. 8 branches. 4A Ground Floor, Jeevan Tara Building, Parlia-ment Street, New Delhi (tel: 312008; telex: 031 3207)
SITA, begun by an American in 1933 as Student International Travel Association. In India since 1954 and claims the highest turnover. 15 branches. Head office: F-12 Connaught Place,

New Delhi (tel: 3311122/3314181; telex: 3162732; fax: 3324652)
TCI (Travel Corporation (India) claims to be the biggest Indian travel agency conglomerate. 24 branches plus representatives in another 23 cities. Head office: Travel Corporation (India) Ltd, Chander Mukhi, Nariman Point, Bombay (tel: 2021881; telex: 2366/3983; fax: 2029424)
Trade Wings founded in 1949, now covers India and boasts the greatest number of tickets sold through any agency. 16 branches. Head office: 30 K Dubash Marg, Fort, Bombay (tel: 2044233/ 2044219)

INTERNAL FLIGHTS The golden rule is to re-confirm your seat as soon as you arrive in the town where you are to take a plane. This way, you are assured of your seat. At the moment, it is impossible to confirm from another city. For instance, if the flight is from Jaipur, it must be confirmed in Jaipur. Therefore, if your journey requires two or three flights, you cannot con-firm right through. You just have to hope all will run smoothly. Sometimes it does not and you may have to wait for a second flight or, more usually, stay overnight. This is one reason why a timetable in India must be flexible. Indian Air-lines are computerised but still overbook their inadequate number of flights; Vayudoot, not yet flying the heavy tourist routes, often have seats.

If you want to get on a flight and do not have a confirmed seat, it is usually quite easy, except on the week-end flights out from and back to the big cities. It is best to arrive at the airport in good time as seat allocation is on the first come, first served basis. Each would-be passenger is told his place in the cancellation queue. Even very high numbers often get a seat.

If an Indian Airlines flight is full and Vayu-doot operate the same route, it is worth seeing if they have spare seats. (See air routes diagram.)

Both Indian Airlines and Vayudoot bookings can be done by the hotel travel desk or by a local travel agent. Vayudoot flights can also be booked at their airports or one of the five regional offices:
Air India Building, 1st floor, Nariman Point, Bombay (tel: 2048585)
Neelanda Building, 28b Shakespeare Sarani, Calcutta (tel: 447062/433091)
Malhotra Building, Janpath, Delhi (tel: 622122/ 623056)
Samrat Complex (2nd fl), Saifabad, Hyderabad (tel: 234717)
26 Wellington Estate, Commander-in-Chief Road, Madras (tel: 869901/861442)

CAR HIRE A car always comes with a driver and costs Rs600-800 for an eight-hour day. Price is measured according to hours and distance.

Petrol is very expensive in India. A hired car may be relatively expensive but it is the best possible sight-seeing investment: you can go where you want, when you want, stop when you want and look out of the window non-stop without having an accident. To keep a driver for a few days, you can strike a good bargain for a round sum that works out well below the local daily rate. On tour, he should be given over-night money (about Rs50). If the car is hired through an agency, it is best to tip a good driver direct as his share of the fee is very little (about Rs30 a day). If the driver is clearly hopeless, or the car unlikely to make the journey, it is best to return to the agency immediately and ask for another. The manager will provide a replace-ment without embarrassment and will respect you for knowing what you want and for issuing clear instructions.

Beware: hotel in-house travel agents often have ridiculous tariffs, so it is wise to get other quotes before booking. A recent traveller in Mysore found the hotel quote was halved in town.

The Automobile Association of India has offices in all the major cities. They are especially useful for up-to-date advice on car hire and routes, and they stock excellent maps. Also, for more rural trips they know where the Dak bun-galows or Circuit houses are for an overnight stay. Membership may be taken out on the spot; there is a reciprocal agreement for members of the AA elsewhere in the world. The five regional head offices are:

Bombay: Federation of Indian Automobile Associations, 76 Via Narinam Road, Bombay 400020 (tel: 2041085)

Delhi: Automobile Association of Upper India, Shivan House, 14F Connaught Place, New Delhi 110001 (tel: 3312323); postal enquiries to C8 Institutional Area, South fi IIT Building, behind Qutub Hotel, New Delhi 110016

Madras: Automobile Association of South India, temporary address at C8 Raghariah Road, T'nagar, Madras (tel: 442705) and 187 Anna Salai.

Calcutta: Automobile Association of Eastern India, 13 Promothesh Barua Sarani, Calcutta 700019 (tel: 759012)

Bangalore is another principal city for care hire. The AA's office there is at India Garage Build-ing, St Mark's Road (tel: 575701)

COACHES AND BUSES There are various very good air-conditioned coaches, particularly connecting the Rajasthan cities. Some have become very smart and show videos on the journey. Tourist offices have the coach time-tables and routes and will tell you where to catch the bus. It is always worth taking the most expensive coach available and affordable, not only for the added comfort but also to avoid the crowded cheaper buses which may look tempt-ingly colourful but are tiring after the first 8 hours or so. It takes very little time to learn to avoid the crammed facilities of everyday India. Local buses are very slow, extremely crowded and, for some people, uncomfortable. But a short trip on one is worth experiencing once.

TRAINS A train journey is an essential part of any trip to India. There are 60,666 kilometres of railway in the country, and trains with romantic names like Himalayan Queen, Pink City Ex-press and the Grand Trunk Express pass through glorious countryside and right beside rural villages. India's first train steamed off from Bombay to a 21-gun salute on April 16, 1853, for its 34-km-long journey; today, its longest route trundles 3,974km every week from Gawahati to Trivandrum. Soon, the princes laid their own local lines; the innovative Maharaja of Baroda was first, and the Gwalior one still runs round the city. India's first superfast train was the Rajdhani Express running Delhi-Calcutta at 130kph; and now the Shatabdi Express zips equally fast between Delhi and Bhopal, via Agra, Gwalior and elsewhere, and between Delhi and Kanpur (not far from Lucknow); miraculously it is usually on time. For train addicts, the Railway Museum at Delhi has some fine old locomotives.

Some of the Victorian stations are magnifi-cent, bubbling with Indians on the move – ones at Bombay, Calcutta and Lucknow are espe-cially grand. As they are located in the city centres, they are quicker to reach than airports and infinitely nicer to arrive in. Travelling by train has strong Raj overtones. Apart from the depressing modernised food systems on a few trains, meals are ordered at one station, mes-sages sent up the line, trays of piping hot dishes picked up at the next and delivered to your seat. There is everything from early morning tea, known as bed tea, and full breakfast to after-noon tea and a three-course dinner, always washed down with a hot, milky, sweet and strong cuppa, delivered with all the ingredients already added.

Some of the best train journeys are suggested in the Getting There: Getting Away sections of the chapters below. An Indrail pass is excellent value, even the seven-day one (see above, p. 9). There are three main classes of ticket: air-conditioned, first class and second class, each with subdivisions. Second class has two- and three-tier sleepers (two is better) and some air-conditioned sleepers. First-class may or may not be air-conditioned and may or may not have chair-cars, carriages with reclining seats. Clearly, first-class air-conditioned is best, and a good way to travel overnight to make the most of sight-seeing if time is short, but it is not available on every train. Again, queuing may be avoided by using a travel agent. Alternatively, the train reservation offices in the big cities have Tourist Guide Assistants who are excellent. They hold tickets reserved for tourists for some popular trains that will be booked out at the normal ticket counters. They give advice and help with bookings throughout India.

Out and about

ORGANISED TOURS   The government and state tourist offices run city tours, usually covering almost identical ground. It is well worth swallowing all coach tour phobia since they are often an extremely good introduction to a city, with transport between widely scattered monuments. Favourite monuments can always be visited again later. The tours tend to be quite exhausting, lasting up to five hours, with a guide. There are also longer, full-day trips to surrounding sights, again cheap and well-run. For both types, the coach picks up and delivers back to the main hotels of the town (except in the big cities). Booking is through the hotel front desk or travel desk, or by telephone or in person to the local tourist office. The Government of India Tourist Office publishes the useful booklet, *Conducted Sightseeing Tours*.

The tickets for a tour often have seat numbers rigidly enforced by the tour leader. The leader is also strict about timing at each place, in order to keep to his schedule which may end at a bad shop, so insist upon more time sight-seeing if all the party want it. At big tourist sights it is worth noting the registration number of the bus so that you can find the right one.

GUIDES   The government and state tourist offices hire out properly trained guides for half and full days. Rates for a party of up to four are about Rs75 for a half-day (four hours), Rs150 for a full day (eight hours). However, a large number of the 800 million or so Indians have become self-taught guides. They pop up everywhere, behind the most remote temple. Usually they are awful, reeling off a few facts and generally intruding upon any enjoyment of the sight. And when you try to get rid of them, they threaten you with a calamity, such as being attacked by monkeys or eaten by a tiger. Sometimes, however, they are charming and become life-long penfriends.

SOLO SIGHT-SEEING   All the bother of finding transport is easily avoided. In a town with scattered monuments, you can hire a bicycle rickshaw or three-wheeler auto rickshaw for several hours. Just agree a flat fee (the going rate will vary from town to town) with the driver, and he will wait for you at each monument. You then pay at the end. Up-market hotels do not allow bicycle or auto rickshaws up to their front doors but there are usually some lingering at the gates. Sensitive visitors from the West may balk at the idea of a scrawny, bare-foot child pedalling them around in a comfortable rickshaw. First-time visitors have been known to pay up and walk the rest. More seasoned travellers can argue to themselves that it is better generously to exploit them – being sure to pay a decent amount at the end of the journey – than not to employ them in favour of an auto rickshaw. Auto rickshaws should have a working meter. If the meter does not work, it is best to agree a price before setting off.

For longer distances, a hired car is better. If you take a taxi to a remote or residential area where taxis are scarce, the driver will wait and then take you to your next destination; if you intend staying at a site for, say, two hours, tell the driver when to come back for you, but do not pay him until the end of the day. Taxi waiting charge tends to be Rs10 per hour, but need to be checked locally. In more out-of-the-way places, there are delightful tongas, two-wheeled carriages drawn by a pony or horse.

ANCIENT MONUMENTS   If protected by the Archaeological Survey of India, there should be a dark blue plaque announcing this. There should also be at the minimum a chowkidar (watchman) but often a substantial staff. In addition, the whole site usually has a fence or wall and neither hawkers nor unofficial guides are permitted to enter. This creates oases of glorious peace in otherwise exhausting popular tourist cities, notably Agra. There may be a small charge for entry, for which a ticket is given, together with a charge for a camera and more for a video or a camera with tripod; flash is often forbidden. Where video and/or tripod are forbidden (which currently includes the Taj Mahal), they can be checked in with security on site. A chowkidar who takes special care in showing the way to a hidden treat or view, or who helps visitors up steep steps, deserves a small tip.

RELIGIOUS BUILDINGS   To visit a mosque, the head and legs should be covered, the shoes removed – some Muslims are more particular than others about women's legs being covered. Hawkers are to be found in many mosques, and officials should help if they are too persistant. To visit a Hindu temple, the shoes should be removed. Temples are at their most interesting on the day of the week especially devoted to their particularly god. On these days there are likely to be processions, music and special food and trinket stalls outside. For instance, Hanuman the monkey god is worshipped on Tuesdays; Shiva's day in Monday.

At both mosque and temple, it is customary to give a tiny coin, a 20 or 50 paise piece, to the shoe guardian; visitors are not obliged to give to the mosque, its school or its saint, nor to a Hindu god or saint.

To know a little more about Islam and the mosque, see p. 53; for more on Hinduism and the temple, see Varanasi, and for temples see Khajuraho (in the North) and Kanchipuram and Thanjavur (in the South).

CONSERVATION GROUPS India is gradually becoming aware of the need for organised and campaigning conservation groups. INTACH (Indian National Trust for Art and Cultural Heritage) is India's answer to the National Trust. It has a network of regional offices, some better than others – Jodhpur's is particularly good and has printed a charming walk pamphlet. Its headquarters are at 71 Lodi Estate, New Delhi 110003 (tel: 611362). Delhi also has a very active Delhi Conservation Society who organise regular walks; find them at N-7/c Saket, New Delhi 110017 (tel: 668118).

SIGHT-SEEING SUPPLIES AND TRICKS It is wise to take the basic pack (see What to Pack in Chapter 1, above), plus extra camera film – it is maddening to finish a film and then bump into a colourful wedding procession. On a long journey, a map is useful, as are some bottles of mineral water, although you can buy both water and fizzy drinks water at most big tourist sites. For meals, either stop at a roadside café and join the lorry drivers for delicious fresh vegetables, bread and steaming tea or ask your hotel to provide a picnic lunch. You can specify its contents: hard-boiled eggs, chicken tikka, rice biryani and fruit cake are usually good; sandwiches are awful; fruit such as bananas and oranges are best bought in bazaars en route.

STREET-WISE SECURITY Street crime is low in India, but rises in the big cities where there are drug problems. Pickpockets tend, as elsewhere, to take advantage of chance. So it is wise to keep all money and documents in a closed bag or buttoned-down front pocket.

STREET-WISE PHOTOGRAPHERS In addition to the tips on when to take pictures (see Manners, above), the wise photographer carries extra film and extra batteries (which can be bought in larger or more touristy towns). But it is best not to have films developed in India, however tempting. Tales of woe abound, and it would be very sad to lose those carefully snapped memories.

Food and drink

These are the biggest worries for most visitors. Although there are one or two golden rules, the dreaded diarrhoea, fondly known as Delhi Belly, can strike anywhere, anytime. One woman who had travelled throughout India over seventeen trips remained unaffected until the night following a smart diplomatic cocktail party in Delhi.

However, to discourage any disease, it is vital to take the preventive measures before leaving home, to take the daily and weekly doses during and after a visit to India and to be careful while there. At first, such details as washing your teeth in sterilised or boiled water are a nuisance, but they quickly become a habit. If Delhi Belly hits you, the stomach will welcome plenty of liquid and settling foods such as curd (yoghurt), lemon juice, bananas, rice and eggs. Hotels in cities have good in-house doctors. Remote areas do not. (See also pages 12-13.) On the whole, hygiene in Indian hotels and restaurants is much improved.

FOOD

India has so many different cuisines, each of great sophistication, that it is a pity not to try the local dishes. In the following chapters, the local specialities and where to find them are given where possible. However, the best Indian food is most certainly served in the home. Indians are disarmingly hospitable, so you are very likely to be invited to eat in someone's home.

Restaurant menus often boast three cuisines: Indian, Chinese and Continental. The Indian food varies; the Chinese can be very good, and tends to be spicy Szechuan dishes; the Continental is usually awful. Such a variety is termed tri-cuisine in the following chapters.

The only two cities with a wide range of restaurants are Delhi and Bombay. But in all restaurants, to avoid the omni-present 'hotel culture', you need to impress upon the head waiter that you want the real local dish, not a watered-down version; it is assumed that a Western palate cannot take the mildest spices. Continental food tends to be bad, institutional, overcooked and tasteless; but vestiges of Raj puddings no longer found in Britain can be excellent, such as spotted dick and custard or caramel custard.

DANGERS In general, eating off the street is madness and eating fried food, salads, unpeeled fruits and ice-cream is risky in most places. However, some people cannot resist the occasional deviation, which is less risky in some parts of India than others. For instance, everyone, quite rightly, warns against ice-cream because it may be frozen and thawed several times before it reaches you. And, in any case, freezing does not kill the typhoid bug. But in Gujarat, a relatively clean state with substantial dairy farming, ice-cream is so delicious and so much a part of Gujarat life that supply seems only just to keep up with demand, reducing the risk. Both local street snacks and ice-cream are listed below, where they are good, leaving you to weigh up temptation against risk. The best rule to follow is: if in doubt, don't eat it.

If your stomach feels delicate, south Indian vegetable dishes with plenty of curd (yoghurt) and rice will probably soon settle it. You can just ask for a thali and the whole meal comes on a tray (see p. 210). It may be tempting to eat familiar European food but it is not necessarily going to be very settling. Meat is less likely to be fresh than vegetables and it is much heavier to digest in a hot climate. Too much rich Mughlai food is like a constant blow-out on French classic dishes washed down with cream and claret. It really should be eaten in small doses, with plenty of the many delicious breads.

THE EATING PROCESS Dishes tend to be served all at once instead of a long string of courses. From a huge menu, you select such goodies as something cooked in the tandoor oven: some meat, fish and vegetable dishes, a variety of rice and breads, a dhal (pulse) and a curd to cool down the spices. When it all arrives, quite the nicest way of eating is with the fingers, pulling off pieces of freshly baked bread and wrapping them around a piece of meat or mixing the spicy juices into rice. As breads are best hot, you can order more as you go. It is important only to eat with the right hand. There is always somewhere to wash and many restaurants bring bowls of hot water to the table afterwards.

FISH Delicious and very fresh all around the coast. The tandoor-cooked pomfret is in a class of its own. In the south, there are plenty of lobster, crab and giant prawns. Where there is inland fresh-water fish, that is very good too. But it is not such a good idea to eat fish where it has had to be transported, such as in Delhi.

PUDDINGS Usually very sweet and often rice-based. Otherwise, there is kulfi (Indian ice-cream with pistachio nuts) and fresh fruit. You only find hard cheese in the hills; cream cheese is added to vegetable dishes.

FRUIT A fantastic variety throughout the country, from Kashmiri apples to the delicious pink bananas of the south. Bazaars have piles of fruit and often a better selection than the hotels. The absolute rule is to eat peeled fruit only. If grapes and tomatoes are irresistible, they

should be washed in sterilised water first.

SWEETMEATS Developed to a high culinary art in India, much as great pastries in the West. Different towns have their own special sweet-meats. Religious festivals, marriages and other celebrations have theirs. They are given as temple offerings and presents. Women who do no other cooking will make the important family sweetmeats, whose quality is dictated by both how long they take to make (the longer the better) and what they taste like. The smartest have a thin sheet of real silver paper on top. (You can buy boxes of the silver papers in grocery shops and impress friends back home.) Although they are rarely served in restaurants, every town has good sweetmeat shops. Local specialities are mentioned in the chapters below.

PAAN This is the digestive taken after an Indian meal. It is also the cause of all those red-stained lips and teeth. Paan is a mixture of spices, slaked lime and the mildly addictive betel nut wrapped in a leaf. It is chewed. When you have had enough, you do not swallow it but spit it out. All sorts of potions can be added to make the paan mixture sweet or sour, a little intoxicating or very intoxicating. The contents dictate the huge price range. In smart restaurants, the paan is made up from a beautiful paan box of ingredients. On the street, the paan seller sits amidst a collection of tins and trays. An Indian has his regular paan seller who makes up his particular mixture.

DRINK

WATER Bisleri now make reliable bottled water. Apart from this, it is to be strictly avoided unless you are sure it has been boiled or filtered, however parched with thirst you are. The rule is: if in doubt, don't drink. Indians have an equally wary attitude to their water and carry thermosflasks when on the move. And, remember, ice is just frozen water.

HOT DRINKS To avoid being served instant coffee, you need to ask for freshly brewed Mysore coffee. It is delicious and served throughout the South and in good hotels in the North. However, it is almost never available in moderate hotels. In small restaurants, it is served with milk and sugar already added. Chai (tea) served in a simple restaurant or on a train is made by boiling up water, milk, sugar and tea leaves together to produce a reviving army-style brew. To achieve this in an up-market hotel, ask for ready-made tea.

COLD DRINKS As post-independence protectionist trading begins to loosen up, the great mogul Pepsi Cola has finally managed to get into India, adding to the huge variety of fizzy drinks which can be bought anywhere with relative safety. They include bottled soda water, Limca and Sprint (lemonades), Campa Cola and Thums Up (India's own versions of Coca Cola), Fanta and Gold Spot (orangeades), tonic waters, etc. However sweet, they are better than nothing. For those who hate fizzy sweet drinks, the least offensive is Limca. In some places, bottled pure mango juice is on sale. You should always witness the top being taken off, otherwise the flies may have been buzzing about.

Still draughts are best taken where the hygiene is reasonably dependable. A nimbu soda (or nimbu pani) is the most thirst-quenching. It is fresh lime juice diluted with soda water and served either straight or with sugar or salt. Whatever fruit is in season can be pressed for a fruit juice, from mango and sweet lime to papaya and orange. In the South, coconut milk is very refreshing. The top is slashed off and the whole coconut served with a straw. In dairy areas, the milk is delicious. It is served straight, as exotic milk shakes or as lassi, usually a thin yoghurt but in western Rajasthan and Gujarat a rich, creamy concoction.

ALCOHOL   Almost all hotels, except in Gujarat state, currently serve beer and spirits in their bars and restaurants, which is part of their attraction for locals. Outside hotels, the prohibition laws of each state are different and are strictly enforced, with the major exception of Gujarat state, which is completely dry. State dry days even hit the hotels and alcohol is then only available on room service. On prohibition, see p. 13 and individual chapters below. Check current restrictions with your hotel or local tourist office.

To buy your own supplies, 'liquor stores' sell bottles of wine and spirits at good prices and often stock a selection of whiskies to rival the best Scottish off-licences. Locals are always happy to give directions to the nearest store, where shopping at their little windows gives a stimulating frisson of wickedness.

INDIAN BEER   Similar to lager and quite gassy. It is both thirst-quenching and suitable to drink with spiced food. Favourite brands are Kingfisher and Haywards, especially in Bombay and the South, and Rosy Pelican in the North. London Pilsner is also made in India.

WINE   Not the best drink in India. Imported wine has often suffered en route; home-grown wine is very variable. Both are expensive. French film crews are known to bring their daily supplies with them. There are three principal Indian labels: Bosca, Anjou and Golconda. Anjou is made in Goa. Bosca grapes are grown in Maharashtra. Golconda uses grapes grown on the hot Deccan Plateau of Andhra Pradesh and Karnataka. Jancis Robinson, a Master of Wine, was surprised by the quality of Golconda Ruby; she described it as 'clean and balanced. It looks and smells quite mature and, although it is very sweet, there is enough acidity to balance it. Considering the heat, it is quite impressive.' If there is something to celebrate, India now makes its own champagne, Koh-i-noor.

SPIRITS   There are various types. Imported liquor is available in hotels and very expensive, which is why it makes a good present. Indian liquor is cheaper and confusingly known as Indian Made Foreign Liquor, or Foreign Liquor for short. For whisky, imported Scotch concentrate may be blended with home-grown malt; the preferred labels are Peter Scott, Diplomat, McDowell No. 1 and Dunhill. Indian gin is not very good and best drunk as a Tom Collins cocktail, a sort of alcoholic numbu soda; good labels are Booth's and Carew's Blue Ribbon. Indian rum is excellent and cheap. It is made in most states, using the Indian-grown sugar-cane. Khoday dark rum is a good brand; Old Monk is matured in a cask; White rum from Sikkim is very good. The local drink store usually stocks a wide selection; but hotels serve expensive foreign brands, unless asked; some hotels do not even stock local brands. To buy your own, see Alcohol, above.

LIQUEURS AND LOCAL DRINKS   There are numerous local potions, often very powerful. Feni, made from the cashew tree or coconut palm, comes from Goa. Toddy is the coconut spirit of the South. In Sikkim they make tea- and paan-based liqueurs.

Keeping fit

OUTDOOR ACTIVITIES   There is a huge range, all serviced to a degree rare in the West. Walkers and trekkers have their food and luggage carried, their tents carried and pitched – some with a separate washroom – and delicious meals cooked for them over the fire. If a walker tires, there is often a spare horse to ride. Fishermen have their tackle carried, the bait put on the fly and even the rod cast if they wish. And, of course, the catch is cooked for them on the spot.

GOLF   India was the first country outside Britain to lay golf courses – the Royal Calcutta Golf Club, established in 1829, is India's oldest golf club. Courses are often spectacularly beautiful, and may be dotted with wooded dells as at Shillong, Mughal monuments as at Delhi, or have the backdrop of snowcapped mountains, as at Gulmarg. At most courses, visitors are welcome and given temporary club membership. Caddies, clubs and shoes can be hired. The clubhouse will advise on caddy payments. In some places, drinks and snacks are brought to golfers on the course. Hotels will assist with necessary introductions.

TENNIS Where hotels have tennis courts, they usually have both balls and ball boys. Some provide a marker (partner) for a single player. Rackets and balls supplied by hotels have rarely stood up to the Indian climate, so keen players should bring their own. Where a hotel does not have a tennis court, the management can usually make arrangements for guests to use one nearby.

SWIMMING POOLS Pools in hotel grounds are usually very well chlorinated, making them entirely safe. A cool plunge after a day of sweaty sight-seeing or business dealing is a joy. In the big cities, the daily dip is an almost essential treat when the weather is hot. But beware: some hotels decide to empty and clean their pools sometime between November and February – just when a European is likely to be wanting them – as this is, of course, winter time in India. Also, some pools close at 7pm, the very time you are likely to return from a steamy day of sight-seeing. Poolside barbecues are excellent at most hotels, showing off the north Indian tradition of meat and fish cooking at its best.

SEA SWIMMING AND BEACHES The balmy waters are deceptive. There is often an undertow, especially on the east coast. Hotels have life guards who advise on when and where to swim. On other beaches, the local fishermen should be consulted. Scanty bikinis are OK at tourist beaches and around hotel pools, but in less Westernised places it is more tactful to wear a teeshirt as well, to avoid upsetting the locals. To go topless, let alone totally naked, is frowned upon in India, except at one or two hippy beaches. Either a group of people will arrive and stare, or someone will bluntly ask you to cover up.

BOATING A hired boat comes with a rower and is always very cheap. In Kashmir, if it is 4 o'clock on a shikara (a boat like a floating double sofa), the servant brews up tea and serves it with fresh macaroons, scones and lotus-blossom honey.

Health and beauty

HEALTH CLUBS AND BEAUTY SALONS Found in top hotels such as the Taj, Oberoi and Welcomgroup chains, these are some of the most luxurious in the world, with low prices. In their labyrinth of marble-lined rooms, trained masseurs give body, head and back massages, using a variety of oils. There are masseurs for men and masseuses for women. As men have stronger hands, a woman can ask to have a masseur. There are gymnasiums, saunas, jacuzzis, yoga lessons and every sort of beauty treatment from hair coiffeuring to pedicures for tired tourists' feet. As hygiene is particularly important, it is best to keep to the hotel parlours which are used by all the locals, too, unless you have a personal recommendation.

Respecting and caring for the body is part of the Indian tradition. And massage is part of family life, whether rich or poor. A wife will often give her husband a massage. A mother massages her children from when they are babies right into adulthood. There are special women who come to the house to massage babies. Girls use oil and a mixture of turmeric and gramflour paste to remove body hair. Massage after childbirth is used to help restore the body's shape. It is not unusual for a busy working woman in her thirties to have a massage from her mother as part of her week-end relaxation. Massage is sometimes part of the ritual of a festival or a religious occasion. The oil varies according to what is available locally. In the South, it is coconut oil; in the North, mustard oil. These are absorbed better than the thicker almond oil which is used on the feet.

ARYAVAIDYA MASSAGE Of the three main types of massage in India, this is the most common. The other two are siddha and unani, but elements of each overlap. Herbs collected by student masseurs are boiled, pressed or ground, then mixed with certain powders, saps of medicinal plants and oils. The oils are expensive and need careful preparation oil so, as one Kerala masseur explained, 'our treatments do not come cheap. . . . [but] what intrigues people today is that it works, and nothing unpleasant happens'.

Different combinations are used according to the purpose of the massage, such as to relax an athlete's muscles, keep a dancer's hands and feet supple or to soothe the whole body. The principles of a massage are to open the skin pores so that the oil enters and lubricates the skin tissues, veins and muscles. The pressure of the massage promotes blood circulation and removes congestion, thus easing digestion and circulation and eliminating toxins. Even a general massage is good for the skin, joints, veins and nerves. To follow the full aryavaidya medicine – based on theories devised some 5,000 years ago and yet banned by the British as heathen and superstitious – massage is combined with a special diet.

Most big towns have an Aryavaidya College where you can go for advice and treatment. Full treatment consists of a controlled diet, oral medicines and various oil applications, such as oil baths and warm oil pressed on the body. As with the increasingly popular homeopathic medicine in the West, both Western and Indian people have found aryavaidya medicine to be the cure for migraines, headaches, depression, low blood pressure, poor circulation, arthritis, rheumatism, asthma and diabetes. See telephone directory for local colleges; see also Trivandrum, below.

HEADS AND HAIR With the heat and humidity, hair needs more attention. Again, women wash, comb and massage one another's heads. The massage is with oil, yoghurt or egg, or with lime and salt to get rid of dandruff. When it also includes the neck and back, it is the best of all massages, as it works on the nerves of the spinal chord to relax the whole body. Beauty salons can usually take care of Western perms. It is best, however, not to have a haircut on the street; just watch other people.

FEET Open sandals or no sandals at all mean the feet need regular attention. Pedicure and foot massage are a post sight-seeing treat. Some of the Bata shoe shops in big cities give good pedicures; so do the large hotels.

COSMETICS Herbal oils and creams, often home-made, are also a part of Indian life. For instance, dried and ground orange peel is used as a face pack cleanser, as are honey, milk and gramflour. Of the packaged herbal cosmetics, Cheriss Products and Sharnaz Husain's range are the best. They are available in health clubs, beauty salons and some chemists. Miss Husain's herbal cosmetics have an international reputation; she has a Delhi salon and a health club nearby (see p. 65).

YOGA Fitness, mental calm and beauty at the same time. As people increasingly take up yoga in the West, more visitors to India are keen to start or keep up their lessons. Yoga institutions are everywhere, even inside hotels and on beaches. (The Kovalam Hotel in Kerala has a particularly good one.) The exercises bring physical, mental and emotional relaxation. It is not at all a waste of time to take one or two lessons, as you feel the difference very quickly. You learn a few simple postures and exercises for breathing and for flexing body joints and organs. As you repeat them daily, the relaxation increases; and the yoga clinic gives advice on how to continue. The important thing is to learn slowly and carefully, and to stick to one system.

Yoga is often used medicinally in conjunction with massage to maintain energy, improve sleep and relieve high blood pressure, asthma and other ailments. And diet is an integral part of cleansing and reviving both body and mind. Ashrams, in or near every town, are the best places in which to follow intensive courses. Many Indians look forward to unwinding for an annual two weeks at their favourite ashram in the same way as Westerners long for their fortnight's skiing, sailing or lying on a beach. The Bihar School of Yoga at Monghyr, Bihar, is currently one of the foremost systems. The school has many publications available by post and is extremely reliable to visit.

If you want to go to an ashram, it is best to go to one frequented by Indians rather than one full of tourists. Since the sixties, several ashrams have sprung up in India aimed to entice Westerners and fleece them of considerable amounts of money. Many Indians believe that these are fraudulent and betray the principles of the true ashram, so beware. To get reliable advice, consult your hotel management or the local Tourist Office.

Night life

Night life is not great in India. However, the day tends to start early for everyone and the early morning light is magical everywhere. And, during the hot months, the hours between dawn and mid-morning are the best of the day. Where there is any night life, it tends to be early evening.

CINEMA Almost as essential a part of a trip to India as taking a train or seeing a festival. Despite the advent of the video, the cinema survives even if there are fewer screens than there were. Film shows run all day, the last one usually between 8 and 9pm. See Bombay, Calcutta and the beginning of the South chapter for more on the massive Indian film industry.

DANCE, THEATRE AND MUSIC India is very rich in high quality contemporary performers, but they are not easy to find in their places of origin. Delhi, Bombay and Calcutta have plenty of halls with constant programmes during the winter months. Down in the South, there are regular performances of Kathakali dance-drama at Cochin and Trivandrum and of Bharata Natyam classical dances at Madras. Other cities have sporadic festivals: Varanasi, Lucknow, Gwalior, Khajuraho, etc. (see following chapters and Festivals calendar). Performances are advertised in the daily paper and usually start between 6 and 7pm. If you are particularly interested in attending the smaller, often private concerts, the hotel can usually help. Top hotels stage 'Dances of India' programmes, usually of poor quality. Some restaurants have Indian dancers and musicians. Despite it being considered very detrimental to a serious career, there are some good performers. But a proper concert in a hall is best of all.

NIGHT CLUBS AND DISCOTHEQUES The former, also called supper clubs, are usually restaurants serving Continental or Chinese food (occasionally Indian) to the Western music of a live and raucous band. The latter, also called night spots, are little more than discotheques, very thin on the ground, so exclusive they are empty half the time, and mostly equipped with archaic lighting and music. The best options are in Bombay, Delhi and Calcutta. Most are attached to deluxe hotels and charge a nominal entrance fee to residents but a very high membership fee to restrict local patronage to high society.

Shopping

WHEN TO SHOP There are two schools of thought on shopping in India. One says, when you see something you like, buy it as you may not find it again. The other says, save up your shopping until the end. A combination of the two gets the best results. Rare local craftsmanship certainly needs to be snapped up when it is found. On the other hand, most people leave India through Delhi or Bombay, and both cities have excellent shopping for high quality goods produced throughout the country – indeed, a leading producer of chikan work (white embroidered muslin) in Lucknow frankly admitted that he sends his best work to Delhi, where he can get the best prices. Wherever you shop, be sure to keep all bills in case customs want to see them on your return home. And while shopping, it is worth bearing in mind that for UK customs India is rated a 'developing country' and therefore there is no duty to pay, just the regular VAT.

TAXES For some items, there is a sales tax to pay. But it should be subtracted from the bill if it is settled in foreign currency (and this includes foreign based credit cards).

INDIAN CRAFTSMANSHIP In all fields this can be of very high quality. The craftsmen serve an Indian public who still keep their money in gold, gems and silk. It is worth buying the best and avoiding the junk produced for tourists and sold from stalls beside monuments. Top-quality silk, cotton, jewellery, leather and carving can be as much as five times the cost when bought abroad. And there is much more choice in India. Also, items can easily be made to order on the spot, or sent on later. As Malcolm Muggeridge observed of an Indian woman in 1934: 'She loves money in an Oriental way, not as money but translated into expensive jewels and exquisite silks.'

Whatever skill you want, it is available. Tailors will run up a dress, shirt or suit almost overnight and can copy any design expertly. Dhurries (flat-weave rugs) cost little and can be made to specific designs, colours and sizes, then shipped home (and they do arrive). Carpets are bigger buys and should be undertaken with caution: it is wise to go only to a shop recommended in person by the local tourist office (and to check out carefully any shop recommending itself as 'authorised' or some such); to compare prices, to bargain hard and, if making a purchase, to sign the carpet on the back yourself and measure it yourself and, if possible, take a photograph of it. You should also have a full descriptive receipt. Then, when it arrives home (usually in three months' time), you can be sure it is the one you chose.

Furnishings and dress fabrics of the highest quality cotton and silk are cheap, come in an endless variety and can even be woven to order. If you buy curtain fabric, the curtains can be made up and sent on by ship. Craftsmen will make up the fine pearls and Indian gems into any design in a week, or less. You can even have your favourite shoes copied.

GOVERNMENT EMPORIA Every state has its own chain of shops, called emporia. They are stocked with a good variety of crafts produced in that state, the quality depending upon the ability of the buyers. For instance, the Gurjari emporia of Gujarat are superb and found in Delhi, Calcutta and Bombay. The buyers do the hard slog, going around the villages to get supplies and commissioning craftsmen to make pieces. The expanding chain of the Central Cottage Industries Emporia at Delhi (see Delhi shopping section), Bombay and Calcutta stocks pieces from all over India. If you prefer to shop in the bazaars, a quick recky in the emporia gives an idea of a price to aim for when bargaining. By doing this research you can sometimes strike a better deal in a bazaar than in an emporium where prices are, supposedly, fixed – but you need to inspect goods carefully for quality.

Although prices at both types of shop may be slightly higher than in the market place, the quality can be very high and they enable you to shop quickly. In addition, the assistants usually know all about their stocks and can direct you to see the local craftsmen at work. The emporia shipping services are usually reliable and not expensive. The price depends upon a combination of volume and weight. A huge crate arrives back home after about three months.

HOTEL SHOPS Unlike their counterparts in the West, they are often of high quality and yet have reasonable prices. Significantly, they are heavily patronised by locals. Their clothes, leather and jewellery shops stock copies of the latest European designs. And there are quality Indian crafts. Clothes shops sometimes have tailors on call who can whip up garments overnight, although the cost will be high by Indian standards and low by European ones. They take credit cards too.

JEWELLERY Except in a few cases, stores in deluxe hotels are the safest places to buy big items, although the price might be slightly higher. Good buys include garnets, topaz, amethyst and black stars, all from India, and pearls which are sorted and pierced in India (see Hyderabad); silver is a good buy, while gold is relatively expensive because of its status in India. Gems can usually be authenticated by a government office. Jewellers will give a certificate of authenticity and usually offer to buy back the gems when you next come, should you wish to exchange them or change their setting. Judging by the number of tales of woe, it is impossible to stress strongly enough that stones should be bought from a reputable shop, such as the few suggested in the text below; if in doubt, stick to costume jewellery found in the markets.

FABRICS The wealth of handloom fabrics throughout the country is impossible to resist, from the woollen shawls of Kashmir to the heavy silks of Kanchipuram. The bazaars have a good selection of cheaper pieces, but the more special weaves are found in some of the shops suggested below. A sari length varies around the country, so it is worth checking the local length if you are thinking of having it cut and made up. Cotton, wool and silk are also woven in long pieces. It is sold by the metre length, but the width is still described in inches.

ANTIQUES Not always as old as they look. Ageing help is sometimes given to newly made objects sold in shops and bazaars, so beware. A reputable antique shop will give a guarantee; in the big cities, this opinion can be endorsed by officials (see next section, Packing to come home). It is illegal to export works of art more than 100 years old (textiles and wood are exempt) without written permission from the Archaeological Survey of India. On the whole, antiques are very expensive, and nice things take time to find. There is a larger range of quality old paintings, bronzes, textiles and sculptures to be found at the dealers and auction houses of London, New York and Paris. Run-of-the-mill art has a high premium within India

and is expensive. If in doubt, stick to buying new crafts, bearing in mind that they will be subject to VAT but not import duty on entry into the UK.

WHAT NOT TO BUY With the need to conserve its rich but vulnerable wildlife, India officially discourages, restricts and in some cases bans the sale of products of threatened species. These include ivory, snakeskin and other animal skins – which also have UK import restrictions for the same conservation reasons. However, unofficially a tourist may well be offered items.

Packing to come home

As it is highly likely you will have picked up things along the way and also had a shopping blitz at the end, packing is an event.

If you make a list of what you have bought and ensure that all the bills and currency exchange receipts are in your hand luggage, customs clearance both out of India and into your home country is quicker.

There are several restrictions on what can be taken out of India, including large pieces of ivory, snakeskin, peacock feathers, animal skin and objects more than 100 years old (see also Antiques, above). For instance, the current restriction on gold jewellery applies to pieces worth up to a maximum total of Rs10,000. The restriction on precious stones is the same amount. The local tourist office or government emporium should have the most up-to-date list. If in doubt, the local Customs Office will help. To ascertain whether your treasures are 100 years old or not, the following authorities can be consulted:
Director, Antiquities, Archaeological Survey of India, Janpath, New Delhi
Superintending Archaeologist, Antiquities, Archaeological Survey of India, Sion Fort, Bombay
Superintending Archaeologist, Eastern Circle, Archaeological Survey of India, Narayani Building, Brabourne Road, Calcutta
Superintending Archaeologist, Southern Circle, Archaeological Survey of India, Fort St George, Madras
Superintending Archaeologist, Frontier Circle, Archaeological Survey of India, Minto Bridge, Srinagar.

If still in doubt, the best policy is to declare your goods at the airports both when leaving India and entering back home.

So that you can roughly gauge the overweight charges and dispose your packing as well as possible, the hotel will weigh your baggage for you. You may need rupees to pay for overweight baggage (see p. 8). Currently, Airport Tax is Rs300.

The disarming thing about travelling in India is that you are unlikely to carry your luggage often, if at all. Only when you reach your home airport will you realise the enormous weight of all the treasures and memories packed inside.

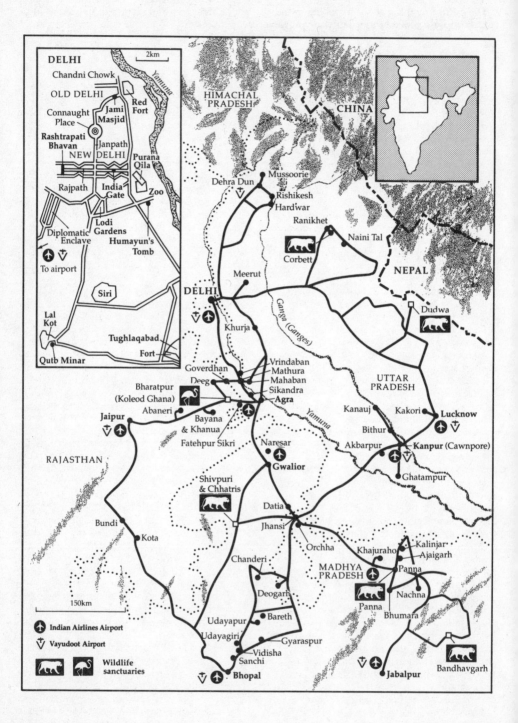

Delhi and Agra:
Power, politics and a trip to Pakistan

Delhi lives, breathes, eats and sleeps politics; politics hits every facet of life. The difference between Delhi and Bombay is India's version of that between Washington and New York. Indeed, one Delhi gentleman looked down his knowledgeable nose, dismissing Bombay as a 'cheap imitation Manhattan'. As the saying goes: Delhi is structured red tape, Bombay is money – to which Calcuttans add, optimistically, Calcutta is living.

Social rank in Delhi is measured solely by political power. A new-boy politician is several rungs above an eminent lawyer, and certainly above any out-dated nonsense like maharajas. Indeed, Delhi is the only city where the former princes are most definitely former. In provincial towns, citizens doff their caps to His Highness and parade him on elephants at festivals; even in up-to-the-minute Bombay, the titled certainly retain their panache. But in Delhi, former aristocrats have to go where the power goes, into Parliament. Indian film stars do not fare much better here, a unique experience for them; in a magazine article on the dining haunts of ten Delhi celebrities, four were politicians and six were writers, painters or performing artists – but not a single film star. They, too, must perform on the political stage to win attention in the capital.

Delhi's day-to-day social life-style is controlled by politics, accompanied by the relevant status symbols. The scheming and gossiping is non-stop, round the clock, often behind the white walls of those peaceful-looking bungalows of New Delhi; and sharp Delhi gossip can truly break a man. It is for chosen ears only. So, political Delhi, which one way or another includes almost everyone of means, has less use for Bombay's hotel-culture, developed for the moneyed to see and be seen – the one public place for vibrant discussion is the India International Centre. However, Delhi is by no means above materialism. Status symbols are flaunted as are a young child's best Christmas present. Driving a Maruti, the Indian-made car, used to provide street cred; but as one knowing and successful man said bluntly, 'Marutis are now too common to carry status. It has to be a foreign car'. The same applies to portable phones; now it is the home fax and the car phone which counts. In the kitchen, where a fridge used to carry status, a washing machine does now – even though the electricity supply is so unreli-

able that dirty clothes are likely to be washed more often by the dhobi, the laundry man.

Even night life is politically determined. Delhi may bulge with museums, hum with performing arts and positively groan with history and monuments. But, for the capital city of what amounts to a continent, night-time Delhi is depressingly dead except in private homes. There, where the hospitality is modest or grand, politics invariably comes up in the conversation. Dinner may be simple vegetables and dhal prepared by the lady of the house or a lavish buffet concocted by a fully staffed kitchen, but it will certainly be spiced up with the latest scandals. And an evening with MPs is a caricature of Delhi life, the men standing drinking whisky, the women sitting chattering in a corner, food gobbled down in two seconds long after midnight. Then everyone goes straight home.

Lunchtimes, long light evenings and weekends, when club-life might blossom, are similarly hit. Whereas Pall Mall lunches and Sunday golf are part of British politics, they have little place in Delhi's scheme of things. Clubs here are either open to all and sundry, like pleasure parks, or stiflingly elite. And none has the welcome warmth and social style of the Bombay Willingdon or the Calcutta Tollygunge, which bubble with families and friends at week-ends. It is not that Delhi is deserted. Far from it. Few people dare leave in case they miss a move in the political game, be they big shot or acolyte. Even the privileged – the Gandhis and hotel millionaire M. S. Oberoi included – who have 'farms' outside the city have a surprisingly reliable telephone line. A farm has nothing to do with collecting warm hens' eggs for breakfast; it is more like a country house set in several acres of (possibly) tilled land, carrying immense snob value just as a dacha does in Russia.

In industry, political influence is everything to any firm, determining whether or not a factory is built, goods imported or licences granted. Influence can speed up the countless hops, skips and jumps through hoops needed to penetrate successfully the tangled, overgrown labyrinth of government bureaucracy which baffles even its administrators.

Each process demands more signatures, authorisations, forms and written permissions than the last – each one extracted from a different office. As job creation goes, it is brilliant. But for those on the other side, it demands powers of patience, persuasion, intrigue, name-dropping and baksheesh (present-giving) that would have impressed the Mughal court. This is why most big firms based in Bombay, Calcutta, Ahmedabad, Madras or Bangalaore have a Delhi office with on-site Men of Influence. And it is why many MPs constantly have to desert their states to be always on call and to be seen in Delhi. For those not seen are not heard. And it is why a Hindu businessman will be found at sacred Tirupati fulfilling an outstanding vow he made six years before to go on a special pilgrimage when his business was eventually set up. Plainly a bureaucratic mire which is increasingly centralised is destructive to this vast and diverse country where each area has its own specific needs; but to change direction would require the charisma, energy and momentum of a Mahatma Gandhi. As one journalist-turned-diplomat remarked: 'As long as Delhi is where the purse is, there will be too much centralisation'.

The basic workings of this all-pervading political machine were set down in the Constitution, which came into force on January 26, 1950, now celebrated as Republic Day. India had become Independent in 1947. The official transfer of power was made by the last Viceroy, Lord Louis Mountbatten, to India's first Prime Minister, Pundit Jawaharlal Nehru, on August 15. That day is now celebrated as Independence Day, when the Prime Minister delivers an address from the ramparts of Lal Qila (Red Fort).

In 1947, Nehru made an optimistic speech, the Union Jack came down, the star of India went up. Nehru then went to Viceroy House (now called Rashtrapati Bhavan) where the two leaders merrily toasted each other in port, the Englishman with 'To India', the Indian with 'To King George VI'. Meanwhile, the Mahatma, who had fought so hard for this moment, was saying his prayers in Calcutta; he was to be assassinated in Delhi the following year.

The previous day, August 14, Mountbatten had attended the creation of a new neighbouring country, Pakistan. All this happened just sixteen years after Lord Irwin had inaugurated Lutyens's New Delhi, designed and built (at vast cost; the bill for the central building alone was $1.25 million) as the new British capital of her Eastern Empire. While the British packed their trunks to go home, some five million Hindus and Sikhs uprooted themselves to move east out of Muslim Pakistan, to be replaced by Muslims from India, amid horrendous bloodshed.

The Indian Constitution outlined a democracy with a President as Head of State, a Prime Minister as Head of Government and a two-house parliament (Lok Sahba and Rajya Sabha) elected by universal suffrage of the then 170 million Indians. The official residence for the President, the head of this pyramid, is Viceroy House, re-named Rashtrapati Bhavan meaning Government House. Its first occupant was Dr Rajendra Prasad (1950- 1962); its current occupant is R. Venkataraman (since 1987). The Constitution was loosely based on Westminster, but also drew on the 1935 Government of India Act and looked to the United States by incorporating a Bill of Rights spelling out basic liberties.

The system of law and administration, the civil service, the railways, roads and irrigation systems, all left by the British, provided a basic infrastructure – as did the English language which, despite all efforts, is still the main lingua franca throughout India. Added to which, India had abundant raw materials and, as Francis Watson observed, 'human resources incalculable in their potential administrative and managerial experience awaiting only the opportunity of expansion'. This was the equipment to transform an agricultural country in debt into, hopefully, a modern dynamic economy.

On January 26, 1950 the Republic of India was inaugurated. The event is celebrated annually with ironically British-style parades in Delhi, then Beating Retreat three days later (see below). The whole city is spruced up like the preparations for the King and Queen in *Alice In Wonderland*. Fairy lights are tested; blossoming trees are trimmed or coaxed.

With all the former princely states incorporated into the 3,287,263 sq km of Independent India, from huge Hyderabad to pocket-handkerchief dominions like Devas Senior in Madhya Pradesh, boundaries were rejigged to create reasonably balanced states. There are now 25 states and seven Union Territories and Special Areas (of which Delhi is one). Each state has a Governor advised by the Chief Minister and his Council of Ministers, a legislature and a High Court (which is sometimes shared between states); each territory has a President. The princes were at first allowed to keep their titles and were given privy purses and privileges, but all these were abolished in 1971 to make every citizen equal before the law. (Although you would not think so in most areas; feudalism dies hard.)

Language was always a problem, and still is. Of perhaps 1,652 languages and dialects spoken in India, most belong to either the Indo-Aryan or Dravidian families. Some streamlining was essential. Hindi written in Devanagari script was proclaimed the national language in 1965, with English as an associate language; and 15 other major languages were recognised. But resentment to Hindi, a northern language, was immediately strong in the South. Disturbances in Madras threatened national unity. And today's traveller still finds English more useful than Hindi. Classical Hindi, spoken by the cultured, is a Sanskrit-based language. The official Hindi used for administration is the everyday language spoken in the North, with some simplifications. As a means of expression, this version is proving inadequate. When the erudite All-India Radio staff were told to broadcast in this more cockney Hindi, they were not pleased. And, despite government backing, there is little quality modern literature in official Hindi.

To ease the conflict, both Hindi and English are official languages today. Of the remaining 3,000 or so languages and dialects, 15 are recognised as national regional languages. To promote the use of Hindi at government level, the law has had to dictate that an officially Hindi-speaking state must communicate with a non-Hindi-speaking state in Hindi – but with a full English translation. In 1983, the eminent lawyer Nani Palkhivala, described India as 'the largest experiment ever undertaken in the art of democratic living. Never before, and nowhere else, has one seventh of the human race lived together in freedom as a single political entity.'

Population growth is another problem. At Independence, the population was 170 million. Today, according to the 1991 census, it is about 850 million. (North and South America's total population is around 623 million while Europe's, excluding the USSR, is a mere 485 million.) The dramatic increase is only partly to do with the lack of birth control. Great strides in medical care have substantially reduced child mortality at one end of the life span and greatly increased logevity at the other. For instance, at the beginning of the century, birth and death rates were roughly the same, so the population remained fairly constant. Today, helped by the pioneer work in fast and painless contraception, the annual birth rate is in fact lower – down from an estimated 4.2% to 3.2% – but the death rate is right down to 1.2%, so that life expectancy in just the last decade has increased from 46 to 54 years. Only when mothers are convinced their children will achieve adulthood and that their lives can be of a higher standard with fewer, rather than more, children will population growth begin to stabilise again. Naturally, education plays a large part in this knowledge and confidence. This is most evident in Kerala, where literacy has reached an all-time high, leaping from 70% to over 90% in a recent literacy drive, compared with a national average of 36%, and where the birthrate is the country's lowest.

Taxes are raised at state and national level and exacerbate the central-state tensions. Each citizen votes for a representative for his state's own legislature and for a national member of parliament. Both then have a tricky job of keeping in touch with local needs and fighting for them in far-away Delhi. Inadequate state taxes force them to go cap in hand to the centre for funds; for instance, while the state is responsible for education, most of the funds for higher education have to be extracted from the centre.

Where the state does rake in the rupees is from lotteries. The two-rupee tickets are sold on the street and bought regularly by every citizen who can, if only just, afford it. Around Connaught Place in New Delhi, street vendors tempt passers-by with wads of brightly coloured tickets which will fill the coffers for Rajasthan, Haryana, Uttar Pradesh or places further afield which the buyer is unlikely ever to visit. The weekly prizes are dreamworthy – often Rs100,000. Even the rich buy tickets, since the prize money carries a flat 30% tax and is not added to earnings. But both central and state governments fleece the tourist. The state Sales Tax (10-15%) and State Luxury Tax (which varies enormously, soaring to 30% in some Gujarat hotels) are levied by hotels and restaurants on top of a central tax on total annual profits. In modest restaurants, one wonders if there is any part of the bill left for the chef.

With life dominated by politics whose juicy Delhi tentacles stretch out to the most rural village, electioneering is a major event, as colourful as a religious festival, and as much show-business as it is in America. To reach India's illiterate – more than 60% – each political party has a symbol. Congress (I), the party of Mrs Gandhi, has a hand. (Nehru's Congress Party split in 1969 into Congress (I), for Indira, and several other smaller Congress parties). The rising Bharatya Janata Party (known as the BJP) has a lotus; the Janata Dal Party has a wheel.

These and other symbols, which may include a pair of yoked bullocks, a sickle, a flower or a rising sun, are chosen by the Election Committees of the parties and are painted on walls throughout the country. In the run-up to an election, politicians address a succession of vast public meetings by roaring around the countryside in cavalcades of tooting cars, or covering their huge constituencies by train and even by plane. It is a measure of the size of the 542 constituencies, each represented by one Lok Sabha seat, that in 1977 the victor of a Bihar constituency won by a margin of 424,545 votes. But, despite the symbols, voting can be confusing since there is no restriction to the number of candidates. In 1985, there were 301 names and symbols listed on the newspaper-sized ballot paper from which Belgaum voters had to make their choice for the Karnataka Legislative Assembly.

Film stars are wheeled out to support candidates, drawing vast crowds - although their intervention in politics is not always reflected in the votes. A film director's charisma once drew 40,000 to a rally, but the candidate lost his deposit at the election. In the South, actors stand themselves, with success: Tamil Nadu, Andhra Pradesh and Karnataka have all had big movie stars as Heads of State.

On polling day, an electorate of about 400 million sallies forth, often en famille, to vote for their choice of more than five thousand candidates at one of the 480,912 polling stations, singing along the way. The women dress in their Sunday best. Bullocks and cows are garlanded, carts decorated. There are fairs, entertainers and plenty of dancing and music. And after the results, there is more fun for the celebrations.

The shadows of Jawaharlal Nehru and of his daughter, Indira Gandhi, still hover over Indian politics – both of their Delhi homes are much-visited public museums vested with an almost sacred atmosphere. Apart from short interventions they were between them prime minister from 1947 until Mrs Gandhi's assassination on October 31, 1984. Then her son, with no political experience, was catapulted into the family seat for five years.

For both Indians and foreigners, it is hard not to think in dynastic terms. Photographs of Nehru and Indira still adorn offices and restaurants. And Indira's personality lingers in the popular mind. Like the decade-long reign of Mrs Thatcher in Britain, her image was surreal for many of her electorate. Her family life, her likes and dislikes were reported as minutely as her political life – she wore handloom saris but no make-up or perfumes; she did not drink nor smoke and, like her father, she took a keen interest in the garden.

She travelled widely and was remarkably accessible to her people and to visitors. Remote villages hailed her as 'Mother'. In Delhi, she held a morning open audience in her garden, a practice begun by her father and continued by her son. And she had an intimate knowledge of Indian culture and wildlife.

This remarkable woman was groomed for her career from an early age. The daughter of Jawaharlal Nehru, a Kashmiri of the Brahmin caste, she received an international schooling. Her marriage to a parsee, Feroz Gandhi, gave her the incalculable advantage of the Gandhi surname. Even in India many people had no idea she was not related to the Mahatma. When her father was Prime Minister, she was first his hostess, and then his political aide from 1957 until his death in 1964. The following year her husband died.

In January 1966, aged 48, she became the second woman ever to be elected Prime Minister of an entire country. Eleven years later, in 1977, her authoritarian ways and her unpopularity (and that of her son, Sanjay) forced her to take the country to the polls. She lost, but remained constantly in the public eye, achieving a landslide victory back to power in January 1980. The same year, Sanjay was killed in an aeroplane accident. Her elder son, Rajiv, was reluctantly dragged into political limelight to stand for parliament for Uttar Pradesh, his home state. Less than four years later his mother was assassinated in her beloved New Delhi garden. And, while India mourned, President Zail Singh swore in the 40-year-old son as her successor at Rashtrapati Bhavan. At a general election held on December 24, 1984, the voters overwhelmingly confirmed him as their leader when Congress won 401 of the 508 seats.

Rajiv threw himself energetically into launching India into rapid and radical industrialisation. His government's first budget drastically cut taxes and relaxed import controls to encourage entrepreneurship and industry – Rajiv's early nicknames were Mr Clean and Computer-ji.

Born August 29, 1944, Rajiv was schooled at the posh but progressive Indian public school, Doon. He then went to Britain where he read mechanical engineering at Trinity College, Cambridge, met his Italian-born wife, Sonia, and trained as an airline pilot before returning home to work for Indian Airlines. But the tragic deaths of his brother and mother totally changed his life. The formerly quiet man soon wore a bullet-proof vest and was being courted by Thatcher, Reagan and Gorbachev. He, Sonia and their teenage son and daughter, Rahul and Priyanka, lived public lives in their heavily fortified home at 7 Race Course Road, around the corner from Indira's house.

But while Rajiv's youth, energy and optimism for India's future won him immediate popularity, five years later the voters called him to account. In the November 1989 general election Vishwanath Pratap Singh, leader of his newly formed Janata Dal Party, came to power, soon to be replaced by Chandra Shekhar. But, faced by the rising, strongly Hindu-biased Bharata Janata Party, known as the BJP, he called another election in May 1991. As the country voted, Rajiv was killed in a bomb explosion at Sriperumbudur, near Madras in Tamil Nadu, on May 21. While India mourned another Gandhi tragedy, Narasimha Rao led Congress (I) through the rest of the election and back into power.

Meanwhile, the big issues of the day remain unresolved: Kashmir, the Punjab and the Mandal Commission's recommendations for more university places and jobs to be reserved for the Scheduled Castes and Tribes which make up 23% of India's population. Then there are the Hindu-Muslim tensions currently focused on the dispute over the Ram Janma Bhumi Temple and Babari Mosque, both claiming the same sacred land at Ayodhya, Bihar. The north-eastern areas, in particular Assam, simmer with discontent and moan for independence, as does the South which harks back to its Dravidian roots to substantiate similar independence claims.

And yet, almost half a century after Independence, despite its own internal problems and the derogatory 'third world' label given by the West, Delhi is the capital of a richly varied but united country which ranks among the top 15 economies of the world. It is self-sufficient in food, has some (but not enough) good education and medical facilities, and has an advanced national science programme – in 1975 India's first own satellite was launched, and in 1984 India sent its first man into space in the Soviet spacecraft Soyuz T-11. Its trade is also vibrant, but businessmen who benefitted from Rajiv's early attempts to liberalise and privatise are now demanding an urgent further dismantling of what is known as the 'licence raj' – the mind boggling array of regulations, taxes and licence controls closing India to foreigners and even, to a great extent, to non-resident Indians and Indians of foreign nationality.

Mrs Gandhi liked to think of herself as 'one of the monuments of Delhi'. But she was also responsible for several more long-lasting landmarks: a vast and superb sports complex for the Asiad in 1982, an impressive arts complex, and a plethora of hotels and fly-overs for the international government meetings. In addition, Connaught Place has lost its sedate neo-Bath stucco character and is now dominated by dramatic high-rises. This overdose of concrete was compensated by the clearing and cleaning up of the capital and its airy, green parks and avenues – a situation now being reversed by the recent acceleration in uncontrolled traffic pollution matched by uncontrolled demolition of New Delhi bungalows and their life-giving surrounding trees. The first went in 1984, to make way for dozens of hideous but lucrative flats. If planning laws remain lax, the ruthless contractors will soon have destroyed this century's best purpose-built city. As one remarked over a glass of imported whisky: 'Lutyens's Delhi is a passing phase. . . . By 2050 – at the very latest – it will all have gone. Delhi will be a modern, multi-storeyed city at last.' So enjoy it while it exists.

If the political pace is too much, residents and visitors can lose themselves in the Islamic monuments built by successive empires and scattered across the city, tucked behind residential homes or surrounded by beautifully kept parks; or they can wander along the blossoming boulevards of New Delhi. For a taste of the old Muslim city, there are the alleys of Old Delhi and Nizamuddin. As the painter, Edward Ardizzone, noted in 1952, Delhi is a 'combination of extreme newness and age, with nothing in between'.

When to go

Delhi's prettiest months are February and March. Despite growing pollution, flowers and trees blossom in Lutyens's spacious city amid the fresh air and sunshine of an English summer. October-November are also green and pleasant but other months bring the extremes of the plains. The debilitating post-monsoon mugginess lifts during September; December-January are distinctly chilly – adored by locals who throw open every window while unprepared tourists shiver. With the intense heat of May-June come dust storms and the hot 'loo' winds, and then the July-August downpours.

FESTIVALS There are festivals to head for and festivals to avoid. People celebrating Holi (March) in Delhi have recently taken to throwing stones instead of harmless pink powder and water. Republic Day , January 26, is a matter of choice. Politicians and tourist offices make a big fuss of it. Everything closes across the country. In Delhi anyone of interest disappears to make family visits to other cities and find some fun, leaving the capital socially dead. The morning parade is led by the President in his ceremonial coach, escorted by the President's Body Guard, founded as his personal body guard by Warren Hastings in 1773, the most senior unit in the Indian Army. Then follow the impressive floats from each state, folk dancing, quantities of gaily caparisoned elephants and camels, and even a helicopter in full elephant fancy-dress showering rose petals. But it continues with a massive and seemingly endless display of guns, tanks and military strength. Each evening that week the strings of lights outlining the Rashtrapati Bhavan are switched on (as they are for Independence Day, August 15), best seen from the rooftop restaurant of the Taj Mahal hotel. The Folk Dance Festival fills every hall for the next two days, followed by Beating Retreat, on January 19, a picturesque sunset parade of massed bands of the armed forces which ends, strangely, with Gandhi's favourite hymn, 'Abide With Me', magical for the few who manage to get seats. Since the Republic Day parade and Beating Retreat are televised live, and since Republic Day is a national holiday with museums and shops closed, it is perhaps not worth planning an itinerary around. Republic Day seat tickets can be obtained from travel agencies and tourist offices.

But, if you are in the area, stay in Delhi for Dussehra (October). It is celebrated in different ways throughout India, and in Delhi as Ram Lila (Rama play). Plays, classical dance, contemporary dance and music recitals fill every hall. Each evening an episode from the Ramayana epic is recounted to commemorate Rama's victory over the demon Ravana and thus the freedom of his captive wife, Sita. Ornate chariot processions daily pass through Old Delhi. On the tenth day, there is a grand procession of huge, firework-stuffed, painted paper effigies of ten-headed wicked Ravana and his relatives which proceeds to the Ram Lila maidan (the open ground between Old and New Delhi). Amid the seething masses of people, the battle of Lanka is re-enacted, Sita is freed and the effigies are burned with bangs, cracks, whoops and a jolly fair. The best way to enjoy the broad outline of the entire Ramayana is to attend a performance by Shobha Singh's troupe: a combination of wit, dance, mime, splendid costumes and headdresses and ingenious scenery staged nightly at the Ram Lila Ground north of New Delhi. *Diwali*, also nationwide, follows three to four weeks later (October-November). Oil lamps in every spring-cleaned house simultaneously light the way for Rama and Sita to return home northwards from Sri Lanka and welcome Lakshmi, the goddess of prosperity, wealth and pleasure, to the start of a new Hindu financial year. (Official New Year is April 13, a public holiday with fairs.) People put on new clothes, eat special sweetmeats and, for nine days or so, the Diwali Mela (fair) is alive with stalls, entertainment and fireworks.

Delhi and Lucknow, both great Mughal centres, celebrate Muslim festivals with feasts and jollity: *Muharram*, commemorating the martyrdom of Imam Hussain, grandson of the Prophet Mohammad; *Id-ul-Fitr*, celebrating the end of Ramadan, the ninth month of the Muslim calendar when there must be rigid fasting during all daylight hours; and *Id-ul-Zuha*, when the sacrifice of Abraham is remembered with prayers, presents for children and new clothes. At Muharram, for nine days the huge tazias (tinsel, silver or brass replicas of Husains's tomb) are paraded by mourning men, accompanied by drummers. There are passion plays; men lash themselves in sorrow; Ulema (religious scholars) read from pulpits in the mosques. It is seen at its most spectacular at Lucknow. See Calendar of Festivals for more festivals.

ARTS Delhi is very lively around Republic Day, Ram Lila and Diwali. In addition, there are the Sangeet Sammelan music festival in November and four important festivals in February: Tansen (music, named after Akbar's court composer); Dhrupad (strictly orthodox music); Maharaj Kalka Bindadi Kathak Mahotsave (classical Kathak dance); and the Shankar Lal Festival (music).

SOCIAL CALENDAR Reaches its height in February-March too. There is the Horse Show, polo, the vintage car rally and the Northern India Golf Championship. India's answer to the Chelsea Flower Show is the Delhi Flower Show, when the air around Purana Qila is heavy and sweet with the scent of thousands of blooms. Of course, being India, there are entertainers as well. It is held in February, after the December-January Rose Show and Chrysanthemum Show. The January International Film Festival, run from Delhi, is held here in alternate years (Delhi 1993). In Delhi it is competitive; when it visits Bombay, Calcutta and elsewhere it is non-competitive.

Getting there: getting away

Hitting and quitting Delhi is easy by air or train. The sparkling new Indira Gandhi International Airport is a quick 30 minutes south-west of New Delhi. However, crossing the city to a central or northern hotel is another story and can take an hour in the daytime. The international airport operates a fixed-rate centralised taxi service for going into Delhi; its taxi drivers should be checked out carefully, particularly for night journeys. Its departure lounge has a bad, over-priced restaurant (usually closed) and fair tourist shops. But the domestic airport, 4km from it has a good restaurant to the right of the check-in desks.

Train is even easier. New Delhi Railway Station lies between Old and New Delhi, and is where the Shatabdi Express leaves; the older Delhi Railway Station, which looks like a Scottish castle, lies north of the old city. Short hops are quicker by train than plane. If the holiday is short, this is a good place to slip in the essential Indian train journey, to Agra on the wonderfully named Taj Express or the speedy Shatabdi Express or to Jaipur on the Pink City Express. The classic inter-city trains – with names like Frontier Mail and Rajdhani Express – take longer than a flight but give an opportunity to see rural life and the landscape and to feel the vastness of the country.

Most international airlines serve Delhi. Indian Airlines and Vayudoot then feed passengers into the rest of the country, especially the surrounding states, major cities and the hills. The daily early morning Rajasthan shuttle stops at Jaipur, Jodhpur and Udaipur. Other daily services include Agra, Ahmedabad, Aurangabad, Bangalore, Bhopal, Bombay, Calcutta, Gwalior, Hyderabad, Khajuraho, Lucknow, Madras, Nagpur, Vadodara, Varanasi. For the hills, daily flights to to Amritsar, Chandigarh (for the narrow gauge railway to Shimla), Jammu and Srinagar as they do up to Kathmandu in Nepal. The weather in Leh determines all flights there (from Delhi or Srinagar). For other places, connections may or may not fly out the same day. And if two flights are necessary, these too may be staggered. Go via Bombay, Madras, Bangalore and Hyderabad for southern cities; via Bombay for Gujarat (except Ahmedabad) and Goa (Dabolim airport, daily); via Madras or Bombay for Sri Lanka (Colombo). The Maldives (Male) are three hops away, via Madras or Bombay, then Trivandrum.

Short train journeys mostly leave early and serve an excellent breakfast of scrambled eggs on toast, bananas and tea, although the Shatabdi Express meals make an abortive attempt at doing something more chic. Go to Agra (2-3 hours) and Gwalior (3-5 hours) on the Shatabdi or Taj Express (New Delhi station); Jaipur (5 hours) and Ajmer (8 hours) on the Pink City Express (Delhi station). Lucknow railway station should be experienced: arrive overnight (10 hours) on the Lucknow Mail or by day (10 hours) on the Gomti Express (both from New Delhi station). Reach the hill cities via Jammu on the overnight (12 hours) Jammu Tawi Mail (Delhi station). For a longer, inter-city journey with excellent arm-chair sightseeing and formidable but safe meals, go on the Rajdhani Express II to Bombay (17 hours) and the Rajdhani Express I – the fastest train in India, hitting 120kph – to Calcutta (16 hours), and on the Tamil Nadu to Madras (32 hours).

Where to stay

Delhi is the best equipped of the big cities. Hotels mushroomed in Delhi in the 80s and now several new or refurbished ones can be recommended. Of the older Delhi hotels, the Imperial has undergone a model restoration. Of the more recent hotels, the flamboyant refurbishment of the Oberoi is effectively a grand rebuilding. Of the new atrium glitzies, the Meridian is probably Delhi's ugliest landmark but the rooms are good. It very much depends upon what you want out of Delhi, what you want out of your hotel and what your budget is as to where you stay. Delhi is the only city with this range of choice.

In such a sprawling capital, location is as important as quality of hotel. Top modern hotels (Taj Mahal, Maurya Sheraton, Oberoi, Taj Palace) are sited in or south of New Delhi's Raj Path, with the exception of the Meridian just north of it, the Holiday Inn right by Connaught Place, and the Hyatt way to the south and nowhere near the monuments. Older hotels with good character and varying facilities are scattered: Ashok south of Rashtrapati Bhavan,

Oberoi Maidens north of Old Delhi, and the Imperial bang in the middle. This, with the Holiday Inn and the more modest Connaught Place hotels, are the best bases for Old and New Delhi sight-seeing. To avoid soaring taxi bills, use the auto-rickshaws usually waiting at the gates of grand hotels (they are not allowed inside).

Another important criterion is food and night life since the best are found in the newer hotels. Delhi's night-life is centred on what locals call 'hotel culture', and it is much better in some hotels than others. To help gauge how a hotel relates to the city, its distance both from Connaught Place and from the airport are given below. Book early for October-March (many tourists are not deterred by the cold), especially if there is also some big international event. Hotel swimming pools are usually emptied in the winter so, if a daily plunge is essential, check that the pool is in action. Even in Delhi, where electric power is reasonably constant, all good hotels have their own generators, 'Otherwise', as one manager pointed out, 'guests would first get stuck in the lift, then check out'.

THE MODERN DELUXE
Taj Mahal Hotel, 1 Mansingh Road, New Delhi 110011
Tel: 3016162; Fax: 3017299; Telex: 31-66874/61898 TAJ DIN
Airport 18km; Connaught Place 3km
300 rooms, including 28 suites, bath attached. Single Rs1,750; double Rs1,900; suites on application.

Every service including travel counter, car rental, bank, business centre, pool, health club, beauty salon, chemist, baby sitter, Khazana shopping arcade, CNN TV service.

Often referred to as Taj Mansingh, Delhi's most friendly deluxe hotel, opened 1978, is well-established and ideal for both holiday-makers and businessmen. Best located of the luxury hotels, and the least ostentatious. Dazzling white marble lobby with fountain and miniature paintings complements the safe-but-smart refurbished rooms (good city views from high floors). Standards and most services meet the Taj Group's high reputation. Sumptuous health club with separate facilities for men and women, from gym to jacuzzi; large swimming pool; a heavily tested and recommended travel counter; and an exemplary shop, more like a department store. Chinese and Indian restaurants good, as is the coffee shop with forest murals; at lunchtime, the bar's little fish buffet and the rooftop Italian restaurant's sumptuous buffet (and views), possibly the only buffets in India whose food can be recommended, make excellent mid-sight-seeing stops. Be warned: reserve dinner tables and make health club appointments. Discotheque

47

mediocre.

Oberoi, Dr Zakir Hussain Marg, New Delhi 110003
Tel: 363030; Fax: 360484; Telex: 3829/74019 OBDL IN
Airport 20km, Connaught Place 5km
350 rooms, including 30 suites, bath attached. Single Rs1,850; double Rs2,050; suites Rs3,000-6,500.

Every service, including travel agency, car rental, bank, business centre, services, pool, health club, yoga classes, beauty parlour, baby sitter, shopping arcade, CNN TV service.

The pioneer Indian high-rise luxury hotel, opened in 1965 and now totally and extravagantly refurbished to make it the classiest, most international deluxe hotel in town, but one whose formal atmosphere is more suited to the businessman than the holiday-maker. Highly efficient and experienced dark-suited staff; a service directory so comprehensive it is a hardback book for bed-time browsing.

Excellent site: all rooms overlook lush golf course or zoo, each dotted with Mughal and Lodi monuments. The mirror-bright marble lobby with jali-work screen now leads via the Art Deco-style black and gold lift to plush rooms: buttoned, salmon pink upholstery, dark wood, vast televisions, walls hung with prints, light switches galore, sumptuous chestnut-brown granite bathrooms with baths to take the largest body – one suite even has a jacuzzi. The five restaurants, 3 bars and discotheque include a rooftop Taipan that vies (with the Maurya's Dum Pukt) for top Delhi restaurant position, and spacious lobby bar overlooking excellent pool. The health club, with separate extensive equipment for men and women, is considered by some globe-trotters to be the best in Delhi, if not the world.

Maurya Sheraton, Sardar Patel Marg, New Delhi 110021
Tel: 3010101; Fax: 3010908; Telex: 31-61447 WELC IN
Central Reservations for the Welcomgroup are here (see p. 13).
Airport 10km; Connaught Place 7km
500 rooms, including 8 suites, bath attached. Single Rs1,725-2,500; double Rs1,925-2,700; suites Rs4,250-7,000.

Every service including travel counter, car rental, bank, business centre, baby sitter, solar heated swimming pool, health club, beauty salon, discotheque, shopping arcade, Executive Club.

Built and run by the Welcomgroup, owned by India Tobacco Company (ITC). The huge, stepped building and its adjoining more private Towers section is adorned with quality contemporary Indian art inspired by the Mauryan Empire and commissioned from prominent painters and sculptors – J. Swaminathan, Akbar Padamsee, M. F. Husain, Tyeb Mehta, Ramachandran, Meera Mookerjee (hers is the Ashoka in front of the hotel) and Krishen Khanna (who oversaw the project). Throughout, strong India-inspired designs avoid the brash anonymity of most Indian hotels.

Its major disadvantage is being slightly too far out; its advantage is closeness to the airports. Facilities and atmosphere good; service variable. Executive Tower rooms and fun suites with sauna or large terrace good; other rooms again vary and need checking on arrival. Health club good, pretty pool and lawn, shopping arcade excellent. (In-house astrologer, Mohinda Chowpra, will 'reveal the heights to which you may rise'.) Food in three restaurants some of the best in town – Dum Pukt vies with Oberoi's Taipan for top place, so book. Pleasant coffee shop and bar; jolly discotheque.

Taj Palace, Sardar Patel Marg, Diplomatic Enclave, New Delhi 110021
Tel: 3010404; Fax: 3011252; Telex: 31-62761/61673 TAJS IN
Airport 10km; Connaught Place 7km
431 rooms, including 33 suites, bath attached. Single Rs1,600; double Rs1,750; suites on application.

All mod. cons including travel agency, car rental, bank, business services, health club, beauty parlour, pool, shopping arcade.

With a honey-coloured marble lobby big enough to play elephant polo, this hotel is for the athletic guest. Fresh rooms; some suites with terraces.

Opened in 1983, this impeccable machine is located next to the Maurya (with those pros and cons) and geared to conference businessmen, complete with a slightly down-market version of the sister hotel's Khazana shopping arcade and an assortment of restaurants including one verging on gimmicky: a replica carriage from the Orient Express train serving over-priced Continental food. Lightning fast room service, excellent health club and pool.

Hyatt Regency, Bhikaji Cama Place, Ring Road, New Delhi 110066
Tel: 609911; Fax: 678833; Telex: 31-61512 HYT IN
Airport 12km; Connaught Place 10km
535 rooms, including 23 suites, bath attached. Single Rs1,727; double Rs1,903; suite Rs2,150-9,000.

Every mod. con including travel agency, car rental, bank, health club, beauty parlour, pool, extensive shopping arcade, tennis courts, discotheque, plus the Hyatt Regency Club and Hyatt Business Centre.

An all-gleaming, all-computerised, mostly-marble businessman's toy. The Regency Club fills a whole floor: super deluxe guests of its 65 rooms have special staff, free breakfast and cocktails in their special lounge and a special key to the floor to keep the hoi polloi at bay. Newish, but now settling down and has a good pool and health club, spacious 24-hour café, and delicious North Indian and Chinese Szechwan food. But atmosphere and location are geared to the worker; the holiday-maker thinks he is still in the office.

Le Meridian, Windsor Place, Janpath, New Delhi 110011

Tel: 383960; Fax: 384220; Telex: 31-63076 HOME IN

Airport 23km; Connaught Place 2km

375 rooms, including 59 suites, bath attached. Single Rs1,850; double Rs2,000; suites Rs4,000-12,000.

All mod. cons include business centre, health club (Universal equipment), beauty parlour, shopping, baby-sitter, pool, travel desk.

Designed by a certain Mr Raja Aderie, the solution to this monstrous landmark (how did it ever get planning permission?) is to be inside it. There, the giant atrium is stocked with bar and coffee shop from which to be mesmerised by the fountain and the four capsule lifts silently rising and falling the full height of the hotel like giant fairy-lit lanterns. Shopping is on the 1st floor; restaurants on ground, 1st and rooftop (with the nightclub). The rooms are in between, full of light, surprisingly peaceful and with stunning views over the core of Lutyens's New Delhi; suites at the corners on every floor. The circular pool with large terrace on the 4th floor hovers above Delhi's traffic; tennis court but no other garden.

Holiday Inn, Barakhamba Avenue, Connaught Place, New Delhi 110001

Tel: 3320101; Fax: 3325335; Telex: 31-61186 HIND IN

Airport 24km; Connaught Place 1km

500 rooms, including 55 suites. Single Rs1,700-1,900; double Rs1,850-2,000; suites Rs2,500-10,000

Every mod. con including heath club, gym, pool, beauty parlour, baby-sitting, travel counter, shopping, business centre, two-floor Club Select for businessmen, Presidential Tower of suites and rooms with special check-in and private business centre.

Opened in 1988, this aims to out-gadget and out-chic the Oberoi and Hyatt. The best description of the building is the management's: 'A 25-storeyed, triple tower building with a 4-storeyed Atrium Lobby'. The lobby can be added to any tourist trail: an atrium that looks as if it has been conceived by a clever child with giant white marble building cubes; sci-fi capsule lifts zip up and down one side, a waterfall tumbling down from on high like the Victoria Falls fills the other – and fills the whole atrium with a thunderous din so that lip-reading for key num-

bers is an essential skill of reception staff. Rooms spacious (children under 12 years sharing with an adult are free) with 'pulsating shower heads' and 'work activity desks'; classy shops, 6 restaurants (including Gourmet Health Food Cafe), 2 bars (one with zebra-skin furniture and wallpaper) and the optimistically named Annabelles discotheque. Unashamedly elite Presidential Tower with Club Privé and its very own atrium. Despite newness, a jolly atmosphere.

Hotel Kanishka, 19 Ashok Road, New Delhi 110001

Tel: 3324422; Telex: 31-62788/62736

Airport 20km; Connaught Place 2km

317 rooms, including 17 suites, bath attached. Single Rs1,050; double Rs1,200; suite Rs2,000.

Services include travel agent, bank, car rental, beauty parlour, business services.

This and the following hotel, the Park, are not in the same class as those listed above. But both are well located and well run. This one has especially good views of New Delhi's centrepiece from high rooms, and has a good pool and surrounding terrace and gardens. It also has an excellent adjoining shopping centre where many states have their tourist offices on the upper floors.

Park Hotel, 15 Parliament Street, New Delhi 110001

Tel: 352477; Fax: 352025; Telex: 31-65231

Airport 14km; Connaught Place ½km

234 rooms, bath attached. Single Rs1,450; double Rs1,550; suites Rs3,000-4,000.

Services include business centre, travel countrer, pool.

As with the Kanishka, above, a practical and central hotel for sight- seeing; some rooms overlook the Janta Manta. Rooms and service fine; pool area unglamorous.

THE OLD WITH STYLE

Imperial, Janpath, New Delhi 110001

Tel: 3325332; Fax: 3314542; Telex: 31-62603 HTL IMP

Airport 18km; Connaught Place ½km

175 rooms, including 3 suites, bath attached. Single Rs1100, double Rs1200, suites Rs3000.

Facilities include bank, car rental, beauty salon, tennis, pool, garden, shopping arcade.

Easily the best of Delhi's old hotels; also the most central. Rooms now almost all sensitively restored and refurbished, keeping their original furniture of cane chairs, hardwood writing desks, bold floral carpets, standard lamps, period dressing tables and Daniells prints. Built to the latest designs in 1933-35 by Raibahadur Ranjit Singh, grandfather of the present owner Mr Jasdev Singh, on an 8-acre site facing on to Queensway (Janpath), the north-south nerve of New Delhi. Italian marble, London silver and crockery and European chandeliers were piled into the white building ready for the grand banquet and opening by Vicereine Lady Willingdon (Lord Willingdon was Viceroy 1931-36), which launched it as a social and political focus. Reluctant air-conditioning, stored in vast trunks, blows hot air in winter and cold in summer 'eventually', says the smiling manager. Every meal, from breakfast onwards, can be taken on the extensive lawns shaded by soaring royal palms. A haven of peace and relaxation amid city bustle. Beware: 120 new rooms being built, so go for old ones.

Ashok, 50-B Chanakyapuri, New Delhi 110021
Tel: 600121/600412; Fax: 6873216; Telex: 31-65647 ASOK IN
Central Reservations for the Ashok chain are here (see p. 13).
Airport 12km; Connaught place 5km
571 rooms, including 111 suites, bath attached.
Single Rs1,450; double Rs1,600; Suites Rs2,250-12,500.

All mod. cons include travel agent, car rental, bank, health club, beauty salon, baby sitter, tennis, pool, shopping arcade. Federico Fellini swears by the in-house astrologer.

ITDC's showpiece hotel of their vast, and usually very disappointing, chain. This hotel is good. Built in 1954, with huge ordinary rooms (with floor-to-ceiling opening windows) that would satisfy the most claustrophobic designer; even more space in the suites and public areas, plus big lawns. Dale Keller refurbished a dozen suites, each with the crafts of an individual state. And his restaurants are some of the prettiest in Delhi – a tented French one, gloriously green and white garden bar, a spacious and sunny coffee shop overlooking the pool and extensive lawn dotted with trees like a private garden. Charming old retainer staff; good Indian buffet for lunch and dinner, shopping arcade merits a detour.

Oberoi Maidens, 7 Sham Nath Marg, Delhi 110054
Tel: 2525464; Telex: 66303/78163 OMDL IN
Central Reservations for the Oberoi chain are here (see p. 12)
Airport 24km; Connaught Place 7km
46 rooms, including 20 suites. Single Rs1,250; double Rs1,350; suites on application.

Facilities include fridge in every room, car rental, baby sitter, tennis court, pool, garden.

Built just north of Old Delhi (Shahjahanabad) in 1900 by Mr Maiden, this is one of Delhi's oldest hotels, modest but charming. Lutyens stayed here while his new city was going up. Colonial building; spacious rooms ('double suites' particularly good) with renovated bathrooms, period furniture and wide verandahs set in eight acres of peaceful, bird-filled garden with hard tennis court, pool (complete with

ornamental bridge) and big shady neem, pipal and banyan trees; a true rus-in-urbis atmosphere. Well-placed for exploring in Shahjahanabad and Civil Lines; not so good for nipping to a business meeting or the airport.

Ambassador, Sujan Singh Park, New Delhi 11003
Tel: 690391; Telex: 31-3277
Airport 12km; Connaught Place 5km.
69 rooms, including 5 suites, bath attached.
Single Rs750; double Rs975; suites Rs1,150-1,800.

Services include fridge in each room, room service, travel counter.

Built in 1951 by one of the New Delhi engineers, Sir Shoba Singh, father of the eminent journalist Khushwant Singh, in the Sujan Singh Park of residential apartments, just south of the Taj Mahal hotel. Still extremely period; no hint of the anonymous international hotel culture. Spacious rooms with huge fridges in equally huge bathrooms; plenty of original furniture – panelled corridors, underlit curved bar and the great circular, domed and immensely popular South Indian restaurant, Dasa Prakash. Minimal garden.

Note: Claridge's, an old hotel under fairly new ownership, has recently dissatisfied so many guests that it can only be recommended for its restaurants.

THE GOOD VALUE AND CENTRAL
These simple, no-frills hotels are mostly right in Connaught Place and often on top of their own good, public, ground-floor restaurant. The nearest peaceful lawn would be at the Imperial, for the price of a drink or meal. All are about 20km from the airport.

Hotel Marina, G59 Connaught Circus, New Delhi 110001
Tel: 352419; Telex: 62969
93 rooms, including 2 suites; bath attached.
Double Rs775; suite Rs1,100.

Posh lobby with white marble floor, plaster columns and chandeliers leads to long, long corridors of rooms; so try for one not too far along and overlooking Connaught Place (those facing inwards are dark and viewless).

Nirula's, L-Block, Connaught Circus, New Delhi 110001
Tel: 3322419; Telex: 31-66224 NCHS IN
29 rooms, including 4 suites; bath attached.
Single Rs399; double Rs700; suites Rs750-795.

More famous for its street-level restaurant. Has the advantage of being easy to find your way back to in the circular confusion of Connaught Circus.

York Hotel, K-Block, Connaught Circus, New Delhi 110001
Tel: 3323769; Telex: 31-63031 YORK IN

28 rooms, each a double with bath attached. Single tariff Rs395; double Rs560.

Clean and simple, with room service from the good street-level Ginza and York restaurants.

Hotel Fifty-Five, H-55, Connaught Circus, New Delhi 110001
Tel: 3321244/3321278
15 rooms; bath attached. Single tarrif Rs600.

Found up steps beside a tailor and near Grindlay's Bank, the small rooms benefit from Mr Mohan Joshi's homely atmosphere.

Central Court Hotel, N-Block, Connaught Circus, New Delhi 110001
Tel: 3315013
36 rooms, including 11 suites; 19 with bath attached. Single Rs225; double Rs350; suite Rs550.

Right beside the Amber Restaurant. Claims to be the oldest Connaught Place hotel, opened in the early 50s; deluxe rooms open onto a wide terrace.

OTHER ACCOMMODATION

The following are all well located and excellent value. Rooms are clean, atmosphere friendly and the single male or female traveller would be safe and well looked after. Services are adequate but not extensive; and some rooms have bath attached.

India International Centre, Lodhi Estate, New Delhi (tel: 619431); single Rs325; double Rs530; particularly nice grounds, plus good library, regular lectures and good restaurant and bar patronised by Delhi's journalists, writers, academics and gossips.

YMCA Tourist Hostel, Jai Singh Road, New Delhi (tel: 311915); single Rs125-215, double Rs285-370.

YWCA International Guest House, Parliament Street, New Delhi (tel: 311561/311970); single Rs140; double Rs230.

Information and reservations

If you enter India through Delhi, this is the moment to acquire countrywide information and to book as much as possible. It is maddening to arrive at Sanchi, in Central India, and be told the guidebook is only available in Delhi. There are offices representing everyone and everything here. The capital's obsession with bureaucracy is catching, however, resulting in slowness and inefficiency, the notable exception being the Janpath Tourist Office. But whatever you need is here somewhere. The usual government office opening hours are Mon.-Sat., 10am-5pm; closed every Sun. and the second Sat. of each month.

Delhi Tourism Development Corporation, N Block, Connaught Place (tel: 3313637). Also desks at New Delhi Railway Station, Delhi Railway Station and airports. All open 7am-9pm, except the airport one, which is usually open 24 hours. Good city tours.

Government of India Tourist Office, 88 Janpath (tel: 3320005), known to many as the Janpath Tourist Office. Extremely good. Knowledgeable assistants on Delhi and every part of India – although if a place is not considered a 'tourist destination', such as Jaunpur, they may need persuading that it exists with the help of a map. Also has desk at airports. Mon.-Fri., 9am-6pm; Sat.9am-1pm. City tours leave from L Block, Connaught Place.

Each state has a tourist office in Delhi, usually very ungrand but with staff who are mostly extremely helpful, and occasionally useless. Most stock lots of information, plus the state map. And most are conveniently bunched together in three big groups and best visited in person on weekdays between 10am and 5pm; some close for lunch. Assam, Gujarat, Karnataka, Maharashtra, Orissa, Tamil Nadu and West Bengal (not good) lie behind their respective state shops on Baba Kharak Singh Marg; Bihar, Jammu & Kashmir, Kerala and Madhya Pradesh are in the Kanishka Hotel Shopping Plaza, all very helpful; and Haryana, Himachal Pradesh, Rajasthan and Uttar Pradesh are in Chanderlok Building at 36 Janpath – this last group could be more helpful. The remainder are Andhra Pradesh, in Andhra Bhawan, 1 Ashok Road; Goa in Goa Sadan, 18 Amrita Shergil Marg; Meghalaya at 9 Aurangzeb Road and Sikkim in New Sikkim House Building, 14 Panchsheel Marg.

The Andaman & Nicobar Liaison Office is at Curzon Road Apartments, Kasturba Gandhi road (tel: 387015).

While getting organised for the rest of the trip, visit the Archaeological Survey of India, next to the National Museum, which has the most authoritative area maps and guides (that is, the ones in print) to all the major archaeological sites (usually sold out on site). The Indian headquarters of the Worldwide Fund for Nature are at C-570 Defence Colony. The special Project Tiger office is at Shastri Bhavan.

There are plenty of newspapers in the capital. *The Times of India, The Indian Express, The Hindustan Times* and *The Statesman* are the principal ones, full of news of the Government's doings, plus daily lists of main events. *The Times of India* runs 'The Week That Will Be' on Fridays, an exhaustive list of forthcoming cultural events. *The Indian Express* also has a preview cultural section and has the biggest circulation of all Indian English-language newspapers. *India Today,* published fortnightly in Delhi, provides spunky political, economic and social commentary. *Delhi Diary* (free from hotel bell captains) is packed with arbitrary lists of cultural events, exhibitions, restaurants and shops, lacking any criticism. The tourist office's fortnightly *Programme of Events* gives skeleton information.

Best of the several guide-books is *Guide to Delhi*, 2nd edition published 1982 by ITDC. Ensure the free map from the Janpath Tourist Office is the latest edition. Otherwise invest a few rupees in Delhi Road Map 1990 edition, on sale at bookshops and from street vendors. See also the bibliography for a selection of the many books on Delhi. See shopping section for bookshops.

Delhi has several excellent libraries including the American Library, 24 Kasturba Gandhi Marg (tel: 44251); the British Council Library, All India Fine Arts and Crafts Society, Rafi Marg (tel: 381401); Max Mueller Bhavan, Kasturba Gandhi Marg (tel: 384956/382792); Delhi Public Library in Old Delhi; the excellent Rama Krishna Mission Library in New Delhi and the three government-funded cultural academies: Lalit Kala Akademi (tel: 387243), Sahitaya Akademi (tel: 388667) and Sangeet Natak Akademi (tel: 387248), all in Rabindra Bhavan, Feroz Shah Road.

TRAVEL AGENTS

American Express, Wenger House, A Block, Connaught Place (tel: 344119/344485); to replace lost or stolen travellers' cheques requires a photocopy of the police report, one photo of the cardholder, the counterfoil slip issued with the cheques and the cheque numbers; if the last ones are also lost, a telex is made to the place of issue. Cox & Kings (India), Indra Place, H-Block, Connaught Circus, New Delhi (tel: 3320067/3310343); Mercury Travels, 4A Ground Fl, Jeevan Tara Building, Parliament Street (tel: 321403/321411) and at Oberoi (tel: 69571); SITA World Travel, F12 Connaught Place (tel: 3311122/3314181); Tiger Tops Mountain Travel, 1/1 Rani Jhansi Road (tel: 771055/731075; fax: 9111 777483; telex: 3163016), especially for wildlife parks and for Nepal; Trade Wings, 60 Janpath (tel: 321322); TCI, Hotel Metro, N-49 Connaught Circus (tel: 3315181/3315834).

AIRLINE OFFICES

Indian Airlines, Kanchenjunga, Barakhamba Road (tel: 3310052); the first floor, reached via steps at the back of the building; when found at last, huge queues of elbowing and shouting people that do not move for hours. Conclusion: pay a travel agent to do the work, particularly for several bookings on a rover ticket, and go off and enjoy Delhi. There is a small Vayudoot office at Malhotra Building, F-Block, Janpath (tel: 622122/82305/623056).

The major international airlines offices cluster round Connaught Place, but a few are further afield. Aeroflot, MBC House, 1st floor, N-1 Connaught Place (tel: 3312843); Air France, Ashok

Hotel, (tel: 604691); Air India, Jeevan Bharati, 124 Connaught Circus (tel: 331225); Air Lanka, Hotel Imperial, Janpath (tel: 3324789); Alitalia, 19 Kasturba Gandhi Marg (tel: 3311019); British Airways, 1A Connaught Place, (tel: 3317428); Japan Airlines, Chandralok Building, 36 Janpath (tel: 3324922); KLM, Tolstoy Marg (tel: 3315841); Lufthansa, 56 Janpath (tel: 3323206); Pan Am, Chandralok Building, 36 Janpath (tel: 3325222); PIA, Kailash Building, 26 Kasturba Gandhi Marg (tel: 3313161); Royal Nepal Airlines, 44 Janpath (tel: 321572); SAS, 12A Connaught Place (tel: 392526); Thai International, 12A Connaught Place (tel: 3323638).

TRAIN RESERVATIONS

Foreigners go to Baroda House, Kasturba Gandhi Marg (tel: 387889), where Tourist Guide Assistants advise and help book trains for anywhere in India and sell Indrail Passes. They also have a special tourist quota of seats. Northern Railway Reservation Office, opposite K Block, Connaught Circus (tel: 344877) for air-conditioned and first class tickets on trains from New Delhi and Delhi stations, plus Indrail Passes. Much queuing. Open Mon.-Sat. 8am-8pm; Sun. 8am-1pm. As with flights, a travel agent will obtain tickets for a token fee.

FOREIGN MISSIONS

Embassies, high commissions and consulates are concentrated in Chanakyapuri (Diplomatic Enclave), specially reserved for them when New Delhi was built, including UK (tel: 601371), USA (tel: 600651) and West Germany (tel: 604861), all on Shantipath. France is at 2 Aurangzeb Road (tel: 374682). For neighbouring countries, Bhutan is on Chandragupta Marg (tel: 609217), Burma (Myanmar) at 3/50F Nyaya Marg, Chanakyapuri (tel: 319461), Nepal at 1 Barakhamba Road (tel: 3811484), Pakistan, 2/50G Shantipath (tel: 600604) and Sri Lanka at 27 Kautilya Marg, Chanakyapuri (tel: 3010201). For others, see telephone directory. Foreigners' Registration Department is at Hans Bhavan (first floor), Tilak Bridge (tel: 272790).

PERMITS FOR RESTRICTED AREAS

Very much better obtained before leaving home. However, it is possible to try and get them in Delhi in person or through a recommended travel agent who will plough through the forest of paperwork. Those longing to experience Indian bureaucracy at first hand get permits for Darjeeling from Foreigners' Registration Office (see above). But they go to the Ministry of Home Affairs, Lok Nayak Bhavan, Khan Market for Sikkim and other restricted north-eastern areas, and the Ministry of Home Affairs, North Block for Andaman and Nicobar islands. Nepal, Bhutan and Burma consulates issue their visas. Janpath Tourist Office issues All India Liquor Permits.

There is a big General Post Office and inland Telegraph Office at Eastern Court, Janpath. Overseas Communications Service, Bangla Sahib Road, sends cables abroad. But both telephone and cable are more easily tackled through the hotel. If you are ill, the recommended hotels have good in-house doctors or can call one quickly. There are good chemists at Connaught Place (the one in the underground Super Bazar is open 24-hours) and, near the Taj Mahal hotel, in Khan Market.

The city by day

Delhi is made up of about fifteen cities, spanning the period from the 11th to the 20th centuries. There is little left of the early cities. They litter the plains, some still living, some deserted ruins. Rulers tended to build drastically over the city they inherited or abandon it for a fresh power-house on virgin soil. This luxury of space, unknown to any other historic capital, continues to be explored for housing and industry. In the smart residential areas south of New Delhi, often called colonies, houses are surrounded by large, leafy gardens, far different from cramped Bombay. Thus Old Delhi (Shahjahanabad) and New Delhi, the two most recent cities and the heart of modern Delhi, are relatively intact – although M. M. Kaye, author of *The Far Pavilions*, remembers well the open vistas of the 1940s, dotted with Mughal buildings that are now destroyed or cluttered up with concrete.

The capital is best seen city by city, outdoors. There are few opening and closing times, lots of parks to pause in, and only the very centre gets jammed up with traffic. Compared to Bombay and Calcutta, it is a spacious dream. Furthermore, most roads are known by a single name, unusually straightforward for an Indian city. Explore Mughal Shahjahanabad's tiny streets, markets and fort on foot; expansive Imperial New Delhi, now India's government headquarters, by car or auto rickshaw, stopping here and there (drivers wait quite happily). Ruins of Purana Qila and Feroz Shah Kotla cities are just to the east, a rickshaw ride away. But first take a car out south to the remains of the oldest cities, glorious for a sunny ramble among the monuments and hillocks and a picnic. Delhi's many indoor museums and museum houses are excellent; most close on Mondays.

ITDC and DTDC (Delhi Transport Development Corporation) do morning tours to New Delhi (but not inside Rashtrapati Bhavan) and out to the Qtub Minar etc. (see p. 55); afternoon tours to Old Delhi (Shahjahanabad) include the Red Fort. Taking both gives a good idea of the overall layout, even if the chronology is thrown out of gear. Prices are cheap, guides good and pauses at monuments not too short – to cover that ground costs ten times as much by taxi and takes far longer by any other transport. Book ITDC tours at L Block, Connaught Place (tel: 350331); DTDC tours at Scindia House, opposite N Block, Connaught Circus.

The Janpath Tourist Office rents out guides for a half or full day. The recommended travel agents can arrange a car and a good driver. A taxi can take five people before there is a surcharge. Auto rickshaws weave through in-town traffic quickest of all. As Delhi is so spread out, it is worth paying the small charge to keep your transport waiting to avoid being stranded and having a long walk.

ISLAM Delhi is a good place to see some of the earliest and most magnificent Islamic buildings in the sub-continent – and visits to nearby Agra, Lucknow and to Lahore in Pakistan (all covered in this chapter) give a fuller picture. A succession of invaders pouring over the Hindu Kush introduced Islam to north India. Muhammad bin Qasim came first, in 711. Mahmud of Ghazni followed in 1001, encouraging mass conversion. But neither became rulers of Delhi, whose stategic position made it the key to power in north India. Then, in 1192, the Turkish invader Mohammad of Ghor's slave general Qutb-un-din Aibak defeated the Hindu ruler of Delhi, Prithviraj III; and when Mohammad of Ghor was assassinated in Lahore in 1206, Aibak, merely governor until then, assumed control there and then made Delhi his power base for the first major Muslim kingdom in India. His rule marked the beginning of the Delhi Sultanate to be succeeded by the Mughal Empire. For the next six centuries, Islam was the dominant social and cultural force in Delhi, creating a rich Indo-Islamic culture (see also p. 46).

Delhi's hundreds of Islamic buildings and ruins help trace the story. Landmark ones begin with the Quwwat-ul-Islam Masjid, India's first mosque; and continue with the nearby Qutb Minar, Ghiyasuddin Tughlaq's tomb at Tughlaqabad, the Sayyid and Lodi tombs in Lodi Gardens, Sher Shar Sur's Qila-i-Kuhna Masjid at Purana Qila, Humayun's nearby tomb, the remaining core of Shah Jahan's Lal Qila (Red Fort) and his Jami Masjid; Aurangzeb's pretty but weaker Moti Masjid and finally the 18th century tomb of Safdar Jang, reflecting a culture in decline.

Muslims (which means 'those who have submitted'), believe in the total surrender of the self to the will of Allah (God). This fatalistic acceptance of God's will is coupled with a belief in equality of all in life and death and in a caste-free society – hence its early popularity with lower social groups. As a monotheistic religion, to avoid the danger of any profanity Islam permits no images of Allah; indeed, idolatry is an unforgivable sin.

The Prophet Muhammad, born in Mecca around 570, is believed to be the last and greatest of the prophets; it was he who consolidated Islam (which means 'submission to God') and preached that there was one God and that there should be one community of believers whose jihad (sacred duty) was to spread the word, if necessary by war. Muhammad died in 632, and by the time the Muslims reached India just 80 years later they had conquered Syria, Iraq, Egypt, Turkey, Iran and had reached the borders of southern France. Today, 11% of India's population is Muslim, some 80 million people, which makes it the largest community of Muslims in any country.

The Quran, Islam's sacred book, records the Prophet's revelations. In them, there is much that is similar to the Old Testament of Jews and Christians (Jesus is recognised as just one of many prophets). For instance, God is creator of the universe, God rewards the faithful and punishes the wicked, God can bestow renewed life after death.

A Muslim has five duties, or pillars: Belief in one true God with Muhammad as his Prophet; the reminder of this by showing humility and praying five times daily; alms-giving and other charitable works; observing a fast from dawn to dusk during Ramadan, the month Muhammad received his revelation; and going on hajj (pilgrimage) to Mecca at least once in a lifetime. Since the aim of marriage is primarily to have children, a Muslim man is permitted to take four wives at any one time. Muslims are not to drink wine, eat pork or display pride, arrogance or ostentation.

Shortly after the death of the Prophet, there was a doctrinal split over who was his legitimate successor, his Caliph. The Sunnis insisted that the Caliph be elected; the Shias that succession should be by descent from the Prophet through his son-in-law. The majority of Indian Muslims have been and still are Sunni.

Sufism is the mystical thread in Islamic thought. Most Muslims on the sub-continent have followed the Sufi path which could assimilate many local religious customs, such as singing and dancing. Also, Sufism echoes many Buddhist and Hindu ideas such as the fundamental belief in the individual's relationship with God and in the release of each person's spiritual awareness. This mystical idea arose in the 10th century and was practised by holy men of various customs and traditions within society, not a separate sect. The Sufi order a traveller to northern India is most likely to encounter is the Chishti. Begun in 966, it was brought to India by the saint Khwajah Muin uddin Chishti who reached Delhi in 1192 (with Aibak's army) and was buried at Ajmer in Rajasthan, to be visited by most of the great Mughal emperors. Another is Hazrat Nizamuddin Aulia, buried at Nizamuddin in Delhi, who promoted the avoidance of temporal power.

The masjid (meaning 'place of prostration'), or mosque, is the most important building for Muslims. In essence, its plan is derived from the Prophet's house at Medina. It has a large open courtyard with a vaulted hall at one end. The courtyard has a tank for ritual washing; the hall has a mihrab indicating the direction of Mecca, for prayer, and a pulpit; and sometimes there is a minaret from which the muezzin summons the faithful to prayer – the muezzins in small towns still call, but in Old Delhi many mosques play a recording through loud-speakers.

Although a Muslim believes that all men are equal in life and in death, and tomb-building and veneration of graves is frowned upon, tombs of the Muslim powerful are some of the greatest contributions to Islamic architecture, and are some of the world's greatest funerary monuments. In the sub-continent, a Muslim's tomb is usually a single vaulted chamber, sometimes with a mosque attached. It may have a surrounding walled rauza (garden) with symmetric parterres divided by streams of water, the whole known as a char bagh (four-garden) and reflecting the Quran's description of paradise. The cenotaph lies in the centre of the chamber, above the grave or tomb, and while a man's has an arched ridge along the top, a woman's is flat. Inside it, the body lies with the head to the north and on one side to face Mecca in the west. The vault enables the body to sit up in response to the angels; its dome on the outside symbolises eternity.

Early cities, Lal Kot to Jahanpanah Quite the nicest introduction to Delhi is a mini-rural trip, a visual history of early Delhi seen through the cities and monuments set in fields, villages and parkland. On the way to the site of the first cities, down Sri Arobindo Marg, a detour left down Kidwai Nagar leads to the grand tomb of Darya Khan, who served all the Lodi sultans (the keen can go on to see the Sayyid ruler Mubarak Shah's tomb and the Lodi period Moth-ki-Masjid, as good as those in Lodi Gardens). Back on Sri Arobindo Marg, another road left, Khael Gaon Marg, leads to scanty ruins of prosperous *Siri*, Delhi's second major city. It was built by Ala-ud-din, Afghan Turk and Sultan of the second Delhi dynasty, the Khiljis (1290-1320), although none of the palace remains. Its water came from Haus Khas. This haus (reservoir) was later, under Feroz Shah Tughlaq (the Tughlaqs ruled 1320-1414), surrounded by a university (1354, see fragments of the fine two-storeyed colonnade on south and east banks) and Feroz Shah's own tomb – the village cottages are mostly newly transformed into upmarket boutiques, with the delightful Village Bistro serving excellent food and drink among them.

The rather insubstantial ruins of Mohammad Tughlaq's *Jahanpanah* city (begun 1325) adjoin Siri to the south, but it is worth taking a final left off Sri Arobindo Marg, beside the Aurobindo Ashram, to find Begampur Mosque (1387), a fort-like structure with kirkis (perforated windows) probably built by Firoz Shah's prime minister.

Out at *Lal Kot*, very little remains of the first citadel of Delhi, built around 1060 and won from the Tomar Rajputs by the Chauhan Rajputs. (The Tomars' city of Dillika was founded in 736.) Their 12th century ruler, Prithviraj III, extended the city and renamed it after himself, Qila (citadel) Rai Pithora. Then came the Turks. In 1206, the great builder and former slave Qutb-ud-din Aibak proclaimed himself the first Sultan of Delhi – he had been governor since 1193. This Sultanate period, under various dynasties, lasted until 1526. Aibak's Slave dynasty (1206-1246) marked the start of the all-pervading Islamic influence in India and laid the foundations of the future Imperial style of Islamic architecture.

Already, in 1193, having demolished 27 or so richly and delicately carved temples in Qila Rai Pithora, he built the first mosque in India, Quwwat-ul-Islam Masjid (Might of Islam Mosque). But although the structure is Islamic and the carving restricted to floral and geometric patterns, it feels very Hindu. Hardly surprising as most of the stonework, including the beautiful columns, is second-hand, taken from the demolished Hindu temples. But the grand, five-arched maqsura (screen) added in 1199 and covered with verses from the Qur'an in deep, tracery-fine carving was entirely new and marks the start of a happy combination: Islamic design and Indian labour. How the Gupta iron pillar with its 4th or 5th century Sanskrit inscription arrived in the courtyard – let alone the technical feat of casting it – is a complete mystery, thick with legends. One is its ability to grant the wish of anyone who can encircle it with his arms behind his back.

Aibak also built the exquisitely carved, red sandstone, five-storeyed tower, the *Qutb Minar* (begun 1199). One of the symbols of Delhi, it is in fact modelled on the tower at Ghazni. The Qutb (pole, axis) signified the pivot of justice, sovereignty and, of course, the Islamic faith – a highly symbolic tower of victory doubling as a minaret for the muezzin to summon the faithful to prayer. According to its inscriptions, it was intended 'to cast the shadow of God over the East and over the West'. Its present height of 72.55m has a story behind it: Aibak built the first layer; his successor Iltutmish added three more; when the top one fell off in the mid-14th century, two layers replaced the fallen one; and when the British added a cupola it was jeered at so much that it was removed (and still stands forlorn in the enclosure). The great art historian Percy Brown expounded on the tower: 'unique . . . made possible by the inspired vision of Qutb-ud-din Aibak, and realized through the creative genius of the Indian workmen'.

The British sketched it endlessly, the Indians rushed up and down it until there was a tragic accident with many killed in 1981, since when the stairs have been temporarily closed. See also the very richly carved tomb of Aibak's son-in-law and successor, Iltutmish, built by himself in 1235, and the buildings put up under Ala-ud-din of Siri fame: a cloister around the mosque, the Alai-Darwaza (south gateway), his unfinished rival tower and his tomb (in the ruins of his college for Islamic studies).

More monuments are scattered across the plains south of the enclosure, including Dil-kusha (Sir Thomes Metcalfe's country house built around a Muslim tomb in 1844 while he was Commissioner of Delhi), the Jamali Kamali complex of mosque and tomb (with fine tiles) built for a 16th century poet-saint and, for the keen, Balban's Tomb and the Madhi Masjid. To see more, go a kilometre on along the main road (past a cluster of good shops on the right), and into Marauli village. On the right stands the tomb of Adham Khan (son of Akbar's wet-nurse, killed by Akbar in 1562 after Khan had murdered a minister); down a lane to the left, almost disguised by the scrub, lie rarely visited mosques, palaces and pavilions built by Delhi's early Muslim rulers, including a splendid baoli (step-well) and the Lodi pleasure palace Jahaz Mahal. For a final treat, seek out Zafar Mahal, one of Delhi's last Mughal buildings, a palace gateway built by Bahadur Shah Zafer in about 1850. All this is excellent picnic country.

East of the Qutb Minar lie the rampart ruins of the city after Siri, *Tughlaqabad*. This massive, 13-gate, fort was built by Ghiyasuddin Tughlaq (ruled 1320-25), first of the Tughlaq dynasty (1320-1413). They established the strongest and most dynamic of the Sultanate states, the beginnings of an Indo-Islamic culture on which the later Mughal rule built. Tughlaqabad, whose substantial ruins are fascinating to explore (from the highest point, the wide horizon takes in both the skyscrapers of Connaught Place and the Qutb Minar at Lal Kot), was abandoned five years after it was built, when Ghiyasuddin's eccentric son, Sultan Mohammad, committed patricide. Mohammad first built a new city, Jahanpanah, between Siri and Lal Kot. Then, like the grand old Duke of York, he marched the whole population down to the new capital of Daulatabad in Maharashtra and, several years later, marched them back again. The Tughlaq's third city was Ferozabad (see below). Opposite Tughlaqabad is Ghiyasuddin's simple warrior's tomb (1320) with sloping walls and white marble dome, and Adilabad Fort, possibly built by Mohammad, who presumptuously called himself Al-Adil (The Just).

Suraj Kund, a vast amphitheatre possibly built by the Tomar Rajputs in the 10th century, is 2km south and a good picnic spot. On the road back into town are the recently discovered rock edicts of a Mauryan king (3rd century BC), probably aimed at travellers passing along the trade route. Do this trip in the early morning for fresh sunlight and peace before the tour buses arrive at Qutb Minar, or in the afternoon after they have gone; avoid Sunday picnickers. Haus Khas and Qutb Minar complex have opening hours: sunrise to sunset. Ensure your driver is briefed, as not everything is obvious tourist stuff.

Ferozabad The rather more stable Feroz Shah Tughlaq – builder, intellectual and antique collector – succeeded mad-cap Mohammad in 1351 for a long reign of 37 years. The city of palaces, mosques and gardens he founded on the banks of the Yamuna River stretched right to Haus Khas where he built the college. It was the richest city in the world and a magnet to scholars. Only ruins of his palace, the Kushk-i-Feroz (with tank (man-made lake) and mosque), and the Ashoka Pillar he brought from Ambala survive. The 3rd century BC inscription on the pillar was the first of the Mauryan emperor's many edicts for peace to be deciphered. James Prinsep cracked the ancient Brahmi script, fore-runner of modern devanagari, in 1937.

East of Ferozabad are memorials to Mahatma Gandhi and India's prime ministers. Raj Ghat is where Gandhi was cremated the day after his assassination (January 30, 1948); Gandhi Museum nearby (open Tues.-Sun., 9.30am-5.30pm). Shanti Vana (Forest of Peace) is where Jawaharlal Nehru (died May 27, 1964), his daughter Indira Gandhi (assassinated October 31, 1984) and her son Rajiv (assassinated May 21, 1991) were cremated (Indira's other son, Sanjay is remembered too), the open land now a tree and rock park. Vijay Ghat is dedicated to Lal Bahadur Shastri (died January 11, 1966). West of Ferozabad is Khuni Darwaza, one of Sher Shah's gateways; south is the International Dolls Museum (5,000 of them), (open Tues.-Sun., 10am-6pm).

Lodi Gardens After the Tughlaqs, the surviving buildings of the Sayyids (1414-51) and Lodis (1451-1526) are mostly tombs – notable exceptions are the baoli and Jahaz Mahal down at Maruali and Hailey's baoli found in a lane off Hailey Road, off Kasturba Gandhi Marg. More than 50 large octagonal and square memorials plus dozens of smaller ones survive from this period, testifying to great building programmes. Some of the most majestic are here, set amid the lawns, ponds, flowers and trees formerly called Lady Willingdon Park. Now a favourite jogging and walking spot for Delhi's influential, from police chiefs to diplomats, political speech-writers to foreign office civil servants – and even the odd puffing, sari-clad, portly Delhi wife.

There are the Bara Gumbad (large dome) and Sheesh Gumbad (dome of glass), still with blue enamelled tiles and painted floral designs; the tombs of Mubarak Shah Sayyid (died 1434), Mohammad Shah Sayyid (died 1444), and Sikandar Lodi (died 1517). The last has the newly imported Persian double dome; excellent rooftop views found up steep steps. It was Sikandar Lodi who moved his court to Agra in 1502, initiating 146 years of royal oscillation between Agra and Delhi that ended with the building of Shahjahanabad. Especially pleasant at sunset, Aashiana café in gardens (open 10am-10pm).

Safdarjang Tomb Off-track historically but just across the road from Lodi Gardens. The last of the grand Mughal garden tombs, built 1753-4 for Safdar Jang, Nawab of Oudh and also prime minister to the Mughal emperor Ahmad Shah (reigned 1748-54). Just as Emperor Humayun's great tomb marks the ascent of Mughal funerary monuments in Delhi, so this weak one with frilly cusped arches and effeminate bulging dome marks the descent and foreshadows the architecture of Lucknow, Oudh's capital, which became the major Islamic power centre of Northern India as Delhi waned. Materials are pinched from Khan-i-Khanan's tomb; fountains splash in the gardens; good views from the roof. Just south is Safdarjang Airport, where Mrs Gandhi's son, Sanjay, was killed in a plane accident in 1980.

Nizamuddin Medieval Sufi village, the oldest living area of Delhi, full of atmosphere. Described by archaeologist Mitch Crites as having 'the most important concentration of Indo-Islamic architecture in India'. It evolved around the dargah (shrine) of the Sufi saint Shaikh Nizamuddin Chishti (Hazrat Nizamuddin Aulia) who died in 1325 – the tomb has been repeatedly rebuilt, but the mosque in whose courtyard it stands survives unchanged. Since it is believed that a saint's grave emanates a special spiritual energy, disciples try to be buried near their master. Among the crowd of graves here, many of them nobles', are the court poet Amir Khusrau (died 1325), one of whose couplets Shah Jahan would make famous in his Red Fort, Shah Jahan's daughter Jahanara, emperor Mohammad Shah (died 1748) and the poet Ghalib (died 1893). In a corner outside the enclosure stands the casket-like tomb of Ataga-Khan coated in tiles and carving – son of another of Akbar's wet-nurses, this was the minister whom Adham Khan murdered, (see Early Cities, above). Today, a hereditary family of priests runs the Jamat Khana Masjid, built by Ala-ud-din Khilji, which is crammed with worshippers for Friday noon prayers. See also the jali screens of the Chaunsath Khamba (1623), Jahangir's all-marble building foreshadowing Shah Jahan's taste.

In the narrow lanes little Muslim buildings survive; women still live in purdah; boys attend daily scripture lessons; women wash in the sacred water of the large baoli (step well); stalls sell typically Muslim items of rose petals, incense sticks, embroidered verses from the Qur'an. On Thursdays qawwalis, Khusrau's creation of choral songs to heighten religious experience, are sung around his and Nizamuddin's graves, the air scented with the spices of delicious biryani (rice and meat dishes) sold from steaming cauldrons.

At Urs festival there are qawwalis, poetry readings and fairs. Qawwalis are mystical poems set to the classical raga modes. It was Khusrau who introduced many of the innovations into the modes and established the first and truest synthesis of the Indo-Islamic music culture. He was certainly an inspiration for the mass Hindu conversion to Islam that began in the 14th century. Today, qawwalis still follow Khusrau's pattern and often use his words; it is well worth coming to hear them sung here.

Money given to the shrine tends to reach other pockets; a project for the desperately needed conservation is under way. To get there, take the narrow lane by the police station on Mathura Road.

Purana Qila Final cities before the big stuff of Old Delhi (Shahjahanabad). Babur (The Tiger), a Barlas Turk descended from both Timur-i-Leng (Tamburlaine) and Jenghiz Khan, defeated Ibrahim Lodi at the battle of Panipat in 1526, and the following year crushed the Rajput confederecy at Khanua. (Timur had made a brief visit to Delhi in 1398, conquering the city and then walking out the next year with a tidy ransom of 120 elephants, sacks of gold and Delhi's renowned stonemasons.) The Delhi Sultanate ended; Mughal rule began – and yet the break was not that fierce, for to the local population this must have seemed at first to be just another Muslim conqueror inheriting an Islamic administration already centred at Agra. Babur died four years later, leaving a few gardens in Agra, nothing in Delhi.

His son, Humayun, erected the first buildings of the budding empire. Dinpanah (Shelter of the Faith) Fort was constructed on the sacred site believed to have been the Pandavas' city of Indraprastha (city of the God Indra), founded and fought over by Arjuna, hero of the epic Mahabharata, and replacing the totally mythical first city of Delhi, Khandavipuri (of which excavations on the southern slope revealed stratified levels dating back to 1000 BC, the period of the epic). The massive walls and three double-storeyed gateways survive, Indian pavilions perched on the Islamic arches.

But Humayun preferred designing carpets, writing poetry, commissioning astrological treatises and feasting to consolidating his inheritance. So obsessed was he by astrology and superstition that it governed his political and military decisions. Thus, in 1540, with Humayun's weakness aggravated by his jealous brothers, the Afghan, Sher Shah Sur, was able take Delhi and run a highly efficient city for five years before his death. Having made the Purana Qila (old fort) bigger and stronger, he naturally renamed it Shergarh. Two of his gateways stand, Kuni (or Kabul) Darwaza (opposite Ferozabad) and Lal Darwaza (just outside Purana Qila). Inside, this early Mughal rival ironically built two buildings which are landmarks in Mughal architecture. The Qila-i-Kuhna Masjid (1541) has Islamic hallmarks such as good proportions, clean lines, fine pointed arches, elaborate decoration inside and outside, and a facade of black and white marble on red sandstone, soon to be a favourite Mughal device; it also has the more Hindu elements of jarokhas (projecting balconies), chajjas (deep eaves) and chattris (domed, octagonal kiosks). Nearby is his Sher Mandal, a two-storeyed octagonal building more famous for its association with Humayun than Sher Shah. Sher Shah also laid down the blue-print for administration with which Akbar would build and consolidate his empire – he laid out the Grand Trunk Road and devised a workable system for land revenue. (Those going to Varanasi or Patna can visit Sher Shar's tomb at Sasaram, judged by some as 'one of India's most wonderful buildings'.)

After defeat, Humayun had wandered around India before going to Shah Tahmasp's court in Persia. He stayed for ten years, paying for his keep with the Koh-i-Nur diamond and, perhaps more importantly, by converting from the Sunni to the Shia faith of his host (see Islam, above). With an army supplied by Shah Tahmasp, Humayan won back first Kandahar and Kabul in 1545, then Delhi in 1555. He converted the Sher Mandal into his library but a year later tripped on the steps as he answered the muezzin's call to prayer, dying from his wounds three days later. Open daily, 8am-6.30pm.

Khair-ul Manzil Masjid Built in 1561 by Akbar's formidable and influential wet-nurse,

Maham Anga, Adham Khan's mother. Once decorated with enamel tiles like those on buildings in early Mughal miniature paintings. Sher Shar Road, opposite the Purana Qila. Also in this area are the Zoo and the Crafts Museum.

Zoo The most important zoo in India, founded 1959, 1,500 occupants. Open-plan (water channels instead of bars), verdant, dotted with Mughal pavilions, superb views of soaring Purana Qila and Humayun's tomb. Contents hit both extremes; rare white tigers of Rewa (first one bred in captivity here) and an elephant that plays the harmonica. Plus tigers, lions, bears and monkeys and incredibly exotic, brightly-coloured birds. Mathura Road. Open Sat.-Thurs., 9am-5pm; summer 8am-5pm.

Crafts Museum Director Jyotindra Jain's oasis of peace and knowledge is a vast collection of traditional crafts displayed in three ways: as regional buildings of India, in large exhibitions and by craftsmen brought from all over India to work on site for weeks at a time. There may be wood-carving, brass-casting, picture-painting, silk-weaving, terra cotta sculpting, etc., with people on hand to explain the techniques, and sometimes items to buy. Delightful atmosphere, providing a good peephole into rural India; the café is used by discerning locals interested in India's contemporary crafts. Aditi Complex, Pragati Maidan. Open daily, 9.30am-4.30pm; special shows on Sunday, 11am and 3pm.

If your crafts appetite is whetted, O. P. Jain's Museum of Everyday Art is a special treat: a wide-ranging collection of pieces from all over India housed in the large basement of his stunning modern home whose structure incorporates some old carvings; Sanskriti C-6/53 Safdarjang Development Area, open Tues.-Sun., 11am-5pm.

Tombs of Humayun and Khan-i-Khanan Nine years after his death, the most important early Mughal monument in Delhi was built to Humayun by his senior widow, Haji Begum. Percy Brown rhapsodises over it: 'Not only one of the most arresting examples of the building art in India, but an outstanding landmark in the development of the Mughal style. In spirit and in structure Humayun's tomb stands as an example of the synthesis of two of the great building styles of Asia – the Persian and the Indian.'

On the long pathway to the tomb, a doorway in the wall on the right leads to a row of dormitories, probably the living quarters of the Persian craftsmen working on the mausoleum, and the Afsarwalal Mosque and Tomb (1566), built by one of Akbar's officers. Further along, the first great gateway (housing the booking office) was the entrance to Bu Halima's Garden, which existed before Humayun's complex was laid

out; and on the right of the next part of the pathway stands the nobleman Isa Khan's octagonal, Sayyid style tomb and its mosque (1547, well worth a look to compare with Humayun's).

Humayun's red sandstone and marble tomb follows the form of the Delhi sultans' tombs (octagonal plan, high central arches, etc.); but it is much bigger, incorporates a garden, and has finer proportions and richer carved detail. As such, it is the first Mughal tomb in char bagh (four-garden) and set the pattern for Mughal memorials that culminated in the Taj at Agra: an ornamental gateway piercing a high wall leads to a formal, symmetrical garden where the domed memorial is set on a broad podium. It was constructed 1565-71 to designs by the Persian architect Mirak Mirza Ghiyas (probably one of the spoils of Humayun's exile), who applied the spatial concepts of Timurid and Safavid architecture to already proven local architectural forms and materials. He also consolidated the double dome (used for Sikander Lodi's tomb) as an important Mughal device, whose two skins resolve the problem of achieving a lofty exterior while keeping the internal proportions in balance. Local Hindu architectural elements include, as in other Mughal buildings, the chajja (deep eaves), chattri (domed kiosk), jarokha (balcony window) and star motif.

Among the other Mughal royals buried here is Dara Sikoh, Shah Jahan's favourite son. And here, in 1857, the last Mughal Emperor, Bahadur Shah Zafar, hid and then surrendered to the British. To the left of the entrance are the beautiful gardens of Sundar Nursery. And outside, down to the left on Mathura Road, the heavy tomb of Khan-i-Khanan (1627) follows the Humayun blue-print; the son of Akbar's early mentor Bhairam Kahan, he was a distinguished poet, military commander and adviser to Akbar and Jahangir. Although the exterior facing was carried off for Safdarjang's tomb, the interior still preserves its finely incised and painted plaster work.

Old Delhi (still known as **Shahjahanabad**, its original name, by some): Agra, not Delhi, benefitted from the creative genius of Humayun's son, Akbar. Akbar's son, Jahangir, and grandson, Shah Jahan, further embellished it. But, after ten years of rule, while the Taj Mahal was being built for his beloved wife, Shah Jahan got itchy feet and moved the capital back to Delhi. Here, between 1638 and 1648 he built the splendid capital that is still the true throbbing heart of Delhi. The empire's top masons and craftsmen worked on stone brought from Fatehpur Sikri, obliterating most of Ferozabad and Shergarh. And, on completion, the empire's administration and the gold, jewel-encrusted Peacock Throne, made for Shah Jahan and a symbol of his phenomenal wealth, were ceremoniously brought to the Red Fort.

Whereas in the previous cities an overdose of imagination is needed to back up accounts of the many mosques, palaces, markets and gardens, in Shahjahanabad it is all here – and all alive and kicking. Even the Lal Qila (Red Fort), with two-thirds destroyed by the British and the remainder now a protected monument, has the lively covered market at its gateway which Mughal nobles would have enjoyed – although Shah Jahan's palace of white marble, once encrusted with silver ceilings and precious stones, is cold and desolate. As one Delhi connoisseur puts it: 'They've picked out everything, but one has to go there'. And as recently as the 1940s, M. M. Kaye saw many more sparkles on the walls.

It is traditional to go to the Red Fort first, but far better to start at Shah Jahan's last building, the *Jami Masjid*, which is full of life. The faithful stream in and out from the surrounding bazaars and the present Imam is directly descended from Shah Jahan's Imam. The red sandstone mosque, with bold marble and brass inlay, is one of the largest in all Islam, built 1644-58 to designs by Ustad Khlil. From the courtyard there is a memorable first view of the Red Fort through the arcade, especially under early morning sunlight. And from the minaret, up spiralling, dark stairs, the whole city shape is clear – although to define any street, except possibly wide Chandni Chowk which is the nerve-centre running from the Red Fort to Fatehpuri Masjid, is impossible. The narrow lanes and their alleys seem all the narrower because home-owners have added extra storeys over the years. Rooftop life is fascinating to watch: children flying kites, mothers preparing food, tethered goats being milked, and men caring for their beloved pigeons. To the south the sleek Connaught Circus sky-scrapers contrast harshly with this medieval view. Open to Muslims at all times, to non-Muslims at restricted times which vary but currently include prayer times. These change according to the lunar calendar. For example, the mosque is usually open to non-Muslims in March at 7am-12.30pm (noon on Fridays), 2-4.45pm and 5.15-6pm, but these times move earlier in summer, later in winter. Entry is up the north or south steps. Minaret open to all, regardless of faith, 9am-6pm but not at prayers times; women and children must be accompanied by a man; binoculars are not permitted.

For action, the best time to visit the Jami Masjid is on Fridays and during Muslim festivals. Throughout *Ramadan* all Muslims over the age of twelve do not eat or drink during the day. As the Qur'an decrees, they must 'strictly observe the fast from dawn until nightfall and touch them (wines) not but be at (their) devotions in the mosque'.

In addition to praying five times a day during Ramadan, Muslims attend tarawih (congregational prayers). A pole is put high up on the mosque with a light on the end which blazes red for fasting, green for eating and drinking. When the green light shows, it is time for iftari (breakfast). There is a mad rush to carts of food lined up along the walls of the Jami Masjid – special dishes include malpuva (sweet egg pancake) and, in Delhi and Lucknow, kebabs, breads, pakoras and sweetmeats. Nights are lively, right until sehri, the pre-dawn meal. But the climax of gourmandising and celebrating is at Id, the end of Ramadan.

Lal Qila (Red Fort) entirely reflects the grand but stultifying court etiquette of Shah Jahan. His income was treble that of Akbar and Jahangir, but he managed to spend four times as much. Edward Terry (chaplain to the sixteenth-century English ambassador to India, Sir Thomas Roe) observed he was the 'greatest and richest master of precious stones that inhabits the whole earth'. From the moment he woke, the whole palace revolved around a minutely strict programme of pomp, ceremony and ritual.

Entry is through the Lahore Gate, now obscured by Aurangzeb's later bastion. Immediately beyond is the Chatta Chowk, the princes' private Burlington Arcade of court jewellers, goldsmiths and weavers, somewhat lower grade today but with good shops at the far end on the right. Across the courtyard is the Naqqar Khana (Royal Drum House), the official gateway to the palace, where top-floor musicians heralded important guests. Immediately inside is the Diwan-i-Am (public audience hall), a huge, columned, open hall with magnificent inlaid white marble throne built in high so that the emperor's subjects could see him from the large courtyard. Behind, across gardens, are the six mahals (palaces) overlooking the river. (Look out for excellent views; musicians and acrobats are often down below.)

From the right, the palaces start with Mumtaz Mahal (now a small museum, open Sat.-Thurs. 9am-5pm) and Rang Mahal (the painted palace), whose silver ceiling was put to use when the coffers ran low. The cooling Nahir-i-Bahisht (Stream of Paradise) used to end here, in the marble lotus-shaped pool, having trickled through all the palaces to cool the air and reflect their dazzling interiors. Next door is Khas Mahal, the emperor's three private marble apartments for eating, sleeping and worship, still richly decorated (and its pietra dura being restored now) – at sunrise he would show himself to his people from here.

The Diwan-i-Khas (private audience hall, currently undergoing full-scale restoration) was the inner and luxurious sanctum for the highest princes. The most important decisions, the best parties and the most tragic events happened here. Listening to music, the candlelight playing on the jewel-inlaid silver ceiling and silk brocades, Shah Jahan is reported as cooing: 'If on earth there be a paradise of bliss, It is this, Oh! It is this! It is this!', quoting a couplet by the poet Khusrau which is inscribed in gold above the arches. Less happy events include Mohammad Shah's surrender to Nadir Shah in 1739. Nadir Shah took the Peacock Throne kept here off to Iran, together with the Koh-i-Nur diamond which had somehow got back into the Mughal treasury after its previous trip to Persia. In 1858, the British exiled Bahadur Shah to Rangoon from here.

Next come the hamams (baths) where merry hours were passed and affairs of state discussed in the hot and cold rooms with their exquisitely inlaid marble floors and walls (although closed to the public, a peep through the window gives an idea). The tiny, white marble Moti Masjid (Pearl Mosque) was built by pious Aurangzeb (1659) so that he could pray five times daily without that long trek to the Jami Masjid. Beyond was the Hayat Baksh Bagh (life-bestowing garden) which had saffron, crimson and purple blooms surrounding the Zafar Mahal, and pavilions around the edges. All are open sunrise to sunset, the red sandstone glows best under late afternoon sun; avoid free-lance guides; buildings prettily lit for sound and light shows, twice daily after sunset (English and Hindi); times, which language and bookings from Fort booking office by the Naqqar Khanna or Tourist Office or ITDC (tel: 350331). Delhi's flea market, the Kabari Bazaar, is held every Sunday on the river side of the fort.

Chandni Chowk Literally, moonlit crossroads. One of the most vibrating and interesting areas of Delhi. Shopkeepers squat in cubicle shops with green and blue painted doors and carved projecting balconies above. Between the houses, whose topmost floors almost meet, are squeezed polychrome temples where the faithful drop in throughout the day. Easy to lose hours wandering in the maze of alleys off the main thoroughfare, thronged with people, bullocks, cows and horses, air scented with fresh breads, cauldrons of thickening sweet milk, spices, perfumes and curries, tame pigeons fluttering down from old havelis (courtyard mansions), cries of shopkeepers, coolies and rickshaw wallahs, clatters and whirrs of furious industry.

The fair has gone on non-stop since 1648 when Jahanara Begum, Shah Jahan's favourite daughter, laid out the 21-metre wide street, lined with lofty old town-houses for merchants

and noblemen, with a refreshing water channel down the middle. In 1663 Francois Bernier reckoned it was the biggest commercial centre in the East. At the top of the chowk, opposite the Red Fort entrance, is Digambar Jain Mandir (1656), the Jain temple whose inmates wear mouth masks and sweep the ground before them lest they harm an insect, and whose adjoining hospital is exclusively for birds – complete with Out Patients section.

Moving down, past the much reduced Pul-ki-Mandi (flower market) that used to spread over the whole street, you find Dariba Kalan on the left. This is a lane of very old shops good for hunting down old and new silver and gold (sold by weight) from jewellers whose forefathers served the emperors; for buying Lotus and Moonlight attar (perfume, see p. 88 for more) from Gulab Singh (he also has a newer, wood-panelled shop on the main chowk); and for chewing exceptional jalebis (sweets) from the shop on the corner of Chandni Chowk, or hot halwa from the stall opposite. Almost facing Gulab Singh, an alley called Kinari Galli stocks all the pagdis (bridegroom turbans), plumes and tinsel a Hindu boy needs for his wedding day, plus papier mâché masks for the Ram Lila plays and glittering brocades for bride and groom. (Dariba Kalan leads on to the Jami Masjid.)

Back on Chandni Chowk, Gurudwara Sisganj (open to all), on the same side, is dedicated to Tegh Bahadur, a Sikh guru beheaded by intolerant Aurangzeb, who also deposed his brother, Dara Sikoh, paraded him around Chandni Chowk dressed as a beggar, murdered him and exhibited his corpse here. Further, on the same side, are two gruesome sites: the kotwali (police station) where nationalists were hanged and the Mughal princes exhibited after the British retook Delhi in 1857; and Sonehri Masjid (1722) where Nadir Shah stood in 1739 watching his soldiers massacre 30,000 Delhi inhabitants. Ghantewala sweetmeat shop, established in 1790, is on the same side.

Then comes another treat: Paratha Wali Gali (Alley of Unleavened Bread), where the lofty old houses leave just enough room for two people to pass, and where cross-legged cooks sit in tiny restaurants and prepare fresh stuffed parathas, served with yoghurt to cool the spices.

Back on to Chandni Chowk and off again down Nai Sarak (by the taxi stand), the air is sickly sweet from shops selling perfumes, incense and tobacco. Other shops specialise in hand-made paper. Return once more to see Fatehpuri Masjid marking the end of Chandni Chowk, built in 1650 by Fatehpuri Begum, one of Shah Jahan's queens. Surrounding it are the stalls for dried fruit and nuts, essential ingredients for the rich Mughlai food, and adjoining the back of the mosque is the action-packed wholesale spice market.

Civil Lines For the British, Delhi was a backwater until 1911. Calcutta and Bombay were where the action was, the power wielded, the fortunes made. Thomas Metcalfe, Agent and Commissioner 1835-53, lived in Ludlow Castle (restored after a fashion) on Mahatma Gandhi Road. He filled it with antiques and devoted an entire room to his hero, Napoleon.

His friends living around him in huge Victorian bungalows included Colonel James Skinner (*c.* 1778-1841), son of a Scotsman and a Rajput lady, who created Skinner's Horse regiment and later built Delhi's first church, the well-kept Greek Revival, St James's, consecrated in 1836. It stands just outside Kashmiri Gate, which saw some of the bloodiest fighting when the British retook Delhi in 1857. Inside are monuments to Colonel George Fraser, Skinner and Metcalfe. Skinner's preserved home is found nearby, through the middle gate of Sultan Singh. Not far away is the thoroughly Raj Nicholson Cemetery (recently cleaned up), where Brigadier-General Nicholson was buried after his heroic death during the retaking of Delhi in 1857; and the better kept Mughal Qudsia Gardens, laid out in 1748 by Qudsia Begum, whose path from slave rags to riches led to marriage with Emperor Mohammad Shah.

Jantar Mantar Giant, abstract, salmon-pink sculptures that look newer than New Delhi but were actually built back in 1724 by mad keen astrologer Maharaja Jai Singh II of Jaipur as masonry versions of brass astronomical instruments – he thought that large sizes would give greater accuracy. Built when he was revising the calendar and astronomical tables for Emperor Mohammad Shah, this brick and plaster observatory is the first of five dotted about India (see p. 111 for more). Sansad Marg, open sunrise to 10pm.

New Delhi The British contribution to Delhi's string of cities is the most successful 20th century planned city yet built. Designed by Edwin Lutyens to administer an empire, it is now government headquarters for a single country of about 850 million people who speak over 1,650 languages and dialects. The whole city is full of trees, air and space – all now threatened by traffic pollution and by the lack of building controls and conservation regulations. Politicians, seemingly blind to these dangers, plot their own careers from elegant bungalows set in large gardens behind avenues lined with lemon- and flame-blossomed trees. Very grand and, for the visitor, very anonymous; the antithesis to the bustling honeycomb lanes of Old Delhi. And quite the opposite of throbbing Bombay, which Robert Byron described in 1931 as 'that architectural Sodom', reserving the word 'magnificence' to describe New Delhi.

On December 12, 1911, George V, King and Emperor, announced at the Delhi Durbar that the capital of India was to move from Calcutta back to Delhi – a Durbar where each of the 562 maharajas had an average of 9.2 elephants, 11 titles, 5.8 wives, 12.6 children, 2.8 railway carriages, 3.4 Rolls Royces, and a bag of 22.9 tigers. And, in true Delhi tradition, nothing existing was good enough. A new city was to be built from scratch. The whole project was either the blindest act of pomposity by the soon-to-dwindle British Empire or its greatest gift to future independent India. Perhaps both.

A northern site was selected and George V and Queen Mary happily laid the foundation stone. However, when the Planning Commission of Edwin Lutyens, J. A. Brodie and G. S. C. Swinton arrived from England, it rode around on an elephant in the boiling heat and chose another site. So, in the middle of one night in 1913, the foundation stone was put in a gunny bag and trundled on a bullock cart to Raisina Hill. Countless similar incidents, much argument and quantities of building later, this 'Anglo-Indian Rome' was inaugurated on February 9, 1931.

Lutyens, assisted by Herbert Baker, had designed a city to reflect the power and size of the British Empire, to accommodate 70,000 people and to have endless options for future expansion. Viceroy Lord Hardinge, who had been behind the transfer, took a keen interest in the plan; his successors Lord Chelmsford and Lord Reading watched it being realised; Lord Irwin, who became Viceroy in 1926, saw the completion and inauguration, just sixteen years before Independence. To level the land, build roads, bring water and electricity, transport stone from Dholpur, employ 30,000 unskilled labourers and sangtarashs (stone cutters) from Agra, Mirzapur and Bharatpur, and plant 10,000 trees, the bill was a cool £15 million. And that was just for putting the official buildings up. If the move from Calcutta had been a subject for hot debate, the phenomenal and ever-spiralling costs did not last long. The rest of the plan was firmly modified.

Volatile arguments included the fundamental question of architectural style: should the city be Indian, Western classical with Indian elements, straight Calcutta classical or Bombay gothic? The second style won. Lutyens did not think much of Hindu architecture – apart from Datia Palace (see below, p. 82), which he thought one of the finest buildings in India. But he admired and was influenced by the Buddhist monuments of Sanchi – as the Rastrapati Bhavan dome shows.

One gaffe that messed up Lutyens's concept

had been the steep gradient of Baker's hill which effectively ruined the view from India Gate up to Lutyens's Rashtrapati Bhavan (Viceroy's house), digging deeper the rift between the two architects and causing Lutyens to wail that he had met his 'Bakerloo'.

Rashtrapati Bhavan, the Prime Minister's official residence, built as the Viceroy's regal home, covers the 330 acres of Raisina Hill and dominates the city. It looks down over the administrative buildings along the broad green vista of Raj Path (road of those who govern) to India Gate and, originally, beyond to Purana Qila – a view wrecked by the next Viceroy, Lord Willingdon, and his 'interfering philistine' wife who allowed a stadium to block out the Purana Qila view. A road either end of Raj Path and one in the centre (Janpath, road of the people) run north to the brick and (peeling) plaster collonnades of Connaught Place, designed to link Old and New Delhi. This area, full of shops and restaurants, has caught some of the liveliness of Old Delhi (Shahjahanabad). It is the focus for the jean-clad young Delhi crowd who follow any Western habit, from hamburgers to faded jeans.

Lutyens and other architects filled the triangle whose points are Rastrapati Bhavan, India Gate and Connaught Circus with bungalows (he called Baker's designs 'bungle oh!s'). Of the projected houses for the important independent Indian princes, only five were built. The excellent 10-acre Rashtrapati Bhavan Mughal garden was the brainwave of Lady Hardinge after a trip to Srinagar (possibly inspired by a certain Constance M. Villiers-Stuart who in her book about Mughal Gardens, published in 1913, pondered how nice it would be to have a modern Mughal garden in the newly planned capital). Lutyens designed it with the help of discussions over breakfast about plants with William Robertson Mustoe (ex-Kew Gardens and Punjab Horticultural Department). Mustoe and W. S. George landscaped the rest of the city, Mustoe choosing and supplying the trees. He planted the big trees, called rai haman, on Raj Path, the blossoming laburnum and gulmohur, and the fragrant tamarind.

There is a good overall view from Baker's unfortunate slope (and the rooftop restaurant of the Taj hotel), particularly good in the late afternoon sunlight. Difficult to visit the superb Rashtrapati Bhavan surrounding buildings, but possible and well worth seeing the Mughal garden which is open for about five weeks following Republic Day (January 26); the Tourist Office has the precise dates.

With a handful of exceptions, other buildings are also tricky to get into, often because they are government- or diplomat-occupied and sensitive to prowlers. However, see the exteriors of Lutyens's Staff Quarters, the large bungalows on Willingdon Crescent (Lutyens stayed at no.1 for his 1923-28 visits); the Imperial Record Office and War Museum along Raj Path, the War Memorial at India Gate and nearby Hyderabad House; and the 'stripped and rather brutal' Baroda House (now the Railway Booking Office, so open to the public).

Buildings by other architects worth looking at include Sansad Bhavan (by Baker, see below), Jaipur House (by C. G. Blomfield, now the National Gallery of Modern Art, see below); No.1 Janpath, built for one of the main contractors for the city, Sirdar Sir Sobha Singh, and St Stephen's College, which fosters some of the most successful and high-powered brains in India (both by W. S. George); and Teen Murti House (where Nehru lived) and no.1 Safdarjang Road (where Indira Gandhi lived), both now museums, see below.

New Delhi churches worth seeking out include H. A. N. Medd's Cathedral Church of the Redemption (completed 1935) on Church Road; funds for it were raised by the Anglo-Catholic Lord Irwin (Viceroy 1926-31) and the finished building is eulogised over by Philip Davies as 'infused with the spirit of Palladio and Lutyens'. Medd also designed the Roman Catholic Cathedral Church of the Sacred Heart (completed 1934), found at Ashok Place, at the top of Pandit Pant Marg. If security permits, it is well worth going to New Delhi's cantonment area to see St Martin's church (1928-30), designed by A. G. Shoosmith who was Lutyens's full-time India representative 1920-31. Built of 3½ million red bricks, Gavin Stamp calls it 'one of the most remarkable of 20th century churches: a sublime mass of brick', but Penelope Chetwode remembers only its nickname, 'The Cubist Church'.

Chanakyapuri (Diplomatic Enclave) is the area south-west of Rashtrapati Bhavan specially reserved for foreign missions. Plots on virgin soil have been taken up by various countries who have mostly, sad to relate, failed to build a mission of architectural note. A lost opportunity to create a showpiece collection by the world's most interesting architects, it is pervaded by a bizarre atmosphere of international diplomatic sterility which echoes the way Raj cantonments kept themselves quite separate from the 'native' towns. Its oddness makes it worth driving through to glimpse the few exceptions: the Indian architect Satish Gujral's masterpiece for Belgium, the very Bauhaus Austria, whacky Sikkim House, cream-coloured and cubist Italy, terraced Kuwait and the gloriously blue-tiled and domed Pakistan.

Rail Transport Museum Found at the southwest corner of Chankyapuri and an essential stop for train buffs. Here is the Fairy Queen, built in Leeds in 1855 and now the world's oldest surviving locomotive. Other locomotives and coaches, signals and tunnels, recount the story of railways in India, including the Oudh and Rohilkhand Railway engine built in Manchester in 1870, the Rajputana Railway engine of 1878, and the Maharaja of Patiala's unique monorail for which locomotives had wheels for track on one side and for road on the other. Shanti Path, open Tues.-Sun., 9.30am-7.30pm in winter; 8.30-11.30am and 4-7.30pm in summer.

Sansad Bhavan (Parliament House) Lutyens's idea but designed by Baker. Circular, colonnaded building with domed central hall and three semi-circular halls designed to house the Chamber of Princes, the Council of State and the Legislative Assembly. Now houses the Rajya Sabha (Upper House) and Lok Sabha (House of the People), with offices for MPs along the corridors and a very fine library (former meeting hall for the princes). Parliament sits eight months of the year. Sessions can be as heated and entertaining as at Westminster (see below, p. 72). South end of Sansad Marg; visits easily arranged through any Embassy or MP.

Nehru Memorial Museum One of the nicest museums in Delhi. One of the few New Delhi houses open to the public. Fine building, with many of the original fittings; lawns, shrubberies and rose-walks maintained by an army of gardeners. Built for the British Commander-in-Chief of India. Occupied by Jawaharlal Nehru, first Prime Minister of India, from 1948 until 1964 and now a museum devoted to him: library, bedroom, drawing room exactly as he left them. Vases of fresh roses – Nehru wore a rose buttonhole every day. Celebrations here and at India Gate on November 14, Nehru's birthday, which is also National Children's Day. Teen Murti House, Teen Murti Marg. Open Tues.-Sun., 10am-5pm. Sound and light show in the garden daily at 9pm (English), mid-September to mid-July, information from the house (tel: 375333) or Cottage Industries Emporium (tel: 311931/311506).

Indira Gandhi Museum This modest, immaculate bungalow set in a lush and mature garden was Indira Gandhi's official residence after her father, Nehru, died in 1964 until 1977, and again from 1980 until her assassination. Visitors move through rooms hung with photographs recounting her life – as a child with the Mahatma, as a chic young woman in Prague, as a playful grandmother – then around the exterior to glimpse her living rooms furnished with restrained simplicty. Then, down the garden path to pause quietly before the glass plaque engraved: 'Here, Indira Gandhi was martyred by two assassins, October 31 1984.' 1 Safdarjang Road. Open Tues.-Sun., 10am-5pm. Nearby is Birla House, where Mahatma Gandhi was assassinated, see Museum Round-up, below.

National Museum Devastatingly rich for a collection founded only around 1950 – ravishing sculptures in the entrance lobby include a sandstone woman holding a fly-whisk (on loan from Patna Museum). Its nucleus is the fabulous Indian art exhibition held in London 1947-48 which drew on public and private collections throughout India. Sir Marc Aurel Stein's magnificent collection of booty found at the close of the 19th century along the Silk Road, whose golden age was the 7th and 8th centuries, is divided between this museum and the British Museum. Find this and much more on the first floor; also very interesting are the Harappan, Mauryan, Sunga and Gupta finds (ground floor) and the Heeramaneck collection of Pre-Colombian art (second floor). The new wing houses Sharan Rani Backliwal's extraordinary collection of over 300 classical, folk and tribal musical instruments. Good publications. 11 Jan-path. Open Tues.-Sun., 10am-5pm.

National Gallery of Modern Art Built by Blomfield as the Maharaja of Jaipur's town house. Like many other 'modern' galleries, its real treasures (first floor) are the aquatints by the uncle and nephew team, Thomas and William Daniell, and other European artists working in India and, amongst Indian painters, the strong Bengali School exponents Abanindranath Tagore, Jamini Roy, Amrita Shergil and Nandalal Bose (the gallery owns 6,000 of his paintings). There are also the bizarre Europeanised portraits by Raja Ravi Varma and examples of post-Independence movements in Baroda, Calcutta, Bombay, Delhi and Madras. But recent Indian art is depressing in the light of the heights of the 16th to 19th centuries and modern Western developments. Touring international shows visit here. Sculptures in the verdant garden. Jaipur House, India Gate. Open Tues.-Sun. 10am-5pm.

Museum Round-up There are as many museums as there are parks in Delhi. In addition to the three general ones listed above, these below have collections of interest for specialists.

Mahatma Gandhi has four special places in Delhi: the serene *Raj Ghat*, where he was cremated, designed by Vanu G. Bhuta; *Mahatma Gandhi Park*, lined with swaying palms, off Chandni Chowk in Old Delhi; *Gandhi Memorial Museum*, Raj Ghat, open Tues.-Sun., 9.30am-5.30pm; and *Hall of the Nation Buildings* (a museum to Gandhi and the freedom struggle; memorial to Gandhi in the garden near where he was assassinated on January 30, 1948), Birla House, Tees January Road, open Tues.-Sun., 9.30am- 5.30pm. The last three attract flocks of pilgrims daily, bearing garlands.

Air Force Museum, Palam, open Wed.-Mon.,

10am-1.30pm. *National Museum of Natural History*, FICCI Building, Barakhamba Road, open Tues.-Sun., 10am-5pm, Sat. until 7pm. *National Philatelic Museum* (rich collection), Dark Tar Bhavan, Sardar Patel Square, Sansad Marg, open Mon.-Sat., 10.30am-12.30pm; 2.30-4.30pm. *Tibet House* (Tibetan art), 1 Institutional Area, Lodi Road, open Mon.-Sat., 9-5pm.

Exhibitions of contemporary art are found in the performing arts centres grouped on Delhi's cultural campus at the south end of Barakhamba Road (Sri Ram Centre, Triveni Kala Sangram), the Lalit Kala Gallery, Rabindra Bhavan, Feroz Shah Road, open daily 10am-1pm and 3-7.30pm; and Kunika Chemould Arts Centre, Cottage Industries Emporium, Janpath, open Mon.- Sat., 9.30am-6pm. See Delhi Diary and daily newspapers for others.

Space and peace

In Delhi there is a luxury of green open space found in few other capital cities. If you cannot stand the bustle another minute, it is never far to a park or garden. And, even more surprising for India, peace is plentiful too. Many of the best places surround the monuments described above. And as coach tours stick rigidly to their well-worn track and schedules, even the standard sights are havens for most of the day, especially early morning and late afternoon.

Top favourite is an early morning or late afternoon stroll in Lodi Gardens, with nearby Safdarjang's garden tomb and the National Rose Garden. Particularly refreshing in this southern area are the zoo with Humayun's garden tomb and Purana Qila flanking it. There are quiet strolls in the back lanes of Nizamuddin. Not far from here is the Golf Course (see Clubs, below) where the greens are dotted with strutting peacocks and surrounded by bottlebrush, shade-giving silver oak, neem and kikar trees as well as the inevitable Islamic tomb remains (Sayyid Abid's is by No.1 hole), all kept spruce by 50 malis.

Moving west, Nehru Park and Buddha Jayanti Park are both pleasant, with good views from the second which was laid out on a ridge by the Japanese (women should not go to either alone). Go further out to Haus Khas or on to the plains around Lal Kot for assured calm, except Sunday when Delhi goes picnicking. The Mughal Qudsia Garden, to the north, is a forgotten overgrown gem.

Right in the centre, there are always people sleeping, relaxing, eating ice creams and chatting on the two kilometres of lawns beside Raj Path and India Gate, favourite meeting places for locals. Rastrapati Bhavan gardens, when open, are very beautiful but also very popular. **Roundabouts** Unexpected spots for locals,

where they take their tiffin cans for picnic lunch, play a game of cards or simply sleep, are the roundabouts. In the graceful geometry and order of Lutyens's city, whenever a spacious avenue crosses another one there is a roundabout. Their gardeners, allotted to specific circles of flowerbeds, are highly competitive. They plant pansies, marigolds, poppies, phlox and other favourites from the British period among the bouganvillea and jasmine, then nurture them into blossom ready for Delhi's annual glut of flower shows and for the prestigious roundabout awards, when the best islands of blooms will have a proud signpost erected, such as 'First Prize, Middle-sized Roundabout'.

Keeping fit and beautiful

With all its gardens, parks and leafy avenues, the best exercise is walking – fanatics can jog. Smart club life in Delhi is more exclusive than in Bombay or Calcutta and does not welcome foreigners with such open arms. Nor are clubs the social focus, since Delhi residents prefer the privacy of their own gardens for gossip and scheming. A visitor who wants serious exercise must select a hotel with a good pool and gymnasium and the ability to arrange outside sports. For example, the Maurya can fix golf, riding, archery and tennis; the Oberoi is bang next door to the Delhi Golf Club and will book a game; the Maidens and Ashok have their own tennis courts. Alternatively, you can use the Delhi sports clubs which are open to everyone (see below). Long-stay visitors should apply to the club secretaries.

Swimming pools In Delhi, pools are often emptied in December-February, so check when booking. The Maurya's is solar-heated and open all the year round. The Taj Mahal, Oberoi, Holiday Inn and Imperial have the biggest and best pools; the Imperial's is nicely secluded from the social life of the lawn. Pools at the Maurya, Hyatt and Taj Palace are good but smaller; the Meridian's circular one is for cooling off rather than hearty exercise. The Ashok, Claridges, Imperial and Maurya open their pools to non-residents for a nominal charge (Rs10-25). For controlled relaxation, there are several good yoga centres, including Vishwayatan (tel: 3718866), Delhi Yoga Sabha, Bhamashah Marg (tel: 222997) and Shri Vaidyanath Yogashram, 172 Tagore Park, Model Town (tel: 715401).

Health clubs The sumptuous, marble-lined complexes in the top hotels can indulge and beautify every part of the body with oils, creams, jacuzzis and steams, by massage, pummelling, pedicure, manicure and coiffeuring – top quality, top to toe titivation. The best are at the Taj and Oberoi hotels, all with separate equipment for men and women and instructors for gym and yoga. The Maurya's has improved, and the new deluxe hotels of Hyatt, Meridian, Holiday Inn are all equipped; the Ashok is rebuilding its clubs. Sharnaz Husain (see p. 36) has her clinic at 13b Connaught Place (tel: 331-6433) and her Raj Haus Health Resort is 40 minutes' drive from Delhi, at Suraj Kund in Haryana State.

CLUB CHECKLIST
Chelmsford Club, Raisina Road (tel: 384693).
Delhi Flying and Gliding Clubs, Safdarjang Airport (tel: 618271 and 611298 respectively). Temporary membership available. Open 1-6pm. Sanjay Gandhi did his ill-fated flying here. Gliding season March-June, September-November.
Delhi Golf Club, Dr Zakir Hussain Marg (tel: 361236). Temporary membership available. Clubs for hire. The North India Championship is held in Delhi. The amateur Golf Championship (est. 1892), the most important golf event in the east, alternates between Calcutta, Bombay and Delhi (1985 Bombay, 1986, Delhi). There is also an 18-hole course as well as fishing and boating at Suraj Kund near Tughlaqabad.
Delhi Gymkhana Club, Safdarjang Road (tel: 375531). Membership mostly for government and defence services. Very exclusive compared with its friendly Bombay brother but excellent facilities (squash, tennis, etc) and nice bar and restaurant in crumbling period buildings.
Delhi Polo Club, President's Estate, Rashtrapati Bhavan (tel: 3015604). Temporary membership available from the Secretary c/o The President's Body Guard. Wooded and open land, high season mid-December to end-January when matches are played on Jaipur Polo Grounds, inside the racecourse.
Delhi Riding Club, Safdarjang Road (tel: 3011891). Open to all. Information from the Club Secretary. Book the previous day for early morning (6.30-9.30am) or late afternoon (4-7pm) riding – too hot in between.
Roshanara Club, Roshanara Road (tel: 712715), Old colonial cricket club with cricket ground. Pretty enough to be a set for the film 'Gandhi'. Delhi Test matches are held at Feroz Shah Cricket Ground.
Delhi Lawn Tennis Association, Africa Avenue (tel: 653955).

Good Eats: Night lights

Delhi entertains at home in spacious bungalows and gardens where no-one eavesdrops on the political gossip or, increasingly, in the mushrooming good restaurants. But there are few night spots apart from the hotel discotheques.

However, the cultural scene is more lively. Here is the greatest concentration of performing arts in north India, attracting all the great Indian exponents, so this may be the moment to catch some good Kathak dancing. For lighter entertainment, there are the mega-stars, psychedelic colours and sing-along intervals of a block-buster Hindi movie followed by a good hotel nightclub.

Prohibition in Delhi reflects the government's half-hearted commitment to eventual total prohibition in India. Currently, the first and seventh day of every month and national holidays are dry but these should be confirmed with your hotel or at the Tourist Office. Liquor stores are closed and hotels serve alcohol only through room service. Otherwise, hotel bars and restaurants serve spirits and wines. Other places do not.

RESTAURANTS
There is some very good food to be had in Delhi, particularly the Mughal- (and thus Persian-) influenced north Indian food and the classic Mughlai court cuisine: meat and vegetable dishes cooked in exotic combinations of gentle spices and thick cream, equal in richness to any classic French dish. So eat a variety of freshly cooked, layered and stuffed paratha and kulchai breads to avoid over-taxing the digestive juices.

Mughlai meat dishes include the classic biryani, meat cooked with spices and then put in a sealed pot with rice which cooks slowly in the meat juices. Then there is murg methi (chicken with fenugreek, cashewnuts, coriander, chilli, etc.) and Patharka gosht (marinated mutton cooked on a stone). Some Mughlai vegetable dishes date back to Akbar's time, when doctors advised the 42-year-old emperor to become vegetarian, but royal chefs still had to produce an array of tempting and succulent dishes. Try baingan mumtaz (stuffed aubergine), khatte alloo (potato) or goochi pulao (mushrooms and rice).

North India also produces kebabs of every kind, the meat tenderised in spiced yoghurt and papaya paste. Tandoor cooking is at its best in Delhi. A clay oven is used to cook marinated chicken, mutton or fish (pomfret is best) and spiced or stuffed breads.

You will find good cooking in some top hotels (notably the Maurya Sheraton, Oberoi and Ashok) and in many small restaurants that amply reward a spirit of adventure. Restaurants in between are disappointing. A deluge of bad, live Continental music tends to accompany Continental food. Be sure to reserve a table at the hotel restaurants; the city-wise Delhi socialites leave tourists queuing and hungry.

Local savoury snacks are sold from roadside stalls and in some hotels. They include chole bhatura (fermented fried bread and chick-peas) and puri bhaji (fried bread with tomatoes and potatoes). Mobile and fixed chaat (savoury snack) stalls making lentil-based or fresh fruit-based concoctions doused with a masala of spices are found both on roadsides and wherever there are shops. They also serve snacks such as pakoras, dosas, samosas and thirst-quenching lassi (thin yoghurt).

RESTAURANT SUGGESTIONS

The big hotels constantly change their restaurants, so ask about latest developments. **North Indian** *Bukhara, Maurya;* sensational North West Frontier food eaten with the fingers, seated on the most uncomfortable stools at low tables (awkward even for someone small) in Pathan-style surroundings. However, it is worth every discomfort for the magnificent Rashmi (silken) chicken kebab, Burra mutton kebab, Afghan-style lamb – and what breads! Praised by Shashi Kapoor (and many other world-weary eaters) for 'the best north Indian food in India'.

Handi: Taj Palace; also ethnic, with very good food, 'delicious, just like it is in north Indian villages' (Kapoor again) but in comfortable Gujarat surroundings of carved wood and patola canopies. There is a buffet of a dozen north and west Indian dishes cooked in the traditional handis (brass cooking pots with a tight-fitting lid, so food cooks slowly in its own steam). Also tandoor food and a wide range of exotic, stuffed breads.

The *Frontier Restaurant* of the *Ashok* does not compare with these two but the *Tandor, Hotel President*, Asaf Ali Road, is of a consistently high standard and remains a firm favourite among journalists and diplomats who eat mostly tandoor cooked chicken to the sound of Indian musicians.

The following have much less swish surroundings but very good food. *Degchi*, 13 Regal Building, Connaught Place; run by the grandson of Shobha Singh, principal contractor for New Delhi. Tandoor and dishes cooked in a degchi, similar to a handi. *Kaka's Restaurant*, Plaza Building, Connaught Place; modest upstairs dining room serves good handi dishes and delicious green masala fish. *Gaylord*, 7 Regal Building, Connaught Circus; the original restaurant, started 1952, followed by Bombay 1956, now has two branches in London and one in Hong Kong (the one in New York is closed). Would-be classy mirrors and chandeliers, solid Indian (and Western) menu. (Gaylord also has a delightful open-air restaurant at the north end of Willingdon Crescent, ideal for lunch.) Other Connaught Circus restaurants to recommend include *Minar*, L-11 Connaught Place, Mughlai, M-17 Connaught Circus. *Khyber*, Kashmir Gate; excellent Peshawari dishes, often cooked in a

kadhai (Indian wok); another favourite with foreign correspondents. The formerly good *Moti Mahal, Darya Ganj*, may have gone downhill but its courtyard setting and evening ghazel singers make eating there an event.

Mughlai *Dum Pukt, Maurya Sheraton;* pronounced by several Indian devotees across the country as 'the best restaurant in Delhi, and probably the best in India'; essential to book a table to enjoy this particular cuisine of cooking long and slow in sealed pots; the list of tried and appreciated dishes is so long that it appears pot luck will bring a good meal; if in doubt, consult neighbouring Indian eaters.

Kandahai, Oberoi; part of the revamped hotel and considered by regular patrons to be good enough to remove the need to cross Delhi to the Dum Pukt.

Haveli, Taj Mansingh; top for food and social scene, but lighting dim to obscurity; try tandoor-cooked kebabs, rich murgh shabnam (chicken cooked in cashewnut and cream), korma and gosht dishes such as Achar gosht, a very Mughlai biryani (meat tenderised in herbs, spices, nuts, raisins, coconut and cream, then cooked with rice), a selection of breads and, to finish, a Mughlai sherbet (like a sorbet water-ice) flavoured with gulab (rose) or chandan (sandalwood).

Mayur, Maurya; also excellent Mughlai and Hindustan cooking, tables well spaced in fresh, Mughlai-ish decor, with live Indian music and ghazels (light songs) good enough to entice local patrons to linger longer, listen in silence and applaud. Try murg gulmar (chicken and lamb's brain, fenugreek, egg and cream), malai kofta vegetables and bhawan kulcha (a bread). They also serve the special raan-e-mirza, supposedly reserved for royalty: leg of lamb cooked very slowly in curd, cardamoms and cumin, garnished with almonds. The recipe is said to come from Bahadur Shah Zafar, the last Mughal emperor.

The *Peacock, Ashok* (Indian musicians) serves Mughlai cuisine, but with a lower reputation. However, *Gulnar, Janpath Hotel* is popular with locals; good atmosphere from live qawwali and ghazels (check performance is on). On no menu does one find Shah Jahani pulao, a truly royal biryani of spiced saffron rice steamed with mutton or chicken, garnished with boiled eggs wrapped in silver foil. But, if ordered in advance, a good chef will prepare any dish.

North Indian and Mughlai for the adventurous *Karim's* has two branches: avoid the atmosphereless one in Nizamuddin West and head for the original one in Gulli Kababian (Alley of Kebabs), on the south side of the Jami Masjid. Some of the best Mughlai and tandoor food in Delhi for the ambitious eater, and plenty of chefs to watch making kebabs and bread and stirring great deghs of stews. Especially good kalmi chicken kebab, burra mutton kebab, biryani and bhakar khani (a very rich bread kneaded with ghi and dried fruits); quite hot spices, so order some dahi (yoghurt). Very modest but extremely atmospheric restaurants, packed out at lunch and supper, merit every effort to visit – best combined with exploring in Chandni Chowk. Other little café-restaurants in this immediate area, equally difficult to find so ask constantly, include *Jawahar* and *Maseeta*, right by Jami Masjid, both feeling as if they started when Shahjahanabad did, both with mouth-watering breads; and *Floral* (in Urdu Bazar).

South Indian Many, all very clean, very vegetarian, very good for delicate stomachs newly arrived in India. Here are five good ones. *Dasaprakash, Ambassador Hotel*, Sujan Singh Park; described as a 'cross between a film set and a church', wide menu, especially delicious fresh grape-juice, butter dosa and honey and fig ice-cream. *Coconut Grove*, Kanishka Hotel; so good that MPs for Kerala constituencies take foreigners for delicious blow-out lunches here. The *South Indian Boarding House*, opposite Shanker Market; filled with south Indians who say it's the best. *Sona Rupa* Janpath; south Indian and Bengali. *Woodlands, Lodi Hotel*, Lala Rajpat Lai Marg; order a thali. See South chapter for more on thalis.

Chinese Several excellent places, all widely praised, usually Chinese chefs. *Taipan, Oberoi*; vies with the Maurya's *Dum Pukt* for Best Delhi Restaurant award. Essential to book and to dress up to dine here in Delhi's designer restaurant with equally designer and delicious food at every course. *House of Ming, Taj Man Singh*; Ming vases, the smartest. *Bali Hi, Maurya Sheraton*; Chinese and Polynesian with rooftop views but European band. *Mandarin Room. Janpath Hotel*; good decor. *Chinese Room, Nirula's*, Connaught Place; oldest Chinese restaurant in Delhi, very fresh. Try also *Tea House of the August Moon, Taj Palace*: a dim sum tea house and restaurant serving Cantonese, Szechwan and regional dishes in pretty Chinese garden decor.

Continental Not often good. These are the exceptions. *La Rochelle, Oberoi*; immensely swish, formal, French and spacious. *Casa Medici Rooftop Restaurant, Taj Mansingh*; much-improved, produces a splendid meat and vegetable pasta buffet at lunchtime, and pasta with night-time views for dinner. *Orient Express, Taj Palace*: bit of a gimmick, the bar a station waiting room, the tables in a railway carriage, the prices high, menu spans the London-Constantinople journey; clients seem happy with this concoction. *Williamsburg Room, Qutub Hotel*, off Sri Aurobindo Marg; more American than Continental, good steaks. *Captain's Cabin, Taj Man Singh*; basically a bar, with good fish dishes. *Takshila, Maurya*; rooftop views go with Mediterranean pâté and pasta.

Lebanese *El Arab*, 13 Regal Buildings, Connaught Place; enjoyed by the young. Full menu from hummus to dolmas.

Japanese *Tokyo, Ashok Hotel*: Delhi's first Japanese restaurant, beautifully built with tatami mats upstairs, regular tables downstairs, delicious food selected from a fan-shaped menu and cooked on the spot and a bill considerably lower than it woul be in Japan.

Lunch specials Around Connaught Place, head straight for the *Imperial* and have chicken tikka, nan (soft bread) and a nimbu soda on the expansive lawn sheltered from the bustle, with the band playing gently. (Their garden room is pretty for breakfast, too, but the dining room is dowdy.) Or go east from Connaught Place to enjoy the café atmosphere and delicious food and fresh fruit juices at *Nathu's* in Bengali Market. In Old Delhi (Shahjahanabad), go to one of the suggested modest Indian restaurants around the Jami Masjid (see above). In the deluxe hotels, either have a barbecue around the pool (huge prawns, lobster, tandoor chicken) or taste an array of dishes at the lunch-time buffet – the Taj Mahal's rooftop one is currently the best in India; the Ashok's Indian one is not bad.

Sweetmeat shops Mughlai sweets are very, very sweet and equally sticky and heavy. Bengali sweets, the aristocrats of sweetmeats, made of milk and cheese, are easier to handle (see p. 183 for more). Best shops are *Nathu's*, Bengali Market, which serves all sorts of other quick meals from South Indian to Chinese, has memorable milk shakes and an equally good atmosphere; *Malik*, Connaught Place; *Bengali Sweet House*, Gole Market, Connaught Place. In Old Delhi, *Gantiwalla* on Chandni Chowk, and *Annapuran* opposite; further down, *Naim Chand Jain's* jalebis and the hot halwa stall are on the corners of Dariba Kalan; and *Giani Ice-Cream* for hot carrot or dhal halwa is near Fatehpuri Masjid.

Tea Delhi lacks the colonial and club tradition necessary for good teas. Those who know go to the lawns of the *Imperial*. *Aap ki Pasand*, 15 Netaji Subhash Marg, opposite the Golcha Cinema, for sipping and buying India's best teas.

Cocktails Restricted to middle and upmarket hotels, and the *India International Centre* by Lodi Gardens. With few high-rise buildings, sunset-over-city cocktails are restricted to the *Oberoi's* rooftop bar (members and residents only) – their spacious ground-floor bar has a glass wall overlooking the swimming pool. The *Holiday Inn's* zebra-decorated bar is central, as is the Imperial's which serves boozy cocktails in the bar and non-alcoholic ones on the lawns. The *Meridian* provides in-house entertainment of the bubble lifts and fountain; the *Maurya's* is cosy. The beauty of Lodi Gardens compensates for the non-alcoholic cocktails at the outdoor café there, the *Aashiana* (also serves food, 10am-10pm).

Drink Chaas is special to Delhi and very refreshing. It is thin lassi (yoghurt) flavoured with ginger, coriander, green chillies and roasted cumin powder.

24-hour coffee shops All the deluxe hotels have them, usually serving Indian and European food, and usually overlooing the hotel pool or garden. They make good, quick-service, round-the-clock cafés for meeting people or having a light meal when adjusting to jet lag or before leaving for an international plane when the next meal is far, far away.

NIGHT LIFE

Discotheques Frequented by Delhi's bright young rich. The best are in the deluxe hotels. Current favourite amongst the Delhi elite is the Hyatt's; but the arrival of the Holiday Inn may change that. Also good are the Oberoi's and Maurya's, with Taj ones coming back up: well designed, good lighting and reasonably up-to-date music tapes, plus a jolly Friday and Saturday night atmosphere of friendliness since membership is so exclusive and expensive for locals that most people know one another. All are open to residents for a nominal charge, to other visitors by arrangement.

CULTURE

Delhi and Bombay are the places to catch good classical dance, drama and music and regional folk dance. Music recitals are often privately sponsored, even if they are held in a public hall, and so tickets are by invitation; the hotel management may be able to help find a concert. Otherwise, to find out what is going on where see the local newspapers or current *Delhi Diary*. Performances usually start 6-6.30pm. Central ticket office at Cottage Industries Emporium, Janpath.

Venues The cultural campus is at the south end of Barakhamba Road and in the adjoining Copernicus Marg. Here are the Sri Ram Centre for Art and Culture (theatre, art gallery, café, art book shop and Sutra Dar Puppet Theatre, shows Saturday evening and Sunday morning); the trendy Triveni Kala Sangram (three art galleries, theatre for plays and dance, café-theatre); FICCI Auditorium (major concerts); Sapru House (theatre); Kathak Kendra (dance); Rabindra Bhavan (National School of Drama theatres, Lalit Kala and Yavanika Sangeet Natak galleries); Kamani Auditorium (plays, dance, music), with Little Theatre Group next door; Bhartiya Kala Kendra (theatre, café).

Not far away are Gandharva Mahavidyalay (music and dance) and Max Muller Bhavan, Janpath. Elsewhere there are the India International Centre, by Lodi Tombs, on Lodi Estate Road No.2, some ticketed shows (i.e. open to the public) very good for catching opening performances in all arts; Gopal Sherman's Akshara Theatre, 11 Baba Kharak Singh Marg (two auditoria) the only theatre with an all-year resident company; and the Fine Arts and Crafts Society, Rafi Marg (amateur theatre, galleries, British Council Library on top floor).

The Exhibition Grounds and Ram Lila Grounds are also worth checking out. They produce a monthly list of events and several free shows (two cinemas, performance venues). In September-October, during Dussehra, Shobha Singh continues what her father began and stages a magnificent Ram Lila, recounting the whole epic each evening with mime, dance and splendid costumes (information from 26 Sardar Patel Marg, New Delhi, tel: 3012405). Entrance to grounds Rs1.

Rabindra Bhavan In the mid-1950s, the government set up various academies to encourage the somewhat imperilled Indian arts. They included the Lalit Kala Akademi (1954), to encourage contemporary visual art and the study of art history – its two journals concentrate on these two aspects; Sangeet Natak Akademi (1953), to survey and stimulate performing art forms throughout India (auditoria plus galleries of musical instruments, puppets, masks); and Sahitya Akademi (1954), to encourage literature in Indian languages. The National School of Drama, established at the same time, is affiliated to the Sangeet Natak Akademi. All these came under the umbrella of Rabindra Bhavan when the government initiated a string of art centres throughout India in the centenary year of Rabindranath Tagore's birth, 1961.

Dance venues There are regular 'Dances of India' programmes (classical, tribal, folk) at Taj Man Singh and Taj Palace hotels, cheap and with explanatory commentary, but of mediocre quality. Similar show daily at Parsee Anjuman Hall, Bahadur Shah Zafar Marg, 7pm. For Kathak, see below. A lighter form of Kathak, the ras lila, recounts the Krishna legend in song, dance, mime and words. It is performed at the Natya Ballet Centre but is best seen in temple courtyards around Mathura at Janmashtami (Krishna's birthday) (see Calendar of festivals).

Theatre Before Independence Delhi was a cultural backwater, staging only amateur adaptations of Broadway and London West End productions. Bombay and Calcutta led the way (see pp. 147 and 184). After Independence Sapru House (inaugurated by Nehru in 1955) and Rabindra Bhavan became the main cultural hiring halls, stimulated by the lively Bengalis. When the dynamic Ebrahim Alkazi came up from Bombay to run the National School of Drama, things changed. He injected a sense of professionalism and had many plays translated into Hindi, even if 90% were still adaptations. But official language Hindi theatre acquired the reputation of being sarkari (government) theatre and the NSD has had a chequered reputation since Alkazi.

Look out for Bengali and Punjabi plays at Sapru House. Dramatists to catch: Vijay Tendulkar (Mahrathi, see p. 147), Badal Sircar (Bengali) and Mohan Rakesh (Hindi). Gopal Sherman's Akshara Company, formed in 1966, range from contemporary plays, musicals and political satires to classical texts such as the Sanskrit Upanishads, drawing on India's rich classical and folk heritage. Amal Allana directs (while her husband designs) ambitious productions whose latest sensation is a new translation into Hindi by the poet Neelabh of King Lear, set in Rajasthan (to know what they are planning next, contact them at E30 Greater Kailash II, New Delhi, tel: 6411804).

To see some vibrant, indigenous theatre, telephone Habib Tanvir whose acting families from Madhya Pradesh stage mime plays in a courtyard near his home in South Delhi (L-15 Ber Sarai, New Delhi, tel: 650894); and Aloke Roy whose Jagran troupe play pantomime theatre in the village, slum and industrial areas of Delhi (E-7/10-B, Vasant Vihar, New Delhi, tel: 601141).

Kathak dance Kathakaras, story-tellers attached to temples in the Braj region in Uttar Pradesh (east of Delhi), were probably behind the emergence of a northern classical dance form. Their devotional recitations used mime and music. The dance that evolved at the Mughal court lays equal emphasis on mime and dance, although now radically refined and secularised. The solo dancer, a man or woman, usually recounts an episode from Krishna's life with a feat of mime, supple twirling and dazzlingly speedy footwork (layakari) whose frenetic rhythms compete with the percussion music. The two main schools are: Bhatkhande Sangeet Vidyapath, Lucknow, and the Jaipur Gharana. It is the Lucknow-school style that is practised in Delhi, at Kathak Kendra (whose dancers also perform at the Kamani Theatre).

In particular, look out for performances by Birju Maharaj, a spell-binding male dancer whose Lucknow family have practised Kathak for centuries, who directed both dance sequences in Satyajit Ray's film 'The Chess Players'. Saswati Sen, a woman and one of the foremost of his many disciples, did the actual dancing. Other dancers to notice are Sitara Devi, Damayanti Joshi, Roshan Kumari and Uma Sherma.

What to buy where

Delhi and Bombay have the best shopping for goods from all over India. But while the Delhi cognoscenti are prepared to give Bombay precedence for restaurants, they claim supremacy for shopping, substantiated by Calcuttans and Bombayites who come to Delhi for their shopping sprees. Mala Singh, founder of the Delhi-based *India Magazine*, only goes to Bombay for restaurants and to buy books, dismissing all else there as 'tatty mock-western junk'. Indeed, Delhi has thousands of good shops, often tidily grouped together by subject – antiques, crafts emporia, European fashions, etc. Spending is so easy it is almost impossible to avoid; and people flying out from here have only their extra baggage on the plane home to worry about.

The biggest centre is Connaught Place, where the fixed price government emporia jostle with chemists, bookshops and the bargain Shankar Market (fabric, wicker baskets, cheap tailors), the Palika Bazar (underground, 300 shops), Panchuian Road Market (lamps, brass, wood) and the Super Bazar. Chandni Chowk is much more fun, but needs hard bargaining. Sundar Nagar (see below) has good art and antique shops.

Then there are hundreds of markets, a shopping centre for each residential area and the big hotel shopping arcades – Khan Market is one of the nicest, with good bookshops, hardware stores, children's clothes boutique, chemists, etc, very lively in the evenings. A good local shopping area is South Extension (open Sundays) with a huge Metro shoe shop next to the best children's western clothes shop in town, Little Kingdom. Of the hotels, which unlike Europe have good-value quality arcades heavily patronised by locals, the Ashok is hard to beat for variety and quality. The Kanishka is also good, as is Taj Man Singh's smart Khazana (treasury), more like a small department store (but inadequate on books) – the same is true of Taj Palace's Collection. The Maurya has excellent arcades, and those at Oberoi and Imperial are good; the grandeur of the Meridian and Holiday Inn shopping floors have yet to prove themselves. Look out also for the permanent trade fair at the Exhibition Grounds: since crafts are a serious industry, there are often state craft pavilions (advertised in the daily papers).

Shops tend to be open Mon.-Sat., 9am-7pm, closed 1.30-2.30pm for lunch. Markets are more often areas of firmly established shops rather than ad hoc stalls put up on the street once a week. The shops either side of the Central Cottage Industries Emporium on Janpath are permanent, yet known as Janpath market. Weekly markets include Chow Bazaar, behind Red Fort

(Sun.) and the bazaar by Hanuman Temple, Baba Kharak Singh Marg (Tues.). As elsewhere in India, fixed prices are only truly fixed in government-run shops – and these do not include 'government approved' shops. Almost nothing opens on Sunday, with the notable exception of South Extension.

The following are just a tiny selection of what is on offer. See also Chandni Chowk above.

Crafts in general To get some idea of the range, pop into the Crafts Museum (see above) which has examples of old and new crafts in various media from all over India. Then see what is on offer in the government-run emporia around Connaught Place. After that, equipped with a fair idea of what should be what in quality and price, the city is yours for tracking down the best.

A good first stop is Central Cottage Industries Emporium, Janpath, a craft department store par excellence. The quality and range is good enough to furnish a complete home, from tiny brass trays to furniture. Highly knowledgeable and helpful assistants run a section for each state, bursting with fair-priced crafts and fabrics (often better than the individual state emporia). Goods can be made to order and then shipped (e.g. curtains made up for an amazing Rs12 per length including lining). Gift-wrapping, packing and shipping are quickly arranged. There is a bookshop, restaurant, booking counter for theatre/dance and an office of the Archaeological Survey of India upstairs for maps. See shopping sections of other chapters for suggestions of what to find in each department.

And a good second stop is to browse down the row of state emporia on Bab Kharak Singh Marg, two roads round Connaught Place from Cottage Industries, going clockwise. Most of these shops are now very good, with helpful staff. Beware: wealthy Delhi ladies come here in gaggles in the evening and, while amusing to watch, can jam up shops and take a long time over making their choices.

These state emporia are arranged in three blocks, A, B and C, with the excellent Coffee House café between blocks A and B, for coffee, sambar and idling for weary, dazed shoppers. To make shopping easier, this is their order, moving east-west. Block A: Gramshilp (khadi fabric), Manjusha (Bengal), Bharati (Delhi), Ambapal (Bihar), Gurjari (Gujarat – especially good), Zoon (Kashmir) and Trimourti (Maharashtra). Block B: Pragjyotika (Assam – silk), Rajasthali (Rajasthan), Purbasha (Tripura), Urkalika (Orissa), Gangotri (Uttar Pradesh – for Varanasi silk and Agra marble), Lepakshi (Andhra Pradesh – silk and bidri ware), Kairali (Kerala) and Mrignayani (Madhya Pradesh). Block C: Poompuhar (Tamil Nadu – for brass, sculpture and silk), Nagaland (Nagaland – for bright,

woollen shawls), Himachal (Himachal Pradesh), Cauvery (Karnataka – for more silk), Phulkari (Punjab), Panthoibi (Manipur) and The Black Partridge (Haryana).

Opposite the complex is Hanuman Temple where there are special pujas (worshipping) on Tuesday afternoons and a bazaar (toys, bangles). Almost next door, Man Singh's makes the best lassi in town. Round in Barakhamba Road is the Central Cottage Export House at G6, New Delhi House, a general emporium plus gallery.

Fabrics For the broadest selection, it is back to the large emporia; those with especially good silk have been indicated above, and usually have metre-lengths as well as saris. Handloom House, 9-A Connaught Place, is disappointing. Cottage Industries is well stocked. The first floor is an Aladdin's cave devoted to fabrics of every kind from every region, from block-printed cotton to fine silk wedding saris; cotton, silk and wool by the metre; braiding up to 15cm wide embroidered wth dancing elephants; and the special Orissa double ikat, Gujarat patola, Murshidabad shot and Varanasi brocades. There is silk of every quality including shot, in a rainbow of colours (about Rs90 per metre; dry clean only), also plain fine wool by the metre and every sort of sari.

Downstairs, Kashmiri crewel-work furnishing fabric. Go to Bihar Emporium for fine raw silk; to Benares Silk, Connaught Place, for brocades.

Khadi Gramodyog Bhawan, 24 Regal Building, Connaught Place, is heavily subsidised by the government to promote rural industry, so prices are low. Khadi is cloth that is spun, dyed, woven and printed by hand as opposed to handloom cloth which is mill-spun, then handwoven. Good khadi buys include Kashmiri tweeds made from merino sheepswool or mixed with Rajasthan wool. There is no tailoring service, but assistants know how much would be needed, such as 7 metres for a 6-foot tall man with a 44-inch chest (a typical Indian mixture of measuring systems).

There are also brightly coloured, checked car rugs from Harayana (price depends upon quality) and cosy old-fashioned dressing gowns of striped or checked wool. Punjab and Himachal Pradesh emporia also stock good tweed; that from Kashmir emporium is over-priced. For cheap and cheerful fabrics, with good-value tailoring on hand, go to Shanker Market to such shops as Memsaheeb at no.58. For very good Kashmir chain-stitch embroidered fabric (crewel work), make an appointment with G. M. Butt at his home, A-2 South Extension Part II, tel: 6445388/6449715).

Lavish, sparkly Hindu wedding saris, silks and tinsels come from Kinari Galli, an alley off Chandni Chowk. FabIndia, N-Block, Greater

Kailash, has some of the highest quality and most imaginative weaves. Worth the detour. It also stocks ready-made clothes, takes orders and ships reliably.

Linen White cotton sheets and towels are a quarter of their London price, although not the finest of fine. Pandit Bros., Connaught Place, has good stock. Bombay Dying is a quality brand name. Smart Bombayites buy their European design, hand-printed table and bed linen with matching lampshades, towels and bedspreads at Xquisite in South Extension Market (open Sunday, closed Monday). For the best traditional table linens, go to FabIndia (see above) and The Shop, 10 Regal Building, Connaught Circus. For the fine chikankari (white embroidery on white muslin), Tandon of Lucknow sell some of the best table linen and kurtas (long, loose-fitting shirts) at their shop in the underground Palika Bazar at Connaught Place.

Books Both Oxford Book and Stationery Co, Scindia House, Connaught Circus and the bookshops in Khan Market, for a wide choice of new books; the second often have export editions of paperbacks printed in England before the English publication date. On Janpath, right near Central Cottage Industries Emporium, the Famous Bookstore groans with books and has more which can be fetched quickly from their godown (warehouse); shops and pavements around Regal Building on Connaught Circus south side are piled with old and new volumes, especially novels. Urdu Bazaar, behind Jami Masjid, for Urdu books, journals and manuscripts, old and new. (Also behind Jami Masjid are the fireworks shops, stocking huge Catherine wheels and enormous rockets which fire into clouds of twinkling stars and then parachute plastic images of Hindu gods down to earth.) For contemporary arts, the Sri Ram Centre is good (see Culture section, above). The best second-hand bookshop is Prabhu Service at Gurgaon village, a few kilometres beyond the airport, owned by Vijay Kumar Jain – a book collector's dream: seven rooms lined floor to ceiling with fascinating volumes; best to phone first, and to take a torch (tel: 20588/01272).

Art, jewellery and antiques If in doubt or if big money is involved, have art objects authenticated at the National Museum or the Archaeological Survey of India, on Janpath; jewels and stones at the Government Gem Laboratory in Barakhamba Road (open 10am-3pm); remember that ivory, reptile skin, tortoise shell and any part of a wild animal is prohibited for export; and in the further interests of conservation it is best to avoid ivory. Also, objects over 100 years old cannot be exported without a licence (see Survival Guide). The best group of antique shops fills the square of Sundar Nagar, beside the Zoo

– wood, paintings, jewellery, bronzes and especially brass from nearby Moradabad. Bharany's, La Boutique (high quality goods, but barter a bit) and Kumar Gallery (also branches in the Ashok and Maurya hotels) are all good. All will supply a certificate for objects less than 100 years old. Chawri bazar, leading west from Jami Masjid, and alleys off it operate more in the Portobello Road tradition of rummaging among old and new, good and bad. Tibetan jewellery and curios are found at stalls outside the Imperial hotel. Locals also go to the covered market of the Red Fort, to the three or four shops at the far end on the right including Tula Ram.

Western clothes Ever-entrepreneurial, Indians do not waste any time. Either side of Central Cottage Industries Emporium, the shops of Janpath Market have the latest European styles, either export rejects (so inspect for faults) or identikit copies of exports destined for smart stores such as Harrods or Bloomingdales.) The shops are in big competition with each other, so barter hard for simple summer dresses, pretty shirts and grander stuff. Jain Bros at shop number 70M have very jazzy high evening fashion with acres of sequins and beadwork.

Lots more in the hotel shopping arcades, at higher prices and sometimes higher standards. Upstairs in Cottage Industries Emporium are very pukka tweed jackets being bought by classy Indians off to the hills, and glorious kids' clothes made of dazzling plain silk. For quality bargain children's clothes, go to Little Kingdom in South Extension or to Khan Market. For the latest in high, high Indian fashion – which is now thoroughly international – phone to make an appointment to see the designers' latest creations at Mutiny at W-127 Greater Kailash (tel: 6411356). The Haveli, at Vasant Goan off the Ring Road, stocks chic ethnic clothes, but prices are rising.

Tailors Find the fastest and most clued up for European styles in the hotel shopping arcades – a 24-hour turn-around is quite possible; if the plane leaves, they lose. Copying is often best, or bring a picture from a fashion magazine of what is wanted; for women, good lining fabric is hard to come by, so it is best to use cheaper silk bought by the yard; the tailor must be supplied with all the fabric he needs. Shanker Market behind Connaught Circus has many tailors working for the fabric shops and prices are much lower (give clear directions for sleeve lengths, double cuffs, collar type, etc.).

Leather The latest designs are copied and made up in Madras, centre of the leather trade, Kashmir (jackets) or Agra (shoes) – but they are usually difficult to buy in the city of origin. At Khan Market in Delhi (also good for books) find the latest Italian shoes at a fraction of their Milan prices, and have shoes made to order; Metro and a cluster of good shoe stores are in F-Block, Connaught Place. For leather clothes and brief-cases, best quality and choice (and highest prices) are in the deluxe hotel shops, Central Cottage Industries Emporium and at Bharat Leather Shop, opposite Nirula's, Connaught Circus. Smooth smart briefcases in analine (a small goat) leather are priced according to their lock; Indian ones are cheap, German and Swiss best and most expensive. There are handbags, hold-all bags, belts, soft men's shoes, women's sandals, wallets. At Cottage Industries, the Kashmir sheepskin leather shop uses north Kashmiri artisans living in Delhi to make the latest off-the-peg European designs in leather and suede, special styles made up in four days (sales tax is exempt if goods are shipped). Furs are excellent buys. In all purchases, be sure the leather has been properly cured and tanned.

Rugs and carpets Daunting for the uninitiated, but tempting as prices are considerably less than in Europe or America. See shopping tips in Survival chapter, above. At Central Cottage Industries no customer should be taken for a ride. Carpets range from all-wool to all-silk and come in every size and pattern. To help, each one should have a descriptive label on the back providing a list of information. One such reads: item (where made): Kashmir; size (in feet): 6 × 4; (knots per square inch): 18 × 18 (=324); contents: 10% silk, 70% wool, 20% cotton (called silk touch); design (each traditional pattern has a name): Kirman; price: Rs5,500. And assistants will help further. For some exquisite chain-stitch rugs made in Kashmir, make an appointment with Meenakshi Devi who designs each one (tel: 611762/4626394).

Dhurries (the Hindi name for flat-weave floor covering). Mostly made at Agra, Mirzapur (near Varanasi) and in Rajasthan – see Agra shopping information, below. Come in all sizes, with current European pastel colours and designs as found at Habitat and Conran. As with carpets, it is wise to sign your choice, measure it carefully, note its pattern (preferably by taking a photograph) and then ship it. Prices are the same for cotton and wool since a cotton dhurrie takes more work. The more light-weight rugs, known as shuffles, are very cheap, all colours, often striped – from Andra Pradesh for loose weave but rougher finish. All may run disastrously if not dry-cleaned. Khadi house has jolly, striped Gujarat shuffles, mini-dhurries with narrow stripes of turquoise, red, yellow and black from Punjab, and jazzy dhurries with a bobbled texture from Uttar Pradesh – all very cheap. See also p. 78.

Tea Indian tea gardens in Assam, Darjeeling and down in the Nilgiri Hills grow some of the world's best leaves. Good fresh teas are sold at Aap ki Pasand Tea Taster's Centre, 15 Netaji Subhash Marg.

Pottery Delhi blue-glazed pottery, mostly made at nearby Kurja, can be found at the Central Cottage Industries and Rajasthan state emporium, but the slightly different Jaipur work is of much higher quality in shape and craft. The Jaipur work is sold at The Shop, Regal Building, Connaught Circus.

See how it's done: Politics and Crafts

Parliament The major industry of Delhi is politics. To see the machinery of Indian government at work, always lively and generally good value entertainment, sit in on a session at Sansad Bhavan, arranged through an Embassy, High Commission or an MP. Debates and cross-banter are in English and the Indian Constitution is loosely based on the Westminster model. India has a President, who is Head of State, and a Prime Minister, who is Head of Government. The two houses of Parliament are Lok Sabha (House of the People, Lower Chamber) and Rajya Sabha (Council of State, Upper Chamber). Lok Sabha, composed of 525 elected members from the States, 17 Union Territories members and 2 Anglo-Indian representatives, sits eight months in the year and elects its own Speaker. The ruling party draws its Prime Minister and Cabinet from this house. Like the American Senate, membership of Rajya Sabha is not for life, as with the House of Lords, but by election (except for a dozen appointments by the President). A third of the 244 members retire every two years. It lacks a Speaker but has the Vice-President as Chairman. Parliament legislates, approves all government spending, amends the Constitution, elects the President and Vice-President (and can oust them) and must approve a Proclamation of Emergency.

Water-pots This is a good business to run throughout India, since a pot's life apparently depends less upon not being broken than upon its failure to work for long. The pot is a natural fridge, keeping water cool and fresh but, so locals claim, only for a few weeks. Then a new one must be bought. The pretty, unglazed earthenware khumba matkas (water-pots) piled high around New Delhi Station are made locally. According to Hindu legend, the first pot was made to store amrit (the water of immortality) thrown up while Vishnu was cleaning out the oceans. Thus the khumbas, the name also given to the potting community, were held in high esteem. But, as plastic and tin are the last word in India today, few khumbas survive. However, there is a thriving workshop opposite the station, tucked behind the main road. Here, smoking hookahs and dressed in dhotis, khumbas throw the matkas (basic pots). After drying in the sun, the women dip them in red slip, fire them in the communal kiln, then sell them across the road. Quality depends upon no cracks, proved by a deep resonant bong when tapped.

Glazed pottery It was probably the Pathan potters from Afghanistan who introduced their glazing techniques to the Muslim court. Kurja, an old town about 80km from Delhi, is still full of Muslim potters living in the tiny alleys of the old town. They use the inky Persian blue known as Jaipur blue (it is used there too), as background for floral designs on Muslim shapes. They also make tiles, use mould casts and do pottery cut-work. A journey to Kurja is well worth the effort for pottery enthusiasts. For contemporary ceramics, stay in Delhi. Gouri Khosla, who did the huge peacock mural at Palam Airport, and Nirmala Patwardhan, who has worked with Bernard Leach, both pot at Lalit Kala Akademi studios which are built in a large medieval fortress at Garhi, East of Kailash in south Delhi. Two other lively potteries are Purush Potteries, 4 Vail Lane and Delhi Blue Art Pottery, 1 Factory Road.

Awaydays

Fortunately, Delhi is a pleasant, open city and the need to escape should not prove too acute. Although it is feasible to go to Agra or Lucknow for the day – even Khajuraho for a four-hour flip around the temples – all three deserve far longer and are much more interesting and beautiful under quieter light than the noonday sun. For instance, the Taj works a different magic by moonlight, dawn light and every other light and each phase should not be missed. Nearer Delhi, the most enjoyable days are passed ambling around the early cities on the southern plains, mentioned above, or heading north to seek out British remnants north of Civil Lines. And there really is nothing much in between these two extremes. When it gets hot and you have to be in Delhi – the temperature hits 47°C in early June – do as one jet-set English businessman does: holds meetings and receives clients sitting in the hotel pool, with a nimbu soda in his hand.

TIME CAPSULE TAJ TRIPS

Round trip 394km. However short a visit to Delhi, it is incomplete without setting eyes on the Taj. For those high flyers who cannot spare a few days in Agra, there are several solutions, all bookable through the travel agents recommended above.

BY CAR Rent a car and driver to go by road, enjoying yet more early monuments strung along the very direct route (3hrs either way, faster at dawn). If there is no release from daytime Delhi, drive down in time for sunset, stay at the *Mughal* or *Taj View* Hotels and eat a delicious dinner of Mughlai food, and return to the Taj once more at purple dawn before sleeping on the drive back.

BY COACH Deluxe bus or air-conditioned coach are cheap and practical ways of doing this journey. The Maurya Sheraton runs the Sheraton Express service daily and, among the many travel companies' Taj deals, Travelite of 36 Janpath (tel: 3327243) currently run a good one at Rs375 to include hotel pick-up, lunch at a good Agra hotel, Government-approved guide, entrance fee.

BY TRAIN The Taj Express leaves New Delhi station at 7.05am (3hrs 10mins). The new Shatabdi Express is speedier: it leaves New Delhi Station at 6.15am, arriving at Agra at 8.05am. The railway follows the road route. Breakfast in the Shatabdi Express is fair, so it is wise to bring extra fruit and perhaps a Fruti fruit juice packet (usually on sale on the platform). After a short snooze, the journey is done. It is a good idea to sign up with the Agra guide who does his rounds during the journey. His tour is cheap and good. (By coach to Fatehpur Sikri for the morning, Fort and Taj for the afternoon.) If the trip does not appeal, rent a car or use bicycle rickshaws to spend the day alternating between the Taj, the Fort, more Taj, taking sustenance from the rooftop restaurant of Clarks hotel (brilliant views), yet more Taj, then the evening train back. The Taj Express leaves at 6.45pm, arriving 10pm; the Shatabti Express leaves at 8.21pm, arriving 10.20pm.

BY AIR This is the most expensive method and, if delayed for morning mist, no faster and extremely annoying. The plane leaves at 7am (check-in time is 40 minutes beforehand), arriving 7.30am, when it is best to rent a car and driver through extremely charming tourist desk at airport and go direct to the Taj, then continue to a hotel for breakfast and a rest. More Taj viewing, on site and from the Fort, before the return flight at 3.40pm.

Note: The Taj is open from dawn until dusk. Sadly it is impossible to visit the Taj at night, even at full moon.

Forays further afield

Delhi is a good springboard for leaping off in every direction. Agra, to the south, is not only a magnet drawing thousands to the Taj but a good base for surrounding Mughal, Hindu and nature sights. For total escape, Khajuraho's temples are isolated on a peaceful, rural plain. To the east, Lucknow preserves its Muslim grandeur, bazaars and atmosphere. All three have good hotels and make perfect breaks. And if the Mughal monuments of Delhi and Agra captivate, it is only a short flight to their third capital, Lahore in Pakistan.

For longer trips, Central India lies further south, whose treasures more than compensate for simpler accommodation (see Bombay chapter). If the hot weather and plains aggravate, Ranikhet and Naini Tal are not far away, nor are Dehra Dun and Mussoorie, both good for gazing at snow-capped peaks; to get nearer those peaks, go further into the cool Himalayas for sports ranging from mountain climbing to tiger-spotting (see Hills chapter). To the west, the hot plains become increasingly desert-like. Shekhavati, an area of villages and deserted forts crammed with painted houses, lies just inside Rajasthan, 150km west of Delhi and good for a week-end break. The other princely states that make up Rajasthan, a succession of palace-filled desert cities each more beautiful than the last, are further away (see Rajasthan chapter).

There are some very good flight deals. For instance, Delhi-Agra-Khajuraho-Varanasi-Kathmandu costs round about the same as Delhi-Kathmandu. A good travel agent will seek out the best deals.

Agra, Uttar Pradesh

The complement to Delhi, Agra fills the gaps in Delhi's Muslim history that begin with Sultan Skandar Lodi taking a fancy to Agra in 1502 and end with Shah Jahan's preparations to return in 1648. Indeed, the principal monuments – the Taj, Fort and Fatehpur Sikri – were built when the Mughal Empire reached its peak in wealth, power and enlightenment, and Agra was the capital and focus of attention. The rulers fulfilled its Mahabharata name, Agrabana – paradise. Akbar (ruled 1556-1605) built extensively, Jahangir (ruled 1605-27) continued, and Shah Jahan (ruled 1627-58) lifted court lavishness to new heights before moving it lock, stock and barrels of jewels to his sparkling new Delhi city of Shahjahanabad in 1648. Agra today is a bustling town as thoroughly geared to tourism as Jaipur.

There are not only Mughal monuments. The legacy of the British Cantonment dominates Agra's spacious character: wide roads lined with bungalows set in large gardens, fine community churches and particularly interesting graveyards. Since Agra lies at the meeting point of three states, Madhya Pradesh, Rajasthan and Uttar Pradesh (which it is just inside), other nearby sights include Bharatpur bird sanctuary, Deeg Hindu palace, Mathura and Gwalior Fort.

Datia and Orchha, just beyond Gwalior, are even more stunning. Agra is by no means a one-night stop.

THE HARD FACTS 197km from Delhi. Season mid-September to mid-March (beautiful gardens blossom January-March), then it gets very hot until the deluge starts at the end of June – some say this is when the Taj is at its most mysteriously beautiful. There is colourful and serious kite-flying every Sunday, with local betting. From Delhi, go by car, train or plane (see Delhi awaydays for Time Capsule Taj trips). There are also daily direct flights from Khajuraho, Varanasi and Lucknow. Connect with Jaipur direct by train or via Delhi by plane; this is dacoit country and so road travel should be during daylight hours.

Choose between two unusually good hotels, bursting with facilities, and a spare third. All have travel counters, car rental, pool, garden and can arrange golf (Agra has three golf courses) and tennis. For a middle-market room, a cluster of less grand but clean hotels hovers along Fatehabad Road. Other hotels less satisfactory, so book early. The old British favourite, Laurie's, is in total decay.

Note: Agra is not known for its hygiene, and complaints from visitors staying in almost all the hotels mention anything from dirty floors and bathrooms to a repeated complaint of food-poisoning, usually after eating fish. The solution: rooms can be specially cleaned while you go out; fish, buffet food and European dishes are best avoided in favour of fresh Indian-cooked vegetables or simple egg dishes such as an omelette.

Mughal Sheraton, Tajganj (tel: 64701; telex: 0565-210). One of the best designed modern hotels in India. Showpiece of the Welcomgroup of hotels, opened in 1976, designed by Ramesh Khosla in the Mughal tradition, using brick and marble for low-lying buildings around garden courtyards with Mughal water channels. It is all set in huge, mature gardens. 282 rooms, including a new Taj view wing. Extensive facilities with health club, beauty salon, baby sitting, croquet, mini-golf, archery, elephant on call for rides. In keeping with Agra, there is top quality Mughlai food accompanied by Indian musicians in the Nauratna restaurant.

Taj View, Tajganj (tel: 64171; telex: 0565-202 TAJV-IN). New and now entirely settled into efficient, Taj-orientated lifestyle. Lives up to the group's reputation. 100 rooms include 5 suites, excellent dawn room service so lazy stayabeds in front rooms can watch the Taj come to life (possibly essential after noisy main road night noises). Back view quiet and over large garden, but no Taj. Mr Modi, who describes himself as an 'Astrologer (For Sceptics & Non-Believers)', lurks in the lobby and will give happily optimistic forecasts.

Clarks Shiraz, 54 Taj Road (tel: 72421; telex: 0565-211). An unexciting pink building with flat but colourful garden. 145 rooms, dreary decor but distant Taj view over Agra from 4th-floor rooms, rooftop restaurant and cocktail bar.

In this busy tourist city, the following middle-market hotels are all fine and well-located:
Amar, Fatehabad Road (tel: 65696). 39 rooms, clean and simple.
Mayur Tourist Complex, Fatehabad Road (tel: 67302). 30 simple rooms, with a large and pretty garden.
Mumtaz, 18½ Fatehabad Road (tel: 65696). 40 rooms, higher front ones with Taj view; quite smart.
Ratan Deep, Fatehabad Road (tel: 63098). Small and modest but cheerful, kind staff and unusually good supplies of hot water.

Note: The only passable colonial hotel is the *Grand,* 137 Station Road (tel: 74014), 31 rooms, simple, friendly and cheap but located west of The Mall. Unless it has improved out of all recognition, the ITDC's Agra *Ashok* should be avoided.

Tourist information is tricky since each state is autonomous and denies the existence of other states. For Agra and Mathura, go to Uttar Pradesh Tourist Office, 64 Taj Road, charming but vague, with a counter at Agra Cantonment Railway Station. For Bharatpur and Deeg, go to Rajasthan Emporium in Taj Mahal Precinct; for Gwalior, in Madhya Pradesh, go to Usha Kirin Hotel. ITDC, 191 The Mall (tel: 72377), has a broader view on life and rents out guides. But it is best to get equipped in Delhi.

TCI travel agency is at Clarks hotel (tel: 3611212/3); SITA is at A-2 Shopping Arcade, Sadar Bazar (tel: 64978/65376); Mercury Travel is on Fatehabad Road (tel: 65365). In addition, Travel Bureau, excellent for UP and MP travels, is next to Taj View Hotel, Fatehabad Road (tel: 68568); postal address PO Box 124, Agra.

There is a large selection of books on the monuments in hotel bookshops (Taj View bookshop is especially well-run) plus at Modern Book Depot, Sadar Bazaar. UP State Road Transport Corporation runs the good tour to Fatehpur Sikri, Fort and Taj, leaving Agra Railway Station daily at 10.30am. Excellent guides allow sufficient time at each place. Bookable at 96 Gwalior Road (tel: 72206), Platform no.1 at the station, or on the Taj Express. Move around Agra by bicycle rickshaw. Currently, there is no prohibition in UP or MP. The Archaeological Survey's office is on Mall Road; theirs are the best guides to Agra and to Fatehpur Sikri, if they are in print.

OUT AND ABOUT **The Fort:** For a sensational first view of the Taj, across the bend of the Yamuna River, start here. (Although winter mist may cloud the good view until about 10am, there is plenty to look at first.) The fort is also associated with all three emperors who erected Agra's important buildings. Ramble all over this *Boy's Own,* unkempt fort city with high walls and wide moat; on to roofs, up and down stairs, in and out of palace rooms – now undergoing major tidying up and conservation.

Agra's Mughal history began the day of the battle of Panipat in 1526, when Babur immediately sent his son Humayun off to guard the Lodi treasury at Agra. There Humayun found the Maharaja of Gwalior's family who, the story goes, placated him with a golf-ball-sized diamond, now believed to have been the Koh-i-Nur (mountain of light) which Humayun later gave to Shah Tahmasp of Persia. Two years later Babur held a grand feast where guests heaped piles of gold and silver on to a carpet laid before him. Mughal splendour in Agra had begun. And when Akbar, aged 14 and brilliant but illiterate (as he remained), succeeded Humayun, the real building and embellishment began.

Akbar's rule was marked by religious tolerance for which he set the example. By marrying a Rajput princess from Amber (whose rulers became the grand Jaipur maharajas) in 1562, he began to turn the warrior Rajputs into allies, killing two birds with one stone. To curry favour, the Rajas of Bikaner and Jaisalmer, and rulers as far off as Tibet, presented pretty relations to Akbar's harem. He eventually had 300 wives living in a harem of about 5,000 women in a complex court hierarchy.

Luckily, Akbar enjoyed building. By 1565 he had pulled down the Lodi brick fort at Sikandra and five years later his new riverside fort of dressed red sandstone was built. Some of his rooms remain including the spacious Jahangiri Mahal, overlooking the Yamuna where he would watch elephant fights on the shore. While it was being built, he lived in a pleasure city 10 kilometres to the south where, among other games, he played polo at night using a ball of wood embers. Then, just as the fort was finished, Akbar began his palace, Fatehpur Sikri, keeping Agra as its citadel.

Next, it was the turn of Jahangir (literally Seizer of the World, although he was in reality politically unambitious). Edwin Binney III, collector of Indian miniature paintings, called him: 'The greatest of art patrons of this highly distinguished family'. His eye was trained in the royal atelier at Fatehpur Sikri. He encouraged greater realism, single-artist paintings rather than shared works, and the signing and dating of pictures. He employed the brilliant artists

Bichitr, Abu'l Hassan, Mansur and many others. However, he was happy to adopt for himself the symbolic nimbus found on saints in European paintings which were highly fashionable at the Mughal court after the Jesuits gave some to Akbar. When Sir Thomas Roe, England's first ambassador to India, visited Jahangir at Ajmer, the only diplomatic gifts truly to impress the emperor were English paintings, especially portrait miniatures. These inspired the many miniature portraits of Jahangir at a window – in some he even holds an icon of the Virgin.

Jahangir lived in the fort, bound by the rigid daily royal programme maintained from Akbar to Shah Jahan and described by Roe as: 'Regular as a clock that stricks at sett howers'. His contributions to Agra's buildings were the facade and adjacent rooms of the Jahangiri Mahal in the Red Fort, the completion of his father's tomb at Sikandra and, indirectly, his marriage to Nur Jahan. For his wife he laid out Shalimar Bagh, the finest Mughal garden at Srinagar in Kashmir.

This love-marriage to the clever daughter of a self-made courtier had a bearing on the two near-perfect Mughal tombs in Agra. The woman was a Persian widow, Mihr-an-Nisa, later known as Nur Jahan (Light of the World). She strengthened the power of her father, chief minister Itimad-ud-Daulah (Pillar of the Government); and married her niece, Mumtaz, to the next emperor, Shah Jahan. Itimad-ud-Daulah's equally influential son and grandson were the next two chief ministers. Nur Jahan added to her family's strength by, it is said, discovering how to preserve attar (perfume) from roses, much to the delight of Jahangir. (For more on attar, see p. 88.)

Shah Jahan (Ruler of the World) spent like mad and built like mad in Lahore, Delhi and Agra. Here, in the fort at Agra, he destroyed some of Akbar's simple sandstone buildings to build a cluster of rich, pietra dura inlaid marble palace rooms along the river front (1628-37) and the exquisite Moti Masjid (Pearl Mosque), begun in 1646, just two years before his new city at Delhi was ready. There is a Diwan-i-Am (public audience hall), Diwan-i-Khas (private audience hall), the emperor's private Khas Mahal with vineyard in front, the Shish Mahal (Mirror Palace) and the Musamman Burj (octagonal tower). This last, exceptionally fine and pervaded with romance, is the best place from which to view the Taj. Shah Jahan built it for his beloved Mumtaz-Mahal (Chosen One of the Palace – real name Arjumand Banu), who went with him on all his campaigns. Then, when he was deposed by his son Aurangzeb, he lived the last eight years of his life here as a prisoner, gazing across to the mausoleum he built for Mumtaz.

Of the few missing details of his buildings, the inlaid colonnade of his bathroom, behind the Diwan-i-Khas, has recently been identified in the Victoria and Albert Museum, London. It has had a remarkable history. It was torn out by the Marquis of Hastings (Governor-General 1813-23) to be given to the Prince Regent (later George IV). However, it failed to be despatched and was sold at auction by a successor, Lord Bentinck, to be presented to the V&A by Sir Alfred Lyall after the Royal Colonial and Indian Exhibition of 1886. The fort is open daily, sunrise to sunset. No sound and light show. Good café; excellent postcard and book stall.

Taj Mahal The greatest monument to love and the strongest magnet to any visitor to India. Irresistible to see on each trip, and more lovely each time. The white marble reflects every change in the light, so go as many times as possible – and it really is worth being there when it floats in soft mauves and pinks at dawn. (Book up with a rickshaw boy the day before. Much nicer than a taxi.) While on campaign with Shah Jahan in the Deccan, Mumtaz died giving birth to their fourteenth child (of which seven survived) in 1631, after 17 years of blissful marriage. He was heartbroken. For the rest of his life, his only other love was architecture.

The following year he began building her mausoleum, the masterpiece of his reign. Shah Jahan was the most energetic and successful patron of architecture of all the Mughal emperors, and took a keen interest in the design and construction of the Taj, drawing on the best minds and best craftsmen of the day – he took a similar interest in his new Delhi city. The Taj is the ultimate refinement of the Mughal tomb design first seen at Humayun's Tomb in Delhi. It took 21 years to complete and employed 20,000 labourers and craftsmen drawn from all over his empire and even beyond it. From the gateway across the garden, the overall shape is perfect; close up, the pietra dura, marble screens and all the craftsmanship are of astounding precision.

The cenotaphs of Mumtaz and Shah Jahan are inside the vaulted chamber; their tombs are below in the dark – beware of pickpockets. (The macabre theory that Shah Jahan planned a black version of the Taj for himself was put about by the not entirely reliable traveller, Jean-Baptiste Tavernier, but has no firm substance.) Good views of the Fort from the platform. In the garden, the mosque is to the left of the chamber; the left-hand central pavilion houses the little Taj Museum. Open daily, sunrise to 7pm; ticket office at west gate. Moonlight Taj visits are currently impossible.

The Taj is particularly beautiful at dawn and dusk. Coach trips arrive for hard afternoon light when the dazzling marble hurts the eyes.

Crowded on Fridays, since this is the tomb of a Muslim queen.

Akbar's Mausoleum At Sikandra, 10km from the Agra Fort. (Worth stopping off to see the fascinating RC cemetery on the way, see British Agra, below.) Tomb and lush garden built over the Lodi city of Sultan Sikandar (ruled 1488-1517) – one or two Lodi remains in the corner. Designed by Akbar in 1602, it supposedly reflects his din-i-Ilani (religion of God), his mixture of Hindu, Muslim, Sikh and Christian thought. However, as Mughal historian Giles Tillotson points out, Jahangir seems to have interfered in the design: see how the arched basement is then followed by pillar and beam upper storeys, making a rather gawky building. Also, what begins as modest sandstone is swapped for lavish white marble. Fine polychrome mosaic designs on the great gateway, together with minarets, are considered to precede those of the Taj; and Jahangir's delicate floral painted vaults inside are nicely restored. Sometimes possible to climb right to the top for good views through finely carved windows of Jahangir's white marble courtyard – a taste of Agra building to come. Open daily, sunrise to sunset.

Itimad-ud-Daulah's Tomb The jewel of Agra, with fewer visitors and greater serenity than the Taj. Like a large reliquary, it is the first Agra building entirely coated with white marble and smothered in pietra dura inlay. The craftsmanship is more refined, delicate and precise than even that on the Taj. It was built by his powerful daughter, de facto empress Nur Jahan and completed in six years flat, in 1628. Not to be missed. Reached through the old town and over a two-tiered, rickety bridge (in a bicycle or auto rickshaw, the best route), over a stronger but further away bridge by car (the longest route) or, rarely now by boat, when the post-monsoon water is high and there are boats for hire behind the Taj. 3km north is Ram Bagh, probably the earliest Mughal garden, built by Babur in 1528, now being restored. Both open daily, sunrise to sunset. For the most romantic views of the Taj, go straight ahead after crossing the two-tiered bridge and follow the twisting lane to Nagla Kachhpura Village and down to the river bank – heavenly at sunrise and sunset.

British Agra Particularly interesting and relatively easy to see, since most tourists are at the Fort or Taj or sleeping off dawn visits to them. The British seized Agra in 1803 and it became capital of Agra Province (later North West Provinces) 1833-58. At the west end of The Mall find Queen Mary's Library, the Central Post Office and the Club; south of it lie Colonel J. T. Boileau's cantonment church of St George (1826), the Havelock Memorial Church (1873), the cantonment cemetery and Metcalfe Hall. North of the old city, towards Sikandra and Mathura, find St John's Church, then the Roman Catholic Cathedral with its high, landmark tower (reminding locals of the Catholic mission founded in Akbar's time), and then Sir Samuel Swinton Jacob's fine St John's College. Beyond lies the Roman Catholic cemetery (land given by Akbar) housing some of the oldest and best Christian monuments in India: a mini Taj Mahal built for the Dutchman General Hessing (1803), the European adventure Walter Reinhardt's tomb and north India's earliest Christian tomb, to John Mildenhall (1614), envoy of Elizabeth I. Others follow the latest architectural styles to reach India, or mix classic cenotaphs with Islamic and Hindu motifs. The episodes of family histories carved on tombstones testify to the perilous life here. St Paul's church is near here, not far from the Protestant cemetery where the tombs date back to three 17th-century factors.

SHOPPING AND CRAFTS It is difficult to emphasise strongly enough that Agra and nearby Jaipur are rip-off cities for naive shoppers. There are hundreds of shops, every other one confusingly professing to be 'official approved' or 'approved Emporium'. They are all highly competitive, so barter everywhere. Apart from at the shops listed below, almost no price is fixed here and shoppers should be very careful. Agra is the worst place for rickshaw boys/taxi drivers/guides offering to show you the best shops. Invariably you pay more and they get a rake-off. Deluxe hotels' shops should be reliable for bigger buys, and quality should be good, if slightly more expensive. For treasures and junk, explore the bazaars in the area west of the Fort. Kite-sellers cluster along one lane, selling cheap ready-made ones or making them to order in just a day. Most shops open 10am-7pm.

Good marble shops are Oswal Emporium, 30 Munro Road and Subhash Emporium, 18/1 Gwalior Road, who take care and time over clients and are happy to show them an atelier where the work is done. Shop for the local Agra rugs and dhurries at Mangalick and Co, 5 Taj Road, Sadar Bazaar; totally reliable, big stock and takes orders for designs, colours and sizes, then ships them when woven; has recently started making brightly coloured dhurries and reviving Mughal floral carpet designs. Mangalick is in a good cluster of shops. His neighbours are Jaiwal (brass), Modern Book Depot, Singh and Sons (chemist) and Agra's Kwality Restaurant. (Sadar Bazaar closes Tuesday.)

For jewellery, go to the well-established Munshi Ganeshi Lall and Sons, whose shop at 13 MG Road is well worth a visit, or to equally well-established Kohinoor Jewellers, also on MG Road. The Handicraft Emporium, 16 Gen. Carriapa Road, is OK for inexpensive buys such as small boxes of inlaid local marble, brass, copper and jewellery, simple dhurries (still made by local prisoners) and brightly coloured bed-covers woven by local women. Other state emporia – UP, Rajasthan, Kerala, Haryana – are in the Taj precinct.

Marble pietra dura Some 500 families in Agra – about 5,000 craftsmen - work the hard, durable and non-porous (so non-staining) marble from Macrana, near Jaipur. The process is the same now as in the 17th century. Apprenticeship begins at the age of 8 and takes 15 years, each student learning all the processes. He then specialises, choosing between being a marble-cutter, gem cutter, gem setter (with secret adhesive recipe) or chiseller, and he makes his own tools.

The shop owner buys the marble and brings it to the craftsmen. A design is agreed on paper and the marble is cut. Using a pointed tool, the design is drawn through a coat of red powder paint covering the marble; stones are selected and placed; the holes are chiselled (slow, precise work); stones are fitted, the final adjustments done with an emery paste wheel; stones are glued and, finally, polished with increasingly fine emery.

Dhurrie weaving Dhurrie in Hindi, kilim in Persian. Whereas it seems pile carpet weaving was introduced into India by Akbar, the flat dhurrie weaving seems to have been an indigenous craft. In the 19th century, it was introduced into prisons to relieve the boredom of inmates who also took up silk-weaving, cobbling, tie-dye, basket-work and horticulture. Prison officers kept a tight control on standards; the prisoners hardly needed to turn out slap-dash work for a quick return. Finished dhurries were sold in bazaars or presented to local maharajas, any proceeds going to the prisoner and his family. They reached a peak of technical skill, sophistication and design between 1880 and 1920. Today, the quality work is done in villages, not jails, although for some time young village women have woven their dreams into the panja (wedding dhurrie).

The women of a dhurrie-weaving family work at a horizontal bamboo loom set a few inches off the ground, inside or outside their home. As they chat and gossip, a senior aunt or grandmother, in the centre, keeps a fierce eye on each team member's work. Materials and designs are supplied by an agent employing up to 100 families in widely scattered villages. But while his designs are just variants of the traditional stars, diamonds, crosses, chevrons and diagonal patterns, he has introduced new materials and modified the palette. Formerly, dhurries were of cotton; now wool and even silk are woven. The strong indigo, red and saffron are

often supplanted by soft blue, ice-cream pink and peppermint green.

Both changes pander to the European market, but old and new can be found. The traditional Agra design of stripes going to a point at either end, leaving a plain surrounding field, is woven with a shuttle, wheras the more complex designs need a lot of finger work. To see weaving around Agra, contact Mr Mangalick (see above), whose nearest weaving families are only 5km away. There is no obligation. As he says: 'You are a guest of my city and my country.'

Forays out of Agra

These suggestions include day trips. Some link up well to make a longer day or a mini-break, stopping overnight.

FATEHPUR SIKRI, UTTAR PRADESH
37km. Essential to visit. The most perfectly preserved and complete Mughal palace city of all, built by Akbar using the highest quality workmanship, then abandoned by him 14 years later when he went to defend the north-west frontiers of his empire. Without its mentor, the city faded and although the royal buildings were kept in order for a period, the houses of unburnt brick soon collapsed. Akbar returned there once, briefly, in 1601; later, Jahangir stayed longer, with Prince Khurram (later Shah Jahan); later still, the Jhats plundered Fatehpur Sikri and despoiled Akbar's tomb at Sikandra. Today, the palace core echoes with the ghosts of Akbar's remarkable court, his foreign ambassadors, his scribes, his mullahs, his craftsmen and the ladies of his harem.

Aged 26, Akbar had no heir, despite all those wives. After the defeat of Chitorgarh in 1568, he made his annual pilgrimage to Ajmer – notice the kos minars (brick tower milestones) still standing en route. He also visited the holy man Shaikh Salim Chishti at Sikri who told him he would have three sons. The prediction came true. The next year a Rajput wife bore Salim (later Jahangir); legend tells us it was the Amber princess who sealed the first Mughal-Rajput alliance. After a pilgrimage of thanks to Ajmer a second son was born and, in 1572, the third son. This was impressive. By 1571 Akbar had decided to build a totally new capital at Sikri and moved his masons there.

Of the town, only the ruined walls remain. But the magnificent palace complex stands, the elaborately carved red sandstone and marble as crisp as it was 400 years ago, still carrying the atmosphere of Akbar's cultured and enlightened court. The building style is closer to the pure Indian of Gwalior Fort, keeping to the column and slab principle, than to the Mughal

Persian-Indian mélange. But the complex motifs of Gwalior decoration fuse happily with Persian jali work and decorative motifs such as the vase of flowers.

Shaikh Salim's white marble tomb with delicate jalis (finely carved screens) added by Shah Jahan is still visited by childless women who tie a cotton thread in the hope it will help them become fertile.

The palace buildings are alive with a mirage of palace life. But the names by which they are known do not necessarily refer to their original function, particularly since the lack of large pieces of furniture in Mughal rooms allowed for a room's function to change or to serve several jobs simultaneously. Through the large and open Diwan-i-Am lies a large courtyard. Here the so-called Diwan-i-Khas is possibly where Akbar sat above the central pillar, his ministers on the balconies, spectators standing below; the Ankh Michaeuli (hide and seek) was possibly used for storing records or the state treasury; and the pattern like ludo on the ground is for playing pachesi, a game like ludo, using giant pieces or real people, like giant chess games in Germany today. Up the other end, one of the most beautiful buildings of all here is the so-called Anup Talao, or Turkish Sultana's house, exquisitely carved outside and in, as if it was a piece of Kashmir wood-carving. In the harem, the so-called Jodhbai Palace and Miriam's House are also jewels of building, carving and painting, and the Panch Mahal (five-palace) is like a five-layered wedding cake of spun sugar. Outside this core, there are countless buildings to explore before crossing the courtyard to the magnificent Jami Masjid with its steep royal steps up to the courtyard where Shaikh Salim's tomb lies and where Akbar added the majestic Buland Darwaza gateway. Fun anecdotes from local guides. Open daily, sunrise to sunset; stay overnight at the on-site bungalow built by Curzon (bookable at Agra's Archaeological Survey office).

KOLEOD GHANA NATIONAL PARK, BHARATPUR, RAJASTHAN

54km from Agra, 17km from Fatehpur Sikri. One of the finest bird sanctuaries in the world, established 1956. 29 sq km of fresh water swamp developed by the Maharaja of Bharatpur for his famous duck shoots where enormous bags were taken; Kitchener and Curzon were at the first shoot in 1902, Viceroy Lord Linlithgow was the guest of honour for the biggest bag of all, 4,273, in 1938.

Today, there are more than 360 species of birds; spot breeding September-October, spot migratory birds November-February. Best time dawn or dusk. It is best to take a jersey and a pair of binoculars. As the mist lifts at sunrise,

take a rowing boat around the islands on the still water. Morning bird songs and flapping, yawning wings are the only sounds. There are water-dancing Chinese coots, gliding eagles, large painted and black-necked storks on treetops, electric-blue kingfishers on low branches. The rare Siberian crane visits here (December-January only), its only known winter home. There are hunchbacked herons, dazzling white egrets and many more. Then take a hot breakfast at the Forest Lodge. At dusk, there are non-water birds, pythons and animals – sambhar, chital, nilgai, pig. Worth hiring a bicycle in town to bike around the sanctuary.

To enjoy both dusk and dawn, stay overnight. Since the lake is often dry these days, it is worth checking before a visit. Inside the park, by-pass *Bharatpur Forest Lodge* in favour of *Shanti Kutir Forest Rest House* (book in writing). Outside, *Golbagh Palace Hotel*, Bharatpur (tel: 3349) is the delightful guest house of the Maharaja's palace and *Saras Tourist Bungalow*, Bharatpur (tel: 3700) is new, clean and a few yards from the park entrance. Best to arrive with Salim Ali's *Book of Indian Birds*. See also the stern early 18th century Lohagarh fort (open daily, 9am-5pm), palace and museum (Sat.-Thurs.) in Bharatpur.

Those going on to Jaipur from here can make two adventurous detours on their journey, one before and one after the Mid-Way café. First, after 70km, a left turn leads to *Bayana*. Those hooked on the Mughal trail can find a fine gateway surviving from a garden Akbar built in 1601, and a 12th and 14th century mosque now turned temple. Nearby is the evocative *Khanua*, the place where on March 16 1527 Babur defeated the Rajput confederacy led by Sangram Singh of Chitorgarh. The second stop is a right turn leading to Abaneri where carved remains of a 9th century Pratihara temple stand next to a deep tank, also with carved panels (see more from here at the Amber and Jaipur museums.)

DEEG, RAJASTHAN

90km from Agra (via Bharatpur or Mathura). Krishna's gopies (milkmaids) had their clothes woven and embroidered here. Walled summer palace of the Maharaja of Bharatpur, completed 1750, a grand complex of buildings with slightly overgrown Mughal gardens set between two huge tanks (artificial lakes). One of the few Rajasthan palaces open to the public yet not tarted up for visitors. Furniture and the occasional aged servant give a feeling that the family has gone for an extended holiday.

The facade of Gopal Bhavan (main palace) looking out over the tank has carved and painted balconies. Inside, there is European furniture on the ground floor and a vast black marble bed and a built-in horse-shoe dining table upstairs. The marble swing outside is booty from Delhi. Find frescoes in Nand Bhavan. The marble-lined Suraj Bhavan and Sawan and Bhadon pavilions are islands amid the surrounding ponds and fountains in the gardens. Keshav Bhavan, the open pavilion, is across the central garden. Purana Mahal, the old palace, is along the south side. The huge exercise room opposite would have had its floor dust mixed with perfume.

The 500 fountains, which used to splash coloured water as a backdrop to lavish firework displays and mock thunder storms with full sound, are now turned on for the August festival. M. C. Joshi's excellent guide book available on site. Open daily, 8am-noon; 1-7pm.

MATHURA, UTTAR PRADESH

On the Delhi-Agra Road, 147km from Delhi, 56km from Agra, 34km from Deeg. Krishna country. Birthplace of the mischievous, blue-skinned, human 7th incarnation of the god Vishnu who subsequently moved to Dwarka in Western Gujurat (see p. 165). As Krishna scholar P. Banerjee has written: 'The love and adoration of Krishna sank deep into the heart of India . . . He is so fundamentally the God who is human in everything.' Thus, a major centre of Hindu pilgrimage and Krishna worship at least since the 4th century BC. Subsequently a prosperous trading centre under the Shunga and Kushana dynasties. Then, a Buddhist centre developed under the Guptas (350BC-465AD) with 3,000 monks furnishing 20 monasteries. Today, one of the seven sacred Hindu cities.

At one end of the town stands the superb museum, packed with sculptures, terracottas, bronzes and coins, the items well-displayed but minimally labelled, with a pretty garden in the middle. With luck students studying there will be keen to practise their knowledge. Shunga, Kushana and Gupta stone pieces have been found nearby. Especially lovely are the Kushana carvings of Kanishka and of a prince from the nearby Kushana capital, Mat (Mathura was a later capital); the Kushana carved railing posts from Sonkh; and the Gupta head of Buddha and standing Buddha (Tues.-Sun., 10.30am-4.30pm; April 16-June 30 7.30am- 12.30pm).

The old town hugs the Yamuna River. Through the majestic gateway and down the narrow lanes lie the bathing ghats. Vishram Ghat is where Krishna rested after killing the tyrant king of Mathura (morning and evening riverside puja by pilgrims); Sati Burj (1570) is a tower commemorating a Jaipur royal's sati (a widow's self-immolation). Here too are Raja Man Singh of Amber's ruined Kans Qila Fort, Aurangzeb's Jami Masjid (1661) built with his usual tactlessness right on the spot where Krishna was believed to have been born, and

the fun Dwarkadheesh Temple (1914) built by Seth Gokuldass of Gwalior, dedicated to Krishna and decorated like a Christmas tree for the big festivals (open 6-10.30am; 4-6pm).

Near the town are several sacred villages. *Vrindaban* (10km) is where Krishna flirted with the milkmaids. The many temples here include the exceptional Gobind Deo (Divine Cowherd, 1590) (all temples open 8-11am; 5-9pm). Other villages are *Mahaban* (11km) where Nanda, Krishna's foster-father, tended the young god; *Gokul* (10km), where Krishna was brought up in secrecy; *Barsana* (47km) where Radha, Krishna's consort, was born; *Goverdhan* (26km) the hillock Krishna lifted on his finger for a week to protect the cowherds of Braj from the god Indra's storms.

It is well worth coinciding with a big Hindu festival such as Holi, Diwali, Janmashtami (Krishna's birthday, a time for the Krishna ras lila dances in the temples) or Annakut, when Mathura and all these Braj villages take turns in the celebrations. For instance, at Holi in Vrindaban, Krishna's life is daily enacted by young, painted and tinselled Brahmin boys at Ashram Sri Caitanya Prema Sansthan for 14 days before Holi night. The Holi water is made by steeping flowers in vats, not by chemicals. Those who visit Banki Bihari temple are pelted with rose petals. People get merry on a concoction of clotted cream, nuts, rosewater and bhang (hashish). Cows are dressed up in heavy brocades. There is ritual bathing in the Yamuna. Women chase men in a mock battle, throwing dung and brandishing sticks. Surrounding villages take their turn during the following days. At Barsana, likened by artist Andrew Logan to Bethlehem, men from the neighbouring village lie down under shields to be thwacked with huge sticks by veiled women. As well as mounting plays, the Ashram at Vrindaban is making important music recordings including the old masters of the classic dhrupad form. It is possible to stay overnight.

GWALIOR, MADHYA PRADESH

118km by road from Agra; direct daily flights connect Delhi and Bhopal (in central India, see p. 157), or take the fast Shatabdi Express train. Spectacular fort built on a narrow sandstone outcrop some 3km long that 'quite stunned' India connoisseur Mark Zebrowski, who puts it high in his priorities of places to visit. Cunningham praised it as: 'the noblest specimen of Hindu domestic architecture in northern India'. No wonder in its heyday it influenced Akbar's Fatehpur Sikri. Since a Rajput built the first fortress in the 8th century, it has been contested by various powers – Tomars, Sikandar Lodi, Babur, the Mahrathas and the British. The Tomar family rose in 1398. Man Singh, the strongest Tomar, ruled 1486-1517. Today a royal mother and son of the Scindias of Gwalior (Marathas) are prominent in Indian politics. She, a strong personality always swathed in her widow's white sari, has been the Vice-President of the Bharata Janata Party since 1980 and twice Vice-President of the All-India Women's Conference. He, educated at Winchester and Oxford, is another ex-Maharaja to be voted to the Lok Sabha on the Congress (I) ticket.

Visit the *fort* first, if possible picking up as a guide Yashwant Singh or his son, who live at the Hindola gateway below the museum and whose charm, eloquent English and knowledge about the fort transform a visit. Approach by the south-west road, passing the colossal Jain statues in the rock, spanning the 7th to 15th centuries (found indecent by Babur who obliterated the faces), through the 10 metre high walls.

Inside is Man Singh's palace, built with vast pieces of stone cut and carved as if they were wood. Exterior embellished with glorious lapis blue tiles of ducks, elephants and palmyra palms; interior carved with dancers, peacocks and fabulous beasts. The natural air-conditioning system would have passed over perfumed water in the summer rooms. Two floors are above ground level; two below, where in the dark, cool rooms Mughal emperor Aurangzeb had his brother Murad killed in 1659 and where, it is said, the women could watch for the flag of victory or defeat and, if necessary, immediately commit sati on the fire already prepared.

Next door, see the Karan, Jahangir and Shah Jahan palaces (with views down to Gujari Palace). Nearby stand the two 11th century Sasbahu temples (currently being well restored) – the most spectacular of all the views is from here – and the 8th century Teli-ka-Mandir, with delicate sculptures on the exterior of amorous couples, flying Garuda and a river goddess, considered by Robert Skelton to indicate its dedication to various famous goddesses. The Archaeological Survey office, near the Man Singh Palace, has padlocked trunks full of guide books to various parts of India but only occasionally to Gwalior.

The good museum is found inside the Hindola Gate and housed in the Gujari Palace (*c.* 1500), built by Man Singh for his favourite wife Mringanaya from Gujarat: established 1913, fine collection of inscriptions, Shunga and Gupta sculptures, miniature paintings and, for those heading south from here, samples of more Madhya Pradesh buildings to be seen en route to Bhopal, at Udayagiri, Udayapur, etc. Good guide book. (Open Tues.-Sun., 8-11am, 2-5pm; April 1-September 30, 7-10am, 3-6pm).

Down in the *town*, seek out the grand Gwalior royal chhatris (and a modern one on the edge of town) amid huge three-wheeler taxis that lumber and lurch along the road, pumping their squeezy horns. There are also two important non-royal tombs. One is the very finely carved sandstone tomb of Muhammad Ghaus (late 16th century) who, it seems, assisted Babur in acquiring Gwalior and later became a spiritual adviser to Akbar; as an early Mughal imperial building in the provinces (it was paid for by Akbar), the tomb is exceptional. The other, right next to it, is of the great musician Tansen (b.1506), whom Akbar made Master of Music at his court in 1562. He is the focus of an annual music festival in December when India's greatest living musicians play round the clock for several days and nights in huge, brightly coloured tents (the Delhi Tansen festival is in February). The stately dhrupad form of Hindustani classical vocal and instrumental music, of which there are few practitioners today, was developed by Raja Man Singh Tomar, then elaborated by Swami Haridas and his disciple, Tansen. Tansen was also crucial to the development of the open-throated simple Gwalior gharana singing (easier on Western ears). Agra, Jaipur and other cities each have distinctive gharana schools but Gwalior's is the oldest and the fountainhead.

Now that the Gwalior family squabbles have concluded, the Scindias' *Jai Vilas* pile of a palace is open again. The ornate, Italianate design was prepared by Lieut.-Col. Sir Michael Filose of the Indian Army for the sly Maharaja Jayaji Rao, who borrowed money from the British but died leaving wealth, precious stones and treasure valued at 62 million rupees. It was completed in three years flat, 1872-4, to be ready for the Prince of Wales's visit. Before the two vast chandeliers were hung in the Durbar hall – claimed to be the biggest in the world, 248 candles each – three elephants were hoisted on to the roof to test its strength. The rest of the interior continues in the same vein, with imaginative details such as a silver train set that circulated cigars and port round the dining-room table, added by the next ruler, Madhav Rao. He drove his full-sized train himself, 'in a dashing fashion' according to E. M. Forster, who also noted in 1921 that this 'shrewd man of business' but 'vigorous and vulgar prince' nicknamed his children George and Mary, the ultimate compliment to the British. Shabby, but amusing to visit.

If Gwalior fort impressed you, then don't turn back, for south lie Datia and, just beyond Jhansi, Orchha. Stay overnight in Gwalior at *Usha Kiran Palace*, Jayendragunj (tel: 23453, telex: 566-225 GARG; cable: USHAKIRAN); a modest Jai Vilas guest house in the palace grounds, run by the Welcomgroup but maintaining all the Maharaja's 1930s high-style furniture: standard lamps, geometric rugs in pastel shades, coloured glass wall-lights, even his curtains. 27 rooms, some more air-conditioned than others; pleasant, relaxed atmosphere, not grand. Garden being restored. Tennis, riding and badminton on palace estate; golf by arrangement. Good local food, best ordered well in advance before sight-seeing.

DATIA-ORCHHA, MADHYA PRADESH

A memorable day-trip from Gwalior to Datia (69km) and Orchha (120km) – and hardly a tourist in sight. Leave at the crack of dawn by car or by the Shatabti Express. At Datia, the fine, seven-storey hilltop Gobinda Palace (1614) is one of the few Indian buildings Lutyens admitted to admiring. More recently, John Keay compared it to Delhi and Agra as 'more integrated and imposing than either'. Above the cool, dark first two storeys, behind the pierced screens, there are sun-dappled verandahs, pavilions and pillared corridors, and lofty rooms, their walls still holding mosaics and paintings. This and Orchha palace were built by a Rajput ruler, Bir Singh Deo, based at Jhansi, whose wealth and influence as a firm favourite of Prince Salim (later Jahangir) leapt after he did him the favour of assassinating Akbar's personal friend and close adviser, the high-powered Abul Fazl (author of the Akbar-nama and Ain-i-Akbari). Abul Fazl was at the time very disapproving of the wayward prince, and his concern about Salim's ability to succeed to the throne would have fuelled Akbar's worry and encouraged Salim to consider Abul Fazl an enemy threatening his future.

Speed on to Orchha, the perfect medieval city, if crumbling a bit, extolled by an India buff as 'very special; by far the least changed and most unspoilt Rajput city I've seen in India', and by another as 'rather like Jaisalmer used to be'. A village survives beside the wooded island fort which was deserted in the 18th century. Inside the fort, find several palaces: the tiered Jahangir Mahal (built for Jahangir; good views); the Raj and Sheesh Mahal. Brightly coloured paintings coat some walls and ceilings; others have finely carved brackets, jali screens and vestiges of tilework. Well worth climbing the hill to Lakshmi Narayan Temple for its murals and for the view, putting on trousers and good shoes to explore the many ruins dotted among the prickles and bushes, and spending a sunset across the river gazing back at the royal chhatris.

To have more time, stay at the charming *Hotel Sheesh Mahal*, 8 rooms, in a corner of the palace – the Maharaja would stay overnight in the large one upstairs with Victorian furniture. Now run by MP Tourism. Book in writing or through MP Tourist Office, 19 Ashok Road, New Delhi (tel: 351187); slow but charming service, and delicious vegetarian food best ordered well in advance. If no rooms, try *Jhansi Hotel*, Shastri Marg, Jhansi (tel: 1360); or return to Gwalior. Avoid night driving: dangerous dacoit country.

West of here lies Shivpuri, which it is possible to visit en route to Gwalior-Jhansi. Outside the wildlife sanctuary (see end of this chapter), there is a cluster of most remarkable white marble chhatris built for recent Gwalior royals. The Rajmata comes here regularly to pay her respects, visiting the house-like mausolea overlooking an ornamental lake. Each is elaborately carved, and the god living inside is woken, fed, clothed, read to, sung to and danced to daily, except during his afternoon nap. More than a hundred people are fully employed to serve them. Closed noon-3pm.

For a wonderful drive down into Central India from Datia and Orchha, punctuated by superb but little-visited architectural treats, see Sanchi in the Bombay chapter, and do the suggested trip in reverse.

Khajuraho, Madhya Pradesh

The temple sculptures, inspired by the ecstatic pleasure of life and deep admiration of female beauty, are famous in the West merely as an A to Z of erotic naughtiness, to be ogled and sniggered at. Nothing could be further from the aims of the builders, as is apparent the moment the carvings are seen. On a rural plain, with birds singing and fields of wheat swaying in the breeze, stand the 25 survivors of a temple city built by the rich and powerful Chandella rulers in the 10th and 11th centuries. The sculptures covering the temples celebrate with human warmth and utter frankness the sublime joy of life and love, reflecting an entirely open society, free from all prudishness or Western sexual neurosis. They express the highest spiritual experience open to man: the Hindu theory that when all the senses give fully, there is total union physically and mentally, arrived at through love-making. The Hindus of Khajuraho loved without shame, uninhibited by the Western concept of original sin. Their sculptures celebrate woman in all her sensuality and vanity, from yawning at daybreak to laughing with her lover at a playful monkey. They could not be further from voyeuristic pornography. They are vivacious and optimistic. Just a plane-hop away, they should not be missed. And the peace: few hawkers, no false guides, no beggars, and bicycle rickshaws instead of cars.

THE HARD FACTS Central India plains get very hot indeed. Avoid April-September; the July-August downpour can be very beautiful or utter misery. Essential to stay overnight as the eyes get cultural indigestion coping with solid temples in a five-hour spin. The Western Group are gloriously serene at sunset and sunrise. In fact, it is tempting to stay several nights for complete relaxation, perhaps visiting some nearby treats.

The seven-day dance festival falls in early March. It has a good reputation. Top dancers perform classical dance-drama against temple back-drops. Although it disturbs the peace of the temples, this is a chance to see dance in its original setting. Apart from the temples, a tiny village, two classy hotels and a few modest ones, there is an airstrip and one road but no railway station. Daily flights from Delhi, Agra and Varanasi; connections to Calcutta and Kathmandu. The two very good, new hotels each have full facilities and a clean pool, garden, good food, good atmosphere and, between them (they are back-to-back), two well-stocked bookshops (other shops are touristy).

Jass Oberoi (tel: 66; cable: OBHOTEL); sparkling 1980s new, quite small, beautifully designed with huge white marble lobby and central sweeping staircase. 54 rooms, each with balcony, all mod. cons, baby sitter; meals served inside or outside; peaceful atmosphere; service good but lacks the usual Oberoi polish.

Chandela (tel; 54; cable: CHANDELA); got here first, built in 1969 by Shyam Poddar, who also organised the airstrip; managed by his sixth son; now owned by the Taj Group. Bigger than Jass with the same pros and cons; more white marble and huge lobby. 102 rooms, each with verandah, simple decor; all mod. cons and big shopping arcade, health club, very good herbal beauty parlour, hair-dresser (all open to non-residents); tennis court, mini-golf – even a temple; efficient and sensitive service (delicious fresh coffee).

The Tourist Office is not useful. The Archaeological Survey book on Khajuraho by Krishna Deva, sold at the Western Group gateway, is essential. Opposite, at Raja's café, there are excellent guides, especially Brijendra Singh whose world revolves around the temples: half-day Rs35; full day Rs65. Beware of buying 'old' brass, much of it made in Delhi the previous week.

THE HINDU TEMPLE As there are just temples at Khajuraho, and they are some of India's most sophisticated and sublime, this is a good moment to look at the story of the temple.

The main religious buildings of Hindus and their offshoots, Buddhists and Jains, have much in common. This is because all follow principles laid down in the Shastras, the ancient architectural manuals compiled by priests. The Shastras set out building forms, techniques and the astronomical and astrological information which relates them to the universes of the cosmos. For instance, a temple often has an east-west axis to follow the rising and setting of the sun; and if its proportions successfully follow the structure of the cosmos, then this harmony with universal order will be good for the whole community. As architectural historian George Michell points out, one Shastra assures the architect that world harmony can be achieved through perfect building proportions, another that 'only work completed according to the rules can gain the desired merit for the patron and worshipper'. In addition to the Shastras, the design of a sacred monument may also derive from a mandala, a geometric diagram describing the pattern of the universe – perhaps based on the shape of an egg or a square.

The temple was not India's earliest sacred building form. That was the stupa, a funerary mound whose earliest survivors date from the Mauryan emperor Ashoka's rule in the 3rd century BC. Small votive stupas were housed in two ways: in chaitya halls where the stupa was in the rounded apse at the end of a long nave; and in viharas, used by Buddhist monks, where the stupa was kept in one of a string of monks' cells surrounding a central courtyard. Both these could be built of wood, cut into rocks or built of freestanding stone.

Unlike these, the temple houses an image of a deity or saviour. It is kept in the sanctuary, the place whose sacred nature is, as George Michell notes, revealed in its name, garbhagriha (womb-chamber), implying its role as 'ritual kernel of the temple'. Other temple chambers, or mandapas (halls), lie in a row, so that this kernel can be seen from the doorway. As the worshipper moves through the temple, he moves through increasingly sacred and dark spaces, usually dimly lit with small windows, each doorway carved with protective figures – carving other than this tends to be restrained, and restricted to columns and ceilings. All the while he sees the deity from an auspicious viewpoint. The mandapas end at the vestibule and then the sanctuary, which only the priest can enter; but when there is a passage round the sanctuary the worshipper continues round it clockwise. All this is part of his worship.

The temple exterior reinforces the symbolism inside. Conceived as the mountain abode of the gods, small sikharas (peaks) at the porch end rise to the highest sikhara over the sanctuary, while the lower, horizontal storeys are called bhumi (earth). To give a soaring, energetic character, the sikharas were built higher and higher. To give an increasingly exuberant and baroque effect to the whole, the exterior surface was punctuated with bold projections, deep niches and abrupt changes of plane. Then, in contrast to the relatively simple interior, any decorative restraint is unleashed and every surface is carved with divine beings, lively animals, lush foliage and ornate patterns.

From timber to rock to free-standing stone construction, the temple maintained its pillar-and-beam technique, without arches or vaulting. On this basic engineering, the stone-carvers ran riot.

Some temples stand on their own. Others are part of a walled complex with subsidiary buildings for minor divinities, including perhaps the consort of the god worshipped in the main temple. Larger complexes would need administrative buildings, libraries, sleeping rooms, food storehouses, kitchens and a purification tank for the temple inmates. Puja items such as flowers, sugar, coconuts and spices would be on sale inside the temple or at its entrance. In the south, these rooms were built as encircling enclosures round the central temple, the outer one with vast pyramid-shaped gateways.

In all, the temple shows just how different the Hindu philosophy is from Islam's. For a Hindu, the temple is a mysterious and vastly complicated experience from porch to sanctum. The exterior is highly symbolic in shape and carving, running the gamut of the Hindu pantheon; in the interior, each dark room has its own symbolism and feels increasingly enclosed and internal, indeed womb-like, as it moves towards the deity. The mosque, however, is open, functional and has its surface coated with flat, non-figurative decoration, often just calligraphy, and concentrates the mind on the one invisible God.

OUT AND ABOUT See the two main groups of temples, Western and Eastern, and a few to the south. Linger on the green lawns surrounding the Western Group. The Rajput Chandellas' rise to power in Central India at the beginning of the 10th century led to a vigorous literary and architectural flowering, patronised by the rulers and focused on their capital, Khajuraho. Their belief was that to build a temple was to reserve a suite in heaven. But the temple city may also have been planned as a non-monastic centre of learning and religion.

The 85 temples erected by them reached the peak of Central Indian temple architecture and sculpture, comparable to – if not surpassing – the Orissan temples at Bhubaneswar, south of Calcutta. Visvanatha and Parsvanastha, two of the finest, were constructed under Dhanga (c. 950-1002). Chandella power, built on diamonds and booty from conquests, waned from the mid-11th century, but the religious centre thrived for another 200 years. Fortunately, their remoteness protected them from Muslim destruction. They were rediscovered in the mid-19th century by the intrepid British.

The Khajuraho temples follow the distinct temple pattern. Each is a compact mass of porch, hall, vestibule and sanctum, the walls surmounted by beehive sikharas (peaks) which, seen from the side, make a rhythmic pattern up to the highest, over the sanctum. The whole temple stands on a high platform, facing east. One explanation for the platforms suggests that the land was flooded to make a lake of temples.

Exuberant sculpture rampages over every surface, inside and outside, modulated to become surprisingly easy to read. Thus, large figures in full light are offset by flat stones or geometric patterns set back in shadow. Friezes of continuous narrative run around the platform but the sikharas have lace-fine geometric cutting to give them feathery lightness.

The technological feat of constructing such marvels, mostly between 950 and 1050, is mind-boggling. Although the flat granite land, birthplace of the first Chandella king, was an ideal site, the sandstone was dug from the Ken River, 20km away, then transported by river and by wooden rollers hauled by elephants. This explains the crispness, for river sandstone is harder than quarried. Notice the women's flesh creases, their delicate finger nails, the droplets of water on the skin, even the mark where she is scratching herself. The system was to cut and carve every stone for the temple, then assemble it in a mathematical triumph of dry-stone interlocking; a 3-D puzzle that makes frivolity of those 5,000 piece cardboard jigsaw puzzles.

It is a short rickshaw ride to the Eastern Group to see *Parsvanastha Jain temple*, an architectural masterpiece. Charming sculptures include a woman applying eye make-up, another removing a thorn from her foot. By going through tiny Khajuraho village and into the fields visible from this temple, it is possible to see a few more of this group. Yet more are dotted around the countryside.

In the Western Group, every temple is worth looking at, especially the early *Lakshmana* (c. 930-950), the most complete, retaining its corner shrines, *Visvanatha* (c. 950-1002) and the magnificent *Kandariya Mahadev* (1025-50), the most sublime of all both in architecture and sculpture, the zenith of Chandella art. There are friezes of elephants, horses and soldiers on campaign, fighting and having a ball on their return home; upsaras (seductive women) stretching, squeezing out water from their hair after a bath, preening in the mirror, awaiting their lovers, swaying invitingly and coyly; mithunas (couples love-making) in dalliance, embracing and fondling. All temples open sunrise to sunset.

For yet more, see the southern group and visit the museum (open Sat.-Thurs., 9am-5pm, entrance by ticket to Western Group enclosure).

Trips out of Khajuraho

The ideal way to enjoy this rural spot is to stay several days. If a temple overdose needs rebalancing, there are diamond mines, the Panna National Park (see end of chapter) and Rajka Falls to visit. Keen historians and archaeologists will find the plain littered with interesting sites. To see some of these, invest in hiring a car, driver and possibly a guide. Then, with picnic, bottled drink and map, set off on these two trips to little-known places.

For some Gupta remains, head south-eastwards through Panna town (see below) to *Nachna* to seek out carved Parvati Temple (5th century), with its sanctuary and passage, and the nearby later Chaturmukha Mahadeva Temple (9th century) with its curved tower and beautifully carved lingum. Then to *Bhumara*, where the Shiva Temple (5th century) has a door finely carved with river goddesses leading to another good lingum. This trip combines well with a visit to Panna National Park.

For some more substantial monuments, again head through the National Park's teak, tendu and ber trees to Panna town (46km) where the Bundella ruler Rudra Pratap Singh employed an English architect to design first the whacky Baldevji Temple (1880s) modelled on St Paul's Cathedral and then his palace (1886) – best view over the town from the bizarre Circuit House. Other buildings to seek out include the 17th century Maharaja Chatrasal's Prannathji Temple for his guru and Kishoreji Temple for a Krishna idol brought from Mathura.

The adventurous and fort-crazy then go north on the road to Banda to find first Ajaigarh Fort, perched above teak forests on a granite outcrop whose cliff face has elaborate rock carvings. The 9th century fort was built by the Chandella kings – its stonework is richly carved with palm, lotus petals and other sacred Hindu motifs – and later held by the Bundellas, Marathas and finally the British (whose artillery is still scattered about). Another 26km reaches the magnificent Kalinjar, one of India's oldest forts, mentioned by Ptolemy. Originally a hill shrine in the Vindhya mountains, invaders have included Mahmud of Ghazni, Qutb-ud-Din Aibak, Humayun and Sher Shah Sur who in 1545 died here of burns when a live shell lit the gunpowder supplies (his tomb is east of Varanasi). The only approch is from the north (that is, from the modern city), through seven gateways to find Sita Sej (a stone chamber with couch), Patalganga cave, Budha Badra tank, the Mrigdhara building (with rock-cut deer), plus scattered Bundella remains, Muslim tombs and an incongruous monument to Andrew Wauchope, a Scot who was the first Commissioner of Bundelkund.

Lucknow, Uttar Pradesh

Surprisingly low-key capital of Uttar Pradesh, India's most populous state whose 111 million inhabitants number more than the whole population of all but six countries in the world (Brazil, China, Indonesia, Japan, the US and USSR). Although 70% of Lucknow's population is Hindu, the old core is, in essence, a quiet Muslim city whose grand decaying monuments and busy bazaars still carry touches of 18th century decadent courtliness – perhaps this is because, rarely in India, government policy has kept heavy industry 20 miles outside the city. In the older areas, it seems that a servant could easily trot past, carrying his master's hookah to prepare it at the house where he is dining, wondering if he will offer a puff to some fellow guest, the ultimate gesture of friendship. Here in Lucknow, the huge palace gardens are restored, the Muslim arts of attar (perfume) preparation and chikankari (white-on-white embroidery) are alive and well, and festivals celebrate the fine musical tradition.

If you are tired of the hassle of Agra, the dazzling colours of Rajasthan, the majesty of Mughal buildings and the relentless hawkers of more popular tourist haunts, come to Lucknow for calm, subtle colours and space.

The population is Shi'ite, rather than Sunni as found in Delhi, Agra, Gurajat and Hyderabad. The Shi'ite Nawabs of Oudh (today Avadh, in Bihar) rose to power in the 18th century as the Mughals declined. So, whereas Safdar Jang, son of Sa'adat Khan (who rose from rags to nawabhood), was stylishly buried in Delhi (see above), his successors made first Farrukhabad, then Fyzabad and then Lucknow (from 1775) their capital.

Asaf-ud-Daula (1775-97) and Sa'adat Ali Khan (1798-1814) were the best of the ten lazy, plump, pleasure-loving and debauched Nawabs. But Muslim culture benefitted. To enjoy themselves, they built with aplomb, employed Mughal artists and craftsmen, encouraged Hindustani music and Urdu poetry, and, of course, led the legendary cult of the Lucknow courtesan-dancing girls to its peak of sophistication. Two good films depict the height and deterioration of Lucknow court life. One is Muzaffa Ali's 'Umrao Jaan', adapted from a 19th-century Urdu novel about a contemporary courtesan's abduction as a child, her training and rise to fame, and then her attempts to get free; set during Lucknow's cultural and nawabi zenith. The other is Satyajit Ray's 'The Chess Players', based on a short story by Prem Chand.

Quite the most head-in-the-sand Nawab was the last, music-loving Wajid Ali Shah (1847-56), whose blind extravagance and indolence led the British to exile him to Calcutta, one of many contributions to the 1857 Rebellion (known by the British as the Mutiny) which staged some of its bloodiest scenes at Lucknow, in and around the Residency. But Wajid Ali Shah should be remembered rather for his music. Sitting in his marble palace, he composed and patronised the light-weight thumri love songs, inspired by the Krishna-Radha romance. Music, like courtesans, was crucial to all the Nawabs. After eating, ghazels, light songs of Urdu poetry, were sung.

The courtesan, or tawaef, was quite different from the basic prostitute, or takaiyan. She was an integral part of Nawabi society. She entertained the Nawabs with dance and song for substantial gold rewards. She could write tolerable Urdu poetry. And she was famed for her guftagoo (art of conversation). The accomplished Bacchua sang ghazels at royal weddings, Addha Biggam was known for poetry, Mushtari for her wit. Although often born into a humble family and amusing her patrons with a good romp as well as a song, the courtesan would become so cultured that the nobility sent their children to be educated by her. But education and pleasure were kept quite separate. The son of a big Lucknow family recently educated by a tawaef was scolded by her when he returned to enjoy other amusements. At the height of tawaef culture and influence in the 19th century, a Nawab gave enormous gifts for the exclusive use of a tawaef's pleasures – jewellery, gold, mango groves, whole estates and a grand town haveli.

THE HARD FACTS Extremes again. Avoid the April-early September scorching heat, but beware of the chilly winter days. Colourful celebrations of the Muslim festivals (see p. 46 and p. 59). The sound and light show at the Residency during winter months is judged 'damn good'. The fortnight-long *Lucknow Festival* (February) attracts India's top musicians and dancers who perform qawwalis (group songs), ghazels, thumris (light, classical song), kathak dance (see p. 69) and classic dramas; there is also the All-India Kite Flying Tournament, fireworks and a film festival. *Bhatkande* festival (September) is pure music. Some of India's many great artists take part in these: Ustad Amjad Ali Khan (plays sarod), Birju Maharaj (from a Lucknow dancing family of many generations), Ustad Ali Akbar (plays sarod) and Ustan Vilayat Khan (plays sitar). Great Varanasi musicians might include Bismila Khan (plays shahnai, a wind instrument) and Pandit Kishan Maharaj (plays tabla). Ravi Shankar now performs as much outside as inside India, introducing his sitar skills to Western ears.

Go by train or plane. Train is more fun: arrive from Delhi on the overnight Lucknow Mail (departs 9.25pm, arrives 7.25am) or the Gomti Express (departs 2.55pm, arrives 10.22pm) at the overpoweringly gigantic Charbagh railway station. Planes connect with Delhi and Calcutta (daily) and with Agra (Tues., Thurs., Sat., Sun.). To see the monuments of both the Nawabs and the British, it is best to stay at least two nights. For a bed, go for concrete and efficiency, or character; both have car rental; the first has operating business services.

Hotel Clarks Avadh, 8 Mahatma Gandhi Marg (tel: 40131-3; telex: 0535-243; cable: AVADH); part of the reliable but unshowy Clarks chain; 98 beds, all mod. cons plus library and golf. Ground floor restaurant simple. Rooftop Falakmuna one can, if asked in advance, serve good Lucknow food, the richest Mughlai cuisine of all, with lots of cream, almonds and pistachios. Try Lucknowi specialities such as the kebabs – kakori (finely ground meat), malai, khati and tangri (leg of chicken), eating them with mughlai paratha or romali roti breads. Try also dum aloo (potato cooked in a sealed pot) and dum pukt (meat cooked in rich spices in a sealed pot), murg nawabi (chicken), mali chutney wala (fish), noormahal biryani (mutton and rice), baingan mumtaz (stuffed aubergine) and Lucknow dahl. Shahi tukri (a richer, sweeter version of bread pudding), seviyan (vermicelli cooked in sweetened milk) and firni (also milk-based) are the classic puddings.

Carlton Hotel, Shahnajaf Road (tel: 44021-5; telex: 0535-217; cable: CARLTON); lots of character, even if in bad need of a lick of paint; old, rambling, former palace with columns, pillars, wooden staircase and a wonderful garden; 51 rooms, mediocre food – eat at Clarks.

The good UP Tourist Office is at 21 Vidhan Sabha Marg (tel: 29214). A good travel agent is Travel Bureau, A-8/3 Paper Mill Colony, Nishatganj, Lucknow (tel: 70046/75689); good cars and guides – Ragnish Vats is especially knowledgeable. Monuments tend to open 6am to 5pm.

OUT AND ABOUT There are two themes to Lucknow: the Nawabs and the British. First the Nawabs. A good place to start is at Asaf-ud-Daula's Great Imambara, mosque and tomb where Muharram is celebrated (1784), built as a famine relief project and designed by architect of the day, Nifayat-ullah and considered by Philip Davies as 'one of the most impressive buildings in India'. Through the great gateway lies the tranquil garden with mosque to the right, baoli to the left and tomb ahead. The Nawab and his wife are buried in the Wedgwood blue central hall decorated with vast mirrors, a dozen great chandeliers and what looks like spray cream squirted all over the scalloped arches. Locals claim it is the largest room in the world unsupported by pillars. Stairs adjoining the tomb reach the bhul bhulaiyan, a labyrinth of galleries, corridors and rooms. There are excellent views from the top across the city, laying out before you some other sites to visit: the Jami Masjid; the Small Imambara with silver pulpit and a forest of chandeliers in its glitzy interior and a replica of the Taj Mahal in its large garden; the three-storeyed Tower (1830s) for watching the moon at Id; the Clock Tower built at the same time as London's Big Ben; the Picture Gallery with a parade of gaily-dressed Nawabs and Kings (as they became under the British); Aurangzeb's white mosque on a hill behind the Imambara's gateway, and the red minarets of Hardinge Bridge.

Wandering the garden, or taking tea from the little stall, the atmosphere is one of civilised see-diness and peaceful order. Fairy-tale turrets, onion domes and minarets of smokey grey, pinkish beige and clotted cream-coloured weatherworn plaster form backdrops to every view like fragile stage sets, with every wall per-forated with arches, arcades, niches and win-dows. All looks deceptively insubstantial; but all this withstood the British guns of 1857.

The Residency Complex represents the British side of Lucknow. It is a frozen reminder of the 1857 Rebellion (known to the British as the Mutiny) which concentrated its attention on Delhi, Cawnpore (later Kanpur) (see p. 89) and Lucknow and became a year when 'savagery on both sides was unparalleled in the British asso-ciation with India' (Moorhouse). It broke out in Meerut, 50 kilometres northeast of Delhi, on May 10. Forty-seven battalions of the Bengal army mutinied, angered at the Company's in-sensitive order to bite cartridges, whose grease was rumoured to be of pig and cow fat, before putting them into their rifles. This was a double insult: pig is forbidden to Muslims, cow to Hindus. The next day the mutineers marched on Delhi (relieved in September); the rebellion quickly spread to Cawnpore (now called Kan-pur, which suffered the great massacre of June 27), and then to Lucknow. The following year, 1858, British India was placed under direct governorship of the Crown instead of through the intermediary East India Company.

The British fort at Lucknow is tidied but mostly untouched since the double sieges and the terrible British retribution which, as Geof-frey Moorhouse writes, 'was vile when it came'. Like the Nawabs' buildings, it is intensely atmospheric.

Huge banyan, neem and bel fruit trees shade the complex. Near the entrance stands the Trea-sury (used as an arsenal in 1857). Then follows the once sumptuous Banqueting Hall, Dr Fayr-er's House where Lucknow's Chief Commis-sioner Sir Henry Lawrence died, and Begum Kothi where Mrs Walters, a wife of the King of Oudh, lived. The elegant Residency building itself (1800), with battered towers, now houses a good little museum on the ground floor, com-plete with a full model of the position in 1857 and plenty of horrific prints; the cool, dim base-ment is where the women and children stayed for the duration of the siege – after three months, Sir Henry Havelock and his small force retook the fort on September 25 only to lose it immediately, and the final relief was not until November 17 under Sir Colin Campbell. A Re-sidency population of 2,994 on June 30 had shrunk to 979. Havelock died of dysentry a week later. In the Cemetery, find the modest graves of Lawrence and of General J. S. Neill, whose Cawnpore revenge (see below) could not be repeated at Lucknow since he was killed here on September 25, 1857.

Reflecting on the Rebellion today, an elderly local Nawab confides, without malice: 'Nothing was the same after 1858'. Indeed, Lucknow played an important role in India's freedom struggle. With one foot in the past and one in the future, this Nawab has conflicting memories – of his grandfather 'coming out of the palace in his coach and horses, preceded by a woman ser-vant who would cry out "His highness is com-ing! His highness is coming! Clear the way!"'; and of attending the 1916 sessions of the Con-gress and Muslim League parties held at Luck-now. They resulted in the significant Lucknow Pact, by which both parties jointly framed a con-stitutional scheme on the basis of Dominion status and also proposed separate electorates (Hindu and Muslim). As a political activist at university, threats of jail made no impact on the young aristocrat – 'Gandhiji went to jail, Jawaharlal Nehru went, Motilal Nehru went. It was normal.' And now, dressed in old chikan-kari and holding his small, silver paan box, this man who can also remember losing hours lounging against bolsters, drawing on his hoo-kah and playing chess on his Chinese lacquer set, sums up Lucknow's recent past. 'One peasant said to me later, after Independence, "If you nawabs had given your peasants just a beaker each, to show you knew we existed, there would have been no uprising." He was right.'

For an oddity, the Iron Bridge near the Re-sidency was designed by Sir John Rennie in 1798, based on one at Boston, Lincolnshire, and cast just 20 years after the first iron bridge in England.

To imbibe even more lazy atmosphere, it is sometimes possible to persuade a local boat-owner at Hanuman Bridge to row up the Gumti, giving a totally different perspective to the city – this is how people used to arrive.

Also in town: the good Archaeological Museum in Kaisarbagh Palace and the State Museum on Barnarsi Bagh (both open 10am-4.30pm, Tues.-Sun.). The State Museum is found through the Zoo and its park (open 5am-5.30pm) and has glorious sculpture on the ground floor (Shunga bull rider and Bodhisattva from Mathura, huge stone Gupta horse), Awadh (Oudh) art upstairs and, round the back of the buildings, statues of appropriately banished overlords including two each of Victoria, George and Mary. Countless other British buildings remain, their rich red brick and clean lines contrasting with the Nawabs' romantic monuments. One good cluster is nearby Government House (1907, to visit, apply at the gateway, asking for the Personal Secretary), the domed Legislative Council building (1928), the public library built like a Scottish castle and Christ Church (1860) which was built as a memorial to the 1857 Rebellion dead.

On the outskirts of the city lies the spacious, affluent cantonment with tidy red-brick bungalows and tiled, pitched-roof public buildings like Tuscan farmhouses. In the middle, the Dilkusha is a nawab's hunting-box which, during the 1857 Rebellion, was taken by Havelock and then Campbell; it was here, on November 24, a week after the final relief, that the hero Havelock died.

Don't miss the French-Indian pile of La Martinière school. Originally called Constantia, it was built as a country residence by French adventurer Major-Gen. Claude Martin (1735-1800), who made a tidy fortune working concurrently for the Nawab, the East India Company and the indigo business. It is huge ('too big for the camera lens'), partly designed by Martin who threw in everything that tickled his fancy: semi-circular wings, bastions, statues, gargoyles, a central stair-tower like Blois – and, tactfully, the huge heraldic lions of the East India Company. He died before its completion, but endowed it as a school; the school Kipling's Kim attended was based on this one. Today, 1500 students aged 6 upwards are being groomed for Indian life in this dilapidated flight-of-fancy, buffaloes grazing beneath the park's feathery-leafed tamerind trees.

SHOPPING AND CRAFTS Chowk is the old market area, a maze of alleys full of the aroma of spices and paan ingredients. In small upper rooms aged ex-Nawabs pensioned off by the British live stylishly in penury. Here lived some tawaefs, but many more takaiyans. In addition to watching craftsmen, find good bidri work (also made in Hyderabad, see South chapter), paper kites and Qur'an bookstands of carved wood – and keep looking up to catch the odd surviving house facade with carved upper storey and projecting balcony. Shami avadh, as the traditional evening stroll was called, began at the chowk crossing. Today, the aristocrats' sweetmeat stalls (presents for the tawaefs), paan kiosks, silver-and-pearl jewellery shops, brocade sellers, parrot sellers and chikankari merchants testify to its stylish past.

Lal Behari Tandon stocks very good **chikankari**, the dying art of extremely skilled and delicate white embroidery on fine white muslin practised by Muslim women and children in their mud-floor homes. Merchants supply the cloth to the workers already woodblock-printed with the design; women and children work it in the villages, but very fine pieces go to a specialist worker for the netting areas and the scalloped edges; the merchant has it washed and ironed and sells it.

The spider's-web fine work, adored by the Nawabs who attracted master craftsmen to Lucknow, can be bought as saris, kurtas, table linen and bedspreads. Alternatively, choose a design in the shop, decide what is to be made and where the emboidery is to be worked – wide border, dotted flowers, etc. – and have it sent on. Totally reliable, it is even possible to send specific orders from abroad. (His Delhi shop is in the underground Super Bazar.) To see another chikankari manufacturer, go to Chikan Mahal, the Rastogi Chikan Emporium at 1 Subhash Marg, near the Medical College, where old Mr Rastogi will show not only the embroidery of his 4-5,000 workers but will take out some old 1960s work so fine the fairies seem to have woven it.

Attar, the art of distilling perfume, is made to a high standard in Lucknow. Asgar Ali Mohammad Ali has moved out of Chowk to New Hyderabad colony and renamed his business Azam Ali and Alam Ali. Alternatively, go to Hafizmohamed Kamil in Aminabad Bazar. Nearby Kanauj is the centre of the exotic Indian perfume industry, but some of the finest are sold here. They are distilled in the traditional way, as introduced by Akbar, who built a perfumery where potions containing pearls, opium, gold and amber were concocted. Basically, essential oils are distilled out of sandlewood, lemongrass, ginger, cintronella, deodar wood, etc. They are then used as carriers for the aroma. This is first distilled from the flowers, or whatever, by heating, when its vapours are absorbed by the oil. There are no additives.

Men make the attar but men and women wear it, the men on special occasions such as poetry readings and marriages. It is a vital part of Indian life: rose-water is used in cooking and sprinkled at festivals, and attardans (boxes of perfume bottles) are circulated at weddings. A good rose-water uses petals picked before sunrise (for the strongest oil) from the Damascene,

Bulgarian or Indica bushes. But a smart lady gives off the expensive musk, saffron or agarwood attar.

Aminabad Bazar is less formal than Chowk. Here in the tiny gullies, you can find everything from saris to fruit. In Nakhas, one of the oldest areas, live more than 5,000 bird-sellers. It is the centre for collectors to buy, sell and exchange parrots, doves, pigeons, budgerigars and cocks, a legacy from the nawabi addiction to kabootabaazi (pigeon flying) and game bird fighting (using quail and cocks). Today, a Sunday market might stock cocks (trained or untrained), lovebirds, pigeons (trained or trained) and lalmunias – tiny birds kept in the house for good luck. Akbar was so keen on kabootabaazi that he renamed it ishq-baazi (love-play). He owned some 20,000 pigeons, took some on campaign and taught them mid-air acrobatics. The 19th century Gaekwad of Baroda, Khanderao, gave his pet pigeons a sensational wedding party, attended by princes and nobles, caparisoned elephants, with presents of jewels for the happy couple.

Near here, good Lucknowi food is found on Chowpatia Street, at Haji Arim cafe near Akbari Gate (famous for his kebabs), near noisy craftsmen bashing silver between waxed paper sheets in a leather binding to make the exotic sweetmeat decoration, and near the men making zari thread for sumptuous sari decoration and the perfume maker Hafizmohamed Kamil. On the roadside stalls, the thick, circular abi roti are a Lucknow speciality.

The tazias of Lucknow, paraded at Muharram, are justly famous. The finest are stored in the imambaras. To see craftsmen making them, using multi-coloured mica, visit Kazmein in Saadatganj area where they work busily most of the year.

For more regular shopping, go to Hazaratganj to shops next to and opposite Royal Restaurant. Gangotri, the state emporium, stocks bedspreads from Faziabad, black pottery from Nizamabad, brass and Varanasi silk.

TRIPS OUT FROM LUCKNOW

If Lucknow has few tourists, the various interesting spots in surrounding areas remain virtually unvisited except by historians of British India. With a car and a driver – or a quick train journey to Kanpur – a couple of trips into the rural countryside make good picnic outings.

For an idea of what a country house used to be like, Mussabagh is just 10km away to the northeast. A turn right off the Kakori road marked 'Mussabagh Park' and then a walk across the fields leads to a romantic 19th-century country house partly built underground for summer coolness (clamber down to explore), with two pavilions; now under Archaeological Survey care; good picnic spot. On another 10km to Kakori village, where European inspection buildings and Muslim buildings are all in good condition.

The trip to Kanpur is longer. As one of the most important British garrisons on the Ganga, its train station is the twin to Lucknow's grand one, and its interesting sites are Rebellion-related. There is Sati Chaura Ghat, hardly changed since 1857, where survivors of the siege were massacred despite Nana Sahib's truce – best found by walking along the riverside. There is the site of General Wheeler's entrenchment during the siege, the line of defences and principal buildings inside them marked with pillars. Nearby stands All Souls' Memorial Church (1862-75) with campanile, spire, stained glass window, marble and memorial tablets. Memorial Gardens is now ironically renamed Nana Rao Gardens (the Indian nickname for Nana Sahib, the local who encouraged the Kanpur siege and massacre). This is where Carlo Marochetti's mourning angel has been placed which originally stood over Bibighar Well. This well, whose site is in Municipal Gardens, was where the few survivors of the ghat massacre were butchered and thrown down. When General J. S. Neill reached the devastation, he led a British retribution which was, as Geoffrey Moorhouse writes, 'vile'. Mutineers were first captured, then made to lick the bloody ground where the British had fallen, sometimes forced to eat pork or beef to break their caste, then hanged. Finally, for a potted history of the town's early history, visit Kacheri Cemetery on Civil Lines.

To see more outside the town, go north-east 24km to Bithur, where Nana Sahib lived, to see the ruins of his and his minister's palaces, the pavilion-dotted river front and some romantic ruins of indigo factories; beyond lies Kanauj, where Sher Shar Sur defeated Humayun in 1540, an ancient town originally the 7th century capital of the area. The remains of the ancient fort lie east of the modern town (sculptures found here are in the town's Archaeological Museum), and there are a fine Jami Masjid and various tombs. South of Kanpur, equipped with a good driver hired through the Meghdoot Hotel, you can explore the old Mughal route which passed through Ghatampur and Akbarpur, lined with deserted elephant tanks, serais and pavilions.

Best to stay overnight at the Meghdoot, The Mall, Kanpur (tel: 211999/211949; telex: 325-282 A/B MGDT); all mod. cons. including snooker table and card room; this is where the Test cricketers stay; patrons claim it has 'the best food in India'. Alternatively, seek out The Attic on Civil Lines, Santosh Mahindrajeet Singh's small, family-run guest house.

Pakistan

On August 14, 1947, the day before India won Independence, Muhammad Ali Jinnah achieved his aim and Pakistan was born. His new land had a readymade combination of beautiful landscape and remarkable history.

This relatively small country – just double the size of the state of Madhya Pradesh in India and triple the size of the United Kingdom – has a conveniently compact variety of dramatic countryside. It stretches from the 1,000-kilometre-long Arabian Sea coastline up through arid plains and the rich Indus valley to the jagged, magnificent mountains of the Hindu Khush, Karakoram and Himalayan ranges – the last two being the world's newest mountains. Here, in the thin, exhilarating mountain air are the romantic passes through which waves of invaders poured down in search of the sub-continent's fabled wealth; and here is the world's greatest concentration of high mountain peaks – K-2, Nanga Parbat, Gasherbrum I, Broad Peak and Gasherbrum II all soar to more than 8,000 metres.

Despite its newness, Pakistan is the custodian of substantial remains of some of the world's most ancient and most remarkable communities. Here, in impressive preservation, lie the Harappan ghost city of Moenjodaro which traded with Ur, the port of Banbhore associated with Alexander the Great, and the three cities of Taxila where one of the greatest universities of the ancient world thrived in the 4th century BC. Here, too, in the vital north-west Mughal capital of Lahore, are buildings to compare with those at Agra and Delhi, a walled city better than both, and British buildings to compare with those at Bombay and Delhi. Finally, it was through this area that Islam and, equally importantly, Sufism, the Islamic spiritual life exemplified by the saints, were introduced into the sub-continent. So, for mountain scenery and cultural links, Pakistan is the logical addition to a trip to Northern India.

Indeed, Pakistan's history seems almost indecently rich for its size. If you are not keen on archaeology and later history when you arrive – for even an adventure into the mountains brings you on to the Silk Route – you most certainly are when you leave. It is everywhere, inescapable. And it is inseparable from Pakistan's religious history.

Current archaeological thought is that some two million years ago man, the species homo sapiens, evolved in this area of the world. Later, in a more formalised way of life, the great Indus Valley Civilisation of 3000-1500BC had its capitals here, at Moenjodaro (astounding remains) and Harappa (less impressive remains

since the British used them as a convenient brick source when building the nearby railway). The Aryans began to arrive around 1700BC, but it was not until the sixth century BC that this area, known as Gandhara, became an eastern, semi-independent province of Darius the Great's Persian Empire, with capitals at Taxila and Pushkalavati (today's Charsadda). That indefatigable traveller Alexander the Great conquered Gandhara in 327-325BC but, with less indefatigable soldiers, left soon afterwards. Gandhara then became part of Chandragupta's new Mauryan Empire, founded in 324BC, and under his grandson, the great Ashoka, was imbued with Buddhism.

Persians, Afghans, Bactrian Greeks, Scythians, Parthians, Kushans, Sassanians, White Huns, Turks and other invaders succeeded one another, the successful ones either stopping to set up as ruling merchants in the lucrative silk trade for the Roman empire or hurrying on to snatch the riches of the deeper sub-continent. By the second century AD, the Kushans ruled a substantial empire, made Gandhara the foremost Buddhist centre (from which it spread to China and Tibet), patronised the Gandharan school of art and made Peshawar their summer capital.

Hinduism, which takes its name from the Indus River, had evolved in communities living along the river banks after the Aryan arrival. It was later consolidated by the fifth-century White Huns (who were possibly absorbed into the Rajput warrior caste), the sixth-century Turki Shahis (when it overtook Buddhism) and then again by the Turki Shahis in the 9th-10th centuries.

Islam, described by Isobel Shaw as 'the binding force of the nation' in Pakistan today, arrived just under 80 years after the Prophet's death in 632. In 711, Muhammad bin Qasim, an Arab, arrived by sea and conquered Sind. Later, Mahmud of Ghazni, a Turk, arriving by land from the north early in the 11th century, finally made Lahore his capital. It was he who hit the sub-continent with what Philip Davies calls 'the full shock of Muslim military might'. Mass conversions began, to be consolidated by the succeeding Afghan Ghorids, whose ruler Mohammad of Ghor swept on down to Delhi where he defeated the Rajputs in 1192.

But well before this, Muslim mysticism arrived, to be of lasting and profound importance. Sufism, an ascetic or quiet way of life adopted by Muslim men or women, grew out of latent mystical elements in early Islam, to develop rapidly in response to prevailing political and social conditions during the two centuries following the Prophet's death. These emphasised military and materialistic life and promoted rigid orthodoxy. The reaction was towards asceticism, quietism, spiritual feeling and emotional faith; or, as a recent writer explained, the Sufi saints 'were virtual embodiments of all the finest moral teachings of Islam. Their lives were devoted to the cause of Love, Peace, Progress, Perfection and the uplift of the down-trodden'. The great Afghan saint and scholar Data Ganj Bakhsh (died 1072) came to Lahore during Mahmud of Gazni's rule and is considered the father of Sufism in the Punjab. One of his pupils was the 12th century saint, Khwajah Muin-ud-din Chishti, who went south into India, to be buried at Ajmer and later revered by the Mughal emperors. Shrines and tombs of Sufi saints are scattered throughout Pakistan, and the Urs (death anniversary) of each saint is celebrated at the shrine with several days of music, singing, fairs and sport.

From the time of the Afghan Ghorids, the area that was to become the Islamic state of Pakistan was predominantly Muslim. The Delhi Sultanate's empire incorporated Lahore and Multan. Under the Mughals, most of present-day Pakistan was part of their empire and Lahore was the vital, strategic defence against greedy invaders from the north-west. But when Nadir Shah of Persia sacked Delhi in 1739, he left with not merely Mughal booty but also with the lands west of the Indus, which later, with the Punjab, became part of the Kingdom of Afghanistan.

Then, early last century, the Sikhs under their hero Ranjit Singh, pushed the Afghans back to the Khyber Pass. From 1799 until 1839 Lahore was their political capital, while Amritsar (in the Indian part of the Punjab) was, and is, their religious capital. Lahore is in fact at the core of Sikhism. Guru Nanak (1469-1539), its founder, was born near there. Introducing Islamic elements into Hinduism, he advocated that there is one God who is truth, the equality of all and the importance of military prowess. It was the sixth Guru, Gobind Singh (1666-1708), who introduced baptism by water stirred with a dagger (after which an initiate was given the name Singh, meaning lion). He also introduced the five kakkars by which Sikhs could recognise each other: kesha (uncut hair), kangha (comb), kachha (shorts), kara (steel bracelet) and kirpan (sword). At Partition in 1947, the Sikhs migrated to India, mostly to the Punjab, but they have special dispensations to make pilgrimages to the many Sikh shrines in Pakistan.

The final pre-Pakistan chapter was British. Mughal power waned in favour of the British, who then turned their attention to the Sikhs controlling the north-west. First, and controversially, they annexed Sind (1843); then they won the First Anglo-Sikh War (1845), the Second Sikh War (1849) and control of Hunza on the Chinese border (1891); finally, when Afghanistan eluded them, they established the Durand Line (1893) which divided British India from Afghanistan and survives today. With Lahore as their elegant, fresh cultural capital, the British built schools, a university and a fine museum there, all inherited by Pakistan together with red brick cantonments and public buildings, roads, railways and canals, and the administrative and legal systems.

Pakistan's road to creation followed India's to Independence. The events of 1857 lit a fire of hostility against the British across the sub-continent, to be quenched only by their leaving India entirely. Feelings were at first united in the Hindu-biased Indian National Congress (founded 1885); but in 1906 Muslims broke away to safeguard their own interests and formed the All India Muslim League. Dr Muhammad Iqbal, poet and philosopher, was the first to propose a separate state for Muslims, in 1930. And it was this idea which was adopted by Muhammad Ali Jinnah (1876-1948), a British-trained lawyer who was born and had received his early schooling in Karachi. Land division was inevitably unsatisfactory for both sides, the western and eastern (now Bangladesh) wings. It divided the fertile, multi-religious Punjab in half, it left predominantly Muslim Kashmir in India, and it created irrigation problems since all Pakistan's rivers pass through India first.

Following the creation of Pakistan, Jinnah became its first head of state. He instantly faced violence and appalling bloodshed as six million Muslim refugees crossed into Pakistan from India, while some four-and-a-half million Sikhs and Hindus left the new Islamic state for India. Later, following Zulfikar Ali Bhutto's policy of nationalisation and increased democracy, General Zia-ul-Haq kept the country under martial law for nine years until 1986. Pakistan returned to democratic rule but then, as now, it is one which is feudal in its operations and still revolves around the twelve great families. When a plane crash killed Zia in 1988, free party elections brought Bhutto's daughter, Benazir, to power as the first female leader of an Islamic country. In 1990 she lost power to Mian Nawaz Sharif who comes from Pakistan's wealth bowl, the agricultural and industrialised Punjab – much of Lahore's beautification is due to his efforts while Chief Minister.

Today, Pakistan's population of 105 million is almost entirely Muslim, and Urdu is the official language. The country is divided into four provinces: dry Baluchistan, river-fed Sind and Punjab, and the mountainous North-West Frontier Province. There are also the Northern Areas (Gilgit, Hunza,Chilas and Skardu) and Azad Kashmir and Jammu. Pakistan's great Indus River tumbles down from the Himalayas, to be fed by the Jhelum, Chenab, Ravi and Sutlej rivers – hence the name Punjab, meaning Land of Five Rivers. And it is with the rich heritage of the Punjab's capital, Lahore, that the most rewarding journey pre- or post-India begins.

HARD FACTS If Pakistan is on the itinerary before leaving home, read Isobel Shaw's *Pakistan Handbook*. The Bartholomew's World Travel Map no.15 of India includes Pakistan. Since there is so much to see and to do in Pakistan, choices are difficult. But tourists are still few, so apart from specific trips into the mountains using small aircraft, it is possible to have a flexible itinerary. Moreover, the climate will reduce some options. The best time for the plains and their monuments is September to March, wearing pullovers in December-February. Then the sun hots up, to become punishing in June-July before the monsoon reaches Islamabad roughly a week after it hits Delhi. But summer heat is easy to beat by going increasingly higher up the mountains. Higher passes tend to be open May-October, and the best moments to visit such cloud-kissing spots as Gilgit and Hunza are for April flowers or autumn colours.

Essential behaviour tips: As a mark of respect, it is the custom to cover arms, chest, legs and, for women, head (a small scarf is enough), and to remove shoes before entering a mosque (some mosque attendants offer overshoes as an alternative). Elsewhere, it is best to keep well covered in local bazaars and town centres. It is also best to ask locals whether they wish to be photographed or not.

Essential trekking tips: Currently, the trekking ceiling is 6,000m, with open (no permit required) and restricted (permit required) zones – Chitral, Gilgit and Skardu are currently restricted zones, for which the Tourism Division issues permits within 24 hours. For more, see Hills chapter, below, and be sure to consult a reputable travel agent in Pakistan such as Walji (see below) before setting out. To fish, for example for trout in the Chitral or the Swat Valley, the season is April-September, a permit is necessary and it is best to bring tackle.

Festivals: Lahore has a glorious kite festival, the Mela Chirghan celebrating the mystic folk poet Madho Lal Hussain (spring) and the National Horse & Cattle Show (end Feb). For religious festivals, probably the most interesting for non-Muslim visitors are the Urs held at the shrines of Sufi saints (simply ask on arrival at a city if there is an Urs taking place at one of the nearby shrines).

Visas: UK, US and most other passport holders require a visa, obtained from your local Pakistan mission. Israelis and South Africans are not admitted. Indians are carefully vetted.

Customs: Alcohol is prohibited in Pakistan and must not be brought into the country. Non-Muslim residents of a few Pakistani hotels may, with a liquor permit obtained through the hotel, buy alcohol, usually only by the bottle. There are several liquor stores, for which a permit is required.

Money: The currency is Pakistani rupees. Only Rs100 cash may be brought into or taken out of the country; and only Rs500 may be changed back into foreign currency.

Travel to and from Pakistan: Three options: air, train and road. By air, flights depart from Delhi and Bombay for Lahore, Karachi and Islamabad; on leaving Pakistan, the airport tax for an international flight is Rs350. By train is more complex: a Delhi-Amritsar ride (the moment to stop off and see the Sikhs' religious centre), then change trains for Amritsar-Wagah border check-post to Lahore old town. By road is the most complex. Before leaving Delhi, travellers should either organise a car to meet them the other side of the border (bookable through a good Delhi travel agent), or catch a bus – it is barely 15km from the border to Lahore.

Travel within Pakistan: Pakistan International Airlines (PIA) run a cheap (subsidised) and efficient internal service to more than 30 airports, some of them closed during winter months; airport tax is Rs10. By car or bus, the main highways, such as the Grand Trunk Road from Lahore up to Peshawar, are excellent – and the gloriously decorated Pakistani lorries provide a constant art show; more off-beat routes have equally off-beat roads. Trains are excellent.

Tourist information: The Pakistan Tourism Development Corporation (PTDC) has offices which, in the big cities, are run by knowledgeable locals and stocked with good information sheets, maps, special interest brochures such as the excellent *Journey into Light*, about Sufi shrines. The principal ones are at 13 TU Commercial Area, College Road, Islamabad; Club Road, Karachi; Faletti's Hotel, Lahore; Flashman's Hotel, The Mall, Rawalpindi; and Dean's Hotel, Islamia Road, Peshawar; plus outposts at Chitral, Gilgit, Skardu, Taxila and elsewhere.

Travel agents: Travel Walji's are efficient, knowledgeable, give reliable advice and have a network of offices and good guides. Their headquarters are at 10 Khayaban Suhrawardy, PO Box 1088, Islamabad (tel: 823963/828324-6; fax 51-823109). Offices also in Lahore, Karachi, Peshawar, Gilgit and Skardu.

The cities

Since the choice is so wide, here are a handful of suggestions for a pre- or post-India visit. They are springboards for your own exploration. It is well worth taking advantage of the internal flights to enjoy several quite different aspects of Pakistan.

Punjab

LAHORE

Season October-March, after which it is hot.

The great thing about Lahore is that, despite being the Punjab's capital, it has retained the gentle atmosphere, spaciousnes and manageable size of a provincial university town such as Cambridge. If Islamabad is politics and Karachi is commerce, then Lahore is culture. Best to begin with an early skip up the *Minar-e-Pakistan*, the tower in Iqbal Park which commemorates the All India Muslim League's Resolution to create Pakistan taken here on March 23, 1940 (open 8.30am, lift works sometimes); Akbar's Mughal *fort-city*, begun in the 1560s, is laid out beneath you. Then down to see it. First, his Mughal Fort (good sound and light show in English on Fridays), with Aurangzeb's great *Badshahi Mosque* opposite the entrance. Then to the fort's encircling, romantic walled *old city* which is the best surviving Mughal city and one of the best collections of bazaars on the subcontinent. Enter it at Delhi Gate (where a car or rickshaw will wait) to explore a ribbon-thin lane of spices, dried fruits and nuts (from Kabul), tobacco ropes, shawls and splendid scissors leading to tiled *Wazir Khan Mosque* (the shoe-keeper can open the door for climbing up the tower; good view); go inside Mori Gate to find the much-revered tomb of the Sufi saint Data Ganj Bakhsh (splendid qawwali singing at his Urs); go to Masti Gate at sunrise to see mud wrestlers training. (The keen can seek out the shrine of Mian Mir, a 17th century Sufi saint whose devotees included emperors Jahangir, Shah Jahan and Aurangzeb, as well as Aurangzeb's brother Dara Shikoh; these last two built his shrine at Dharampura, 5km from Lahore old city.)

Across the Ravi River lie Jahangir's magnificent *tomb* back-to-back with Asaf Khan's crumbling one, with Nur Jahan's simple one nearby. To the north-east, along the canal built to feed them, are Shah Jahan's great *Shalimar Gardens* (fountains play morning and afternoon for an hour, except during frequent cleaning; charming kiosk serves tea and fruit cake beneath the trees). The fine red-brick British buildings lining The Mall include the *Museum*, founded by Kipling's father (the Zum-Zum gun made famous in *Kim* stands outside it) who stocked it imaginatively with quality objects (do not miss the miniature paintings, Kashmir shawls, Gandhara sculpture, Harappan finds and the Queen-Empress's statue).

For bazaar shopping, the old city is more fun than Anarkali Bazaar. Classy carpet shopping is safe, good quality and good value at the factories of Shalimar Carpets and Pakistan Panjab (sign on the back, measure it, check description on invoice and either take it or have it sent). Weavers work in the traditional way, using the old Shiraz, Bukhara, Baluchi, Turkish, nomadic and even Chinese designs. Lahore is known for its food – 'Lahore bazaar is better than anything in Delhi' claims the gastronome Yasmin Hosain; try murgh chola (chicken & chickpeas) or tikka kebab and plain naan, bought off the stalls in the old city and other bazaar areas; it is quite safe. For a more formal restaurant, Gulberg Kabana, Main Boulevard, Gulberg. To stay, the best is *Pearl Continental Hotel*, Shahrah-e-Quaid-e-Azam (tel: 69931), splendid outdoor barbecues, and near the Jinnah Gardens (the botanical gardens) for cool morning and evening strolls; or the old Faletti's, Egerton Road (tel: 303660), atmospheric but rather run down.

TRIPS OUT *Harappa* is 204km away, a hard day trip, but it is better to make the effort to go to the infinitely more preserved Moenjodaro. Alternatively, go to *Multan* (350km, about five hours drive), a goal of many invaders which Isobel Shaw claims 'is full of unexpected treasures'. Now a successful industrial city, so these have to be sought out, but it is well worth it to see a variety of early Muslim mosques and tombs. Try first for the easily found Tomb of Rukn-e-Alam, whose turquoise and deep blue tiles show why Multan was tile-supplier to the subcontinent. For more tombs, see Syed Yusuf Gardezi's, Ali Akbar's, and the popular Sufi saint Shah Shams Tabriz. For mosques, find the Savi and the Eidgah. Also worth seeking out the Tomb of Baha-ud-din Zakaria, the Lohari Gate to enter the old city's bazaars (for textiles), Saddar, or Cantonment, Bazar (for dhurries). By staying overnight – advisable unless you do a day trip by plane – it is possible to drive on from here through the cotton fields and past plenty of old monuments and locals in brightly coloured turbans down to Karachi via Sukkur and Moenjodaro (583km). A fair hotel is the Mangol, LMQ Road, Dera Adda (tel: 30164/74916).

Sind

KARACHI

Season November-February, then it gets hot and humid.

The capital of Sind is Pakistan's largest city and its commercial and industrial centre. In 1843 Sir Charles Napier made it Sind's capital, developed the port and laid out a new town; surviving British buildings litter the city, from the Masonic Hall (1845) and Holy Trinity church (1858) to Mereweather Tower (1887) and the High Court Building (1929). Jinnah made his home town Pakistan's initial capital, but its location and debilitating climate led to the decision in 1958 to found Islamabad.

The most atmospheric outing is to the great natural *port* where vast ships are busy loading and unloading, where dock-workers commute in overloaded boats to outlying residential areas and where it is easy to bargain for a boatman to take you crab fishing in the harbour. As the sun sets, the boatman cooks up a delicious, spicy crab stew, then returns to the quay under the twinkling stars. Daytime treats are more down to earth: the *National Museum* is essential for those intending to go to Moenjodaro; the *Mausoleum of Quaid-e-Azam Mohammad Ali Jinnah* is grand and impressive and its underground museum fascinating (ask to hear tapes of his speeches); and the old British area in and around *Clifton* breathes grandeur past and present – Clifton Beach is a favourite week-end outing with a Blackpool atmosphere: camel rides, food and souvenir stalls, a 1920s pier and locals, often fully clothed, jumping the waves.

As this is an international businessman's city, there are good hotel restaurants or the more fun little café-restaurants in every bazaar. Having seen the famous green turtles on Sandspit Beach, there are green alabaster ones to buy in hotel shops – Karachi's white and green alabaster mines are some of the world's best. Several deluxe hotels include the *Pearl-Continental*, Ziauddin Ahmed Road (tel: 515021); *Karachi Sheraton Hotel*, Club Road (tel: 521021) and the *Holiday Inn*, Abdullah Haroon Road, (tel: 512309).

TRIPS OUT Apart from whacky Clifton Beach, there are two vital trips for culture enthusiasts. The first, to Moenjodaro, requires either seats on the one plane up and down there daily, or a 510km drive (which for safety should be done by day). The second, a package of treats, is strung out along the highway east of Karachi.

MOENJODARO

To wander the streets of a city which thrived perhaps 50-60 centuries ago, stroll along the narrow lanes, pause at shops and peer down corner wells, inspect the public baths and the state granary, nose around the courtyards and rooms inside private homes, is to experience something unique in the world. The highly cultivated inhabitants of the capital of the Indus Valley Civilisation, which covered most of present-day Pakistan, had a city to compete with the Italian Renaissance ones. And it all survives. It seems as if they have just nipped off leaving their sophisticated town-planning, health-preserving drainage and conveniently placed wells to go into the surrounding countryside for a picnic. (Indeed, it is not clear why it was abandoned.) So strong is the atmosphere that it

would not be surprising if a bullock-cart laden with cotton bails rumbled round the corner. A museum of objects found on site such as seals, jewellery and children's toys reveals more about the people's advanced society; the elusive script is currently being cracked by academics round the world. Probably best to explore the ruins before the sun gets hot, and to imbibe the atmosphere; then visit the museum and take refreshment; then return to the site and imagine how British archaeologist Sir John Marshall felt when he rediscovered it in 1922.

It is a good idea to take a guide book, or read the latest theories before leaving home, since the on-site guide book is often out of print; equally essential to take plenty of food and drink since on-site supplies unreliable. Helpful on-site Archaeological Survey representative, who knows about local potters' villages, but he is not a guide. Best to spend at least a full day, either flying up and back from Karachi (book well in advance, or check for cancellations), or going by train or car and staying overnight at the simple, on-site Archaeological Department Rest House (tel: 3), booked in advance or, during off-season, on arrival; order meals on arrival or, better still, take some supplies. (The Harappan sea port of Lothal is in Gujarat, see Bombay chapter. Keen archaeologists should also check out the newest finds in Pakistan, made by Professor Jarrige of the Musée Guimet in Paris; his digging at Mehrgarh, near Quetta in Baluchistan, has revealed a pre-Moenjodaro civilisation.)

CHAUKUNDI TOMBS, BANBHORE, MAKLI HILL AND THATTA

Best, in fact, to see these in reverse, setting off early with food and drink supplies, and a hat. The well-restored, magnificently tiled Shah Jahan mosque at *Thatta* (100km) was built by the Mughal emperor in 1647; this and nearby Shah Bazaar (with carved balconies and rooftop wind catchers) testify to Thatta's former greatness. *Makli Hill*, the great ridge just before Thatta, is further testimony. Possibly the world's largest necropolis, these gloriously bold and sturdy mausolea with fine carving and some vestiges of tilework are strewn over the eight-kilometre-long ridge. The grandest belong to the 14-16th century Sammah rulers and the 16-17th century Tarkhans – don't miss Sultan Jam Nizam-ud-din's (d.1509) or Isa Khan Tarkhan II's (d.1644). Many of the important Sind Sufi saints have their shrines here, too, including Shah Inayat and Pir Patho Debali. The really keen can stay at the Archaeological Rest House bookable through the Archaeological Department in Karachi (tel: 431821); the Rest House gives permission to drive along the ridge to reach the Sammah tombs.

Having picnicked here, the return journey is via the equally amazing *Banbhore* port, at Gharo Creek on the left. Plenty to see at this archaeological site suffused with atmosphere. Sited at the mouth of the Indus, Greek-influenced pottery suggests it was possibly founded by Alexander the Great in 325BC. After the Buddhists and Hindus brought it to greatness, it seems the 17-year-old Muhammad bin Qasim, the first Muslim invader into this area, took Banbhore in AD711. Later, in 727, the earliest known mosque on the sub-continent was built here (floor and foundations survive). Wander round the site on paths carpeted with ancient pottery shards, right down on to the sands to see the fortifications. Finally, to sunset at the more modern *Chaukundi Tombs* (15-19th centuries) on a ridge to the right of the highway, 27km from Karachi. Covering several acres of scrub, this is just one of more than a hundred graveyards in southern Pakistan left by the Baluchi and Burpat tribes. Exquisite relief carving on honey-coloured stone reveals the sex buried inside: a man is given a turban on the grave top and weapons and horses round the sides; a woman often has stylised jewellery. Animals and humans suggest a pre-Muslim influence, as do the rosettes which suggest sun worship.

North-West Frontier and Northern Areas

THE GRAND TRUNK ROAD LAHORE-PESHAWAR

An easy and varied long drive (436km), with plenty of good stops for forts, archaeology and even a Mughal garden. It can be done either way, northwards or southwards, stopping overnight at Rawalpindi and, for keen archaeologists, at Taxila; use train or plane for the reverse journey. The *Grand Trunk Road*, originally laid out by the Afghan Sher Shar Sur (his Rohtas Fort is on the way), runs from Kabul to Calcutta via Lahore and Delhi. He followed the ancient trading and invading route down through the Himalayan passes through what is still today lawless Peshawar and on to tamer Lahore. Built to improve communications and defence, it was lined with shade-giving trees and equipped with wells, milestones and separate serais (inns) for Hindus and Muslims, where news was exchanged and the emperor's spies eavesdropped. The Mughals and then the British improved the road. Today, this Pakistan section is still a true highway: its surface is motorway smooth and along it thunder outrageously decorated lorries.

Out on the open road from Lahore, through lush Punjab fields of wheat, rice, sugar-cane and cotton and over the Chenab and Jhelum rivers, another 16km reaches Dina. Down a track on the left, the awe-inspiring walls and gateways of Sher Shar Sur's magnificent *Rohtas Fort* (1540-50) are silhouetted high on a natural bluff reached across a river bed (to get there, either wade across or hitch a lift in a passing jeep).

Rawalpindi makes a good overnight stop – the *Pearl-Continental* (tel: 62700) is good; old *Flashman's* might improve once renovated (tel: 581480). Brought to prominence when the Sikhs took it from the Ghakkars in 1765 and made it a trading centre, Rawalpindi's bazaars such as Sarafa (gold, silver, brass), Moti (ladies'), and Bohr (medicine) are still vibrant networks of tiny lanes; and the quite separate British cantonment is good for colonialists. Its twin town, the newly laid out *Islamabad*, is 15km away. Conceived in 1958, begun in 1961 and confirmed as Pakistan's principal seat of government in 1962 (to be shared with Dacca, now Dhaka), it has been the full capital of Pakistan only since 1971. The Greek firm of Doxiadis Associates designed it as eight zones (diplomatic, commercial, educational, etc.), using a grid system with its apex facing the Margalla Hills. They hoped it would grow to gobble up Rawalpindi. Fortunately, it has not. Rawalpindi retains its atmosphere, spirit, spicy smells and cheery people. The kindest words yet heard of Islamabad are 'spacious, lots of greenery, clean, no drama, very diplomatic'; the more general reaction is that it is 'probably the most sterile, artificial city on earth; no bazaars, no rickshaws, no heart, no atmosphere'. Students of contemporary architecture and town planning might be fascinated. The one building worth a look is the Shah Faisal Mosque, symbolising a desert tent and surrounded by four 90-metre-high, rocket-like minarets. Currently the world's largest mosque, it was designed by a Turk, Vedat Dalokay, funded by donations from Saudi Arabia and can hold 100,000 worshippers. (Islamabad airport serves the valley of Swat and the mountains of Skardu and Gilgit; and the Karakoram Highway starts here; see below).

Back on the road northwards, the *Margalla Pass* is worth a pause to find a short section of Sher Shah Sur's original cobbled road on the right leading up to the very point where Babur invaded and where later Mughals passed on their annual springtime trip up to the sweet cool air of Kashmir.

One kilometre beyond, down an unmarked road on the right for 3km, lie the extraordinary remains of the three cities of *Taxila* (thrived 516BC-AD600) – Bhir Mound, Sirkap and Sirsukh. Another of Pakistan's great treasures rediscovered by Sir John Marshall in 1913, this was a great Gandhara city and a melting pot for various cultures. Bhir Mound (6th-2nd centuries BC) was the first city, at whose famous university Panini compiled his Sanskrit grammar in the fourth century (sited by the Museum, few remains). Sirkap (185BC–AD80) was the second city, with an acropolis, a grand 700-metre-long main street, 20-roomed houses with painted and panelled rooms set round central courtyards, a Jain or Buddhist stupa for each area, and an Assyrian-influenced royal palace (sited 30 minutes' walk along the ridge from the Dharmarajika, plenty of remains). Sirsukh (AD80–460) was the last city, built by the Kushanas (sited 700 metres north of Sirkap, near Jandial Greek Temple, little excavated so far).

Taxila Museum, housing fine Gandhara Buddhist sculptures, coins and everyday objects, is not to be missed, and makes looking at the less obvious remains more rewarding. Of the 50 or so sites in the valley, the best to start with are Jaulian (a Buddhist monastery), Sirkap and Dharmarajika (huge Buddhist stupa). Taxila is better serviced than Moenjodaro: there is an information centre (although it is best to arrive with the essential map and guidebook, since stocks vary and on-site labelling is minimal), reasonable cafeteria, two Archaeological Rest Houses (bookable at Taxila Museum or through the Archaeological Department, Karachi) and a Youth Hostel.

Back on the GTR, as it is fondly known, another 14km reaches the tranquillity of ruined *Wah Garden* right beside the road on the left. Laid out by Akbar, it is said he exclaimed 'Wah!' (How beautiful!) when he saw the gurgling river in its lush dell with mountain backdrop. Today, the ruined bathhouse, decaying waterfall and elegant cyprus and plane trees give it a magical, secret garden quality. Nearby, at *Hasan Abdul*, roadside cafés serve the fresh, local fish, much enjoyed by regular travellers. Here, too, is *Panja Sahib*, an important Sikh pilgrimage place where Guru Nanak used his bare hand to hold back a boulder tumbling down the hill; the rock bearing his hadprint is in the gurdwara. Beyond here, landmark *Attock Bridge* spans the narrow, deep Attock Gorge where the River Indus gushes far, far below. For Babur, crossing this river by raft was a hairy military operation using a bridge of boats. Sher Shar Sur built the first bridge, and his great serai (inn) survives beside the new bridge; Akbar built the fort (1581–6) as his base for campaigns against Kabul.

PESHAWAR

This last great city before the wild mountain passes is in frontier country, an incongruous mixture of film-set medieval town, elegant British cantonment and modern university campus. Together they make up the capital of the North-West Frontier Province, known as NWFP.

The way to get the feel is first to wander the *old town*, which is as interesting as Lahore's, with plenty of old, carved wooden houses surviving. It is quite safe to pause in a café to tuck into some of Peshawar's justly famous food – tikka and sikh kebabs, balti ghost (lamb or chicken cooked with onion and green peppers) or chapli kebab (flat beef), eaten with a fresh, hot roghni naan which, according to Peshawar-born Yasmin Hosain, is the acknowledged queen of Pakistani breads. Wash it down with green tea which, when made with Peshawar water, is claimed by locals to be 'inimitable'. Refreshed, a good wander starts in Chowk Yadgar, the open main square lined with money-changers and barbers, and dives into the covered Sarafa Bazar (tribal and formal jewellery, lapis lazuli from Afghanistan and Chitral). Another good area to explore is Qissa Khawani Bazar (dried fruit and nuts, birds, tea, gold and jewellery), formerly the place for professional story-tellers which explains the quantity of tea-houses with their samovars hanging outside. From here, find the coppersmiths, then Peepal Mandi Bazar (fresh chickens and vegetables) and, behind it, Posth Bazar where the special chitralis (Peshawar woollen hats) and chughas (Peshawar long woollen, handwoven coats) are sold.

The atmospheric old bazaars, perfumed with constant spicy cooking aromas, seem to be trapped in time. Barely changed over the centuries, except for the addition of a few cars, here you can watch the traders, tribesmen, travellers and, now, the Afghan refugees. Most mesmerising of all are the tall, broad-shouldered, ferocious-looking *Pathans* who meet on the streets or in tea-houses to do their staple trade in drugs, arms, smuggled goods and vast wads of currency, as well as gold jewellery, fancy leather slippers and their beloved woollen hats and shawls. With rifles slung over their shoulders and their faces partly covered by the loose ends of their turbans, it is easy to believe that these men still abide by Pukhtunwali (the Way of the Pukhtuns, or Pathans), the ethical code which demands that every insult be revenged, every guest protected, summed up in the forthright proverb 'He is not a Pathan who does not give a blow for a pinch'. Meanwhile, their women, ensconced in maroon and black burkas, glide silently in and out of jewellery shops where they supervise meticulous weighing of a pile of gold strings and baubles, barter hard and long, and pay up with cash. The tall, fearsome and warlike Pathans, converted to Islam by Mahmud of Ghazni, are one of the world's largest tribal societies. Today, numbering about 15 million and spread over both sides of the border, most live quietly. But just here, in the mountains around Peshawar, the Pathans have never been subdued. This is a truly lawless zone. Natural and fearless guerrilla fighters who are crack shots and know their hills intimately, their proud honour and passion for independence have kept them free from all would-be conquerors – Mughals, Afghans, Sikhs, British and Russians. They still dress in colours known to them as khaki (meaning dusty) which blend with the mountain scenery and which inspired the British army, when fighting here, to abandon brightly coloured uniforms for quieter tones.

By comparison, the *Cantonment* area across the railway is tame indeed. But it is atmospheric. Amid the tree-lined avenues find the Museum (for the best Gandharan art in Pakistan), St John's Church (1851), Khalid bin Walid Bagh (an old Mughal garden with surviving chenar trees) and Peshawar Club. Then, perhaps, take tea beneath a parasol in the garden of the old mud and brick Dean's Hotel. Locals' eyes will sparkle when you ask the way to Bara (stream) Bazar, the fascinating local smuggled goods market; and they are likely to offer to come and eat a kebab at the favourite local restaurant, *Notia*. To stay here, choose between the modern *Pearl-Continental*, Khyber Road (tel: 76361-9) and the atmospheric old *Green's*, Shahrah-e-Pehlavi (tel: 72404) or *Dean's*, Islamia Road (tel: 76483-4), both in the Cantonment.

TRIPS OUT TO PASSES AND VALLEYS
It really is worth every effort to go out into the surrounding countryside. But, since it is no exaggeration to say this is a truly lawless country and kidnapping or shooting is a very real possibility, it is essential to obtain the necessary passes in Peshawar from the Home Secretary's local Civic Secretariat, near the Pearl-Continental Hotel; they are given if prevailing political conditions are calm.

DARA
A permit is needed to visit this fascinating gun-making town (42km), lined with mini-gun foundries and shops, with prospective shoppers testing possible purchases by firing them into the air on the crowded pavement.

KHYBER PASS
Another permit is needed to go up the desolate, twisting Khyber Pass which begins at Jamrud Fort, 18km from Peshawar, and goes up and up past heavily defended, mud-walled, homes of Pathan smugglers and bandits. From its summit, Landi Kotal, the spectacular view on a clear day is across jagged mountain ranges into Afghanistan, towards Kabul just 150km away.

SWAT VALLEY
No permissions needed to make a memorable outing in any season into this beautiful valley (177km), claimed by the well-travelled Shafiq-uz-Zaman to be 'the most beautiful valley in Pakistan'. In the lush, lower part, there are wheat fields and orchards producing some of Pakistan's famous sweet oranges – which are sold to thirsty drivers from great piles on the roadsides. In the upper part, against the backdrop of snow-capped mountains, Swat river cuts down through pine forests. Walking, both hearty and relaxed, can happily mix glorious countryside with trout fishing, gasping at breathtaking mountain views and exploring quantities of Buddhist monastery and stupa remains. The motto is 'the higher you go, the more beautiful the valley becomes'.

Either drive up via the Malakand Pass, Takhte-Bahi (near Mardan), Pakistan's best preserved Buddhist monastery, and Udgram and Birkot Hill (both visited by Alexander the Great); or, less interesting, fly up to Saidu Sharif (the best way during hot May-September) and drive up the valley from there. In winter, snow comes down to Bahrain. To stay in Saidu Sharif or neaby Mingora, *Swat Serena Hotel* (tel: 2220) or Pameer, Grand Truck Road, Mingora (tel: 4926) are both fine. In winter, snow comes down to Bahrain, so Miandam and Madyan are the last overnight stops. Good handicrafts to be found in the village bazaars. In summer, it is possible to drive right up to Kalam and then trek across to Chitral or Gilgit valleys. First-time and more ambitious trekkers should take a guide.

CHITRAL VALLEY
Quite different from Swat. The beauty of this long, narrow and isolated valley nestling beneath the Hindu Kush mountains and accessible only April-October lies in its contrasts of oases of green surrounding stone houses, terraced fields of wheat and maize, barren hillsides, and snow-capped mountains. Until 1970, Chitral and its 250,000 people were a separate kingdom ruled by a mehtar. And in the Kafir Kalash Valleys live a fast-dwindling 3,000 Kafir Kalashis (Black Infidels) whose pale skin, fair hair and occasional blue eyes sustain the legend that their ancestors came over the Hindu Kush with Alexander the Great. To get there, either fly to Chitral town or do a gruelling drive of 12-15 hours. Once there, enjoy the town and its polo matches (June-November), good trout fishing in the Lutkho River (April-September, permit from Chitral town) and walk the Birir, Bumburet and Rumbur valleys lived in by the fascinating Kafirs (photography needs payment).

THE MOUNTAINS: UP THE KARAKORAM HIGHWAY TO GILGIT AND HUNZA
If Moenjodaro is Pakistan's ancient wonder, then the Karakoram Highway is its modern one. Against all odds, it follows the old and tortuous

middle route of the three ancient Silk Routes that ran between China and the West (see Auriel Stein's finds in Delhi's National Museum and London's British Museum). Until the 1950s, travel here could accurately be described using the words of the Chinese pilgrim Fa Hien written in 400AD: 'The way was difficult and rugged, running along a bank exceedingly precipitous. When one approached the edge of it, his eyes became unsteady; and if he wished to go forward in the same direction, there was no place on which he could place his foot, and beneath were the waters of the river called the Indus'.

This man-made feat, fondly known as KKH, has notched up a mixture of proud and tragic figures. Completed in 1978, it has taken 20 years, 8,000 tons of explosives, 80,000 tons of cement and 15,000 Pakistani and 30,000 Chinese labourers to win the 795km of road, at the expense of almost 900 lives. Pack horses carried equipment; Pakistani soldiers built the road, the Chinese the bridges. Engineers worked suspended by ropes down sheer cliff faces, rockslides were frequent, and glaciers, strong winds and extreme temperatures ranging from 48C in summer down to minus 30C in winter all hampered construction.

Today, the KKH starts at Havilian, 100km from Islamabad, and then zig-zags up through Kohistan, Gilgit and Hunza to Khunjerab Top, beyond which lies Xinjiang Province of China. There, another tract of highway stretches to Kashgar. Twisting round three great mountain ranges, the Himalayas, Karakorams and Pamirs, it hugs the Indus River for much of its journey, winds round Nanga Parbat (the world's ninth highest mountain), passes through high-altitude desert where there is barely any rainfall, crosses dramatic gorges, skims along shelves on cliff faces 500m above the Indus, and is maintained by a constant force of 1,000 Pakistani soldiers.

For all its technology, it can be as bloodwarming now as it was for Fa Hien. When Alexander Frater drove it in 1986, he reported that 'the journey along the massively pot-holed KKH was made at Formula One speeds, our vehicle swerving wildly to avoid the rock falls . . . the road had a stony, corrugated surface which the drivers took very fast . . . avoiding lorries whose drivers teasingly attempted to push us into the riverbed below . . . the final stretch, on a wildly undulating switchback through the Takla Makan, was completed at 80 m.p.h. At Kashgar, aching and dust-covered, we ate melons [which] perfumed the air'. Probably the world's most spectacular drive, it is perhaps worth the discomfort.

WHEN AND HOW TO GO When to go poses a

dilemma. The Khunjerab Pass is open to foreigners May 1-November 30, weather permitting. On the other hand, the best times to go to Gilgit and Hunza are for April blossoms and October autumn colours; July is hot.

To travel through the Khunjerab Pass, a visa for China is necessary; a 3-7 day one is available from the Chinese Embassy in Islamabad. It is wise to carry altitude sickness pills and warm clothes, plus food and water.

To drive the whole way to Kashgar takes a comfortable four days; alternatively, fly up to Gilgit and spend two-three days driving to Kashgar. Weather permitting, there are two flights up to Gilgit daily, but it is best to go for the earlier one as it is the most likely to depart. Flying either up or down is agreed by globetrotters to be 'one of the world's most spectacular flights'.

Driving one way might well be enough. So, for an ideal, ten-day-long trip which need not go into China, drive Islamabad-Gilgit and stay at *Gilgit* for at least four nights (at *Serena Lodge*, Jutial for good views and food). In Gilgit, enjoy the travelling traders in the bazaars, fishing (permit obtainable in Gilgit) and rafting, a variety of walks and treks, and excursions to Chitral (see above), into the upper Swat Valley (see above) and the Baltistan Valley for a good variety of landscape. Continue up through the *Hunza Valley*, described by Alexander Frater as 'a secret, enchanted valley where fields of ripening buckwheat glowed pink in the evening light and luminous silk banners fluttered among the walnut trees'. At Hunza, enjoy the famous water, apricots dried on rooftops and home-made wine, before going on to *Gulmit* for two nights (*Silk Route Lodge* has hot water). Here, visit the charming local museum run by the ex-ruler, take local walks and do a day-trip to the Chinese border, spotting stunning glaciers and peaks. Return to Gilgit to fly back to Islamabad. Alternatively, do the trip in reverse. Essential to book flights in advance; there is a refund if they do not go.

Wildlife sanctuaries in India

There are some good sanctuaries in north and central India, although they are not always easy to reach. There are also seven in Pakistan. However, the fine bird sanctuary at Bharatpur is right by Agra and has reasonable accommodation (see above), although if the lake is dry there will be fewer birds. Royal Chitwan Park in Nepal, one of the best-run Asian parks, is very acccessible (see Hills chapter). North-east of Delhi, Corbett UP has superb new facilities, while deep in Madhya Pradesh Kanha National Park has the well-established and well-run Kipling Camp (see Bombay chapter). The selection below are the most accessible and/or interesting.

CORBETT, UTTAR PRADESH
Season November-June, best January-March; closed during monsoon. Go by good road, via Moradabad (to buy brass), 297km (about 6hrs); or by train to Ramnagar 8km away; or by Vayudoot's thrice weekly flight to Pantnagar, 2 hours' drive away.

Best place to stay is Tiger Tops Mountain Travel's new *Tiger Tops Corbett Lodge*, by the Kosi River; 20 rooms with bath and balcony overlooking mango and lychee trees; swimming pool; excellent public areas; explore on elephant, in four-wheel drive vehicles or on foot; trained guides; also run 7-day excursions into the Kumaon Hills for trekking on foot or pony and for mahseer fishing (bookable through ExploraAsia in London, or at Tiger Tops offices in Delhi and Kathmandu). The others, at Dhikala, have confusingly similar names: *New Forest Rest House* (rooms with attached bath), *Old Forest Rest House* and *Forest Rest House Annex*, all bookable through UP Tourist Office, Chandralok Bhavan, 36 Janpath, New Delhi (tel: 322251), which also runs week-end package tours; or through the Chief Wild Life Warden, 17 Rana Pratap Marg, Lucknow (tel: 32). Good guides and many machans (watch towers). Explore by elephant or jeep.

With one of the best tourist infrastructures of the Indian sanctuaries, the park is particularly beautiful and well worth visiting. 520 sqkm of sub-Himalayan foothills, covering the Patlidun Valley of the Ramganga River and the lower slopes of the Shivalik range. Established in 1935, it is India's oldest wildlife sanctuary and is named after Indian wildlife champion Jim Corbett, who grew up here. In 1944, he was already concerned about the threat to India's wildlife and championed the conservation awareness of Indians. Explore miles of open country by car or elephant. From the machans spot the many tigers. This is a Project Tiger park, so successful, according to the director, Mr Singh, that the territorially possessive tigers are now fighting each other to the death (9 tigers killed in 1983), so more land must be found for the increasing tiger population (a tiger needs up to 80 sqkm). Also plenty of elephant, Himalayan black bear, leopard, ugly hog deer and handsomely antlered chital. In the Ramganga river see the large river tortoise and, in spring, fish for fat mahseer and goonch (permit from Dhikala Game Warden). Rich bird life (over 500 species).

DUDHWA NATIONAL PARK, UTTAR PRADESH
Season November-May, best January-March. Go by road, 430km from Delhi (about 10hrs), 215km from Lucknow (or daily train). Stay at *Tiger Haven*, the home of wildlife expert Arjan (Billy) Singh, where all charges go towards the wildlife work; or at *Forest Rest House*. Both bookable through Wildlife Warden (Kheri Region), Dudhwa National Park, Lakhimpur Kheri District, UP. Explore by elephant or jeep.

490 sqkm lying on the India-Nepal border, run by Arjan Singh who was one of the first committed wildlife conservationists to attempt to re-introduce the tiger and other big cats into the wild. Established in 1977, it was awarded the World Wildlife Gold Medal for rehabilitation of captive-bred tiger and leopard into the wild. In addition to big cats, the park forests hold sambhar, various deer (swamp, hog, barking, spotted), sloth bear, nilgai, elephant, hyena, jackal and porcupine. Also rich bird life and reptiles. Some fishing.

BANDHAVGARH, MADHYA PRADESH
November-June; closed July 1-October 31 for monsoon. Fly to Khajuraho, then 210km by road; to Jabalpur, then 175km by road; or overnight train to Satna, met by park jeep. Stay at *Bandhavgarh Jungle Camp*, run by naturalist Mr K. K. Singh with Tiger Tops India, bookable through Tiger Tops Mountain Travel, 1/1 Rani Jhansi Road, New Delhi (tel: 523057/771055). If full, stay at *White Tiger Forest Lodge*; 8 rooms, bookable through Tours Manager, MP State Tourism Development Corporation, Gangotri, T. T. Nagar, Bhopal (tel: 62173; telex: 0705-275) or, if less than 10 days in advance, through MPSTDC, Railway Station, Jabalpur (tel: 21111).

Established 1968. Currently harbours one of the highest density tiger populations of any Indian park (22 counted in 1982), plus a not too dense landscape, so a good place to spot them. (The other two most likely tiger spotting parks are Kanha and Ranthambhore.) And there is a camp good enough for up-market package tours to use. The first white tiger was found just outside the park in 1951. The park stretches across the heart of the Vidhayan mountain range of central India, with sal forest and valleys, prehistoric caves and ancient clifftop Bandhavgarh fort (see the Vaisnavite sculptures showing all Vishnu's incarnations). By elephant and jeep see plenty of tiger, langur, sloth bear, wild boar and gaur (Indian bison), deer such as chital, sambhar, barking deer and chowsingha antelope.

SHIVPURI, MADHYA PRADESH
Season February-June. Fly or drive to Gwalior, then 112km. Stay at *Sakhya Sagar Boat Club* in the park or *Shivpuri Hotel Circuit House*, both bookable through The Collector, Shivpuri.

160 sqkm of deciduous plains forest, former summer capital of the Scindias of Gwalior who went on tiger shikar (hunting). Spot the occa-

sional tiger, leopard and bear today, and many sambhar, chital, nilgai, chinkara and chowsingha pig. Good lake birdlife includes flocks of demoiselle cranes.

PANNA, MADHYA PRADESH

Season October-April. 48km by road from Khajuraho. Stay in Khajuraho.

543 sqkm of 'incredible wilderness' of valleys and gorges bordering the Ken River; countless post-monsoon waterfalls. One of India's newest National Parks, dotted with living temples of a bizarre Spanish style that amused the Maharaja of Panna. Formerly some of the best, but highly controlled, shooting for the local rulers; then, after Independence, indiscriminate shooting had a devastating effect. Teak forest harbours tiger, leopard, blue bulls, sloth bear, panther, cheetah, cheetal, sambhar, chinkara (Indian gazelle) and chowsingha (four-horned antelope). The rare gharial and mugger crocodiles can be found in the Ken, which passes through the park for 50km. There is a profusion of paradise fly-catchers, MP's state bird. Ken Crocodile Sanctuary nearby.

Wildlife parks in Pakistan

Here is a brief outline of the parks, each in a different climatic and geographical region of the country. To find out more, contact the National Council for Conservation of Wildlife, Islamabad, the Wildlife Conservation Foundation of Pakistan, Karachi, or the World Wide Fund for Nature (Pakistan), Lahore, with regional offices at Karachi and Gilgit.

AYUBIA NATIONAL PARK

All seasons. In the Murree Hills outside Rawalpindi, Punjab. Possible to spot leopard at night and pheasant by day, among the monumental oak and fir trees. Chairlift provides good views.

CHITRAL GOL NATIONAL PARK

April-October. High up in the North West Frontier Province's Chitral Valley. Keen hikers will see the Kashmir markhor, urial, wolf, birds of prey and perhaps snow leopard and black bear. Conducted tours available.

CHILTAN NATIONAL PARK

March-May, September-October. On the Afghan border outside Quetta, Baluchistan. Chiltan markhor and wolf live in grass, shrubs and trees of the grand hills, although they need patience to spot. Two good and peaceful rest houses with glorious views.

KHUNJERAB NATIONAL PARK

May-October. High up near Gilgit, Northern Areas. The Karakoram Highway passes through the park where Marcopolo sheep and Himalayan ibex are common but the snow leopard elusive.

KIRTHAR NATIONAL PARK

October-May. 150km north-east of Karachi, Sind. Hide-outs for watching urial, Sind ibex and chinkara at sunrise in winter. Rannikot Fort, one of the world's largest, is inside the park. Conducted tours available.

LAL SUHANRA NATIONAL PARK

October-March. 30km from Bahawalpur, Punjab. Probably the best park for variety of animals and birds. See black buck, chinkara gazelle, blue bull antelope, hog deer, nilgai, migrating birds, possibly the one-horned rhino and much more, amid the man-made eco-system of forest plantation, desert and wetland. Large children's area with playground, boating lake and small motel. Four good rest houses. Park administrator also runs three- to five-day camel safaris into the Cholistan Desert, which blossoms after the August rains.

MARGALLA HILLS NATIONAL PARK

October-April. On the outskirts of Islamabad, Punjab. Panoramic view of the Potohar Plateau, where monkey, kalij pheasant, goral and barking deer live, and where the rich birdlife include ducks migrating to Rewal Lake. City-dwellers come walking at weekends, often staying at the rest houses at Pir Sohawa and Pharilla (bookable at the Directorate of Environment, CDA, Sitara Market, Islamabad).

Find out more

Countless books have been written on Delhi and on the Mughals. The few included below are highly readable and have good bibliographies. The contemporary diaries and accounts, stocked by good libraries (see p. 18), are fascinating and bring the whole period alive. On the British, the material grows annually, too. To find out more, write to the British Association for Cemetreries in South Asia (BACSA), 135 Burntwood Lane, London SW17; their newsletter has plenty of book reviews on all aspects of British India.

Alexander, M.: *Delhi and Agra, a travellers' companion*, London, 1987

Ansari, M. A.: *Social Life of the Mughal Emperors*, Allahabad, 1974

Barton, G. and Malone, L.: *Old Delhi, 10 Easy Walks*, Delhi, 1988

Beach, M. C.: *The Grand Mogul, imperial painting in India 1600-1660* , Williamstown, 1978

Beach, M. C.: *The Imperial Image, Paintings for the Mughal Court*, Washington, 1981

Bence-Jones, M.: *Palaces of the Raj*, London, 1973

Brand, M. and Lowry, G. D.: *Akbar's India: Art from the Mughal City of Victory*, London, 1985

Corbett, J.: *Man Eaters of Kumaon*, Oxford, 1948

Edwardes, M.: *A Season in Hell*, London, 1973

Fazl, Abul: *Akbar-nama*, trans. H. Beveridge, 3 vols, Calcutta, 1907-39

Fazl, Abul: *Ani-i-Akbari*, trans. H. Blochmann and H. S. Jarrett, 3 vols, Calcutta, 1873-94

Frykenberg, R. E.: *Delhi through the Ages*, Delhi, 1986

Gascoigne, B.: *The Great Moghuls*, London 1979

Godden, R.: *Gulbadan*, based on the Humayun-nama written by Babur's daughter, London 1980

Hutchins, F. G.: *Young Krishna*, New Hampshire, 1980

The Indian Heritage: *Court Life & Arts under Mughal Rule*, Festival of India exhibition catalogue, Victoria and Albert Museum, London, 1982

Irving, R. G.: *Indian Summer: Lutyens, Baker and Imperial Delhi*, Oxford, 1981

Jahangir: *Tuzuk-i-Jahangiri*, trans. Alexander Rogers, ed. H. Beveridge, 2 vols, London, 1909-14

Kaul, H. K.: *Historic Delhi, an anthology*, Delhi, 1985

Kaye, M. M., ed.: *The Golden Calm; An English Lady's Life in Moghul Delhi*, London, 1980

Lall, J.: *Taj Mahal and the Glory of Mughal Agra*, India, 1982

Lawrence, J.: *Lawrence of Lucknow*, London, 1990

Llewellyn-Jones, R.: *A Fatal Friendship: The Nawabs, the British and the City of Lucknow*, Delhi, 1985 and 1991

Masani, Z.: *Indian Tales of the Raj*, London, 1987

Moraes, Dom: *Madhya Pradesh*, India, 1983

Nicholson, L.: *The Red Fort, Delhi*, London, 1989 and *The Romance of the Taj*, exhibition catalogue, Los Angeles County Museum, 1989

Rai, R.: *Taj*, Singapore, 1986

Sharma, R. C.: *Mathura Museum of Art*, Mathura, 1967

Sharma, Y. D.: *Delhi and its Neighbourhood*, Delhi, 1964

Singh, B. A.: *Tiger Haven*, London, 1973

Singh, K. and Rai, R.: *Delhi: A Portrait*, Delhi and Oxford, 1983

Singh, K. and Basu, S.: *Nature Watch*, Delhi, 1990

Spear, P.: *Twilight of the Moghuls*, London, 1951

Tillotson, G. H. R.: *Mughal India, Architectural Guides for Travellers*, London, 1991

Welch, Stuart C.: *Imperial Mughal Painting*, New York and London, 1978

Yalland, Z.: *Traders and Nabobs: The British in Cawnpore 1765-1857*, Salisbury, 1987; her other publications include a *Guide to the Kacheri Cemetery* and the *Early History of Kanpur*.

On Pakistan (See also general books suggested above and at the end of Chapter 1).

Ahmed, A.: *Discovering Islam*, London, 1988

Amin, M.: *Journey through Pakistan*, London, 1982

Bhutto, B.: *Daughter of the East, an Autobiography*, London, 1988

Burki, S. J.: *Pakistan under Bhutto, 1971-1977*, New York, 1980

Caroe, Sir O.: *The Pathans*, London, 1958, reprint Karachi, 1975

Churchill, W.: *My Early Life*, London 1930, reprint 1959

Duncan, E.: *Breaking the Curfew*, London, 1989

Ingholt, A., and Lyons, I.: *Gandharan Art in Pakistan*, New York, 1957

Keay, J.: *When Men and Mountains Meet*, London, 1977

Keay, J.: *The Gilgit Game*, London, 1979

Jamal, M.: *The Penguin Book of Modern Urdu Poetry*, London, 1986

Maraini, F.: *Where Four Worlds Meet; Hindu Kush 1959*, London, 1964 – splendidly illustrated

Matheson, S. A.: *The Tigers of Baluchistan; A Woman's Five Years with the Bugti Tribe*, London, 1967

Marshall, Sir J. H.: *A Guide to Taxila*, Delhi, 1936

Mumtaz, K. K.: *Architecture in Pakistan*, Singapore, 1985

Murphy, D.: *Where the Indus is Young*, London, 1977

Naipal, V. S.: *Among the Believers*, London, 1981

Newby, E.: *A Short Walk in the Hindu Kush*, London, 1981

Polo, M.: *Travels Retold*, London, 1958

Qutaeshi, S.: *Legacy of the Indus; A discovery of Pakistan*, New York, 1974

Schofield, V.: *Bhutto: Trial and Execution*, London, 1979

Schofield, V.: *Every Rock Every Hill*, London, 1984

Singer, A.: *Lords of the Khyber*, London, 1984

Singh, K.: *Last Train to Pakistan*, New York, 1961

Stein, Sir A.: *On Alexander's Track to the Indus*, London 1929 and 1975

Stephens, I.: *Pakistan*, London, 1963

Wheeler, Sir M.: *The Indus Civilization*, Cambridge, 1972

Wolpert, S.: *Jinnah of Pakistan*, London, 1984

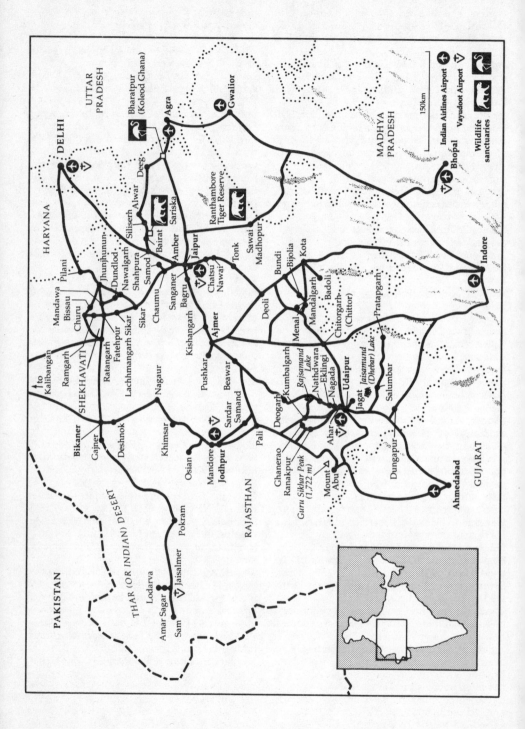

Rajasthan:
Pleasure and palaces and desert villages

Rajasthan is classic fantasy India at its best. Palaces built on dreams glow in the fiery desert setting sun. Fortress cities conceal treasure-trove bazaars of jewellery, precious stones, enamelling, embroidery and mirror-work. Piles of spices sweeten the air. Women bring colour and sparkle to every city alley and village well: shy, smiling girls and laughing ladies draped in splashes of raspberry pink, lapis blue, saffron, pillarbox red and tangerine, weighed down with silver rings on their noses, ears and toes, bangles around their arms and ankles. Snooty camels haul cartloads of fire-wood along the road and jam up the city alleys. Bhopas (folk balladiers) and their families, swathed in long, tomato-red tunics and turbans, sing ballads about Rajasthani heroes and lovers. And the polo-playing maharajas are alive and well, joining with their citizens in the constant round of festive gaiety.

The princes of India may have lost their titles, land and revenues since Independence, but feudalism lives on. Their former states maintain their individuality. Both rural and city people, on the whole, have a profound sense of belonging to the order and show love and respect to their maharaja – whom they call just that. Some even elect him as their member of parliament, endorsing his former position as their protector.

But gone are the days of pomp and ceremony that outshone Croesus in their mad extravagances. When the ship from England carrying furniture for the new 347-room 1930s Jodhpur palace sank, the Maharaja merely ordered replica sets to be made.

When Maharaja Madho Singh of Jaipur went to England for Edward VII's coronation, in 1902, he had a temple built in the P&O liner he chartered. He threw bags of gold, silver and silk into Bombay harbour to invoke a safe journey from the oceans. In England, he drank nothing but Ganga water, stored in gigantic silver pots, and he and his retinue filled three large Kensington houses.

Each prince now lives in just one or two of his several palaces. His other past pleasure houses lie decaying across his state. But the canny Rajput often puts his luxurious legacy to commercial work to replenish his revenue-starved coffers. His product is his homes, households and sometimes himself. His market is the delighted tourist, who can, for a few days, live like a maharaja or his maharani, enjoying their amusements, pampered to distraction.

The palaces, like real-life Piranesi capriccii, were built during the British protectorate and are more like overblown country houses than fort palaces. They dominate each city and boggle the mind with their massive size, their hotchpotch styles and their splendid interiors. But they are just a recent amusement of the Rajput princes, the majority built in the 19th or even 20th centuries. Before then, war was their game. The tall, proud, moustachioed Rajput warriors, all excellent horsemen, make no bones about their pedigree: they claim descent from the sun and moon via the hero gods of the Ramayana and Mahabharata epics.

On a more mundane level, they were probably descended from the Huns who settled in north-west India, rising to power in the 9th and 10th centuries. After Mahmud of Ghazni's Muslim expansions of the 11th century, those in the west built clifftop forts and lived dacoits' lives, raiding valleys for food and booty. They fought hard; they drank hard. When a battle was clearly a loser, they donned saffron and fought to the death, never fleeing. Their women were equally heroic. When Chitorgarh was lost in 1535 the Queen Mother led 13,000 women to the pyre to commit johar, mass ritual suicide by burning. Finally, they gained supremacy over the area that became known as Rajwarra, Rajputana and now Rajasthan, land of princes.

It took Akbar to subdue them, one by one, with countless marriages to Rajput princesses (see p. 75) but even then he gained only alliances, not subjugation. Under this shaky Mughal security, the Rajput court culture – hunting, miniature painting, etc. – continued, influenced by the Mughal court. Rajput inter-state rivalry persisted, to be taken advantage of by first the Mughal emperors (who put Man Singh of Amber in command of the Mughal army sent against his neighbouring Mewar Rajputs) and their rebelling sons (Prince Akbar allied with the Jodhpur rulers against his father Aurangzeb), and then, later, by the British.

Stability under the Mughals ended when Marathas, Sikhs and others rebelled against Mughal supremacy. Then, at the beginning of the 19th century, the canny British watched as each state was forced into a corner by its enemies. A Rajput alliance was inconceivable. When each was weakened sufficiently, the British came to the rescue. They offered protection in return for loyalty. And they later rewarded the princes for their support during the Rebellion of 1857 (known by the British as the Mutiny). When British India came under Crown rule in 1858, the Rajput princes remained independent, along with about half the country which became known as Princely India – the other big tracts were Hyderabad and Mysore.

To encourage loyalty, the British heaped privileges on the princes: titles, medals, honours and their own special military units. They encouraged them to modernise their states and to play them at polo and cricket. The British also set up Indian versions of British public schools for their sons, like Mayo College at Ajmer. Founded in 1875 by political agent Colonel Walter who wished 'the sons of the aristocracy' to have an 'Eton of India', it quickly followed the British public school tradition of gaining most renown for its sportsmen, in this case polo players.

But the young princes maintained their Indian standards. Officially, boys were allowed three personal servants, but many pupils kept separate households with quantities of servants and stables with dozens of horses. Photographs of the Maharaja of Jaipur, a Mayo College product, holding polo trophies at Windsor Great Park line the walls of the cocktail bar of the Rambagh Palace hotel. Other public schools, still thriving, included the Doon School at Dehra Dun, where Rajiv and Sanjay Gandhi were educated, and Sherwood College, in the hills at Naini Tal.

The British ploy worked well. The princes forsook war for peace. To live in peace was to build and live as ostentatiously as possible, which they did with a crazed fervour. The Maharaja of Baroda hails the palaces as 'a testament to the princes' power, wealth and capacity for self-indulgence'.

The benefit for the rest of us is that visitors to Rajasthan can now stay in fairytale palaces. There are rooms with murals of dancing girls and black marble bathrooms. Those with a large family or holidaying with friends can take a suite of seven rooms surrounding a tinkling fountain. It is possible to take an indoor dip in a palatial indoor swimming pool. There are dazzling gold and gems set in the walls of city palaces. There are chances to ride velvet-caparisoned elephants and to wander among princesses' gardens amid peacocks and cooling fountains. Rajasthan offers a glorious variety of luxurious pursuits: to go out to a royal game park dotted with pretty pavilions; to explore the painted Marwari havelis; or to visit desert villages by jeep and camel, sleeping under the stars. If the time is right, there is the Pushkar Camel Fair, or the Holi festival in jewel-like Jaisalmer or the Muslim festival of Urs at Ajmer.

But Rajasthan is not just palaces. There is a different, but equally exotic daily life being lived in its bazaars, villages, even along the roads. Here the rich diversity and colour of the traditional charm are really found. Monuments and museums cannot be missed, but it is also worth poking around the back alleys and getting out on the road to the tiny surrounding villages. As the artists Tim Lovejoy and Christian Peltenburg-Brechneff recently found: 'We felt the remote isolation of rural India 10 minutes out of any town or city, like travelling back 100 years or more; the road is like a tunnel, your car is zooming through not just the past but a whole other time zone.'

When to go

Season September-March, beginning with post-monsoon stickiness and clouds, ending with desert dryness. Best months visually are September-October when trees blossom and pleasure lakes are full; actual monsoon, July-August, can be stunning, even if wet. Flowers blossom November-March, peaking February-March. November-January evenings are cold and the locals wrap themselves in brightly coloured woollen shawls. March is sunny and hotting up, but there are fewer package tours – an important consideration in Rajasthan tourist traps.

FESTIVALS The best of the Hindu religious festivals to see in Rajasthan are Dussehra (September-October), Diwali (20 days later) and Holi (March-April), all public holidays when everything closes. There are big fairs and often huge firework displays. At *Dussehra*, 10 days of plays, processions and firework effigies celebrate Rama's victory over the demon Ravana and coincide with the harvest (but it is best of all in Delhi and Varanasi). At *Diwali*, women don black veils edged with gold tinsel. Oil lamps (clay pots holding lighted wicks in oil) are lit in every home and put outside on window and garden ledges to show Rama the way home from exile and to welcome Lakshmi, the goddess of wealth. Five days of jollity begin with the new year. It is a big time for gamblers – those favoured by Lakshmi to win at Diwali should keep a lucky hand for the whole year. For trading communities, such as the Marwaris of Shekhavati, this is business new year as well. Many put coins, an earthenware lamp, a weapon, a book and other objects before the youngest child who selects one, indicating the course of the following year. The next three days are devoted to Krishna, Shiva and the demon Bali, a monkey king son of the temperamental god Indra. On the fifth day, sisters put the red tikka mark on their brothers' foreheads.

Holi celebrates the arrival of spring. Rajasthan is the place to be, with pure enjoyment for everyone in every city, even commercial Jaipur. In the days running up to Holi, children get deliriously excited. On the eve, at sunset, bonfires of unwanted or dirty possessions symbolise the end of the year and a fresh start for the new one; householders tie a bunch of fresh green lentils on to a stick, singe it in the purifying bonfire and take it home to eat ceremoniously. On Holi itself, laws and social conventions are suspended from dawn until noon. Men and women flirt, playing holi by squirting pink water at one another or throwing clouds of pink, mauve, green and saffron powder. The men, often a bit merry on alcohol and bhang, sing and dance through the streets, banging the dramatic, repetitive rhythm out on a chang (huge drum). Having slept off the excitement, the keener shop-keepers open in the evening.

Holi celebrations at Nathdwara are unique but, unlike those at Mathura (see p. 80) have little to offer the visitor as they centre on the temple, which is closed to non-Hindus. Here, the black Krishna icon, called Srinath, is dressed in turmuric yellow, a diamond natha on his forehead. On Holi and other days the pichwai (cloth-painting) is drawn back so that hundreds of pilgrims can worship him. Srinath images and pichwais fill the markets of Nathdwara and Udaipur.

Then there are Rajasthan specialities. *Gangaur* (March-April, about two weeks after Holi) is the most important, especially in Udaipur (see the splendid murals of it in the City Palace). Gauri (another name for Shiva's wife, Parvati) is the goddess of abundance and fertility. Gauri also means yellow, the colour of ripened wheat. After a fortnight of light-hearted prayer for married bliss and faithfulness to painted wooden images of Gauri, a singing procession of ladies takes the Gauri image from her temple for a ceremonial bath in the nearest lake. Shiva then arrives to collect his bride in a pageant of caparisoned horses and elephants. There used to be a big water pageant on Pichola Lake at Udaipur.

Teej (July-August), when there is singing and dancing and women (wearing striped green veils) and children play on flower-bedecked swings hung from trees, is a double celebration: the onset of the monsoon and the reunion of Shiva and his wife, Parvati. This is best at Jaipur, where gaily caparisoned elephants escort the Parvati image from her parents' home to her husband's. The *kite festival* on January 14th is also spectacular, although kites are flown to a lesser extent at other festivals too. Men and boys expertly fill the sky with bobbing splashes of vibrant colour.

Head for Ajmer for the Muslim saint's *Urs* festival; to nearby Pushkar for the *cattle fair* (November-December); India's biggest livestock fair at Nagaur in the Thar Desert, 130km from Jodhpur (January-February); and *Nag Panchami*, in honour of Naga, the serpent king, at Jodhpur (July-August), when women worship the visiting snake charmers. The recently established *Desert Festival* at Jaisalmer (January-February), with camel polo, camel races and desert music and dance, has its merits but since it is run by the tourism officials rather than being indigenous, it is a bit self-concious.

Getting there: Getting away

Indian Airlines serves Rajasthan at three airports: Jaipur, Jodhpur and Udaipur; the daily early morning shuttle runs Delhi-Jaipur-Jodhpur-Udaipur-Aurangabad-Bombay (and vice versa), and there are other flights during the day. Vayudoot serves these three plus Jaisalmer, and is extremely useful since IA flights in this area are often fully booked. Be sure to book at high season. Otherwise travel between cities by car, train or speedy air-conditioned buses. All three airport cities make good bases for touring. Alternatively, it is a good idea to arrive at one and leave from another. Car hire gives the most freedom and is not exorbitantly priced. Distances are not huge, roads are quite good, and the rural daily life is packed with colour and tradition. Unless the luxurious Palace on Wheels train, consisting of ex-maharajas' carriages, improves its programme (which rumour says it may), it does not stop long enough anywhere. Passengers enjoy superficial glimpses of Rajasthan on a memorable train journey, but to see Rajasthan properly, they must come again. Far better, on a short holiday, to take one or two ordinary trains. For instance, the Pink City Express from Delhi to Jaipur (departs 5.55am, arrives 11am); the overnight train from Jodhpur to Jaisalmer; the overnight Super-Fast Express from Delhi to Jodhpur (departs 6.10pm, arrives 6.55am); the morning express from Agra to Jaipur (5hrs).

Information and reservations

To set up a trip after arrival in Delhi or Bombay, go to the recommended travel agents in those cities. To set up a trip on arrival in Rajasthan, Jaipur is the area headquarters for several good agents who have outposts throughout the state: Aravalli, 43a Bhogat Vasko, Civil Lines, Jaipur (tel: 72735/52130); Mayur Travels, Mirza Ismail Road, Jaipur (tel: 77284); Rajasthan Tours, Rambagh Hotel, Jaipur (tel: 521041); Sita, D-Villa, Station Road, Jaipur (tel: 68226/66809); TCI, A-3 Jamnlal Bajaj Marg, C-Scheme, Jaipur (tel: 65371) and Travel Plan, 4 Daulat Niwas, Hari Marg, Civil Lines (tel: 65532). A travel agent can book trains, cars, hotels and find out precise current bus times. His fee is small. It saves hours of effort, or the disappointment of arriving at a full hotel. Always carry food and drink when driving.

Two package tours can fill up the biggest palace hotels, so winter visitors should book well in advance. On the whole, the government and state tours in each city are good: quality guides give thorough introductions to scattered palaces and forts, and the coach collects from the hotel and delivers back. Food is not wildly exciting in Rajasthan, except in one or two hotels which make a special effort to serve local dishes (see below); it is rarely up to Delhi standards. Several Indians even say they stick to vegetarian food in Rajasthan. If you are in any doubt about hygiene, head for a town's South Indian restaurant. Rajasthan has partial prohibition, in this case meaning that national and religious holidays are dry. Night life apart from local folk entertainment organised by hotels is usually pretty poor, but the English fortnightly, *Rajasthan Echo*, and the monthly *Jaipur Vision* carry details of what there is. Local tourist offices help find folk dancing and music. Uma Anand's *Guide to Rajasthan* is excellent, as is the *Guide to Rajasthan*, published by the ITDC. Shopping is irresistible in Rajasthan, but bargain hard in the bazaars and shops, and make large purchases with care: this the centre of Indian tourism and lies on an old trading route peopled by tough, experienced traders.

See – and hear – how it's done

Despite the onslaught of tourism into Rajasthan, heavier than anywhere else in India, the vast fund of traditional music, folklore, ritual and crafts thrives across the state. Communities add their own idiosyncrasies to general Rajasthani traditions. It is important to stress that the way to encounter them is to explore the back streets of cities and, even more so, to go out to the villages, keeping a beady eye on the roadside and not being afraid to ask the car driver to stop if there is something interesting. Here are just a few things to look out for. (Those special to one city are mentioned with that city's attractions.)

To find a particular sort of musician, dancer or craftsman, just ask. Tour guides, museum keepers and tourist offices should know what's what. Shopkeepers are especially helpful about where their stock is made and will give precise directions and even sometimes play escort in their spontaneous kindness.

Bhopas The most familiar musician is the itinerant bhopa (balladier), originating from Marwar. Clad in vermilion with matching or saffron turban, he sings and dances with his heavily veiled wife and often his young son, playing his rawanhatta stringed instrument with a short bow tinkling with bells. They perform ad lib, proud to be able to produce the right song for the moment, a birthday, honeymoon, wedding aniversary, etc. They are delighted by requests. Pabuji ka bhopas are a special class (found everywhere except Alwar and Bharatpur), who use the prop of the 13-metre-long cotton Pabuji Ki Phad (scroll-painting ballad) to elaborate upon each scene as they sing heroic poetry and mime-dance, holding an oil lamp up to each intricately painted scene as the story of Pabuja unfolds. The subject is a 13th century hero from Rathore and performances of his deeds are supposed to remove evil influences from homes. Phads, densely illustrated in dominant red, yellow and green, are produced in Chitorgarh and by the joshis of Shahpur. It is best to avoid the smaller panels produced for the tourist in poster colours.

Folk dance In the days leading up to Holi, Gangaur, Teej and marriages, wealthier women dance the ghoomar in streets and villages, moving round in circles and twirling their ghongras (very full skirts). And during the fortnight before Holi, everyone, irrespective of caste, dances the gingad. Men dance the gair to the beat of the chang drum. The ghoomar-gair dance is much faster, the dancers twisting and turning as they strike each others' sticks. The Garasias tribe love dancing, often after a day's work and for days and nights together before Holi. Teratal is closer to ritual acrobatics than dancing. The men sing while the women dance and accompany them simultaneously, playing the 13 cymbals (teratal) tied all over their bodies.

Itinerant entertainers These ply their trade at any wayside hamlet, fair or festival. A man with a dummy silk horse fitted to his waist dances the lok nritaka to the beat of his partner's huge drum. A folk musician plays the morchang (like a Jew's harp). A man dressed up as a monkey amuses passers by; another as the monkey god, Hanuman, howls and chatters and mimics his audience. Acrobats walk the tightrope or bend an iron bar with their foreheads.

The nomadic Kalvelias tribe of snake charmers, the women heavily bejewelled, sing, dance and play the been (or punji, made of a gourd) to entice the snake to rise and sway. There are different tunes for different snakes. The Kalvelias have milked the snakes' poison sacs and return them to the wild when the sac refills.

The Kangujri wears a tight pyjama, flowing skirt and conical hat, and calls himself both Radha and Krishna at once, singing songs about them as he travels from door to door. And there are puppeteers and all sorts of bhopas, some with bells, others playing the mashak (a bit like Scottish bagpipes) and others performing feats like piercing a needle through the tongue.

Mendhi The leaves of mendhi (myrtle) have an astonishing array of properties. Dried, crushed and dissolved in sugary water, they are painted on women's hands and feet. The fine, lacey designs are highly symbolic, usually related to prosperity and happiness, and are an essential part of Hindu ritual at ceremonies and festivals. Woe betide the woman who forgets her mendhi. It can bring sterility. Failure before Teej festival by a wife whose husband is abroad means he may not return. The mendhi paste put between the palms of a bride and groom at their wedding must turn crimson, or their marriage will be a disaster. A good design on a woman's hand improves her luck and is essential to avert tragedy: the satiya, a reverse swastika motif, is applied just before a mother gives birth. After birth, she will only recover if mendhi is applied to her nails. (It does not stop at humans: when a cow gives birth, both cow and calf are painted.) Who applies the mendhi is vital: a barber's wife brings prosperity, especially if five married women sing menhadi songs at the same time. A widow is such bad luck that she cannot even paint herself, let alone others. And so it continues, touching every corner of life. Each motif has a meaning: the scorpion for love; the parrot for separated lovers (it carries their messages); the peacock to be a companion to lonely love; lotus and fish for women's eyes. It is used as a perfume, a medicinal cure for headaches, a dye for cloth or to prevent hair turning grey, and is drunk by singers to improve the voice. It is quite obviously the wonder drug for which the West has been searching.

Kathputli Puppeteering, one of the oldest entertainment forms and possibly the source of Indian drama. Formerly entirely nomadic, the puppeteers now spend the monsoon at their homes – villages in the eastern desert areas, where their yajamans (patrons) are. They spend eight months of the year on the road. The cot, or stage, for the performance has an embroidered curtain, gloriously known as Taj Mahal. The shows are at night, about two hours long, performed by the kathputliwala (puppeteer) and his wife. He pulls the strings, she plays a drum and sings the story. Puppeteers carve their own big, wooden puppets (a metre or more tall), then paint and costume them beautifully. Old and new puppets can be found in the bazaars, especially in Jodhpur, although the tradition used to be that a puppet no longer fit for use would be floated off downstream, to release its spirit. Short, delightful shows are staged almost daily in Jaigar Fort, Jaipur, and at several hotels.

Kavad Brightly painted, wooden, mobile temples of all sizes, with lots of little compartments closed with doors, are carried from village to village by the itinerant kavadia bhat to perform kavad. As he narrates the Ramayana, he opens each door to reveal little paintings of the gods in the story, the finale being, of course, Rama, Lakshmana and Sita. There is a coin slit in the temple for offerings. Old temples are found in antique shops; new ones in Udaipur, Jodhpur and Jaipur.

Barbers Shaving is a public activity, as is dentistry which draws good crowds for tooth extraction. The barber sharpens his knife on a stone (which also cleans it), rubs water on the beard, shaves it off to a silken finish, tidies up the eyebrows and avoids at all costs the carefully nurtured, thick, drooping Rajasthani moustache. As he shaves he wipes the hairs off the knife on to his leg. In former days the hairs would be weighed and the barber would exact an equivalent fee in gold from a rich man, in kind from a poor man. Barbers give a luxuriously smooth shave, almost never breaking the skin. But, because of those exceptions, it is better just to watch.

Teeth beauticians An equally public activity. For 50 paise, the beautician will rub ointment on to a patient's teeth and gums, then clean and improve the teeth, shaping them with a strange assortment of files. If necessary, he replaces a missing tooth – or wrenches out a bad one.

Meenakari The art of enamelling. The highest quality and quantity crafted is to be found at Jaipur, the meenakari centre. Delicate patterns of birds and flowers in ruby red, deep green and peacock blue on a brilliant white ground are fired on to elaborate gold earrings, pendants, cosmetic boxes, attardans (perfume holders) and other objets d'art. The grander ones are then made more glittering with white sapphires and dangling natural pearls; the cheaper ones use silver or copper in place of gold.

The art is also practised in other Rajasthani cities, such as Amber and Nathdwara, and in Delhi and Varanasi. Indian meenakari, similar to European champ-levé work, was introduced by the Mughals – although Queen Aahhotep of Egypt was adorning herself with enamel jewellery in 1700BC. Heights of perfection were reached in the Mughal court ateliers, the envy of all. Towards the end of the 16th century, Raja Man Singh lured five meenakaars (enamelwork craftsmen) from Lahore to his capital at Amber. Their descendants still work in the new capital, Jaipur.

The method is painstakingly slow, precise and demands top quality materials – a master meenakaar takes 15 days just to enamel both sides of a pendant. First, the goldsmith copies old designs to make the object. He uses 23½ carat gold and a touch of copper, so that it does not melt during firing. On to the surface he solders tiny moulds for the gems. Then the meenakaar takes over. His aim is to achieve the most glowing colours, mixing secret potions of metal oxides (cobalt for blue, iron for green) in a vitreous base. He used to use finely ground precious stones. Each enamel colour is pulverised, then made into a paste. The meenakaar engraves his miniature arabesques and birds on to the gold, chisels out tiny flat fields and fills them with the enamel paste, applying it dot by dot with a stylus. As each colour is completed, the piece is fired, starting with red, which sustains heat best, and ending with white, which is liable to run. The firing is extremely tricky: too hot and the gold will melt; too cool and the enamel will not melt enough to fuse. After the kiln, a bath of water and acid reveals the success of the colour.

When all the colours are done, they are buffed with a corrundum stone (like a sapphire) to smooth the surfaces. Then to the gem setter for kundan (gem setting) in pure gold leaf. After several months and considerable skill, the object is complete.

Craftsmen can be found most easily in Jaipur back streets. Master meenakaar Deen Dayalji's sons and pupils live and work in his haveli, Gopalji ka Rasta in Memiyon ki Gali, a very narrow alley of Johari Bazar. Kudrat Singh is another Jaipur master meenakaar. Nathdwara work tends to use silver, making it cheaper. Cheaper meenakari can be found in the bazaars. A jeweller is best for bigger buys.

Lacquered brassware A combination of applied lacquer and engraving to decorate brass trays, bowls, dishes and vases, the grander pieces of which are silver or gold plated. To make the object, shapes are cut from brass sheets, soldered together and refined with tools. For the complicated patterns (the more refined and intricate the better), the engraver first sketches the scheme on the brass. With his tools he chases the pattern, raising parts by repoussée, indenting parts by embossing, engraving fine arabesques and details. The craftsman makes his own sticks of lac for colour and, after applying them, buffs them up to a metallic shimmer.

Leatherwork Mojadis (slippers), often made of camelskin, are decorated with embroidered designs, the cobbler working in his bazaar shop. Shoes can be made to order, with special designs, as can water bottles and handbags. Rajasthani mojadis are famous for their variety, bright colours and designs, each special to one town.

Pottery In the villages, potters make the big storage and water pots. The clay is a rough mixture of earth, water and dung (for fibre and strength), pounded by a woman of the household. The potter throws the clay on a huge stone, perhaps a metre in diameter, whirling on just a wooden peg. The stone's weight maintains the momentum for a good long spin, sped with a stick if necessary. He then roughly

shapes about 30 pots in the early morning, leaving them to dry for about eight hours before beating them into exact shape, using a hammer on the outside and a pummel inside. After more drying, the women decorate them with simple designs, using mineral paints. When the kiln is full, they are fired, then distributed around the village. The surplus are taken to market where there are always buyers, not through careless breakages but because the cooling properties of the pot apparently diminish after a few months.

Bandhana The ancient Indian technique of tie-dyeing fabrics, seen throughout Rajasthan and Gujarat. Rajasthani women wear bandhana or wood-block patterned odhnis or pilos (head veils) over their cholas (short-sleeved, tight-fitting blouses) and ghongras (very full skirts), some ten metres round. Every community has its own designs, the man drawing the patterns, the women and children tightly binding all his dots, some pinhead small, before dying the fabric. The strings are then untied to reveal the pattern. The more complex the design, the tinier the dots and the more precisely tie-dyed, the more the article is worth. But the colours have universal significance: yellow for spring and fertility; nila (indigo) for Krishna; hari nila (a paler blue) for water; gerua (saffron) for the wise man and poet who renounces worldly things.

In towns, the merchants supply the fabric and designs to families, usually Muslims. Women and children as young as six work them, their nimble fingers tying a whole veil in one day for about Rs2. The fabric then goes to the dyer before the merchant sells the veils at Rs60 a piece – a tidy profit. There is an enormous variety of patterns and quality: cheap bandhana work can be found in markets; top quality in shops. Tying and dyeing can be seen in the backstreets; drying on the flat rooftops.

Block-printing Fabric printed with carved wooden blocks on borders, in circles or all over. Practised in Gujarat, Rajasthan and neighbouring states, and in the South, but most lively in Rajasthan. In its heyday, the tiny village of Sanganer, outside Jaipur, was known as the 'Metropolis of Calico-Printing'. The colours of the design are separated on to tracing paper, then pricked on to the wood by the block-maker. He then cuts it out with hammer and chisel. Precision is essential: one mistake and a new block must be cut. The cheepas (hand block printers) really prefer vegetable and mineral colours and boil up their evil-smelling witches' brews. To make black, they take iron, charcoal, molasses and flour and boil them together for 15 days – one feels they might well throw in a frog and chant a spell for good measure.

Printing is often done in a long, barn-like building with high windows and built-in niches to store the blocks. The whole length of fabric – fine muslin to heavy cotton – is pinned on to long, spongy-padded table tops. The first colour is printed right along, by which time the beginning is dry enough for the second colour, then a third, fourth, even fifth shade. The printer depends entirely on his eye and a steady hand to get the flowers, trees, animals, houses, birds and stripes clear and accurate. After boiling and exposure to the sun to make the design fast, the fabric is sometimes khari printed.

Khari-printing Embossed printing in gold or silver, usually in delicate floral designs, each motif individually printed by the chipa (khari-printer) on to plain or printed fabric. The process is usually done in a special room, the air twinkling with gold, like dust caught in a sunray. In bazaar lanes, the khari printers will emboss borders on people's skirts, blouses and dresses very quickly for a tiny charge.

Screen-printing The modern, speedy version of block-printing. Whereas it takes four people to block-print eight four-coloured saris in a day, those same four can screen-print 160 similar saris in a day, increasing output 20-fold. In addition, a wooden block wears out fast and even on day one has a fuzzy outline compared to a screen-print. The practical set-up is much the same as for block-printing but the printer just hooks the printing frames on to alignment pegs on either side of the long tables to ensure a precise match.

Dhurrie-weaving see Agra.

The cities

If possible, it is nicer to stay at least three days (preferably longer) in the bigger cities to feel their very different atmospheres and to see their old fortresses, museums, palaces, bazaars and surrounding forts and villages. And it is important to leave time for amusement and relaxation staying in the dream palaces of princes and the homes of nobles.

Eastern Rajasthan

JAIPUR
259km from Delhi, 228km from Agra. Bustling, monkey-filled, oleander pink, toytown capital of Rajasthan. A perfect piece of humanist town planning laid out in 1727 by Maharaja Jai Singh II (1699-1744) and his architect, Vidyadhar Bhattacharaya. A grid system of very wide tree-lined avenues, and a surrounding crenolated wall with seven gates, follow the principles of a Hindu architectural treatise, the Manasara. Airy, flat and ordered, it is a complete contrast to the old hilltop fort capital, Amber, where the rulers had accumulated vast wealth and in-

fluence, substantially increased from the moment the wily Mughal conqueror Akbar created his first Rajput alliance by marrying the charming Amber princess in 1562.

Jai Singh II, enthroned at the age of 13, was a precocious and shrewd politician who, within the year, had won from Emperor Aurangzeb the hereditary title Sawai, meaning one and a quarter, to indicate his superiority over his contemporaries. He was an aesthete, architect, engineer, astronomer, inventor, mathematician and patron of art and music. In his new city, traders and craftsmen had their own areas and distinctive architecture, painted a variety of colours. The city's coat of warm pink follows the original plan – in the 19th century, there was an experiment to paint the different quarters different colours, but no-one liked it. The pink was chosen not as a symbol of welcome but to imitate the expensive red sandstone used by the ruling Mughals at their impressive Agra and Delhi forts – the rubble and plaster walls of Jaipur imitate the structure of those at Delhi built a century earlier.

In addition to its monuments, several floodlit at night, Jaipur is the Rajasthan city best equipped with hotels, restaurants, information and shops. It is also the final point of the fly-by-night tourist's Golden Triangle, Delhi-Agra-Jaipur, of which the local citizens can take undue advantage. Beware of over-pricing and over-booking. Hotels are best booked in advance and it is advisable to arrive clutching the written confirmation.

THE HARD FACTS There are two top-notch places to stay, one for playing princes, the other for central location.

The Rambagh Palace, Bhawani Singh Road (tel: 75141; fax: 73798; telex: 365254 RBAG IN); former main palace of Maharaja Man Singh II (1911-1970, known as Jai to his friends) who, in 1957, was the first to enter the palace hotel game; run by the Taj chain since 1972. Maharaja Ram Singh (1835-80) developed a small hunting lodge out of some pleasure pavilions outside the city walls, embellished by Madho Singh II (1880-1922). Besotted with England after attending Edward VII's coronation in 1902 (see introduction to this chapter), he added the deep herbaceous borders (glorious January-March), squash and tennis courts, indoor swimming pool and, being a polo fanatic, a private polo field next door. (After breaking an arm, he turned to flying and built his own aerodrome.)

His adopted son and successor, Jai, became Man Singh II, the last Maharaja (ruled 1922-49). He lived here and, while away at Woolwich Training Academy in 1931, had it enlarged and modernised to be his official residence, with further up-datings when he married his third wife in 1940, Gayatri Devi (Ayesha to friends).

A beautiful princess from Cooch Behar in North-East India, she shot her first leopard at the age of 12, enjoyed London society as a teenager and returned to marry the Maharaja. After Independence, she was elected MP in 1962 for the opposition Swatantra Party with a majority of 175,000, the largest ever in a democratic country, and now lives at Lillypool, a house in the Rambagh gardens. In her autobiography, she recalls being vastly impressed when she visited the Maharaja's first two wives there in the winter of 1932, not expecting 'the furnishings . . . would be so modern and have such an air of sophistication; they could have been anywhere, in England or Europe or Calcutta'. Some of the larger suites are almost the same today: the latest and most boldly stylish rugs, lamps, built-in electric fires and chaises-longues that high 1930s design could produce. Unfortunately, much of the delightful period atmosphere has been destroyed in the recently refurbished rooms (new fitted carpets, etc.).

110 large rooms including 15 suites, plus modest health club, beauty salon, business services, good travel agent (Rajasthani Tours), car rental, shopping arcade (Anokhi and Mr Jain the bookseller), camel riding and golf on request, and magnificent manicured gardens with Lalique fountains, folk dancers and musicians performing during the day and evening. It is best to go for a room overlooking the gardens and to check out a room before accepting it; and it is worth splashing out on one of the 16 suites, such as the Maharaja's, with superb fittings and black marble bathroom, and the Maharani's, both decorated in honour of his 1940 wedding. Service can be sleepy. Sipping a nimbu soda on the lawns, lolling on the deep verandahs, or enjoying a cocktail in the Polo Bar are the perfect relaxation after a day of dusty bazaars and forts. Lofty dining room with Indian musicians (lunch and dinner) accompanying variable food (Indian and Continental); the fresher, simpler coffee shop does good samosas and huge club sandwiches.

Mansingh, Sansar Chandra Road (tel: 78771; telex: 0365-2344WLCO IN). Central (just off Agra Road, good for shops). 100 rooms, all mod. cons include travel agent, car rental, beauty salon, shopping arcade, good newish pool, golf/ tennis/riding/polo by arrangement; basement restaurant OK, rooftop Shiver restaurant and bar excellent, with Jaipur views, top quality Mughlai and vegetarian food accompanied by good Indian ghazals (light songs) at lunch and dinner. Locals' requests keep the musicians and singer going into the early hours. Friendly service.

Jai Mahal Palace, Jacob Road, Civil Lines (tel: 68381; fax: 68337; telex: 3652250 JMPH IN).

Slightly less rambling than the Rambagh and totally refurbished, this palace is well managed and still has the charms of a painted bar and pretty dining room. Part of the Taj Group. 120 rooms, all mod. cons include car rental, shopping arcade, pool, tennis, riding and peacocks in the garden.

Rajmahal Palace, Sardar Patel Marg (tel: 61257; fax: 73798; telex 036 313 JAI IN). Used as the British Residency from 1821; later used by the Maharaja after leaving the Rambagh. Feels like a large family home. 11 rooms, all mod. cons including a swimming pool.

Note: If this is not enough royal living, the little 1920s *Ramgarh Lodge* at Jamuva Ramgarh (tel: 75141; fax: 73798), 45km north-east of Jaipur, has just 9 rooms, spacious gardens and overlooks Ramgarh Lake.

The thakurs (nobles) of the maharaja lived in fine town houses when they came from their estates to attend the Jaipur court. Some of the descendants are now hard-up and, having sold land and possessions, run their family homes as small hotels. Great charm, original furnishings, painted walls, libraries, gardens and often very interesting hosts to listen to. All rooms have fans (a few have air-cooling systems) and bathrooms (usually just shower, not tub). A few of the especially pleasant ones are listed below.

Narain Niwas, Kanota Bagh, Narain Singh Road (tel: 65448). Rajput haveli built in 1881 by Narain Singh Ji, now run by Mr Mohan Singh. Rich fin de siècle interior with four-poster beds, chandeliers, Afghan carpets, paintings and East India Company furniture. 22 rooms (one with wall-paintings of fantasy colonnades), rooms air-cooled, clean throughout, terraces, garden, swimming pool. Good food cooked as and when requested.

Achrol Lodge, Civil Lines Road (tel: 72254). Gentle Mr Mahandra Singh runs his handsome, simply furnished, peaceful family home with big lawns, shady trees. 8 rooms, all with fans, some with delicate tracery wall-painting. They only serve breakfast and Indian dinner.

Bissau Palace, Chandpole Gate (tel: 74191/ 67728). Excellent location for walled city. Run by Mr and Mrs Sanjay Singh, descended from the Bissaus, a Rajput family from Shekhavati. Beautifully maintained library and drawing rooms; swimming pool, tennis court. Lively atmosphere. 30 rooms, all with fans. Good food includes Rajasthani dishes.

Haveli Hotel, Statue Circle (tel: 75024). Mr Vinay Poda lives upstairs in his 1940s haveli where rooms surround a small courtyard; beautiful, extensive gardens. 10 rooms.

Samod Haveli, Gangapole (tel: 42407). Just inside the north wall of Jai Singh's city, found through a painted gateway. Colourfully painted and furnished public rooms behind a large courtyard (open to non-residents for meals). 11 rooms.

Mandava House, Sansar Chandra Road (tel: 75358). Rambling old family house 1km from the railway station, with 17 new rooms.

Postscript: To stay simply but right in the hub of the Pink City, *LMB Hotel* in Johari Bazar (tel: 48844) has 33 simple, clean rooms above its famous vegetarian restaurant and ice-cream/ sweetmeats parlour. The Jaipur *Ashok* and *Clarks* Amber hotels, both modern, are emergencies for upmarket hotels.

Tourist information from the Information Centre, Sawai Ram Singh Road (tel: 72345), the Department of Tourism, Rajasthan, 100 Jawaharlal Nehru Marg (tel: 74875/73873) and the Railway Station (tel: 69714). Government of India Tourist Office at Hotel Khasa Kothi (tel: 72000). Both RTDC and ITDC run good five-hour tours with the focus on Amber Fort and then the City Palace, Observatory and City Museum. Recommended. RTDC also do a full day tour. Both offer inexpensive guides. Rajasthan Tours at the Rambagh will help with specialist guiding, such as to nobles' houses, or around the back streets or to see crafts. Cultural programmes are held in Ravendra Manch, near Albert Hall. To find out what's going on, read the *Rajasthan Echo*, *Jaipur Vision* or ask at a tourist office. Several good bookshops on the west side of Chaura Rasta (Usha, Arvind, Best Book), plus Mr Jain in the Rambagh.

Sports facilities are the best in Rajasthan. All hotels can arrange tennis/squash/riding/polo. Polo is especially important in Jaipur: the season is January-March, when five big tournaments are held. There is also elephant polo (the day before Holi), camel polo and bicycle polo. Fishing at Ramgarh Lake (45km), used for the Asian Games yachting competitions, stay at Ramgarh Lodge (see above), permits from Gangaur Tourist Bungalow (tel: 74373) or Fisheries Project Office, Tonk Road (tel: 76253). Jaipur Flying Club (affiliated to Delhi Flying Club). Rajasthan Mounted Sports Association, Dundlod House, Civil Lines (tel: 66276/66147), run by young locals, can set up a wide range of sports and safaris: polo, riding, horse safaris through Rajasthan (7-12 days) and to Pushkar Fair (3 days). They can also set up re-creations of Holi, Diwali, even a complete 'Princely Wedding' for up to 50 people to attend, with caparisoned elephant and horse procession, 14-man band, fireworks display, 20 actors in the full dress and jewellery of princes and princesses, the wedding ceremony performed by a Brahmin, and a dinner – yours for only $4,000. But there is no restriction on numbers for their elephant spectacle: a procession of 20 caparisoned elephants, 9 camels and much more, followed by elephant racing and elephant polo. It costs $2,400.

OUT AND ABOUT There is a lot to see in and around Jaipur but it is nicest to start by going out of town up to the old fort city of Amber (11km, see below), the capital before Jaipur was built. On return, start with Jai Singh's model palace. **City Palace complex** Described by the Maharaja of Baroda as 'the most daring and successful synthesis of Moghul and Rajput styles'. Begin on the outside with the *Hawa Mahal* (Palace of the Winds), a lace-like five-storey building in the palace wall, one room deep, built in 1799 so that the royal women in purdah could watch the world outside from its 593 niches and windows without the world watching them. Open daily, 9am-4.30pm (closed Friday), climb to the top for views.

Inside, visitors can see the principal palace rooms containing the museum, Jantar Mantar (Observatory) and Govind Devi Temple, set in gardens and courtyards – part still occupied by the Maharaja. White marble elephants guard the Diwan-i-Khas where silver urns that stored Ganga water for Madho Singh's trip to England stand. The two-tiered doorways of the Peacock courtyard are totally encrusted with coloured stones, while above it, in the beautifully painted, seven-storeyed Chandra Mahal (Moon Palace), lives the former Maharaja and his family. In the *Maharaja Sawai Man Singh II Museum*, founded 1959 and housed in various scattered palace rooms, do not miss the textiles and musical instruments in the Zenana, the carpets and paintings in the Diwan-i-Am, the transport collection, the changing exhibitions from the vast and fascinating collection of royal photographs and, of course, the armour, probably the finest in India. Good publications. Open daily, 9.30am-4.30pm, except public holidays and festivals.

Outside the large gateway is the strangely contemporary-looking *Jantar Mantar* (Instrument Formula). Jai Singh II was the first Indian astronomer to depart from the Hindu emphasis on theory in preference to observation; the first to build an observatory in India; and the first to make contact with European astronomers. (The Jesuit expedition Jai Singh II sent to Europe in 1730 returned with the latest astronomical gadget, the telescope.) Mohammad Shah entrusted him to revise the lunar calendar and correct the astrological tables, for the smoother working of religion and empire alike. He made daily observations, sent astronomers abroad on research, consulted with his guru Pandit Jagannath, and translated Euclid and read Ptolemy before he began building five sets of outsized astronomical instruments resembling cubist scuptures for a children's playground.

The first was at Delhi (1724-27). The one at Jaipur (1728-34) is the largest and best preserved, because of its marble lining. Ujjain, Varanasi and Mathura (destroyed) followed, being the ancient centres of religion and learning. Jaipur's device has recently been restored to look even more like cubist toys. Each structure has a different purpose: the large, circular Ram Yatras are for reading altitudes and azimuths (distances in the sky); the 12 Rashivilayas for calculating celestial latitudes and longitudes; the Samrat Yantra (Supreme Instrument) is a vast gnomon (right-angled triangle) that acts as a sundial for measuring solar time by reading its shadow on the quadrants either side (accurate to within 15 seconds). Open daily, 9am-4.30pm.

At the *Govind Devi Temple*, it is possible to see puja (worship) being performed: devout locals hurry there between work and especially at the end of the day to wait for the temple doors to open, then witness the images of Krishna and Radha enacting their daily lives, such as waking up (5.15am) or being dressed (10.30am), or for evening prayer (6.30pm), followed by jolly music and processions. Ceremonies, lasting about 30 minutes, are daily at 5.15am, 8.15am, 10.30am, 12 noon, 5.15pm, 6.30pm, 8pm in winter, slightly different in summer.

Central Museum The collection begun in 1833 and housed in the gloriously named Albert Hall (1887, referring not to the Queen-Empress's husband but to her son, Prince Albert Edward, later Edward VII). Founded by a surgeon, Thomas Holbein Hendley (who was instrumental in reviving Jaipur's blue pottery tradition), and designed by Samuel Swinton Jacob (architect of Bikaner's great palace). Both men were prime movers in the late 19th century revival of quality craftsmanship and of the specifically Indian decorative arts and crafts being submerged beneath Western influences and fashions (John Lockwood Kipling, Rudyard's father, demonstrated similar beliefs in Lahore, see above). So the museum houses delightful examples of everything connected with Rajasthani life, from puppets and costumes to brasswork, woodwork, jewellery and models showing how a horse works, all very well labelled. Ask to see the Carpet Museum, housed in the detached Durbar Hall at the front of Albert Hall and kept under lock and key. Fabulous carpets include the huge Persian Garden Carpet of *c.* 1632, the design a bird's eye view of a garden, with water, ducks, birds feeding their young in trees and sporting animals. (Ask for the good booklet on it, by H. P. Vaish.) In Ram Niwas Gardens, open Sat.-Thurs., 9.30am-4.30pm, closed Friday, packed on Sunday.

There are other Jaipur palaces and forts to see. The *Nahargah (Tiger) Fort* was mainly built by Jai Singh II in 1734 as a retreat for his maharanis. It is reached by car (6.5km) or, for a sunset walk, up a steep, paved path found down Nahargarh Fort Road, off Chandpool Bazar, past descending goat-herds. Superb views (small café, and even a two-roomed, very simple hotel in the old walls).

En route to Amber, the impressive *Jaipur chhatris* (cenotaphs) are at Gaitor (8km), down a dusty road to the left; Jai Singh II's has a dome, pillars and peacock carvings; open daily, 10am-4.30pm. The ladies' chhatris are back on the main road, on the right. Just beyond is Jalmahal, a ruined pleasure palace built in Man Sagar Lake, now usually dried up. Beyond here, a road to the left twists up on to the ridge where a left turn leads to Nahargarh Fort, a right to the magnificent *Jaigarh Fort* whose great walls hold vast guns, underground passages, a fascinating museum, a gun-foundry set up by Man Singh when he stole the secret of gunpowder from the Mughals in Kabul, and a cooling summer palace where puppeteers play almost daily; open daily, 10am-4.30pm; café.

At the east end of Jaipur, the charming little *Sisodia Rani Palace* (8km), murals on the exterior, terraced gardens below, with fountains and pools, was built in 1774 by Maaji Chundawt Sisodia, Jai Singh's Udaipur queen. Near here, the sacred monkeys of Hanuman Temple are fed their banana tea daily; while almost opposite the palace stands the unkempt Uidyadhar Bhattacharaya garden honouring Jaipur's hero builder. *Ramgarh* (25km), the stronghold before Amber, overlooks Ramgarh Lake (good for fishing) whose Art Deco villa is now a quiet hotel in the Taj Group.

RESTAURANTS The *Mansingh's* rooftop *Shiver* is without doubt the best for Mughlai food, and the *Jai Mahal* is good too. The *Rambagh* is lovely for a snack or tea. In the dining hall, ask for Rajasthani sulla (barbecued mutton). If in Johari bazaar, go to *LMB* for excellent vegetarian food and the best sweetmeats in Jaipur (local specialities are firni, misri mawa and, in winter, halwa) and a selection of home-made ice-creams big enough to impress queues of discerning American travellers. In Mirza Ishmail Marg (known as MI Marg), which flanks the south wall of the city, *Niro's* and *Chanayka* (formerly *Kohinoor*) have good reputations for north Indian food – kebabs, tandoors, etc. – and *Kwality* is safe, clean, run-of-the-mill.

SHOPPING AND CRAFTS Crafts still thrive from the days of Jai Singh's patronage, when he designed special areas for the bandhanas, cheepas and meenakari workers. The bazaars are concentrated to the south of the walled city. Other shops are on MI Marg and Agra Road. Opposite Hawa Mahal find the charming raconteur Pritam Singh, who sits on the pavement selling handfuls of agate and moonstone for a twentieth of the price in the shops behind him; and find good Rajasthani shoes; bargain hard for the clothes. Do beware of antique shops in Jaipur. As one shopkeeper said, a twinkle in his blue eyes: 'Some of my things are really old. But what I do is make new pieces with old designs and then treat them to give them the antique touch.' Faith Singh's shop, Anokhi, is an essential stop, found on Tilak Marg near the Rambagh (which has an outpost).

At Sanganer Gate, there are the kite shops. To be the patang-undane wala guru (master kite-flyer of the community) is a big thing in Rajasthan. Nearby Bapu Bazar (closed Monday) has cheap, fun meenakari jewellery (see above) plus some of the more expensive pieces; and bandhana, block and screen print fabric shops, including work from Sanganer, sold by sari length and by the metre. Colour ranges are both the traditional sombre earth reds, oranges and browns as well as shocking stripes and large polka dots in citrus yellow, hard red and bright green. Good selections at Yashdev, no. 7, and Mona Prints, no. 28 – shop owners will direct you to craftsmen. There are embroidered mojadis (leather slippers) in Nehru bazaar (closed Wednesday).

In the wide Johari bazaar plain cotton, in dazzling peacock blue, sunshine yellow, April green and magenta, and bandhani work are sold by weight in various qualities of cloth (the cloth bazaar is down a covered alley on the west side, near the top). On the same street and in two tiny alleys off it, Gopalji Ka Rasta and Haldiyon Ka Rasta, there are silversmiths and semi-precious stones (bargain hard); lapidaries turn stones using just a bow attached to the grinding wheel, and metal discs and abrasives to cut the facets.

In the back streets, poke into the courtyards to find leather-workers and sweet-makers, look up to see women's co-operatives printing on roof-tops, and notice the pretty facades, with delicate designs on the pink plasterwork and overhanging balconies. Chaura Rasta and Tripolia bazaars stock fabrics and quantities of tin for jolly costume jewellery bangles.

On MI Marg, serious jewellery and stone buying can be done at Jewels Emporium, Gem Palace, established for generations, or Lall Gems and Jewels, all reliable. Fair prices (about 50% of London prices) for semi-precious stones; find a smoky topaz as big as a pigeon's egg for a few rupees, cut and polished garnets, yellow topaz, amethyst, black stars, most of them brought down from Kashmir. Away from here, find Bhuramal Rajmal Surana, off Haldion-ka-Rasta, one of Jaipur's finest jewellers; and Yogi Durvabhji's Emerald House, Subhash Marg, C-Scheme (tel: 72318/64171), both shops patronised by discerning Indians.

To see block-printing (see p. 108) without going to Sanganer, visit Maharaja Textile Printers sited conveniently on the road to Amber, on the right.

For dhurrie-weaving (see p. 78), ask at the emporia or go to Art Age, C-34 Lajpat Marg, Bhagwandas Road (tel: 75726) and Mr Vijaivargia will take you to some of his weaving families working in Jaipur. His weavers will make dhurries to order using traditional or modern designs.

Jaipur blue pottery It is an irony that the two surgeons Maharaja Sawai Madho Singh brought to Jaipur to modernise the medicine and irrigation of the state spent their leisure time energetically reviving Jaipur's flagging crafts. While Dr Hendley founded the City Museum (see above), Dr de Fabeck founded the School of Art in 1866. One craft to be revived quickly was the local blue pottery, made into blue and white pots of all sizes as well as tiles. Originally influenced by the delicate Persian shapes and designs of Mughal pottery, and sharing that love for rich lapis blue, the revived art is now one of the best buys in Jaipur. And Kripal Singh (see shopping, above) and his 15-man studio use the traditional methods to turn some of the nicest pieces, decorated in lapis, turquoise and ultramarine with floral and geometric patterns incorporating birds and animals. His studio and shop is at B-18a Siva Marg, Bani Park (Anokhi also stocks his work).

SANGANER

16km south from Jaipur on the Tonk road.

In addition to the different fabric printing techniques, the meenakari work, brasswork and leatherwork, all practised in Jaipur, anyone interested in crafts should nip out here. The ruined palace can be found through the triple gateways, and there is an interesting Jain temple. But the small, sandy, camel-filled town's lifeblood is its river whose fixing powers made it the centre of block, screen and khari printing (see above). Block cutting is done in the bazaar, and paper-making using cloth offcuts is done in the few house-factories not printing cloth – find one off the main street, just after J K Arts.

Paper-making Practised in the Kagazi mohulla (area), mainly by Muslims. Paper-making complements the cotton and silk rag trade as it uses its waste (some comes from work for the European shops Monsoon and Anokhi). The stone machinery is in rooms off family homes whose courtyards are reminiscent of the Merchant-Ivory film, 'The Householder', with chickens pecking, children playing, women cooking and weaving straw jalis (mats). The rags are churned with water and bleached in a circular stone vat until they are pulp; strained, sieved and dried; then moved to square vats for dying and rinsing. Then a wooden ladder and a jali are floated on the liquid surface while the slurry is stirred furiously with a wooden stick. It settles between the wood and the mat which are removed, the slurry clinging to the mat. The mat is then placed on a thin muslin sheet and drawn away with a quick twitch. When the pile of wet sheets between the muslin is high enough, it is pressed. The sheets are then pegged up to dry, perhaps dyed, then painted with starch, trimmed and finished (in many grades from silky to rough). The beautiful gold and silver speckling, seen on the album leaves of Mughal paintings in museums, is done last.

Saadh Textiles and J K Arts, both on the main street, have a good stock of printed goods; Khadi Ghar on M I Road in Jaipur stocks speckled paper. Anokhi's fabrics are printed here and at Bagru.

AMBER

11km from Jaipur on the Jaipur-Delhi road, past Gaitor, past hills whose every peak is fortified, between cliffs and wild bougainvillea to the magnificent *fortress-palace* which seems to grow out of the rocky hill rising above Maota Lake, sadly dry most of the year now. Former capital of the extensive Jaipur state until Jai Singh II moved down to the plains, the site was won by the Rajputs in 1037. But the fort was not built until 1592, by Raja Man Singh I, commander in Akbar's army, and continued by his successor, Jai Singh I, who gave it its Mughal character in the Diwan-i-Am and Diwan-i-Khas.

The stern exterior of ramparts (further protected by Jaigarh Fort perching above) belies the jewelled interior whose richness increases as the small rooms rise higher, up to the Sheesh Mahal (Hall of Mirrors, recently well-restored). There are taks (niches) for gold and silver ornaments; coloured glass windows depicting Krishna; walls painted with floral patterns and religious and hunting scenes (older ones in the zenana); and dados of carved marble. Everything is star-spangled and shimmering. Don't miss the fine views from the rooftop.

To make the walls shine, powdered marble, egg shells and even pearls were added to the last coat of paint. More lavish apartments have ceilings and walls encrusted with pachikari-kakam, convex pieces of coloured mirror glass set in patterns in the plaster, and with kanch work, larger pieces of mirror outlined with vermilion, gold and silver. This mirror work is found also at Jaipur and Jodhpur, but the finest is here, outlining cyprus trees and delicate arabesques.

At the white marble Sila Devi Temple, puja is regularly performed with clanging bells and beating drums. Beyond the square where

people take elephant rides and pause at the café, a path found through an arch runs down past the old deserted palace to the pretty village; through it, past the mosque Akbar built and past gemstone cutters, you can clamber up the ramparts to watchtowers. Open daily, 9.30am-5.30pm, best to go early to avoid queuing for an elephant; don't miss the elephants' café at the bottom or the little Archaeological Museum by Maota Lake; further up the slope, the road to the left leads up to Jaigarh Fort (see Jaipur, above).

ALWAR

143km from Jaipur or Delhi. Driving between the two cities, Alwar is a stop on the slightly longer and much quieter and prettier route which goes through Sariska Wildlife Sanctuary (see p. 131). Turning off the main road at Shahpura it is worth stopping at *Bairat* where the remains of the 3rd century BC Buddhist shrine with stupa is the only known piece of Mauryan architecture in Western India, proving Buddhism's early presence here. Sariska merits a stay, and the pretty *Siliserh Lake* beyond has waterside chhatris and a modest, off-beat 20th century palace with wide terrace for a lake view drink (*Lake Palace*, Siliserh, Alwar, tel: 22991; 11 rooms, boating and bird-watching for the energetic).

Crowned by another hilltop fort, Alwar only became free from Jaipur in 1776, forming one of the last Rajput states. Alliance with the British considerably helped its dynastically unstable life during which, somehow, a cluster of fine palaces were constructed at the foot of the hill, extravagant tiger shoots were held on hunting elephants, and elaborate pageantry filled the streets.

Vinai Vilas, the City Palace (1840), is a sensitive marriage of Mughal proportions with Rajput decoration; stables could hold 3,000 thoroughbreds from India and England, and the treasury housed state jewels that included a cup cut out of a single diamond. Now it has a musty but fascinating museum on the top floor, found by wandering through the palace labyrinth now housing hundreds of civil servants which makes it more lively and evocative of royal days than most Rajasthan palaces. Good miniature paintings (if on view), armour, textiles and musical instruments. (Open Sat.-Thurs., 10am-4.30pm). To go up to the *old ruined* fort, seek permission (usually given instantly) from the Superintendent of Police at the City Palace, then hire a jeep and driver from the courtyard and set off by noon, taking a picnic. See the Purjan Vihar garden and summer house, the royal chhatris, the temples and pavilions beside the tanks. Also worth seeking out is Yeshwant Niwas, an Italianate palace built by Maharaja Jey Singh. Disliking it on completion, he never lived there but instead built in 1927 Vijay Mandir, a 105-room palace beside Vijay Sagar (Lake of Victory), where the ex-royals still live (partly open to the public). To stay overnight, go to *Phool Bag Tourist Palace*, opposite New Stadium (tel: 2274), central, clean and set in a lush garden.

Bharatpur: 174km from Jaipur, see p. 79. On the main road, just near the excellent mid-way café, shop and garden, the temple-keen can detour northwards to Abaneri to find the remains of Harshat Mata Temple and tank (9th century), the stone carved with amorous couples, dancing and sporting scenes. More remains in Amber and Jaipur museums.

Deeg: 192km from Jaipur, 89km from Alwar, see p. 79.

SHEKHAVATI

Literally, Garden of Shekha, a 15th century ruler of this area in north-east Rajasthan which lies within the triangle of Delhi, Bikaner and Jaipur. Recent pioneer work by Ilay Cooper, Francis Wacziarg and Aman Nath has put the area on the map (see bibliography). Here, in more than 360 villages lived the wealthy Marwaris who, in the 19th and 20th centuries, built themselves grand havelis and covered them inside and out with lively frescos, like life-size miniature paintings. They are a catalogue of their lives, fashions, habits and the latest news. They show the camel as a means of transport forsaken for a horse carriage, a car, a train and finally the 'flying ship' of the Wright brothers. Queen Victoria in mourning is recorded, as is the visit of King George V and Queen Mary to India. Views of the cooling Venice waters are as acceptable as British soldiers, local romantic folk stories and Hindu devotional scenes, all imbued with spirit, colour and zest for life which contrasts with the uninviting, hilly, scrubland landscape.

The *Marwaris*, originally from Marwar further west, were the merchant communities who prospered on the caravan trade routes between Delhi and the coast and between central Asia and China. Their name later became synonymous with the Rajasthan merchant class. With their money they financed and served the princely courts which in turn protected them, so there was mutual benefit. They were also extravagant patrons and had an in-built philanthropic sense, building not only immensely grand painted havelis to impress their friends and amuse their women, who were not permitted to go outside, but also schools, wells and reservoirs.

Then, in the mid-19th century, came problems. The British, who had overshadowed the princely courts, created customs barriers to cut off their entrepot markets and introduced new British goods to compete with Indian products. At the same time came the Opium Wars (1839-42), a decline in indigo trading because of German synthetic dyes and the replacement of overland trade routes by water and rail.

So the canny Marwaris upped sticks and went off to the ports, where the money was. They did not make for Bombay, where competition in the 1870s was stiff, but east, taking with them their strong business traits of financial conservatism, social orthodoxy and generous willingness to promote others in their community.

And they prospered. So, when the British began selling out in Calcutta, the buyer was often a Marwari. G. D. Birla was one who left his family in Pilani to go to live in Calcutta; his descendants are now one of the richest families in India. The Poddars and Goenkas are two other powerful Marwari families. Indeed, Thomas A. Timberg estimated that 'more than half the assets in the modern sector of the Indian economy are controlled by the trading castes originating in the northern half of Rajasthan'.

However successful a Marwari is, he often feels Shekhavati is still his home, so many havelis are maintained there – or at least have guardians. These walled town mansions have rooms facing inwards to two or more courtyards, the mardana for the men, the zenana for the women. The main doorway may be fortress-like, of heavy carved wood embellished with brass and iron fittings. There was not much furniture, but the facades, gateways, courtyard walls, parapets and ceilings were covered with paintings worked in a quality fresco technique similar to the Italian method, that has kept many remarkably well preserved.

The paintings date from the 18th century but the majority were produced 1830-1900, often by men who had followed their fortune to the ports but left their hearts – and, initially, their families – in Shekhavati where they continued to build and decorate. Early images of local legends and religion feature portraits of Krishna and Radha, Hanuman, Lakshmi – all Rajput favourites – and always Ganesh above the entrance. The Birla ancestral home, Shiv Narayan Birla (now a small museum), at Pilani, built in 1864, has a parade of elephants on the facade. The paintings of the later Goenka haveli in Mandawa, about 1870, show the development to more ornamental designs, every inch covered with polychrome floral patterns, tromp l'oeil architecture and pictures.

THE HARD FACTS Essential to have Ilay Cooper's guide, on sale at Mandawa Fort and elsewhere; otherwise, or perhaps in addition, take a local guide as specific buildings are tricky to find.

Drive around the area for two or three days,

looking at havelis and forts tucked behind crowded bazaars, staying in a choice of converted old buildings. *Castle Mandawa*, loved by Delhi diplomats, built 1755, beautiful rooms, original furnishings; sunset or sunrise from the roof magic, and staff will deliver tea there. (The unused half is to become an Oberoi hotel.) The owner also runs an enchanting hill-top Indian village hotel complex nearby (basic comforts). Also in Mandawa, Ramesh Janjit and his family run a *guest-house haveli*, reports of good food and care. *Dundlod Fort*, same period, slightly less grand but comfortable. *Roop Niwas Haveli*, Nawalgarh, built in the 1930s, less character but clean, good food and in a wonderful town. Booking by cable or letter; the two forts get busy at week-ends. Take picnic lunches. Winter nights get cold. Be sure to rent a good car with a driver who knows the area and how his car works; garages are scarce; driving from Delhi, there is a delightful garden café at Jhunjhunun, 30 minutes before Mandawa; driving from Jaipur, stop at Samode.

OUT AND ABOUT A trip from Jaipur could include some of the following. Day one, take a picnic and set off for Fatehpur, 160km away. Just out of Jaipur spot *Chaumu fort*, then take a detour right to *Samode*, through the narrow lanes to the remarkable palace with its elaborately painted rooms, gilding, meenakari work and louvred windows so that the women could listen without being seen (*Samode Palace Hotel*, Samode, Jaipur, book in Jaipur on tel: 42407, 20 rooms).

Then pause at *Sikar* to find the old quarter near the Clock Tower, with the Biyani havelis of Wedgwood blue, the Jubilee Hall, the temple converted from a palace and the fort (with a portrait of Queen Victoria as Empress of India). Stop at *Lachhmangarh* for a picnic inside the hill-top fort – asking the chaukidar (keeper) to close the gates for peace; glorious views over the town below and Shekhavati beyond.

To *Fatehpur*. Lively, many painted havelis include superb Devra and Singhania havelis, with mirrorwork and Japanese tiles. Then backtrack via Lachhmangarh to *Mukundgarh*, built around the temple square, local handicrafts in market. Then to *Mandawa*: to stay in the huge fort (*c.*1755). Stunning views and old frescoes, havelis in the bazaar, more havelis of Chokhanis, Goenkas and Sarafs.

Day two, to *Ramgarh* (the Poddar chhatri) via Fatehpur; to *Mahansar* for the best haveli of all – Soni Chandi Ki Haveli, the showroom of the gold and silversmiths; to *Bissau* (painted chhatris, havelis plus fort); and to *Jhunjhunun* to see Modi and Tibdiwala havelis, the Chhe (six) Haveli complex and the Rani Sati Temple where the Marwaris gather for the annual fair. (North-

east of here is *Pilani*, the Birla haveli museum, about 80km; Delhi is 180km beyond.) *Nawalgarh* has hundreds of havelis. Catch the frescoed telephone exchange and the aerial view of Jaipur painted in the fort dome (ask for it to be unlocked) and finally to *Dundlod* (another Goenka haveli).

Bissau connects with Bikaner (205km); from Nawalgarh, the road returns to Jaipur via Sikar (138km) or to Delhi (230-260km, depending on the route chosen).

Central and southern Rajasthan

AJMER

131km from Jaipur; 198km from Jodhpur; 302km from Udaipur. Sacred Muslim shrine in a crowded, walled, lakeside town beneath Taragarh Hill, an important Muslim pilgrimage centre in Hindu-dominated Rajasthan. Mahmud of Ghazni may have sacked it in 1024 and Mohammed of Ghor in 1193, but for the Mughal emperors it was a place of religious pilgrimage to the shrine of a particularly favoured Sufi saint. Akbar, who annexed it in 1556 for strategic and religious reasons, built a palace there and came annually, often partly on foot (see p. 78). Sir Thomas Roe presented his credentials to Jahangir here in 1616, marking, according to some, the first official contact between Britain and India (although he failed to gain a personal audience with the emperor). From 1818 it was a small area of Rajasthan controlled directly by the British and not via the princes.

THE HARD FACTS Best place to witness the Muslim festival of Urs. Travel by car, stopping at *Bagru* (20km from Jaipur) to see vegetable dyeing and printing, and at *Kishangarh*, 27km outside Ajmer, for a picnic beside the deserted lakeside palaces and a visit to the romantic, decaying Fort housing some of the highly stylised, effeminate miniature paintings for which little Kishanger state is so famous (to stay in the *Maharaja's Palace* contact Mr Veer Singh, Marjhela Palace, tel: 1). There are good trains from Jaipur, Delhi, Jodhpur and Udaipur. Tourist Office at Khadim Tourist Bungalow (tel: 20490). Best to stay at gentle Pushkar (11km, see below); in Ajmer, use the new, *Mansingh Palace* (run by Jaipur's Man Singh hotel group) overlooking Ana Sagar lake, at Vaishali Nagar (tel: 30855/6), 60 rooms and all mod. cons.

OUT AND ABOUT See Akbar's fort-palace (1570), housing the museum's collection of Mughal and Rajput armour (open Sat.-Thurs., 10am-5pm); and the Arhai-din-ka-Jhonpra (The Hut of Two and a Half Days), a fine mosque said to have been built in that amount of time by Mohammad of Ghor in 1193 after he had blindly destroyed 30 Hindu temples and a Sanskrit College, exquisitely carved prayer hall ceiling and screen (best in late sunlight, full of the faithful on Fridays). Beyond, a rough path leads steeply up to Taragarh (Star) fort (views). There is a Disneyland-style 19th century Nasiyan (Red) Jain temple; beyond are Shah Jahan's white marble pavilions in a delightful park on the east banks of the man-made Ana Sagar Lake (1135-50), overlooked by the old Residency. Southeast of the town lies the famous Mayo College, school-time home of boy princes.

Urs mela (festival, dates vary) is even better here than at Nizamuddin in Delhi. It is held in the old town in the Dargah, begun by Iltutmish of Delhi, completed by Humayun and known as *Dargah Sharif* (Holy Shrine) or Dargah Khwaja Sahib (remove shoes before entering). It is the tomb of the Sufi saint, Khwajah Muin-ud-din Chishti, who came to India in 1192, and later to Ajmer. Akbar aded one mosque (c.1570); Shah Jahan added another. Wealthy first-time pilgrims pay for a sumptuous feast to be cooked in the huge iron deghs (cauldrons) in the courtyard, eaten by them and afterwards gorged by the locals.

The festival, commemorating the saint's death, is six days of continuous music and fairs attended by Muslims from all over India and the Middle East: qawwalis are sung through the night, while dervishes elect their king. Rare opportunities to hear quality Urdu music that was born in the courts and shrines. Roses cover the tomb, washed on the final day by women rubbing rose water over it with their hair, then squeezing it out into bottles, to be taken as medicine by the sick. Out of festival time, there is singing most days.

PUSHKAR

11km north-west of Ajmer, over Nag Pahar (Snake Mountain); 149km from Jaipur. After the frenzied atmosphere of Ajmer, this is a total contrast. A quite extraordinary and magical quality of light hovers over the lake, bouncing off the surrounding ghats and temples. The music of bells, drums and worship from some of the thousands of tiny lakeside temples softly reverberates across the water. The faithful quietly perform their ablutions in the holy water, said to have sprung from a lotus blossom carelessly dropped by Brahma as he was contemplating where to perform a Vedic yagna (sacrifice); other versions are more complex (pushkar seems to be Sanskrit for both lotus and full to the brim). Certainly, the lake is second only to Mansarovar in the Himalayas in sanctity. From the hills above, the eye sees only desert. The deep fiery red sunsets are sensational.

This gentle village is peaceful and soothing for most of the year, but thrown into raucous and colourful confusion for the annual cattle and camel fair at Kartik Poornima (November-December full moon), amplified by equally colourful pilgrims who believe that to wash in the holy waters on these days is to be cleansed of sin. In both moods, it is worth visiting.

THE HARD FACTS Normally, go by car from Ajmer or Jaipur. To stay overlooking the lake, choose between *Sarovar Tourist Bungalow* and *Pushkar Hotel*, the two most comfortable and clean, or the simpler *Lake View Hotel*. Essential to book in writing. During Pushkar fair, stay in the tented village erected for tourists: double tents with shower and lavatory, communal dining tents, food included in tent price – 2 camps: stay in the RTDC one. Take woollen sweaters. Surprisingly, there is apparently no smell of camel. *Pushkar Fair* 10-day hubbub of colour, noise, commerce and faith as the desert tribes and camel caravans meet to trade cattle, camels, goats, sheep, cloth, shoes, jewellery and spices beside the sacred lake and to perform their rituals in its waters. 500,000 or so attend, with their 120,000 camels, horses and cattle. Tourists have increased, and so diluted a little of the raw tradition; but it is still worth going.

Best are the last five days. There are camel races to show off and encourage buyers – and gamblers. The Ladhu Unt (loading the camel) race has whole teams (up to 10 men) clambering on to each camel before a chaotic race. Camels for sale are groomed, then examined, prodded and probed before the long negotiations over price begin. There is splashing in the ghats, folk dancing, bazaars selling every kind of adornment for humans and camels (beautiful wool rugs), magicians and a circus.

Temple music wafts through the night, as the fires die down and the Rajasthani melodies played on the stringed ek-tara come to a close. On the night of the full moon, the pilgrims bathe by moonlight, then send marigold and rose petals floating across the lake on green plate-like leaves. It is worth getting up early to see the camels and tribes rousing themselves in the pink of the dawn desert light.

South-west of here, towards Jodhpur and Chitorgarh, *Beawar* is an oddity, a stone-walled town of ordered plan with wide avenues, founded by Colonel C. G. Dixon while he was Superintendent of Mewar, 1836-48; his tomb is worshipped by locals.

BUNDI

200km from Jaipur, via Deoli; 142km from Ajmer; 156km from Chitorgarh. In 1820, even 19th century palace know-all, Lieut.-Col. James Tod, who knew Rajasthan inside out, was vastly impressed by the romance and prettiness of Bundi. In 1983, India buff Shalini Saran wrote on approaching the city: 'I had known that Bundi would be beautiful, but I hadn't imagined anything quite as beautiful as what now lay before me'.

Rarely visited by tourists, this lively backwater town nestles in the narrow valley of Bandoo beneath its protective fort and within massive, castellated walls, looking just like one of the delicate miniature paintings produced at its court. Inside the walls, tiny shops like window ledges pierce the maze of narrow street walls at eye level. They sell traditional Rajput wares, such as green and brown afion (opium) pellets symmetrically arranged on a thali (platter). Spot the surviving sandstone gateways which divided the different mohallas (areas) and could be closed for protection. A sprawling pile of palaces growing out of the hillside at the top; their interior walls are covered in astonishing 18th century frescoes – the much-needed restoration is revealing even older paintings, pushing back the fresco tradition even further.

Backward Bundi reluctantly changed its method of marking time from a bowl of water and a gong to the new-fangled clock at the beginning of this century. And the modern palace, constructed to entertain British guests with British customs such as balls, and built in most other states at the turn of the century, was only begun in 1945, just two yars before the British left – and is still unfinished. As the thoroughly modern (ex-)Maharaja of Baroda writes: 'Bundi is deliciously behind the times.'

THE HARD FACTS It takes about six hours to drive to Bundi, but the route is pretty and the arrival breath-taking. Leave early, taking a picnic to enjoy on arrival at Bundi. Those coming from Jaipur pass the great hilltop forts near Chatsu and Nawai and can pause at *Tonk* to see the Sunehri Kothi (golden mansion). Those coming from Chitorgarh can picnic at *Menal*, where some 11th-century temples perch on the edge of a lush gorge with waterfall; and pause at *Bijolia* where, behind the fort, some more temples include the Undeshvara whose lingum shrine is surrounded by water; the fort-keen can seek out the Mandalgarh remains (with Chitorgarh and Kumbalgarh, the third great fort built by Rana Khumba).

Try to stay at the *Circuit House* (government officials take precedence over tourists); again, book in advance. Alternatively, stay in Kota (see below). Move about town in tongas.

OUT AND ABOUT Go up to the ruined Taragarh (Star) Fort, built 1372, for fine views. Visit the *palace* below, really a conglomeration of palaces built by successive rulers and named after them. Rao Chattar Sal (1631-59), a warrior hero and Governor of Delhi under Shah Jahan,

made the last addition, the Chattar Mahal. In keeping with Bundi's backwater tradition, it is all pure Rajput with few of the Mughal touches of order, proportion, arches and columns but plenty of romantic-looking drooping roofs, richly carved brackets supporting projecting balconies, and an abundance of lotus flower and elephant motifs.

In the mid-18th century, after a spot of territorial warring, Maharaja Umed Singh (1744-71) was a great art patron. It was he who had the splendid murals painted in the Chitra Shala, a cloister-like courtyard. They coat the walls and ceilings, depicting in the bold and fresh Bundi-school style: Krishna dancing with the cowgirls; enthroned rulers; tiger chikar in the local forests; ladies swinging at Teej festival; military triumphs; elephants giving a princess a shower; and much more. It is all enlivened with ducks, symbolising lovers, dabbling in lotus-filled lakes, and is painted in a cool palette of blue, cream and shades of green. See also the magnificent views, the very deep Sabirna-Dha-Ka-Kund (square, stepped water tank (reservoir)) built in 1654 to cope with the considerable changes in water level, and another well, the Nathawatji-Ki-Baoli, outside the east gate. The on-site chaukidar will need a tip.

Then hie off to explore out of town: to the new but traditional *Phool Sagar* (3km) with fine gardens and lake and interiors described as 'near-Deco', where the Durbar (the title by which the ex-ruler is still known) lives (permission from his Secretary, telephone number 1, of course) – it was here that Kipling wrote part of *Kim*; *Shikar Burj*, a royal hunting lodge; and the chhatri in the well-kept *Kohak Bagh* (gardens) nearby.

KOTA

38km south of Bundi. Not quite such a time-warp as Bundi. Kota is Rajasthan's fastest growing industrial city, with an Atomic Power Station, India's largest fertiliser plant, etc. The old part is not polluted, but full of glorious buildings, an even more grandly decorated palace and two museums, reflecting the time when in 1579 Rao Ratan Singh, ruler of Bundi, gave his son, Madho Singh, the tiny principality of Kota that blossomed into a powerful, cultured city.

THE HARD FACTS Kota is a short drive from Bundi, so it is possible to stay here in the 1930s riverside *Brij Raj Bhavan Palace* (tel: 3071). Not the swishest of palace hotels but air-cooled and full of atmosphere, with furnishings of royal photographs and shikar trophies. Comfortable, with good food. Guests are tended by aged family retainers who also look after the former royals living in another part of the palace. Tourist Office at Chambal Tourist Bungalow (tel: 6527), should be able to help with unlocking the city palaces.

OUT AND ABOUT The excellent Maharao Madho Singh Museum is housed in the equally brilliant and very Rajput *palace*, entered through a Hathi Pol (Elephant Gate), flanked by a mural of a wedding procession. There are armour, textiles, miniatures dating from the height of the Kota school of painting (18th-19th centuries) and sculptures – and the rich and busy decoration that covers every surface of the palace rooms. See especially the 18th century decoration in the Durbar Hall, including lamp niches; a chequerboard of Kota miniature portraits of equestrian, enthroned and standing nobles, the doors inlaid with precision mirrorwork and black and white inlay using ebony, ivory and elephants' teeth. Also in the palace is the Government Museum of coins, manuscripts and sculptures rescued from Baroli. (Open all Sat.-Thurs., 11am-5pm).

Apart from the palace, have a look at the Umed Bhavan, designed for Umed Singh II by Samuel Swinton Jacob (see Jaipur Central Museum) and soon to be another hotel; see the royal chhatri outside the northern city walls; take a stroll in Chambal Gardens; go boating here or on Kishor Sagar.

Outside the city, visit *Badoli* (16km), a deserted city with crumbling fort and fine remains of three of the many 10th century, Pratihara period carved temples that formed one of the earliest temple complexes in Rajasthan (see especially the great mandapa pavilion standing alone); and, an oddity, Tod's Bridge (8km), built by the infamous Colonel Tod.

CHITORGARH (CHITTOR)

156km from Bundi; 115km from Udaipur; 187km from Ajmer. One of the most stunning forts in Rajasthan, former capital of Mewar. It has everything a Rajput fort should have: legend, historical drama, courage, romance and desolation. The legend is that the fort was built on the precipice by Bhim, one of the Pandava hero brothers in the great epic, the Mahabharata. The historical fact, here almost better than legend, is that the capital of the Sisodias, the number one family in the Rajput hierarchy of 36, was sacked three times, and three times the warriors donned saffron robes and rode into battle to die while their wives performed mass suicide by fire, known as johar, to preserve themselves from the conquerors.

In the second sack, in 1533-5, 32,000 warriors and 13,000 of their women died. There is romance in that the first sack, in 1303, was by Ala-ud-din, the Kilji Sultan of Delhi, to win the beautiful Padmini who, when defeat was imminent, followed her women on to the burning pyre, dressed up in their wedding finery and singing merrily.

After the third sack, by Akbar in 1568, 8,000 warriors rode out to their death. Maharana Udai Singh, forgoing Rajput tradition, fled to Udaipur where he established his capital, never to return to Chitorgarh. Meanwhile, Akbar uncharacteristically killed thousands of inhabitants, leaving it a ghost city.

THE HARD FACTS Excellent mid-way stop between Bundi or Kota and Udaipur, or a day trip from either, taking a picnic. If necessary, stay overnight at the *Panna Tourist Bungalow* (tel: 273), modern, modest and clean. (Their restaurant is OK for lunch.) Tourist Information at Janta Tourist Rest House, by the railway station (tel: 9); runs 3-hour conducted tours, starting at 7.30am and 2.30pm. Archaeological Survey of India Office in the Fort (tel: 14), opposite Rana Kumbha's palace, supplies approved guides (can be good) and, sometimes, publications. Move around by tonga.

OUT AND ABOUT The romantic remains of temples, palaces and towers date from the 7th to 15th centuries and are scattered through the walled city of 5 sq km, jutting up 180m above the surrounding plain. See the seven pols (gates); the rambling palace ruins of Rana Kumbha, 15th-century enlightened ruler who built 32 fortresses to further defend his kingdom (the women are said to have performed johar in a vault here); the palace of the heirs apparent, opposite (together with museum and Archaeological Survey office); the Jain and Hindu temples; the Jaya Stambha (Tower of Victory) to the south, an architectural feat and probably a religious building but traditionally believed to have been built to commemorate Kumbha's victory over the Sultan of Malwa in 1440 (you can climb to the top); and the smaller Kirti Stambha (Pillar of Fame). Then there are other palaces: Patta of Kelwa's delicate balconies; Padmini's palace and water pavilion; Ratna Singh's palace (with lake, good for a picnic) – every building drenched in Rajput romance.

UDAIPUR

115km from Chitorgarh; 264km from Ajmer; 275km from Jodhpur; 185km from Mount Abu; 262km from Ahmedabad (for launching into Gujarat, see Bombay chapter). As romantic as Chitorgarh but this time very much alive: a thriving provincial city with bustling bazaars, fountains playing in princesses' gardens, royalty – albeit officially former royalty – living in part of the City Palace, two excellent museums and a centrepiece lake suffusing all in an exquisite light. There is even an island dream palace to stay in. A warm, friendly atmosphere pervades all and, despite a number of tourists, it is far less commercially aggressive than Jaipur. Udaipur has pedigree splendour too. When Udai Singh made this his Mewar capital in 1567, he brought with him the honour and pride of the top Rajput family clan, the Sisodias, descended directly from the sun via the god Rama (see Chitorgarh, above). His oasis town of lakes and streams set in the Girwa Valley of the Aravalli mountains had a good water supply and excellent natural defences. On the advice of a sage, Udai Singh built a temple above Lake Pichola, then his palace around it.

Successive rulers added more rooms to make it the biggest of all Rajasthan palaces, yet it is harmonious in its overall Rajput character, with jharokahs (projecting balconies), inlaid walls and coloured glass windows. Above it all rises the gold kalash (pinnacle), the privilege of only the gods or independent kingdoms.

There is a story that superior pride led one heir apparent, Maharana Pratap, to display the height of chivalrous one-upmanship. Disapproving of the Amber subservience to conqueror Akbar through a marriage alliance, he invited Raja Man Singh of Amber to a picnic beside Udai Sagar Lake, then left his son to play host. Afterwards he had the ground Man Singh had trod on washed with Ganga water and insisted that his generals take purification baths, for which insult Man Singh (himself a general under Akbar) reaped appropriate revenge at the Battle of Haldighat (1576) and Pratap lost Udaipur to Mughal occupation for a decade.

A later ruler, Amar Singh, bowed to Jahangir's Mughal might in 1614. But intrigue continued and Maharana Karan Singh gave refuge to Jahangir's rebellious son on Jagmandir Island in Pichola Lake where he proclaimed himself emperor when his father died. Royal chivalry raised its head again when Aurangzeb threatened to marry the neighbouring Princess of Roopnagar: the Mewar hero, Raj Singh, swooped down to marry her, and then had to face the emperor's fury and his revival of the jizya (tax on all non-Muslims) which led, of course, to war. In 1818, like so many other Rajasthan states, Mewar came under British paramountcy but managed to avoid almost all British cultural influence.

THE HARD FACTS Arrive by air (airport about 25km out of town, so share taxi), train (for instance, Chitorgarh-Udaipur trains leaving at 5.50am arrive 9.10am and at 3.40pm arrive 8.30pm), or car. As this is one of the most relaxing and atmospheric places in Rajasthan, here are three royal palaces to stay in, of varying grandeur, plus some simpler but charming ones.

Lake Palace Hotel, Pichola Lake (tel: 23241-5; telex: 203 LPAL IN); a dazzling, white marble fantasy island in the deep azure Pichola Lake, built about 1740 (some earlier and later bits) as a summer palace for the Maharana to frolic with his ladies, with guardian crocodiles in the lake; still used for royal coolness up until Independence. Wall-paintings of dancing girls and hunting scenes and crystal and silk furnishings typical of Indian royal taste decorate rooms surrounding courtyards of lotus pools and terraces (now suitable for stunning sunset cocktails). Built for pleasure; now run as a pleasure hotel since 1962. Under the auspices of the Taj Group since 1971. Coloured glass and mirrorwork now beautifully restored. Known as 'the James Bond hotel' after location shooting for the 007 movie, 'Octopussy'. Reach it by tiny, bobbing, rowing boat.

85 rooms, including 10 suites. All mod. cons plus marble swimming pool, painted and inlaid bar, boating. The suites have the murals: most other rooms have lake views; otherwise, explore the many terraces at various levels. Sports are swimming, boating and watching sunsets; pigeons are now kept under control; atmospheric bar. The disadvantages: the food is improved but still dreary, use the coffee shop in preference to the restaurant, or snack round the lily pools.

Shiv Niwas (tel: 28239, 28240; fax: 23823); Josceline Dimbleby found it 'swish beyond anything', 'terribly grand', with 'the best views of any hotel anywhere'. But reports are mixed. Here guests stay in the royal guest house of the top-notch Udaipurs, the east end of the vast and rambling city palace overlooking Pichola Lake. Built by Maharana Fateh Singh, with carved pillars, mosaics, ponds, delicate wall-paintings, carved balconies and lavish space, it has been given a dusting and furnished with Udaipur surplus treasures. The result is royal opulence with modern additions and facilities.

31 suites; all mod. cons, large central courtyard with marble-lined swimming pool, circular turret bar, stunning banquet lounge and crystal room (only for looking), food can be good. Excellent for peace, poolside relaxation and proximity to the town; bad for lake views (unless you have one of the special suites).

If those do not match your wishes or your purse, try the Laxmi Vilas Palace Hotel (tel: 244112/3; telex: 033-218). Rather stern building, with unexciting 1960s-style interiors and food but good lake view over Lake Fateh Sagar, and swimming pool; mixed reports of standards. Then there are the modest but charming hotels. The Rang Niwas Hotel (tel: 23891), 20 rooms, is a guest house built around a courtyard garden, on Lake Palace Road underneath the City Palace, run by K. Arjun Singh and his son, Vikaimaditya Singh, who grow their own vegetables and serve the best food in Udaipur (restaurant open to visitors). For real peace, spend a few days out at Lalit Bagh, Naharmangra, their country farm, not far from the airport. Disadvantage: no lake view. Two hotels centre town: *Hotel Jagat Niwas*, 25 Lal Ghat (tel: 23128), 18 rooms, right on the lake, simple, relaxed, roof terraces; and *Hotel Sai-Niwas*, 75 Navghat (tel: 24909), 7 rooms, behind Jagat Niwas, newly built in the traditional style, with murals by the owner, S. K. Singh, lake views, good local food. As an extra, the old *Badi Haveli* is much more modest but is clean and has a 360 degree city view from the rooftop. One hotel across the bridge and outside Chandpole, facing the main ghat: *Lake Pichola Hotel* (tel: 29197), simple, clean large rooms overlook the lake. And finally the option of staying outside town at *Shikarbadi* (tel: 83200/4), 25 rooms, the Maharaja's 1930s hunting lodge, with stuffed tigers and pretty garden, view over a little lake, nearby scrub for walks to spot nilgai, spotted deer, wild boar and birds.

The Tourist Office at the railway station (tel: 3605) supplies guides. RTDC (tel: 3509) run excellent five-hour morning tours of scattered monuments, gardens and museums, recommended; and afternoon tours to Nathdwara, Eklingi and Haldighat. For travel agents, seek out the local office of those listed on p. 105.

OUT AND ABOUT There is plenty of the City Palace left after the former royals and the paying would-be royals have taken their chunks. It houses the museum and, like other palaces, is itself a museum, every wall and ceiling decorated (some by Hindu craftsmen who had worked under Shah Jahan but were booted out by bigoted Aurangzeb). Visitors enter through the Tripolia Gate (1725). Inside, do not miss the original shrine around which the fort was built, the great painting of the Battle of Haldighat, the exceptional Indian miniatures, the 3-D peacock mosaics in Mor Chowk, the view out over *Pichola lake*, the great marble bathtub for ceremonial royal bathing, and the dazzling royal breakfast room. Pure Hindu throughout; not a concession to Mughal influence. Open daily, 9.30am-4.30pm. A separate museum stocks armour, open daily, 9.30am-4.30pm.

The lakes and gardens are the joy of Udaipur. Join the daily sunset boat ride to go around *Pichola Lake*, enlarged by Maharana Udai Singh, past the merchants' havelis, women singing and washing on the ghats, temples, a royal hunting lodge, the exquisitely beautiful and romantic Gul Mahal pavilion (1621-28) on Jagmandir Island whose stone elephants greet visitors, ending with a nimbu soda or cocktail at the Lake Palace which forms Jagniwas Island.

The lakes to the north are also lovely: see them all from the Pratap Memorial on high Moti Magri (Pearl Hill), open daily 9am-6pm. It is sometimes possible to go boating on Lake Fateh Sagar (dug out by Fateh Singh), stopping off at Nehru Island, a garden with restaurant; the lake edge is dotted with parks. Udaipur's lush gardens are, for Rajasthan, exceptional. At Saheliyon ki Bari, Garden of the Maids of Honour (in fact, a clutch of Delhi damsels sent by the emperor as a peace offering), the boys used to be turfed out after they reached eight years of age. Fountains play over the lotus pools, marble kiosks and life-size marble elephants – one of the few gardens in India where the water, so essential to the total effect, is switched on; open daily, 9am-6pm. The views from Sajjan Garh (Monsoon Palace) over the whole city are sensational, especially at sunset; Gulab Bagh (Rose Garden), Sajjan Niwas Gardens, has tropical and sub-tropical trees and plants (some labelled) and is considered the best herbarium of Northern India, plus good birds, nicest early morning.

RAJASTHAN FOLK ARTS Anyone interested in Rajasthan folk arts, crafts and traditions should visit the exemplary *Bhartiya Lok Kala Mandal*, a museum housing puppets, masks, costumes, instruments, kavads (mobile temples), Pabuji Ki Phads (scroll-painting ballads) and much more, with daily shows using the treasures, and workshops around the back where craftsmen carve and rasp puppet heads, paint kavads or tailor clothes for puppets. Good publications. Open daily, 9am-6pm. Another, newer organisation is the *West Zone Cultural Centre*, one of seven centres set up in 1985-6 to 'present to the people an aspect of the richness and diversity of our cultural heritage'. Udaipur's is by the main ghat, in a large haveli where there is a little museum, gallery and sometimes theatre and dance in the courtyard; open 10am-5pm, contact Vilas Janve, Programme Officer (tel: 23305/23858); the centre's specially created village of rural craftsmen, *Shilpgram* (3km), near Havala, is well worth visiting, open daily, 10am-sunset (major winter festival). Finally, the *Meera Kala Mandir*, near Paras Cinema, stages dances every Tuesday, Thursday and Saturday at 7pm.

RESTAURANTS Not many, in keeping with Udaipur's provincial atmosphere. Best food in town is at *Rang Niwas Hotel* (see above), try the local makki (maize), bajri (millet) or misi (gram, barley and wheat) roti with seasonal sabsi (vegetables). The *Roof Garden Café*, above some shops on Lake Palace Road, is also good, open all day. Others in town, at Chetak Circle: *Park View*, *Berry's* and *Kwality*. *Lovers' Paradise* Restaurant does a good dosa special; the *Heritage*, Hospital Road, has good vegetarian; and

Sunrise Bakery makes chilli puffs 'out of this world'. Go to *Lake Palace* for courtyard tea and terrace/bar cocktails – moonlit boat rides back to and from the Lake Palace are heavenly.

SHOPPING AND CRAFTS Three good areas: Bapu Bazar (from Suraj Pol to Delhi Gate), City Palace Road and Jagdish Road (the two roads run from the City Palace down to Hathi Pol and then to Chetak Circle), and the more touristy but good shops on Lake Palace Road. All worth exploring to find silversmiths (old and new stock), the odd surviving toy-maker (sets of military bands, birds, animals), puppet-makers, sweetmeats bubbling in iron cauldrons, bookshops, pawn shops, old coins, wood carving, musicians, khari printing (have a dress decorated on the spot, see p. 109), bandhani prints, meenakari and brasswork, and plain woollen shawls for slashes of vivid colour; and you may well spot a wall-painter on the way. There are also dark images of Sri Nathji and pichwais (cloth paintings, usually bad quality), both from nearby Nathdwara (see below). At Suraj Pol, find Chawla Achaar Centre (near National Medical Agencies), a stall-like shop selling the best pickles in Rajasthan – an outpost of the family's headquarters in Jodhpur, and Krishna Beej Bhandar (near Bansal Medicals, the chemist) who stocks all kinds of exotic vegetable seeds; at Delhi Gate, Jyoti Stores stocks Ayurvedic medicines; good fabric and clothes shops in Bapu Bazar include the Lucky Cloth store patronised by some of Udaipur's smartest ladies. For crafts, try Chelawat Art Gallery on Jagdish Road, and Shreenath Emporium and Ganesh Handicraft Emporium, both on City Palace Road; the excellent Rajasthali is at Chetak Circle (stocks the incongruous floating stone ducks from Dungapur).

OUT OF TOWN Visit *Shikarbadi* in the hills, a turn-of-the-century hunting lodge; fun to stay overnight (see above) and to ride. For sunset peace, go to *Ahar* (3km) where the Mewar chhatris stand amid a ruined city. For nearby temples, *Nagada* (25km) has the important 10th century Sasbahu temples and the *Eklingi* temples, always thronged with pilgrims, house the guardian deity of the Mewar rulers. North of here on Highway No.8 lies *Rajsamand Lake*, with Maharana Raj Singh's pretty marble pavilions; and north again (some three hours driving from Udaipur), by Deogarh Midway Restaurant, is *Deogarh*, where paintings of this important miniature school coat the walls of the fort (seek out the chaukidar to open up). Southwards, for a beautiful picnic go to *Jaisamand Lake* (48km), built by Maharana Jai Singh in the 17th century (and still the second largest artificial lake in Asia), surrounded by chhatris guarded by mar-

ble elephants, with summer palaces for Udaipur queens on either side. On the way, near Kuraba, lies *Jagat*, where temple addicts can find a 9th-century Pratihara temple with plenty of elaborate carving. (To continue to Jaisamand Lake on foot or horse, make plans with a travel agent such as Travel Plan before setting out.) At *Dungapur* (another 50km, south-west of Salumba) are two stunningly decorative and lavishly decorated palaces, perfectly preserved (private, but try writing in advance).

NATHDWARA

48km from Udaipur, via temples at Nagada and Eklingi (22km), the battle site of Pratap versus Akbar (1576, Pratap won) at Haldighati (40km). A black stone image of Vishnu, called Sri Nathji, was brought here from Mathura in 1669. It is kept in the temple of Sri Nathji and is an object of pilgrimage for many Hindus. Although non-Hindus are forbidden entry, the bazaar around the temple is interesting.

See pichwais (cloth paintings hung in front of the Sri Nathji image when he is sleeping or being washed) being made, images of Sri Nathji, and the extraordinary temple sweets: about 20 varieties of sweeter-than-sweet prasaad made in the temple, blessed, sold to pilgrims who take them home to those who could not go on the pilgrimage – so delicious that Indians have them sent to far-flung addresses. Rajsamand Lake lies beyond (18km) (see above).

RANAKPUR, KUMBALGARH AND GHANERAO

A visit to some or, better still, all of these makes a fascinating trip out of Udaipur or a good Udaipur-Jodhpur stop-over. Ranakpur is 98km from Udaipur; 197km from Mount Abu; 160km from Jodhpur. An exceptionally beautiful drive through mountain, desert, villages and farmland to a cluster of Jain temples at one of the five most sacred Jain sites (see Mount Abu, below). Probably the most beautiful of all Jain temples, these lie in a remote valley surrounded by the wooded Aravalli hills instead of hilltop Palitana, Girnar and Abu.

The central, enormous temple, built in 1439 and dedicated to Tirthankara (Jain saint) Rishabdeo, contains a three-storey chaumukha (four-faced shrine) dedicated to Adinath, 29 halls supported by 1,444 pillars, a riot of carving on every surface, the whole capped with quantities of domes and spires; open daily, noon-5pm. To eat, try a delicious Jain thali at the *dharamsala* (possible to stay, too), or have a picnic in the surrounding hills or at *Maharani Bagh Orchard Retreat*, just nearby; they serve drinks and, if the countryside seduces, there are rooms to stay in and good vegetarian food to eat.

For a real marathon day, go on through very rural villages to the impressive 15th-century

Kumbalgarh Fort (rated second after Chitorgarh by Rajputs) and hike up the citadel and round the walls and return on the Rajsamand Lake and Nathdwara road. But Kumbalgar deserves more. Stay over at Mr Mohindra Singh's Aoudhi Resort outside the walls (a dozen little cottages, hot water, clean, book in writing) to explore with him on horseback the wild surrounding countryside soon to be a panther national park. Even more wonderful is Ghanerao Fort north of here, an unchanged 17th century fort-turned-hotel run by Mr Singh's brother, Thakur Sajjan Singh and his graceful wife; very simple, set in an atmospheric town of traditional craftsmen (shoe-making, spinning, etc.) – as one London globe-trotter revealed, 'if my job went tomorrow, I'd go and live there for six months'; book in writing; riding, Land Rover trips to sanctuary with Forest Lodge good for spotting game; take a bearer to do the great walk, three hours with a steep climb, to the view 'so ravishing that it was well worth it', according to Bruce Palling, who found Ghanerao 'sublimely romantic'.

MOUNT ABU
185km from Udaipur; 197km from Ranakpur; 222km from Ahmedabad; 264km from Jodhpur. The only escape from the dusty, desert heat of Rajasthan and eastern Gujarat. Here, on a large, 1200m-high plateau, are lungfulls of fresh air, a feast of green trees, viewpoints by the dozen and lakes and lush gardens.

Very fashionable with Indian honeymoon couples who take rolls of photographs of each other and dutifully go to the Honeymoon Point at sunset 'to watch', as Josceline Dimbleby's family did, 'the sun dropping down into the earth miles away across the huge flat valley'. Important to Hindus because Nakki Lake was dug by the gods, using only their nakks (nails); because the serpent Arbunda, son of the Himalayas, rescued Shiva's bull, Nandi, from a chasm here – hence Abu. Important to Rajput Hindus because the sage Vasishta lived here, from whose fire Brahmin priests performed Yajna and created a race of warriors, the four primary Rajput clans. But it is most important to Jains for its group of temples, of which Vimal Vasahi (1031) and Tejpal (1230) display some of the finest architecture and carving of all Jain art.

THE HARD FACTS Season March-June (after that, rain) and September-November (after that, cold). Stay at one of the small hotels, run like provincial English guest houses, with English gardens and smiling welcomes for guests and their dogs, all rooms with bath. *Palace Hotel* (Bikaner House), Delwara Road (tel: 2123), 28 rooms, each huge and softly decaying; the Scottish baronial building was built as the British embassy's cool escape, became the holiday home of the Bikaner ruler, and now serves boarding-school food, has a wonderful overgrown garden and is full of atmosphere. Also try *Mount Hotel*, Dilwara Road (tel: 55) 7 rooms; or *Hotel Hilltone* (tel: 137/237; cable: HILLTONE), 44 rooms.

Tourist Office (tel: 51), opposite bus stand, can supply approved guides. The RTDC runs identical five-hour morning and afternoon tours, bookable at the Youth Hostel. Sightsee by car or on foot. Mount Hotel's food is about the best; otherwise stick to Gujarati fare of vegetarian thalis and delicious ice-cream found at a string of modest but very clean restaurants on the road to Nakki Lake.

OUT AND ABOUT Head out of town up to the five Dilwara *Jain Temples* (5km). See especially Vimal Vasahi and Tejpal temples, both built by ministers to Gujarat rulers, the first dedicated to Adinath (first Tirthankara) and built of Makrana marble, entered through 48 carved pillars, past a procession of carved elephants, to a courtyard of 52 cells, the central shrine and an octagonal dome, all richly carved; the second dedicated to Neminath (22nd Tirthankara), every facet of the marble carved with delicate, lace-like figures and patterns. Do not miss the huge, almost transparent lotus suspended from the dome.

For views, go to *Guru Shikhar* (15km), at the end of the plateau and, at 1,725km, the highest point in Rajasthan; to the *Durga Temple* (3km), up 200 steep steps; *Achalgarh* (11km) to see a Shiva temple; and, nearer town, Robert's Spur and, of course, Honeymoon Point (at sunset and sunrise) and Sunset Point. In town, there are Nakki Lake (like an Indian Brighton, with peddaloes on the lake), the public gardens and small museum on Raj Bhavan Road (open Sat.-Thurs., 10am-5pm). Apart from that, go for hillside strolls and relax.

From here, there is a good rural trip south into Gujarat, via fine Solanki Hindu and Jain temples (see p. 163 and 167).

Western Rajasthan

JODHPUR
275km from Udaipur; 264km from Mount Abu; 300km from Jaipur; 290km from Jaisalmer; 240km from Bikaner. Lying on the edge of the Thar Desert – although locals will say firmly it does not start for another 100km – the flat, sandy, colourful, slow-paced city is dominated by two massively huge palaces, totally out of proportion, one a city-fort stronghold built on a high natural bluff, the other, one of the finest large buildings of the 1930s, erected by a remarkably unimaginative ruler as his solution to unemployment during famine. Jodhpur does

not seem very grand now, but it certainly was. As capital of Marwar, on both the trading routes and the strategic Delhi-Gujarat route, the Marwaris reaped fortunes from the passing camel caravans and their loads of copper, dates, silks, sandalwood, dyes, opium, spices, coffee and much more. These were the trading Marwaris who later moved east to Shekhavati (see above) and who now dominate Indian commerce.

Jodhpur was founded in 1459 by Rao Jodha, although the 35,000 square mile territory was won by the Rathores back in 1211. Jodha was chief of the Rathore Rajput clan, firmly descended from the sun god, Surya, and the most powerful prince in Rajasthan.

The rock must have been an irresistible site, although the sati buffs testify to the usual Rajput female valour at moments of defeat. By the time Akbar was suing for peace with the Rajput clans, Rao Udai Singh (died 1581) was able to win wealth by helping him begin to add Gujarat to his conquests. (His son completed the job and moved on to tackle the Deccan.) He then gained influence at court in 1580 by marrying first his sister to the emperor, then his daughter to Akbar's son. Finally Akbar pronounced him King of the Desert.

Maharaja Jaswant Singh (died 1678) led Shah Jahan's armies and, unfortunately, Dara Sikoh's against Aurangzeb, the winner. Hot on the heels of defeat came disaster, murder and patricide, leading to endless internal feuds. It was not until the strong personality of progressive Pratap Singh emerged in the 1870s that Jodhpur regained credibility. A younger royal son but three times regent, he was a fanatical royalist (he went to London to meet Queen Victoria in 1885), a fervent huntsman (fought hand to hand with jungle boars), had impeccable manners and tried to toughen up the royal heirs by making them wrestle with muzzled leopards.

Maharaja Umaid Singh (died 1947) had a topsy-turvy understanding of Pratap's progressiveness. When in 1929 the monsoon failed for the third year, famine struck and Jodhpur was living up to its name of Land of Death, he buried his head in the plentiful sand and served his people by employing 3,000 of them each day to build him a vast palace to the latest designs and with all mod. cons, completed in 1945, on the eve of Independence. Today's former ruler has turned it, contents and all, into another of Rajasthan's fantasy hotels.

THE HARD FACTS This is desert country, so expect much dry dustiness and heat after midMarch. The hot Thar Desert, divided between the Jodhpur, Bikaner and Jaisalmer Rajputs (with a tract in Pakistan, too) is known by a contraction of marust'hali, meaning abode of death. It is no joke forgetting to take a water

bottle or some cold drinks on trips out into the villages. Jodhpur's airport is just 4km from the city; excellent time-saving overnight trains connect with Delhi, Ahmedabad and Jaisalmer, Choose between two princely homes: the vast and wondrous Umaid Bhawan and the relaxed, friendly home of royal cousins – each offers something entirely different and there is a good case for staying two nights at each. Each is a fundamental part of Jodhpur and each gives a completely different aspect of the city.

Umaid Bhawan Palace (tel: 22316; telex: 0552 202 UBP IN) exemplary use of a palace as a hotel, total period feeling maintained by careful restoration where necessary, such as re-upholstering sofas with the correct fabric. Run by the Welcomgroup. Looks over the town from Chittar Hill, a site dictated by the astrologers but as ridiculous as the whole project. It lacked any water supply and, even today, the deep wells mean that the alkaline water sometimes tastes very odd. A 12-mile railway had to be built to carry the sandstone from the quarry at Sursagar. An estimated half a million donkey loads of earth had to be carried up for the foundations alone. And rock had to be blasted so that trees could take root. The sandstone was cut and interlocked, without using mortar.

Goodness knows what the starving labourers thought of the finished project in 1945, when the family moved in. The 195 × 103 metre rose sandstone palace was designed by British architect H. V. Lanchester, president of the Royal Institute of British Architects, its massiveness bearing the mark of his Delhi work under Lutyens and his experience in town hall architecture. His other India work included planning in Lucknow, Madras and Calcutta.

The design was symmetrical, in the beauxarts tradition, each section with its own courtyard for privacy. Modernity had to compromise with strict purdah, so the pillared corridors were hung with bamboo curtains to allow the women to move around the palace.

The interior was also high European 1930s tempered with local Indian traditions and a royal taste for gilt. Massive brass front doors, good enough to rival contemporary ones in New York or Paris, led to courtyards and 347 rooms which included eight dining rooms and a banquet hall to seat 300. Carved big cats raced up the sweeping marble staircase to suites for Their Highnesses and visiting princes. The furniture was fated. The ship bringing the first set from England sank. A second order was placed but the factory was bombed. Finally some imitation European furniture was made locally and mixed with what had been obtained elsewhere.

Then there were all the latest toys for the progressive prince. The double dome (the outer skin 24m above the inner) of the huge central courtyard uses reinforced concrete. Inside the dome is a whispering gallery. Below it lies a marble floor and gilt furniture. 40m below the courtyard is the magnificent swimming pool, the walls painted with fish and a continuous seabed for an underwater rather than underground feeling. Air-conditioning throughout is part of the original plan. There is a billiard room and a cinema/theatre. During the Second World War, vast Christmas balls were given for all the troops, when dancers overflowed from the ballroom into the gardens. The Maharaja gave each guest an embossed pewter mug one year, a leather wallet another.

The palace is now divided into three: the hotel takes the lion's share; the present ex-Maharaja Gaj Singh II has a part; and the main halls are a museum well worth visiting. The museum includes the fine Durbar Hall with 1940s murals by a palace-hopping Polish painter who forgot to seal his plaster, so that it peels. There are good miniature paintings (a fraction of the huge collection – ask to see more) and armour, and a fine clock collection (clock catalogue recently published). Open daily, 9am-5pm.

The hotel part has 78 very spacious rooms, including 6 suites of up to 7 rooms apiece, fully decorated with original furnishings and furniture, giving an entirely period feeling. Facilities include all the mod. cons noted above plus travel counter (including booking the Jodhpur royal carriage to Jaisalmer), car rental, doctor on call, badminton, squash and tennis courts; golf on request. Peacocks screech in the gardens. Worth taking a suite as it is relatively cheap and enormous fun, with high 1930s lighting and decor. The suite Peter O'Toole stayed in while filming 'Kim' is designed like a ship. The two enormous royal suites have fine views, beds big enough for a zenana, glorious art deco mirrors, paintings, bathtubs and a tinkling Belgian crystal fountain in their courtyard. The Gaj Singh suite has a completely subsidiary bathroom suite (with a choice of squat or sitting lavatory).

Service slowish, especially room service; it must be half a mile to the kitchens (worth ordering breakfast the previous evening). Food can be very good, especially the delicious western Rajasthani dishes, so talk to the chef. Moonlit courtyard barbecues are a romantic delight. Local bhopas and their families sing and make merry music every evening. Try to take tea, thick milkshakes or cocktails on the verandah gazing at the stunning sunsets. For sightseeing, consult with Baiji, the knowledgeable public relations lady whose grandfather was Pratap Singh and who knows everything about Jodhpur.

The disadvantages: it could simply be too huge and impersonal for some. Forty years on, some would prefer new light fittings and curtains; others want comforts like new mattresses. For others, it is a pure period piece and should not be missed.

Ajit Bhawan, near Circuit House (tel: 20409). Delightful family house built for Umaid Singh's younger brother, Maharaja Ajit Singh, crammed with furniture, hunting trophies, family mementoes and warm atmosphere. About 50% of the palace rates. Run in the guesthouse tradition by two of Ajit's descendants, Maharaj Sobhag Singh and Maharaj Swaroop Singh, who are dedicated to giving visitors a chance to see something other than forts, palaces and bazaars. They host their guests as if they were private friends, giving them homemade chilli chutney, fussing over them if they do not eat breakfast, advising them with care on their sight-seeing and even taking them out into the surrounding villages themselves – a great treat.

50 rooms scattered around the house, all double with bath and air-cooling; some around the central courtyard, others in charming, purpose-built cottages in the gardens (might be too small for big or tall people). Each cottage is a room and bathroom, designed like a traditional villager's home, the furniture and fabrics made locally to complement the old family pieces (note: quite small for two big people). Room price includes food, good home cooking, usually local Rajasthani dishes cooked in degchies (big pots) in the courtyard or pretty garden. Golf, squash and camel riding by arrangement. The owners play golf, using a mat to tee off because of the sandiness. The disadvantages: Ajit's could be a little claustrophobic and lack privacy.

Apart from these two, *Hotel Karni Bhawan*, Defence Lab Rod (tel: 32220), 15 rooms, is a new, sandstone, family-run hotel, run by Thakur Sunder Singh and considered by India connoisseur Brendan Lynch 'charming, with excellent Rajasthan vegetarian food served in thatched huts in the garden'. (Mr Singh's son-in-law runs Pokaran Fort, on the Jodhpur-Jaisalmer road, see below.)

Tourist Office at the Tourist Bungalow, High Court Road (tel: 21900), open daily, 9am-7pm; Information Centre, Government of Rajasthan, High Court Road (tel: 20493), neither very good. Better to use the in-house knowledge of Umaid and Ajit's. Universal Book Depot, at Jalori Gate, is good. The charmingly written and useful *Jodhpur, a traveller's guide*, is available from the bookshop and the shops inside the fort gateways. Move around by tonga and bicycle rickshaw but take a taxi up to the fort. To find out more about the rich music and dance traditions, contact Rajasthan Sangeet Natak Academy, B-Road, Paota Area, open Mon.-Sat.,

10am-5pm. Asha Medical Hall, Sojati Gate, is a good chemist.

OUT AND ABOUT **Meherangarh** (Majestic) **Fort** is magnificent. It is really a fort city inside a 10km wall. Local musicians serenade visitors' arrival up the winding road. The handprints made by devoted and proud women before committing sati mark the wall beside Lohapol (Iron) Gate. Well worth the surprising Rs10 entrance fee. 18 sections, guided by charming old retainers with impeccable English and memories. The maharajas' paraphernalia is laid out by subject: howdahs, including a huge glass one to be carried by 12 men, booty from Gujarat defeat; cradles including the present maharaja's, with a portrait of his father on top – early training in respect; festive tents; very fine miniature paintings, especially Jodhpur rulers such as Bakhat Singh, who built the fort; exceptional armour; Durbar Hall; temple; dazzling white inner courtyard for Holi celebrations; painted playroom with swing, coloured balls hanging from the ceiling, pachesi boards; and everywhere the most delicate jali work (pierced screens), each with a different pattern. From the ramparts you can see the city beneath the sheer drop, with blue-painted houses belonging to Brahmins and the gurgling of life, music and shouting wafting up. The musicians strike up again as visitors leave, earning their baksheesh. Open daily, 9am-5pm. Of the shops, Sunderam Art Emporium is definitely OK, see below; and the owner can help find the INTAC (Indian National Trust) pamphlet which is a guided walk round the old town hugging the fort walls, starting from the painted building at the U-bend above his shop. The blinding white Jaswant Thada cenotaph, built 1899, is on the route down to the town.

If staying at Ajit Bhawan, it is worth visiting the Umaid Bhawan palace museum and having a swim (very welcome amid the sand), a verandah drink and the courtyard barbecue, if it is on that night. If staying at the Umaid Bhawan, it is a good idea to telephone the Ajit Bhawan to arrange to go on the jeep trip for the day, ending with dinner at Ajit's, if they are not too full with guests. Jodhpur really is a two-horse or, rather, two-camel town.

RESTAURANTS AND FOOD   In addition to the three hotels, try *Kalinga*, near the railway station, and the vegetarian *Pankaj* at Jalori Gate. West Rajasthani cooking uses the locally grown millet, so dishes are quite heavy. Sogra is a thick, millet chapati served with plenty of ghi (clarified butter). Sohita is mutton cooked with millet. Sulla is another mutton dish, the pieces marinated then cooked on skewers over charcoal. Khud khar (rabbit) gosh is whole rabbit

cooked very slowly. Krer kumidai saliria is three desert beans cooked with cumin, chillies and other spices.

Local food to buy in the markets includes mirchibada, a large chilli whose centre is scooped out and mixed with potato and spices, then put back and deep fried, eaten with the very necessary cooling dahi (curd) and known locally as dynamite. Local sweetmeat specialities include mawaki-kachori, an immobilising meal of pastry stuffed with a mixture of nuts and coconut, with a syrup poured through the hole at the top when it is bought. It is best found at *Misthra Bhander*, an old establishment quite near the clock tower in Sardar bazar. And do not fail to drink SPL (=special) Makania Lassi at *Sri Mishri Lal Hotel* at the main Sardar bazar gateway, the thickest, richest, creamiest in India – the spoon stands up in it. And, if asked, they will grind up bhang (local hashish) and stir that in, too, turning the lassi green.

SHOPPING AND CRAFTS   Jodhpur is rich in both. There are nice wooden boxes, speckled ones made at Jaisalmer, plain ones here, circular for cosmetics, small for opium, rectangular for money and jewels. And there are huge puppets – this is a big centre for puppet-making; painted horses, originally made as toys for the horse-crazy maharajas; ink-wells; silver pipes, where the tobacco is smoked through hot coals; and, of course, bandhana-printed textiles. Within Meherangarh Fort, Sunderam Art Emporium has some nice boxes and the manager, Mr Pathan, will tell – even show – visitors where the craftsmen are, such as the Muslim bandhana families in Bambamola area and other bandhana workers around Siwanchi and Jalori gates; the shoe-makers of Udaimandel and around Mochi (shoe) Bazaar; the wood-turners; the ivory workers; wooden horse-makers (one made a life-size horse for a rupee-millionaire Bombay wallah); and the delightfully honest Gujarat furniture-maker who ages his lovely carvings to make them 'duplicate antiques – the French and Germans do not like new carving'.

Lalji, on Umaid Bhawan Palace Road (tel: 22472) is the Aladdin's cave for anything old, from small pieces of silver, wood, brass or ivory to huge appliqué wall-hangings, all stocked from the surrounding villages, with very knowledgeable staff, entirely fair prices and reliable shipping. Many a treasure in a smart Delhi home was found here. The Rajasthan Emporium is good too. Avoid Albani Handicraft Emporium, which is over-priced.

The best bandhana is found at the big shops outside Sojati Gate, at Bhagatram Ishwarlal, Lucky Silk Shop and Prakash Silk Stores. To see dhurrie weaving, go to Salavas village (18km); and for more bandhana, and leather and woodwork, go to Pipad (70km).

The central Sardar Bazar is full of colour, with no cars and almost no begging. Enter by Sojati Gate and head directly for Sri Mishri Lal Hotel, in the right-hand part of the main market gateway, for some milk-of-the-gods lassi. Then on, into the market: street barbers and dentists by the clock tower landmark; past piles of earthenware pots beyond and through a gateway. Here is the Krishna temple, Gulab Sagar Tank and an old palace (now a girls school).

Back to the clock tower and turn right to find a maze of alleys, each with its own theme, so the shops are highly competitive and shout against each other to vie for custom, be it flowers, sweetmeats, shoes, wool, silver or bandhana. The craftsmen work behind. Just outside Sojati Gate, women sell bangles and there is a gold and silver market; and Maharaja Handicrafts, which is good. Finally, on the main road outside Sojati Gate, the famous Achaarwalla pickle shop makes and sells the best garlic, lime, lentil and mixed chutneys in Rajasthan.

OUT OF TOWN To the east, lie desert villages, best visited with Ajit Singh or another knowledgeable local (see below). South-east, through several other interesting villages, lies *Sardar Samand*(55km), summer palace of the Maharaja with a wildlife sanctuary. To the north is first *Balsamand* (7km), whose lake and garden were constructed in 1159. The modern palace dates from 1936 (open daily, 8am-6pm, nice for picnics). *Mandor* (2km beyond) is the old capital of Marwar, where the fine temple-like chhatris of the Jodhpurs are set in lush, terraced gardens outside the ruined city. See especially the 15 rock-cut figures in the Hall of Heroes and Ek Thamba Mahal, a delicately carved, circular, three-storeyed palace. Take the steep winding path to the right, cross the reservoir to find about 60 chhatris of the Ranis. *Osian* lies 60km north of here, but is well worth the effort (perhaps en route to Khimsar and Bikaner) to see Rajasthan's largest group of early Hindu and Jain temples – about a dozen of them, built during the 8th and 9th centuries, centred round the still living Sachiya Mata Temple.

Day trips to villages in family jeeps Meet and talk to villagers. Be the guest of handsome Jhats for lunch. Witness the weekly barber's visit. See potting and weaving and discuss marital customs. Take tea with smiling Bisnoi tribeswomen, brightly clad, heavy bangles up the whole length of their arms; their men wear pure white. All Bisnois believe in the sanctity of animal and plant life, as laid down by the 15th century Guru Jambeshwar in the form of 29 basic tenets, hence Bis (twenty) noi (nine). They further believe their ancestors are reincarnated

as deer, so there are usually herds of deer found near Bisnoi villages. Spot the wildlife and, if very lucky, a white buck in the scrub.

And sample a draught of afion (opium). It used to be given to Rajput runners and to warriors before battle. It is still taken as an umlpano (infused in water), to be drunk by a guest from the cupped hand of his host. But, in the 19th century, Tod observed of the Rajputs that 'the hookah is the dessert to the umlpano; the panacea for all the ills . . . and with which he can at any time enjoy a paradise of his own creation'. He found the Bhatti Rajputs of Jaisalmer 'as addicted as any of his brethren to the immoderate use of opium . . . inhaling mechanically the smoke long after they are insensible to all that is passing around them'. (Trips organised by Ajit Bhawan cost Rs250 per person, well worth it, but check carefully that the itinerary is what you want.)

KHIMSAR

100km north of Jodhpur, or 130km via Mandor and Osian; 150km south of Bikaner. A remote 15th century Rajput stronghold in the Thar Desert, its castle the hotel. Excellent for a quiet escape or a night or two between Jodhpur and Bikaner.

It is a good journey from Jodhpur or Bikaner. From Jodhpur, go by car via Balsamand, Mandor and Osian (see above). From Bikaner, stop off first to see Karni Mata Temple at *Deshnok* (32km), where holy rats frolic freely, sip milk and are cared for by the faithful who believe they will be reincarnated one day as holy men. If your stomach cannot take the rats (which hop over your toes; this is not for the faint-hearted), the next stop is *Nagaur* (110km), another medieval desert town with a very fine fort. It also has a mosque built by Akbar, the shrine of a disciple of Khwajah Muin-ud-din Chishti of Ajmer (see p. 91). There are a cluster of chhatri outside the town gates. And a huge, colourful four-day cattle fair takes place in January/February with camel races, cock fights, horse and bullock competitions and lots of puppeteers, folk dancing and singing.

At Khimsar, it is best to stay at the moated *Royal Castle* (tel: 28, or book through Umaid Bhawan Palace, Jodhpur), 14 rooms. Built as a fortified thikana (home of a local thakur, ruler), by Karam Singh, fifth son of Rao Jodha, founder of Jodhpur. It was named Fateh Mahal after a Sufi saint buried there. Repairs over the centuries mean the present Thakur Saheb, Onkar Singh, lives in the 18th century part. Watchmen still guard the heavy gates. The hotel run by the Welcomgroup; 10 rooms in the 1920s wing, all with bath and hot and cold water; folk dancing, music, West Rajasthan food, barbecues in the Maharaja's tent, 6-seater jeep for sightseeing. A good idea is to drive out into the desert for sunset, to spot antelope, blue bull and quantities of peacocks and deer. (The nearby villagers are Bisnois.)

Postscript: for total escape, go south from Jodhpur to stay at *Rohet Ghar* in District Pali, bookable through Rohet House, PWD Road, Jodhpur (tel: 31161); similar to Khimsar in its isolation, with a glorious village described by palace hotel chronicler Michael Sugich as 'a great place. The village is pristine and the villagers look like they were all born from the same Adonis'.

BIKANER

240km from Jodhpur; 280km from Jaisalmer; 150 from Khimsar; 205km from Bissau (Shekhavati). Right out in the desert, the principal town of north-west Rajasthan is a heavily fortified, pink sandstone fort-city famous for its camels and colourful inhabitants, set amid the arid sand and scrub, under scorching, relentless sun. The state was founded in 1488 by Rao Bika and was, as Naveen Patnaik writes 'the size of England, . . . a sandy plateau with no rivers, peopled by desert nomads and peasants tilling parched fields. There was little rain, but still the bards sang: "Out of the silken darkness of a desert dawn, Emerged the dream of Bikaner".'

It derived its wealth from being sited on the trade route and its security from an effective team of military camels. The rulers could safely lounge about smoking opium and drinking their favourite aphrodisiac tipple, asha, made from gold, silver, pearls and sheeps' and goats' brains. When these pleasures were threatened, they gave the British 200 camels for their Afghan warring in 1842 and acquired political standing.

Then along came the inventive and progressive Maharaja Ganga Singh (ruled 1887-1943) – quite a different type from his would-be progressive fellow prince in Jodhpur. With a combination of military, industrial and sporting entrepreneurship, he lifted backward Bikaner into the 20th century and became the most pukka prince of all. In 1898 he founded the colourful Bikaner Camel Corps, called the Ganga Rissala (seen at Delhi Republic Day Parade). He built a railway and encouraged coal-mining, a combination that trebled the state's income and resulted in a spate of public building and his own spectacular pink pile of a palace, built outside the walls to Samuel Swinton Jacob's design.

Then he instigated an essential event in the social calendar: the annual shoot for imperial sand-grouse, followed by roaring about in a Rolls Royce after black buck, a military tattoo by camels in black chainmail and a huge banquet, attended by the Prince of Wales in 1905. The day's bag for 40 guests could be 10,000-12,000 birds, the highest count being achieved by the guest of honour, of course, sometimes surreptitiously ensured by tucking two good marksmen behind him.

THE HARD FACTS   Arrive by road or take a train from Jodhpur, Jaipur or Delhi. It is best to stay at the **Lallgarh Palace** (tel: 312); begun in 1881 to designs by Sir Samuel Swinton Jacob and smothered in the results of both his work at Jaipur, where he had published a catalogue of Rajput architectural decoration, and his study of Bikaner fort. There is delicate jali work, friezes cover every surface, archways are scalloped, romantic cupolas break the skyline. Building and gardens are a bit run-down now. As at Jodhpur, the ex-royals still live in a wing, some rooms are a museum (much gilt, vast carpet made by Bikaner prisoners, a zoo of stuffed animals, bronzes and shooting photographs galore, open 9am-6pm) and the remainder is hotel. 14 rooms, meals included in the room price; golf and squash by arrangement.

Alternatively, stay out at **Gajner Palace** (32km, book through Lallgarh at least 24 hours in advance, so preparations are made); a royal summer palace of the 1890s, with original Waring and Gillows furniture and fittings. If the electricity fails, water is heated by huge log fires burnt beneath the water tank. Try to arrive by dusk, to enjoy the huge terrace and, if the lake is full, watch the duck and possibly spot imperial sand-grouse – now in greater safety. 18 rooms, old retainers tend to guests, out of town but quiet. Good for spotting wildlife. Best to stay at Lallgarh first, explore Bikaner, then stay at Gajner for total relaxation before the long desert journey to Jaiselmer. Both hotels brimful of charm, but slow service and mediocre food. Tourist Office in Tourist Bungalow, Pooram Singh Circle.

OUT AND ABOUT   The glorious **Junagarh Fort**, entered between two life-sized elephants, was built 1588-93 by Raja Rai Singh, one of Akbar's generals. It can compare with Jodhpur's fort. The emperor made one of his many Rajput marriage alliances with a Bikaner princess. The fort has a magnificent Mughal Durbar Hall. Its pretty surrounding palaces – Har Mandir (for royal weddings), Karan Mahal, Durgar Nivas, Chandra Mahal (Moon Palace), Phool Mahal (Flower Palace), Anup Mahal – with exteriors of pavilions and balconies and interiors of carved marble, wall-paintings (including fake pietra dura), lacquer work and mirrorwork, and a small, choice museum (manuscripts, armour), open Thurs.-Tues., 9.30am-5pm; no guide book.

It is worth exploring the Lallgarh palace and museum, wandering through the dazzlingly colourful bazaars (spotting the nomads visiting from the desert) and visiting the *Ganga Golden Jubilee Museum* which houses a fine collection of archaeological stone carvings (pre-Harrapan, Gupta and Kahsan), quality Bikaner school miniature paintings, local crafts and, of course, armour, open Sat.-Thurs., 10am-5pm. Good antique shops between Lallgarh Palace and the fort, stocking old photographs, carvings, locks, weights and local crafts. In the old area of the city, *Kotharion ka Mohulla*, seek out the old piazza surrounded by merchants' houses such as Rampuriyon ki Haveli. In contrast to Jaisalmer's honey-coloured stone, these are of red sandstone with shops for local needs on the ground floor.

The best trip out of Bikaner is to the local *camel-breeding farm* (10km), run by the government. Go at about 5pm, ride camels, then watch hundreds of the proud beasts being brought in. Notice their eye lashes which breeders try to make grow longer to keep the dust out of their eyes. The beautiful royal *chhatris* at *Devi Kund* (8km) are also worth visiting. Those on the Indus Civilisation trail (see Pakistan section) can go north to *Kalibangan* (200km, by car or train) which, with Lothal (see Bombay chapter), makes up India's best Harappan remains: here are remains of pre-Harappan residents and of Harappans – citadel, a grid of houses, pottery and engraved seals.

JAISALMER

280km from Bikaner; 290km from Jodhpur. The most western city in Rajasthan, and the most perfect Rajput walled desert city, is a golden jewel shimmering above the hard sand, like a fairytale mirage. Satyajit Ray called his film set there 'Shonar Kella' (Fortress of Gold). Consistent wealth from lying on the trade route – the city had five camel caravanserais to cope with the through traffic – was lavished on domestic architecture. Every building is a joy. The ethereal havelis have astonishing carving of the highest quality – as the Keeper of the Palace of Westminster put it: 'No tat here. The rest of India is full of tat.' The women and children, dressed in vivid Rajasthan brightness, smile and giggle in the narrow streets. Others carry water jugs with the grace of classical ballet dancers. There is extraordinary elegance and style everywhere, all bathed in a desert light that starts each day at dawn with membrane-pale mauve and ends the day at sunset, hot and livid red. The only sadness is the general low quality of new building outside the walls.

THE HARD FACTS During the much-lauded Desert festival (first held in 1979), when prices soar, accommodation and train seats are difficult to find. But Holi (February/March) is charming here. In addition, there are the big Ramdeo fairs in August-September and November-December and the other big Rajasthan festivals of Dussehra, Diwali and Gangaur, all celebrated with traditional jollity.

To get there from Jodhpur, two options: road or rail. The road is unexciting unless miles of hot empty desert bring a thrill. If so, stay overnight at the romantic, 14th-century *Pokaran Fort* (book through Pokaran House, PWD Road, Jodhpur, tel: 30614); 168km from Jodhpur, 110km from Jaisalmer, 240km from Bikaner, believed to be one of Humayun's stops during his flight to Persia after Sher Shah Sur unthroned him; 4 old and 10 new rooms, old fort furnishings, good local food, camel safaries, village visits, and animals such as spotted and pen-tailed sand-grouse, houbara bustard and chinkara to spot.

Train is easier. The railway line was built when the city became strategically important during the Indo-Pakistan wars of 1965 and 1971. Take a sleeper to Jaisalmer, either the regular one or the Maharaja's two dazzling white carriages, his coat of arms painted on the side: one has 7 coupés and 2 baths, for 14 people (Rs50,000), the other has 3 coupés, a sitting room and bath, for 6 people (Rs9,000). Prices include cooks, butlers and escort from Umaid Bhawan Palace (see p. 124) and 2 nights (there and back) plus breakfast, lunch and dinner in Jaisalmer. Book well ahead. Taking the regular sleeper, the Umaid Bhawan will lend pillow and blanket, to be put in the left luggage office at Jaisalmer station when confirming the return sleeper on arrival, then used for the return journey. A jeep bus service runs between the station and city. Jaisalmer is a pedestrian city; to explore the surrounding desert, use a taxi.

To get there from Bikaner, there is no train, so go by road or, for the keen, by camel – it takes about two weeks and tremendous potential saddle soreness, so perhaps two days is enough, and the rest by road.

To stay in Jaisalmer – and it certainly deserves more than one day – hotels are mushrooming to serve increased tourism. Current best is *Hotel Himmatgarh*, 1 Ramgarh Road (tel: 225), built by the women's chhatris, overlooking the city, rooms as individual cottages, family run, dine under the stars as the moon rises. *Hotel Jawahar Niwas Palace* (tel: 2208) is on the outskirts of town, 15 rooms in an ex-royal guest-house originally built for the political agent (c.1884). To stay in town, *Shri Giriraj Palace Hotel* (tel: 2268) is in a nice old building, Nagpur House in Manak Chowk, 'one minute's walk from the First Gate', run by the friendly Neembdan Barat who also runs a good little travel agency; the rooftop restaurant is delightful. Then there is the very modest *Jaisal Castle* (tel: 62; cable: JAISAL CASTLE) in an old courtyard guest-house, 11 small rooms, simply furnished, cold water only, rooftop sunset views; or *Narayan Nivas Hotel* (tel: 108), a converted caravanserai at the bottom of the town, 24 rooms, each with shower, set round a deep open hall, like a giant verandah, where the camels used to sleep – the men slept on the cooler roof. Local Langas, Mangniyars and Dholis play and sing music in both hotels each evening. Local food can be good, but ask for it.

Tourist Office at the Tourist Bungalow on the road into the city from the station. The guide book *Jaisalmer, The Golden City*, by K. N. Sharma, is charming. Jaisal Tours operates from Jawahar Palace (tel: 97).

Both hotels can arrange camel and jeep tours, run by Mohendra Singh, whose family also breed and own about 100 camels. To go on a camel tour for a few hours, go directly to Narayan hotel on arrival by train and they can be ready in one hour. For a longer tour, sleeping overnight in the desert, the party consists of camels (one each plus one for luggage), cook, bedding, tent, onions to keep the snakes away, night watchman and wireless contact with the police (this is well-guarded territory bordering on Pakistan). It takes 11 days to reach Bikaner; seven to Pokaran. A camel covers 20-30km a day. Beware of cheap camel marketeers: their beasts will not be trained, the saddles will not be good. And their treks will not be safe. For faster exploring, take a day's jeep safari and visit 10-12 villages, possibly sleeping out overnight.

OUT AND ABOUT On arrival by train, go to *Gadisar Tank*, the large natural oasis that attracted Rawal Jaisal to the site. See early morning light on the Jain temples, women with chaori (rings of ivory) up the length of their arms collecting water; left of the beautiful archway (supposedly built by a prostitute), climb on to temple roofs for views and see the little local museum. Then off up to the *fort* on Trikuta (three-peak) hill. Built in 1156 by Rawal Jaisal, of the Bhatti Rajput clan, it is the second oldest fort in Rajasthan, after Chitorgarh. Within the fort, see the seven-storey palace just inside the thick gateway, and the four other mahals (palaces); the highly decorative Jain temples are near the entrance (open daily until noon).

But the nicest thing to do is wander through the alleys seeking out the magnificent *havelis*. These are quite different from the Shekhavati havelis: they are very tall to catch the breeze; very thick-walled to keep cool; their jali screens are still used today because Jaisalmer women still observe purdah; and instead of paintings, their exterior walls have been carved to honeycomb delicacy with a feverish energy; and several of the interiors are painted and decorated too.

See especially *Nathamal ki Haveli* (1885), a prime minister's home. It was carved by two Muslim brothers, Hati and Laloo. There are sandstone elephants at the door. Inside is the beautifully painted first floor. The five *Patwa* havelis stand in a row, built 1800-60 by five brothers on the proceeds of opium-dealing and smuggling and gold and silver trading. Now two are owned by the government (open daily, 10.30am-5pm), one is rented to a shopkeeper who encourages people to ramble over it, one is lived in by some Patwa descendants, one by another family. *Salim Singh ki Haveli*, built by Salim Singh in 1810 when he was prime minister, has a superb facade but there is almost nothing left inside. And do not miss the time-warp *Mandir Palace*, a giant carved reliquary built at the end of the 19th century in Rajput style with Islamic elements brought by passing traders, furnished entirely with silver – for only that can reflect the moon, the Jaisalmer ancestor (small area open daily).

Shopping around the bazaars and alleys can turn up constant treasures, since this is the central market place for all the surrounding villages. Find the local bandhana (made at Kadi Bundar), including very lovely wool-work. There are also silk shawls, wool jackets, camel leather mojadis (slippers), camel-hair carpets, goat-hair weaving, jewellery, the huge Rajasthan gathered skirts (up to 7 metres), and some nice old clothes with good embroidery. The shop in one of the Patwa havelis has some particularly nice things, if it is still there. (The future use of the house is uncertain.)

OUT OF TOWN Take a camel to the ladies' chhatris for sunset – the view back to the city is unforgettable – or take a car or camel to the men's magnificent chhatris 3km away, many of them with hero stones. Further afield lie *Amar Sagar* (6km), for pretty Jain temple and ruined garden, and *Lodarva* beyond (another 7km), more Jain temples amid the ruins of the pre-Jaisalmer ancient capital. Heading west from Amar Sagar, find first *Mool Sagar* (another 3km), a garden and tank, then Sam sand dunes, as seriously desert as Rajasthan gets.

Wildlife sanctuaries

Despite the arid land, the princes nurtured their forests to ensure lavish, status symbol chikars (hunts). The three main sanctuaries in Rajasthan evolved from this tradition.

KOLEOD GHANA NATIONAL PARK, BHARATPUR, RAJASTHAN see p. 79.

RANTHAMBORE TIGER RESERVE, RAJASTHAN
November-May; best March and even better April-May but very hot. 160km from Jaipur by

car or train, nearest station Sawai Madhopur. Directly accessible on the Delhi-Bombay train. To stay at the *Maharaja's Lodge*, Ranthambore National Park Road, Sawai Madhopur (tel: 2541; fax 0141 73798), book direct or through any Taj Group hotel; 16 rooms in the former royal hunting lodge, plus large gardens, 20 minutes' drive from the park, 2km from the railway station. To stay in the *government lodge* it is essential to book in Jaipur (see above). Alternatively, stay in a tent at the *Indian Adventure Camp*, approved by one smart Londoner as 'quite fun'. Note: with the success of this park, visitors are now controlled in the interests of conservation, so be sure to book ahead.

400 sqkm of dry deciduous forest, perfect natural habitat for tigers. Set in the Aravalli and Vindhyan hills, dotted with pavilions and dominated by the hilltop Ranthambore fort. Plenty of tigers and other game to be seen in a very picturesque landscape. Favourite hunting haunt of the late Maharaja of Jaipur, who built the lodge and entertained, among many others, the Mountbattens and the Queen and Prince Philip. Other guests were given elaborate tents. Tiger, leopard, hyena, bear, blue bull, sambhar and other deer were spotted or shot from elephants. When the royal party was there in 1961, the Maharani recalls that Prince Philip 'bagged a large tiger with a beautiful shot'.

Today the tigers are being saved, not shot, and Prince Philip is an ardent conservationist. Since Project Tiger was launched by the World Wildlife Fund in 1973, the estimated Indian population of tigers has risen from a disastrous 2,400 to about 3,300 in 1984 – in the 15 tiger reserves alone, the increase is from 268 to 1,069. National parks and sanctuaries cover 75,763sqkm – 2.3% of all India and 19% of India's forest. But it is a misconception to blame India's wildlife problems on the princes and the Raj. They observed strict sporting rules and guarded their wildlife preserves ruthlessly, even if they did occasionally dull tigers' senses with opium-laced water and hold big chikars to impress visiting Viceroys and fellow royals. The real damage came after Independence when sporting rules were ignored, villagers had guns, there was widespread poaching and, worst of all, colossal deforestation. A tiger population of around 30,000 in 1947 (unchanged since 1930) dropped to 2,400 in 23 years.

The 900 increase during the first decade of Project Tiger was described by Guy Mountfort, Vice-President of the then World Wildlife Fund, as 'probably the most successful conservation project for wildlife ever launched'. The tigers are breeding well. Their food of wild boar and deer are also multiplying. Protected forest areas are increasing. The problem is the competition for space between tiger and man – a tiger needs up to 80 sqkm and defends it to the death. Fellow tigers are thereby endangered and, occasionally, so are humans. Not all conservationists are optimistic about the big cats' future.

SARISKA, RAJASTHAN
February-June; April best for tiger. On the Delhi-Jaipur road, 200km from Delhi, 96km from Jaipur. Essential to book the park visit in writing, booking a machan and guide, too, with the Wildlife Warden, Sariska. Stay at either *Tiger's Den*, the clean and well-organised lodge at the park gates run by Rajasthan State Tourism Corporation; or at *Hotel Sariska Palace* (tel: 22), 27 rooms in the royal and palatial hunting lodge right opposite the park entrance, with large gardens, original furnishings, evening barbecues and peace.

800 sqkm of deciduous forest near Alwar, a sanctuary since 1958 and also a Project Tiger reserve. Formerly enjoyed by the Maharajas who held highly organised tiger chikars, when VIP guests mounted their well-trained hunting elephants while the Alwar soldiers and cavalry acted as beaters with military precision. See tiger, leopard, sloth bear, wild boar, nilgai and chital from jeeps and two machans (watch towers) overlooking water-holes, especially at dusk. During the monsoon, the sanctuary is very lush, beautiful and full of birds. Explore this rambling park which takes in local villages, temples and Kankwari Fort by jeep with a guide; the lucky spot a tiger at dawn or dusk.

Find out more

Archer, W. G.: *Indian paintings from Rajasthan*, London, 1957; rev. ed. Calcutta, 1962

Baroda, Maharaja of: *The Palaces of India*, London, 1980

Beach, M. C.: *Rajput Painting at Bundi and Kota*, Askona, Switzerland, 1975

Beny, R.: *Rajasthan*, London, 1981

Brunel, F.: *Rajasthan*, London, 1985

Cooper, I.: *Guide to the Painted Towns of Shekhawati*, Churu, Rajasthan, 1980s.

Crewe, Q.: *The Last Maharaja: A Biography of Sawai Man Singh II*, London, 1985

Devi, G. and Rau, S. R.: *A Princess Remembers. The Memoirs of the Maharani of Jaipur*, London, 1976, reprinted 1984

Hendley, T. H.: *Rulers of India and Chiefs of Rajputana*, London, 1897

Masters, B.: *Maharana: The Story of the Rulers of Udaipur*, Ahmedabad, 1990

Mountfort, G.: *Saving the Tiger*, London, 1981

Pal, P.: *The Classical Tradition in Rajput Painting from the Paul F. Walter collection*, New York, 1978

Patnaik, N.: *A Desert Kingdom: The Rajputs of Bikaner*, London, 1990

Singh, R.: *Rajasthan, India's Enchanted Land*, Hong Kong, 1981

Tod, J.: *Annals and Antiquities of Rajasthan*, ed. W. Crooke, 3 vols, Oxford, 1920

Topsfield, A.: *Paintings from Rajasthan in the National Gallery of Victoria*, Melbourne, 1980

Topsfield, A.: *The City Palace Museum, Udaipur*, Ahmedabad, 1990

Wacziarg, F., and Nath, A.: *Rajasthan: the painted walls of Shekhavati*, Delhi, 1982.

Bombay, Central India and Gujarat: Big city to quiet villages

Bombay has vitality. It throbs with action and money. It is positive and forward-looking. It is India's only modern international city. A single Indian working woman can lead a more liberated life here than elsewhere in the country, even in Delhi. The top Indian businessmen, merchants, dealers, actors and all those who make their worlds go round are here – with powerful Delhi representatives who crack through the ever more centralised bureaucracy. Even if the politics of commerce and industry is dealt with in Delhi, the activity is here. Gujaratis, Parsees and Goans contribute to the immigrant population of 9 million, swollen by 40% over the last decade by immigrants from the surrounding countryside to make it the second largest city in India. In addition, there is a floating population of other Indians and foreigners, some working, some just having a good time. For the Bombay rich, the coffers of rupees are emptied and replenished quickly and with panache; for the poor arriving with dreams, the rupees are few and life is squalid. Bombay is India's most ostentatiously rich city; it also possesses India's largest slum, Dharavi, where an estimated 290,000 people live in some 55,000 hutments in an area of just 175 hectares.

Bombay is the country's financial, industrial, commercial and trading centre. It has about 15% of India's factories, 45% of her textile mills, handles 50% of her foreign port traffic and is responsible for a third of her income-tax receipts. The cash economy, known as 'black money', thrives here like nowhere else. As one Malabar Hill resident remarked: 'There are two economies in India, white and black. Nothing happens without the black. We could not sit here having tea and cakes without it. And when the tax man swoops, you do a deal with him, too.'

Bombay has by far the highest cost of living in India, the largest film industry in the world, and property values on a par with New York. It is the centre of the Indian gold and diamond markets, has excellent quality shopping and the best night life, and is the only Indian city to have an extensive network of good restaurants.

It all grew on seven boggy, malarial islands acquired by the British for next to nothing. Mumbadevi, the largest, was part of Catherine of Braganza's dowry when she married Charles II in 1661. But London was neither impressed nor aware of what it had acquired. Pepys termed it 'that poor little island'. Lord Claren-don believed it had 'towns and castles therein which are very little distance from Brazil'. Four years later the British took possession of the remaining islands and in 1668 leased the lot to the East India Company for £10 in gold per annum. The 'Company', which had received its trading Charter from Queen Elizabeth I in 1600 and had a base up the coast at Surat, knew just what a good deal it had got. It could collect all Bombay's revenue (then estimated at £2,833 per annum), make the laws and, when its headquarters were moved there in 1687, the city soon became the centre for the west coast trade.

Trade fed Bombay's progress from seven-island swamp to single-island city, as it did that of Calcutta. Both grew and prospered to become great cities and centres of British administration. Both were – and still are – magnets for immigrants. But whereas Bombay continues to absorb newcomers and to create wealth, Calcutta, formerly so much grander and flashier, can offer its floods of immigrants little today. In Bombay things get done, telephones work and appointments are kept (almost) on time.

But this wealth came slowly to Bombay. Gerald Aungier, known as the father of Bombay and Governor 1672-77, established the Courts of Justice, began the Company militia which became the East India Company Army, and started the practice of encouraging all religions and nationalities to settle in Bombay. He welcomed Parsees, merchants from Gujarat, Banians (Hindu traders) fleeing Jesuit oppression in Goa, and Arab traders. But, for the British, life was pretty grim. There was little amusement, few women, a bit of racing but plenty of corruption, and often too much Bombay punch. This consoling concoction was a mixture of local toddy (coconut-based spirit), sugar, lime-juice, spice and water, the five ingredients called punch from the Mahratti word for five, panch. Even by the end of the 18th century, when the population had grown to about 120,000, there were probably barely 1,000 Europeans and life was not bright.

Then, at the beginning of the 19th century, things began to hot up. In 1813 trade restrictions relaxed when the Company lost its monopoly of trade between Britain and India. The new P & O steamers brought women out to India. Later on, batches of young women arriving in search of husbands were known as 'the Fishing Fleet'. The railway came in 1853 (the first east of Suez),

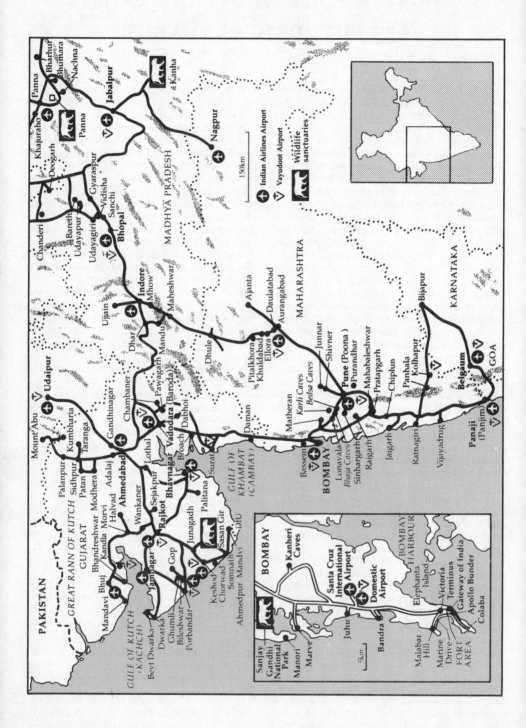

150km

Indian Airlines Airport
Vayudoot Airport
wildlife sanctuaries

PAKISTAN

Bharhut
Bhumara
Nachna
Panna
Khajuraho
Deogarh
Panna
Kanha
Jabalpur

Nagpur

MADHYA PRADESH

Chanderi
Bareth
Udayapur
Gyaraspur
Udayagiri
Sanchi
Vidisha
Bhopal

Indore
Mhow
Maheshwar

Ujjain

Dhar
Mandu
Pawagarh
Chambaner

Dhule

Ajanta
Daulatabad
Aurangabad

MAHARASHTRA

Bijapur

KARNATAKA

Mount Abu
Udaipur

Palanpur
Kumbharia
Sidhpur
Patan
Taranga
Modhera
Adalaj
Gandhinagar
Ahmedabad

Pitalkhora
Khuldabad
Ellora

Junnar
Shivner

Pune (Poona)
Purandhar

Mahabaleshwar
Pratapgarh
Chiplun
Panhala
Kolhapur

GOA
Belgaum

Bhandreshwar
Kandla
Morvi
Halvad
Wankaner
Sejakpur
Rajkot

Lothal
Vadodara (Baroda)
Dhaboi
Bhavnagar

Daman

Matheran

Karli Caves
Betsa Caves

Panaji
(Panjim)

GULF OF
KHAMBAT
(CAMBAY)

Ratnagiri
Vijayadrug

Jaigarh
Raigarh
Sinhargarh
Lonavala
Bhaja Caves

Bassein
BOMBAY

GREAT RANN OF KUTCH
GUJARAT

Mandavi
Bhuj
Jamnagar
Gop
Junagadh
Palitana
Surat
Broach

Chumli
Bileshwar
Porbandar

Keshod
Chorwad
Somnath
Ahmedpur Mandvi

Sasan Gir
DIU

GULF OF KUTCH
(KACHCH)
Bevt Dwarka
Dwarka

BOMBAY

Kanheri
Caves

Santa Cruz
International
Airport

Domestic
Airport

BOMBAY
HARBOUR

Sanjay
Gandhi
National
Park

Manori
Marve

Juhu

Bandra

Elephanta
Island

Victoria
Terminus
Gateway of India
Apollo Bunder
Colaba

Malabar
Hill
Martine
Drive
FORT
AREA

5km

134

the telegraph in 1865, the first cotton mill opened in 1857. The vast docks were begun that would take decades to complete.

Under Sir Bartle Frere, Governor 1862-7, new streets were laid out and the great Victorian Gothic public buildings rose which still dominate the city centre. Bombay needed space so, once the islands were joined together, projects were begun to reclaim land from the sea by throwing in Bombay's hills and much else. By the 1950s, the city's total area had increased by a third.

Reclamation continues today – so maps are constantly out of date, with buildings where the sea is painted. But it is insufficient and now there is to be a new twin city across the harbour, designed by India's architect king, Charles Correa. Correa's other buildings include Bharat Bhavan, an arts complex at Bhopal in central India, (see below), the Cidade de Goa beach hotel in Goa and the Kovalam Beach Resort in Kerala (see Sun chapter), and in Delhi recently a sky-scraper at Connaught Place and the new British Council building. In 1984, the Royal Institute of British Architects awarded him their Gold Medal for his architectural work.

The wealth and expansion of Bombay were the fruit of trade that had begun to blossom in the early 1800s. After a famine in China in the 1770s, much cotton-growing land was given over to grain. India began to supply cotton as well as opium to China, exchanging them for tea, which was catching on in Britain with the reduction in import duty. In 1859, opium took 42% and cotton 30% of Bombay's total trade. In 1863 the railway linked the city to the cotton-growing Deccan. Six years later the Suez Canal opened, making Bombay the uncontested premier western port of India, vying with Calcutta on the east coast.

The early 1860s were a period of enormous prosperity. The American Civil War boosted an already surging cotton trade when the Confederacy ports were blocked, halting cotton exports to Manchester. India immediately stepped in, cotton prices soared for four years – nothing but pint mugs of champagne were drunk – and then crashed in March 1865 when news reached Bombay that the war had ended and American trading would resume.

Small communities and strong individuals have built Bombay. They brought with them their own food, customs, architecture and languages which, to an extent, they still retain. The so-called 'cages' of the red-light district around Falkland Road are considered by some to be traditional Gujarati houses whose box-like rooms have slatted facades on the ground floor. Bombay still has no common language and is full of variety, making it truly cosmopolitan.

One such strong individual was David Sassoon, whose family later spread to Europe and America. He was a Sephardic Jew from a Baghdad family of bankers and community leaders. He arrived in Bombay in 1833 and within 25 years had built up an empire that covered every aspect of trading, from the goods to the docks. He put his eight sons in key world trading cities, took British citizenship in 1853 and, the final symbol of social success, in 1872 his son was created a baronet, Sir Albert Sassoon of Kensington Gore.

But the best-known group of immigrants are the *Parsees* who arrived in the 1670s. This phenomenally successful but tiny community of Zoroastrians (fire-worshippers) migrated from Persia when the Muslims came to power, finally landing at Sanjan in Gujarat in 745 AD. The story goes that their emissaries to the king of Surat returned with a full glass of milk, indicating that Gujarat was a land of prosperity but full up. The Parsee captain dropped a teaspoonful of sugar into the milk and sent it back, indicating they would add the sweetness of life. (Less romantic variants have a coin dropped in and claims of greater prosperity.) Whatever the truth, the Parsees were accepted.

They remain a very tight-knit community. Following their prophet, Zarathustra (golden light), they seek knowledge and illumination through worship of fire and sun and follow the path of Asha – good thoughts, words and deeds. Their scriptures are in Persian, they speak Gujarati, and the bodies of their dead are laid in towers of silence for vultures to eat rather than be allowed to pollute the sacred fire or earth. They seldom marry outsiders because the children would not be true Parsees. In a small and elite community this means inter-marriage and so, whilst the sane tend to be intelligent and successful, there is a certain amount of battiness about.

The Parsees came to Bombay as traders, shipbuilders and bankers. Both at work and at play, they made instant friends with the British, on whom they increasingly modelled their lives, from learning Shakespeare and wearing top hats to playing cricket and golf. Some of the first Indian undergraduates at Oxford and Cambridge were Parsee. There were the shipbuilding Wadias, the Camas, Pestonjis, Readymoneys and Jeejeebhoys. Jamshetji Jeejeebhoy (1783-1859) was the first Indian to be created a baronet. Streets, statues and institutions named after the families litter the city.

The most talked about Parsee family today is the Tatas. Jamshetji Nusserwanji Tata (1839-1904), father of the dynasty, first reaped his rupees from the cotton trade. Although his fingers were severely burned when the cotton bubble burst in 1865 and he was stuck on a ship bound for London, he recovered to build mills, a hydro-electric works, a steel works, open iron-ore mines, start a shipping line – and build a huge memorial to himself, the Taj Mahal Hotel.

His descendants have pushed out the feelers of the House of Tata even further: into tea, trucks, scientific research. It was Tata Airlines, founded in 1932, that went public as Air India in 1946, and two years later became Air India International, the first joint undertaking between the government and the private sector. Like Value Added Tax in Britain, Tata is impossible to avoid. Today's leading Parsees are often lawyers, writers or doctors. One is Nani Palkhivala, one of India's leading lawyers, who served as Ambassador to the United States from 1977 to 1979.

Bombay's gleaming sky-scrapers on the newly claimed land at Nariman Point have a Manhattan air about them. Their symbol of wealth is in harsh contrast to the crowded old bazaars and seedy suburbs that constitute most of Bombay. As Correa says: 'Every day it gets worse and worse as physical environment . . . and yet better and better as city . . . every day it offers more skills, activities, opportunities on every level.' Nevertheless, there is a rising trend to opt for the spaciousness of Delhi. For the Westerner arriving in India, Bombay is a relatively easy city – crowded and humid but with the rough corners smoothed off. A more challenging India lies beyond, in the cities of Calcutta, Madras, Delhi and Ahmedabad, in the Kulu hills and Tamil Nadu temples, in lush Kerala and desert Rajasthan.

When to go

Between October and February the air is fresh, the skies blue. Bombayites rival the British in their talk about the weather, praising the 'glorious cold winter' (which resembles a Continental summer). But in March, heat and humidity start rising and their previous banter makes sense. By June it is boiling hot. Then comes the drenching monsoon until September – known as 'three-shirts-a-day-weather'. After that, the stickiness decreases slowly.

FESTIVALS *Ganesh* (or Ganapati), the benign elephant-headed deity, is the subject of the biggest festival, celebrated on his birthday in September. Ganesh's abilities to smooth the path to success in anything from writing a letter to starting up a business or going on a journey is eminently suited to money-making Bombay. The city is filled with gaudy, pink, garlanded clay images of the fat, sweet-toothed god of prosperity and wisdom – each with a morsel of last year's figure added to this year's clay mixture. More than 6,000 images are made annually, the largest ones by factory workers who compete

fiercely, collecting funds months in advance. Traditional idols are sometimes jazzed up with flickering multi-coloured lights or electric fountains, like a Hindi film prop. There is even a society entirely devoted to Ganesh Utsav (festival).

The ten-day celebrations begin with much puja performed to the images set up in homes and on street corners. Women buy new saris and bangles, prepare kheer (a special rice pudding) and spruce up the home. On the tenth day, full-moon day, half the city parade their idols down to Chowpatty beach, which is already adorned with multi-coloured Ganesh sand sculptures. The images are carried on high – the huge ones on trucks – amid clouds of pink gulal (powder), music and dancing, and then finally immersed in the water to bob out into the Arabian Sea. In 1894, when the British banned crowd assemblies, Lokmanya Bal Gangadhar Tilak successfully claimed that this was a religious festival and his political messages, disguised in dance and drama, stirred Bombayites to fight for independence.

There are good celebrations for Diwali, Dussehra, Holi, Gokulashtami and Coconut Day, as well as the big non-Hindu festivals (see Calendar of festivals, p. 283).

SOCIAL CALENDAR Keeps to the cool months, October-March. It revolves around racing (see p. 143) which culminates in the Derby in February-March, cricket which peters out in March, gloriously vulgar weddings which peak in December-January, and the big festivals from Ganesh until Christmas and New Year. Grand Hindi film premières are in the winter too. (The government funds the Indian Film Festival, keeping it on a short rein in Delhi, and lengthening the leash for other cities to act as host on alternate years.)

Getting there: Getting away

Arriving at Bombay's new International airport at Sahar is not the joy it should be – nor is leaving through it. If India is keen to attract tourism (and thus foreign currency), this method fails. Baggage is unbelievably slow to arrive, the lavatories resemble paddling pools, telephones rarely work, there are few chairs and queues for the bank never move. (Officially, all rupees are in India, so it may be essential to change money before taking a taxi into town.) To depart, it takes up to one-and-a-half hours to reach the airport through daytime traffic snarls (reduced to 40 minutes when traffic clears after midnight), and well over an hour to check in before embarking upon the emigration and security checks.

Arriving on domestic flights at Santa Cruz airport is better. But to connect a domestic with an international flight means taking a taxi for the 5km between airports as the bus service is erratic.

There are two roads from the airports over Mahim Creek on to the central Bombay isthmus, both unattractive, lined with squatters' meagre housing and jammed with traffic except in the middle of the night. It takes ruthless fare bargaining, with help from the officials (see Survival chapter).

Internally the nicest way to arrive or leave Bombay is by train at the majestic Victoria Terminus (but some arrive at the other station, Bombay Central). With the demise of the Bombay-Goa steamer, the more adventurous could drive up from Goa by car (for a route, see Sun chapter). From Pune, there is the choice of car, bus or train.

Most international airlines serve Bombay. Many of them have late night departures, allowing passengers to avoid the traffic and hanging around in the airport amid crowds and heat. Internally, Indian Airlines makes excellent connections, especially to Gujarat, Rajasthan, and central and southern India. Daily direct flights go to all major cities including Ahmedabad, Aurangabad, Bangalore, Belgaum, Bhavnagar, Calcutta, Cochin, Dabolim (for Goa), Delhi, Hyderabad, Jamnagar, Keshod, Madras, Mangalore, Nagpur, Pune, Rajkot, Trivandrum and Vadodara (Baroda). The daily morning Rajasthan shuttle stops at Udaipur, Jodhpur and Jaipur. Daily flights go north to Srinagar via Delhi. Colombo (Sri Lanka) is accessible daily except Fridays, either direct or via Trivandrum or Madras. Male (the Maldives) is reached via Trivandrum on Mondays or Thursdays.

The best train to and from Delhi, the Rajdhani Express (17hrs), runs five times a week but uses Bombay Central, whereas the Punjab Mail arriving at Victoria Terminus takes 29 hours. For Calcutta the Gitanjali Express and the Calcutta Mail both use Victoria Terminus. But the Madras Express (27hrs) and Madras Mail (31 hours) and trains for Pune (3½hrs) and Hyderabad (18 hours) leave from a third station, Dadar. Sadly, the wonderful steamer journey between Bombay and Goa is currently suspended; but it is worth checking.

Where to stay

Fortune seekers and fortune spenders, with all their hangers-on, have been passing through rich and fashionable Bombay in large numbers for over a century. And they continue to do so. It should be stuffed with good hotels, both the bright 'n' brassy and the comfy colonial. Indeed, more than 130 are listed in *Hotel and Restaurant Guide India '90*. But few give the comfort that cures jet-lag and strengthens for culture shock and sub-continent travelling and, as one knowledgeable London-Bombay tour operator confided, 'even my budget travellers tend to swallow their pride and go to the Taj'.

At the top end of pampering, downtown Bombay has one Taj and two Oberois, with top services, matching prices and heavy bookings. The Welcomgroup's SeaRock, Leela Kempinski, Sun-n-Sand and Holiday Inn, all technically in the same league, are way out at Bandra and Juhu, but well-located for a beach and the airport on an overnight stop (avoid the Centaur). Most other hotels are a dozen rungs down the ladder. Inexpensive but pleasant and central are – in descending order of price and sophistication – The President, Ambassador, Fariyas, Natraj, Ritz, Grand and Diplomat. For more privacy, the Royal Bombay Yacht Club and the Cricket Club of India have rooms but require a little pre-planning. There are no rooms at the Willingdon Club or the Bombay Gymkhana. Since Bombay is long and full of traffic jams, the distance from hotel to airport and railway station are given in the list below to help planning and minimise travelling.

In the commercial and trading capital of India, with the best links to the rest of the country and the world beyond, hotel beds are hot property and rights to reservations can be contested. So book well in advance and arrive clutching the hotel's letter of confirmation.

CENTRAL HOTELS

Taj Mahal and *Taj Mahal Inter-Continental*
Apollo Bunder, Bombay 400039
Telephone: 2023366; Fax: 287-2711; Telex: 3837/6176/2442/6175
As headquarters of the Taj Group of Hotels, the Central Reservation System is here (see p. 12).
Airports 34km; railway station 4km
599 rooms, including 49 suites, attached bath. Single Rs1,800-1,995; double Rs1,950-2,150; suites on application.

Every service including travel agency, bank, airline offices, business services, pool, health club, hairdresser, florist, chemist, babysitter, shopping arcade, eight bars and restaurants, discotheque.

Quite justifiably an institution and a thriving memorial to the father of the Tata clan. But the difference in the two hotel titles is crucial. The red-domed Taj Mahal Hotel was built in 1903 by Jamshetji Nusserwanji Tata, designed by a local English architect named Chambers, constructed the right way round, contrary to popular myth, cost £500,000, had its own Turkish baths and electric laundry and is the one to stay in. The Taj Mahal Intercontinental is the modern skyscraper annex, used by aircraft crews who want to sleep in peace and by Arabs happy to waive character for carpeted corridors.

Although all facilities are common to both parts, the greatest facility is Tata's building. To stay here in a spacious old room – or better still in one of the dottier old suites with rooms for the guest's manservants and maids – is to stay at 'The Taj'.

Built to outdo the fashionable and exclusively European Watson's (which no longer survives), it was a roaring success from the start. Sited to welcome with panache the linerloads of visitors, its doors open to all races, it was instantly on a par with Raffle's, Shepheard's and the Peninsula.

Aldous Huxley may have called its style a mixture of 'the South Kensington Natural History Museum with that of an Indian pavilion at the International Exhibition', but high society continues to know it more intimately than its namesake in Agra. Somerset Maugham, the Beatles, Duke Ellington, Gregory Peck and Mohammad Ali have all stayed here. It is the place to be seen, anywhere, any time – even just hanging around the lobby. It rivals the up-to-the-minute Oberois in everything and outdoes them in some things – it has the best art book shop and newsagent, the nicest swimming pool and tea lounge. The Oberoi may have the edge on service but the Taj has a character and smell (cruelly likened to fish by an American-born lady) it is difficult not to get hooked on. See other sections for more.

Oberoi Towers Marine Drive (Netaji Subhash Road), Nariman Point, Bombay 400021
Telephone: 2024343; Fax: 2043282; Telex: 11-4153/4154 OBBY
Airports 28km; railway station 2km
650 rooms, including 48 suites, attached bath. Single Rs1,950; double Rs2,150; suites Rs4,000-8,000.

The most modern of mod. cons. plus travel agency, bank, airline offices, business facilities, pool, health club, beauty salon, baby-sitter, massive shopping arcade.

Probably the most efficient hotel in India. Certainly the tallest building in the country when it went up in the late 1980s. (Mr Oberoi was not hampered by such trifles as height restriction, nor was the Maharaja of Gwalior for his skyscraper built on the sea front beyond the racecourse, next to his blue-domed palace.) The Lego-rigid 35-storey block perches on top of a base shaped like a concrete liner. Totally refurbished following the tragic 1990 fire, the block contains the bedrooms, each with identical cleanliness and comfort and most with stunning views over Bombay and the Arabian Sea. The higher the floor, the better – lightning fast lifts avoid long waits. The very modern suites, well decorated using regional Indian crafts, nobble the best views at the top. The concrete

liner contains the facilities. They start at the bottom with the Cellar discotheque (avoid), and rise through a good health club, exceptional beauty salon, 6 eating and drinking haunts (2 more on top of the tower) and a two-storeyed, 200-shop bazaar attempting to combine Knightsbridge and Oxford Street, topped by a swimming pool shaped like a clover-leaf. Like the Taj, the Oberoi is a social focus for Bombayites and is acquiring a distinctive and friendly character rare in a modern hotel. See other sections for more.

Hotel President 90 Cuffe Parade (Capt. P. Pethe Marg), Colaba, Bombay 400005
Telephone: 4950808; Fax: 495 1201; Telex: 11-5769/4135 PRES IN
Airports 32km, railway station 5km
299 rooms, including 16 suites, attached bath. single Rs1,100; double Rs1,300; suites on application. Facilities include travel counter, bank, business services, pool, health club, hairdresser, baby-sitter, shopping arcade.

Built on the reclaimed land of Back Bay (still printed deep-sea blue on some city maps). Modern, non-architectural, 18-storey block in the developing business area. Better placed for businessman than tourist. Part of the Taj Group, with their solid comfort and good service. Known for its good food: Gulzar restaurant is best, and there is Italian, Continental, Chinese food.

The Oberoi Nariman Point, Bombay 40021
Telephone: 2025757; Fax: 2043282; Telex: 11-4153/4154 OBBY
Airport 28km, railway station 2km
350 rooms, including suites, attached bath. Single Rs2,200; double Rs2,400; suites Rs4,000-12,000. The Oberoi Group's second, newish and immensely swish Bombay hotel sited bang next to the Oberoi Towers. All mod. cons and computerised telephones; large rooms, 24-hour butler service on each floor, business facilities, pool, health club, beauty salon, baby-sitter, extensive shopping arcade.

Opened in 1986, this unashamedly up-market arrival is presumably an attempt to today's answer to the Savoy, London. It supplies its 16 storeys with traditional on-call butler, period furniture, polished granite showers and baths, and a choice of four bars and restaurants. Then it adds the contemporary: computerised fitness equipment and 'environmental units' in the Health Club, 'The Belvedere' private Executive Club, and a business centre to satisfy gadget-freak businessmen.

Natraj 135 Marine Drive (Netaji Subhash Road), Bombay 400020
Telephone: 2044161; Telex: 11-2302 RAJA IN
Airports 27km, railway station 1km
83 rooms, including 10 suites, attached bath/shower. Single Rs925; double Rs1,050.

On the plus side are the central site, recent renovation and excellent views in the rooms overlooking the bay. Minuses are dreary tri-cuisine food, an ice-cream parlour (it is better to eat out) and general atmosphere.

Ritz 5 Jamshedji Tata Road, Bombay 400020
Telephone: 220141, 220116; Telex: 2520 RITZ IN
Airports 28km, railway station 2km
72 rooms, including 7 suites, attached bath. Single Rs860; double Rs985; suites Rs1,560-1,800.

Old, central hotel with character, newly painted, nice atmosphere. Indian and Italian and Continental food.

Fariyas Hotel 25 Off Arthur Bunder Road, Colaba, Bombay 400005
Telephone: 2042911; Telex: 3272 ABAN
Airports 26km, railway station 3km
80 rooms, including 5 suites, attached bath. Single Rs825; double Rs935.

Well established and well located, with friendly staff sending satsified guests off on their Indian travels.

Grand 17 Sprott Road, Ballard Estate, Bombay 400038
Telephone: 268211
Airports 25km, railway station 1km
72 rooms, attached bath. Single Rs355-395; double Rs485.

Old hotel with corridors around central courtyard with potted flowers. Newly green-painted, 3rd and 4th floor rooms have view over harbour, nice gentle atmosphere.

Hotel Diplomat 24-26 B. K. Boman Behram Marg, Colaba, Bombay 400039
Telephone: 2021661
Airports 25km, railway station 2km
52 rooms, atached bath. Single Rs375; double Rs475.

Recommended by one well-seasoned traveller used to comfort as 'much preferable to the Taj: dead cheap and simple but far better service. I go to the Taj to eat and drink'.

CLUBS

Neither of the two Bombay clubs with good rooms enjoys the social swing of Calcutta clubs. They offer peace, privacy, space and a certain charming refinement.

Royal Bombay Yacht Club Apollo Bunder, Bombay 400039
30 rooms. Single Rs350; double Rs605 (price includes all meals), plus a temporary membership fee of Rs250 for 28 days. To apply for membership and to book, write to The Secretary, including introductions from two members and advanced payment in Indian rupees. Library, billiards, table tennis, garden.

Stained-glass windows and steel engravings of ships decorate the spacious Yacht Club Chambers. With the room comes a bearer (Rs10 per day) to molly-coddle the guest with breakfast, bed-making, laundry etc.

Cricket Club of India D Vacha Road, Bombay
Telephone: 220262
40 rooms for men only. Rooms let by the week, single Rs200, double Rs400, plus temporary membership fee of Rs200 for 8 days, open to anyone. To apply for membership and booking, write to Major-Gen. Michigan, Secretary.

Affiliated to the Royal Overseas League, London and the Caledonian Club, Edinburgh.

Cricket, badminton, tennis, pool, squash, table tennis, cards. Huge grounds, very efficient, central and thus popular, so book well in advance. Good restaurant. The Cross Bats, a group of mainly first-class cricketers, fondly nicknamed the Blind Bats, meets here regularly for lunch.

Note: As in Delhi, the best budget accommodation for central location and clean but simple comfort are the YWCA, Madame Cama Road (tel: 2020445) and the YMCA, 12 Wodehouse Road (tel: 2020079).

AIRPORT AND BEACH HOTELS

Welcomgroup SeaRock Sheraton Land's End, Bandra, Bombay 400050
Telephone: 6425454; Fax: 6408046; Telex: 71230/71140 ROCK IN
Airports 10km, railway station 15km
398 rooms, including 9 suites, attached bath. Single Rs1,300-2,100; double Rs1,450-2,250; suites Rs3,500-5,000.

Extensive facilities include travel and airline counter, bank, business service, Executive Club, baby-sitter, health club (sauna, Turkish bath, yoga), beauty salon, shopping arcade, sports (tennis, squash, billiards, gym), 2 pools (adults and children), discotheque, 24-hour room service and restaurant.

Part of the Welcomgroup chain, recently refurbished rooms. Superb site, the hotel almost in the sea. Go for a high room and choose it for sunrise or sunset views. Enough amusements, pampering and sports on hand to save the most direly delayed air passenger from boredom. Six small restaurants each serving different cuisines: excellent North West Frontier, seafood, Dumpukht (as at Delhi's Maurya hotel), Continental, Far Eastern (revolving at the top) and 'shudh' vegetarian.

The Leela Kempinski Sahar, Bombay 400059
Telephone: 6363636; Fax: 6360606; Telex: 79236 KEMP IN
Airport 1km, railway station 15km
280 rooms, including 30 suites, attached bath. Single or double Rs1,850-2,100; suites Rs3,000-11,000.

Extensive facilities include all the regular services plus Privilege Club rooms, quantities of telephones in each room, fitness and racquet centre (gym, sauna, steam and Jacuzzi), tennis, squash and badminton courts, swimming pool, 2 bars and 3 restaurants.

New, equipped with every device to pamper the travelling holiday-maker or businessman with a day to spare to get brown or get into shape before taking a plane to the next stop. Reports of satisfied customers. The group has an equally swish new hotel in Goa (see p. 274).

Holiday Inn Balraj Sahani Marg, Juhu Beach, Bombay 400049

Telephone: 6204444; Fax: 6204452; Telex: 71266/71432

Airports 6km, railway station 12km

210 rooms, including 16 suites, attached bath. Single Rs1,250-1,700; doubles Rs1,400-1,700; suites Rs2,500-6,000.

Facilities include Executive Floor, travel desk, health club and beauty salon, shopping arcade, 2 swimming pools (adults and children), discotheque, 4 restaurants, 24-hour room service and coffee shop.

Sun-n-Sand Hotel, 39 Juhu Beach, Bombay 400049

Telephone: 6201811; Telex: 71282

Airports 7km, railway station 15km

118 rooms, including 6 suites, attached bath. Single Rs700; double Rs800; suites Rs900-1,800. Facilities include pool, health club and movies.

Information and reservations

Maharashtra Tourism Development Corporation, Express Towers, Madame Cama Road, Nariman Point (tel: 2024482/2026713/2027762/2024627). Best on trips out of Bombay, e.g. whether the steamer to Goa is operating; the best way to go to Ajanta and Ellora.

Government of India Tourist Office, 123 M Karve Road, Churchgate (tel: 293144), open Mon.-Sat., 8.30am-5.30pm (closing 12.30pm on the 2nd Sat., of the month and public holidays). Extremely knowledgeable and helpful staff. Issue Liquor Permits, essential for Gujarat (see below). Also have desks at both airports (open 24 hours) and at Taj Hotel, Mon.-Sat., 8.30am-3.30pm (closing 12.30pm on the 2nd Sat. of the month and public holidays).

Government of Gujarat Tourist Office, Dhanraj Mahal, C. Shivaji Road (tel: 243866).

Government of Goa, Daman and Diu Tourist Counter, Bombay Central Station (tel: 396288).

Government of Rajasthan Tourist Office, 230 D N Road (tel: 267162).

The Times of India, *The Indian Express*, *The Financial Express* and *Economic Times* are all good for news and local information, as is *The Sunday Observer*, headquartered here. *The Daily* is for gossip. The fortnightly semi-glossy, *Bombay*, has a 'briefing' section for films, performing arts, exhibitions, sport. The Government of India Tourist Office publishes *This Fortnight for You!* (free from their office) carrying much the same information in minimal form.

The best guide book to Bombay is a package by Miriam Kaye called *An Illustrated Guide to Bombay and Goa* (1990). The Government of India's free 28-page booklet is a survival kit of names and addresses. Their map is best (although not good). *The Latest Road Map of Bombay* is hopelessly out of date, even leaving reclaimed land and its buildings under the sea. But excellent journals and books on Bombay have been accumulating since the last century (see Bibliography).

TRAVEL AGENTS

American Express, Majithia Chamber, Dadabhoy Naoroji Road (tel: 266361/260629); Cox & Kings (India), Grindlays Bank Building, 272 Dr D N Road (tel: 2043065/653209); SITA, 8 Atlanta Building, Nariman Point (tel: 240666/233285/233584); TCI Chander Mukhi, Nariman Point (tel: 2021881/2027120).

AIRLINE OFFICES

Indian Airlines, Air-India Building, Nariman Point (tel: 2024142); Vayudoot, same address (tel:2048585). International airlines offices on Veer Nariman Road include Aeroflot (tel: 221743); British Airways (tel: 220888) and Swissair (tel: 222402). In the Taj hotel are Air France (tel: 2025021), Pan Am (tel: 2024024) and Cathay Pacific (tel: 2025234). At Nariman Point are Air India (tel: 2024142), Japan Airlines (tel: 233215) and Singapore Airlines (tel: 2023365), all in the Air-India Building, and Lufthansa (tel: 2023430) in Express Towers. Thai International (tel: 219191/215207) is in the World Trade Centre, Cuffe Parade.

TRAIN RESERVATIONS

Victoria Terminus Station, Bori Bunder (for trains to the east, south and a few north), open 9am-12.30pm, 1-4.30pm. Western Railway Reservation Office (for the west and north), Churchgate, open 8am-1.45pm, 2.45pm-8pm. These are for first-class bookings and Indrail Passes, and have Tourist Guide Assistants who hold the quota of seats reserved for those paying in foreign currency.

FOREIGN MISSIONS

UK: 2nd floor, Hong Kong and Shanghai Bank Building, M Gandhi Road (tel: 274874); USA: Lincoln House, Bhulabhai Desai Road (tel: 8226417); France: Tata Prasas N Gamadia Road, off Peddar Road (tel: 4949808/4948277); West Germany: 10th floor, Hoechst House, Nariman Point (tel: 232422). Most countries represented in Delhi have smaller representation in Bombay and are listed in the telephone directory. Foreigners Registration Office, Annex 2, Office of the Commissioner of Police, Dadabhoy Nao-roji Road, by Mahatma Phule Market (tel: 268111).

British Council Library, Mittal Tower A Wing, Nariman Point (tel: 223560). Bombay GPO is on Bori Bunder, near Victoria Terminus. The Central Telegraph Office is at Flora Fountain. If illness strikes, the top hotels have doctors on call and the others can find one quickly. There are several hospitals; chemists include Kemp & Co. in the Taj hotel and Wordell on Veer Nari-man Road.

The city by day

From Monday to Saturday Bombay is action-packed. Deals are struck. Mountains of rupees are made; more mountains are spent. The streets are full of businessmen scurrying to appointments. Merchants and traders race to keep up supplies in shops and markets. Cars blast their horns. Well organised beggars – some with devilish charm – earn the family wage at traffic lights. On Sunday, Bombay is silent except for the sound of the cricket bat. The smart spend the day en famille at the Willing-don or Gymkhana clubs, play cricket or golf and go to the races. The less smart play cricket on the maidans and go to museums and parks. It is the best day for seeing the Fort area architecture without getting run over.

Bombay's past and present are business, not culture. Unlike Calcutta and Delhi, there are few museums. And, although immigrants built every sort of temple, mosque and church, it is their secular buildings which are significant. So Bombay is an outdoor city made familiar by wandering the streets of the Fort area, where past tycoons are remembered by their own grand buildings and other people's monuments to them. Bombay's cosmopolitan entrepreneu-rial spirit is most lively in the huge network of bazaars. Late afternoon is the time to spy on Malabar Hill's grand homes before joining Bom-bayites for a sunset stroll along Chowpatty Beach or, more spectacular, watching the sun go down and Marine Drive light up from Naaz café opposite the Hanging Gardens.

The MTDC (state) and ITDC (central) tourist offices both run city sight-seeing tours. Neither are worth taking. Some of their stops are with-out interest, others need more time. The scat-tered itineraries mean more driving than see-ing. Far better to explore one area on foot, moving to the next by public transport. Bombay is swarming with taxis – check the meter works before hopping in. The courageous can take a double-decker bus, but avoid the rush hour. Although roads have old and new names (which get renewed), everyone except govern-ment employees uses the old ones.

Apollo Bunder From the opening of the Suez Canal until aeroplanes took over from liners, this is where most arrivals took their first step on Indian soil – ironically, it would be where the last of the British officially left. Drenched in early morning sunlight, the sparkling Gateway of India and the Taj hotel represent Britain's final imprint on the city and an early monument to the rising influence of the most successful Bombay Parsee tycoons, the Tatas.

Apollo Bunder has always been fashionable. A modest iron gazebo amused 19th century pro-menaders. All changed in 1911 when King-Emperor George V made the first-ever State visit to India by a reigning monarch. First a hugely decorative white plaster arch, with dome and minarets, was hastily erected for the King and Queen's arrival on December 2. Then, when they had gone, the good idea was made permanent and the visit commemorated with a yellow basalt arch based on Gujarati styles, de-signed by the Bombay Government architect, George Wittet. It was built in 1927, just 20 years before the final British parade through the arch and out of India. For the Taj building, see Where to Stay section. Inside the hotel, up the grand staircase, is the Sea Lounge for gracious morn-ing coffee and elegant afternoon tea. Around the building are displayed art works collected or commissioned by the Tatas. Early birds can see great activity on Sassoon Dock when the fisher-men unload their catch at dawn.

Fort area The area stretching from the remains of Fort St George westwards to the Maidans and from the Prince of Wales Museum north to Victoria Terminus. Fort is a rather loose term for the present core of Bombay which expanded from the original fort and still goes like a fair throughout the day, businessmen, shop-workers and students packing out the restaurants at lunchtime, then leaving en masse for the suburbs at night. Some of Bombay's old-est and finest buildings are here. Two of the old-est stand east of the arcaded Horniman Circle (formerly Elphinstone Circle, now named after an anti-Raj newspaper editor), the classical Mint and Town Hall (behind which are the Fort St George remains, exceedingly difficult to visit, and the old docks). The Mint, with its Ionic Portico, was built on reclaimed land in 1829 (to visit, apply to the Mint Master).

The purer Doric *Town Hall*, designed by Col. Thomas Cowper, fulfilled a double function: municipal building and a home for the Asiatic Society library. It was funded partly by public lottery and took 15 years to build, finishing in 1833. One hitch was the columns sent out from Britain for the 260ft facade: they were too big but fortunately found use in Byculla Church which was then being built. Building and library are open to the public. Inside, men perch at high newspaper racks. Around the grand, book-lined rooms stand statues of Bombay big-wigs: Mountstuart Elphinstone and Sir Charles Forbes, both by Chantrey; Lord Elphinstone; Sir Bartle Frere and Sir Jamsetji Jeejeebhoy.

Frere was the Governor who brought Bombay architecture up to date. He had James Trub-shawe draw up the plan and imported British architects for individual buildings. Frere cham-pioned the Gothic Revival, fashionable in Britain, and under him (1862-67) the newly affluent Bombay became, in the words of Gavin Stamp: 'the finest Gothic City in the world with a remarkable concentration of Gothic public buildings'. And it still is.

The grandest are on *K. B. Patel Marg*, past the Cathedral of St Thomas (begun by Aungier in 1672) and across the Piccadilly Circus of Bom-bay, Hautatma Chowk (formerly Flora, and before that Frere, Fountain). They stand looking across the Maidan, although buildings on the reclaimed land beyond the green now block their sea view – and the consequent impressive land view for arrivals by sea. There is Trub-shawe's old GPO (now the Central Telegraph Office); Col. Wilkins's Public Works Office (1869-72); Lt-Col. Fuller's High Court (1871-9); Sir Gilbert Scott's University (1869-78) with the huge Rajabai library clock tower (good views from the top) and Cowasjee Jehangir Hall; and Wilkins's Secretariat (1865-72).

At the north end of the Fort area is Frederick William Stevens's masterpiece, Victoria Termi-nus (1878-87), showing 'how the Gothic of Scott and Burges could be adapted to India and make a really impressive public building' (Stamp). F. W. Stevens's Municipal Buildings (1893) and Begg's domed GPO (1901) complete this group.

Two other facts account for Gothic Bombay's success: the good local polychrome building stone and the delightful, spirited animal and bird carvings by Indian craftsmen working under the direct stimulus of Lockwood Kipling, Rudyard's father, who was head of sculpture at Bombay School of Art and responsible for carry-ing William Morris's arts and crafts ideals to India. (he also founded Lahore's splendid museum, see Delhi chapter.)

Prince of Wales Museum Another building de-signed by Wittet to commemorate the globe-trotting George V, this time his first visit to India in 1905 before he became king. Shielded from the surrounding roads by a mature garden, the museum was begun in 1905, became official in 1909, took in visitors from 1914, officially began to work in 1921 and was completed in 1937 – a glorious example of the workings of Indian bureaucracy.

The four sections – art, archaeology, natural history, forestry – now form one of the most im-portant collections in India, well displayed and

a joy to visit. From the beginning, locals gave generously: the families of Tata, Hydari, Jehan-gir, Gupta and Latifi. The nucleus of the fabulous art section is the Purshottam Vishram Mawji Collection – don't miss it. The miniature paintings are upstairs. Good guide book, pamphlets and reproductions available. Open Tues.-Sun., 10.15am-5.30pm (July-Sept. to 6pm; March-June to 6.30pm). Closed on public holi-days. Jehangir Art Gallery, reached by a dif-ferent entrance, exhibits what is, sadly, the best in contemporary Indian art, but the Samovar Café is good, and fashionable among the liter-ati.

Markets Concentrated in the area between Victoria Terminus and Maulana Shaukatali (Grant) Road. A maze of action and colour in narrow lanes full of temples, mosques and tall, rickety Gujarati-style houses, whose carved, projecting balconies almost meet. Actually buy-ing something is an added extra, see shopping section. Beware of pick-pockets. Inside *Crawford Market* (bas-reliefs by Lockwood Kipling on the front) are flowers and fruit, piles of pomfret and Bombay duck, and future meals of chickens, goats and birds squawking, scampering and hopping around sacks of grain, mini temples and astrologers' hide-outs. (Have a fresh mango, pineapple or pomegranate juice at the Badshah Cold Drinks House.) Pillow Corner is across the road. To visit by car, the driver will drop you and arrange a collection time, since there is no parking.

Just north is *Zaveri bazaar*, off Abdul Rahman Street. Here, in mirrored, floodlit caves of gold and silver guarded by electric doors, koli fishing wives jostle with Parsee princesses to hand over fat wads of rupees to even fatter shopkeepers. The brass and copper bazaar (with the up-to-date stainless steel bazaar) is at the top of Kalba-devi Road, by Mumbadevi temple and tank, home of the goddess who gave Bombay her name. To the west is the bangle bazaar on Bhu-leshwar.

Further north, centring on Mutton Street, is *Chor Bazar*, stocking everything from new linen and old lamps to Staffordshire figures and san-dlewood sweetmeat boxes. In the parallel Dha-boo Street is the leather market.

Marine Drive Only claimed from the sea in 1920 – hence the austere buildings lining it. But at night its superb sweep from Nariman Point to Malabar Hill twinkles prettily, earning it the cli-ché: the Queen's necklace. It is the last British contribution to Bombay's town plan, designed as 'Ocean Way' to follow the whole of the west shore, but still incomplete. Bombayites prome-nade here, watching cricket on the green by day, couples bashfully holding hands for sun-sets and stars by night. It is a great meeting place.

Chowpatty Beach, at the far end, is the focus for political meetings and festival jollifications as well as daily street entertainment (extra on Sunday), yoga, gossip and snoozing. Sample belpuri, the Bombay snack of murmuras (puffed rice), sev (crisp gram flour strings), onions, herbs and spices made up at stalls according to your taste. The stall-holders are often third generation Uttar Pradesh immigrants, but the ice-cream-wallahs of the stalls behind come from the Punjab. The rich, creamy pineapple and mango ice-cream is delicious. To finish, the paan-wallahs of Chowpatty are famous, their concoctions starting at 50 paise for a simple digestive and rising to Rs500 for an exotic aphrodisiac. The nearby Aquarium is good (open Tues.-Sun., 11am-8pm).

Malabar Hill Still the smartest place to live, with plenty of elegant old bungalows in leafy gardens, despite the double enticement of the Juhu-Bandra jet-set and developers' cheques. Those who sell out to high-rise builders often get the penthouse apartment as part of the deal. Old Parsee families and former maharajas now have diamond dealers, construction magnates and film-stars for neighbours. On the southern tip, Malabar Point, is Raj Bhavan, a complex of bungalows serving as the seaside Government House until Frere made it the official headquarters in 1885. (It is closed to the public, best seen from Marine Drive.) Nearby is Walkeshwar Temple, where the god Rama stopped overnight en route to save his wife Sita from the evil clutches of Ravana.

On top of the hill are the Parsee *Towers of Silence*. Although they are behind a wall and cannot be visited, they are one of India's most famous tourist monuments. Also here are the Hanging Gardens, reminiscent of municipal gardens at Worthing but with amusing topiary of elephants, ploughmen, camels, etc. The nicer Kamala Nehru Children's Park (named after the first Prime Minister's wife), is opposite. The best views of all are from the top terrace of Naaz café next door.

Haji Ali's Tomb The mausoleum built at the end of a 500-yard long, beggar-lined causeway is supposedly named after a rich Bombayite who, after his pilgrimage (haj) to Mecca, gave away his wealth and lived here. At low tide, when the causeway is not submerged, Muslims come with their servants to pay homage. They exchange rupees for piles of paise with the moneychangers, then run the gauntlet of the beggars, giving paise to each as the servant ladles home-cooked rice from a cauldron into his metal bowl.

Mahalaxmi Race Course Named after the goddess of the nearby Hindu temple who, aptly in Bombay, concerns herself with wealth. The British may have brought the racing habit to Bombay (having held their first race in Barasat, near Calcutta, and built their first proper race course at Madras in 1777) but the Parsees have been its strength and are still prominent. It was Dorabji Rustomji who helped establish the original course at Byculla and was an energetic member of the Bombay Turf Club, founded in 1800.

With the expansion of Bombay, the new course opened here in 1878. At the same time, Bombay became well-known for horse-trading, especially in Arab horses. But in 1948 the government banned racing Arab horses in India, thus stimulating the breeding industry which now has more than 70 studs across the country. The Stud Book is kept at the Royal Western India Turf Club in Bombay. The top race of the whole Indian racing calendar is the Derby held in Bombay in February-March.

One of the most successful horse owner/breeders of Bombay is Ranjit Bhat who already had 4 Derby winners by the time he was aged 37. The 1977 winner, Squanderer, was trained by Rashid Byramji of Bangalore, trainer of the most Derby winners in recent years. Jagdish, the top prize-winning jockey, rode Squanderer, making this his fourth Derby win. But while Squanderer is considered one of the best ever Indian-bred horses, it is Own Opinion who holds the stakes-earning record, a total of more than Rs18.5 lakhs. Other big owner/breeders include Y. M. Chaudhry, London Pilsner beer baron Noshir Irani, Bombay industrialist Sunit Khatau (whose Track Lightning won the 1981 Derby and the Invitation Cup), and Mr M. A. Ramaswamy of Madras who owns more than 80 horses including the most valuable, Own Opinion.

The course is charming: immaculate flower beds surround the green and white grandstand, where fusty aged colonials and fashionable Bombayites stroll, gossip and lay quite heavy bets. During the season, November to March, meetings are on most Wednesdays and at weekends. As India's most popular race course, with a grandstand seating almost 5,000, all race days are well-attended with an average crowd of 8,000. You can bet, too – who knows, if you stay for the season you may pip Rajendra Kisha's record of Rs48 lakhs winnings in 1971-2. The jockey to watch is Pesi Shroff who, aged just 22, won 61 races in the 1987-8 season and has made more than 600 wins in all.

Victoria and Albert Museum and gardens Inspired by the other V&A in South Kensington in London and built by public subscription raised by Sir George Birdwood, a physician and authority on Indian crafts who became the first curator, the collection recounts the history of Bombay with prints, maps and charming model groups of trades and crafts. Open Mon., Tues.,

143

Fri. and Sat., 10.30am-5pm; Thurs., 10am-4.45pm; Sun., 8.30am-4.45pm, closed Wed. Outside, the statue of Prince Albert and the clock tower were given by Sir Albert Sassoon. Elephanta Island, in Bombay harbour, was named by the Portuguese after a stone elephant they found there. The elephant now stands to the right of the museum.

There is nothing municipal about the excellent 34-acre Victoria Gardens, a mature and serious horticultural park laid out by Birdwood in the 1850s on drained swamp land. A list of currently blossoming trees and shrubs is chalked up on a blackboard at the entrance. The Minton tiles, terracotta panels and entrance turnstile were all imported from England. Inside, banished from M G Road, is Noble's marble statue of Queen Victoria, mostly paid for by the Gaekwad of Baroda. The zoo is here, with elephant, camel and pony rides for children. Open Thurs.-Tues. 8am-6pm.

Space and peace

Not plentiful in Bombay. The expansive sweep of Marine Drive gives a feeling of space, and the breeze brings welcome fresh air, but there is little peace. Right in the city, the maidans provide both space and peace in the early morning. Victoria Gardens are green and quiet; the Hanging Gardens are dull and quiet. At Mahalaxmi Temple, on a promontory below Malabar Hill, the air smells sweet and the devotees arriving to perform puja also find a breeze and certain peace. Entrée to the Gymkhana or Willingdon Clubs means quantities of space, peace and service. During the afternoon, there are more snores than splashes on the walled lawn of the Taj pool area. All these are jam-packed on Sunday, when the streets and lanes are quiet for architecture addicts.

Keeping fit and beautiful

If the pace of Bombay is not exercise enough, the sports facilities are good and better than in Delhi. The sea surrounding Bombay is definitely not for bathing. If a swim is essential to survival, the best pools, open to residents only, are at the Taj (set in large, walled lawn), Oberoi Towers (7 floors up, stunning views over bay and city) and SeaRock hotels, and at the big social clubs. These also provide more serious sports amid extensive grounds, wicker chairs, and club-houses with libraries that take *The Daily Telegraph*, *The New Yorker*, etc. Clubs usually offer temporary membership to foreigners. The good hotels can arrange some games for guests: the Taj manages tennis, golf and sailing, the President tennis and golf. Joggers can take on Marine Drive.

Health clubs The body beautiful can be pampered to an extraordinary level in Bombay. Both the Taj and Oberois have scrupulously clean health clubs and beauty salons housed in a never-ending warren of rooms. The Kempinski is good, too, while the President has less extensive facilities. Taj, Oberois and Kempinski also have the latest gadgets and facilities, including massage, sauna, jacuzzi and Turkish baths, gym and yoga (some available to each sex at different times, so check); their beauty salons are excellent and open to non-residents, offering every sort of hair, face, hand and foot treatment. A head and back massage works wonders on the nerves and relax the whole body; a foot massage renews sight-seeing enthusiam. Indians from other cities spend whole days here being rubbed, scrubbed and titivated from head to toe, with food and drink on call.

CLUB CHECK LIST
Bombay Gymkhana, M G Road. For temporary membership (up to 6 months), apply to The Secretary in writing or on arrival, preferably mentioning a member for proposal (from a firm or hotel). The word gymkhana is a corruption of a word meaning ball-house, probably created in the Bombay presidency to describe an essential ingredient of Raj life: a public place for athletics and sport.

The Bombay Gym was established in 1875 on land in the city centre leased from the government. The first Indian test match was played here. They are now held at Wankhede Stadium. Bombay is the centre of cricket in India. Several matches may be played on one green simultaneously, a single player fielding for two matches – but no accidents to date. The 1,400 members tend to be young or with families. There is cricket, of course, plus hockey, swimming pool, football, tennis (6 courts, 3 floodlit for night play), snooker, billiards, squash, and table tennis. The multi-verandahed mock Tudor clubhouse has a relaxed, friendly atmosphere.
Chambur Golf Club, Chambur. At least an hour out of town, but a nice course. Apply through hotel.
Cricket Club of India, D Vacha Road (tel: 2040250). Known as the CCI, see hotel section for membership and facilities. Reliable restaurant. Apply here for details of test matches throughout India and for the two big Indian inter-state competitions: the Duleep Trophy and Ranji Trophy, named after two great Gujarati cricketers. Bombay used to win the competitions regularly. Its team included Sunil Gavaskar, who has achieved the most runs in test cricket. But now Haryana, with Kapel Dev in the team, is stronger.
Maharashtra State Angling Association, c/o Safe Glass Corporation Ltd, 97/99 Dhanji Street.

Contact the Secretary for temporary membership. Fishing is at Powai Lake outside the city, boat, rod, tackle and bait provided. Possibility of catching katla, rahu, mirgil, kalbos, betki, gorami.

Royal Western India Turf Club, K. Khadye Marg, Mahalaxmi. Apply to the Secretary for the season's fixtures list.

United Services Club, Cuffe Parade. Run by the army. Golf and swimming.

Willingdon Sports Club, K Khadye Marg, Tumsiwadi. Apply to the Joint Secretaries for temporary membership (weekly fee, maximum 4 months) and, as with the Bombay Gym, try to acquire a proposer. Founded in 1917 and, notably, open to Britons and Indians from that moment. Those Bombayites not at the Gym on Sunday are probably here. 3,000 members, all believing they belong to the most exclusive club and many passing the week-ends in its extensive grounds, playing golf, tennis, squash and badminton, swimming or just lazing around the gardens and rambling clubhouse. Raj food.

Good eats: Night lights

Eating is a treat here. Bombayites often eat out, especially at lunchtime when workers living in the suburbs can meet their friends. And as each immigrant community brought their own cuisine, there is a huge variety to choose from. It is easy to avoid the awful live European bands in some hotel restaurants, often misleadingly called supper clubs or night clubs.

Cultural entertainment is on a par with Delhi. As well as the avalanche of films, especially classic Bombay talkies, India's top performers in theatre, music and dance fill the concert halls nightly. Moreover, there are pleasant bars for sun-downers and, later on, a choice of discotheques. If this is the first stop in India, take advantage: such a variety of evening entertainment is rare outside the big cities.

Partial prohibition currently operates in Bombay, meaning that, although there is no dry day and beer is served everywhere, a permit is necessary for buying spirits outside hotel bars and restaurants.

RESTAURANTS
Even in Delhi, where people are loath to admit to Bombay's supremacy in anything and where eating out has improved enormously in recent years, the mention of Bombay restaurants sends hands to stomachs as their owners crow: 'I put on pounds when I go there', 'There's this South Indian place – better than anywhere down south', 'Ooh, the fish curry from City Kitchen – but they run out if you are late', 'There's a little place near the Metro Cinema . . .'. On and on. And with justification. It is the only city in India

with the money and lifestyle to support an extensive network of good restaurants. There is excellent Iranian, Chinese, Continental and Portuguese-Goan food in addition to every cuisine of India, from Bengal to Gujarat, from North-West Frontier to deep South. Although some of the best are in the hotels, here is a rare chance to choose from dozens of street restaurants and eat fresh, excellent food, even if the decor is basic. The few listed below are just a springboard for gastronomic exploration. The one cuisine it is difficult to find is the truly local Maharashtran, best cooked in private houses.

As well as the distinctive cuisines, the Bombay kitchen melting-pot has produced certain dishes associated with the city. Local pomfret, Bombay duck and shellfish (including lobster, but over-priced) are caught off Bombay. Bombay duck is the dried small bummelo fish. The Parsee dish dhansak (demanding some twenty-four vegetable, spice, herb and pulse ingredients) is a chicken or lamb dish cooked with lentils and vegetables. It was traditionally eaten for Parsee Sunday lunch but has now entered the general Bombay repertoire (best eaten at Irani cafés). In season (April-June), the west coast Alphonso mangoes, the king of mangoes, are eaten straight or spiced with cardomon, in a dish called aamras. Belpuri (see above, Chowpatty Beach) is the classic Bombay snack.

West Indian food of Maharashtra and Gujarat starts with pudding. A thali of light vegetable dishes follows, served with a constantly replenished variety of freshly baked puris and roti (breads), rather than the rice of the South, and shrikand (thick, sweetened curd flavoured with saffron and nutmeg). Both states produce quantities of milk and make exceptional curd (yoghurt) and exotic fruit ice-creams. The local Aarey Milk Colony and Worli Dairy are much-plugged, over-rated tourist attractions.

Typical Bombay and West Indian dishes are served in the big restaurants.

RESTAURANT SUGGESTIONS
The big hotels constantly change their restaurants, so ask about latest developments. **General Indian** Tanjore, Taj; top of the market, excellent regional dishes, will prepare any others on request. Eat lounging on low sofas entertained by quality Indian dancers and musicians. Gaylord, Veer Nariman Road; open 1956, the second in the chain after Delhi, 1952, tables inside and outside (all too rare). Delhi Durbar, 197 Falkland Road; in the red-light district, better than its branch at Colaba. Best dishes, biryani and dabba gosh. Copper Chimney at Dr Annie Besant Road, Worli; merits the effort to get there, better than its sister branch at K Dubash Road in the city. Khyber, Kala Ghoda, Fort; whacky decor for smart, spicy Punjabi

food. *Sheetal*, 648 Khar Pali Road; one of the best places to eat fresh shellfish.

Mughlai Indian *Moghul Room, Oberoi*; setting and atmosphere up to Tanjore (see above), meat in rich sauces of spices and cream. *Gulzar, President*; equally rich Hyderabadi and biryani dishes.

Gujarati West Indian *The Village, Poonam International Hotel* (near Mahalaxmi Racecourse); set up like a Gujarati village, modelled after Vishalla, outside Ahmedabad, overlooks the sea. Jolly atmosphere, food good. *Samrat*, behind Eros Cinema, off J Tata Road; very Gujarati, heavy thali dish, pudding first. *Thacker's*, corner of M Karve Road and 1st Marine Street; same as Samrat. Chetana, 34 K Dubash Marg (Rampart Row), Kala Ghoda, sited opposite the Jehangir Art Gallery and serving Gujarati and Rajasthani vegetarian dishes. *Thaili*, Tara Baug Estate, Charni Road, home cooking and family recipes from the Kutch owners. Various cheaper vegetarian 'clubs' in Kalbadeve, open to all, include *Ram Club*, above a sweet shop, opposite the Corn Exchange; supposed to have the best Rajasthani food in town, although the place is not pretty. Try lassi, vegetables, chapattis and rice. Others are *Friends' Union, Joshi Club* and *Thakker's Club*, described by gourmand Mala Singh as producing thalis 'out of this world'.

South Indian *New India Coffee Shop*, Kittridge Road, Sassoon Dock; claims to serve the only real Kerala breakfast. *Purohit*, Churchgate. *Woodlands*, near the Opera House; dosa and pongal recommended.

Irani cafés and Parsee food Not many straightforward Parsee restaurants. Even Parsee wedding receptions have forsworn the legendary spreads. If invited, go to the Parsee club, *The Ripon*. Otherwise, Parsee food, with lots of meat and egg dishes, can be found in the Irani chaikhanas (tea houses), the equivalent of a Parisian café. They are mostly run by Zoroastrians who came to Bombay from Iran early this century. Some have fine interiors of stained glass, mirrors and tiles – and photographs of the late Shah of Iran.

Best for breakfast (from 5am, most cafés stock the daily papers), lunch and tea. Eat Mawa (cakes), khara (biscuits) or a dibbe wala meal of chicken or mutton covered with thick, spicy soup ladled from a huge witch's cauldron. Dunk in pieces of bun (hard bread), and wash them down with phudina (mint tea made with milk and sugar) or beer. During the 1950s there were about 3,000 cafés in Bombay. Among the few remaining, the best and most beautiful include *Bastani, Kyani* and the *Sassanian Restaurant and Bakery*, all at the north end of M G Road, at Dhobi Talao; *Merwan* on M Shakatali (Grant) Road; the *Bombay A1* (eat Parsee dishes of mutton dhansak, fish patia and sali boti), *Vazir's*,

Pyrkes at Flora Fountain (modern), *Byculla* and *Regal*, both near Byculla railway station, near Victoria Gardens, *Military Café*, Meadows Street, Fort area, and *Paradise Snack Bar*, Sindh Chambers, Colaba, opened in 1956. Less pretty is *Piccolo*, Homi Mody Street, an outlet of the Ratan Tata Institute.

Goan If Goa is not on the itinerary, a good Goan meal is the next best thing. Try *Martin's*, Colaba. *City Kitchen*, Fort Market; best for fish at lunchtime; so go early they tend to run out. Plus three hotel restaurants: *New Martin Hotel*, 21 Glamour House, near Strand Cinema, Strand Road; *St Mary Hotel*, 120 St Mary Road, Mazgaon; and *Saayba Hotel*, Bhatiya Building, S V Road, Bandra.

Maharashtran *Sindhugurg*, R K Vaidya Road, Dadar; local patrons eat thalis and will help recommend favourite dishes. *Tambe Arogya Bhavan*, N C Kelkar Road, Dadar; opened in the 1940s and popular ever since.

Chinese *Nanking*, Shivaji Marg, Colaba; the best of many, justly lauded in London (by Bernard Levin, among others) and New York, simple, clean, cheap, everything (but especially whole Pomfret Nanking for two) is delicious. *Chop Sticks*, Veer Nariman Road; good food and outside café tables with local paan stall. *The Golden Dragon, Taj*; Szechwan, also renowned, reviving its flagging reputation. *Kamling*, Veer Nariman Road; one of the oldest in Bombay, opened 1938, Cantonese, twelve Chinese cooks prepare good, simple food. Packed out for lunch and dinner. *China Gardens*, Om Chambers, 123 August Kranti Marg, Kemp's Corner; current favourite of the smart set who eat Chinese, Thai and Japanese there.

Polynesian *The Outrigger, Oberoi*: So far, the only one in Bombay. Lunch is a buffet.

Continental Can usually be persuaded to serve Indian food too. Worth investigating as they often pinch the best rooftop views. But cooking almost like home and often comes with live European bands. *Ménage à Trois, Taj Mahal*; currently the best in town, set up by a London restaurateur. *The Society, Ambassador hotel*; Bombayites consider it to have the best Continental food, also serves Indian. *La Brasserie, Oberoi*; upmarket coffee shop; and *La Rotisserie, Oberoi*, upmarket restaurant.

Italian *Trattoria, President Hotel*; the hotel's 24-hour coffee shop, reasonable pasta.

Breakfast specials In addition to the Irani cafés (see above), try *Gulshan-e-Tran*, Palton Road, Crawford Market, which opens at 7am and runs all day.

Lunch specials Excellent buffet spread at the *Moghul Room, Oberoi* – similar one at the Taj is remarkably bad. More fun are the Irani cafés and lunchtime haunts of businessmen in the Flora Fountain area which often close at night. Try the

Khyber, M G road (tandoor); *Vienna Hotel*, near Metro Cinema (ask for fish lunch). If by chance you are in Juhu, eat very fresh fish from the small shacks on the beach.

See also SeaRock and Chowpatty Beach, above. In Colaba, near the smart Taj Mahal, *Bade Mian Sheekh Kabab Stall* in Tulloch Road is recommended for a quick kebab.

Sweetmeats *Mathura Dairy*, near the Ambassador hotel; especially for the renowned Bengali concoctions. *Princess Kulfi House*, Samaldas Gandhi Marg (Princess Street); freshly made sweets and ice-creams. *Parsee Dairy*, Princess Street; ice-cream so thick it needs a knife to cut it.

Tea *Sea Lounge, Taj*: the Fortnums of Bombay, deep sofas, the smart meeting between shopping sprees. Tea, sandwiches and cakes. *Gaylord*, Veer Nariman Road; sit outside, café informality, delicious milkshakes, tea, beer and cakes. *Poolside, Taj*: as guests wake from siesta, waiters scurry back and forth delivering trays of tea and fresh lime sodas.

Cocktails *The Ambassador* hotel for best 360 degree views from bar above revolving restaurant. The *Taj's* rooftop bar is good, but the *Oberoi's* has strange windows – it is almost impossible to see out of them. Colonial cocktails in the wicker chairs of clubs have great style.

24-hour coffee shops The big hotels have these rather useful cafés. Those in the *Taj*, *Oberois* and *President* are good for quick, light meals.

NIGHT LIFE

Discotheques (Sometimes known as 'night spots' in India.) A discotheque only lives when it is full of people. The Indians have missed this vital point and persist with their elitism, making membership very expensive and exclusive. So several potentially good discotheques playing pacey, imported tapes, are half empty except on Fridays and Saturdays. To find candid views on the current best, talk to the Guest Relations Desk in your hotel; with Juhu and Bandra the fashionable residential areas, you may well be sent on a 30-minute taxi ride up there. Membership is on the door.

CULTURE

It cannot be stressed strongly enough that regular opportunities to see the top exponents of classical Indian music and dance-drama are confined to Delhi, Bombay and Calcutta. Notable exceptions are Madras, where there are performances of Bharata Natyam dance, and Cochin for Kathkali dance. See Information section for how to find out what is on where.

Performances are usually at 6.15pm or 7pm. The Taj and President hotels have classical dancing at the earlier time, but it is not very good. Public halls used by visiting artists include Birla Matushri Sabhagar, Tejpal Auditorium, Patkar Hall, Rabindra Natya Mandir, Shivaji Mandir, the huge Shanmukhananda Hall, Lokmanya Talik, the Tata Theatre and the Homi Bhaba Auditorium. The acoustics for the Tata Theatre and the Lincoln Centre in New York are, inappropriately, by the same designer: good for European chamber music but no good for Indian.

Theatre The Maharashtrans and Gujaratis have a strong creative thrust, like the Bengalis, but Bombay is a cultural slave to the West and to its Hindi film world. Thus, direct imports such as 'Evita' and 'Death of a Salesman' run for months in packed houses, while traditional Indian plays in Hindi or English fill the remaining theatres. The now highly commercial Parsee theatre, developed from the British touring companies, once full of the literati and an inspiration for early films, produces lightweight comedies. The contemporary, often vibrant, Marathi and Gujarati plays, performed in their own language or in English, attract thinner audiences and may only pop up for a day or so before the troupe disappears on tour – these and the Bengali theatre are now the most lively in India, playing to enthusiastic, knowledgeable audiences and often using keen amateur actors who do a job by day and act by night. It is these companies who also stage Shakespeare. Alyque Padamsee recently put on 'Othello' starring Kabir Bedi. Well worth finding, so inquire at the National Theatre and the National Centre for the Performing Arts. Simple folk drama is sometimes at the Hanuman Theatre, Delisle Road.

After Independence, Indian theatre underwent radical changes and by the 1960s was acquiring a national character. The main exponents were four dramatists: Sombhu Mitra from Bengal, Girish Karnad from Karnataka, Mohan Rakesh who wrote in Hindi, and, perhaps the most important, Vijay Tendulkar, a Maratha. For their texts they went back to Indian classical Sanskrit works or historical events, but they gave their plays a new flexibility, allowing for plenty of music and dance and often incorporating folk traditions. Tendulkar's 'Ghashiram Kotwal', set in a period of Marathi history but injected with contemporary analogies, is one of the most impressive of these plays. Habib Tanvir (now based in Delhi, see p. 69) used folk tunes and techniques to present Hindi versions of Sanskrit texts, so following a play is not difficult.

The lively Marathi theatre continues to evolve at Pune, where both Tendulkar and Mohan Agashe write and direct. A trip to Pune could take in a performance at the Bal Gandharva, Nehru or Tilak Smarak Nidhi theatres. Otherwise, plenty of productions are brought to Bombay.

Contemporary Hindi plays are found at various lively centres. One is the slightly controversial Prithvi theatre, out at Juhu (with adjacent restaurant). The late Jennifer Kendal and her husband Shashi Kapoor were actively involved – they met when they were each acting in their parents' unconventional family theatre companies. Shashi then forsook his family to be with Jennifer in the Kendal's Shakespearana. Funded by the trust left by his father the great actor Prithviraj Kapoor (which also supports cancer hospitals in Goa and Bombay), Prithvi promotes a national Hindi theatre by putting on its own productions and offering visiting theatre companies low rents.

Cinema Bombay revolves around films. The video may have arrived in most households, but films are still the raison d'être of Bombay social life and a large chunk of its financial life. For a tourist to miss seeing a Hindi film is like missing the theatre on a visit to London. A regular Hindi film is a sophisticated, slick and perfectly timed mixture of heroism, romance and fighting on wildly extravagant sets, interspersed with seductive song and dance (the dancer miming to someone else's voice), all filmed in dazzling hues that give new meaning to 'glorious Technicolor'. They combine the talents of Busby Berkeley, Fred Astaire and Ginger Rogers.

The story is immaterial, although the audience gets completely involved, shouting to warn the hero of an enemy, cheering when a battle is won.

The film is three or four hours of pure escapism and great entertainment, which is why an Indian spends the first part of his wage on the weekly 'philum'. And it is why a humble servant reasoned with his mistress, with astonishing profundity, that he should have his wages a day early to pay for his film ticket: 'Because you have everything, memsahib, but we have nothing, so we need films for our dreams'.

Naturally there are hundreds of cinemas (some showing Western films), a few surviving from the 1930s-50s, including the Metro on 1st Marine Street, Eros on J Tata Road and M Karve Road, and the very dilapidated but pretty Opera House, in from Chowpatty Beach (with Tea Rooms next door). There are at least three shows a day, at about 3pm, 6pm and 9pm, and some morning shows at 9am and noon. Balcony seats are best. *Bombay* magazine has a round-up of the principal films, with criticisms. Newspapers give minimal details; giant hoardings even less. The avalanche of film magazines give no details but are almost as entertaining as the films, full of gossip about the gods and goddesses of the film world, and phenomenally bitchy. Among the juiciest are *Ciné Blitz, Star Dust, Star and Style* and *Film World. Screen* is considered the best magazine/trade paper.

India produces the most films in the world, about 800 films in 12 languages every year. Bombay is the centre today and Bombay is where it all began. The Lumière Brothers' Cinematographe was first demonstrated here on July 6 1896, at Watson's Hotel, Esplanade Mansion, just six months after its first showing in Paris. It was advertised as 'The marvel of the century. The wonder of the world. Living photograph pictures.' Success was immediate. There were special zenana shows for women in purdah. And there was no elitism: from the beginning, tickets were cheap, creating the char-anna-wallah (four-anna-bloke) mass audiences, which have determined the rise and fall of the industry's stars and studios ever since.

Dhundiraj Phalke, affectionately known as Dadasahib (daddy-sir), was India's first great director and once observed, with justification: 'I established the film industry in India in 1912.' This was the year he completed his film 'Raja Harishchandra', to be released on May 3 the following year – the first Indian feature film, Pundalik, by R. G. Torney and N. G. Chitre, came out in 1912. Phalke's film was made in Bombay, and he did its script, casting, direction, photography, developing and printing, using British equipment. The titles were in Hindi and English to reach the char-anna-wallahs and their memsahibs. It did so well that two years later he employed 100 people in his studio, the blueprint for future Indian studios. Of his 20 feature films, 'Lanka Dahan' (Burning of Lanka) was such a box-office bonanza that takings had to be hauled away in bullock carts. The film's plot is an episode from the mythological epic, the Ramayana. These myths, together with lives of saints and Muslim romances, have remained sure winners as subjects throughout Indian film history.

The post-World War I industrial boom in Bombay brought fortune seekers and professionalism to films. Studios and actors desperately imitated Hollywood. After the 'Thief of Bagdad''s popularity in 1925, a certain Master Vithal was heralded as India's Douglas Fairbanks. Prithviraj Kapoor (father of Shashi and Raj), who left Calcutta theatre for Bombay films, earned the nick-name 'Errol Flynn of India'.

But Hollywood films reigned supreme, accounting for 85% of films shown in India. Nevertheless, the 1930s and 1940s were the golden age of Bombay film-making. The first talkie film 'Alam Ara', was made in Hindustani by Ardeshir Irani and released in Bombay in 1931. Bombay Talkies, opened in 1934 by Himansu Rai and his wife, was the biggest studio and its Hindi films were the forerunners of today's commercial successes: a careful mixture of glamour, music, melodrama, song and a tiny drop of social consciousness or moral message.

In Pune the energetic Prabhat Studios turned out earthy, imaginative, intelligent films, often in Marathi with the occasional rather uncomfortable Hindi versions aimed at a larger audience. Films were made fast. E. Billimoria, the first Indian cowboy, starred in more than 300 curry-Westerns – with the added feat of avoiding singing and dancing in any.

Irani's 'Alam Ara', just pipped Calcutta's J. F. Madan to the post. It contained 10 songs and first-night tickets changed hands at 20 times their face value. Elsewhere audiences had to be enticed with promises: 'Hear your Gods and Goddesses talk in your own language'. The enxt year, Irani released the first Indian film in English, 'Noorjehan', about the Mughal emperor Jahangir's ambitious wife. And in 1937 Irani produced another first: 'Kisan Kanya' was India's first film in colour.

The smooth changeover to talkies in India, as opposed to the traumas undergone in Hollywood, was because many actors had stage and voice training. But there were hitches. Men could no longer play women's parts. And when Hindi emerged as the most popular language, some non-Hindi-speaking stars bit the dust. One was the 1920s heroine Sulochana, whose salary had exceeded that of the Governor of Bombay. Inspired by Bengal, theatre playwrights were employed to write the dialogues. Film dialogues are still very important and sell as separate records. In the 1970s one film dialogue sold half a million copies.

But film music was even more important and is still the main criterion for a film's success. Music cuts across language barriers, whips up the emotion of a scene and has anyway always been part of traditional Indian theatre, religion, festivals – even politics. Film songs are the chart hits of India. Singer and actor are usually two different people, but no one seems to mind hearing their favourite voice fronted by a succession of fashionable actresses in various films. Lata Mangeshkar, queen of Hindi film singing, has recorded more than 25,000 songs.

The change in power from the studio to the individual star occurred in the late 1930s, when financially tottering studios had to free their actors from the pay-roll and exclusive contracts. Actors then went free-lance and the good ones could – and still do – call the tune. Currently, Amitabh Bachchan is king and can name the craziest price ever demanded by an actor and get it. When he was injured in 1980, visitors to the hospital included the Prime Minister, Mrs Gandhi. On his recovery the hoardings proclaimed: 'God is great: Amitabh lives'.

In Bombay's next boom, after World War II, independent entrepreneurs developed and refined what Bombay Talkies had begun, creating the present-day Hindi masala (mixture of spices) – a film designed to reach the widest possible audience by containing a little bit of everything, from myth and romance to comedy and song. Even now, there is little difference between a social or costume drama and a mythological film. V. Shantaran made the first Indian Technicolor film in 1955, called 'Jhanak Khanak Payal Baaje' (The Jangle of Anklets). It was a dance extravaganza, starring the great Gopal Krishna. Shantaran also made 'Shakuntala', the first Indian film to be commercially released abroad. Mehboob Khan's finest film, 'Mother India' (familiar to Western audiences) was made in 1957. And another Indian classic, 'Gunga Jumna', was made the next year by Nitin Bose, who with Bimal Roy carried social awareness from Calcutta to Bombay. It was Roy's 'Do Bigha Zamin' (Two Acres of Land), about peasants in Bengal, a prize-winner at the 1954 Cannes Film Festival, which really presented an alternative to the Hindi masala.

At the same time, former clapper-boy Raj Kapoor emerged as the first director of the new generation of commercial Hindi film-makers. His 22-year collaboration with script-writer K. A. Abbas began in 1951 with the internationally triumphant 'Awaara' (The Tramp). Raj Kapoor, son of Prithviraj, immensely handsome, good at romance and comedy and an above-average tabla player, both directed and starred in this film which established him as a screen idol.

Today the masalas continue to pour out of the studios in what has been described as a crisis of aesthetic bankruptcy, a sterile imitation of former success. Despite huge, alluring advertisements, some in 3-D, and slogans such as 'Titillating Hot Stuff' or 'A Hot Box of Sins', these are empty promises as censorship is strict. But they still make a lot of money. The film-making process is intriguing to an outsider. A visit to a studio can easily be arranged by the tourist office. If luck holds, it will be full of action. And as a dozen studios serve the copious film companies, some work around the clock. Several companies hire various parts of one studio to make entirely different sorts of films. A Western may have a classic myth and a modern romance for neighbours. To add to the confusion, a star may be involved in more than 10 films simultaneously, putting in 4 hours as a whimpering, love-sick princess on one set, then, after a quick change, 3 hours as a destructive goddess two doors along. Finally, the lighting experts may come from Madras and only speak Tamil; the film script may be in Tamil, Telugu or Hindi, the three favourite languages for features; the songs will be mimed and sung by someone famous for her voice rather than her looks; and the film will probably be edited in

Madras.

Film finance is equally tangled. Armed with a potential film, the producer goes to the big financiers – in Bombay these may be diamond dealers, or the construction industry, Sindhis and Marwaris. They lend a sum of money at a fiendishly high interest rate of 40-60%, subtracting the interest payment out of the money to be lent. The better the stars already signed up, the more favourable the deal may be for the producer. But this only finances a bit of the film. Then another loan must be found to pay off the first loan and finance the next bit.

Naturally, the ball stops rolling sometimes, leaving incomplete films. However, if the stars are big enough at the box office, the distribution rights can be sold before shooting starts, thus financing the whole film. Consequently, there is not much scope for adventurous, experimental, often loss-making cinema; that is done in Calcutta. The slowly emerging alternative cinema in Bombay is financed by the Film Finance Corporation. It has a small output, even smaller audience and the majority of screenings are at foreign film festivals.

What to buy where

Bombay and Delhi offer the best shopping, although some of Bombay's more up-market boutiques are ambitiously highly priced and clearly aimed at wealthy locals. But there are good shops for quality traditional crafts made all over India. The Government Emporia, though good, are not up to Delhi standards; the markets (see above) merit a good look (clinging on to handbags). To know how hard to bargain in the markets, check out the prices in the Emporia. Conversely, to get an idea of the quality and range available, look in the markets. In addition, Bombay's Taj and Oberoi Towers hotels have exceptional shopping for clothes, shoes, leather, jewellery and books: convenient, perhaps more than in the market but considerably below their Western prices. The Taj shops are scattered down corridors; the Oberoi's are in a 200-shop, 2-storeyed complex adjoining the hotel. New shops at the World Trade Centre at Cuffe Parade and in the Craft Centre at Nariman Point are not yet as good.

Western India crafts Gurjari, the Gujarat Government Handicrafts Emporium, is perhaps the best of the state emporia in Bombay. High quality in everything: tie-dye and printed silk and cotton from Ahmedabad; fun appliqué wall hangings and bedspreads in bright colours; muslin and silk from Surat and Khambat; stuffed, embroidered elephants of every size; brasswork and carved wood. For the best Gujarati skills, which are rare now, the manager will arrange for the member of a Patan weaving family living in Bombay to bring in a selection – but skilled craftsmanship is costly, so beware. However, the cheaper, but still special, Rajkot weaves are in stock. On the pavement around the rear entrance to the Taj, Gujarati women sell Kutch and Saurastra, some good, mostly old pieces.

Other Indian crafts Central Cottage Industries Emporium, Shivaji Maharaj Marg, just behind the Taj; stocks crafts from the whole of India, used by locals, very efficient staff, shipping quick to arrange – and arrives safely the other end. Good range of hand-embroidered Kashmiri furnishing fabric (50% of London prices even when shipped), and other goods from Kashmir, Rajasthan and the South. Quality crafts also found at Jehangir Art Gallery Shop; Contemporary Arts & Crafts, Jagmohandas Marg Road; Craft Centre, Raheja Centre, Nariman Point; Khadi Village Industries Emporium, D Naoroji Road; Kairali, Nirmal, Nariman Point (Kerala crafts); Kashmiri Government Arts Emporium, P Mehta Road; Purbashree, Khira Bhavan, Sandhurst Bridge (North-Eastern states crafts); Fantasia, Oberoi Towers.

Old crafts and antiques See Survival Code Chapter for legal restrictions. Several in the lanes behind the Taj sell hallmarked and old Indian silver; more mixed shops include A. K. Essajee, D. Popli & Sons, Heermanek and Son, all on Battery Street, and Oriental Art Museum in Mereweather Road. Around the Prince of Wales Museum, Phillips Antiques (no relation to the London auction house) has everything from Raj porcelain to rubbish; Natasan, one of the major art dealers in India, has his Bombay branches in the Jehangir Art Gallery complex and the Taj. Upstairs in the Pundole Gallery at Flora Fountain plenty of the nice pieces are small enough for an already stretched suitcase.

High fashion clothes In fashion-conscious and high profile Bombay, designer labels are as important as they are in Paris or Milan. In the Oberoi and Taj hotel shopping complexes, seek out the choicest boutiques and ask to see creations by Zerxes Bhathena, Anna Singh Signature, Hermant Trivedi, Arjun Khanna and Shahab Durazi. But be prepared to pay international prices.

Jewellery For gold and diamonds, keep to large shops and there should be no problems. If the Zaveri bazaar ones are too overwhelming, both Taj and Oberoi have jewellery shops. Indian craftsmanship in gold and silverwork and stone-cutting is regarded as best of all and is very cheap. Stones are good buys, but gold is quite expensive (ideally, bring your own). Diamonds are 15-20% less than in Amsterdam, London and New York and come in two qualities, deluxe and super-deluxe, each sold with a certificate and the promise to buy back the jewellery at any time at the current price (see below). When buying, look out for the four 'Cs': carat, clarity, colour and cut. (Diamonds carry special setting restrictions and tourists taking them out of the country require a certificate and must bay in foreign exchange, so check carefully or your diamond may not be forever.) If the designs of the jewellery in stock are no good, any piece can be made up in about a week. And the customer can bring his own gold or stones. For instance, pearls are very cheap in Hyderabad – a fifth of London prices – but stringing and setting are best in Bombay (for stringing, Hyderabadis go to Rai, next to the Regal, Colaba). A reliable jeweller is Tribhovandas Bhimi Zaveri, who has shops in Zaveri Bazaar, the Oberoi and Opera House; and Gazdar in the Taj. For old and new silver, try the silver bazaar at Mumbadevi (especially nos 17, 39 and 47). Check the day's price first as it is sold by weight.

Fabric M Karve Road has the sari shops, which also stock fabric by the metre and jazzy brocading, some wide enough to have elephants, princesses and camels woven in. Customers are expected to take their time. One good shop is Kala Niketan. In the Taj, Indian Textiles has extremely beautiful (but quite expensive) silk, crêpe de chine, brocade and the rare crêpe cotton. Nearby, at Churchgate, Pride sells fabrics that are all Indian made but use European designs and cost less. To have fabric made up, Smart and Hollywood Tailors near the Jehangir Gallery have been tried, tested and praised for copying in a few days a Calvin Klein suit in fabric and an Aquascutum raincoat in soft leather, the fabric and leather bought in the bazaars. (At the time of writing, Handloom House had been gutted by fire and was closed. Should it have re-opened, it is good.) To have fabric embroidered and made up, go to Adity Enterprises, Sea View Terrace, Wodehouse Road.

Books For art and culture, the Taj bookshop is best. If it fails, try Strand Book Stall, off N P Mehta Road, in the lane opposite the HMV shop. Around the university, the second-hand bookstalls sprawling along the streets from Flora Fountain to the General Telegraph Office are a bibliophile's dream – all manner of goodies waiting to be discovered in the tall, wobbling piles. Mr Merchant has his stall outside the New and Second-Hand Book Shop, founded in 1907, which is so full of volumes it is difficult to get in to browse through them. For rare books, prints and maps, go to Jimmy Ollia, 1st floor, Cumballa Chambers, Cumballa Hill Road (tel: 350649).

Leather The instant the designs come out in Milan and Paris, the Indians copy them. And although shops in the two hotels stock a dazzling array of the latest shoes, bags, belts and jackets at a fraction of the European prices, Dhaboo Street in the bazaar area has more variety, better quality (suede-linings for bags) and is even cheaper. The Muslim wholesalers' shops are bursting with stock, so search out the best, then bargain hard. Belts start at Rs20, wallets Rs50, handbags Rs65 – the shoe selection is limited. There is also leather by the piece. As recommendation, the Italians come to pick up this year's Guccis, the French their Cardins. Since India does not import either make, their copyrights do not extend here, so the blatant piracy is not illegal. To find the tiny street, get somewhere near, then ask. In the hotel shops, Joy shoes in the Taj is patronised by globe-trotters.

See how it's done: Industry and craft

Cinema To visit a film studo (see above), contact the ITDC tourist office.

Cotton mills Much of Bombay's wealth was founded on these. Some still smoke and clatter when not on strike. They are straight out of Dickens, labour-intensive, throbbing with huge, out-moded machinery, the air full of cotton fluff and boiling hot. The cotton goes in one end raw and comes out the other as dyed fabric. The tourist offices can arrange a visit.

Diamonds Some of the most famous diamonds were mined and first cut in India – the 410-carat Regent (in the Louvre), the Great Sancy (belonging to the Astor family), the Black Orloff (somewhere in New York) and the Darya-i-Nur (last seen at the late Shah of Iran's coronation in 1967). The Koh-i-Nur (Mountain of Light), weighing 108.93 carats, probably came out of the Golconda mines before the 14th century. In the 16th century, Emperor Babur calculated its value as 'two and a half days' food for the whole world'. Having sparkled on various rulers' heads, the British claimed it from the Lahore treasury as compensation for war losses. It is now part of the Crown jewels and kept in the Tower of London until the next coronation.

Seven centuries later, supremacy in diamond mining has passed to South Africa but India is still a centre of the highly skilled craft of diamond-cutting and polishing, especially small stones. Most is done at Surat in Gujarat, but some in Bombay, the diamond-dealing port. In addition to native diamonds, small stones are imported, cut and exported, making India the world centre of the cutting industry. To see the fascinating and intricate process, from bruting the rough stone to the final polish, go to Thakurdwar in central Bombay. Poke into the courtyards to find Gujarati boys aged 16 to 30 working at lathes in tiny rooms.

Awaydays

Bombay is neither claustrophic nor dull, so the need for a quick escape may not arise. If it does, the worthwhile day trips around the city are few, mostly focused on the abundant cave-temples, so a tempting extravaganza is thrown in. The bigger hops make better trips (see next section).

Elephanta Island 10km. For those who hate Bombay and are besotted with rock-cut temples. There are four Hindu temples, dated vaguely from the 4th to the 9th centuries, their beautiful sculptures much damaged by the Portuguese. But to see them involves a grim 10km journey bobbing across the harbour, fighting fellow tourists up to the caves, being hit on the head by the football of one of a dozen games being played in and around them, pestered by shoddy stall-holders and deafened by blaring cassette-players, then the grimmer return journey. A much nicer outing is to the other caves (see below) or, better still, fly or take the train up to the Ajanta and Ellora cave temples for two days on a package deal (see below).

Beaches For a serious beach, drive or fly to *Goa* (see Sun chapter). Otherwise, 40km away are *Marve* and *Manori*. Go by car to unspoilt Marve (plus nearby fishing village) and on by ferry and horse-drawn tonga to Manori. Very romantic, and it is tempting to stay overnight at the *Manoribel*, a clean, simple hotel of six cottages right on the beach, but be sure to book at weekends. If desperate for a beach, it is 21km to dirty Juhu beach (do not swim but do eat fish from the little huts and have your fortune told). The smart residents have nothing more to do with it than the odd early morning horse-ride or jog, and a late night gaze at the moon reflected in the sea.

Sanjay Gandhi National Park 35km. Not one of the great wildlife parks, but a big space and plenty of trees. Contains a lion safari park and the formal Krishnagiri Upavan garden. Beyond them the park is wilder, with teak woods, blossoming trees, deer, interesting birds and the *Kanheri* caves: 109 Buddhist rock-cut temples and cells hewn from a huge circular rock during the 2nd to 9th centuries. Biggest cave complex in India, nos 1, 2, 3 and 10 best, not much sculpture, good views.

Bassein 77km. Just across the Ulhas River on the mainland, shortest route by train, then taxi. Rather good ruined city (walls and bits of buildings), historically interesting. Built by the Sultan of Gujarat but Portuguese from 1534 until 1739 during which time it was greatly expanded and rose to become the 'Court of the North', with cathedral, stately homes and the Hildalgos (aristocracy) famous for their grandeur and wealth.

Buddhist caves trail About 250km round trip, or stop with a picnic to see some on the way up to Pune (see below). Best to go by car, including one or two of Shivaji's many forts en route, such as *Lohagan* and *Visapur* (above the Bhaja Caves), and a detour to overnight at Matheran (see Hill Stations, below). The cave remains at *Lonavala* are followed by figurative sculptures in the lushly sited *Bhaja* ones (2nd century BC). 9km south-east of here are the *Bedsa Caves*, slightly later, with jolly carvings on the pillar of the chaitya (prayer hall); while 6km northwards are the rock-cut monasteries of *Karli* (5th century BC). Sedan chairs carry visitors up the steep hill, where Cave no.8 has 'the largest and most completely preserved chaitya hall of the early Buddhist series in the Western Deccan' (George Michell), with bold carvings of lions, elephants and figures, and the 37-pillared hall lit by a sun window.

The other Taj Day trip extravaganza to the Taj Mahal, Agra. Catch an early plane to Delhi (2hrs), drive to Agra (3hrs), ogle the monument to love, swim and eat at the Mughal Sheraton or Taj View hotels, return – or stay over for the magical sunset and dawn experiences. Some travel agencies do a package deal.

Forays further afield

With its excellent communications, some lesser visited places are accessible from Bombay, particularly in Gujarat. But the pilgrimage to Ajanta and Ellora is first priority. Despite all the coastline, only the Goa beaches are really good (see Sun chapter). For the nearer places such as Pune (Poona) and the hill stations, train and bus are both good; they go from the city centre, thus avoiding the drive to (and hanging around at) the airport.

The travel agents listed above will advise and book, but try to give them notice for the popular week-end trips to Goa or the Ajanta/Ellora caves. Good off-season and mid-week deals to both.

AJANTA AND ELLORA

However short the visit to western India, it is worth squeezing in two days to come here. The caves of Ajanta and Ellora are one of the technical and artistic feats of Buddhist art. Like the Taj, the ruined city of Hampi and the Khajuraho temples, they are one of the wonders of India. There is nothing natural about the caves. They are man-made: more than 60 temples cut directly into remote hillsides in the Western Ghats and decorated with sculptures and, at Ajanta, paintings. Since their rediscovery in the 19th century, the air has been fading the exquisite wall-paintings; some caves with paintings may be temporarily closed for conservation.

Indians are as anxious as foreigners to see the caves with paintings before they are closed – or before the paintings fade into obscurity. Good Brahmin parents bring their children to see the pale images they remember with bright hues. So, put on comfy shoes, take a torch (the lighting is erratic), prepare to join throngs of fellow tourists and catch these treasures while you can. En route to Ellora, the *Boy's Own* medieval fort at *Daulatabad* is an added bonus.

THE HARD FACTS As the monsoon is quite light, it is possible to go to Ajanta and Ellora all the year round, but October-November is best when the post-monsoon lushness and plump cows astound those arriving from dry Rajasthan. December-March are pleasant before the work-up to the June rains. There are flights on both Indian Airlines and Vayudoot up to Aurangabad (Ellora 30km, Ajanta 106km); or there is a long train journey up over the ghats. Choose betweeen two hotels in Aurangabad, both newish, with mod. cons. (If both are full, go to the Aurangabad Ashok.)

Ajanta Ambassador Hotel (tel: 82211/82367; telex; 0745-211). 125 rooms, sensitive service, good pool, sports including tennis, excellent restaurant.

Rama International (tel: 822455-7; telex 0745-212. 100 rooms, part of the Welcomgroup chain, next door to the Ambassador and very similar, with same wide range of facilities plus health club; improved.

Both hotels can offer an all-in price of breakfast, packed lunch and dinner. Both are slightly out of town but have travel counters for car hire, tour reservations and flight confirmation; and shopping arcades for literature on the caves.

OUT AND ABOUT The full day trips run daily by the MTDC and ITDC are excellent value, the guides usually good and the time spent at each spot reasonable. Beware: the bus picks up at around 8am, and it takes a full day trip to see each set of caves. So, passengers on a plane arriving after the bus departs must either hire a car (guides available at each site) or stay an extra day. It does not matter which caves are visited first, even though Ajanta's pre-date those of Ellora. Ajanta caves are open 9.30am-5.30pm; Ellora caves from sunrise to sunset. In Aurangabad, buy himroo (silk and cotton mix) shawls, silk saries with elaborate zari work made in nearby Paithan, and bidri work.

Ajanta In the 2nd century BC, at the beginning of the Satavahana dynasty, a community of Buddhist monks came to this remote area and began chipping their retreat out of the semi-circular cliff of a gorge. Over the next 900 years, they carved out 4 chaityas (sanctuaries) and 25 viharas (Buddhist monasteries). Then, in the 7th century, Ajanta was abandoned in favour of a new site, Ellora. It was not until 1819 that a British hunting party, searching out an elusive lion, stumbled upon the pristine caves in the thick forest, then part of the Nizam of Hyderabad's territory. The caves are a pocket history of Buddhist art and thought. In the 2nd century BC a new form of Buddhism broke away from the original exclusive and ascetic Hinayana form which favoured the symbolic and abstract. This new branch, known as Mahayana, went for mass appeal in direct competition with popular Hinduism. It also encouraged the development of a much richer and more realistic art which reached its golden age of maturity under the Gupta dynasty, 320-647. Cave nos 8, 9, 10, 12 and 13 are the simple, Hinayana ones.

Each cave is monolithic. This means the rock has been chipped away from the cliff-face to create the space; nothing has been added. Carving began with the ceiling and worked down, around pillars, monks' beds (with pillow), carvings on capitals, facades and jambs, and huge statues of the Buddha and his consorts in back rooms. The technical feat is mind-boggling. And, in addition, the carving and painting achieves a classical grace. The frescoes of the life of Buddha and the later jatakas (Buddhist fables) are painted in yellow, red, black and a little slate blue, all locally found minerals, with touches of precious, imported lapis lazuli which still retains its brilliance. Benjamin Rowland has observed: 'Nowhere else in Indian art but at Ajanta do we find such a complete statement of indivisible union of . . . sacred and secular art. . . . Here is a turn to a sort of religious romanticism of a really lyric quality, a reflexion of the view that every aspect of life has an equal value in the spiritual sense and as an aspect of the divine.' Best paintings in nos 1, 2, 16, 17 and 19; best sculptures in nos 4, 17, 19 and 26, beautifully lit by the afternoon sun.

Ellora Buddhism was already losing out to the Hindus and Jains when the monks moved to this gentle hillside in the 7th century. So there are caves representing all three faiths: 12 Buddhist (600-800AD); 17 Hindu (around 900AD) and 5 Jain (800-1000AD), the caves numbered in that order. The blasé who have already been to Ajanta will not think much of the Buddhist ones, but note the beginning of Hindu liveliness in nos 11 and 12. The Jain temples, slightly north of the rest, have delicate, highly detailed carvings. But it is the Hindu caves that are spectacular, their profusion of carvings bursting with energy in striking contrast to the static, contemplative Buddhist sculpture.

See especially no. 16, Kailasa Temple, named after Shiva's home in the Himalayas, Mount Kailasa, and built to represent it. A bridge leads through an enclosure to the courtyard where elephants and flagstaffs flank the two-storey temple and Nandi pavilion. Friezes of dynamic carving recount legends of Shiva and episodes from the Ramayana. The complex covers the same area as the Parthenon and every bit is part of the hillside, making it the biggest monolithic structure in the world and one of the greatest monuments of Dravidian art, built at the height of the Rashtrakuta dynasty in the middle of the 8th century. Standing facing it, an especially magical room to the right is carved with bejewelled ladies lounging on benches. As the knowledgeable Arun Acharya remarked: 'India is known for the Taj; it should also be known for the Kailasa Temple'.

Pitalkhora For the cave-keen, just beyond Ellora. Like Ajanta, they date from the early Satavahana period. Overlooking a ravine, most were cut 2nd-1st centuries BC to be monasteries of cells round a central hall, and painted fragments show they were in use until the 5th century AD.

Daulatabad Fort Built on a natural pyramid-shaped hill, with everything from anti-elephant multiple doorways and spoof dead-end corridors to steep, slippery, gravelled pathways and a dark spiral tunnel down which defenders dropped hot coals on their attackers. No wonder Mohammad Tughlaq, Sultan of Delhi, could not resist it and decided to move his capital there in 1327, naming it Daulatabad (city of fortune). A few years later he realised his mistake and Delhi's citizens who had not died on the 1,100km walk there had to trek home. Spectacular views from the top.

Khuldabad The sixth Mughal emperor, Aurangzeb, chose to be buried here in pious Islamic tradition, beneath a simple slab of white stone and surrounded by the tombs and mosques of holy men where muezzins still cry out beautifully to call the faithful to prayer; worth a quiet explore, very atmospheric.

Aurangabad Named after Aurangzeb. Not attractive. The Ellora-Daulatabad tour bus whizzes around the main sights, which is quite enough. The most amusing is Bibi-ka-Maqbara, a tatty, poor imitation of the Taj built for Aurangzeb's wife in 1679; (behind it, there is a pleasant early morning or sunset drive up to some local caves of which the most beautiful is 'Aurangabad 3'). The most interesting is the Panchakki waterwheel, driven by a natural spring, which finances an orphanage.

HILL STATIONS

Matheran 171km at 800m. The best switch-off near Bombay. In the Sahyadri range, made popular in the 1850s by one Hugh Malet (although Ptolomy went there long before). Bombayites who are not grand enough to go to Ooty (or simply don't like it) come here, to nearby Khandala and to Mahabaleshwar for lungfulls of good air. Season October-May (pre-rain June is misty); avoid the deluge of the rainy season and, if possible, week-ends. Go for shady trees (Matheran means mother forest), orchids, views (clock up the panoramas at the Six Points), riding and peace – no cars; no action.

Take the Pune Express to Neral (2hrs), then change into brightly painted, tiny, narrow-gauge carriages (1st class has pink curtains) for the last 21km (2hrs), full of twists, tunnels and monkeys with black or red faces. The nicest place to stay is *Lord's Central Hotel* (tel: 28 or book in Bombay, tel:318008/367776); clean, modest, usual iri-cuisine restaurant. Move around on foot or on horseback – escorts provided if needed. The rickshaws are less fun.

Views of Bombay and sunsets are seen from Monkey, Hart, Echo, Chouk, Porcupine Points and, best of all, Panorama Point; but go up to Duke's Nose (named after Wellington) on the Deccan Plateau for the most spectacular views. For an outing, the caves around Lonavala.

Mahabaleshwar 200km at 1,372m. Highest hill station in western India. In Raj days, the fashionable place where the British cooled off. Sir John Malcolm initiated the hill station in 1828. Go for views, waterfalls, walks, some sport. Season as for Matheran.

The journey is by train or plane to Pune, then taxi, or by car all the way. Of several hotels, the *Mahabaleshwar Club* (tel: 221), period charm, peace (temporary membership for foreigners, write to the Secretary); otherwise, try the *Fountain* (tel: 227; Bombay booking at Foundtain's Food Restaurant, tel: 8227182), or some modest bungalow hotels such as *Fredrick* (tel: 240), *Dina 46* , (tel: 246) or *Race View* (tel: 238).

Walk through the flower-filled woods (April for orchids and lilies); see Dhobi, Chinaman and Lingmala waterfalls and views of Krishan and Koyna valleys from Raj-named spots such as Wilson, Kate, Bombay, Elphinstone and, to make Scots feel at home, Arthur's Seat – one of the best, with a sheer drop of 600m. Keep in shape with golf and tennis at the club, go boating and fishing on Venna Lake. Visit the old village, very holy to Hindus (festival, February-March). Take trips to two of the best Shivaji forts: Pratapgarh and Raigarh. Bee-keepers sell their honey.

PUNE (POONA)

Currently most famous – or notorious – not as the place where the Maratha leader Shivaji was raised, nor for its fine museums and precocious theatre and film work, nor even its race course, but for the Sri Rajneesh Ashram where Westerners (especially Americans and Germans) pranced around in their birthday suits extolling the merits of free love much to the amazement and horror of the locals and, via 'Sex Guru' articles, the rest of India.

Sri Rajneesh had an annual turnover of £2 million at the ashram alone, amplified by sales of his discourses: 33 million words distilled into 336 books and 4,000 hours of tape with titles such as 'Ninety Nine Names of Nothingness'. Then, quite suddenly, Sri Rajneesh disappeared, to re-emerge with a fleet of cuddly Rolls Royces in Oregon, USA., later to die. Meanwhile, the ashram has been rubber-stamped by the government and is now on the official Pune tourist bus route. To visit inside, simply arrive at the gate and ask to be shown round; take your passport and, if you want to eat or drink, an Aids test certificate.

THE HARD FACTS At 580m. The fresh air of this pleasant provincial town is especially welcome during Bombay's sticky months which coincide with the racing season from July to October. Pune was the Bombay Government's hide-out during the monsoon. Get there by the hare or tortoise routes: the hare takes the daily 30-minute plane hop (Indian Airlines or Vayudoot) between slow road and airport queues; the tortoise goes by train, enjoying a leisurely breakfast on the Deccan Express (4½hrs, leaves 6.45am) or tea and toast on the Deccan Queen (3½hrs, leaves 5.10pm); the bus pauses for modest chai or cold drinks on its journey. To leave Pune, either return to Bombay, fly to Goa direct (Vayudoot) or head inland by road.

The best place to stay is the *Hotel Blue Diamond* in Koregoan Park (tel: 28735; telex: 0145 369; cable: BLUEDIAMOND), 114 rooms, concrete, good service, mod. cons, pool, health club, beauty parlour, both tri-cuisine restaurants quite good. Patronised by the nearby ashram's visitors, so good service, newsagent and direct dial telephones which work. Best information counter is on the railway station.

OUT AND ABOUT Spend time in the *Raja Kelkar Museum* where a selection of Shri Dinkar Kelkar's magnificent collection is exhibited in rotation in his old house. (If interested, ask to see pieces not on show.) Especially fine betel nut crackers, musical instruments and everyday objects. Dr Kelkar intends to open a section devoted entirely to women. Excellent illustrated catalogues. (Open daily, 8.30-12.30; 3.00-6.00.) The Bhandarkar Oriental Institute contains an important collection of Oriental manuscripts.

Wander around the Shanwarwada Palace remains, the narrow streets of the old Peshawa town and the elegant cantonment – Pune is still an area military headquarters. Go into Pancheleshwar rock-cut temple (8th century) and catch

a good view from the hilltop Parvati Temple. See the buildings erected under the British: the Council Hall, Wellesley Bridge, Deccan College (Bhandarkar, Edwin Arnold and Wordsworth's nephew taught there; Jeejeebhoy founded it). The pretty race course is in the old parade ground, overlooked by the Club. Film buffs can visit the National Film and Television Institute. Theatre-goers can catch one of Agashe's or Tendulkar's plays at the Bal Gandharva, Nehru or Tilak Smarak Nidhi theatres (several performances daily). Irani cafés are here too (see Bombay food section, above); try Café Good Luck and The Lucky, both near the Deccan Gymkhana.

Trips out on the Shivaji trail To the north, a heavy but rewarding day visits first *Shivner* (80km) to see a great hillfort which is the site of 50 Buddhist cells (3rd century) and the place where Maharashtra's 17th-century Maratha hero Shivaji was born; and then nearby *Junnar* for quantities of simple Buddhist caves (2nd century BC-3rd century AD) and a monument to Shivaji. To the south-west, across more mountains, lies *Sinhargarh* (19km), meaning Lion's Fort, which sprawls over the high hills and has been held by everyone from Muhammad Tughlaq to the Marathas, Mughals and British – Shivaji's leader Tanaji, who took it in 1670, has a memorial near the gorge. To the south-east, impressive *Purandhar* (32km) is a double fort and was one of the Deccan's strongest; begun around 1350, it has been held by the usual succession of Mughals, Marathas and British; its 42km-long wall has three gates and six bastions – a hike round it drums up a healthy appetite.

THE DRIVE TO GOA/KARNATAKA
A memorable drive down through the rugged Western Ghats, with detours to hilltop and coastal forts. Whether starting from Bombay or Pune, and heading for Goa or inland to explore Karnataka state, this is best done with an overnight stop at *Chiplun Riverview Lodge*, Village Dhamandivi, Taluka Khed, District Ratnagiri (tel: 57), owned by the Taj Group, so bookable through their other hotels, 37 rooms each with two queen-sized beds, restaurant overlooking the Vashisti river serves local Konkan food.

The roads from Bombay and Pune meet near the hill station of Mahabaleshwar (see above). Short detours lead to two high Shivaji forts: the spectacularly sited *Pratabgarh* was an important Shivaji stronghold, its massive walls considered impregnable (now reached up 500 steps); and equally impressive *Raigarh* (unimpressive until you arrive), where Shivaji's royal and public building alone amounted to an estimated 300 stone structures; it was here that he was crowned prince in 1648 and here that he died in 1680; with its great walls, bastions and building remains, this is another appetite-inducing fort to explore.

Chiplun is not far down the Goa road, and perhaps worth two nights to see the above forts plus the little seaside village and port of *Jaigarh* with its overlooking fort built by the Bijapur rulers. Southwards lies a crossroads: to coastal *Ratnagiri* or inland over undulating hills to another Shivaji treat, *Panhala*; yet another vast hilltop fort with spectacular walls, surviving Tin Gate and great granaries – most romantic to stay overnight here, at *Panhala State Tourism Hotel*, ordering food on arrival (and defumigating cottage rooms of mosquitoes). *Kolhapur* is 19km from here where in the oddly named Rankala A Ward, the former ruler's *Shalini Palace*, designed by Major Charles Mant, is now a government-owned hotel in the Ashok group (tel: 20401). Bijapur is a day's drive.

On down the Goa road, *Vijayadrug* (48km south of Ratnagiri) is a final Shivaji fort for those who have still not had enough. The strong, ancient seafort was enlarged by the Bijapurs and again by Shivaji who gave it its formidable triple walls, 27 multi-storey bastions and a great citadel, all so strong that not even a joint Anglo-Portuguese force could take it in 1720. The drive on down to Panaji becomes increasingly palm-fringed, the perfect backdrop to lotus-eating Goan life.

Central India – Madhya Pradesh

The lesser-visited cities of Mandu, Ujjain, Bhopal and Sanchi are quick and easy to reach and the rewards are rich. Moreover, in the high tourist season of November to February they remain, so far, delightfully empty compared to the beaten track. The trip north connecting Bhopal to Gwalior (and then Agra) takes in some glorious but almost unvisited ancient cities lying on the Betwa river.

THE HARD FACTS The richly forested, large state of Madhya Pradesh is most pleasant from October to March, with the bonus of constant Hindu festivals. It is best to mix the travel methods. Daily planes (Indian Airlines and Vayudoot) connect Bombay and Delhi with Indore (for Mandu and Ujjain) and Bhopal (for Sanchi); the Shatabti Express zips down to Bhopal daily from Delhi via Agra and Gwalior; and car hire is best done at the airport or hotel, bargaining hard for an all-in price. It is a long, one-day drive to Mandu from Aurangabad, Vadodara or (more manageable) Bhopal. Central Indian hotels are fairly modest, so the fussier must steel themselves. There is no prohibition in Madhya Pradesh at present.

MANDU
Its other name, Shadibad, means 'City of joy'. Former magnificent and courtly capital of the central Indian kingdom of Malwa, now a romantic, ghost city sprawled over a 12sqkm hilltop. Its atmosphere has been described as 'dormant rather than dead'. There are mango, tamarind and banyan trees. The city is particularly beautiful when emerald green and full of waterfalls immediately post-monsoon.

Wander around some of the 70 or so fine Muslim and Hindu monuments built during its heyday from the 11th to 16th centuries, especially under Mahmud Shah (1436-69) and Ghiasuddin (1469-1500), who was devoted to women – his harem was reputed to hold 15,000 pretty maids. Mandu usurped nearby Dhar as capital in 1405, and continued the building style mingling both Gujarat and Delhi elements.

The 500-elephant parade heralding the entry of Jahangir (1605-27) on March 3, 1617, was one of Mandu's last great spectacles. Thomas Roe, Britain's first ambassador to India, had followed the emperor here from Ajmer. He found lodgings in an old building, had his little white Iceland pet dog carried off by a lion and, on September 1, attended Jahangir's birthday party where he was ceremoniously weighed in gold and jewels; but dysentery and piles prevented him watching Prince Khurram's triumphal entry and weighing. The following year, at Ahmedabad, a healthier Roe finally got part of what he wanted: a letter from the emperor to James I including the vital words 'it is my pleasure and I do command that to all the English merchants in all my dominions there be given freedom and residence . . . and that their goods and merchandise they may sell or traffic with according to their own will . . . and that all their ships may come and go to my ports wheresoever they choose at their own will'. The great Anglo-Indian trading link was formally established.

See the magnificent Jami Masjid, outside which local villagers of scheduled castes and tribes now hold their market (and where you can rent bicycles); wander the ruins of Jahaz Mahal; and indulge in a sunset at the palace and pavilion of Baz Bahadur (the last king, defeated by Akbar) and his Rani Rupmati, India's Romeo and Juliet. Baz Bahadur came across the lovely Rajput peasant girl, Rupmati, singing in a forest, fell in love at first sight and brought her to his palace. He erected buildings for her but then had to flee in the face of Mughal defeat. Rupmati, captured for the general's future pleasure, committed suicide by swallowing ground diamonds.

Accommodation is modest; book in advance at monsoon time. Best is *MP Tourist Bungalow* (tel: 35, bookable at Indore Tourist Office but best done in writing direct); otherwise there are *MP Tourist Huts, MP Travellers Lodge or Taveli Mahal Rest House*, a converted palace with a handful of simple rooms (run by the Archaeological Survey). Buy D. R. Patil's excellent booklet on Mandu (with map), published by the Archaelogical Survey of India. To see Mandu's precursor, make an excursion to the less impressive *Dhar* (33km) to see two early mosques (c.1400) and the fort with its palace remains.

UJJAIN

The Gupta king Chandragupta II (380-414) forsook the official capital of Pataliputra to rule here in what his poet, Kalidasa, described at 'the town fallen from heaven to bring heaven to earth'. It was dogged by political upheavals later on. See the riverside temples and ghats, Maharaja Scindia's palace, and go out of the city, past yet another of Jai Singh's observatories, to Kaliadah, the Mandu Sultans' pretty pleasure palace. Ujjain is one of the seven sacred cities of India, and the triennial Kumbh Mela festival takes place here every 12 years, next one 1995, see Calendar of Festivals.

INDORE

Major textile centre but good base for Mandu and Ujjain. Do not miss the museum's major archaeological collection (open Tues.-Sun., 10am-5pm). See also the Jain Kanch Mandir (glass temple), one of the more over-the-top giant Jain reliquaries, encrusted with mirrors, crystal, beads and mother-of-pearl (open 10am-5pm). Stay at *Suhag Hotel* (tel: 33270-9; telex: 735 345; cable: SUHAG HOTEL), 75 rooms plus 8 suites, all with bath; air-conditioning, travel agent, car rental, beauty salon. Tourist Office (tel: 38888) in the bus station, opposite the railway station. Tours to Mandu and Ujjain. Those interested in weaving can go south to *Maheshwar* (60km) to see the ghats, museum, perhaps some Shivatri celebrations and the Weaving Centre which is reviving the famous and exquisite Maheshwari saris; check at the Tourist Office before setting out.

BHOPAL

Capital city of Madhya Pradesh. 187km from Indore; 290km from Mandu. Infamous for the devastating Union Carbide explosion in 1984; but, despite this, still a city of lakes and gardens, and the best base for Sanchi. Named after Raja Bhoj, the 11th-century founder, and the huge lake he built that dominates the city (pal means dam). An Afghan mercenary from Delhi, Dost Mohammed Khan, founded the Bhopal dynasty at the end of the 17th century, a tiny Muslim dot in a predominantly Hindu state.

See remains of Dost Mohammed Khan's fort

and walls; his descendant Shah Jahan Begum's unfinished, pink Taj-ul-masjid (another mosque claimed to be the biggest in India); the Nawab's palace overlooking the lake; the museum (local archaeological findings). Most of all, wander in romantically-named gardens such as Farhatafza Bagh (Enhancer of Joy), catch sunset views of the minareted city from Shamla Hill, and go evening boating on the lake. Charles Correa's new *Bharat Bhavan* building is here. It is one of the leading centres for the performing arts and for the preservation and practice of tribal and folk arts. The centre is also trying to preserve the dying classical music form of dhrupad. Well worth visiting to see craftsmen during the day and, possibly, a performance in the early evening.

The most pleasant place to stay is the *Jehan Numa*, Shamla Hill, Bhopal (tel: 540100; telex: 0705,343); built among the teak forests in the 1890s by Nawab Sultan Jahan Begum's second son (the Begum was Bhopal's third successive female ruler); now restored and opened as a hotel in 1983, and still nicknamed 'Number 10', its old telephone number. The 60 rooms in the basically Italian palazzo style building surround and internal courtyard; nice grounds. The *Imperial Sabre*, Palace Grounds (tel: 72738), a former palace guest-house, seems to have gone downhill; otherwise there is *Hotel Ramsons International*, Hamidia Road, (tel: 72298; cable SETHI-BROS); 22 rooms (6 air-conditioned), small but good, or the bigger *Rajdoot Hotel*, Hamidia Road (tel: 726912; cable: RAJDOOT); 120 rooms (30 air-conditioned), travel agent, bank, car hire. Tourist Office at 5, Hamidia Road (tel: 3400), tours to Sanchi.

SANCHI

Hilltop site of an imposing and unmatched collection of magnificent Buddhist monuments. The buildings span almost the whole range of Indian Buddhist art, from its birth in the 3rd century BC to its decay in the 12th century AD, justifying George Michell's rhapsodising that Sanchi is 'of outstanding significance for the number and variety of its monuments, and also for the quality of its accompanying sculptures'. Here are also the best-preserved stupas (Buddhist relic mounds). All this is very unusual since Sanchi has no connections with Buddha's life. The answer lies in the Mauryan emperor Ashoka (c273-236BC), a zealous convert to Buddhism who probably built the first stupa and pillar, selecting this spot as peaceful yet close to prosperous Vidisha. (Ashoka, in the tradition of keen converts, built 7 more stupas at Sanchi and an estimated 84,000 throughout India; from here his son, Mahendra, took Buddhism to Sri Lanka.) Pious merchants of Vidisa then endowed the monastery, laying the foundation for its energetic and quality building activities. In 1818 General Taylor 'discovered' the deserted ruins, marking the start of some tragic destructions (the pillar of Ashoka was used to build a sugar-cane press), disappearances and restorations (some of the gateway architraves are reversed).

If architectural indigestion comes fast, then start with Stupa no.1 and its four magnificent tornas (gateways), followed by Stupa no. 3, Temple no.17 (the best preserved), Monasteries nos.45-47 and out of the walls, on the western slope, Monastery no.51 and Stupa no.2. The good Archaeological Museum, outside the wall to the north, is well worth a visit. The Buddha's life and teachings are conveyed through symbols in early Buddhist art: the lotus represents his birth, the tree his enlightenment, the wheel his first sermon (see Sarnath), the stupa his nirvana (salvation), and his footprints, throne or riderless horse his presence. Debala Mitra's essential guide to Sanchi (plus map), published by the Archaeological Survey, should be on sale at the booking office. Official guide-lecturers free. Open daily, sunrise to sunset (small museum 9am-5pm). To stay on site, best is *MP Travellers Lodge* (tel: 23); rooms in the *Circuit House* and *Rest House* both depend upon no travelling civil servants wanting them.

DAY TRIP FROM SANCHI OR BHOPAL
A good trip out northwards from Sanchi, with picnic, takes in four local sites. Heading northwards, the patrons of many Sanchi buildings were merchants living near present-day *Vidisha* (10km); good little Archaeological Museum near the railway station. Set on the Betwa and Bes rivers about 3km north of here, present-day *Besnagar* is the site of ancient Vidisha whose mounds and remains date to Maurya and Shunga times, and whose great riverside column has an inscription dating it to 113BC when the Greek ambassador Heliodorus visited Taxila (see Pakistan). Southwest of here, at *Udayagiri* (6km west of Vidisha), the rich carvings on some 20 Gupta cave temples (5th century) provide insights into early Hindu art (with Temple no.17 at Sanchi, these are the earliest datable Gupta buildings). North-east of Vidisha lies *Gyaraspur* where Hindu and Jain remains of Pratihara times (8th-10th centuries) include the hilltop Maladevi Temple, part rock-cut, part built, with one of the earliest known mountain-like sikharas (beehive-shaped tower).

THE BHOPAL-GWALIOR DRIVE
Not a trip for the comfort-fussy, but fascinating for the buildings on the way, lying silent in their rural surroundings. Best done by car; possible but tricky by train.

Having indulged in the Sanchi magic, and made the day-trip out to Vidisha and its surroundings, the big journey starts early. First stops are Udayapur and Bareth. At *Udayapur*, the splendidly preserved Udayeshvara Temple (1080) is, according to architectural historian Christopher Tadgell, 'one of the supreme masterpieces of its type'; according to another, George Michell, "its ambitious scale, rhythmic proportions and rich sculptural ornamentation" make it the finest surviving monument of the Paramara dynasty, comparable to Chandella temples at Khajuraho. For something quite different, seek out the 15th century mosque at *Bareth* 6km to the east, and other scattered Islamic monuments. To *Chanderi*, where the splendid fort on a huge rocky outcrop was the citadel for the northern capital of Malwa; little changed since Babur took it in 1528. As at Lal Kot in Delhi, Rajput masonry was reused for speedy erection of fine, robust Islamic buildings, this time in the mid-15th century – seek out the Khuni Darwaza, the Badal Mahal Darwaza triumphal gateway, the four surviving storeys of the seven-storey Kushk Mahal, the Jami Masjid and, outside the city, the Madrasa and Shahzadi-ka-Rauza. East to *Deogarh*, where a fort overlooking the Betwa contains Jain temples (9-10th centuries) and the 6th-century Dashavatara Temple whose carvings are 'one of the masterpieces of early Gupta decorative art' (Tadgell).

Speed on to stay at Orchha for two nights, to have a full day in this magical deserted city; then visit Datia and possibly Shivpuri en route up to Gwalior and Agra (see pp. 82 and 99).

Gujarat

Gujarat state is a contradictory mixture. Successful, modern businessmen move their rupees out of shot of the fiendish state taxes, while democratised aristocrats of the hundreds of tiny princely states club together to make extravagant marriage deals with big-wigs such as the Mysores. There is the sophistication and enlightenment of the textile millionaire Sarabhai family and the blind ignorance of men who are still mesmerised by cars and mown down so often that local newspapers no longer find it newsworthy. The typical Gujarati has two jobs and makes a tidy fortune, yet the siesta system produces a state of total inertia from noon until 4pm. The Gandhi presence is strong, though sometimes it seems more superficial and self-righteous than truly austere. So, officially there is total prohibition – Gandhi's great ally, octogenarian Morarji Desai, still a political force in Gujarat, threatens death by fasting if it is repealed. But unofficially there is hardly a man who does not have his tame bootlegger, hardly a 'bash' (party) without whisky.

Non-Gujaratis derisively call the state 'a village where they make money and they hoard money'. Certainly the Gujarati merchants are highly successful at home and abroad, although rarely in the Marwari and Punjabi big business league. The Parsees' key into India was the promise of bringing wealth to Gujarat and they still live in every town, their flame-topped pillar burning in Sanjan where they arrived in 745. The money-making Jains concentrate in Gujarat. Their religion has added force to the state's almost total vegetarianism. The Kasturbhais are the biggest Jain family, owning 7 textile mills plus dyeing and chemical works. And, in accordance with Jain piety, they have established educational and religious trusts including a big one at Mount Abu.

Ahmedabad, thick with relics of its Mughal grandeur, is the thriving commercial centre of Gujarat, with fine museums and an enlightened patronage of contemporary and traditional Indian arts almost unique in India. Amid the hubbub of cars, buses and countless bicycles in the fast-moving city centre, camels obediently plod round one-way systems and stop at traffic lights. But the final nonsense in Gujarat is the new town of Gandhinagar, built 30km away from Ahmedabad as the bureaucratic capital. Ahmedabad workers and businessmen are forced to lose a day's wages and make a 64km trip every time they have to collect, complete or sign a piece of paper – which is often in India.

At the same time, the rural areas are hardly industrialised at all. People maintain their traditional dress, skilled crafts (especially weaving) and village lifestyle. To the north lies the Raan of Kutch. To the south is Saurashtra and the Sasan Gir wildlife sanctuary and Jain pilgrimage centres. To the west are the territories of the fun-loving deity, Krishna, and freedom-fighter Gandhi. To the east lies the palace-filled, cultural centre of Vadodara (Baroda). Around it all, the long coastline is dotted with ports which have brought trading wealth since Harappan times.

THE HARD FACTS Gujarat has interesting buildings (Muslim, Hindu and Jain), villages, museums and wildlife, with very few of the tourist trappings (both the good and the bad ones) found in neighbouring Rajasthan. This is because there are still few Western tourists. Gujarat has yet to catch on. Therefore a warning or so is needed. Most hotels are simple and inexpensive, but their charges are subject to a sliding state luxury tax that can add 30% to the bill. Full prohibition is in force. There is not a bar in the state. If the nightly whisky soda is essential, be sure to go equipped with an All India Liquor Permit. It has to be produced at the liquor store, where the bottle will be subject to a 45% sales tax. Obviously, bootleggers are cheaper, but illegal.

The season is November to February; then it hots up. There is an abundance of festivals and village fairs, especially Krishna-related ones.

With so many Gujaratis in Bombay (and perhaps because until 1956 Gujarat was part of Bombay state), there are superb air connections. Indian Airlines fly to 8 cities: Ahmedabad, Bhavnagar, Bhuj, Jamnagar, Keshod, Porbandar, Rajkot and Vadodara (Baroda); Vayudoot flies to 7: Kandla, Porbandar, Keshod, Bhavnagar, Surat, Vadodara (Baroda) and Rajkot. A good mini-tour could start in Ahmedabad, then continue by car for a few days, spending nights in palace hotels and flying out from another city. Below are one or two suggestions of places that might be included. Bombay travel agents can advise and book everything. (Mercury Travels run special Gandhi tours from Bombay.) One of the best things to buy are the superb handloom textiles, avoiding the machine-woven fabrics on which Ahmedabad's 20th-century wealth was founded.

AHMEDABAD

Although a thriving industrial city, much of the town founded by Ahmed Shah in 1411 is still standing and many of the 20th-century buildings are also notable. Peak period was the 16th century, when it was described as 'the greatest town in Hindustan, perhaps the world', and Sir Thomas Roe compared it favourably with London in 1617, adding 'every [English] fleet sends his factors to Ahmedabad'. Indeed, during the Gujarat Sultanate (c.1396-1583), the whole area enjoyed a thriving maritime trade which brought it prosperity and cosmopolitanism. Money was lavished on public and private buildings from the arrival of the Khiljis (1290) onwards, encouraging a specific regional Indo-Islamic style which incorporated more indigenous Indian elements than usual. It reached its peak under the reign of Mahmud Begada (1458-1511) at Ahmedabad and Champaner, his home town.

Today's royals are the textile barons, the Sarabhais, a brilliant Jain family who became cotton millionaires in the 19th century and have now diversified into chemicals and pharmaceuticals. Family members have become top scientists, dancers and art connoisseurs. They mostly live at The Retreat, a leafy compound of art-filled houses surrounding the old Sarabhai mansion. Here is perhaps the most successful of Le Corbusier's private houses, where house, garden, sculpture and paintings intermingle to make a mature and harmonious home. The Ambanis are newer to Ahmedabad. They came from Aden and built up the man-made fibres Reliance Textile group, rags to vast synthetic riches in 15 years flat.

THE HARD FACTS   Try to coincide with the Navrati festival, September-October, 9 days of street dancing and bhavai (lively Gujarati folk theatre), or the Makara Sankranti kite festival on January 14, the biggest of all kite festivals. Kitemakers from across India show off their vividly coloured masterpieces. Ahmedabad is 8km from the airport.

Only two good hotels, both central and looking across the river at Le Corbusier's Mill Owners' Association building.
The Ritz, Lal Dawaja (tel: 353637/8/9); 19 rooms, built by a wealthy Muslim in the 18th century, simple but lots of character and atmosphere, run by knowledgeable Goan, Mr Pereira, whose father started the hotel; lightning-fast room service by smiling uncle figures who instinctively bring the right newspapers with breakfast.
Cama Hotel, Khanpur Road (tel: 25281-5; telex: 012377); concrete, very efficient management, keen young staff; 45 rooms, all mod. cons. including liquor store, fast room service yields delicious fresh coffee, good restaurant but Gujarati food for lunch only.

Copious information from Tourist Office, Ahmedabad Municipal Corporation, Danapath (tel: 36364) and Tourism Corporation of Gujarat, H K House, off Ashram Road (tel: 4496834/49172). The TCG run several half-day city tours, worth considering as monuments are widely scattered; they also run 5-day and 6-day package tours including one to Kutch, another to Dwarka and Somnath. Indian Airlines is on Lal Darwaja (tel: 391737). Best travel agents are TCI, near Handloom House, Ashram Road (tel: 77601/78770) and Sherry Tours and Travels, Lal Darwaja (tel: 26932).

OUT AND ABOUT   Central Ahmedabad has some of the best Indo-Saracenic buildings constructed for the Muslim rulers. They are distinctive for their bold Muslim structure happily married to intricate Hindu decoration carved by locals. Do not miss the Rani Sipri tomb and mosque (1514) or Siddi Sayyad's mosque (1515), bold buildings with extraordinarily delicate jali (pierced stone) windows, hallmarks of the Gujarati style – (merits risking death to reach it on a traffic island). Rani Rupmati mosque (1430-40) is worth seeing, as is the Jami Masjid (1424), where local kids guide tourists up to the women's balcony and then on to the many-domed roof which resembles a sci-fi lunar landscape. The citadel remains and the Sidi Bashir mosque ('shaking minarets') are not as interesting as promised (minarets currently closed indefinitely, for restoration).

Also Muslim and unique to Gujarat are the richly carved, galleried *baolis* (step-wells), also known as vavs, which lightened the drudgery of fetching water. See Dada Hari baoli (1435, closed for siesta 1-4pm) in town and the most beautiful one of all, *Adalaj Vav* (1499), 19km (30 minutes' driving) north of Ahmedabad (almost the only building that does not close for siesta). *Kankaria Lake*, south of the city centre, is where Emperor Jahangir and his beloved Nur Jahan frolicked. It is still a refreshing area, with lakeside cafés and a good zoo. In the south-west suburb of *Sarkhej* are the remains of a more Hindu palace scheme built around 1457 by Mahmud Birgarha, possibly designed by Azam and Mu'azzam whose mausoleum is nearby. In the prevailing aesthetic climate of Gujarat, the chaste elegance extended to every last detail.

Skipping on to the 20th century, visit the riverside *Sabarmati Ashram* (designed by Charles Correa), founded by Mahatma Gandhi (1869-1948) in 1915, who moved here 2 years later. This was the cradle of the non-cooperation movement begun in 1920. It was from here that Gandhi began the Dandi March in 1930, protesting against the Salt Tax. Of all the institutions associated with Gandhi in India, this is the place that gives the clearest idea of the Mahatma's strong and charismatic character, his austere code of living and his mammoth ambition for India's independence and self-reliance, symbolised by the spinning wheel. Romain Rolland described him as 'A small weak man, with a lean face and tranquil brown eyes and with spread out big ears. This is the man who has stirred to action three hundred millions of men, shaken the British Empire and inaugurated in human politics the most powerful moral movement since nearly two thousand years.' Open around the clock. English sound and light shows on Wed., Fri. and Sun., at 8.30pm (tel: 866873).

The museums are a treat – if they can be caught open. Most important is the *Sarabhais' Calico Museum*, the only substantial museum in India devoted entirely to textiles, now housed in the gardens of the family mansion; excellent publications; Shauhi Baug Area (tel: 51001), closed Wed, open Thurs-Tues, 10.30am-12.30pm and 2.30-4.30pm. The mansion itself is now open as a centre for Hindu studies: Jainism, Vishnuism and Shivaism; exhibits from both the textile collection and the Sarabhai Foundation Collection. There are three other not-to-be-missed museums. N. C. *Mehta Museum* of Indian miniature paintings is one of the finest collections, housed in Le Corbusier's Sanskar Kendra Municipal Museum, Paldi (tel: 78369), open Tues.-Sun., 9am-noon, 3-6pm. (Next door is the Tagore Hall designed by B. V. Doshi, a leading Indian architect who worked with Le Corbusier on Ahmedabad and Gandhinagar buildings.) *Vechaar* is a large collection of rare Indian utensils, housed in a newly constructed traditional Gujarat village called Vishalla, on the outskirts of town, at Vasana (see below) (tel: 79845), open Mon.-Sat., 5-11pm; Sun., 10am-1pm; 5-10pm (see also food section below). Another worthwhile museum is the *Shreyas Folk Museum*, holding traditional mirror-work, distinctive tribal clothes and decorations, off Circular Road, open Thur.-Tues., 9-11am; 4-7pm.

FITNESS, FOOD AND ENTERTAINMENT
Apart from the old centre, Ahmedabad is a flat, industrialised and unattractive city to wander in. For pleasant walking, there is the zoo and Kankaria (with boating) and Chandola Lakes. The clubs' facilities of tennis, billiards, badminton and swimming are accessible through the good hotels. In addition, Ahmedabad Gymkhana, Airport Road has the golf course; the Sports Club of Gujarat, Sardar Patel Stadium, Navrangpura, has cricket; Ellisbridge Gymkhana has bowling. All three have pools. Sherry Tours can organise chikar (hunting) for partridge, duck and chinkara (one of the deer family) October-February.

All this and more may be necessary after a Gujarati thali feast at *Vishalla*, Sarkhej Road, Vasana (5km), built as a Gujarati village with museum, crafts, performing arts and restaurant. This is not only the best place to taste the exclusively vegetarian Gujarati cuisine but is one of the most enjoyable restaurants with entertainment in India. On arrival for dinner (not later than 8.30pm), order and pay for 'meal' plus fruit juice before and pudding after (about Rs75 for two). Fruit juices (pineapple, orange, apple, sugar cane, etc.) and entertainment fill the long gap between ordering and being called to eat. People weave, pot and make paan in the village buildings. The excellent museum is open (until 10pm), as is the shop. And outside there are string beds to lounge on, while puppeteers recount legends with huge string puppets, musicians play and dancers perform.

Dinner is an overwhelming feat taken sitting cross-legged on the floor, knees resting on pink-painted wooden leg rests (the stiff-limbed are given chairs). Waiters converge, bearing steaming tin pots and ladle an array of vegetables, pulses and fresh curd on to a platter of leaves sewn together. Millet flour chapati and other hot fresh breads arrive continuously. A dozen or more chutneys and salads are served in separate pottery dishes – onion, lime, green chillies, tomato, coconut. Mugs of buttermilk wash it down. Everything is constantly replenished. Then come the hot, sweet, cardamom-scented, crunchy-and-gooey jalebis (some Gujarats eat the sweet at the beginning of

the meal). Then a rich rice and wheat mixture ladled over with ghi (clarified butter), an irresistable calorie concentrate. Finally, be sure to leave space for creamy, nutty, homemade ice-cream. No need to eat again for a week.

In the town centre, eating is a mundane experience by comparison. But *Hotel Saba* (opposite the Cama) and *Hotel Chetna*, next to Krishna Talkies on Relief Road, should produce a good thali. A revolving sky restaurant called *Patang* (kite) serves the tri-cuisine plus Guja rati food. Dishes can have odd combinations. Khaman dhokla is a chickpea flour cake; undhyoo is a winter dish of aubergines, broad beans, potato and sweet potato cooked buried (undhyoo) under a fire; srikand, signifying hospitality, is hot savoury puris eaten with sweetened yoghurt flavoured with saffron, cardamom, nuts and candied fruit. The special Surat sweet is gharis (thickened milk, butter and dried fruits), best from *Azad Halwai* sweetmeat shop, Relief Road.

Ice-cream eating in Gujarat is serious business and it is tempting to try some. A good parlour competes with the American Baskin and Robbins and Dayvilles chains. There is a good parlour on every street corner. The aptly-named *Havmor* on Relief Road is especially good, where mango and pineapple are in the huge selection of ice-creams and strange flavoured milk drinks.

Good drama, dance and music programmes are held regularly at the Tagore Theatre, Paldi; Surdari Hall, Raikhadi; Sheth Mangaldas Town Hall, Ellisbridge; and Paemabhai Hall, Bhadra. It is worth looking out for performances by the local Darpan Academy. There may also be some bhavai (Gujarati folk theatre), which is undergoing a revival. The Tourist Office or Sangeet Natak Akademi provide information and advice on what is on where.

SHOPPING AND CRAFTS Gujarat's rich tradition of high quality weaving, hand-block printing and tie-dye fabrics has risen to its former heights under the energetic and watchful eyes of Mrs Jaya Jaitly, a champion of all Indian crafts, and Mrs Mrinalini Sarabhai, widow of the brilliant scientist, Dr Virkram Sarabhai, and a dancer by profession. Both are adamant about maintaining the correct colours and crafts – no bastardisations for a quick sale.

Some women who had left their crafts to earn better money as stone-breakers and road labourers have even been persuaded to return to their villages to produce good embroidery. The Gurjari state emporia in Ahmedabad, Bombay and Delhi are well stocked so, unlike Orissan crafts, Gujarat crafts can be bought just before leaving India. In Gujarat itself, the good and easy shopping is in Ahmedabad. Elsewhere, delve into back streets to find nut crackers, silver, wood, brass and other treasures in tiny, dark shops. But some towns, like Bhavnagar, have very little.

Fabrics The endless variety of textiles, at all prices, are the best buys. There is smooth crepe and fine cotton by the metre, screen-printed with small floral motifs. Pieces of cloth are hand-painted with concentric patterns of deities and flowers. Bandhana (tie-dye) silk or cotton is first woven, then tied and dyed to create the pattern, the best produced at Rajkot, Jamnagar and the Saurashtra villages. A special bandhana cotton is the rabari abla with appliqué mirror-work (worn by shepherds, rabaris).

Saris, 5½m long, can be batik-printed, stamp-printed with stars, flowers and mangoes in bright colours on dark ground or block-printed with traditional earth tones. Moving up, silk is grown near Saurat and Patan. The striking silk panatar (wedding sari) is dazzling red and white, often with a crisp checked design and elephants around the edge for good luck; a lagdi patta has a double border, a thick gold stripe and floral field that is either printed or richly embroidered.

The zari (gold thread) work loved so much by the Mughals comes from Saurat and is applied to saris, velvet, evening shoes and handbags. Tanchoi is the tapestry-thick Saurat brocade. Beware: the 'gold' thread is usually metal over a plastic core; possibly Gurjari would have a piece with real gold thread.

The queen of textiles is the *patola* sari, kept under lock and key in the few shops that stock them. It demands accurate planning and skilled craftsmanship. First, the intricate design of rows of figures, animals and patterning is worked out. Then the threads for the whole sari are tie-dyed vibrant colours precisely according to the design. Finally, they are woven, the crispness of the completed design determining the quality and price – less if just the weft is tie-dyed than if both warp and weft are, the true patola.

A few families still practise the true patola weave in Patan. But it is easier to see at the National School of Weaving at Rastriya Shala educational institution in Rajkot, where patola and other weaves are being revived.

There is plenty more besides textiles. At Sankheda, near Vadodara, carpenters make and varnish highly decorative furniture, achieving their deep golden lacquers by using juice extracts from woods. There are glorious swings and rocking chairs which can be shipped or, easier to carry, stools, mirror frames and candle-holders. Gaily embroidered, stuffed toy elephants, horses and camels of all sizes come from Kutch. Brass and wood pataras (chests) come from Bhavnagar, woollen shawls from Saurashtra and silver or brass nut crackers from Kutch.

But leave the new embroidery, beadwork and wood-carving. Old pieces are better, so hunt around the Manek Chowk area of the old city. This is where the jewellery market is, where tiny shops sell cheap'n'cheerful bandhana and where kids sit on the mosque steps doing wood-block printing, their friends spinning cotton nearby. And remember to look up, for here and in Ratan Pole area the houses are beautifully carved. Each is one room wide but 4 or 5 storeys high, the layers cantilevered out on supports carved as swans, musicians or gods, the over-hanging balconies carved with rich floral and geometric friezes.

Find fabrics, furniture and toys at Gurjari, Ashram Road; fabric only at Handloom House, Ashram Road. Among the fabric shops lining Ratan Pole streets, Deepkala has good pieces (ask to go upstairs to see handloom patola silks, avoid their synthetics) and is open long hours, Sun.-Fri., 8.30am-8pm.

Forays into Gujarat

These few suggestions include day trips. The places further away link up to make trips of a few days that can end back at Ahmedabad again, or at one of the several cities with airports, or can lead on to surrounding states. Outside Ahmedabad, Gujarat is immediately very rural and made up of tiny villages. There are blue-eyed shepherds dressed in baggy white jodhpur and kurta (waistcoat) and cerise turbans, and cows, sheep and bullocks with huge curly horns. Dotted among them are some of the masterpiece temples built under the Solankis, who rose in the 9th century to become the dominant power in Gujarat and southern Rajasthan in the 11th-13th centuries. In contrast, this seemingly isolated land has some of India's most extravagant late Raj buildings – at Junagadh, Wankaner, Morvi, Bhuj and the Art Deco seaside palaces of Ahmednapur Mandvi, Chorwad, Porbander and Mandavi. And, for the sightseeing weary, there are two beach hotels.

HEADING NORTH
GANDHINAGAR
30km. India's second planned town, named after the Mahatma and designed, like Chandigarh, by Le Corbusier, assisted by Indian architect B. V. Doshi. Begun in 1960 as the capital of Gujarat after it was separated from Maharashtra. The city is planned as government offices surrounded by 30 residential sectors, each with its own community facilities, all set in green, blossoming parks beside the Sabarmati River. Sounds idyllic but not all inhabitants describe it in such glowing language.

MODHERA

106km, via Adalaj step-well (see Ahmedabad). *Surya Temple*, dedicated to the sun, was built in 1026 under the Solanki king, Bhimdev I. Many parallels with the Shiva Temple at Somnath on the south coast. Both were erected under the Solankis, whose affluence came from east-west trade passing through their coastal ports; both were financed by public subscription and built by voluntary skilled labour; and both were devastated by the Muslim iconoclast Mahmud of Ghazni and then suffered subsequent earthquakes. But the typical Solanki carving, extremely rich yet very refined, encrusts every remaining surface. Sited above a stepped tank, the sandstone Surya Temple glows appropriately in the late sun.

Dawn rays reach into the temple to the spot where Surya's image was placed. In *Indian Architecture*, Percy Brown goes into ecstasies over this building: 'lit with the living flame of inspiration, . . . an atmosphere of spiritual grace . . . its creator a weaver of dreams'. There is also a two-storey, 11th century baoli.

PATAN

130km – 24km from Modhera. Little remains of the Hindu capital Anhilwara, sacked by Mahmud of Ghazni in 1024, but this quiet provincial town has fine carved wooden houses, 108 Jain temples and some master weavers creating the legendary patola weaves. One of the families still creating Patan patolas is the Salvis, whose home is right in the centre – locals give directions. (To visit weavers, consult with Gurjari in Ahmedabad.)

THE DRIVE PATAN-MOUNT ABU, RAJASTHAN

140km. Described by Indophiles as 'unmissable', with Solanki temple-spotting on the way. First, to *Sidhpur* for the Solanki temple of Rudra Mahalaya (12th century) and a townful of ghostly, great, elaborately decorated merchants' houses including Mr Hararwalla's, a magician who transforms persperation into perfume and has birds hatching eggs in mid-air. Next stop is *Taranga*, off to the east, to catch a well preserved and fully developed Solanki temple scheme. Finally, a small detour to *Kumbharia* for the five richly carved Solanki period Jain temples. Just south of Mount Abu (see p. 123), at *Ambaji*, the Gujarat folk drama, Bhavai, is often staged in the temple courtyard (consult Tourist Office for dates). To break the journey, there are various Dak bungalows along the route (again, the Tourist Office has details).

HEADING SOUTH-EAST

VADODARA (BARODA)

120km. Parks, lakes and palace museums still dominate this expanding industrial town, former capital of the Gaekwads (means protector of cows) of Baroda who were so rich last century they had a carpet woven of diamonds and pearls and had canons cast in gold.

See the crazily extravagant *Lakshmi Vilas Palace* with its 500-foot facade, completed in 1890 at a cost of £180,000 for Maharaja Sayajirao. The first architect, Major Mant, designed it and then died insane; the second, R. F. Chisholm from Madras, oversaw its completion. Its facade, with domes, balconies and jali screens, looks Indian; but its plan and rooms are entirely Western, complete with ballrooms billiard room and even imported European marble and French furniture in the true Indo-Saracenic style – just like Jai Vilas at Gwalior and Umaid Bhawan at Jodhpur. The reforming Gaekwad then went on to build roads and railways, to outlaw child marriage, to establish free and compulsory education, to found hospitals and generally to be extremely enlightened. Meanwhile, his Maharani campaigned against purdah and chaired the first All Indian Women's Conference. Museum of armour and sculpture open at erratic times. This is where the current ex-Maharaja lives. Cambridge-educated, former Member of Parliament and minister, mad keen cricketer and wildlife conservationist, this energetic man is now forming a museum of turbans.

The *Baroda Museum and Art Gallery* is set in a fine park: good Mughal miniatures and European oils (open Sun.-Fri., 9.30am-4.45pm; Sat., 10am-5.45pm). Not far away is the *Maharajah Feteh Singh Museum* where Titian and Raphael turn up in a mixed collection of world-wide goodies (open Tues.-Sun., 9am-noon; 3-6pm except April-June, 4-7pm). Other places to see include old Bhadra plus Nazarbagh and Makarpura; an excellent baoli, Naulakhi Well; the Islamic Maqbara for filigree marble screens; and Sarsagar Lake for boating.

Do seek out the superb *Tambekarwada*, a four-storey haveli (merchant's town house) whose walls are covered from top to bottom with murals. Open daily, managed by the Archaeological Survey of India, directions availble from the Tourist Office opposite the railway station. The fine MS (Maharaja Sayajirao) University of Vadodara (Indo-Saracenic designed by his favourite, Chisholm) has especially strong music, dance and drama faculties. Regular evening performances attract the leading artists of India. Vadodara also has a thriving contemporary art school whose painters exhibit world-wide. Outside Vadodara, Sankheda is a centre of lacquered wooden furniture-making. To stay overnight, *Utsav Hotel*, Professor Mankra Road (tel:551415), or Welcomgroup's *Vadodara*, R C Dutt Road, Alkapuri (tel: 323232). An airport connects with Delhi and Bombay.

Champaner 43km north-east of Vadodara. When Mahmud Begada besieged and took the city in 1484, he spent 23 years building a new city only to desert it shortly afterwards. Inside Pavgadh Fort find grass-lined streets, ruined buildings, the Custom House, the Mandir, Nagina Masjid, Borah Masjid and, best of all, the splendid Jami Masjid (1485) modelled on Ahmedabad's. Near here, 45km east of Vadodara, is Pawagarh for Jain temples, Islamic granaries and the ruins of a great fort taken by Akbar in 1573.

Dabhoi 24km south-east of Vadodara. The 13th-century fort, possibly built by the ruler of Patan, has four magnificent gateways with great carved brackets of musicians, dancers and warriors, pilasters showing Vishnu with crocodiles, and much more.

Broach and Surat For those keen on early European remains, this trip south demands stamina, but it is well-rewarded. First stop is Broach, one of India's older ports. Flourishing in the 1st century, it later had an English factory (1614), then a Dutch one; see the great river wall, the fort and its English church, Dutch factory, Civil courts and other public buildings. See also the melée of fine Jami Masjid, interesting Dutch tombs (3km to the west) and fine Parsee Towers of Silence. Surat was possibly the Pulipula mentioned by Ptolemy, but is certainly the port founded in the 16th century by a rich Hindu called Gopi. The Portuguese tried to take it; Akbar did take it, in 1572, when it became a great merchant city and doorway for European influence. In 1612 Jahangir granted the English trading rights in Surat; Dutch and French followed; but the double disasters of fire and flood in 1837 wiped out its strength, leaving it to be the flourishing textile city it is today, as well as a centre for diamond cutting and polishing (see See how it's done, above). Among many interesting buildings, see especially the view from the castle (1546), the English and Dutch cemeteries, and the four 16th and 17th century Islamic mosques. Beware: there are few tourists here, and monuments are not easy to find. From here, the coast road down to Bombay is pretty and easy to drive (see p. 272); alternatively, take a Vayudoot plane.

HEADING SOUTH
LOTHAL

87km. Archaeological find of major significance: an important Harappan port that traded with Egypt and Mesopotamia around 2400-1500BC, and thus the earliest known urban settlement in India. Part of the Indus Civilisation whose capitals were further north at Moenjodaro and Harappa (see Pakistan section in Delhi chapter). Discovered in 1954 by archaeologist S. R. Rao. Excavations reveal a sophisticated port using a scientific understanding of tides; planned streets and bazaar areas, with underground drains; merchants' houses with bath areas and fireplaces; joint burial grounds; dockyards and warehouses; terracotta seals with Indus valley script; fine gold and faience jewellery and children's toys that include a chess set. Excellent on-site museum; the archaeologically keen can stay at the very modest *Taran Holiday Home*.

PALITANA

215km. For Jains, Satrunjaya is the most sacred of their five, temple-covered, sacred hills. Girnar, near Junagadh, comes second. JAINISM developed in the 6th century BC and, like Buddhism a century later, was breaking away from rigid, caste-ridden Hinduism. Like Buddhism too, it was a prince who led. Mahavira (599-527 BC), the 24th and last Tirthankara (saint), renounced his pampered life and lived as a naked ascetic for 12 years before achieving the highest spiritual knowledge. He then became a jina (conqueror) and his followers became Jains.

Jains have no god since they believe the universe was not created but is infinite. However, they do believe in reincarnation and in salvation, to be found through, amongst other efforts, temple building and ahimsa (reverence for all life) which demands strick vegetarianism. Many wear mouth masks in case they should swallow an insect. There are two sects: Digambaras (sky-clad) who have no possessions, not even clothes, and Shvetambaras who are less strict. Jains concentrate in Gujarat, Bombay and Rajasthan to be close to the sacred hills as pilgrimage should be on foot. Like the Parsees, they tend to be bright, commercially successful and exercise power disproportionate to their meagre 3½ million population. Well-known families are the Sarabhais and Kasturbais but, in general, Jains are self-effacing, neither giving money to the community nor spending it ostentatiously on themselves, which would contradict their tenets.

To visit Palitana, arrive through the quiet countryside of shepherds, sheep and flocks of geese by 7am to climb before the heat. The route is already full of white-clad pilgrims, the old or sick carried in dolis (string chairs), the rich on gaily caparisoned elephants. Well worth pausing for tea and fortifying nuts at Oswald Guest House before the climb. It takes about 1½ hours to climb the 4km of steps up Shatrunjaya (place of victory over worldliness) and arrive through a white marble jungle of 863 temples, each in its tuk (enclosure), on to the rooftops, 591m up. If climbing is too much, be carried up in a doli. At the gates, refreshing yoghurt made of creamy buffalo milk is sold in shallow earthenware pots by young girls who have each brought their own supplies from home and urge visitors to taste their personal recipes.

Stunning views, air filled with the scent of jasmine trees. The biggest temple, Chaumukh, was built by a wealthy banker in 1618 to save his soul. But the most sacred is dedicated to Shri Adishwara (or Rushbhadav), the first Tirthankara, where the faithful chant at the image bedecked with gold and enormous diamonds. Coffers groaning with more jewels stand nearby. A successful Ahmedabad merchant might well add a diamond necklace to them. A 'donation' of Rs900 brings the honour of opening them and dressing up the deity in more jewels. They are no longer on public display. Priests hand a pass to each leaving visitor who, many steps down and 45 minutes later, exchanges it for a free, reviving breakfast of ladu (a heavy sweetmeat) and brass dishes of steaming, sweet tea. Open 7am-7pm, when the priests leave. Stay at *Oswald Guest House* here, or at Bhavnagar.

BHAVNAGAR

244km from Ahmedabad; 60km from Palitana. Cotton-exporting port with Gandhi Smitri (museum and library to the Mahatma) and one shop, Gandhisamriti. The splendid palace-like hospital built in the 1930s by Maharaja Takhtsinghji was designed so that a patient could ride up to the operating theatre on his camel.

Stay here to visit Palitana, at *Nilambag Palace Hotel* (tel: 24340/24422). Welcomgroup's unpretentious, small, courtyard palace well-built at the turn of the century, much polished wood and Maharaja's furnishings, private house atmosphere. It was Maharaja Krishnakumarsingh who was the first maharaja to hand over his state to the Union of India and who later became Governor of Madras State (now Tamil Nadu). 14 rooms (suites very spacious), attached bath, big verandahs on upper floors, garden, pool, hard tennis court. To escape the heat, Gujarat's answer to Srinagar is *Mahuva*, lush with coconut palms, but it is not well developed for Western tourists yet. Bhavnagar connects by air with Bombay, by road with Somnath and Gir.

HEADING SOUTH-WEST

RAJKOT

216km, pausing on the way at Sejakpur to see one of the best Solanki temples, Navalakha (12th century), with stepped sanctuary and mandapa and exuberant carving all over. Former capital of Saurashtra, now associated with Gandhi who passed his childhood here when his father was diwan (chief minister) to the Raja. His home can be visited. Other Gandhi connections are the fine Alfred High School where he was educated and the Rashtriya Shala, founded in his presence in 1921 (housing

the National School of Weaving). See also Rajkumar College (built 1870 to educate Gujarati princes, with a fine hall) and Watson Museum (building and contents open Thurs.-Tues., 9-11.45am; 3-5.45pm). Local bandhana, patchwork and mirrorwork are good. Rajkot is the junction for exploring Saurashtra and Kutch, flat areas with colourful tribes and walled kots (village forts), the occasional Kutch one still locked at night. But stay at Wankaner, 38km away (see below). Rajkot connects by air with Bombay.

WEST FROM RAJKOT
JAMNAGAR

87km. 16th-century pearl fishing town, the Rajput Jadeja's capital, whose fame rests as much on producing the two Indian cricketers Ranji and Duleep as on its bandhana fabrics and its Ayurvedic College and Research Centre. Broad streets and old buildings surround the Ranmal lake, whose island Lakhota Palace now houses a museum of Saurashtran sculpture and pottery (open Thurs.-Tues., 9am-noon; 3-6pm). See also the odd Manekbhai Muktidham, a cremation ground covered in statues of Indian gods, goddesses and saints. Several markets to watch the craftsmen and buy their bandhana, embroidery, silver, nutcrackers – and renowned sweetmeats. To stay, the *Hotel President*, Teen Batti (tel: 70516). Jamnagar connects by air with Bombay.

DWARKA

234km. Krishna's capital, regularly referred to as Dwaravati in the great epics, especially the Mahabharata. Intensely holy, therefore, for Hindus who flock to celebrate his birthday, the Janmashtami festival (August-September). Blue-skinned *Krishna* is believed by many to be the 8th incarnation of Vishnu. He was born into a nomadic cattle-herding family of the Yadeva clan who later migrated here from Mathura (near Agra, see p. 80). He spent a gloriously naughty childhood, a wickedly flirtatious adolescence, had a very sexy romance with Radha, defeated various less fun-loving gods and rulers, and is number-one popular hero. Join pilgrims to see first the fine exterior of Dwarkanath temple with its 5-storey spire, the 13th-century Bhadkeshwar temple on the shore and, on the island of Beyt Dwarka nearby, an eccentric 19th century temple in the form of a house for Krishna and his 56 consorts. (Recent Harappan finds here testify to another early port, see Lothal, above.)

PORBANDAR

178km. Port town of narrow lanes, used by Arab traders since the 8th century. Visit the old house where Mohandas Karamchand Gandhi was born in 1869 and the nearby Kirti Mandir memorial to him which blends architectural elements of all India's religious styles. Gandhi's father and grandfather were diwans (chief ministers) of Porbandar.

Take a stroll along the shore to see the turn-of-the-century Daria Rajmahal palace showing (appropriately for the seaside) Venetian, Gothic and Arab influence (now a training college) and the sprawling 1927 Anut Nivas Khambala shore palace built by the cultured Maharaja Natwarsinghji (now a museum of Gujarat history). Plans to open it as a hotel may be realised by now. Incidentally, Natwarshinghji in 1931 captained the first offical Indian cricket team to play in England. Charming 1930s *guest house* nearby for overnight stays. Porbandar connects by air with Bombay.

Out of town, a good country day trip inland takes in early temples (6-7th centuries) at *Bileshwar* and *Gop*, with later Solanki ones (12-13th centuries) at *Ghumli*.

SOUTH FROM RAJKOT
JUNAGADH AND GIRNAR
99km. Archaeological finds push Junagadh back to pre-Harappan times. Later, in the 15th century, it produced the great poet-saint Narshi Mehta, whose devotional songs are still sung throughout Gujarat. But today, the Jains' sacred *Girnar Hill* draws the crowds (although there are Hindu temples and a mosque too). See notes on Palatana above. This hill has a mere 2,000 steps, rising 600m through a wood to the topmost temple, Amba Mata, where couples worship to secure a happy marriage. Just below is the biggest and oldest temple, dedicated to the 22nd Tirthankana, Neminath, in the 12th century. When Gujarat traveller Joss Graham climbed up the hill for the Shivrashti festival, he slept there overnight and woke 'hearing the praying murmurs of the great mass of devotees, 100,000 of them, in their communities and tribal groups; an incredible and strange sensation'.

En route to the hill, see the epigraphically important boulder inscribed by the Mauryan emperor Ashoka (3rd century BC), Rudradaman (150AD) and Skandagupta (454AD) (open 9am-noon; 3-6pm). Visit the fine old city fort, Uparkot, founded in the 9th century by the Chudasamal Rajputs. Inside the triple gateway are 2 more stepwells, a Rajput palace, Buddhist caves with clever spiral staircase, a mosque and Jami Masjid.

In town, see the grand 19th-century Maqbara (Nawabs' mausolea), especially Mahabatr Khan's very Gothic one and, nearby, his rags-to-riches Wazir's. He, named Bahauddin, was extremely bright and progressive and was responsible for the serious Gothicism of the city: the wide straight streets, the arches leading into piazzas, the arcades of shops, the fairytale Italianate palaces, the Venetian Gothic library and the general splendour more suited to a Midlands factory city than an isolated corner of Gujarat. Do not miss the extraordinary (both building and contents) Durbar Hall, nor the Museum in the zoological gardens, where more royal furnishings lie unused (open Thurs.-Tues., 9-11.45am; 3-5.45pm, also closed alternate Sats). Tourist information next door; the Sakkar Bagh Museum; Rupayatan institute for handicrafts and the zoo (for a foretaste of the Gir lions). Find craftsmen working on embroidery and patchwork, sometimes of high quality. For Junagadh seaside palaces, see below. Junagadh connects by air with Bombay from Keshod airport.

SASAN GIR: (58km). See wildlife section at chapter end.

SOMNATH (PRABHAS PATAN)
88km. Although destroyed and rebuilt about a dozen times – early ones including the demon Ravana's in silver and Krishna's in wood – the superb 11th-century shore temple has sufficient still standing, either on site or in the museum, to testify to its legendary beauty; and the fine new carving testifies to a healthy surviving tradition. Pilgrims flood here to worship Shiva and to bathe in the nearby rivers. Shiva is believed to have shed his Jyotrilinga (luminous energy) here (as he did at a dozen places); Krishna is believed to have left his mortal incarnation here, at Bhalka Tirth. Best at 7am, noon or sunset. See notes to the better preserved Modhera, above. The Archaeological Museum is at Surya Mandir, Patan City Bazaar (closed Wed. and alternate Sats).

AHMEDPUR MANDVI, DIU AND CHORWAD
Two good places to stay as bases for this whole area are the beach hotels at Ahmedpur Mandvi and Chorwad, both ex-Junagadh palaces.

Sumudra Beach Resort, Ahmedpur Mandvi, Kathiawar District; sited opposite Diu island, 145km from Keshod airport, also accessible by rail to Delwada station and by bus from Ahmedabad (298km). The main building was a seaside palace of the Nawabs of Junagadh, protected by earthen wall complete with gate, sentries and drummers. Now slowly gaining popularity as a beach hotel. Terraces for lounging; empty, sandy and clean beaches to lie on; hammocks beneath the garden palm trees to snooze in. To maintain the relaxation, pack anti-mosquito repellant. Food good, especially the local thali eaten with bashra (black millet bread), and the kedgeree and local prawns – seen up the beach in mountains being shelled by local women. Possible to go out with the fishermen.

Fellow guests probably all Indian.

The local village is a walk away, with ferries to *Diu* full of friendly locals. The great draw is that, unlike Gujarat, this until recently Portuguese enclave is not dry, so cafés such as Joy Bar abound, as do advertisements for booze. Diu and Daman (another island 160km north of Bombay) were captured by the Portuguese in 1531 and 1534 and, together with Goa, remained theirs until December 1961; the two islands became a separate territory in 1987. Diu is rather shabbily pretty, with its impressive fort, baroque cathedral, surviving Portuguese living in cottages with European gardens, a good market and excellent jewellers. It also has its own beach, Ngaio, with palms, sand and hippies. Sunset on Diu is wonderful.

Chorwad Palace Beach Resort, Chorwad. Nearest airport is Keshod (40km); also accessible by rail to Chorwad Road station and by bus from Ahmedabad (393km). Not as organised as Samudra, nor is the beach as good, but it is just as well sited, and the building is splendid. This ex-Junagadh seaside fun palace (1928), built more like a hotel than a house, is now appropriately a real hotel run by Gujarat Tourism. The sea almost encircles the palace; the beach is long, with rocky outcrops; the fish is delicious and, again, it is possible to go out in the fishermen's catamarans.

NORTH FROM RAJKOT
Not far are *Morvi*, where Thakur Sahib Waghaji (ruled 1879-1948) built first the whacky Dubargadh Waghaji Palace (c.1880) in Venetian Gothic, then, following the European change in taste, his New Palace (1931-44) in stylish Art Deco (1931-44) with tubular-framed furniture, subterranean bedrooms and lift; and *Halvad*, with beautifully carved, lakeside palace.

THE RANN OF KUTCH
The more adventurous should press on north to these salt flats to see the Asiatic wild ass and the largest breeding flamingo area in the world. The capital is *Bhuj*, a kot (walled town) until recently locked at night, with narrow alleys running between carved overhanging balconies, old palaces and royal mausolea. The secondary capital was the extremely lucrative port of *Mandavi*; favoured by the Mughals as a port for pilgrims going to Mecca, wondered at by the British who in 1819 arrived to find more than 800 ships used it, today studded with palaces including Ram Singh's incredible Dutch facade added to the old palace. In Bhuj, see the grand Italianate winter palace, and hunt in the back streets for some of the very best Gujarat bandhana embroidery and silver. To stay, the *Prince* is the nicest; and there are a number of new hotels, too.

Travelling on round the Rann of Kutch is rewarding and extremely atmospheric, but not for those fussy about their comfort. It is best to take a guide from the Bhuj tourist office. At *Bhandreshwar*, see Solanki temple and mosques. North of Bhuj lie *Banni* and other villages. The plains are used by Muslim and Hindu herders who grow a dozen different grasses for animals while they themselves eat millet – these herders wander across the India-Pakistan border, going where the rain falls on this barren land. On the roads notice the pallias (stones commemoratng poets and warriors). Each is carved with a man on a horse, a woman in a chariot or just a hand denoting death by sati (self-immolation), the sun or moon above recording the date of the death or act of bravery. Sati was performed by husbands, wives and mothers here; one man watching his wife commit sati in 1805 complained to Sir Alexander Walker 'not from feeling regret for his loss, but for the expense he was explosed to in his endeavours to procure another wife'.

WANKANER
38km. The base for west Gujarat. Stay at either the grand and glorious Ranjitvilas Palace or the Purna Chandra Bhavan (full-moon house) in the palace grounds, once the royal guest house. *Ranjitvilas Palace* (tel: 363621; cable to Secretary, Yuvraj Digvijaysinh, Palace, Wankaner); home of yet another Rajput family, the Jhalas. Former Maharana Rajsahib Pratapsinhji runs his palace as a country house for paying guests. Set on a hill in 225 acres of flat Kathiawad landscape, it was built 1907-14 to designs of the then Maharana, Amarsinhji. He ruled for 67 years, travelled world-wide and threw all his architectural experience into the palace: Victorian ironwork, Gothic arches, Italianate pillars, Dutch roof and colossal, domed central clock-tower. Inside there is a marble double spiral staircase designed to prevent those ascending from seeing those descending (useful for night-time corridor walking); an indoor swimming pool; a 1930s baoli (one of the last to be built) for air-conditioning and a museum.

12 double rooms, attached bath, palace furnishings, meals included (picnics provided), chikar (hunting) for antelope and small game can be arranged as can visits to rural villages and fairs, Morvi, Halvad and trips to Kutch. Essential to book by letter or cable, indicating time of arrival and first meal needed. The *Purna Chandra Bhavan* (c.1920), with indoor swimming pool, in the palace grounds (now renamed *Oasis Palace Hotel*) is booked through the palace and guests can use the palace facilities. More buildings dot the grounds.

Wildlife sanctuaries

Only two, but both excellent. However, the Karnataka and Tamil Nadu reserves in the South are as near as these and connected by direct flights; see Wildlife Sanctuaries section of South chapter.

KANHA, MADHYA PRADESH

Season November-May. Direct flights from Bombay, Delhi and Calcutta to Nagpur, then by road 270km; or fly to Jabalpur (Indian Airlines or Vayudoot), then by road 175km. Stay at *Kipling Camp*, well-sited, equipped with both tents and chalets built in local style; bookable through Bob Wright, Tollygunge Club, Calcutta or through a travel agent, such as SITA. (Reports say the camp is nicest when Bob Wright is in residence.) Alternatively, stay at the state-run *Kisli Hotel*, bookable through MPSTDC, Bhopal or B. Rekwar, Shakti Travels, Mandla, MP. For local information and other government accommodation, apply to The Manager, Wildlife Tourism, MPSTDC, 1494 Wright Town, Jabalpur (tel: 23906). Explore on elephant.

2,200 sqkm of very rich faunal land in the Banjar Valley right in the middle of India and hunted over until recently. Setting of Kipling's *The Jungle Books*. Set up in 1955 to save the almost extinct hard-ground barasingha (the Indian swamp deer), now numbering around 150. The park is part of Project Tiger and now provides a near certainty of seeing a tiger. The first serious research on tigers was done here by American big-cat expert, George Schaller, in 1963-65. There are also chital, leopard, hyena, blackbuck, barking deer, gaur (Indian bison) and sambhar; plus birds such as crested serpent-eagles and black ibises.

GIR, GUJARAT

Season October-June. Fly to Keshod, then 90km by road. Stay at *Sasan Gir Forest Lodge*, Junagadh, bookable in writing or through ITDC Bomabay (tel: 233343); or at *Forest Bungalow*, Junagadh (60km), bookable direct two weeks in advance or through the Government of Gujarat Office, Dhanraj Mahal, Apollo Bunder, Bombay (tel: 257039) or the Gujarat Information Centre, Baba Kharak Singh Marg, New Delhi (tel: 343147).

1,412 sqkm of Gir's deciduous and thorn forest constitutes one of the most important Indian sanctuaries and the only place in the subcontinent to see lions in the wild.

Here the rare Asiatic lion, once found throughout the Middle East and north India, has been saved (although some find it a bit too tame). Not only did it suffer from Raj guns, but also from the famine of 1899-1900. This led the Viceroy Lord Curzon to cancel his shoot and the Nawab of Junagadh to begin protecting the Gir lions. Meanwhile, the lions, short of food, ate 31 people in the state the next year, and made off with countless cattle. Although there has been controlled shooting since then, Gir now has over 200 lions. See them up close, in their natural habitat, sometimes in prides of more than a dozen together. They tend to mate October-November, producing young in January-February. See also wild boar, deer, antelope, hyena, leopard and the Indian chowsingha antelope whose buck is the only wild animal to have four horns – the female is hornless. Birds include oriole, rock-grouse, paradise fly catcher and flocks of flamingoes.

Find out more

Burgess, J.: *The Temples of Palitana in Kathiawad*, Bombay, 1869, reprinted at Gandhinagar, 1976

David, M. D.: *History of Bombay 1661-1708*, Bombay, 1973

Forster, E. M.: *The Hill of Devi*, London, 1953

Gosh, A., (ed.): *Ajanta Murals*, New Delhi, 1967

Jackson, Stanley: *The Sassoons*, London, 1968

Jain, J.: *Folk Art and Culture of Gujarat*, Ahmedabad, 1980

Jain, J.: *The Master Weavers*, Bombay, 1982

Karkaria, R. P.: *The Charm of Bombay: an anthology of writings in praise of the first city in India*, Bombay 1915

Kulke, Eckehard: *The Parsees in India: a Minority as an Agent of Social Change*, India, 1978

Maclean, J. M.: *Guide to Bombay*, Bombay, editions published 1875-1902

Singh, M.: *The Cave Paintings of Ajanta*, London, 1965

Stamp, G.: 'British Architecture in India 1857-1947', *Journal of the Royal Society of Arts*, Vol. CXXIX, 1981, pp. 357-377.

Stamp, G.: 'Victorian Bombay: Urbs Prima in Indis', *Art and Archaeological Resarch Papers*, June 1977, pp. 22-27

Strachan, M.: *Sir Thomas Roe 1581-1644*, Salisbury, 1989

Tindall, Gillian: *City of Gold, The Biography of Bombay*, London 1982

'Treasures of Everyday Art: Raja Dinkar Kelkar Museum', *Marg*, Bombay, and 'Treasures of Indian Textiles', *Marg*, Bombay, 1980

Yazdani, G., (ed.) *Ajanta Frescoes*, Vols I-IV, Oxford, 1931-46

Yazdani, G.: *Mandu, City of Joy*, London, nd.
Fabric note

The most up-to-date publication is John Gillow and Nicholas Barnard's *Traditional Indian Textiles*, London, 1991.

Since 1972 the unrivalled collection at the Calico Museum has gradually been covered in substantial volumes, edited by John Irwin and published in Ahmedabad. They should be available in good art libraries and include the titles *Historic Textiles of India at the Calico Museum, Indian Printed Fabrics, Indian Embroideries, Indian Pigment Paintings on Cloth, Indian Tie-dyed Fabrics.*

The museum also stocks copies of *The Journal Of Indian Textile History*, ed., J. Irwin, 1955 et seq.

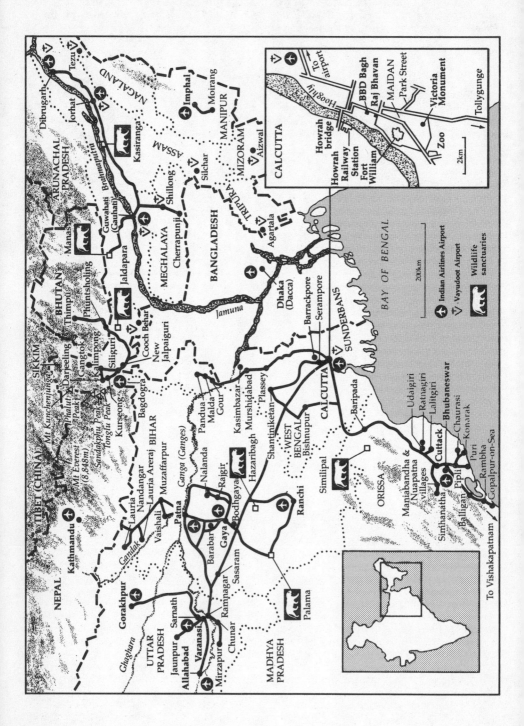

Heading east:
Calcutta, Varanasi and Orissa

The temptation to explore the toytown palaces of Rajasthan on the first trip to India, then, next time, climb up into the hills or plunge down south, leaves eastern India out in the cold. And stories of poverty in Calcutta and death in Varanasi (Banares) do not help.

But whereas Calcutta is certainly not for the tourist who demands a time-warp of paintbox palaces, charming markets and romance, nor for the over-sensitive who prefer poverty and death to be kept conveniently out of sight as they are back home, it is a fascinating city for the seasoned traveller. It is rich in good museums and buildings, both the inheritance of the British – although a lack of conservation enforcement is allowing too many buildings to dwindle away in favour of anonymous, concrete multi-storey piles. Its colonial foundation lives on in social and sporting life. It is the centre of the vibrant contemporary Bengali culture, seen in literature, politics and the visual and performing arts. And it is an excellent springboard for visiting Varanasi, Orissa, the hills of north-east India, Bhutan and Nepal – or escaping to the Andaman and Nicobar Islands. Also, it is from Calcutta that travellers fly to Burma.

However, it is not an easy city for a first-time visitor. The fabric of Calcutta is decaying. Geoffrey Moorhouse called Calcutta: 'A permanent exhibition of decaying English Classical Buildings', while Bombay 'still glories in preposterously confident Gothic Revival constructions'. (Bombay now has its own problems of over-crowding, so the contrast is no longer so sharp.) Yet, by peering through the crumbling masonry and dirt, the former colonial grandeur can be found, conjuring up visions of glittering balls and echoes of William Hickey's wicked gossip.

In Indian terms, Calcutta is a new city. In 1690 Job Charnock, an agent for the British East India Company, leased the three tiny villages of Sutanati, Govindpur and Kalikata, on the banks of the Hooghly River, from Emperor Aurangzeb. They became the Company's safe trading base. Six years later the Company built the first Fort William, named after King William III. It was the beginning of the Indian Empire. After various teething troubles – including Clive the trouble-shooter arriving from Madras in the nick of time to recapture the city from the Nawab of Murshidabad in 1757 – Warren Hastings became the first Governor of British India in 1772.

From then until 1911 when it was announced that the capital would move to Delhi, Calcutta blossomed. And even when it lost the political throne, it maintained commercial supremacy right until Independence, when the Indian economy changed from being colonial-based to Indian. It was at that moment that the new industries sprang up in Bombay. Until then, Calcutta was the headquarters for all the major British firms, from the traditional Jardine Henderson to the modern ICI. For their raw materials – jute, coal, iron ore and tea – came from Calcutta's rich hinterland.

After Clive's triumph the Fort was rebuilt (costing £2 million) and a huge area of jungle cleared so that the enemy could be seen approaching and the British could have a clear aim of fire at them. Around this two-mile long Maidan (open space) rose extravagant Regency mansions with columns, pilasters and porticos, built by the newly wealthy jute and opium millionaire merchants, the nabobs, who might keep a hundred servants for a family of four. Government House and Dalhousie Square formed the administrative centre to the north.

It was James Atkinson who in 1824 first gave it the epithet 'City of Palaces', the title of his poem which includes the lines: 'But we here behold A prodigy of power, transcending all The conquests, and the governments, of old, An empire of the Sun, a gorgeous realm of gold.' Later he continues: 'I stood a wandering stranger at the Ghaut (sic), And, gazing round, beheld the pomp of spires And palaces, to view like magic brought; all glittering in the sun-beam . . .' It was indeed a stuccoed classical city of palaces, likened by contemporaries to St Petersburg and Nash's London, although the climate attacked the buildings, and the people, very quickly. Crumbling Calcutta is nothing new. Many of the great figures of the period are buried in South Park Street Cemetery, a potted history of colonial Calcutta. But many of them may have lived hard for, as Atkinson reasoned: 'Drink again The frothy draught, and revel joyously; From the gay round of pleasure, why refrain! Thou'rt on the brink of death, luxuriate on thy bane.'

The writer Nirad Chaudhuri arrived in Calcutta in June 1910, a year before the British announced their departure, and stayed for thirty-two years. The first impressions this empire capital made upon him were not of glittering palaces. Instead, three particular sky-line features remain in his mind: 'They were, first, chimneys and church spires. . . . [then] the group of five cranes on the site of the Victoria Memorial . . . [and] every thousand yards square or so of the top face of Calcutta had a bamboo mast bearing on its head a bird-table, consisting only of a trellised frame, for pigeons to sit on.'

The British left a thriving legacy: many museums, the university, the Asiatic Society, the Botanical Gardens and, above all, the clubs. Colonial Calcutta parallelled the British development of exclusive social clubs with rigid codes of conduct and elaborate ceremonial, providing dignity and privacy for the rising bourgeoisie, the new elite. Calcutta has more clubs than any other Indian city and they are still the focus of social life, from cricket and cocktails to swimming and Sunday lunch. Prettiest among them is the Tollygunge Club in south Calcutta, the perfect country club on the edge of the city. For the Bengalis, the 19th-century cultural renaissance led to an awakening of national identity that culminated in the 1857 Rebellion, also known as the Bengal Uprising and, by the British, as the Mutiny. Their intellectual and political precocity produced the liberal thinker Rajah Ram Mohan Roy, the literary Nobel Prize winner Rabindranath Tagore and his extraordinary family, politician Subhas Chandra Bose, film-maker Satyajit Ray and now a long-standing but far less radical Communist state government.

But they seem to have abandoned all efforts to cope with their city, either conserving the past or looking after the present – although central Calcutta was scrubbed into spruceness when it hosted the championship international cricket match in 1988. The problems are too huge, the finances too small. Its position as commercial, administrative and political capital of the Indian Empire has long gone. Few people put money into Calcutta. The Indian princes and the European lords of commerce have mostly gone, leaving the once dazzling social season a mere shadow, the pleasures palace either sold off, closed up or used as government offices.

Today the few old families, still using diamonds for buttons on their silk shirts, stylishly dissipate the fortunes amassed by their forefathers, burying their heads in sweet sands of golf, racing and club life rather than quitting Calcutta for the thriving markets of Delhi, Bombay, Bangalore and elsewhere. They are great raconteurs of past family extravagances. One recalled: 'My father had great style. He loved women. At the end of a dinner party, he would give each woman a precious stone to match her dress – emerald, amethyst, etc.'

The most energetic and enterprising of the many immigrants Calcutta has absorbed are the Marwari families from Rajasthan, epitomised by the Birlas. Other big families are the Goenkas, Singhanias and Poddars. Marwaris make up most of the new rich. Having arrived in Calcutta at the end of last century, made several fortunes, often by taking over where the British were pulling out, they now diversify their business interests and their social life throughout India. Their lifestyle tends to emulate anything Western, from French gilt furniture and concrete to jeans and junk-food, rather than offering patronage to the architects and craftsmen working within the Indian tradition. (For more on Marwaris, see Shekhavati in the Rajasthan chapter.)

The Birlas, who are to the Marwaris, what the Tatas are to the Parsees, are an exception. Amongst much else, they own *The Hindustan Times*. (The Goenkas of Madras own *The Indian Express*.) Although they are amongst the richest Marwari families and thus one of the richest families in India, they are devout and keen on education. The not-so-modestly named Birla temples glitter with rich mosaic, precious stones and metals in Calcutta, dazzle with white marble on a Hyderabad hilltop and add to the 2,000 or so other temples at Varanasi. The Birlas have also set up an institute for technology and science, an education trust, a planetarium and the Birla Academy of Art and Culture in Calcutta. Mahatma Gandhi was a close friend of the family. It was at their home in Delhi that he was assassinated.

In a country where normally well-balanced modest men of all ranks fall into a life-time of debt in order to give an impressive wedding and provide dowry enough to upgrade the status of their daughter (and therefore themselves) or strengthen inter-family bonds (or business bonds), the Marwari wedding is the grandest of all. The most ostentatious are held in the extremely lavish new houses, furnished with ex-Maharaja gilt. Lavish public weddings are held at the flashy grand hotels in December and January when it is worth joining the crowd to gawp at the kilos of diamonds and pearls and gold – after all, they are worn to be noticed. The wedding guests may well be honoured with fruit imported from Harrods and orchids from Thailand. However, the ultimate flashy wedding will be transported to Bombay, India's glitz capital.

But the old and new rich are an even tinier minority in Calcutta than in other Indian cities, to be glimpsed at the few fashionable restaurants, the very pukka clubs (more Pall Mall than the real Pall Mall) and the races (in the members' enclosure, of course). What is more immediately apparent on arrival in Calcutta are the sheer numbers of people, like drones of a queen bee, seething and swarming over the pavements and roads. There are millions of them everywhere, in fact about 10 million in all.

From the beginning, Calcutta has accepted quantities of immigrants from the Bengal hinterland, from other states and from outside India. It was Job Charnock who invited the Armenians and many others. The Chinese came much later, in the 19th century, when the enterprising Yong Tai Chao brought 80 families to Acchipur near Calcutta, hoping to start lucrative tea and sugar-cane plantations. When most of them were slaughtered by locals, the remainder moved to the city, to the Tangra area, to do successful business in leather tanning and shoe-making – tanneries still perfume the Tangra air, and Chinese custom-made shoes can be ordered in Bentinck Street. They also supplied the best hair cutters and went into the restaurant trade, formerly dominated by the Italians and Swiss.

Since Partition the city's population has swollen to epidemic proportions, increased again during the Indo-Pakistan war of 1965 and the Pakistan-Bangladesh war of 1972. And the numbers continue to grow.

However, for most arrivals Calcutta has not produced her golden egg. Overburdened with people, the roads are not repaired; the transport system is a disaster; the inadequate water supply has led to the use of polluted water and an increase in water-borne diseases; the sewerage and rubbish collection services cannot cope; and the supply of power is so erratic that, in addition to the hotels and offices, even private flats have their own generators.

There is enormous unemployment and consequent poverty and squalor. A few may be found by Mother Teresa and her Sisters of Mercy who work ceaselessly and selflessly, touching just a tiny fraction of the problem with their love and tenderness, always bringing smiles and making the poor feel wanted. Their work is all the more extraordinary because the suffering is on such a huge scale.

Mother Teresa simply calls her work 'doing something beautiful for God'. In his tribute to her, Malcolm Muggeridge wrote: 'to (choose), as Mother Teresa did, to live in the slums of Calcutta, amidst all the dirt and disease and misery, signified a spirit so indomitable, a faith so intractable, a love so abounding that I felt abashed'. Since 1948, when she stopped teaching at the Loretto Convent School in Calcutta, with five rupees in her pocket, Mother Teresa and her increasing number of helpers have cared for destitute children, lepers and the dying. For she believes deeply that, even more than food and shelter, the poor need to be wanted. And hundreds of other like-minded charities, large and small, work equally hard to conquer the misery and make lives happy.

Even well away from the slums, in the streets off Chowringhee where deprivation is not so acute, the density of slow-moving human bodies winding between the sky-scrapers, the decaying old mansions and the bustees (huts) of the poor is stifling. There are bodies everywhere.

On the pavements they lounge, chat, sleep or set up shop. There are dubious, makeshift kitchens, complete with vegetable preparers, cooks, and washing-up sections. They vie for space with leather, tool and fruit vendors, typists, booksellers and beggars. There is no space to walk. There is no space on the roads either, which are full of nose-to-tail, honking, stationary jallopies, overflowing city buses, cows, rickshaws with jangling brass bells, more people and piles of earth. For those who can afford it, even the shortest journeys are taken by car, to maintain prestige and dignity and to avoid the cluttered, potholed pavements.

The piles of earth are part of the construction of the Underground – a slight misnomer as some of it runs above ground and parts have to be raised. One man who arrived in Calcutta in 1946 remembers wide avenues, elegant vistas, houses with big lawns, streets washed every morning and two new projects: the underground and the fly-over incorporating a second – and much needed – bridge over the Hooghly River. Nearly forty years on, neither is complete, although the Underground is partly open. It runs for 10km from Esplanade down to Tollygunge. Opened on October 24, 1984, it is clean, cheap and runs smoothly. Every train should be full but – a typical Calcutta irony – the poor cannot afford it and the rich would rather sit in their private cars in steamy traffic jams than join their fellow citizens for speedy cool travel. Indeed, the whole story is a typical Calcuttan tale. Meanwhile work on the fly-over is still halted each time the designers wish to modify the plans.

But the administration and labour of both keeps up employment, even if the workmen's dust fills the heavy, humid air so that by 8am you are ready for your first bath of the day.

It takes at least three days to achieve in Calcutta what takes one day in Bombay or Delhi. In a city where every topic can be discussed and debated endlessly, every Calcuttan agrees about that, because communications are so atrocious.

So, the combination of the exhausting humidity, the crowded pavements and the almost standstill traffic means that planning your day is crucial. And Calcutta is big – a city area of 102sq km: the Metropolitan District 1,380sq km – and just crossing the centre can easily take an hour by car. Walking the quite large distances be-

tween interesting places is by no means a picturesque promenade. A successful itinerary goes
for geographical proximity rather than a
personal desire to see a number of sites in a specific order.

The traffic is not the only hurdle in Calcutta.
The telephone system barely works at all, yet
most people have a minimum of three telephone numbers, often more. The solution, even
for a businessman, is just to turn up, which is
what everyone has come to expect.

But this can be tricky since the confusion of
road names is worse here than anywhere else in
India. In Calcutta it seems that every road has
two names, before and after Independence.
'Before' names are known by everyone: 'after'
names are printed on the maps. A few people
know both names of a few roads – and they are
rarely the taxi drivers or hotel staff. Most people
react to both Dalhousie Square and BBD Bagh –
although the full works of Benoy-Badal-Dinesh
Bagh (remembering Bengal's three great mar-
tyrs) might baffle. But Lenin Sarani has not
caught on for Dharamtala Street, and Ho Chi
Minh Street is unlikely to replace Harrington
Street, where the US Consulate happens to
sited.

When to go

The intense humidity, due to low altitude and
closeness to the sea, may deflate the most energetic. November to February is best: from
March, it begins hotting up, reaching a crescendo before the colossal rains which pelt down
from the end of June until mid-September,
bringing slight relief but also flooding, washing
away many homes and most of last year's
efforts on the Underground.

FESTIVALS European Calcuttans say the Season begins with Durga Puja in September-
October and ends with Holi in February-March.
'After that, Calcutta is hell.' Bengalis take a
broader view: 'Baro mase tero parban' (thirteen
festivals in twelve months). In fact they have 20
official – and several unofficial – holidays and let
their hair down at any excuse, be it Diwali,
Christmas, the Muslim Id, a political hero's
birthday or the day bank accounts are closed at
the end of December. Bengali New Year in
April-May is especially fun, if hot. See Festivals
Calendar for more.

Durga Puja is the biggest Calcutta festival, the
Bengal version of Dussehra. The goddess
Durga, destroyer of evil, is one of the many
forms of the great goddess Devi, portrayed as a
goddess riding a lion. (Kali, another form of
Devi, is altogether more sinister.) Riotous celebrations last about three weeks. It is a bad time
for business as the city hardly functions, but

good for spectacle, music, dance and drama. On
the final day, elaborate images of Durga are processed through illuminated streets throbbing
with loud-speaker music, to be dunked in the
Hooghly River at night, with more rejoicing on
the Maidan.

In Tangra, the Chinese district, the old Buddhists and Taoists and their younger Bengali-
speaking children all celebrate the Chinese New
Year and the Moon and Dragon festivals.

SOCIAL CALENDAR Calcutta races are run
from early November to late March on Saturdays or mid-week, about six meetings a month.
There is the Calcutta Thousand Guineas and
Two Thousand Guineas; the Calcutta Oaks,
Derby, St Leger and the Governor's Cup. But
the climax is the Queen Elizabeth II Cup (end of
January). Well worth attending for the pretty
course, the best panorama of Calcutta from the
grandstand, snooping on the Members' Enclosure (entrance fee) where Calcutta's best
banyan tree gives shelter to ladies in the latest
saris, frocks and hats, and chatting to some of
India's most serious punters – the highest odds
offered in India were here, 222 to 1, on Hopeful
Venture on December 28, 1983. Set in 30 acres,
the course was built in 1819. In the days of the
Empire, Christmas race week was a social highpoint when the Viceroy and Vicereine would
drive past the fine grandstand with regal
formality. In 1945, even with New Delhi the official capital, the Viceroy's Cup drew the largest
race crowd yet, 35,343 people. For the season's
fixtures list contact the Royal Calcutta Turf Club
office, 11 Russell Street, Calcutta 700071 (closed
Mon. afternoon and Tues).

ARTS Culturally, Calcutta is one of the most
vibrant Indian cities. A musician has not made it
until he has performed here. The major music
festivals are November-March. The most important are Park Circus (January), Dover Lane
Conference and ITC Music Festival, but there
are countless high-class performances throughout these months. Calcutta is the home ground
of leading Indian musicians such as Ravi Shankar, Ali Akbar Khan and Nikhil Banerjee. The
city also has one of the oldest symphony orches-
tras in Asia.

Getting there: Getting away

The best way to arrive is by train, especially
from Delhi. Howrah station, teeming with
activity, is just across Howrah Bridge from the
centre; Dum Dum airport is an unscenic hour's
drive away, even using the new by-pass built
with funds from the World Bank. The lightning
fast (16hrs) Rajdhani Express, with first-class
air-conditioned coupés and three-course meals

(Indian or European), leaves New Delhi on Mon., Tues., Fri. and Sat. Or there is the more sedate and traditional Delhi-Howrah Mail (22hrs) and the Air-conditioned Express (24 hrs). From Madras, take the Coromandel Express up the coast; from Bombay, the Gitanjali Express or the Calcutta Mail. The shorter trip from Varanasi takes about 12hrs.

Sealdah Station on the east side of Calcutta serves the north and north-east, including Darjeeling.

Dum Dum airport (close to the small arms factory where the soft-nosed bullet was invented in 1898) is, ironically, the only clean and efficient international airport in India. Thai Airways, British Airways and Air India have good timetables for flying in and out. Internally, Indian Airlines connects Calcutta direct with all other major cities, including Bombay, Delhi and Madras daily, Bangalore and Hyderabad Tues.-Sun. There are daily flights to Bagdogra (for Darjeeling) and Bhubaneswar (for connections with Varanasi on Tues., Thurs., Sat. and Sun.). A flight to and from Kathmandu goes daily except Tues. and Sat.; the Port Blair flights (for the Andamans) are Tues. and Fri. The smaller airline, Vayudoot, serves the north-east states.

Sadly, there is no passenger sea service between Madras, Orissa and Calcutta.

Where to stay

The Indian system of awarding stars to hotels is particularly bizarre in Calcutta. There are only two top quality hotels, the Oberoi Grand and the new, competitive Taj Bengal. For good location but less grandeur, there are the New Kenilworth, the improved Park and, for those who gain membership via a member, the very pukka Bengal Club; for a more modest but still central room, the Fairlawn and Astor. But, with the Underground so clean, empty and fast, it is well worth considering the Tollygunge Club for rural peace and fresh air at the beginning and end of each day; rooms and facilities are open to all foreigners and the air is glorious.

In essence, good accommodation is scarce, so book well in advance. For something much more interesting, consider staying in a home. The shortage of accommodation during the 1988 cricket championship stimulated the creation of a paying guest scheme; several participants live in the city centre; details from the Government of in the India Tourist Office.

Note: avoid the Hindustan International and old Great Eastern hotels; the Airport Ashok is good for its café and lavatories if you have a delayed flight.

Oberoi Grand 15 Jawaharlal Nehru Road (Chowringhee), Calcutta 700013
Telephone: 292323/290181; Fax: 29-1217; Telex: 7248, 7854
Airport 16km; railway station 5km
250 rooms, including 8 suites, all with attached bath. Single Rs1,900; double Rs2,150; suites on application.

All mod. cons, including travel agency, bank, shopping, hairdresser, in-house astrologer, safe deposit, baby-sitter, business services. A rare combination of old character and style with modern facilities and high standards. Originally built in the 1890s as the Royal Hotel incorporating the Theatre Royal and run by a former jeweller, Arrathoon Stephen. When the theatre burnt down in 1911, he acquired some adjacent land and expanded.

Since Mohan Singh Oberoi bought it in 1938, it has become to the Oberoi chain what the Taj Bombay is to the Taj chain. Everyone from John F. Kennedy to Princesss Anne has stayed here. Its efficiency is a daily miracle in Calcutta. Not only does it have generators for power cuts but the water is purified ten times before guests receive it and the telephones work quite often. Corridors are hung with prints of Calcutta; newly decorated rooms exude plush comfort. The large swimming pool is pure joy amid the stifling air. Health Club excellent (massage, sauna, Turkish bath, gymnasium); hairdresser patronised by local Europeans. Take cocktails in the newly enlarged, fridge-cold bar or at the poolside café; eat at the Coffee Shop or excellent Polynesian and Mughal restaurants, again much patronised by discerning locals. The jolly Pink Elephant discotheque testifies to the determination of Calcutta's elite to enjoy themselves, whatever is happening in the streets. See also night life section.

Taj Bengal 34b Belvedere Road, Calcutta 700027
Telephone: 494664/494968/494233; Fax: 281766/288805; Telex: 8035.
Airport 26km; railway station 7km.
250 rooms, including a range of suites, attached bath. Single Rs1600; double Rs1800; suites Rs3,250-Rs6,500.

All mod. cons. include full business centre, good pool and health club, shopping arcade, baby-sitting service.

A good, but still not settled, attempt to mix the rural advantages of Tollygunge with a top-class city hotel. Located at the south end of the Maidan in tree-filled Alipore, near the National Library (formerly the Deputy Governor's mansion) with its lovely garden, and the Horticultural Gardens, and opposite the race course and the gates of the lush zoo and gardens. Thus, soothing views from higher windows (across the Maidan and its British landmarks), and good places on hand for fresh-air morning walks. Rooms grandly done-up, if slightly claustraphobic in an effort to be state-of-the-art appointed. These and the outrageously vast, gleaming, trade-mark Taj marble lobby (with obligatory 1980s high atrium so rooms above are reached across Fatehpur Sikri-style walkways) bear the increasingly bizarre stamp of Taj interior design. Rooms mix Raj-style prints of red roses with polychrome pottery doorknobs (where, oh where, is a nice Bengali kantha for a bedspread?), while the lobby is a rum mixture of good carvings, giant pots perched on a stepped waterfall, and a seemingly random selection of contemporary paintings whose only shared quality is the ability to strike anguish or depression into the hearts of worried guests – it is not a place to linger. Around it, though, the bar serves excellent cocktails and snacks, the Esplanade coffee shop and is up to Taj standard and patronised by locals, and there are quality Chinese and Indian restaurants and a poolside barbecue. Service is, on the whole, good. Once settled, this could make the Oberoi quiver in its boots.

Tollygunge Club 120 Deshapran Sasmal Road, Calcutta 700033
Telephone: 463141
Airport 23km; railway station 12km
11 rooms, bathroom attached. Room prices on application. To book, write to Bob Wright, Secretary.

Set in an estate of over 200 acres, facilities include riding (open to non-residents), golf, 8 tennis courts (5 hard, 3 soft), indoor and outdoor swimming pools, 2 squash courts, badminton, billiards, cards. Founded in 1895 to 'promote all manner of sports', Tolly not only offers a beautiful club house, vast grounds, healthy horses and lungfuls of gloriously fresh air, but is run by Bob and Anne Wright who know everyone and everything and share it all with their guests. In 1788 Richard Johnson built the club house which later became the residence of the deposed sons of Tipu Sultan. By the close of the 19th century Tollygunge was already known as Sahibangicha, 'the garden of the white men', where Europeans relaxed outside the city. Today, Calcutta society meets at the club to play sports, gossip over tea, chocolate cake and later cocktails, and wander in the grounds with their blossoming trees, tropical plants and exotic birds. The atmosphere is relaxed, friendly and welcoming.

New Kenilworth 1 & 2 Little Russell Street, Calcutta 700071
Telephone: 448394/448397; Telex: 3395
Airport 18km; railway station 7km
100 rooms, including 7 suites, attached bath. Single Rs650; double Rs750; suites Rs1,000-1,200.
Spacious garden and all mod. cons.

Good, clean hotel located at the south end of the Maidan, off Shakespeare Sarani. Stay in the old wing which has been renovated. Take tea and dinner in the garden.

Park Hotel 17 Park Street, Calcutta 700016
Telephone: 297336/297941; Telex: 3177/7159
Airport 18km; railway station 7km
155 rooms, attached bath. Single Rs1,250; double Rs1,350; suites Rs3,000- 4,000.
All mod. cons. include swimming pool, book shop and what is gloriously described as an 'All weather car park'. Much improved, but still comparatively expensive (the Kenilworth is a better deal). Right on a main shopping street, and not far from that useful but under-used Underground.

Fairlawn 13/a Sudder Street, Calcutta 700016
Telephone: 244460, 241835
Airport 15km; railway station 6km
20 rooms, attached bath. Single Rs500; double Rs550-600, to include meals.
The Kapoors (Shashi, Felicity Kendal etc.) may have enjoyed this hotel for years, but recent comments on Mr and Mrs Smith's hotel have hit extremes of satisfaction and disappointment. You take a chance.

Astor Hotel, 15 Shakespeare Sarani, Calcutta 700071
Telephone: 431931; Telex: 2020
Airport 16km; railway station 4km
32 rooms, all single, attached bath. Single Rs385.
Friendly, well located hotel with large front garden which doubles as a favourite Calcutta restaurant – glorious on hot evenings.

Bengal Club 1/1 Russell Street, Calcutta 700016
Telephone: 299233
Airport 18km; railway station 7km
14 beds, attached bath. Prices on application. Apply for temporary membership through a member. To book, write to Mr S. V. S. Naidu, Secretary.
Facilities include an extensive, well-run library. The oldest survivor of colonial Calcutta's social clubs still retains its period style, although it is reduced to a shadow of its former self. It was established on February 1, 1827, in Esplanade West. In 1845 the Club moved into the house on Chowringhee where Thomas Babington Macaulay, Law Member of the Supreme Council, had so enjoyed living the decade before. A new building replaced it in 1909 but with the decline of British society in the 1960s the club retreated into the back of the building.
Each room comes with a bearer. The club has a reserve list of retired bearers, one of whom is hired on your arrival, fired on your departure. Cocktail parties in the grand room spill out on to the lawn which twinkles with fairy lights. Deep green leather sofas in the reading room; peace in the large library; the London *Daily Telegraph* is constantly perused. Upstairs, five-course set luncheon starts with thick soup and sherry, ends with Kalimpong cheese. Bengal food on

Wed. Downstairs, the well-run Oriental Room is open to families. It is lively and serves à la carte Indian and Chinese food.

Paying guest accommodation in private homes. The following are central and also tried and tested:

Mrs S. Thakur, flat 28, 3rd floor, Harrington Mansions, opposite the US Consulate (tel: 445017)

Mrs S. Ghosh, 3a Loudon Street (where the Institute of Modern Management is on the 1st floor)

Saroj Deep, 16/1 Hindustan Road, Gariahat; less central but a very nice house.

Information and reservations

These are essential both for Calcutta information and for organising trips into the surrounding areas; they are often more helpful and up-to-date than their Delhi offices. It is here that permits for the Andamans, the north-eastern states and for Burma can be obtained, political climate permitting.

Government of West Bengal Tourist Bureau, 3/2 BBD Bagh, east side (tel: 238271), open Mon.-Sat., 7am-6pm; Sun., 7am-2pm. Very helpful. Also have desks at the airport and Howrah station; good for information on trips out of town.

Government of India Tourist Office, 4 Shakespeare Sarani (tel: 443521, 441402), open Mon.-Sat., 9am-6pm (until 1pm on 2nd Sat. of each month). Very helpful; hold list of private homes to stay in; also have desk at airport.

Information centres for nearby states include: Andaman and Nicobar Islands, 3A Auckland Place (2nd floor) (tel: 442604); Arunachal Pradesh, 4B Chowringhee Place, (tel: 236500); Assam, 8 Russell Street (tel: 248341); Bihar Tourist, 26-B Camac Street (1st floor) (tel: 446821); Manipur, 26 Rowland Road (tel: 478358); Maghalaya, 9 Russell Street (tel: 241900); Mizoram, Mizoram House, 24 Old Ballygunge Road (tel: 477034); Nagaland, 13 Shakespeare Sarani (tel: 445269); Orissa, Utkal Bhavan, 55 Lenin Sarani (tel: 243653); Sikkim, 5/2 Russell Street (4th floor) (tel: 247519); Tripura, 1 Pretoria Street (tel: 443856); Uttar Pradesh (for Varanasi), 12A Netaji Subhas Road (tel: 227855). Beware: visas for Bangladesh and Burma cannot currently be obtained here.

Calcutta is a highly literate city and publishes several English language newspapers including *The Statesman*, *Amrita Bazaar Patrika* and *The Telegraph* which carry reports of the city's current controversies and triumphs and details of the day's events and entertainment. The WBTB produces *Calcutta This Fortnight*, a free leaflet (from their office or the Government of India Tourist Office).

Guide-books are scanty: either the WBTB's *Calcutta*, a booklet with selected lists and opening times, or *Calcutta Briefs* (Rs6), a maze of quotes, facts and pull-out maps. But there are a number of good books on Calcutta, see end of chapter.

TRAVEL AGENTS
American Express, 21 Old Court House Street (tel: 236281); SITA World Travels, 3-B Camac Street (tel: 297185/297187); TCI, Everest House, 46-C Jawarharlal Nehru Road (Chowringhee) (tel: 44997174).

AIRLINE OFFICES
Indian Airlines, 39 Chittaranjan Avenue (tel: 260730/1); Vayudoot, Dum Dum Airport (tel: 569582), and Neelambar Building, 29b Shakespeare Sarani (tel: 477062/403091), particularly useful for north-east India. International airline offices on J N Road include Air India at no.50 (tel: 442356); Air France at no.41 (tel: 296161); British Airways, also at no.41 (tel: 293430); Royal Nepal Airlines, again at no.41 (tel: 298534). Cathay Pacific Airways are at 1 Middleton Street (tel: 293211). Thai International and Scandinavian Airlines are both at 18G Park Street (tel: 299846); Aeroflot is at 58 Chowringhee (tel: 449831). Burma (Myanmar) Airways is at 8/2 Esplanade East (tel: 231624).

TRAIN RESERVATIONS
Eastern Railway Booking Office, 6 Fairlie Place (tel: 224356), with Tourist Guide Assistant. South-Eastern Railway Booking Office, Esplanade Mansions (tel: 239530, 235074). For Orissa and Sikkim rail travel, consult their information centres (see above).

FOREIGN MISSIONS
UK: 1 Ho Chi Minh Sarani (tel: 445171); USA: 5/1 Ho Chi Minh Sarani (tel: 442335); France: 26 Park Street (tel: 298314); West Germany, 1 Hastings Park (tel: 459141); Netherlands, 18A Brabourne Road (tel: 225864).

For trips out of India, the following may help. Bangladesh: 9 Circus Avenue (tel: 445208); Bhutan: 48 Tivoli Court, Pramothesh Barua Sarani (tel: 441301); Burma: 67 Park Street (tel: 213200); Nepal: 19 Sterndale Road (tel: 452024); Thailand, 18B Mandeville Gardens (tel: 460836), closes at noon. Foreigners Registration Office, 237 A J C Bose Road (tel: 440549/443301).

Calcutta General Post Office is at BBD Bagh. Long queues, good poste restante.

For medical assistance, your accommodation will recommend one of the numerous English-speaking doctors. Dey's Medical Stores, on Lindsay Street, is a good chemist.

The city by day

The golden rule in Calcutta is 'the earlier the better'. As the people and traffic and humidity increase, so movement and energy slow down. The city centre retains the broad streets of its colonial planning but it is easier to appreciate without the bellowing horns and choked-up traffic.

And there is plenty to do before the many museums reveal their treasures. Temples and churches open early as do the Botanical Gardens and the Zoo. At the other end of the day, the Planetarium and Birla Museum stay open late, early evening strolls are pleasant, most shops stay open until 7pm or 8pm and the Kali Temple only closes its doors at 10pm. Almost no two monuments keep the same hours and the relation between the printed hours and actuality depends upon current 'short staffing'. There is no official siesta in Calcutta; Monday is the closed day for landmarks such as the Victoria Memorial and the Indian Museum, and West Bengal has 20 official public holidays when almost everything shuts up.

In addition, the sights are scattered across this huge, slow-moving city, so a spot of planning, even by the vaguest tourist, pays dividends.

The WBTB and ITDC (at the Government of India Tourist Office) run almost identical full and half-day introductory sight-seeing tours. Go for the morning ones which cover scattered sights. The museums in the afternoon trip are better enjoyed alone. For transport, it is cheaper (and much more convenient here) to hire a car and driver from either tourist office for a half or full day rather than catch taxis. Rickshaws (pulled by wiry, barefoot men who refused to convert to bicycles) are good for short hops. Buses and trams are only for a serious game of sardines.

Botanical Gardens The finest in India and Calcutta's principal lung. Here, amid lakes, lawns and rare trees in 273 acres sprawling along the west bank of the Hooghly, are the Palmyra palm and mahogany avenues; the palm, orchid, fern and cacti houses; the gigantic banyan tree like a complete wood (apparently so-called because the Hindu traders, or banias, sheltered under these trees in the Persian Gulf) and a herbarium of 40,000 species of dried plant.

The Gardens were laid out in 1786, under Colonel Kyd, and the plant collection expanded by Dr Roxburgh; there are memorials to both. The tea-culture of Assam and Darjeeling was developed here. Now in dire need of an injection of funds, but nevertheless atmospheric. Best in the early morning sunlight and fresh air. Go the traditional way, by ferry from Chandpal

or Babu Ghats (checking first that the Botanical Garden Ghat will be open); or by car (about 40 mins), being sure to return over the Howrah Bridge either before the rush hour at 9am – or much later on. Cars carrying foreigners may be driven inside the Gardens. Open 7am-5pm.

Howrah Bridge and Station A single turmoil of moving bodies and overloaded vehicles. The loads carried by humans defy belief: a door balanced on the head with six trunks on top is quite normal. The single-span cantilevered bridge built in 1943 is the only bridge across the Hooghly and carries 2 million people every day. Beneath it, masseurs, barbers and flower sellers do brisk business.

The station was designed in 1906 by Arts and Crafts architect, Halsey Ricardo. Its hall throbs with food-sellers, water-carriers and passengers arriving and leaving, each with hordes of well-wishers and luggage carriers. And, of course, astrologers for the journey, here in the form of neon-lit weighing machines that punch out a person's weight and consequent fortune. Station platforms are wide enough for the gentry to go directly from the train into their waiting cars. Over the platform entrance, a large blue and white neon sign pompously proclaims: 'Godliness is next to cleanliness'.

BBD Bagh (Dalhousie Square) Writers' Buildings, constructed in 1780 for the clerical staff of the East India Company, bear testament to this former powerhouse of the British. The GPO, built in 1864-8, was designed by Walter Granville, one of his many Calcutta buildings. It stands on the west side, on the site of the first fort, indicated with brass markers. The controversial Black Hole incident of 1756 was in a guard-room in the sleeping quarters. It was overlooking this square that Philip Francis, Hastings's great enemy, lived around this time and wrote home: 'Here I live, master of the finest house in Bengal, with a hundred servants, a country house, and spacious gardens, horses and carriages . . .' The WBTB is on the east side; and nearby is 2 Brabourne Road where permission to visit the Marble Palace is obtained. There is a tablet marking Warren Hastings's house in Mission Row, an old street to the east. Clive and Philip Francis lived to the north-west, now the commercial quarter. Lit up at night, and without the cars and people, the square gives an idea of what British Calcutta was like.

Early Calcutta originally extended northwards from here – the smart southern area was developed later and Alipore grew up around the Deputy Governor's mansion, now the National Library. So, northwards lie some of the crumbling old merchants' mansions in and around Shyan, Bagh and Girish bazaars. While seeking out the next four stops, sharp eyes will spot grand old facades and modest narrow alleys almost unchanged.

Asutosh Museum of Indian Art The first public museum in an Indian university, founded in 1937 and named after Asutosh Mookerjee, champion of university Indology studies. The collection concentrates on the rich artistic heritage of eastern India, and includes sculpture, folk art, textiles and an excellent group of Kalighat paintings and terracottas. Well displayed. Informative booklet. In Calcutta University, College Street. Open Mon.-Fri., 10.30am-5pm; Sat., 10.30am-1.30pm. (For books, see What to Buy section.)

Marble Palace After the ethnic Asutosh collection, here are Rubens, Reynolds and Murillo paintings, stuffed birds, Chinese porcelain, vast Venetian gilt mirrors, Belgian chandeliers, a grandfather clock, statues of Pan and the young Queen Victoria – looking disturbingly seductive – all piled into dusty, half-lit rooms. Rajendra Mullick, at the age of 16, began building and filling his Palladian mansion in 1835, apparently using 148 different kinds of marble, which led the Viceroy, Lord Minto, to dub it Marble Palace on his visit in 1910.

In the grounds are an aviary, a menagerie, the family temple and pelicans swimming round the European fountain. Rajendra never left India: his creation is the product of a hybrid culture developed by the Calcutta nouveaux riches under British influence. The Mullicks still live in a wing of the building and continue Rajendra's tradition of charity, feeding hordes of poor who collect at the palace gates daily at noon. The totally run-down palace next door was built by Rajendra for his relations. 46, Muktaram Babu Street, off Chittaranjan Avenue. Open 10am-4pm (except Mon. and Thur.). To visit, obtain a letter of permission from the WTBT, 2 Brabourne Road.

Rabindra-Bharati Museum The ancestral home of the extraordinarily gifted Tagore family, now devoted to the 19th-century Renaissance Movement of Bengal which involved several Tagores. The poet, philosopher and fervent nationalist Rabindranath Tagore (1861-1941), who won the Nobel prize for literature in 1913, was considered the embodiment of modern Indian culture and India's poet laureate. It was he who composed the anthem 'Jana Gana Mana Adhinayaka' for the Calcutta Congress of 1911 which was adopted as the National Anthem after Independence. 6/4 Dwarkanath Tagore Lane, off Rabindra Sarani. Open Mon.-Fri., 10am-7pm; Sat., 10am-1.30pm; Sun., 11am-2pm.

St John's Church Of the many churches in Calcutta this is especially interesting. Modelled on Gibbs's St Martin in the Fields in London (with the local addition of a palanquin ramp) and consecrated in 1787, it later served as the cathedral,

1814-1847, until St Paul's was ready. Inside, pretty wicker-work seating, Zoffany's 'Last Supper' with local residents used as models for the Apostles (given by the artist as the altarpiece, now in the south aisle), and fine marble memorials to distinguished servants of the Empire. In the vestibule, a desk and chair used by Warren Hastings, who headed the building committee and was married here in 1818 to Mrs Marian Imhoff whom he had met on a boat to Madras.

Outside, the churchyard served as the first burial ground of Calcutta, 1690-1767. One of the city's oldest masonry structures is the octagonal mausoleum of Job Charnock who died in 1692, two years after he founded the city. Nearby is the tomb of Admiral Charles Watson who helped Clive retake the city and died a few months later, in 1757. The domed grave belongs to 'Begum' Johnson, a much-loved Calcutta grande dame who died in 1812 aged 87 after an eventful life that included four marriages, being imprisoned by Suraj-ud-Daula and fuelling local gossip with her whist parties in Clive Street.

Indian Museum Largest museum in India, founded in 1814 by a Danish botanist Dr Nathaniel Wallich, having originated in a collection accumulated by the Asiatic Society (established in Calcutta in 1874). The huge collection is basically divided into art, archaeology, geology, zoology and industry. Short-staffing tends to put padlocks on several rooms, but this in fact aids decision-making as everything is worth seeing.

Stars to search out begin at the front door with the 2nd-century BC Sunga stone sculptures. Galleries surround a cool garden courtyard where sculptures stand among the columns and visitors peacefully pause for cultural breath on the seats. Upstairs, find amazing zoology and fossil collections including some thick brass bangles found inside dead, man-eating crocodiles. Past the turtles, crocodiles and gharials on the right-hand (south side) gallery, the Indian paintings are found with some determination on the right, after the textiles and a model of faraway Taj Mahal made at nearby Murshidabad – if you reach bronzes, you've gone too far. Reopened in 1989, it is well worth the effort to find a good selection ranging from Mughal through Rajasthani and Pahari to the Bengali School (Hrishikesh Dev Varma, Sunayani Devi, Jamini Roy, Rabindranath Tagore). Beyond here is the South and East Asian art. Good general guide book, although staff reluctant to admit to the existence of the publications office. Open Tues.-Sun., 10am-4.30pm (March to Nov. until 5pm).

Victoria Memorial George Frampton's statue of the Empress of India set between two ornamental lakes welcomes the visitor to this gigantic reliquary of white marble. From the moment Lord Curzon conceived of a museum to depict Indian history, especially the Victorian era, the project and result epitomised British Victorian attitudes. Sir William Emerson designed a Renaissance building with token Saracenic features. One Prince of Wales (later George V) laid the foundation stone in 1906. Another (later Edward VIII) opened it in 1921, by which time the grandiose plans for the new capital of the Eastern Empire at Delhi were well under way. Faced with Makrana marble from Jodhpur, its dome surmounted by a figure of Victory and its pathway blocked by a statue of the queen-empress, it is one of the more ridiculous bits of British baggage littering Calcutta, only emphasised by the turbaned shepherds grazing their sheep outside the enclosure. Now this city landmark has an energetic committee working to make one or two rooms air-conditioned (and thus at a constant humidity and free from polluted air) in order to house some of its rare collection of pictures which are being restored by an Anglo-Indian team led by restorer supremo Patrick Lindsay.

The pictures have been described as 'one of the finest collections of British paintings, watercolours, prints and drawings in the world'. Certainly, almost anyone who was anyone in the British art world between 1770 and 1825 went to India to seek out the Picturesque and, more to the point, cash in on the extravagant patronage of both British and Indian patrons. Zoffany, Stubbs, Devis, Tilly Kettle and Chinnery all came, as did the uncle and nephew team of William and Thomas Daniell.

The result is that almost anyone who was anyone in British Indian history is remembered here, usually by a top portrait painter. A Royal Gallery of paintings extols the glories of Queen Victoria's reign. Her writing-desk and piano are in the centre of the room. There is a replica marble statue of Lord Clive (the original bronze is in London) and Verestchagin's glorious painting of the Prince of Wales (this time the future Edward VII) making his state entry into Jaipur in 1876. Amid all sorts of odd bits and bobs is 'Finden's set of portraits of the female aristocracy of the Court of Queen Victoria in 1849'; and, much more interestingly, vast oil-paintings of Indians who mattered to the Brits, from the King of Oudh to Dwarkanath Tagore, the first Indian Justice of the Peace. Don't miss the great paintings of Lord and Lady Curzon (who instigated this building) making their thoroughly regal entrance into Delhi for the 1903 Durbar.

Among the many good paintings by British artists, it is well worth looking at Burne-Jones's portrait of Rudyard Kipling; Thomas and William Daniell's oil paintings (the finest collection of their work); Allan Ramsay's portraits of George II and Queen Charlotte; and several of Zoffany's best works, including a portrait of Warren Hastings and his family. This last is on the first floor from which there is a good view over the Maidan. The publications office, when open, has a useful catalogue of the Daniells collection and another on the busts and statuary. Open Tues.-Sun., 10am-3.30pm (March to October until 4.30pm). Closed on public holidays.

Just outside the magnificent gates there used to stand the statue of Lord Curzon, replaced by a missile-like bronze of Sri Aurobindo Ghosh, the cultured mystic of Pondicherrry (see p. 246). **Museum Round-up** Calcutta's strong cultural tradition, combined with the legacy of the Victorian passion for systemisation and public education, has given birth to more than 30 museums in the city. Like the Rabindra-Bharati Museum, they often concentrate on a single topic. In the selection below, opening days and times are merely guidelines: both are very erratic and should be checked with a tourist office before arriving at closed doors.

The Academy of Fine Arts (contemporary and historical Indian art), Cathedral Road, open Tues.-Sun., 3-8pm. *Birla Academy of Art and Culture* (contemporary and historical art collection plus temporary exhibitons), 108-9 Southern Avenue, open Tues.-Sun., 4-8pm. *Birla Planetarium* (second only to London's), 96 J Nehru Road, open Tues.-Sun., 11.30-8pm, with shows and programmes in various languages. *Ethnographic Museum*, Tribal Welfare Department, New Secretariat Buildings, K S Roy Road, open Mon.- Fri., 10.30am-5pm. *Government Industrial and Commercial Museum* (West Bengal handicrafts and cottage industries), 45 Ganesh Chandra Avenue, open Mon.-Fri., 10.30am-5.30pm; Sat., 11am-1pm. *Netaji Museum* (Netaji Subhas Chandra Bose's home), 38/2 Lala Lajpat Rai Sarani, open Mon.- Fri., 6-8pm; Sun., 9am-noon. *Nehru Children's Museum*, 94 J Nehru Road, open Tues.-Sun., noon-8pm. *Regional Handicrafts Centre*, 9-12 Old Court House Street, open Mon.-Sat., 3-5.30pm. *Royal Asiatic Society of Bengal* (fine library of books and manuscripts; good, but flaking, European paintings), 1 Park Street, open for studying only, Mon.-Fri., noon-7pm; Sat., noon-6pm. *State Archaeological Museum*, 33 Chittaranjan Avenue, open Mon.-Fri., 11am-5.30pm; Sat., 11am-2pm.

In south Calcutta (about an hour from the centre) there is the excellent *Gurusaday Museum* (folk art), Bratacharigram, off Diamond Harbour Road, Thakurpkur, open Fri.-Tues., 11.30am-4.30pm; Wed., 11.30am-1.30pm; closed Thur. On the way down there is *Lok Sanskriti Samgranhasala* (folk culture, an annex of the Archaeological Museum), 1 Satyen Roy Road, off Diamond Harbour Road, Behala, open

Mon.-Fri., 11am-4pm.

Maidan area The Maidan may be a two-by-one-mile open space, but it is not quite the refreshing green park the map promises. Main roads criss-cross the tired grass, worn down by trade exhibitions, sportsmen, festival celebrations and the huge, annual Communist rally in January. The quantities of colonial statuary have been removed by the government to Barrackpore. A good time to take a stroll here is late afternoon while locals play cricket, yoga, football and tennis or saunter along Strand Road as the sun sets over the Hooghly. Boats can be hired for a sunset row. Looking across the Maidan from the massive walls of Fort William (still in use, so not open to the public), little remains of Chowringhee (J Nehru Road), once the backdrop of great houses mirroring the wealth and security of imperial power.

But at the north end *Raj Bhavan* (Government House) still stands, designed in 1799 for the Marquess of Wellesley by Captain Charles Wyatt of the Bengal Engineers who, lacking imagination, found an adequately imposing model in Adam's recently completed Kedleston Hall, Derbyshire, built for Lord Curzon. (Now the residence of the Governor of West Bengal, it is not open to the public.)

To the left of the Raj Bhavan are the pretty Eden Gardens. To the right, the bizarre Sahid Minar (Ochterlony Monument), with Egyptian base, Syrian column and Turkish dome, erected to commemorate a man whose enjoyment of everything Muslim ran to taking thirteen wives who would ride out together on a string of elephants. For a superb view from the top of the column, first get permission to ascend from the Deputy Commissioner of Police, Police HQ, Lal Bazaar. The Victoria Memorial, the excellent Birla Planetarium, St Paul's Cathedral (stuffed with fascinating Empire memorials and lit by Burne-Jones's great west window of 1880) and the race course lie to the south.

And across Tolly's Nulla (a canal dug from the silted up Adiganga, the old course of the Ganga, by Major Tolly in 1775) in Alipore is the spacious, 41-acre *zoo* opened in 1876, with good collections of birds, animals, reptiles and fish, and the rare white tiger of Rewa (open daily, 8am-5pm). Near here is the National Libarary, a fine mansion built for the Deputy Governor, and its splendid gardens.

South Park Street Cemetery It is yet another irony of decaying Calcutta that the only thorough conservation job has been carried out on a colonial Christian cemetery. Flowers and blossoming trees surround the restored obelisks, urns, temples and towers of the classical mausolea erected to Calcutta's notable figures. The cemetery replaced St John's churchyard in 1767. It was then some distance from the British town, along narrow Burial Ground Road (later named Park Street after Sir Elijah Impey's deer park – he lived in Middleton Row). Burials were often by torchlight at night or with military pageantry.

Among them were William Hickey's wife Charlotte Barry; Col. Charles Russell Deare, who died fighting Tipu Sultan; Captain Cooke, who died in a sea fight off Calcutta; Col. Kyd, founder of the Botanical Gardens; the linguist Sir William Jones, founder of the Royal Asiatic Society (his is the tallest monument); Thackeray's father; the Anglo-Indian poet Louis Vivian Derozio; and Sir John D'Oyly, a vivacious gentleman whose love of the hookah finally finished him. People often died young, from the heat, cholera, dysentry, tuberculosis, although the disease was often not recognised. Eating too many pineapples was supposed to have killed one Rose Aylmer. There is a piazza of headstones from the French Cemetery, formerly on the opposite side of Park Street, now replaced by a school. Very good booklet available from the custodian. Open all the time, every day.

St Paul's Cathedral The first Church of England cathedral built in the British Empire. Begun in 1839, designed by Major Forbes, the imposing building was partly funded by the East India Company. Lady Dalhousie, wife of the Viceroy, compared the interior to a railway station in 1840. But it is worth going inside to see the Burne-Jones stained glass west window; Francis Chantrey's statue of Bishop Heber; Sir Arthur Blomfield's mosaics around the altar, and the many memorials which in so few words reveal whole lives spent far away from home working the Indian railways, trading in tea or jute or merely arriving in high hopes only to succumb immediately to the climate.

Kali Temple One of the few buildings apart from the Victoria Memorial that people have heard of before their arrival in Calcutta and one of the city's few landmarks of Indian architecture. Kalighat is an important place of pilgrimage and the temple, built in 1809, is only the latest of several. Kali or Kalika (meaning 'the black') is one of the forms of the goddess Devi. Devi is the wife (and therefore female energy) of Shiva and has two characters – benevolent and malevolent. Each is manifest in several forms, but the nasty ones like Kali and Durga are worshipped most often. When the frenzied Shiva was wandering the cosmos with Devi's corpse, Vishnu cut the body into pieces with a Sudarshan wheel (a sort of quoit) and a toe fell here. Paintings of Kali are sold around the temple, the black-skinned goddess shown dripping wth blood, snakes and skulls hung around her neck, her ten arms wielding a variety of weapons. The daily animal sacrifice in the courtyard witnessing to the destroyer goddess's power gives the crowded surrounding market an ugly atmosphere. Open until 10pm.

Space and peace

The Botanical Gardens, especially in early morning, are serene and empty and well worth the journey (slightly busier at week-ends). And Tollygunge Club is a haven at any time. In the city centre there are more escape holes than appear at first: South Park Street Cemetery, the well-planted grounds of the zoo, the Agri-Horticultural Gardens behind the National Library on Belvedere Road (where the annual flower show is held – a great social event), and Rabindra Sarobar lakes and park to the south. Peace and coolness are found in the many churches and synagogues scattered throughout the city; and the small entrance fee for the Indian Museum keeps the courtyard quiet. Despite the drawbacks of the Maidan, Eden Gardens and the Strand are very pleasant from late afternoon onwards and boats up the Hooghly leave from Chandpal ghat.

Keeping fit and beautiful

The humidity of Calcutta may not encourage exercise, but the Bengal sweets may demand it. The Oberoi and Taj hotel pools are the best; and several clubs have one. The Maidan is good for jogging but the horses for hire there should be avoided – go to Tollygunge for riding. For quieter exercise, yoga and gymnasium centres include North Calcutta Yoga Byayam Centre, 9/A Lakshmi Dutta Lane, and Paschim Banga Yoga Byayam Society, 8B Ghose Lane. Gentler still, the Oberoi and Taj hotels have good health clubs; excellent, cheap for residents, with massage, saunas, gym and well-trained staff.

Calcutta is full of wizard Chinese hair-cutters, so on a long trip in India, this is the moment for a trim. Residents go to Fairy Nook on J. Nehru Road, New Ennis and Sunflower on Russell Street, Blue Haven on Park Street, Eve's near New Market and the Oberoi Hotel.

The best sports are found in the lively clubs which perpetuate the colonial combination of social meeting-place, good facilities and great style. At the top of the club hierarchy are the Calcutta Club, Tolly, the Royal Calcutta Turf Club, the Bengal Club and the Royal Calcutta Golf Club. Any friend or business colleague in Calcutta will belong to more than one of the 20 or so clubs and can take guests. Some have reciprocal membership with overseas clubs. But in any case, temporary membership is open to bona fide foreign visitors at most (a notable exception is the Calcutta Swimming Club). If in doubt, contact the Secretaries.

CLUB CHECKLIST

Tollygunge Club See Where to Stay section. Probably the best all-round facilities. They are open to foreigners, but telephone or write first.
Bengal Club See Where to Stay section. Billiards.
Bengal Flying Club, 95 Park Street
Calcutta Club, 214 Acharya J C Bose Road (tel: 443318). The 2,000 members number the most senior Bengalis – another 4,000 are on the waiting list. Tennis, swimming, etc.
Calcutta Cricket Club, 19/1 Gurusaday Road (tel: 478721), also tennis. The first cricket match in India was played on the Maidan. The club is the oldest existing cricket club outside Britain.
Calcutta Ladies Golf Club, 42B J Nehru Road (tel: 443816), founded in 1891 by the furious Mrs Peddler who was not allowed to play on the two men's courses and who won permission to play on the Maidan provided no building was erected – so the club house is on wheels.
Calcutta Polo Club, no club house, contact via the Turf Club, see below. Although it originated in Persia, polo was introduced into India from Manipur where it was played by the tea-planters. Silchar Polo Club was the first of its kind, established in 1859; then Calcutta's in 1863. The season is December, the same month as the Calcutta Horse Show.
Calcutta Rackets Club, by St Paul's Cathedral (tel: 441152). Squash courts.
Calcutta Rowing Club, 15 Rabindra Sarobar (tel: 463343)
Calcutta Swimming Club, 1 Strand Road (tel: 232894)
Lake Club, 29 Rabindra Sarobar (tel: 462538)
Royal Calcutta Golf Club, 18 Golf Club Road (tel: 461288): The centre of Indian golfing and the oldest royal golf club outside Britain. Originally the Dum Dum Golf Club, founded in 1829 near the airport, then moved to the Maidan and finally to Tollygunge in 1910; made 'Royal' the following year, when the king-emperor George V visited. The Amateur Golf Championship, the oldest (est. 1892) and most important annual golf event in the East, alternates between Calcutta, Delhi and Bombay (1985 Bombay, 1986, Delhi). Guests can hire caddies and clubs, playing caddies available. (Other Calcutta golf courses are at the Tollygunge Club and Ladies Golf Club, see above.)
Royal Calcutta Turf Club See Social Calendar, above.
Saturday Club, 7 Wood Street (tel: 445411). Established in 1872 for the juniors of the Raj, still popular with the young. Very large membership. Good swimming, tennis, squash and card room.
Mohan Bagan Athletic Club, CFC Ground (tel: 231634).

Good eats: Night lights

Calcuttans are fond of reminiscing about how sprightly the city was right up to the end of the 1960s. It is not so now. Again, the social centres for eating – lunch, tea and dinner – are the clubs, although the food tends to have remained as Raj as its surroundings. The handful of good restaurants outside the hotels tend to close by 10pm. Supper clubs offer mediocre food and raucous live European music. They fold up around midnight and should be avoided. For a really adventurous evening combining exploration, food and usually some amusing incidents, set off early for Tangra, the Chinese area (see below).

Currently, there is partial prohibition in Calcutta. So, jolliest nights are Wednesday, before dry day on Thursday (when many restaurants close), and Saturday.

However, the cultural scene is very healthy. As in Delhi and Bombay, here is a chance to see top quality theatre, music and dance, and sample the distinctive Bengali cinema, with a wide choice of performances each evening.

RESTAURANTS

In Calcutta, even more than Delhi, people eat in. A Bengali believes his Mum's cooking is best. If a household cannot cope with guests, there are caterers galore. Usually, only the famous Bengali sweets are bought. This is partly tradition and partly because Bengali dishes must be eaten freshly cooked as the delicate herbs and the fish do not wait well. When the smart go out, they want European, Chinese or north Indian food and their friends seated at the next table, in common with the rest of smart India. But moving down-market, the Chinese population supply quantities of excellent restaurants.

RESTAURANT SUGGESTIONS

Bengali *Suruchi*, Elliot Road; the only reasonable restaurant serving typical Bengali dishes – suruchi means 'good taste'. Unflashy decor; fish dishes recommended. The mustard oil used in Bengali cooking gives it a distinctive flavour. Try bekti, rui, Bagda and Golda prawns and hilsa. There is dahi maachh (ileesh or katla curried in yoghurt, ginger and turmeric), malai curry (prawns and coconut) and prawns cooked in mustard oil with garlic and coriander. All are eaten with a variety of rice dishes or with loochi (deepfried bread, like puri) – the local hilsa fish has lots of bones but good flavour. Finish with a sweeter-than-sweet Bengal sweetmeat or with misthi dohi (sweetened curd with raw jaggery – sugar). Then go off to a paan-wallah and sample Calcutta maghai, one of the most special paan concoctions.

North Indian and Mughlai *Amber*, 11 Waterloo Road; Punjabi food on three floors, patronised by local commercial centre and journalists from *The Statesman* and *Amrita Bazar Patrika* at lunchtime, crowded, good atmosphere, large menu, good food. *Kwality* , 17 Park Street; one of the best and most reliable of this large chain. *Moghul*, Oberoi Grand Hotel; excellent Mughlai food eaten lounging on low sofas in a marble-lined room, with good live Indian music. *Sonargaon, Taj Bengal*; named after the terminus of the Grand Trunk Road, a mock rustic setting in this deluxe hotel for reputedly excellent food. *Shah-en-Shah, Great Eastern Hotel*; tandoori dishes recommended, with more live Indian music. But in this hot, humid city, perhaps nicest of all is to chew a kebab or so beneath the stars in the popular front garden of the *Astor hotel*; if it's full, there is an outdoor restaurant at the nearby *Kenilworth*.

Chinese Encouraged perhaps by its eastern location, some of India's best Chinese food is to be found here. *The Bengal Club* has very good dishes, as does the *Ming Room, Trinca's*, Park Street; those not at the Amber for lunch are probably here, exchanging gossip across tables; tables in the front room best; long menu with stars denoting 'pungent' dishes. The *Chinoiserie, Taj Bengal*, is suitably sophisticated in its setting and cuisine. Try also the *Jade Room, Park Hotel*; and the *Chinese Restaurant, Great Eastern Hotel*; food recommended, surroundings not.

For less grand Chinese restaurants, try *Kimwah*, 51/a Garcha Road (behind the tram depot on Gariahat Road); chimney soup at *How Hua* on Free School Street; *Chung-Wah*, 7/1 Chittranjan Avenue; *Coley*, Russell Street and any in the Tangra area. For Tangra, set off early evening (taking alcohol if you want to, since it is rarely available) and seek out one of the small, utterly Chinese café-restaurants.

Polynesian *Oberoi Grand Hotel*; amusing, slightly self-conscious ethnic setting, but food alright.

Continental *Sky Room*, Park Street. No alcohol but fashionable, especially with Marwaris, so book. *The Esplanade, Taj Bengal*; good food, upstairs quieter.

Bengal sweets One is named after Lady Canning. Ishwar Gupta wrote an ode to another, the rossogolla. Recently, a politician was compared to the same sweet: pure, white, soft, sweet and all too soon finished. That is how serious sweets are in Calcutta. Sample rossogolla, rasmalai, sondesh, gulab jamun, shorbhaja and barfi at *K C Das* (who invented rasmalai) on Esplanade Road East, *Gupta's* on Park Street, *Ganguram* on Shakespeare Sarani (plus other branches) or make a pilgrimage to *Girish Dey*, 56 Ramdulal Sircar Street.

Tea A still thriving Raj ritual, performed on the

lawns of Tollygunge Club or Kenilworth Hotel, beside the Oberoi pool or in a restaurant. At *Flury's* tearoom on Park Street, start a full nursery tea with beans on toast and Indian savouries, then end with home-made meringues and chocolate cake. Taj Bengal prides itself on having a Swiss chef for its *La Patisserie*.

Cocktails Nowhere with a view over the city. Hotel bars mostly dowdy, except the Oberoi's fridge-cold *Chowringhee*. The Taj Bengal's *The Junction* is a welcome arrival. But best of all are the bars and lawns of the clubs.

NIGHT LIFE

Discotheques As remarked above, the Oberoi's *Pink Elephant* with its jolly tapes of the latest bopping tunes is yet another of Calcutta's anathemas. Patronised by Calcutta's young elite and their pals – from ex-maharajas to Communist politicians.

CULTURE

Discover what's on offer by consulting the daily newspapers or, for extensive listings, *Calcutta This Fortnight* (from the tourist office). Opposite the Calcutta Club on Acharya J C Bose Road is an excellent information centre and box office for the arts. Main halls include Rabindra Sadan, the Academy of Fine Arts, Birla Academy and the Sisir Mancha. Of the traditional theatres centred in north Calcutta, one of the oldest is the Star, with a revolving stage; the Rangana and Empire are also in the north. Avoid the awful 'Dances of India' programme at hotels. Nandan Theatre is a new cinema concentrating on art films. Visual arts shows often stay open during the evening, so the culture-keen Calcuttans can go after work. At the recent touring exhibition of Henry Moore sculptures, the Delhi venue was all but empty throughout whereas the Calcutta one was a perpetual party of vibrant debate by intellectuals, artists, politicians, merchants and professionals.

As performances start around 6.30pm when the rush hour is in full swing, allow plenty of time to get to the hall.

Theatre Modern Indian theatre has its roots in Calcutta, where performances began in the late 18th century. Plays were often – and still are – adaptations of novels. At the beginning of this century the actors were just as involved in early cinema as theatre. Mime, exaggerated gesture and interludes of dance or cabaret are still staple ingredients, so language need not be a barrier. Since the 1950s the offshoot of modern developments has been towards a greater realism, especially in Bengal where the politics of the left have led to the characters of Karl Marx and Ho Chi Minh being introduced into the traditional folk form. Bengali writers and directors to look out for: Sombhu Mitra, Badal Sircar and Utpal

Dutt.

During the day, lively street theatre still thrives in Calcutta, the ad hoc performances attracting small crowds on street corners.

Dance Performances of the Indian classical dance-dramas are often difficult to find in their places of origin. The top dancers go to the big cities. So it is worth catching whatever is around, be it southern Bharata Natyam or northern Kathak. Closer to Calcutta were developed the strong traditions of Manipuri, Odissi and Chhau – and countless folk dances.

In the lyrical and graceful devotional dances of Manipur the women use delicate steps and gestures for the raas dances, based on the stories of Krishna. But in the pung cholom dance the men leap, whirl and spin as they beat out the rhythm on drums slung from their necks. Look out for top dancers Guru Singhajit Singh and Charu Sija.

The classical Odissi temple dance also favours Krishna, recounting the tales with highly sensuous and lyrical movements of the hips and back, balancing pure dance with story-telling. Leading exponents include Sunjukta Panigrahi, Sonal Mansingh, Madhavi Mudgal, Protima Bedi and Malvika Sarrukai. All these dancers have trained under Guru Kelucharan Mohapatia, who was instrumental in the revival of Odissi and, as a child, was a gotipura (a young male odissi dancer dressed as a woman).

Chhau are the highly expressive folk dances of Bihar, Bengal and Orissa, usually recounting stories from the Mahabharata or the Ramayana. Although some dancers use elaborate clay masks and head-dresses, the whole story is told with body movement – no mime or song – as in Kathakali dance.

Cinema Choose between English, Hindi and Bengali. Bigger cinemas advertise in the press, with screening times – three or four a day. The Bengali film industry played a big part in India's film history and is now undergoing a revival, so it is worth trying a Bengali film.

Moving pictures reached Calcutta in 1896. In 1901 the enterprising Hiralal Sen screened films of plays staged at the Classic Theatre as an added attraction, after the stage performance was over. Jamshedji Framjee Madan, the Parsee owner of a successful theatrical company in Calcutta, became the first Indian movie magnate, with cinemas throughout the land. It was Madan Pictures which showed the first foreign talkie in India, 'Melody of Love', and which in 1931 missed producing the first Indian talkie by one month.

With sound came regional language cinema and naturally Bengal was the first to adapt its literary giants to the screen: Tagore, Bankimchandra Chatterjee and, most importantly, Saratchandra Chatterjee, whose plays 'Devdas',

'Parineeta' and 'Swami' have since been made in most regional languages. With sound came songs too, almost 70 on one 1930s film. New Theatres was the big Calcutta studio. From the start it was more political and cultural than the commercially minded Bombay. It bravely pioneered genuine political cinema such as 'Udayar Pathe' (Awakening), 1944, about the spiralling tension between rich and poor in Calcutta, and Ritwik Ghatak's 'Nagarik' (Citizen), 1952, calling on the working class and refugees not to lose hope after Partition. When the studio broke down, Nitin Bose, Bimal Roy and others went to thriving Bombay, introducing their social awareness into Hindi films.

Since then, despite lack of funding, bad laboratories and constant power cuts, such figures as Satyajit Ray, who made the landmark 'Pather Panchali' in 1955, and the radical Mrinal Sen, have produced an alternative, caring cinema. It is better known in the West than across India, although Ray has a strong cult following in Calcutta. And with the injection of financial support from the government of West Bengal since 1980, a more secure industry is growing, blending the old recipe of colour, action and music with social relevance. Ray's film 'Ghaire Baire' (The Home and the World), released in 1984, is an adaptation of Rabindranath Tagore's novel. It manages to marry the fiercely political theme of the Swadeshi (freedom) movement with a hero and heroine who break into dubbed song.

What to buy where

Shopping in Calcutta is not easy, but it repays effort. The Bengali silver- and goldsmithing is some of the best in India. Books, especially second-hand ones, crafts and fabrics are also good buys, and this is the centre of musical instrument making. But for high fashion, wait for Delhi or Bombay. It is best to shop by area, since the size of the city and its traffic congestion conspire against free movement.

For classic saris from all over India, the shops patronised by knowing locals for their wedding trousseaux are in and around Park Street – their names often begin with the lucky letter 's'. But for high quality modern designs, both sari and dress lengths in silk and cotton are designed and sold by Monu Khemka at Take 'n' Talk, 2/1 Russell Street, while Basanti Ghorsia sells her chic designs at her Razmatazz Boutique, 20 Shakespeare Sarani, next to Seetal.

Lindsay Street has the chemist, Dey's Medical Stores; the tailor, Gulam Mohammed Bros who will copy shirts and suits in 2 days (there are many more tailors on Madge Lane, a side-street); Handloom House for fabrics and the Government Emporia for West Bengal (called Manjusha), Manipur and UP. At the north end

of J Nehru Road (Chowringhee) the Central Cottage Industries Emporium has a much improved stock, with delightful Bengali wooden toys, jewellery and silver downstairs, and silk by the yard plus glorious Bengali saris upstairs. Nearby in Esplanade Road East, weavers from East Pakistan sell their silk and cotton at Refugee Handicrafts. (Down in south Calcutta, a number of state emporia including the excellent Gujari of Gujarat are clustered together in a new complex by Dhakuria Bridge, open Mon.-Sat., 10am-6pm.)

Behari Ganguly street is lined with shops for silver and gold, while the beautiful buttons worn with Bengali kurtas (long shirts) are sold at shops such as Dayal at 1/a Ashutosh Mukherjee Road. Ask in these for silversmiths who will copy old designs, or even make up something from an old Christie's or Sotheby's catalogue. The city's famous musical instrument craftsmen are found working in tiny ateliers open to the road in Lal Bazar and Rabindra Sarani in the old Chitpur area. Avoid the air-conditioned market: 100% imported goods, down to the last pencil.

Books Calcutta University awards the most degrees of any university. The Royal Asiatic Society was founded here. The National Library is here. Calcutta gave birth to the 19th-century literary renaissance and India's national and political consciousness, and claims that one in three of its citizens are poets – see them reading their lines on the Maidan at weekends. There are probably more publishers here than anywhere else in India. So there are a lot of books, old and new, many in English. College Street is a book collector's dream: solid shops and stalls that spill down side-streets. Hours of happy browsing – and always the real possiblity of falling upon a first edition of Murray's guide to India or a Daniell print. For new books, go to Oxford Book Company on Park Street, or to Classic Books, 10 Middleton Row.

Bengal crafts Traditional terracotta figures are made in villages throughout the state: a Bengali lady and babu (old man) may come from Jayanagar or Majilpur; models of occupations from Krisnanagar. Rice measuring bowls made of wood inlaid with brass, often in a shell design, are less fragile to pack. So are the brass oil-lamps in the form of figures or horses.

Delicate, cream-coloured pith work is carved from a dried freshwater plant into a horse, an elephant or Krishna and Radha. There is delicate silver jewellery, conch-shell bangles from north Calcutta and carved ivory from Murshidabad. The local children's dolls are made of papier maché or cotton. Give Kalighat paintings a miss: the artists no longer have the talent displayed with such bold assurance in the 19th century. For all these goods go to Bengal Home Industries Association, 57 Chowringhee and

West Bengal Government Sales Emporium, Lindsay Street.

Fabric The huge variety runs from gaily striped cotton through embroidered bedspreads and woollen blankets to the queen of Bengal silk saris, the Baluchari. Striped cotton comes in all weights and is cheap (Rs21 per metre). The fish, tiger, horse and other Bengali motifs embroidered on to bedspreads and table-cloths were originally applied to cotton shawls used by old women or to wrap a baby – one of several successful adaptations of a dying craft to modern use. The more intricate cotton Kantha embroidery quilts are sometimes further enriched with surface embroidery. For silk, fine Murshidabad saris are woven plain, then printed all over with delicate floral designs. From Dacca, formerly a great Muslim weaving centre, the finest cotton saris have very precise geometric designs woven into their borders.

But a *Baluchari* brocade sari is for the collector. The name derives from an extinct village near Berhampur in Murshidabad district. It has been suggested that Gujarati weavers possibly migrated there in the 18th century, bringing with them the brocade weaving tradition. In the 19th century, the aristocratic Bengali lady's showiest sari came from this area and may have taken six months to weave. The great late 19th century Baluchari weaver was Dubraj, who signed some of his creations.

The highly complicated design of floral motifs with a palo (end border) of bands of figures in compartments covered the whole sari. There might be nawabs smoking hookahs, durbar scenes, ladies giving flowers to lovers – even steam engines. Owners of such treasures used a mixture of neem leaves, dried polas flowers and black cumin seed as mothballs.

Today the designs worked at Vishnupur (see below), are slightly less sophisticated, although prices start at Rs800. Ask for Baluchari palo. These fun designs are also available much cheaper as prints. Buy fabrics at Handloom House on Lindsay Street and Khadi Gramodyog Bhavan (which stocks much more than khadi) on Chittaranjan Avenue.

See how it's done: Crafts, industry and caring

To see the striped cotton and other fabrics being woven around Calcutta, contact the All Bengal Women's Home, 89 Elliott Road.

Idol-makers Near the river in the Kumartuli (Potters') area of north Calcutta, off Chitpur Road, the idol-makers prepare images of Kali, Ganesh, Lakshmi, but most of all Durga. They work all year, stimulated by nips of home-brewed liquor, modelling clay images around straw cores and then storing them in the eaves of their jumble of hutment workshops. The chief kumar gives the goddess her features and expression (often strikingly similar to film star matinée idols); the whole team paint them up in jolly, gaudy colours equally similar to the film-stars' make-up and costumes. Since they are for religious use, they remain unbaked, as terra cruda.

Calcutta port The city's wealth was founded on trade and the port is still one of the most important in the East, despite bad silting in the Hooghly. This started when the current in the Ganga altered some years ago, but may be checked when – and if – the Farakka Barrage is completed. To visit, telephone the Port Authority to arrange a permit in advance.

Jute Fortunes were also made in jute which continues to be a major industry. To visit a factory or mill, contact the Jute Museum, Jute Technological Research Laboratories, ICAR, 12 Regent Park (tel: 464541).

Charity Hundreds of organisations are working to relieve some of the mammoth suffering in Calcutta. They may help the old, the young or the disabled; they may work through existing homes, hospitals, schools or communities, or run their own; and they may range in size from the worldwide Save the Children down to small amateur organisations equally successful in a more modest way. If you want to give, there is sure to be a charity to suit your particular concern and satisfy your particular demands, with a liaison officer in your home country. Best known is Mother Teresa's Missionaries of Charity. Her headquarters at 54a Lower Circular Road (tel: 247115) may be visited. Donations should be made payable to Mother Teresa Missionaries of Charity and delivered there or, outside India, sent c/o Barclays Bank Ltd, Station Approach, Southall, Middlesex, England. Further information from Mrs Ann Blaikie, Chairman of the International Committee of Co-Workers, Missionaries of Charity, 41 Villiers Road, Southall, Middlesex, England.

Awaydays

Probably essential for anyone spending more than a few days in Calcutta. For a gentle day take a picnic to the Botanical Gardens or cruise up the Hooghly (boats seasonal). For something more ambitious, visit Murshidabad or Bishnupur, both reached by pleasant rural drives. Tourist offices and travel agents carry the latest information on when, where and how to travel. For greater freedom, a hired car is usually better than a tourist bus.

Boating on the Hooghly There are several ghats in central Calcutta, so traffic can be avoided at source. Boats can be hired from the ghats on Strand Road to go down to the Botanical Gardens. Trips up to Serampore and Barrackpore are much longer. The tourist offices have up-to-date information.

Botanical Gardens 8km. See Out and About, above.

Sunderbans This is the Ganga delta, an area 2,500 sqkm of estuarine forest, creeks and swamps originally stretching from the mouth of the Hooghly inland for about 300km and full of game. Still the largest mangrove forest in India, watered by the daily tides. Cruise around the mangrove forest for a good chance of seeing some of the 300 or so Bengal tigers, and deer, crocodiles and wild boar; crocodile farm; Sajnekhali Bird Sanctuary; Lothian and Halliday Island Sanctuaries.

There are various ways of going. One is by car or bus (200km) to Basanti, then by country boat up to Gosaba, then by rickshaw or walking across land to more water, and finally another boat to the Sunderbans – in all, about 6½ hours. To stay overnight, sleep on the launch or in the *WBTB Tourist Lodge* or the *Sajnekhali Tourist Lodge* (30 beds, bookable in Calcutta at the WBTDC.) Another way is to take a bargain WBTDC 2- or 4-day tour, run twice a month. For either, a permit is necessary, obtained from the Forestry Department in Writers' Building. Best months: August-March.

Barrackpore 24km. After Richard Wellesley had finished his extravagant new Governor's House in the city, he planned to build a country house here, connecting the two with a 14-mile-long avenue. In fact, only the 'bungalow' was built (and that after Wellesley left), a large classical building beside the Hooghly. The landscaped airy cantonment park has suffered but the house, now a hospital, can be visited. Nicest to go by boat; the road suffers from too much traffic and too many potholes.

Serampore 24km. Facing Barrackpore across the Hooghly, the former Danish colony of Fredericknagore was sold as a job lot with Tranquebar and a bit of Balasore to the East India Company in 1845, for £125,000. Under the Danes it was an important missionary centre. The fine Danish Governor's house, church and college still stand. The college contains an exceptional library of manuscripts and early printed books collected by the Rev. William Carey, including first editions of translations of the Bible into 40 Indian and Asian languages printed in Serampore (open Mon.-Fri., 10am-4pm; Sat., 10am-1pm). The spectacular Car Festival held at Mahesh temple 3km away in June-July is second only to the one in Puri.

Bishnupur 200km. Capital of the Hindu Malla dynasty in the 16th and 17th centuries. The Mallas made Bishnupur a cultural centre of Bengal, then sold it by auction to the Maharaja of Burdwan. It was a centre of sericulture and weaving (see What to Buy section). The dhrupad style of Indian classical music was developed here. And the kings built some outstanding – if odd – terracotta temples, (see especially Shyam Rai and Jore Bangla). In the chowk bazaar and shops see the excellent handicrafts being made and sold: silk, metalware, terracotta horses. It is here that the Baluchari saris are still woven. Bishnupur is also famous for Bengal sweetmeats and flavoured tobacco. At the Jhapan festival in July-August, dedicated to the snake goddess Manasa, the city is full of snake-charmers performing tricks from bullock carts.

Santiniketan 170km. Rabindranath Tagore developed his father's ashram in an open-air school in 1901 (enlarged to a university in 1921). Its aim is to bring man closer to nature – santi means peace, niketan means abode. The Maharani of Jaipur studied there, as did Mrs Gandhi. Worth visiting to see interesting 20th-century art, rare in India. The buildings were designed by Tagore's son, Rathindranath, and the sculptures, frescoes and murals are by Jamini Roy, Ram Kinkar, Nandalal Bose and others. Also Tagore Museum and, during the winter, cultural festivals. Open to visitors Thurs.-Mon. by appointment with the Public Relations Office which the WBTB will arrange. Stay at the modest *University Guest House*.

Murshidabad 220km. Clive described Suraj-ud-Daula's city as 'extensive, populous and rich as the city of London'. What once was the capital of the Nawabs of Bengal, brimful of bustle and grandeur, is now a quiet rural town, living on sericulture and mango cultivation (some connoisseurs say the finest mangoes of all).

But there is plenty to see including the Italianate Nizamat Kila palace built in the 1830s for a Nawab, known as Hazarduari Palace (house of a thousand doors) with armoury, library and Queen Victoria's gift of a gigantic chandelier. There are the ruins of Katra Mosque, modelled on the mosque at Mecca, and the palace of Jagat Sett, one of the richest 18th century financiers. It is nice to take a boat across the river to the Khushbagh (garden of happiness) and see the sunset from Moti Jhil (pearl lake). Local Murshidabad block-printed silk saris can be bought. Just outside the town, *Kasimbazar* (8km) has early English remnants (palace, mansion remains) testifying to former greatness when it was Bengal's leading agency and Calcutta's founder, Job Charnock, was Chief (1681).

The road up to Murshidabad passes *Plassey*, site of Clive's triumph in 1757. Stay overnight at the clean but modest *WBTB Tourist Lodge* at Murshidabad or their one at Berhampore (12km).

Gaur, Malda and Pandua Worth staying on at Murshidabad for a day-trip 120km north. To deserted Gaur, 8km south-west of English Bazaar, an ancient Hindu town that became the capital of Bengal's first Muslim rulers (15-16th centuries), to be envied by Humayun as 'Abode of Paradise', sacked by Sher Shah Sur and finally part of Akbar's Mughal Empire (1576); see the extensive remains, especially mosques, scattered over 51 sqkm of the original substantial city. On to nearby *Malda*, a busy cotton and silk market for the French, Dutch and English in the 18th century; the earlier Islamic buildings have survived better than the European ones. Finally, 11km north-east, lies *Pandua*, Bengal's capital 1338-1500, then deserted in favour of Gaur; see the brick-paved road running through all 9km of the town's length, and the various mosque and tomb survivors.

Seaside If desperate, go to Digha (240km) or Bakkhali (132km). Both have good beaches but bad accommodation and week-end crowds. Better to take a longer break and go down to Orissa (see below).

Forays further afield

As one Calcuttan businessman screeched down a long-distance phone line on a May afternoon: 'Don't talk to me of heat! It's 90 degrees here, the power is down and I'm on my third shirt today'. If the power breakdowns, communication failures, congestion and humidity become unendurable, then getting right away from Calcutta is easy. An hour's flight does it: north into the cool Himalayas; west to the pilgrimage city of Varanasi; south to Orissan temples and beaches; and south-east to the Andaman and Nicobar Islands.

Trips to some of these and all the north-eastern states and to Bhutan and Burma require special permits and visas and therefore need advance planning, preferably well before leaving home – officials talk of 8-12 weeks to obtain a permit for these areas. The travel agencies, information centres and foreign missions listed above have the latest information on these more sensitive areas. They will also help plan and book any trip – it is even more uncomfortable and time-wasting queuing in Calcutta than other Indian cities. For Nepal, see Hills chapter; for the Andamans, see Sun chapter.

European firms with offices in Calcutta often own houses in Darjeeling, Kalimpong or Puri for use by their employees and guests. Their hospitality can reach Indian heights, so there is no harm in asking what they have got and whether it might be available.

DARJEELING
The British bolt-hole from steamy Calcutta. The cool, fresh air, green vegetation and scenery were irresistible. The inquisitive rushed around recording the flora and fauna, playing sports and creating Surrey gardens. The fruits of their energies contributed to the Botanical Gardens in Calcutta and to Kew Gardens in London. The adventurous nipped up mountains – Edmund Hillary left from Darjeeling with his four 'small, sinewy, smiling' Sherpas on his Gawhal expedition in 1951, two years before the Everest triumph. The entrepreneurs planted tea gardens. The civil servants removed the headquarters of the Bengal Government there for the summer. Today, the jungle may be less dense but little has changed. Flowers, mountains, tea and breath-taking views abound. The local population is a hotchpotch of Lepchas, Limbus, Tibetans, Nepalese, Bhutias, Kashmiris and Bengalis, often wearing their colourful tribal costumes. Buddhism flourishes here, described by John Keay as 'the only place where one is conscious of a living Buddhist ambience'.

THE HARD FACTS Darjeeling lies on a spur of the Ghoom-Senchal Ridge, at an altitude of 2,134m, with spectacular views across the Himalayan peaks. The climate is best from April to mid-June (for rhododendra, magnolia and other blooms) and mid-September to December (for views) – clearest skies are in November. Either side there are mists, the winter air drops to 1°C and the monsoon blots out views and blocks off roads. Most festivals are in January and February.

The journey up is part of the trip. First, fly to Bagdogra or catch the Rocket Service night train (which is fun, but one way might be enough, returning by air). Then, either take the narrow gauge toy train from New Jalpaiguri or Siliguri to Darjeeling along the two-foot-gauge line completed in 1881; seven hours of chugging, puffing, hair-pin bends and changing scenery, but relatively safe-feeling; or take a taxi, driven by the road equivalent of a sherpa who, with amazingly precise knowledge of the land, perfect eyesight and equally perfect timing, manipulates the jeep round the road's hairpin bends and just, but only just, hangs on to its mountain slope; not for the faint-hearted or vertigo sufferers. For a more country trip, fly Vayudoot to Coochbehar, then drive up.

Various hotels of which the red-roofed, cream chateau built by Arrathoon Stephen (who built the Oberoi Grand, Calcutta), *Hotel Oberoi Mount Everest*, will be the best if promises of re-opening in 1991 after its revamping come true. Meanwhile:

Windamere Hotel, Observatory Hill (tel: 2841/ 397); 27 rooms. Built as a house around central garden, fires lit in the rooms at night, library, badminton court, food reasonable – children eat at 6pm, adults at 8pm. *The Planter's Club*: ramshackle but fun, right in the town centre. And

Hotel New Elgin, H D Lama Road (tel: 3314); 22 rooms, patronised by discerning trekkers.

The Tourist office, 1 Nehru Road, is not wonderful; wiser to obtain full briefing from a Calcutta travel agency, especially for trekking or climbing. Foreigners Registration Office, Laden La Road (tel: 2261), for permits (see permit note below). Indian Airlines, 1 Nehru Road (tel: 2355).

OUT AND ABOUT   Dawn at *Tiger Hill* (at 2,590m, 11km away), the sun rising over Mount Kanchenjunga – and on a clear day Mount Everest – is truly worth getting up for. Get there by 5am (one hour's drive), clad in jumpers. Views from Tonglu, Sandakphu and Phalut good, too, but further away.

In addition to roaming the hills to see unusual flowers, there are collections in town: Lloyds Botanical Garden (founded 1865), with extensive hot houses (open daily, 6am-5pm); Zoo, mixes mountain plants with animals; Natural History Museum (open Fri.-Tues., 10am-4pm; Wed., 10am-1pm). There is an interesting and well maintained cemetery of Raj residents. The Himalayan Mountaineering Institute, the only one for training mountaineers, comes complete with a museum devoted to the mountains and mountaineering equipment. And there is even a living exhibit teaching there: Sherpa Tenzing Norkay, who accompanied Hillary up Everest in 1953.

The town itself is not especially picturesque. As one keen India visitor summed up: 'damp, muddy, church and schools, sort of atmospheric - but those glasses of filthy Tibetan tea!'. But the mesmerising Himalayas are all around, ever present, and just glimpsing their silent majesty under different lights from sunrise to sunset is wondrous.

The Passenger Ropeway (3km), the first one in India, 8km long, connects Darjeeling with Singla Bazar. Not for vertigo sufferers. To ensure a seat, telephone the Officer-in-charge at the ropeway station (tel: 2731).

FITNESS, FOOD AND ENTERTAINMENT Just tackling the steps and vertical lanes of this hillside town keeps the muscles in trim. But if the additional walking, trekking (on foot or pony) and mountaineering are not enough, try the Senchal Golf Club (at 2,484m, one of the highest); tiny Lebong Race Course (the highest in the world; spring and autumn seasons) and fishing on the Rangeet River at Singla (8km) and Teesta River at Riyand (41km, the District Forest Officer gives permits). Darjeeling Gymkhana Club, Bhanu Sarani West (tel: 2002/2020); well equipped for indoor and outdoor games, offers temporary membership to visitors.

Tibetan food is thoroughly unexciting. The hotels mentioned serve the regular Indian, Chinese and European dishes. Apart from these, go to *Glenary's* for stylish uniformed waiters and unstylish food, or to *Chowrasta* for South Indian food. Kalimpong cheese, rather like Lou Palou, is one of the few harder cheeses made in India. Darjeeling faces west, so sunset cocktails are particularly good. Local ethnic groups perform interesting folk dances, especially during festivals.

SHOPPING, CRAFTS AND INDUSTRY Tea: With 78 tea plantations in Darjeeling employing 46,000 people (the bulk Nepalese) and producing 10.5 million kilos of tea annually, tea-growing takes on a new interest. Although much more tea is grown in the less accessible Assam, Darjeeling is considered to be best because of the favourable climate. It is so expensive that a 'Darjeeling' tea is usually blended with leaves from other areas, which also balances the flavour. It is possible to visit the Happy Valley Tea Estate (2km) to see the orthodox production method, from fresh green leaf through withering, rolling, pressing, fermenting and drying to the final grading (open Tues.-Sat., 8am-noon and 1-4.30pm; Sun., 1-4.30pm). The best tea to buy is unbroken leaves of Golden Flowery Orange Pekoe.

Tibetan crafts When the Chinese invaded Tibet, many refugees came here. At the Tibetan refugee Self-help Centre, established in 1959, the workshops for weaving and carving, etc., are open to visitors and the finished goods are on sale: woollens, carpets, leather, wood-carving. Himalayan crafts: At Hayden Hall in Laden La Road, local women sell their woollen products. Bargain hard for good wood carving and local jewellery (but avoid the mediocre thankas) in touristy Chowrasta, J Nehru Road or the more colourful bazaars off Cart Road. On the road out to Ghoom, Manjusha, the Bengal Government Emporium, stocks Himalayan crafts and Bengal fabrics at fixed prices.

KALIMPONG

(51km from Darjeeling at 1,250m). Currently, no permit needed for a visit of up to 15 days. Reached along magnificent scenic route. Hillside market town lying below the massive peak of Kanchenjunga, formerly a major trading post for wool merchants and still a place where different cultures meet in the bazaar. Glorious views, blossoming flowers throughout the year and colourful markets (Wed. and Sat.) where villagers in local costume sell farm goods and wool. Several Buddhist monasteries, the best being the newly restored, brightly painted Thonga Gompa Bhutanese monastery, founded 1692. Kalimpong is a centre for commercial nurseries that export orchids, cacti, amaryllides, roses, gerbera, dahlias and gladioli. Standard, Sri L. B. Pradhanand and Sri Ganesh Moni Pradhan are among the top nurseries. Arrange a visit to one through the WBTB in Darjeeling. Many good picnic spots with views, especially Durbindras; otherwise to to the Himalayan Hotel or Hotel Maharaja (South Indian food). To stay overnight, the *Silver Oaks Hotel* is recommended; the *Himalayan Hotel* and the *WBTB Luxury Tourist Lodge* are clean and modest.

Other options: *Kurseong* (36km); or a bigger trip to the *Jaldapara Wildlife Sanctuary* in the Dooars (120km from Siliguri). There are also connections to Bhutan and Sikkim.

Sikkim, Bhutan and the North-East Frontier

Trips to see these areas need to be planned in advance and the current required permits obtained (see Permits and Visas, below). Also, a good travel agency is essential. Visitors should not expect fancy accommodation nor, in some cases, great freedom of movement. But the scenery, wildlife and trekking opportunities are exceptional.

THE HARD FACTS Reaching these areas is not easy. The first leg can be flown; then there is a choice of car, train or local bus. Currently, Indian Airlines flies to Guwahati, Tezpur, Jorhat, Dibrugarh and Dimapur in Assam, to Imphal in Manipur and to Agartala in Tripura; Vayudoot currently flies to Guwahati, Jorhat, Dibrugarh and Silchar in Assam, Shillong in Meghalaya, Tezu in Arunachal Pradesh, Agartala in Tripura, Aizwal in Mizoram.

Permits and Visas Provided that some of these areas are open to visitors, foreign nationals will need a separate permit for each state and a visa for Bhutan. The permit may define that only part of the state can be entered. Validity is often short. Only a few can be extended at the destination. Some states require different permits for different districts. Some go further: To go to Darjeeling by air requires no permit, but to go by train or road does. Other states give permits more readily to groups than to individuals, notably Assam which likes groups of four or more. Still others prefer to give a certain length of permit, such as Meghalaya which favours a 7-day one. Finally, any regulations are apt to change.

The moral is to get the latest information from your Indian mission before leaving home and try to obtain all the necessary papers. Apply as early as possible – some states require twelve weeks notice. Then check again at the city of entry into India. If booking the trip in India, go to any Foreigners Registration Office. In Calcutta there is also the Home Political Department, 1st floor, Writers' Building, BBD Bagh. Alternatively, the recommended travel agencies will do all the hustling and paperwork for a very small fee.

It would be extremely annoying to arrive at a frontier or airport and be refused entry. However, should a difficulty arise, as usual in India knowing the right person works miracles and, short of that, just going straight to the top gets miracles started.

For the most accurate information consult the Deputy Secretary, Ministry of Home Affairs, Government of India, (F-1), North Block, New Delhi 110001.

SIKKIM
Go for the mountains, flowers (500 species of orchid alone), painted houses and monasteries. Season February-May and October-December. Fly to Bagdogra, then use a taxi/bus/train combination to cross the border into Sikkim, annexed by India in 1975 to become its 22nd state. Good to stop en route at Pemeyangtse Monastery (8th century), Sikkim's chief and second oldest monastery and one of 60 still active (possible to stay at a nearby tourist bungalow, Hotel Pandim). Then continue to the capital, to stay at the *Nor-Khill Hotel* (tel: 386/720) or *Hotel Tashi Dekel* (tel: 361/458/862). Information: Government of Sikkim Department of Tourism, (tours, car hire, guides); Foreigners Registration Office (visas); Sikkim Himalayan Adventure, Yak and Yeti Tarvels and Snow Lion Treks (essential for trekking).

The town is spectacularly sited on a long ridge overlooking the Ranipool River, with stunning views of the Kanchenjunga range. See a potpouri of house types, the Tsuklakhang palace, the Institute of Tibetology Orchid Sanctuary and Chorten Institute of Cottage Industries; enjoy views fron Enchey Monastery and the deer park. Well worth visiting the Orchid Sanctuary to see some of the 500 species of orchid – driving around Sikkim has been described as 'like driving through a sub-tropical paradise garden: hibiscus, bougainvillea, orange groves, pontsettia, with Kanchenjunga peaks behind; and such beautiful people, too'. Bakkim and Dzongri are outside town, as are the monasteries at Pemayangtse, Tashiding, Rumtek and Phodang, whose painted walls and fantasy butter sculptures are the setting for masked dances. There is nice jewellery and other crafts sold at the Cottage Industries Emporium.

BHUTAN
Go for the mountains and more painted houses, palaces and monasteries. Season March and September-November. Fly to Bagdogra, then it is 380km of bumpy road to the capital, *Thimpu*. Currently all visits are a fixed package, payable

in advance, with high prices for rather basic accommodation. A more comfortable hotel is *Hotel Druk*, in the foothills at Phuntsholing. Built and run by the Indian Welcomgroup, it has a distinctly Bhutanese character. Information: Director of Tourism, Ministry of Finance, Tachichho Dzang, Thimpu; currently, visas are somewhat difficult to obtain, and the monasteries are discouraging visitors who, they say, upset their worship.

NORTH-EAST FRONTIER

Consists of two Union territories, Mizoram and Arunachal Pradesh, and five states, Assam, Manipur, Meghalaya, Nagaland and Tripura. Go for the wildlife (especially Kaziranga Nature Reserve), countryside, rich tribal cultures and their constant festivals of song and dance, tea plantations – and the lack of tourists. As it is close to China, the whole area is politically sensitive. Some parts may be closed; in others, movement may be restricted. But reports testify to every effort being well rewarded. Indian Airlines and Vayudoot between them service the area from Calcutta, and connect Bagdogra with Gauhati. Again, advanced planning is necessary (at least 8 weeks), and a good travel agent essential.

ASSAM

Season October-May. See also Wildlife sanctuaries at end of chapter.

Guwahati (Gauhati) Stay at *Hotel Nandan*, G S Road (tel: 31281), new and central, or the hill-top *Bellerne Hotel*. Information: three tourist offices, on B K Kakati Road, Ulubari and Station Road. See Assam State Zoo (one-horned Indian and two-horned African rhinos), Umananda and Kamakshya temples, sunset over the Brahmaputra River and the anthropology, forestry, crafts and State museums. Visit Sualkashi to see silk-weaving in every house; buy Endi, Muga and Pat silks. Visit Manas wildlife sanctuary.

Jorhat Stay at the ITDC *Kasiranga Forest Lodge* in the sanctuary (tel: 785109). En route, see the Jay Sagar temples and glimpse a bush or so of the 60% of India's tea crop grown in Assam, and visit a tea garden (which can only be done unofficially, by dropping a hint to anyone you meet, from hotel manager onwards, since they will all know tea people). To the east lies Nagaland, where the tribesmen's culture is under government protection. Intrepid travellers will find the Nagas living in tiny villages and see their impressive war dances.

MEGHALAYA

Season all the year round including, for some, the incredible monsoon (end June to mid-August); Its name means 'Abode of the Clouds', and they rarely go away. Shillong's annual rainfall is 241cm. Nearby Cherrapunji's is 1,150cm, the highest in the world, a fact which encouraged the travel writer Alexander Frater to follow India's monsoon here from Kerala and write about it in *Chasing the Monsoon*.

Shillong Pretty, sporty hill station at 1,496m altitude, one of the earliest outpost of the British in the north-east and home of the Khasi tribals. Stay at *Hotel Pinewood* (tel: 3116, 3765, 4176) modest. Arrive via Gauhati airport. Information: four tourist offices, all on Police Bazaar. See waterfalls, streams, pine groves, flowers (such as on road to Cherrapunji) and Khasi tribal dancing (at Smits and Nongkrem). Sports include good 18-hole golf course – the game was introduced in 1898 – and fishing on Uniam Lake and at Ranikor and Dawki.

MANIPUR AND MIZORAM

Manipur's women and most of its men spend hours dancing. When not dancing, they weave. Lands of wooded hills and lakes, with a surprising number of Christians among the many tribes; the Mizos, who have received enthusiastic missionaries since late last century, like variety and may swap from Presbyterian to Anglo-Catholic one week and on to another sect the next.

Imphal Go for the dance, especially Rash Lila festival (October-November). Fly to Imphal. Accommodation basic, best at *Hotel Ranjit*, Thangal Bazaar (tel: 382) or *Tourist Lodge* (reserve by letter to Director of Tourism). See temples, museum, visit Moirang (folk-culture). Buy weaving and crafts in the large Khwairamband bazaar.

Varanasi (Banaras), Uttar Pradesh

(Banaras, or Benares, is a British corruption of a Mughal version of the old Hindu name. This original name was revived after Independence.)

The holiest Hindu city in India and one of the oldest living cities in the world, contemporary with Thebes, Babylon and Nineveh. For the devout Hindu the 2,000 odd temples piled on to the bank of the sacred Ganga make up Kasha (divine light) and must be visited at least once in a lifetime to wash away sins, and, preferably, be visited again shortly before death. To die here is to have the greatest hope for the next life.

Varanasi may be the centre of Hindu culture with fine music and a good museum, but its daily trade is pilgrims, India's most important tourists. Here, every facet of Hinduism is to be seen, from great purity and holiness to the depths of degradation and squalor – and certainly some confidence tricks. An extraordinary quality of light permeates it all.

When the artist Edward Lear arrived here

during his 1873-5 trip, he was at first his usual grumpy self, finding the hotel, people and city all conspiring against his attempts to draw. But, by the end of his brief stay, he was captivated, as his journal shows. 'Got on a boat, a large one, for no-one can have the least idea of this Indian city's splendour without this arrangement. Utterly wonderful is the rainbow-like edging of the water with thousands of bathers reflected in the river. Then the colour of the temples, the strangeness of the huge umbrellas and the inexpressibly multitudinous detail of architecture, colour, etc. . . . I had always supposed this place a melancholy, or at least a staid and soberly-coloured pot. . . . Instead I find it one of the most startlingly radiant of places full of bustle and movement. Constantinople and Naples are simply dull and quiet by comparison.'

It is much the same today. Off the water, the maze of filthy, clattering, cow-filled, narrow city gullies (alleys) swarms with pilgrims, rich and poor, old and young, gurus and pupils, straight and eccentric, sane and batty, whole and limbless, sighted and blind, healthy and sick. Between temple visits they buy puja items (religious offerings) of flowers and spices from tiny peephole shops set high in the street walls. They also buy tourist mementoes of green, plastic, hopping frogs. There are noisy processions following a celebrated priest or a marriage, and quieter ones for the dead who, wrapped in white silk or cotton, are borne to Jalsain Ghat on stretchers, bicycles, rickshaws or horses.

Everyone is heading for the Ganga, the goal of every pilgrim. On the 5km of ghats (water-side steps) leading down to the sacred water they give discourses or listen to discourses – the fat Brahmins sit beneath tatty straw umbrellas. They perform puja. They wash and attend scrupulously to their toilet or live in abject squalor. They read, practise contorting yoga or lounge vacantly and sleep. They beg or give alms, and quite often they die. The less devout gossip, smoke various intoxicants and talk twaddle. There are priests, yogis, widows and philosophers. And there are barbers to shave heads before taking the purifying waters. More secular entertainment comes from akhara (pit) wrestlers and acrobats who climb the mal kham (smooth wooden pole).

Local children entice tourists on to their boats grinning 'Best time see burning bodies' (untrue: they are burnt around the clock). Bigger children propose a 'massage'. And music and chants blare out from a very loud loud-speaker.

In the sacred water the faithful wash, perform Hindu rites, pumice-stone their feet, lather up their hair, have a pee, clean their teeth and wash their dhotis. The city sewers empty out nearby. They also drink the water and, extraordinarily, do not suffer. As Eric Newby writes in *Slowly*

Down the Ganges: 'At Banaras, thousands drink the water every day . . . My wife and I have both drunk the water unboiled in the 50-mile stretch of the river where it first enters the Indian Plain . . . without any unfortunate effects. Yet when we left the river we invariably became ill.' Visitors would not be wise to follow his example, although the Anglo-French project to clean up the sacred water is beginning to take effect.

Both river and ghats are saturated with a serene and holy light. Under this, human activity stirs into prayer at the first glimmer of the pure and magical dawn, gains momentum through the morning, then slumps into a stupour under the glowing, almost tangibly thick, afternoon sunlight before rousing itself for more prayers and night-time temple visits.

Although the word Varanasi is a compound of the two small rivers it lies between, the Varuna and the Asi, its whole raison d'être is the river Ganga whose powers of cleansing can bring salvation. The Ganga rises near Gangotri, at an altitude of 4,000m in the Himalayas, irrigates the north-east plains of India (sometimes with terrible flooding and devastation) and empties into the Bay of Bengal 2,000km later, through a huge delta stretching from Calcutta to Dacca. Most of the temples in Varanasi are dedicated to Shiva. For, when the water goddess Ganga was told to save great souls, Shiva caught her in his thick, tangled hair to prevent her flooding the world. Thus, Ganga's water trickled out over the souls, freeing them to go to heaven.

Varanasi was already thriving 2,500 years ago, when Buddha passed by. It was at Sarnath, 10km away, that he delivered his first sermon after receiving enlightenment, making it as important to Buddhists as Varanasi is to Hindus. From the 11th century, Muslims periodically ravaged Varanasi and its temples, the worst case being Aurangzeb who converted the most famous temple into a mosque. But the city survived. Temples are still being added – the rather flashy Birla one (Tulsi Manasmunda) has just been completed – and its creative and cultural heritage is unbroken. The philosopher Kabir was born here, as was the freedom fighter Rani Laxmi Bai. The thumri melody of Indian song originates here.

Today, Varanasi produces many of the top musicians, including Ravi Shankar, and some of the best tabla players. The city has always been a centre of Sanskrit and classical Hindu studies. Now it is also a centre of modern Hindu studies, focused at the Banaras Hindu University which was founded by the nationalist Madan Mohan Malviya. It is enthusiastically patronised by the present ex-Maharaja.

Around the city schools of gurus continue to

dedicate their lives to interpreting the Hindu epics, the Mahabharata and Ramayana. Each has his pet subject and holds saptahs (weekly sessions) when he sits on a plinth and expounds and elaborates with great oratorical skill on a single stanza from the text. Crowds of thousands may gather to hear a good speaker such as Dr Shri Vats. Smaller saptahs are held indoors (as they are throughout India), mostly attended by older women who take along the younger members of the family to learn the scriptures. Some temples specialise: gurus at the Krishna temple, Gopal Mandir (run by a woman, Sharad Ballabha Betijee), concentrate on the Bhagavad Gita, a philosophical discussion between Krishna and Arjuna before the big Mahabharata battle.

There is little of the Swami cult here that has attracted Westerners to India since the 1960s. The Maharishi Mahesh Yogi's ashram is far upstream, at Hardwar. It was there that the Beatles went and where Mia Farrow's younger sister meditated non-stop for 96 hours. Swami Shivananda, founder of the Divine Life Society, is not here either. The Swami, apparelled in ochre, would give lectures on 'The Exploration of Inner Space' and then pass round chocolate biscuits to eat. Afro-haired Satya Sai Baba seems to have little time for holy Varanasi. He gave a special audience to Delhi diplomats and performed his miracle of making 'sacred ash' materialise between his thumb and forefinger before their cynical eyes. This yoga cult attracts more Western devotees than Indian. Only a small fraction of India's Hindus know of its existence. The majority follow the old traditions seen here at Varanasi.

THE HARD FACTS Varanasi perpetually overflows with pilgrims, but the weather is best October-March; it rains mid-June to September, when the river rises above the ghats and gushes and swirls through a city oddly quiet with only a token faithful. The *Ram Lila* festival (the northern version of Dussehra) in September-October is even more spectacular here than in Delhi: some 30 days of plays and music in honour of Rama, each night a different venue, ending with a massive procession; at this time, the Ramayana is read continously in the temples, the faithful taking turns, while the ex-Maharaja of Varanasi is patron of the whole event. There are no regular concerts, so *music festivals* are a rare chance to hear some of the great Varanasi talents. They include: Lalit Sangit Parishad, December; Rimpa (started by Ravi Shankar), January; Dhrupad Mela, last week of February; music dedicated to Hanuman, played at Sankat Mochan Temple, first week of April; music dedicated to Durga, mid-August.

There are flights to and from Calcutta on

Tues., Thurs., Sat. and Sun.; connections with Delhi, Agra, Khajuraho and Kathmandu daily. Taxis are happy to take more than one customer into town (25km), halving the fare. The overnight train to and from Calcutta or Delhi is excellent, arriving at the central or Cantonment station.

There are only two good hotels and this is tourist territory, so book. One is *Clarks Varanasi,* The Mall (tel: 42401/06; telex: 0545-204); the first of the Clarks chain, a 19th-century core with plenty of character, started by the Clarks who sold out to the local brothers Gupta in the 1930s. 140 rooms, attached bath. Garden rooms in the old block are nicest, with 1930s furniture, huge bathrooms, and views over the garden. Back rooms look across fields to the Varuna river. Shopping, travel agent, health club, yoga classes, pool. Restaurant decor dreary but food has best reputation in town and includes Mughlai and Lucknowi dishes and a full Chinese menu (with Chinese chef). There are lunchtime poolside barbecues with live Indian music and evening garden barbecues; fresh Mysore coffee if you ask for it, instant coffee if you don't.

Taj Ganges, Nadesar Palace Ground, Raja Bazar Road (tel: 42485/42495; telex: 0545-219) New building, opened 1981, with all the Taj chain comforts and much improved management. 104 rooms, attached bath. Fair shopping, travel agent, good big pool, tennis, tiny golf course, restaurant nice with good food (including some rich Lucknowi Mughlai dishes) and a garden buffet dinner.

Government of Indian Tourist Office, 15B The Mall (tel: 43744). Uttar Pradesh Government Tourist Bureau, Parade Kothi, Cantonment (tel: 43486/43413); superb, run by a knowledgeable local team headed by Mr D. K. Burman, a trained archaeologist. It will arrange good guides for Sarnath (not the easiest place to visit unaided), and special music and dance performances. It provides reliable advice on the ghats, shopping and tours (city, Ramnager Fort, Sarnath). For news and entertainment guide, see the *Northern India Patrika* newspaper. Best guide books: *Glimpses of Varanasi* by K. Jaycees or *Banaras* by S. N. Mishra. The Survey of India map of Varanasi sometimes in print. Best book shops: Motilal at Banarsidas in Chowk and New Metrex International, in front of the UPGTB. Partial prohibition currently in force: the 1st and 7th of each month are dry days.

HINDUISM To visit Varanasi is to touch the very core of a religion followed by 83% of Indians. Yet, with alarmingly long texts and a plethora of gods whose family tree is impossible to chart, it is difficult for a non-Hindu even to begin to tackle.

The earliest religious practices on the sub-continent predate the Indus civilisation of the 4th-2nd millennia BC; more will be known only when their script is deciphered. But it was the Aryans, who came down through the mountains around 1500BC, who brought a distinctive religion and set it down in the four Vedic texts. The 1,028 hymns of the oldest, the Rig Veda, are considered the source of Hindu literature. Their script was an early form of Sanskrit, still the sacred language today for Hinduism and all the religions which developed out of it: Buddhism, Jainism and Sikhism.

The brahmins were originally the priests of the Vedas. They sang them and, like Christian priests, they acted as go-betweens offering sacrifices to the gods on behalf of the people. Later texts, such as the Upanishads (philosophical treatises), reveal two developments. At a spiritual level, there is the beginning of the fundamental Hindu belief in karma, the spirit's movement across generations, enduring a series of rebirths. In each, the soul progresses or regresses according to past deeds. Trapped in this perpetual suffering, the only escapes are through nirvana, a state of bliss in which personal identity is extinguished, or in moksha, the final release from the cycle of rebirth.

The other development, at a temporal level, was the growing power of the brahmins. This power increased as rituals became more complex, the abstract philosophy of the Upanishads was adopted and the texts remained always in Sanskrit. The common man was effectively cut off from his religion. The reaction was the birth of two offshoots of Hinduism, Buddhism and Jainism, in the early 5th century BC, which concentrated on simple and practical doctrines preached in people's own languages. (Later, Hinduism would retaliate by making Buddha the 10th incarnation of Vishnu and by promoting Hinduism as a liberal religion permitting worship to any deity in any manner or form.)

As the centuries passed, each Hindu increasingly came to worship a single god or goddess chosen from the multitude of nature spirits, totemic gods and heroes adopted from earlier cults, as well as gods of the Vedas. This worship, known as bhakti, involved total submission to follow a path of love to the ultimate goals, nirvana or moksha. With this evolved the elaborate rituals and the great popular myths. The Mahabharata (which includes the Bhagavad Gita) and Ramayana are the great epics; a body of legends and religious instruction make up the eighteen Puranas. The quite short Bhagavad Gita, written as a dialogue between Krishna and Arjuna, contains the essence of Hindu philosophy: the theory of karma and the immortality of the soul, and the human struggle for love, light and redemption.

The multitude of gods and their hectic adventures and complicated inter-relationships can confuse. At the top there is the Trinity – Brahma (Creator), Vishnu (Preserver) and Shiva (Destroyer). Today's Hindu, although he believes in the existence of the supreme universal spirit of Brahma, often follows Vishnu or Shiva; another favourite is the elephant-headed god of good fortune, Ganesh (son of Shiva and Parvati). Those following Vishnu are known as Vaishnavites, those following Shiva as Shaivites. These two principal cults and a third, Shakti, devoted to various goddesses, co-exist in such harmony that they sometimes join together. The Seven Sacred Cities which pilgrims should visit are each dedicated to Shiva or Vishnu, except for Kanchipuram which is dedicated to both. Of this and the others – Varanasi, Hardwar, Ujjain, Mathura, Ayodhya and Dwarka – it is Varanasi which, blessed with kasha (divine light), can most effectively wash away sins and, if a believer dies here, give greatest hope for the next life.

In sculpture, the gods appear for the first time in the 1st-3rd centuries; in architecture, Shiva is the favourite dedicatee for the first peak of Hindu architecture, the sublime temples of the Chandellas (Khajuraho), the Somavamshis (Bhubaneswar), the Solankis (Gujarat) and the Cholas (Thanjavur), all with elaborate sculpture. Despite the arrival of Islam in North India with the Delhi Sultanate, Hinduism continued to flourish and develop under royal patronage during the 15th and 16th centuries, notably at Vijayanagar and Kanchipuram. Also, the devotion to the blue-skinned god of human form, Krishna, the 8th incarnation of Vishnu and hero of the Bhagavad Gita, increased dramatically – in Orissa, Puri's temple was transformed into a Krishna one, and the Jagannath cult became a state religion. Meanwhile, in the south, the rulers could sponsor almost all the gods in their uniquely vast temple complexes where countless shrines could each serve a different god.

OUT AND ABOUT *The ghats:* Follow Edward Lear's recommendation for seeing Varanasi from a boat and get out on the water both for sunrise and sunset. One 4am start is essential – sleep off the shock around the pool later. As dawn breaks, the notes of the shehna (reed instrument) played by the great Bismillah Khan on the terrace of Shiva (or Shanka) Temple echo across the Ganga. The dawn light on the Ganga is unique. In the half-dark, you take a little boat from Dasaswanadh Ghat and go first up river to Asi Ghat, then back and on at least to Panchganga Ghat. (To feel the atmosphere and peace, avoid going with a group, even if it costs more.)

Pilgrims can be seen on the shore, rousing themselves on the ghats beneath the palaces of the maharajas of Varanasi, Jaipur, Udaipur,

Gwalior, Mysore. They needed salvation too, but in comfort. Some are occupied by squatters now. Boatmen dump the odd corpse in the river, an honour permitted only to a Sadhu (holy man) and those who die of small-pox, because they are possessed by Sitala, goddess of fever diseases who might be injured by cremation. Every year, the powdery remains of the other 35,000 or so bodies are thrown into the water after cremation.

As the sun rises, the faithful flow down to the holy water, washing begins and the city comes alive. Of the 80 or so ghats, each with a Shiva lingum (phallic emblem), five (the panchtirath) are especially sacred and should be visited by a pilgrim in one day, in this order: Asi, Dasaswanadh (where Brahma sacrificed 10 horses), Barnasangam, Panchganga (where the four other sacred rivers of India are said to mingle) and Manikarnika (the most sacred, where Mahadeo dug the tank to find Parvati's earring; also the principal burning ghat, where the most privileged families are burnt on the Charanpaduka slab marked with the imprint of Vishnu's feet).

Other ghats have their own importance and are interesting to visit strolling under the rich, late afternoon sunlight, or in another boat, having slept off the morning's effort.

Starting in the south, Asi Ghat is where pilgrims bathe in the confluence of the Asi and Ganga waters. Next comes Tulsi Ghat commemorating the poet Gosain Tulsi Das who translated the Ramayana and died here in 1623. The sewage pumps out under Janki Ghat. Bachhraj Ghat is Jain. Shivala (or Kali) Ghat has a splendid Shiva lingum and is owned by the ex-Maharaja of Varanasi, who is an accomplished musician and an active force in the city. As a devout Brahmin, he bathes in the holy water daily. Hanuman Ghat is popular with devotees of the monkey-god. Nearby, the Dandi Paths (a cult of ascetics) use Dandi Ghat. Harish Chandra (or Smashan) Ghat, named after a Hindu drama hero who worked on this ghat, is one of two burning ghats (the other is Manikarnika). Kedar Ghat has fine lingums and temple. Mansarowar Ghat is named after a lake just inside Tibet which is near the Ganga's source and at the foot of Kailash Mountain where Shiva lives.

At Someswar Ghat, meaning 'moon-lord', the diseased are cured. Ahalya Bai's Ghat was built by the able Mahratta princess who governed Indore 1767-95. Man Mandir Ghat is beside yet another of Jai Singh's observatories (also at Jaipur, Delhi, Ujjain). Lalita Ghat leads to the Nepalese Temple full of erotic paintings, and further inland to the Golden Temple. The famous burning ghat with a heap of temples is Jalsain (photography forbidden), named after Vishnu's form of Jalsai (sleeper on the ocean). Dattatreya Ghat is named after a Brahmin

teacher-saint believed to be incarnated with the Trinity: Brahma, Vishnu and Shiva. Finally, the Trilochan Ghat is where pilgrims bathe in the specially sacred water between its two turrets. The akhara wrestling and malkham acrobatics are staged near here.

In the city the most interesting thing to do is to wander in the gullies and peep into the temples, especially around the Golden Temple (which is not open to non-Hindus, only partially visible from the balcony opposite and not worth it; the other temples are open to all). If you peep into the dilapidated palaces you will see the carved wood, marble and brass of former grandeur. Paan shops sell the special Varanasi patta, relished throughout India and second only to the Calcutta maghai. There are also bhang (hashish) shops on every corner, selling all sorts of varieties prepared by different rituals – sometimes even in sweetmeats and drinks. To the south is the red-stained Durga (Monkey) Temple next to the Tulsi Manas Temple which has the Ramayana told in relief inside. Beyond is the Banaras Hindu University (known as BHU) where the Bharat Kala Bhavan is one of the finest museums in India, with a magnificent collection of Indian miniature paintings and sculptures (usually open Mon.-Sat., 11am-4pm).

From here, the ferry sets off across the river to the 18th century *Ramnagar Fort* where the ex-Maharaja of Varanasi still lives, complete with pet elephant, vintage Cadillac, court ceremonial and audiences. (Fort and museum open daily, roughly 10am-noon; 2-5pm.) The archaeological digs here have revealed evidence of Varanasi's existence in the 9th century BC.

To eat in town, both the Diamond Hotel at Belupur and the Chinese *Win-Fa* at Lahurabir are reliable. But the local favourite is *Hotel Padis Poonam* in Jagatgunj. Varanasi vies with Calcutta in sweetmeat fame; taste kheer mohan, pista burfi, the delicious chum-chum (oval-shaped, coated with dessicated coconut and sometimes stuffed with mallai-cream) and rasgulla at *Kamdhenu*, *Luxa* in Guruduara Market or *Ram Bhandar* at Thatheri Bazar in the Chowk area. An excellent snack is pati (also called chiky), a sort of sweet bar of jaggery (raw sugar) and nuts.

SHOPPING AND CRAFTS There is no Handloom House in Varanasi, nor good government emporia, except a huge Kashmiri one (with high prices) opposite the Taj hotel. Shopping is done in the bazaars: Satti bazar for saris; Thatheri bazar for silver and traditional Varanasi or Moradabad brass (the pinker the better, showing high copper content; the gleaming buckets are irresistible); Gadolia and the whole central Chowk area for everything (especially toys).

Fabrics The hand-woven, sumptuous Varanasi

silk brocades are the best buy. These were the finest fabrics of the 16th century Mughal court, although at that time Varanasi was famous for its muslins and zari cloth (like cloth of gold) rather than kinkhabs (brocades of metal threads worked on a silk ground). Varanasi brocades are still the flashiest today. Gold, silver and silk threads are woven into heavy, textured saris and stoles, with an all-over design of small motifs. Some can be bought by the metre. The guldasta kinkhab (flower bouquet gold cloth) is so thick it can only be draped as a shawl; a gyasar has Buddhist motifs; a latifa has rows of buti (flowers); a badal me phul has a free pattern of clouds and flowers.

These are classics, so expect to pay for a work of art, a combination of top quality materials (Karnataka silk, real silver and gold-polished silver thread) and master weavers' skills. The finest cost up to Rs20,000, but there are perfectly beautiful cheaper ones. Beware: ignore young men who ask, usually in a single breath: 'Please may I practise my English would you like to come for a cup of tea and see my uncle's silk factory?', often adding, for good measure, 'My cousin will give you very good massage'.

Find the best fabrics at Brij Raman Das (in a beautiful old house) and Ushnak Malmulchan (also branches in Delhi and Madras), where discerning Indian women shop. Mohan Lal Kishan Chan keeps the Bombay film actresses swathed in metres of top quality brocade. More modest spending is at Ram Bhaj Rosham Lal at Chowk and Bhagwan Lila Exports, Sundunagar. If you ask to see the fabric for export, you may be taken across town to the warehouse and have a much better selection. And do not miss the daily silk market, found through an arch off Thatheri Bazar. Here, in a tight-knit maze of tiny alleys, the handloom weavers bring their wares into town in the late afternoon and sell them to plump dealers sitting in little cubicles carpeted in white cotton and furnished with a sari-box, money-box, calculator and telephone. The hardest work is done November to February; there is no weaving in July and August. To visit the weavers, either in the Pili Kothi area or out in the villages, ask at one of the shops or at the tourist office, or contact the Institute of Handloom Technology and Weavers' Service Centre, Chowk (tel: 54534/65294).

The classic, tightly knotted carpets from Mirzapur and Bandoli are big buys and should be undertaken with great care (see p. 72).

ASHRAMS For health in mind and body. There are several around Varanasi, on the whole reputable and not the Swiss bank account variety. Two recommended are Mata Anand Mayi Ashram and Bharat Seva Sangh Ashram.

Forays into UP and Bihar

HEADING NORTH
SARNATH

11km. The cradle of BUDDHISM, whose archaeological remains are suffused with both historical-religious atmosphere and the contemporary peace of visiting Buddhist pilgrims. Here, on a July full moon around 528BC, Buddha preached his first sermon, after he had received enlightenment. Called 'Setting in Motion the Wheel of Righteousness', it set out life's problem and its solution, advocated moderation (the Middle Path) and became the essence of Buddhist teaching. Before this, Buddha was a royal prince, Siddhartha (later known as Gautama), probably born around 563BC, who renounced his family and went in search of peace and an end to suffering. It is thought he was about 35 years old when, after years of meditation at Gaya in Bihar (now called Bodhgaya, see below), he attained enlightenment and began his mission to impart it to others.

After his first sermon here at Sarnath, he toured India as the leading spiritual teacher of his day, preaching and converting, and organising his followers into an ascetic monastic order called the Sangha.

Reacting against the current Hindu brahmins' emphasis on complex abstract philosophy and against detailed ritual, Buddha expounded a practical dogma in everyday language. The essence was dhamma (religion), sangha (monasticism) and bodhi (enlightenment), but no extremes. Buddha proclaimed the Four Noble Truths: sorrow, cause of sorrow, the path to ending sorrow, and the end of sorrow. He reasoned that the root cause of all human misery is desire. Thus, to kill desire would be to have perpetual happiness. And the way to kill desire is to follow the Noble Eightfold Path: right conduct in belief, thought, speech, action, means of livelihood, endeavour, vigilance and meditation – and again, no extremes of luxury or austerity. He also called this the Middle Path, a way of life that working people could follow to find spiritual peace.

After Buddha's death in 483BC, a council of 500 Buddhists was convened who edited his sermons. At the second council, there was a schism and two sects emerged. The Hinayana who regarded Buddha as the Great Master, followed the Eightfold Path and used Pali language for their texts; and the Mahayanas who raised Buddha to the position of Saviour God, worshipped his idols, used Sanskrit and adopted Hindu ideas of bhakti – it was this form which spread to China, Japan, Tibet and Mongolia while Hinayana Buddhism is found in Sri Lanka, Burma and Thailand.

Devoid of any philosophical speculations, Buddha's practical code won great popularity. The Mauryan emperor Ashoka (ruled c.273-236BC), whose capital was at nearby Patna (see below), converted and made it a state religion. It was he who put up monuments at places associated with Buddha, erected the Ashoka columns in far-flung market places to propagate it, and sent monks off to take the new religion to Nepal and Sri Lanka. After the Mauryas, the Shungas (central India), Kushanas (Gandhara and Mathura) and Guptas continued royal patronage.

Of the two sects, the Mahayanas triumphed, partly because they devised a series of Bodhisattvas, close followers of Buddha who attained nirvana but postponed it to show others the way. As in later medieval Europe, Mahayana monasteries were often also universities attracting students from all over the sub-continent and beyond. When they returned home, they disseminated their ideas, so that by the 6th century Mahayana Buddhism had reached the Far East where it would have a lasting impetus.

Conversely, back in India the following century, Hinduism made a new bid for popularity and Buddhism, increasingly complex, began to lose out to it. By the 12th century, Buddhism in India, the country of its origin, was confined to the Himalayan valleys. Today, the small Buddhist revival in India has raised the faithful to 0.7% of the population. Japan is paying for the restoration of holy sites and the building of rest houses, while the Tibetan monks fleeing the Chinese desecration of their monasteries have, with their spiritual leader the Dalai Lama, made India their home.

Here at Sarnath, where it all began, some imagination is needed to bring what was a thriving monastic centre to life. The monastery's 3rd century decline and subsequent Muslim destruction have left little. From the entrance to the left of the museum, find Ashoka's great Dharmarajika Stupa left of the path and, sloping down behind, the Main Shrine, Ashoka's column and various monastic buildings; on the right of the path find a monastery, Jain temple and the cylindrical Dhamekh Stupa, Sarnath's best surviving building. The capital of the Ashoka pillar, carved with back-to-back lions, is now the official symbol of India and is preserved in the excellent (but badly labelled) museum, together with fine Gupta sculptures (open Sat.-Thurs., 10am-5pm). Essential guide-book to Sarnath by V. S. Agrawala available at the ticket office. Buddha Purnima festival celebrates Buddha's birth with a big fair and procession on the day of the full moon in May.

HEADING NORTH-WEST
JAUNPUR

58km. Deemed 'an absolute must' by all-knowing architectural historian Christopher Tadgell, for its four fantastic mosques. Reach there by road or train, taking a picnic ('there's nowhere to eat') to enjoy in perfect peace of what a tourist official in Delhi dubbed 'not a tourist destination'. Once the capital of the large Muslim Sharqui kingdom which, while guarding the eastern borders of Delhi's Tughlaq empire, put up remarkable Indo-Islamic buildings. When Sikandar Lodi (later to be crushed by Babur) sacked it, only the mosques survived devastation. Seek out first the Mosque of Shaikh Barha (1311) at Zafarabad (6km); then head back across the Gumti river over the splendid Akbari Bridge (1564-8), with its elephant milestone. Beyond the fort (1360), the four great mosques start with Atala Masjid (1408). Then, catch the fragmented Jhanjiri Masjid (1430) before finding the next three: the largest ambitious Jami Masjid (1458-79), the Khalis Mukhlis Masjid (1430) and finally the smaller Lal Darwaza Masjid (1450). Architecturally, all have pylon-like, almost Egyptian facades, two-storey arcades and huge gateways.

HEADING SOUTH-WEST
CHUNAR

15km. West of Ramnagar, excellent for space, fresh air and picnic. The old fort on the hill was taken by Humayun in 1537, lost to the Afghans, retaken by Akbar and finally became British. There are fine Mughal tombs and, beneath the fort, a very interesting British cemetery. Until 1860, soldiers who had married Indian women, and therefore wanted to retire in India instead of going home, could take half their pension and come to live at Chunar. Many are buried here, and later generations of an Anglo-Indian community still live on, eking out meagre finances in their beautiful decaying houses. Beyond here lies Mirzapur whose noisy streets, like a festival of percussion instruments in full swing, clang to the sounds of thousands of brass-beaters. Outside, the famous carpets are woven in rural factories and mostly sold for export.

HEADING EAST
INTO BIHAR ON THE BUDDHIST TRAIL

If the Buddhist remains of Sarnath interest you, this is the time to do a trip eastwards to a rich package of holy sites – and a few other treats. But be warned: accommodation may be simple, the roads and facilities in rural Bihar are not geared up to the comfort-conscious traveller. It is wise to travel with food and water supplies at all times. Gaya and Patna have airports.

Those who want to get the most out of this area, which is not an easy thing to do without plenty of reading and, for the remains, plenty of archaeological understanding, might consider doing so with a guide, particularly north of Patna. Shantum Seth, a lay Buddhist and student of the Vietnamese Zen Master Thich Nhat Hanh, leads what he calls 'A Pilgrimage in the Footsteps of the Buddha through India and Nepal' every December and January. Each trip is 2-3 weeks long, visiting at a gentle pace all 8 of the pilgrimage sites associated with Buddha, with optional meditation en route; he also arranges special trips at any time; contact Seth Consultant Pvt Ltd, 40/42 Janpath (1st floor), Peareylal Building, New Delhi 110001 (tel: 3015467; fax: 3323676; telex: 031.61919). For other information contact the Government of India Tourist Office, Room no.151, Tourist Bhawan, Birchand Patel Path, Patna (tel:226721); or the Bihar State Tourist Information Centre, Fraser Road, Patna (tel: 25295) – their Delhi office at 5 State Emporia Complex, Baba Kharak Singh Mark, New Delhi (tel: 343081) is good, too.

Out on the Grand Trunk Road lined with mature trees, the first stop is *Sasaram* (100km) to see Sher Shah Sur's magnificent, five-storey, mid-lake tomb (1540-45), constructed by him to designs by Aliwal Khan, admired by the India cognoscenti and given tops marks by historian Giles Tillotson: 'In terms of compositional harmony and power of form, [this] is one of the finest works of architecture in India'. A good picnic spot, too.

To *Bodhgaya* (130km), where the Buddhist trail begins. This is where he meditated and received enlightenment, beneath the bodhi tree, which then became an important Buddhist religious centre; see Maurya, Shunga, Gupta and Pala remains, plus the great Mahabodhi temple complex (7th century onwards) and the museum. To stay, various simple rest houses include *Travellers Lodge* and *Mahabodhi Society Pilgrims Rest*, a *PWD Inspection Bungalow* (if no civil servants need it) and, the most upmarket, the *Bodhgaya Ashok* (tel: 22708-9).

On to *Gaya* (10km), more important for Hindus who come to perform pujas for the souls of their ancestors, see the museum for Bodhgaya sculptures. From here, there are two routes to Patna. The short one is via the *Barabar* and *Nagarjuni* hills to see three very early Mauryan period rock-cut temples (3rd century BC). The longer one, via Rajgir and Nalanda, is more interesting. The ancient Magadha kingdom, often visited by Buddha, had its capital at *Rajgir*. Its ruler, Bimbisara, was converted and the first council was held here – the city is also sacred to Jains, since Mahavira came often, too; from the present village, it takes a good amount of walk-

ing (plus some imagination) to explore the hilly site of the ancient city. Plenty of modest accommodation. At *Nalanda* (10km), also visited by both Buddha and Mahavira, there are more substantial remains of the great monastery and university which flourished in the 7th century (Hiuen Tsang and I-Tsing studied here) and was the principal seat of learning in Eastern India under the Palas. To stay, *Nalanda PWD Rest House* (civil servants permitting) or three dharamshalas.

Everyone agrees that *Patna* (102km from Rajgir, 178km from Bodhgaya) is not a pretty city, and that its traffic system is such that once inside it, it is hard to escape. But this once glorious capital of the Mauryan empire on the banks of the Ganga is worth plunging into on this trip for its superb museum on Budh Marg. Bihar's state collection includes glorious early sculptures such as Kushana Jain saviours, Gandhara Bodhisattvas, Pala Buddhist figures, a Hindu Vishnu and Ganesh and quantities of quality finds from nearby Nalanda, made there during its 9th-century artistic heyday; open Tues.-Sun., 10.30am-4.30pm. Colonialists can also explore Patna's British buildings, while archaeologists can visit Kumrahar Excavation site where ancient city remains dating between 600BC and 600AD are being revealed. To stay, the best is the Welcomgroup's *Maurya-Patna*, South Gandhi Maidan (tel: 22061; telex: 022-352), 80 rooms, all mod. cons, swimming pool.

The trip can end here, with a flight or train to the next destination.

The hardy can continue on the Buddhist trail. First stop is *Vaishali* (55km), a small village among banana and mango groves and rice fields where Mahavira was born and where Buddha spent his last rainy season. Local Licchavi rulers erected a stupa (5th century BC) over Buddha's relics and Ashoka put up one of his columns (3rd century BC), this one unpolished and lacking inscriptions. To *Lauria Areraj* (150km) for another, better Ashoka column, this one well polished and bearing six edicts. Finally, to *Lauria Nandangar* (100km), where collapsed stupas are scattered over the two sites, with one survivor (in which Buddha's ashes were perhaps enshrined) and another Ashoka column, with seven edicts. To stay, various modest rest houses; railway at Shikarpur (14km).

Orissa

A green, fertile and almost entirely agricultural state strewn with densely carved, beehive-shaped temples and tiny villages of red houses, the exteriors exquisitely decorated with white rice-flour paintings. There is even fresh air, good beaches and a traditional seaside hotel. It is the complete antithesis of Calcutta's stifling, seedy splendour and overcrowding. Indeed, Orissa is so unindustrialised that rural Bhubaneswar hardly seems fit to be the capital of its 25 million Oriyans, 23% of whom live in the hills in more than sixty tribal groups. Some great monuments from Orissa's days of glory are in the capital. Most important are the group of temples built at the height of Oriyan Hindu culture between the 7th and 15th centuries. Through paddy fields and villages lies the Sun Temple at Konarak built in the shape of a huge chariot and covered in carvings.

The seaside resort of Puri is just down the road, where the Jagganath temple's huge and magnificent festival chariot gave its name to the ugly, thunderous juggernaut lorries of Europe. The June-July *Rath Yatra* festival is one of the most spectacular of all Indian festivals, when Puri is over-run with pilgrims. To commemorate Krishna's journey from Gokul to Mathura, the images of Jagganath and his brother and sister are hauled through Puri on vast raths (chariots), so heavy they need the strength of 4,000 temple inmates to pull them. The gods are then left at the Gundicha Mandir (garden house) for their annual week's holiday before being dragged back home. Then, with a healthy religious entrepreneurship, the raths are broken up and sold as instant relics.

THE HARD FACTS Inland, the best season is September-March, and Bhubaneswar's Tribal Fair of arts, crafts and performance arts held at the end of January is well worth catching. Puri is a popular breather for Calcuttans all the year round. Either studiously head for or absolutely avoid the Rath Yatra festival. Other popular times are the October Durga Puja festival, and May to September when Calcutta is unbearable, the courts close and the legal profession along with everyone else head for the sea or the hills. The pre-monsoon breakers (May-June) produce the best surf, but there is a dangerous undercurrent. Bhubaneswar (61km) makes the best base for sight-seeing; Gopalpur-on-sea is a bit far away and best used as a pure beach resort, with the option of some pioneering travel southwards.

From Calcutta, daily flights go to Bhubaneswar. There are direct flights from Hyderabad (Tues., Thurs., Sat.) and Varanasi (Tues., Thurs. Sat., Sun.). Overnight train to Puri is more fun, at least one way. The Howrah-Puri Express leaves Calcutta at 8.50pm, arriving 8.35am; the Puri-Howrah Express leaves Puri at 6.05pm, arriving 5.30am. For Gopalpur-on-sea, the Howrah-Madras Mail leaves Calcutta 8pm, arriving Berhampur 6.42am; the reverse journey leaves at 10.20pm and arrives at 6.16am. Hire a car on arrival or through the hotel, bargaining hard for an all-in flat price until your departure.

THE HOTELS
In **Bhubaneswar,** choose from four hotels covering all prices.
Bhubaneswar Oberoi, Nayapalli, (tel: 56116; telex 0675 348). Opened in 1986, the Oberoi Group's large new hotel imitates local temple architecture. Equipped with 70 rooms, business centre, pool, tennis courts and gardens. 1990 reports of lovely architecture but musty smells, so it is vital to ask for the room to be well aired in advance of arrival; to make up, charming and helpful staff, good picnics produced for the day trips.
The *Kenilworth*, Gautam Nagar, (tel: 54330/1; telex:0675 343); 72 rooms and all mod. cons including swimming pool in this friendly sister hotel to its Calcutta namesake.
Hotel Kalinga Ashok, Gautam Nagar (tel: 53318; telex 0675 282; cable: TOURISM). Clean, pleasant, 64 rooms, attached bath, car rental, mod. cons.
Hotel Swosti, 103 Janpath (tel: 54178/56617; cable SWOSTI).

Government of India Tourist Office, B-21 Kalpana Area (tel: 54203); Orissa State Tourist Office nearby, down the lane beside Pantha Nivas Tourist Bungalow, who sometimes run day trips to Konorak; ask here to see training classes at the Odissi Dance Academy or the College of Dance and Music. Maureen Liebl's *Guide to Orissa* (1989) is excellent, available at either office.

In **Puri,** stay at the *South Eastern Railway Hotel*, Chakratirtha Road (tel: 63; cable: SURF); built as the home of Lady Ashworth, bought by the Bengal-Nagpur Railway with land going right down to the sea. Opened as a hotel in 1925. Still known affectionately as 'the BNR' by Calcuttans, although the BNR was taken over by the SER some 30 years ago. Puri was the Brighton of India, frequented by both Raj and maharajas and, later, ambassadors. J. K. Galbraith came when he was ambassador to India and loved it (the hotel built him an extra long bed): 'I am not what you might call a beach man . . . with the single exception of Puri in India where the main attraction is an excellent hotel set well back from the sand.'

It is now a period piece, somewhat run down but fun if you enter the spirit and have some Indian experience. Guests and staff alike can look as pukka (and slightly worn out) as an amateur cast for an an Agatha Christie play. 37 spacious rooms, some with sea view. Spacious verandahs with green and red cane chairs overlook well-kept lawns and bright flower-beds. Huge Raj nursery meals (saved by the very fresh fish course – they will try to get lobster, if asked) are included in room price – porridge for breakfast, fruit cake for tea.

One is expected to take a siesta: notices upstairs read: 'silence please, 2-4pm and 10.30pm-7.30am' – one recent guest was 'told off for laughing too loudly one night'. There are billiards, table tennis and books; swimming is not advisable (dirty beach, undercurrent), but a walk along the shore to find fishermen is. Note: payment is by travellers' cheques or cash. No credit cards.

If the BNR does not tempt, try this, right on the beach: *Prachi Sun and Beach Hotel* (tel: 638; cable: PRACHI). 37 double rooms, attached bath, car rental, very new but promising, some Oriyan decoration. Ground-floor rooms have small verandah and then sand.

Three hours down the coast the Oberoi chain have a hotel at **Gopalpur-on-Sea**, *Hotel Oberoi Palm Beach* (tel: 23; cable: OBHOTEL); 172km from Bhubaneswar, 16km from Berhampur railway station (the way to arrive from Calcutta). A oldish building of 20 rooms set around a courtyard and strung along the garden facing the sea; car rental, tennis, baby sitter. 100 metres from the sea, where fishermen bring in their catch on to the empty golden sands. Arrangements made for riding, sailing and fishing. Very relaxed and quiet, with good local food on request.

OUT AND ABOUT Once you have enjoyed the Bhubaneswar temples, it is well worth getting out into rural Orissa.

BHUBANESWAR
Known as Ekamrakshetra during the medieval period when it was one of five religious centres in Orissa. The enlightened 7th-8th century Shailodbhava and Bhauma Kara rulers were followed by the 9th-10th century Somavamshis who brought a distinctive temple architecture to its height, to be continued by the Eastern Ganga rulers. The keen temple building in the 7th century both secured a place in heaven and showed off wealth and power to fellow mortals. It maintained its vigour so that by the 15th century, some 7,000 sandstone temples surrounded the main tank alone (glorious at sunset), of which about 500 partly or wholly survived the Mughal conquest of the 16th century.

The temple design was governed by strict mathematical rules down to the tiniest detail. But basically each temple had an entrance (jagamohan) and a sanctum for the deity (deul) which had the bee-hive tower (sikhara) above. Endless extras could be added, from dancing halls to sub-temples and shrines. The earlier small, squat shrines developed into large, ostentatious temples of increasingly slender proportions. Every outside surface was carved with geometric designs, flowers, animals and cavorting or loving gods and humans. Carvings

are modest and story-telling at first, cut in shallow relief. Later, there are more single female figures, cut in high relief and given increasing delicacy and seductive charms. They reach their height of joyful sensuality at the Rajarani and Brahmesvara temples and at Konarak on the Sun Temple. The interiors were usually left plain.

Note: the Lingaraja temple, considered by Hindu experts to be the finest, is not open to non-Hindus, who may peer at it from a platform but can see little. Better to look closely at a range of the other good ones, to see the special Oriyan temple architecture and its decoration: Parasuramesvara, 7th century, tiny, lavishly carved, an early stone Orissan building; Vaital Deul, slightly later, carving freer and more elegant; Muktesvara (10th century), almost perfect proportions coated with vibrant, delicate carving; Rajarani (early 11th century), very fine in architecture and in its spirited and vibrant carvings, especially the nayikas (females); and Ananta-Vasudeva (1278), the form almost a mini- Lingaraja temple, the carving rich and profuse, similar to the contemporary Konorak carving.

Visit also the state museum, with well displayed archaeological and crafts departments, and the Tribal Research Institute (both open Tues.- Sun., 10am-5pm).

Just outside the town, to the south, are the part excavated ruins of *Sisupalgarh*, occupied from the 3rd century BC to the 4th century AD, thick with pottery shards (best reached on foot across the fields from Brahmesvara Temple). At *Dhauli* (8km) are a set of edicts by the Mauryan emperor Ashoka (c273-236BC), one of the earliest inscribed records in India (with an English translation set up nearby). Ashoka was India's Constantine, a fierce, warring tyrant who, after winning the Kalinga wars near here, turned to Buddha and followed the path of peace. In these edicts he states: 'All men are my children'. The elephant boldly carved out of the rock above the edicts symbolises Buddha, 'best of elephants', and is the earliest known sculpture in Orissa. *Hirapur* has the Chaunsath Yognini temple (11th century) whose carved dancing goddesses hold weapons and emblems for identification. Finally, *Pipli* (20km) sells tourist junk in its streets while its good appliqué work is sold in Bhubaneswar.

Also just out of town, but to the north, the extensive and important Jain cave temples (1st century BC) in the *Udayagiri* and *Khandagir* hills (5km) are the earliest known art in the region, best visited at sunset for good views over the surrounding plain.

For eating, Oriyan food is similar to Bengali. There is plenty of fish: bekti, rui and sometimes lobster, prawns and crab; an Oriyan thali has puris, pappa, white rice, fish, vegetable (perhaps kara saag, spinach) and sweet. The Oriyan speciality is chena purda patha, meaning cheese-burnt-sweet, and is just like caramel custard – very settling for the stomach.

SHOPPING AND CRAFTS It is important to buy the superb fabrics and crafts of Orissa now, in Bhubaneswar; a few are available in Delhi, Calcutta and Varanasi; almost none in Bombay. (Cuttack has some fabric shops; Puri has a good bazaar-like town centre; Konorak has just the temple.) There is a riot of choice: good appliqué work (including glorious sun umbrellas), terracotta toys, bold papier mâché masks (elephant, lion, etc., originally used for the epic dramas), playing cards, bell-metal bowls and plates, brass dhokra work (cast by the lost wax method) from Mayurbhanj and Barapali, patta chitra (Puri paintings) on muslin, wood carving using the almost grainless white gumbhari tree and Bhubaneswar's tarkashi (silver filigree) from Cuttack, still showing the flat, intricate Islamic designs brought by the Mughals. Find much of this at Orissa State Emporium, Utkalika (East Tower Market Building).

Fabrics One of India's finest weaves is the cotton or silk weave of Orissa called the *double ikat*. For this, the warp and weft threads for the whole sari are first tie-dyed according to the pattern, then woven together – a technical and artistic triumph. The different designs of each area are still very distinct, unlike Andhra Pradesh where they are losing their individuality. Maniabandha saris often have a pink field; Sambalpuri saris have very clear designs and often a brocade effect in the weaving; but top notch is a Sonepur silk sari woven with rows of clear, small figures, elephants, flowers and fish.

Crafts and some fabrics can be found at Orissa Co-operative Handicraft Corporation, Hall No. 1, East Market Building (where Mr Burma will give directions for seeing craftsmen at work). The best fabrics are at Handloom Weavers' Co-operative, Hall No.2, West Market Building (open Mon.-Sat., 9am-noon; 4-9pm). Other good fabric shops in Market Building, and Gauri Handicrafts in the old town has a good selection. Modern Book Department, New Market stocks books on Orissa. In principle, everything closes for a siesta, noon-4pm, and all day Thurs. Note: Very few credit cards are accepted in Orissa shops. Master weavers can be seen at Maniabhanda and Nuapatna (70km, see below).

DAY TRIP OUT OF BHUBANESWAR
Head north-east to *Lalitgiri, Udayagiri* and *Ratnagiri* (90km) for Buddhist relics, stopping at *Cuttack* to see the Barabati Fort and to wander the delightful Nayasarak and Balu Bazar to find local silver filigree work. Ratnagiri was from the

5th to 12th centuries Orissa's main Buddhist centre, with monasteries and university; see stupas, monasteries and temples, with less substantial Buddhist remains at the two neighbouring sites. On the way back, the temple-keen can detour west from Cuttack through the Buddhist weaving villages of *Maniabandha* and *Nuapatna* to *Simhanatha* where the island in the middle of the Mahanadi river (reached from Baideswar or Baramba) has a beautiful and well-preserved early temple (8th century), well worth the effort.

TOURING INLAND FROM BHUBANESWAR
The hills inland are home for Orissa's *tribals*, the official word describing various indigenous people who have remained outside the mainstream of Indian life. Some still live very isolated lives, others have settled to become agriculturalists, others have become skilled workers and follow a formal Indian lifestyle. For anyone interested in tribal life, this is a fascinating area to explore, but it is essential to have a good guide (ExplorAsia does good trips, see p. 7). As one middle-aged traveller enthused on her recent return: 'Be prepared to wash in rivers and draw your own water from wells, but if you've got gumption and want to get close to the poeple and the land, this is the way'. It is not tough travelling: tenting and camping with a cook, outrider and two drivers. And the rewards are 'a kaleidoscope of memories – short people dressed in nothing but beads, men with long hair scooped up with brightly-coloured plastic combs, women wearing huge brass bangles, people living by bartering for what they need'.

TOURING SOUTH-EAST FROM BHUBANESWAR
A trip to *Konarak* (64km) is a must, taking supplies of food and drink. On the way, make a quick detour after Pipli to *Chaurasi* to catch a good temple (10th century). *Konarak* has one of the finest temples in India which must be clambered over to enjoy the carving. (The inside is filled with sand, to prevent it collapsing.) First stop, however, should be at the small but good museum which stocks Debala Mitra's guide to Konarak (closed Fri.).

The restored temple was probably built in the 13th century to celebrate the Eastern Ganga ruler Narasimha's war victory and marks the peak of Orissan architecture. It symbolises Surya, the sun-god, and looks like a vast stone chariot with 12 pairs of wheels, drawn by 7 galloping horses, every facet richly carved, some very delicate, some equally bold, with scenes of love, royal hunts and military processions and huge, free-standing elephants and beasts.

Then on, down the open coast road to *Puri* (30km), a quiet, slightly has-been resort, full of charm. The stylish Bengali villas are now a bit dilapidated. But it has a lovely seaside atmosphere and feels as if ice-cream and candy-floss should be on sale. A good place to relax and swim. Old Puri town should be visited at sunset. The Jagganath temple, the focus of the town, is not open to non-Hindus, but can be seen by going to Ragunandan library which is on the first floor of the market square opposite the temple. The librarian will show you on to the roof (and supply a stick for warding off the monkeys). The sun setting behind the temple is beautiful. A donation to the library is expected afterwards. It has a good collection of 16th-18th century Pali manuscripts available on request Mon.-Sat., 9am-noon; 4-8pm).

As darkness falls, the whole town twinkles with the lights of shops and stalls and the air is filled with chattering, shouting and delicious smells as the huge bazaar rumbles into action for the whole evening. Holy men take up their positions near the temple. Some sit inside a thorn bush, only the begging hands poking out. In dark side-streets old people queue at the bars of now illegal opium shops that were once so common.

South of here lies *Chilka Lake* (good migratory bird life October-January) and, beyond, Gopalpur-on-Sea for total relaxation (see p. 200) before returning to Bhubaneswar (168km).

SOUTHWARDS INTO ANDHRA PRADESH

From Orissa, the adventurous traveller can go further south to Mukhalingam and Vishakapatnam, both just inside the state of Andhra Pradesh. The road to Vishakapatnam goes via Berahampur to *Mukhalingam* (130km), the first capital of the Eastern Gangas; three good temples in the Orissa tradition: Madhukeshvara (8th century), 'one of the best-preserved examples of the early Orissan style' (Michell); Bhimeshvara (8th century), similar to it; and Someshvara (10th century). It is another 150km to *Vishakapatnam*, now a major east coast industrial town but in the 15th century a port for powerful Vijayanagar (see South chapter). Today, avoid the factories in favour of miles of totally unspoilt beaches, especially Rishikonda and Lawson's Bay; the local landmark is The Dolphin's Nose, a great rock jutting into the sea near the harbour. Locals come to the sea for cooling walks; South Indians come for holiday relaxation; not a European in sight.

OUT AND ABOUT   Vizig, (as Vishakapatnam is known), and its beaches make a good base for several outings. *Simhachalam* (16km) has a magnificent Varaha Narasimha temple (13th century) built by the military commander of Narasimha, the Eastern Ganga ruler who built Konarak's temple; the central temple is very Orissan; the gateway is a giant southern-style gopuram. *Bheemunipatnam* (24km), down the coast, has a calm and especially nice beach plus remains of the charming 17th century Dutch settlement, Hollanders Green (fort and cemetery). *Sankaram* (41km) has somewhat dilapidated Buddhist monuments and interesting rock-cut caves on its pretty hills.

For a very special trip into the countryside, take a picnic to the ancient *Borra Cave* (90km) with their stalgmites and stalactites; then go on to the very beautiful *Araku Valley* (30km) to stay overnight (possible to do all this as a delightful, rural train journey). Araku is a lush green valley in the Ananthagiri hills peopled by almost 20 different tribes who live among the fine trees, plants, Zilda waterfalls and even small coffee plantations; to stay, various guest houses include *Forest Rest House, PWD Inspection Bungalow* (civil servants permitting) and *ATTDC Tourist Guest House*.

For an off-beat day, *Vizianagram* (27km northwest of Bimlipatam), founded in 1712, is where successive maharajas have built a fine fort, palace and town including a commemoration of the Prince of Wales's India visit of 1875. But you might just want to saunter beside the waves of the Bay of Bengal.

To get to Vishakapatnam from Gopalpur-on-Sea, drive down the coast road or take a train; overnight trains from Calcutta come here direct. Flights connect with Calcutta, Hyderabad and Madras. Since Vishakapatnam is an old-established beach resort, there is a wide variety of hotels: *Park Hotel*, Beach Road (tel: 63081; telex: 0495 230) is the swishest in town, with 64 rooms, all mod. cons plus swimming pool; *Ocean View Inn*, Kirlampudi (tel: 54828; telex: 0495 388), 30 rooms, is cheap and modest; and other similar ones with evocative titles such as *Palm Beach, Sea Pearl* and *Silver Sands Inn* seem to beckon with bucket and spade. Simhachalam temple's Chandan Yatri festival is March-April.

Wildlife sanctuaries

Eastern India is rich in wildlife sanctuaries. Here some of the most important research is being carried out on how best to save endangered species and increase their numbers. The gharial crocodile is one current subject. Notable success stories are the great Indian one-horned rhinoceros – called the 'hideous' unicorn by Marco Polo – and the wild buffalo, both to be seen in the uniquely unspoilt tracts of Assam in Kaziranga and Manas. If permits are being issued for either sanctuary, then go if at all possible.

Kanha, Madhya Pradesh: see Bombay chapter.

KAZIRANGA, ASSAM
Season February-May. Fly to Jorhat, then 96km by road. Advance booking (rooms and elephants) and permit essential. Three weeks before your intended departure either go to a travel agent or apply direct to the Divisional Forest Office, Sibsagar Division, Jorhat. If short of time, cable the Officer in Charge, Kohara Tourist Lodge. Stay at ITDC *Kaziranga Forest Lodge* (see Assam and Permits sections, p. 190, 191), and ask for a room with balcony and view, good facilities, occasional dance programmes. Explore by elephant, car and boat.

430 sqkm of forest, swamps, plain and the totally wild Baguri area. The park was established in 1908 when poachers had reduced the rhino count to a mere dozen. The Chinese pay high prices for the blood, skin, urine and bones, believing them to have medicinal and magical properties – and the locals also believe in the rhino's medicinal properties. But they pay highest for the horn which is powdered for medicines to cure fever, etc. – Indians, especially Gujaratis apparently, also credit the horn with aphrodisiac powers. Today about 900 rhinos roam the sanctuary. There are also plenty of wild elephants and wild buffalo, along with swamp deer, hog deer, tiger and Himalayan bear. Around the jheels (swampy lakes) are black-necked stork and ring-tailed fishing-eagles.

MANAS, ASSAM AND BHUTAN
Season January-March, with fishing November-December. Fly to Gauhati, then 176km by road. Best is to stay at the *Forestry Department bungalow*, bookable through the Division Forest Officer, Wildlife Division, Sarania, Gauhati; or at the *Manas Tourist Lodge*. Explore by elephant and boat.

270 sqkm of outstanding sub-Himalayan riverine forest on the south bank of the River Manas which divides India from Bhutan. There are morning and afternoon flights of great pied hornbills; rare waterfowl include white-capped redstart, mergansers, ruddy shelduck and large cormorants. Also to be spotted are elephant, rhino, buffalo and tiger and on the Bhutan side, the golden langur.

JALDAPARA, WEST BENGAL
Season February-May. Fly to Bagdogra, then 153km by road; or by Jamair to Hashimara airstrip 6km away. Trains stop at Hashimara. The place to stay is the pretty *Madarihat Forest Lodge* just outside the sanctuary or the *Holong Forest Bungalow* inside. Information: Forest Utilisation Officer, 6 Lyons Range, Calcutta.

Explore by elephant. Just below Bhutan, 100 sqkm of sub-Himalayan forest and savannah harbouring elephant, rhino, rhesus, hog deer, wild boar, tiger and leopard and rich birdlife (including lesser florican, great stone plover, red junglefowl).

HAZARIBAGH AND PALAMAU SANCTUARIES, BIHAR
Season February-March. Fly to Ranchi, then by road, 100km to Hazaribagh, 150km to Palamau. Accommodation at *Dak Bungalow* or *Forest Lodge* at each.

Hazaribagh Sanctuary is in undulating hill forests in the Damodar valley, abounding in big, healthy sambhar. These are best seen by car at night, as are the nilgai, muntjac, chital and occasional tiger and leopard.

Chital, tiger, leopard, jungle cat, elephant, gaur, langur and the rare wolf live in the dry deciduous Palamau Sanctuary and there is also rich bird life.

SIMLIPAL, ORISSA
Season November-June. About 300km by road from Calcutta or Bhubaneswar. Nearest railway station Baripada. Visitors stay in modest forest bungalows.

The park is part of Project Tiger. So there are tiger to be seen, as well as leopard, elephant, chital and sambhar. They roam over 2,750 sqkm of the Simlipal Hills, with waterfalls and streams in the forest clearings. See Barhepani and Jaranda waterfalls. Good hill birds.
Sunderbans, Bengal: See p. 187.

Find out more

Note: In 1990, the 300th anniversary of Calcutta's European founding stimulated several new publications; a few are listed below, all with excellent bibliographies.

In the *New Cambridge History of India*, one of the first volumes to be published in P.J. Marshall's *Bengal: The British Bridgehead, Eastern India 1740-1828*, Cambridge, 1987.
Anand, M. R.: 'Konarak', *Marg*, Bombay, 1968
Archer, M.: *Early Views of India, The Picturesque Journeys of Thomas and William Daniell 1786-1794*, London, 1980
Archer, M.: *Indian and British portraiture, 1770-1825*, London, 1979
Banerjee, Samik: *Calcutta 200 Years, a Tollygunge Club Perspective*, Calcutta 1981
Bose, Nirmal Kumar: *Calcutta; a Social Survey*, 1968
Busteed, H. E.: *Echoes from Old Calcutta*, 1st published Calcutta 1882, reprinted by Shannon, 1972
Chaudhuri, N. C.: *The Autobiography of an Unknown Indian*, London, 1951 and 1987; from 1910 to 1942, he lived in Calcutta.
Chaudhuri, S., ed: *Calcutta the Living City*, Vol.1 *The Past*, Vol.2 *The Present and Future*, Oxford, 1990

Eck, Diana: *Banares the City of Light*, London, 1984

Ghosh, J. C.: *The Bengali Renaissance*, London, 1948

Griffiths, P.: *History of the Indian Tea Industry*, London, 1967

Hickey, William: *Memoirs*, ed. Peter Quennell, London 1960

London, J.: *Calcutta and Its Neighbourhood*, Calcutta, 1974

Losty, J. P.: *Calcutta City of Palaces; A Survey of the City in the Days of the East India Company 1690-1858*, London, 1990

Marshall, P. J.: *East Indian Fortunes: The British in Bengal in the Eighteenth Century*, Oxford, 1976

Mehta, R. J.: *Konarak, The Sun-temple of Love*, Bombay, 1969

Mitra, D.: *Bhubaneswar*, New Delhi, 1978

Mitra, D.: *Konorak*, New Delhi, 1976

Mohanty, B. C.: *Appliqué Crafts of Orissa*, Ahmedabad, 1980; he has also written on patachitras and ikats of Orissa

Moorhouse, Geoffrey: *Calcutta, The City Revealed*, London, 1983

Muggeridge, M.: *Like It Was: The Diaries of Malcolm Muggeridge*, London, 1981

Muggeridge, M.: *Something Beautiful For God*, London, 1972

Newby, E.: *Slowly Down the Ganges*, London, 1983

Newby, E. and Singh, Raghubir: *Ganga, Sacred River of India*, Hong Kong, 1974

Skelton, R. and Francis, M. (eds): *Arts of Bengal*, London 1979

Spear, P.: *Master of Bengal – an Illustrated Life of Clive*, London, 1975

Spear, P.: *The Nabobs – the Social Life of the English in 18th Century India*, London, 1932

Stamp, G.: 'British Architecture in India 1857-1947', *Journal of the Royal Society of Arts*, vol. CXXIX, 1981, pp. 357-77.

Welch, S. C.: *Room for Wonder: Indian Painting during the British Period 1760-1880*, New York, 1978

Wilson, H.: *Benares*, London, 1985

Woodruff, Philip: *The Men Who Ruled India*, Cape, 1953

The sizzling South: Silk, spices and cities of faded splendour

South India is an exotic land. Weddings, festivals and political meetings are celebrated with gusto and with lashings of tinsel, music, gaiety and fireworks. The Hindu faithful sweeten their temple precincts with perfumes of coconut, camphor, incense and garlands of flowers. The temple elephant saunters off for his bath, bucket in trunk, and the temple musicians beat drums and blow trumpets to signal puja (worship). Finest silks of vibrant colours are cultured and woven in mud huts. Pricy spices are nurtured on the Nilgiri Hills and artfully displayed on large platters in the bazaars. Wildlife parks abound with rare animals, birds and flora.

Everywhere there are flowers: the rickshaw boy constantly renews his jasmine garlands; women wear white and orange blossoms woven with tinsel in their hair; heaps of stalkless flowers, sold by weight or strung into garlands, fill the air of flower bazaars with a heady, intoxicating perfume. Everywhere there is colour: bullocks' horns are painted in red and green stripes and bells are fixed to the tips; a scarecrow is given a big, glossy, red and black face.

Even the languages sound exotic, from the elegant Urdu in Hyderabad to the gobbledygook Tamil and Malayalam of the deep South that sounds like someone practising a tongue-twister based on double 'lls'. Words have Germanic multi-syllable length, names are unpronounceable and familiar gods acquire local names, like Padmanabha for Vishnu. And the whole peninsular is encased in the band of coconut palms and white beaches that form the Coromandel coast of Tamil Nadu and the Malabar coast of Kerala.

The South Indian film industry pervades all. The tiniest village boasts a magnificent Art Deco cinema, proudly lettered 'Tirumalai Talkies 1940'. Despite the ubiquitous video, southern cinemas still do good trade. Massive, garish 3-D movie hoardings are tarted up with tinsel and gold. Podgy wooden arms and legs are added to the poster images of the gods and heroes to make them burst out beyond their huge frames. A 20-metre-high Roger Moore, fattened up to appeal to local taste, brandishes an outsize 007 revolver in a Bangalore street.

Cinema neon lights inspire a Kerala coffin-maker to have as his shop sign a remarkably tasteless, blood red, flashing neon coffin. The splashes of crimson, saffron, lapis and deep pink found in Rajasthan make way for the harsh celluloid clashes of gaudy mauve, ice-cream pink, yellow, orange, sky blue and peppermint green. The centuries-old temples, with their riot of leaping gods, are being 'restored' with this same palette, using weather-wearing hard gloss paint, which is causing a great debate among the art historians. And, most telling of all, three out of the four southern states have at some time elected film stars as their Chief Ministers of State: Tamil Nadu, Karnataka and Andhra Pradesh. Furthermore, the delectable and busy Tamil actress Manorama has made it into the Indian version of the Guinness Book of Records (appropriately called the Limca Book of Records) for starring with three successive Chief Ministers of Tamil Nadu in some of her 1,000 or so feature films.

Scene changes are dramatic. Muslim Hyderabad, city of the lucrative pearl trade and decaying palaces, sits on the arid Deccan Plateau. Eastwards lie forgotten buildings and, on the distant coast, unvisited beaches. Southwest, parched, flat Andhra Pradesh and Karnataka are dotted with piles of giant-sized boulders like Barbara Hepworth sculptures. Magnificent forgotten cities of the wealthy Muslim sultanates and Hindu Chalukyan, Telugu and Hoysala kingdoms are now backwater towns or totally deserted. Passengers chugging through on steam trains are confronted with huge advertisements, beautifully painted directly on to boulders, exhorting them to buy Campa Cola or Charminar cigarettes (named after Hyderabad's landmark). Coconut sellers squat at roadside oases ready to slash their wares and offer fresh, soothing milk to dusty throats. Further south, the plains are brightened by mulberry bushes for silk and flowers which will eventually be sold in Bangalore market.

Through the wildlife sanctuaries beyond Mysore lie the Nilgiri Hills, covered with an incongruous mixture of valuable spice forests, coffee bushes, monkeys and waterfalls, topped with tea plantations and mossy, rolling hills like those found in the English Lake District.

Here are Ooty and her sister hill stations. There are sights which seem familiar to English eyes. There are timber-frame houses like those in a South of England county like Surrey. There are horses, hounds and pink-coated huntsmen chasing after a fox, as if across a farmer's field in Lincolnshire. These exist side by side with run-

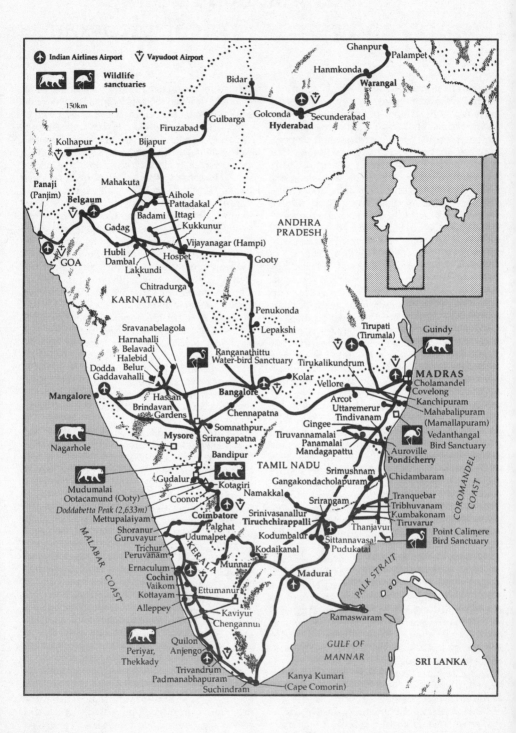

Indian Airlines Airport Vayudoot Airport

Wildlife sanctuaries

150km

Ghanpur
Palampet
Hanmkonda
Warangal
Bidar
Golconda Secunderabad
Hyderabad
Gulbarga
Firuzabad
Bijapur
Kolhapur

Panaji (Panjim)
Mahakuta
Belgaum
Aihole
Pattadakal
Badami Ittagi
Gadag Kukkunur
Hubli Vijayanagar (Hampi)
Dambal Hospet
Lakkundi
Chitradurga
KARNATAKA
GOA

ANDHRA
PRADESH

Gooty

Penukonda
Lepakshi

Tirupati
(Tirumala)
Guindy

Sravanabelagola
Harnahalli
Belavadi
Halebid Ranganathittu
Dodda Belur Water-bird Sanctuary Tirukalikundrum
Gaddavahalli
Kolar MADRAS
Cholamandel
Mangalore Vellore Covelong
Hassan Bangalore Arcot Kanchipuram
Brindavan Uttaremerur Mahabalipuram
Gardens Chennapatna Tindivanam (Mamallapuram)
Mysore Somnathpur Gingee Vedanthangal
Srirangapatna Tiruvannamalai Bird Sanctuary
Nagarhole Bandipur Panamalai Auroville
Mandagapattu Pondicherry
TAMIL NADU Srimushnam Chidambaram
Mudumalai Gudalur Gangakondacholapuram
Ootacamund (Ooty) Kotagiri Namakkal Srirangam Tranquebar
Doddabetta Peak (2,633m) Tribhuvanam
Mettupalaiyam Coonor Srinivasanallur Kumbakonam
Shoranur Coimbatore Tiruchchirappalli Thanjavur Tiruvarur
Guruvayur Palghat Kodumbalur Sittannavasal Point Calimere
Trichur Udumalpet Kodaikanal Pudukatai Bird Sanctuary
Peruvanam KERALA
Ernaculum Munnar
Cochin Madurai
Vaikom
Kottayam Ettumanur
Alleppey Kaviyur
Chengannui
Ramaswaram
Quilon Anjengo
Periyar, PALK STRAIT
Thekkady Trivandrum
Padmanabhapuram GULF OF SRI LANKA
Suchindram Kanya Kumari MANNAR
(Cape Comorin)

MALABAR COAST

COROMANDEL COAST

down princes' palaces and local Indian shacks. The inhabitants and visitors are a strong cocktail of socialite Indian honeymooners (even the newly-wed Jaipurs, with the world their oyster, came here), flashy Bombay and Bangalore film-stars, the primitive Tonda tribe and left-over colonials who cast disapproving glances from horn-rimmed spectacles as they sit reading old copies of *The Daily Telegraph*.

Plunging further south there are the two states that form the tip of India. The viridian green paddy fields of Tamil Nadu, known as the rice-bowl of India, are littered with lifesize, brightly painted, terracotta horses, gods and elephants that look like giants' toys. Here are the great temple cities of the Pallava and Chola kings, with pyramid gopura (gateways) alive with wrestling, dancing and fighting deities and demons.

Across the Cardamom Hills is wealthy Kerala, a narrow, verdant, west coast strip whose backwaters, paddy, rubber and coconuts (Kera means coconut) provide a lush, fluorescent green backdrop for toytown Christian churches, mosques and houses. They are all of crazy designs, looking spick and span and boldly painted in gleaming candy pink, sky blue, mustard, mauve and apple green. Sometimes, whole walls are striped or checked, with some sculpture thrown in as well.

Kerala is very different from the rest of India. It has a tradition of home ownership and distribution of wealth. You rarely see a beggar in Kerala. The state consumes more soap powder than any other. Here, the Christian Church is as politically influential as the film industry. Here also is India's lowest birthrate and highest literacy ¬ from an impressive 70% (twice the national average), an energetic literacy drive in 1990 pushed it up to 93.06% which UNESCO rates as full literacy.

There is a political awareness to rival that of Bengal. It is so intense that no-one dares start an industry without the prior consent of the trade unions. After years of waiting, the up-market Taj Group of hotels has recently taken the plunge; and so far, so good. It is difficult to know if there are more strikes than festivals – they both look much the same and pop up everywhere. Kerala was only created in 1956 (out of Travancore, Cochin and Malabar) and promptly voted in India's – and the world's – first freely elected Communist government the following year.

Its wealth from exporting coconuts, rubber and the Nilgiris' produce, which accounts for some 25% of all India's cash crops, is now further boosted. Kerala has supplied most of the labour for Middle East construction, the workers returning annually laden with outsize videos, cassette recorders and the latest gad-gets. In response to all this comparative literacy and wealth, small bookshops advertise 'school books and bank guides'. With the Middle East demise, this cash injection is already drying up, and half-built grand houses are unlikely to be completed.

In this mixture of rural simplicity and celluloid crassness, natural beauty and architectural marvels, three modern and energetic cities have grown up around colonial Madras, the Nizam's courtly Hyderabad and the cool bolt-hole bungalows of Bangalore. Each threatens to throttle its fine old buildings with pollution and planning. Conservation is ignored in a blind destructive rush for modernism. The Urban Ceiling Act, which applies throughout India and restricts the amount of undeveloped land a man may own within the inner city, seems to have contributed to the damage. Land that has to be sold naturally fetches a better price if it has planning permission. And up go the sky-scrapers.

The provincial cities, in contrast, tuck their industry away, leaving Mysore still looking and feeling like the Maharaja's private city of palaces. The temple city of Madurai is as seething with pilgrims as Vatican City during a Holy Year. In Trivandrum, the older people still go to the main street every morning to doff their caps to the Maharaja as he rides from his palace to the temple for morning puja.

There is a myth that south India consists solely of dreary temple ruins. It is an ugly slander. The deserted temples are in fact splendid remains of whole temple cities. And the living temples vibrate with community life – bazaars, smells, colour, music and worship. But these Southern temples are not as easy to enjoy as the Mughal monuments or Rajput palaces of the North. They demand more effort, even a jot of reading up or a good on-site guide. To find out a little more about Hinduism, the temple and temple life, see Varanasi, Khajuraho, Kanchipuram and Thanjavur sections.

The South also has a variety of scenery, monuments, peoples and traditions to rival anything the North can offer. And it benefits from the added charms of an even more open-hearted people than those in the North, less touched by Western commercialism and ideology. And the way to find it is to brave the heat and dust and hie off into the countryside, stopping overnight in a Mysore palace or an old British Residence or a simple Circuit House, then cooling off in the hills or relaxing on empty silver beaches.

When to go

Apart from the hills, the South is hot or very hot. The season for the Deccan and Tamil Nadu is November-February when winter days resemble a European mid-summer heatwave and nights bring little freshness. From March, the mercury rises to boiling point. Even the locals faint, break out in prickly heat and get sunstroke. The beaches are difficult to enjoy when it gets really hot. Then, with luck, come the monsoons between May and November, depending on the area (see Weather chart, p. 2).

Kerala sun is less ferocious (monsoon from May until October). The hills experience a much softer climate: November-February bring misty mornings, warm sunshine days and cold nights; March-June and September-October are delightfully warm, with spring flowers and then autumn colours; June is windy, July-September wet.

FESTIVALS Amid the constant stream of festivals, there are some worth planning an itinerary around. *Pongal* (called Sankranti in Karnataka) is harvest festival and the most important festival of all. It is celebrated across the South but best in Tamil Nadu. After a successful harvest, crucial to rural India, the land, sun and animals are all thanked.

Four days of holiday celebrations begin on the first day of the Tamil month of Thai (usually January 13 or 14). The first day is Bhogi, on the eve of Pongal, when evil spirits are driven out of homes by removing old pots and clothes and burning them on a village bonfire. Houses are spring-cleaned, whitewashed, some re-thatched and redecorated. Women draw exquisite kolams (religious patterns) with moistened rice flour on pots, stove, front doorsteps and the place where the special offering will be cooked.

On Pongal day, families have baths, massage each other and put on new clothes. Then the newly harvested rice, sugar-cane and turmeric (and other ingredients) are boiled up in the new pots. When the froth is pongu (boiling over, the more it spills the better the year ahead), some is offered to Surya, the sun god.

Day three is Maattu (cattle) Pongal, when the cows and bullocks, so valuable to the farmer, are lovingly washed and sprinkled with turmeric to ward off evil. Their foreheads are anointed with red powder, their long horns polished and brightly painted. Bells and beads are fastened to the tips and heavy garlands of coconut and mango leaves, sugar-cane, palmyra shoots and flowers are hung round their necks. More Pongal rice is offered to them before they are paraded around the village. Then come the very competitive games, including the manja virattu (chase for turmeric) and the jalli kattu, a sort of American rodeo where the young men chase bulls to wrench off bundles of cloth tied round the horns or necks. The winner keeps the contents, of cane, vegetables or even jewellery and money.

Of the big all-India Hindu religious festivals, *Dussehra* (September/October) and Diwali (October-November) have southern versions. Dussehra is best in Mysore (where it is called Dassera) and celebrates the triumph of good over evil in the goddess Chamundeswari's triumph over the demon Mahishasura. (In the North it is Rama's triumph over Ravana.) Ten days of medieval pageantry come to a climax with Vijayadashami, a sumptuous procession of caparisoned elephants, horses and cavalry and garish and garlanded deities (often with faces similar to the latest film-star). The parade ends with fireworks, symbolising traditionally auspicious days when major projects were embarked upon, such as buildings or wars. A celebration of the goddess of learning, music and the arts, Saraswati, is thrown in at the same time, so there is a good cultural programme of yakshagana dance-drama, Bharata Natyam classical dance and huthuri folk dance held in the splendid palace Durbar Hall and grounds.

Diwali follows the North in worshipping Lakshmi, goddess of wealth, but not in celebrating Rama's return to Sita. Here it is the triumph of Krishna and Satyabhama over the demon Narakasura, who had got too big for his boots and abducted some gods' pretty daughters and even robbed the mother goddess, Aditi, of her earrings. The demon was slain at dawn, when the celebrations are held: coloured kolams decorate the houses, effigies of Narakasura are burnt in every village, sweetmeats exchanged, oil baths taken and new clothes donned.

The Muslim festivals of Muharram, Id-ul-Fitr at the end of Ramadan and Id-ul-Zuha (or Bakr-Id) are best seen in old Hyderabad (see Delhi for more on these).

Apart from Pongal festival, there are other southern specialities but they mostly happen in one place only. Madurai has two big ones. The *Teepam* (float) festival (January-February) celebrates the birthday of the 17th century ruler, Tirumala Nayak. Temple gods are dressed up in silk, bejewelled and garlanded and processed to the big tank. They are dragged round on a huge barge, with music and chanting, the tank lit by thousands of oil lamps in built-in niches. *Meenakshi Kalyanam* (April-May), held at the thronged Meenakshi temple that constitutes most of Madurai city, celebrates the marriage of Meenakshi to Shiva. Ten days of jollity lead up to the procession of the deities on a huge chariot that rivals the raths of Puri (see Calcutta chapter).

The most spectacular Kerala temple festival is the *Pooram* at Trichur (April-May), just south of the Nilgiris. It is described by Kerala temple expert Pepita Noble as having 'breathtaking' sights, 'gigantic' crowds and 'stunning, ear-splitting, glorious' music. 'Everything about it is on a grand scale.' Two goddesses, Paramek-kavu and Thiruvambady, and eight other deities are honoured. Fairs are set up as crowds flood in. Vantage points on shop roofs are sold for Rs250. Cars are forbidden as the streets are decorated with coconut leaves, pendants and oil lamps.

The 30 elephants, chosen for their size and beauty of trunk, tail, ears and tusks, arrive on the eve, together with their food – lorryloads of panapatta (palm leaves). On Pooram morning, they are dressed up in nattipattams (like gold-plated chain mail) and Brahmins sit on top of them to hold the symbolic deity, silk parasols, vencharmanrams (whisks) and alavattoms (peacock feather fans). Then the whole party sets off on a slow, glorious day-long procession and ritual, with constant music, cheered along by the faithful with offerings of rice and flowers.

The whole thing is repeated after sunset with different music and flaming torches, ending with a massive firework display which lasts until dawn. At 8am, the elephants assemble again, there is three hours of drumming, then more fireworks.

At Irinjalakuda (30km south of Trichur) there is nightly Kathakali and Karnatic music for 11 days, starting on the second night of Trichur Pooram.

Onam lasts for a week, leading up to full moon day in Chingom (August-September), and is Kerala's harvest festival and New Year. Feasting, new clothes, washed houses and dancing greet the annual visit of the legendary king, Mahabali, who was famous for his prosperous reign. The snake boat races held on the back-waters at Kottayam, Aranmula and Payipad are the climax. Long, low, dug-out boats, with highly decorated beak-shaped or kite-tailed sterns, compete for the Nehru Cup, when up to 100 rowers race in boats along the palm fringed backwaters.

SOCIAL CALENDAR   Dominated by horse racing. Bangalore and Bombay have the main stud farms in India and Bangalore's racing season is May-July and October-February, with meetings most Fridays, Saturdays and Sundays. Ooty's season is April-June, with meetings on Saturdays and Sundays, but mid-May is the climax when the Ooty dog show and flower show are also held. Madras meetings are in December; Hyderabad's July-September and November-February.

Getting there: Getting away

The South has an efficient network of a dozen airports, making it very easy to fly into one, take a short trip by car, then take a second plane hop and another trip. Indian Airlines encourage this

with their discount flight deals (see p. 9). Flights also connect directly to the best beaches (Madras, Goa, Maldives, Sri Lanka) and the off-beat ones (Mangalore, Vishakapatnam, Gopalpur-on-Sea) for a pre-or post-sightseeing rest (see Sun chapter).

The principal direct connections are daily between big cities; two or three times weekly, sometimes via other airports, between smaller ones.

The cities with airports are: Hyderabad, Vishakhapatnam, Madras, Madurai, Tiruchchirappalli, Coimbatore, Trivandrum, Cochin, Kozhikode, Bangalore, Mangalore and Dobolim (for Goa). For Sri Lanka, there are flights to Colombo from Madras (daily, except Fri.) and Trivandrum via Tiruchchirapalli (Tues., Sat.). For the Maldives, fly from Trivandrum to Male (Mon., Thurs.). For the Andamans, fly from Madras.

Some train journeys are excellent for seeing the countryside and often fill a gap where there is no air connection. They chug along the lush coastline or cut across valleys, rubber plantations and the Cardamom and Nilgiri Hills. Good ones include the overnight Madras-Cochin Express (departs 7.20pm, arrives 9.40am); the Madras-Madurai-Quilon Mail (departs 7.05pm, arrives Madurai 6.40am; departs 6.55am, arrives Quilon 2.50pm); the Parasuram Express from Quilon to Trivandrum (departs 4.55pm, arrives 6.25pm). The Madras-Bangalore train journey is not particularly pretty.

But the train up to Ooty is a collector's item: spectacular views from little yellow and blue carriages as they slowly climb the narrow gauge line, locking into special teeth for the steeper slopes. A three-part journey: first to Coimbatore by air, road or overnight train (which is best); then train from Coimbatore to Mettupalaiyam on the Nilgiri Express (depart 6.30am, arrive Mettupalaiyam 7.30am); then to Ooty on the narrow gauge (depart 8am, arrive 12.30pm). Take the 2pm train down from Ooty (only 3½hrs) to connect back to Coimbatore. Train times change, so check on the spot.

The best way to travel part of the Kerala journey is by ferry on the backwaters (see Kuttanadu, below). Sadly, considering the beautiful coastline, there is no ferry service between ports.

Information and reservations

The best way to set up a trip in the South after arriving in India is to go to the recommended travel agents in Delhi, Bombay or Calcutta, listed above, choosing one with offices in the South, or go to one of the big southern cities and book everything from there.

The big, reliable chains are found in the South

as follows:

Cox & Kings are at Highpoint 4, Shop no.4111, 54/1 Palace Road, Bangalore (tel: 260509) and c/o Hotel Connemara, Binny Road, Madras (tel: 860123). SITA are at Sita House, 1 St Mark's Road, Bangalore (tel: 578091); Tharakan Building, M G Road, Ravipuram, Cochin (tel: 353012/363780); Sita House, 3-5-874 Hyderguda, Hyderabad (tel: 233629); and 26 Commander-in-Chief Road, Madras (tel: 478861). TCI are at 9 Residency Road, Richmond Circle, Bangalore (tel: 212826/212990); 1st floor, Telstar Building, M G Road, Ravipuram, Cochin (tel: 351646); 102 Regency House, Greenlands Road, 680 Somajiguda, Hyderabad (tel: 212722); and 734 Anna Salai, Madras (tel: 868813). All three have representatives in the smaller cities.

Many of the hotels are modest and simple, but they often have great charm and, because of the heat, hygiene standards in the South are considerably higher than in the North. This applies to the preparation and consumption of food, too. Night life ranges from limited to non-existent, but it is worth making every effort to see the exceptional classical dance found almost every night in Madras and Cochin and also worth going to a South Indian film (see below). Shopping is best in Bangalore, Hyderabad and Madras.

The state and government sight-seeing tours in the big southern cities are very good, some say better than in the North, but the southern accents can be rather heavy. Local 'approved guides' at remote spots are usually charming but useless, reeling off lists of multi-syllabled gods, interspersed with eccentric facts, spoken in broken English using archaic phrasing.

South Indian food

Many dishes are hotter than northern ones, but that does not mean they have to frizzle up the taste buds and bring on a sweat. Indeed, combined with lots of rice, soothing fresh dahi (curd) and coconut (the important southern ingredient), they are pleasantly light to eat in the heat and easy to digest. The southern cuisine is less rich than the northern and therefore less likely to give tummy trouble. The vegetarian diet can be supplemented with delicious freshwater or sea fish.

It is best to avoid meat, except to enjoy the rich Mughlai food in Muslim Hyderabad and at the top hotel restaurants of Madras, Bangalore and Madurai. Those desperate for a steak will find beef in Kerala where the population has a high Muslim and Christian content. The trading Chettinand tribe of Tamil Nadu have given a spicy chicken dish to the southern repertoire. Cocktail titbits are delicious: fresh, hot cashew nuts, fried prawns and crunchy banana chips.

The South is almost totally vegetarian, as is Gujarat, and many north Indians eat vegetarian at least one day a week – when they often use their abstemiousness as an excuse for a whacking great sweatmeat or rice-based pudding after the vegetables. Thus, the Indian vegetarian cuisine is highly developed, with an almost infinite variety of vegetable combinations cooked with different – and often very gentle – spices.

It is quite possible to eat a different dhal (pulses) dish every day – pure vegetarians have dhal with every meal, for its nutritional value. Sambar is a dhal cooked with several seasonal vegetables. The most common basic ingredients include brinjal (aubergine), okra (lady's fingers), sag (any green leaf vegetable), palak (spinach), mattar (peas), sarson ka sag (mustard leaves), pyazi (onion), aloo (potato), tomato and many others, each turned into a delicious and distinctive dish. Plain boiled potatoes are an abhorrence to Indians, who consider most Western food dreary and unimaginative.

The easiest way to order is to ask for a *thali* (large, circular tin platter). It is delivered with six or so katoris (little dishes), each containing a different vegetable or pulse dish and one katori with dahi (fresh curd, sometimes seasoned and mixed with onion and tomato to make pachadi), one with chutney and one with mithai (sweet pudding). They are usually arranged in order, so you work round the different, complementary flavours, often beginning with rasam (clear lentil soup, later anglicised into mulliga-tanni, meaning pepper-soup, at the Madras Club) and ending with payasham (rice pudding with almonds, raisins and cardamom seeds).

More chutneys and pickles are put on the table, together with salad and possibly a side dish of pakoras (fried vegetables, known as bhajias in the North). Mango pickles can be fire hot, like kadu manga and thokku, or cool, like vadu manga. The substance of the meal arrives separately: a pile of steaming, boiled rice ladled from a big tureen into the middle of the thali dish, replenished as it goes down. The rice comes in many forms: flavoured with lemon or tamerind, cooked with curry patta (leaves) or with coconut.

Those with bigger appetites can also have a constant stream of hot, freshly baked breads and other treats, such as crispy thin poppads (small poppadums, the big ones are known as Punjab poppadums) or a dozen varieties of dosa (paper thin rice pancake a metre in diameter). Other breads are appam (soft-centred, crisp rice and coconut pancake), adais (thick, spicy lentil and rice pancake), murka (deep-fried rice, peanuts and cashewnuts), vadas (a crunchy, doughnut-shaped, deep-fried mixture of dhals and spices) and uppama (seasoned semolina). But these are really better ordered as a light meal in themselves, the huge dosa often served wrapped around a dryish potato filling, then called masala dosa, and served with some freshly ground coconut and chutney. The typical south Indian idlies (steamed cakes made from fermented rice flour), a breakfast favourite, need ghi (clarified butter) or a more liquid sambar (potato, peas, mustard seed and other spices). And there is no fear of lacking the protein of a thick steak: the mixture of cereals and pulses provides it all.

Fish is especially good in the South. The white, flakey bekti is cooked with coconut milk to make fish curry, called molee in Kerala when the coconut milk is spiced with ginger, green chilli and herbs. There are pomfret, lobster, mussels, oysters, prawns, crab and small sharks. Fried mackerel and sardines are excellent. Pickled fish is considered a delicacy. Karimeen, a freshwater fish found in Kerala, is cooked in a fiery sauce of onions, green chillies and spices.

Every restaurant, even the tiniest roadside café, has somewhere to wash your hands which is used by everyone on arrival. (There is often no towel, but the heat soon dries them.) Then, when the steaming food arrives, however smart the restaurant, get stuck in with your fingers (right hand only), mixing sauces with rice, dunking breads, scooping up chutneys and dahi with bread and finger tips, drinking up the rest of the sauces and generally enjoying it all with abandon. Indians claim that to eat with cutlery is as unsatisfactory as to make love through an interpreter.

Wash it down with the very refreshing fresh coconut milk or lassi (yoghurt drink). Other drinks available are fresh fruit juices such as mango, orange, pineapple or guava; numbu sodas or fizzy bottled drinks (Fanta, Campa Cola, Limca, etc.). If the spices are still tingling, have a kulfi (ice-cream flavoured with saffron and pistachio nuts) or, in September, fresh custard-apple ice-cream (found especially in Hyderabad). Fruits include the southern mango varieties of romani or malgoa and several varieties of banana: the small yellow and the big pink both have strong, delicious flavours. Try also jackfruit kernels and fresh toddy, best cut fresh in the market or on the roadside.

See how it's done: Crafts and customs

As with Rajasthan in the North, the essence of enjoying South India is to be adventurous and get out into the countryside. Many of the best historical sights are separated by long, dusty drives, cutting across state frontiers. They are worth every effort to reach but, to repeat, the South is not just temples and monuments.

There is masses to see on the way. Trains go slowly, passing right beside rural villages. Buses stop in villages and towns for the driver and passengers to stretch their legs, eat and drink. Remember, though, that photography in railway stations is prohibited.

But the most versatile way to travel is by car, asking the driver to stop for anything that catches the eye. It is a good idea to set out very early, before sunrise, while it is cool, then stop for breakfast. Here are just a few things to look out for, in towns, villages and along the roads. Take a tip from the Indians and carry plenty of drinks on a trip – the sun gets very hot.

THROUGHOUT THE SOUTH

Small restaurants Unlike in the North, these modest cafés that pop up on roadsides and in side streets of towns are very hygienic. There is no need to take boring hotel picnics, except as a back-up in more off-beat areas. The cafés are known as udipis, vihars, meals, tiffin houses, etc. Some of the best dosas and idlies of all are found where the big lorries stop (just as it is often where the best breakfasts are to be found in Britain).

For something more substantial, order 'meal' or 'special meal'. Watch the food being cooked with acrobatic speed and efficiency. Then, with luck, it will be served on beautiful fresh banana leaves, although the patron is liable to proudly honour his Western visitor with cutlery and crockery. The mountain of rice will be replenished up to four times, under the assumption that a whole pile will be gobbled up with each of the four sauces: ghi, sambar, rasam and finally thayyur (thick curd).

Don't drink the water, which is delivered automatically. Instead, stick to bottled drinks such as Limca or tea or coffee (both well boiled). Coffee is served piping hot in a stainless steel beaker set in a dish (the two together called a davara). This equipment cools and froths up the sweet, milky liquid. You pour it from as high as possible from beaker to dish and back again – a serious ritual known as 'coffee by the yard'.

Rice Miles and miles of green paddy fields are dotted with the vibrant coloured backsides of women bent double planting and transplanting paddy. India's highest rice-producing state may be Bengal, the largest area under rice cultivation may be in Uttar Pradesh, and the highest yields per acre may be in the Punjab, but it is in the South that rice awareness reaches its peak for the traveller.

Oldest records of domestic rice cultivation on the sub-continent have been found at Neolithic sites dating to 7000BC. Considerably later, the Chola dynasty's wealth in the 9th-13th centuries was founded on the Tamil Nadu rice bowl and rice is still a principal southern crop, with two annual harvests. (Three near the Cauvery and other large rivers.) There are many varieties. The small nellore grains are grown in Andhra Pradesh. The up-market basmati rice is grown here but Dehra Dun basmati grown in the North is the queen of rice. Basmati's low yield makes it twice as expensive as the regular white rice usually served. Red rice (with red streaks) is the cheapest and has a better flavour but has to be asked for specially. Hotels usually serve it to their staff, not their clients. Harvesting methods vary. In Bengal, sela is rice that is harvested, par-boiled in the fields and then dried until needed.

But rice is not just the staple diet; it is a fundamental part of social and religious life. A baby's first food is always rice, symbolising the hope that it will never go hungry. There is a rice ceremony to Saraswati, goddess of learning, before a child goes to school to learn the alphabet by drawing with fingers on a tray of rice. At the sacred thread ceremony, when a Brahmin boy enters adulthood, he begs for rice from his family.

A new bride tips over the bowl of rice placed on the threshold of her house, spilling it into the home to bring fertility and prosperity. A pregnant woman is given presents of rice. Rice is a medicine for the eyes, is part of every festival, in Andhra Pradesh is fed to crows (the incarnation of people's ancestors), and is meant to ward off evil. In Tamil Nadu it is showered on brides as a blessing and, mixed with turmeric powder to make akshintulu, showered on children and offered to the gods. Finally, at the sradh ceremony after death, rice balls are offered to help the spirit find peace.

Kolam More rice, this time the ritual decoration of the floor with muggu (rice powder), carried to a fine art in the South (as are the alpanas of Bengal and rangolis in Gujarat, mandanas in Rajasthan and sanjhnis in Uttar Pradesh). The southern woman makes the kolam every morning, after sweeping her home. With great dexterity and years of practice, she skilfully lays a very beautiful and intricate geometric design of dots outside the house to bring prosperity and happiness – and to encourage the plagues of black ants (favourites of the elephant-faced god, Ganesh) to gorge themselves and not bother to come inside.

In Margazhi month (mid-December to mid-January) the kolams are especially huge and intricate. For the January festival of Ratha Saptami, when the sun god steers his chariot towards the Tropic of Cancer, she makes a stylised chariot kolam. For big occasions (festivals and weddings) muggu is mixed to a paste so that it lasts longer, and kaavi (red mud) is used as a border. In Kerala, the glorious kolams around the Onam festival are composed of petals of all the seasonal flowers. Places of worship have specific designs for different areas: the padman is a stylised lotus kolam made where the ceremonial lamp is placed. Kolams can be spotted on roadsides in the early morning.

Cinema Tamil is the most influential Indian cinema after Hindi. What is more, Madras is second only to Bombay in sound film production – Bombay films are often edited in Madras. And, with three out of the four southern states having at one time voted actors as their Chief Ministers, with hoardings that outdo Hollywood, and with film gossip flooding the papers, economic journals and conversation, it might be interesting to sample a southern celluloid stunner and get an insight into this obsession. Screenings are around 10am, 1.30pm, 6.30pm and 9.30pm, and the smarter cinemas are air-conditioned, so it makes for cool, relaxed sightseeing, but a less bubbly fellow audience. Two-star rated films are considered tops, and India has its own set of two-star film-stars. Half the cinemas of India are in the South. Andhra Pradesh is the state with the most, 2,487 in 1987; while the best single street for choice is in Bangalore, where 40 of its 150 cinemas line Kempe Gowda Road. They mostly show films in Kanada and Tamil, but it is the turned-up Technicolor, outlandish sets and incongruous singing and dancing that matter, not the plot or dialogue. (The thriving serious cinema of the 1970s and 1980s is more difficult to find and to understand and English sub-titles are rare.) If curiosity is aroused, the Tourist Office can set up visits to film studios in Bangalore, Madras and Trivandrum.

The political and technical strength of southern film-making began early. With the coming of talkies to the South in the mid-1930s, the Madras studios were hit hard: the four southern languages – Tamil, Telugu, Kanada and Malayalam – belong to the Dravidian family, quite different from the Indo-Aryan Hindi, Bengali and Marathi of the North. So the South went its own way, developing a flourishing, flamboyant cinema at such Madras studios as Gemini, Modern Theatres, AVM and Vauhini and perfecting dubbing techniques into the four main languages – hence their sound supremacy now. By the late 1950s, half the Indian cinemas were in the South, and half the Indian films were made in the four southern languages.

Even today, Asia's largest studios are Nagi Reddi's Vijay-Vauhini in Madras, which has 20 sound stages plus ground for outdoor shooting. Furthermore, the Keralan actor Prem Nazir holds the world record for playing the hero in more than 600 films (Tamil, Kanada, Telugu and Malayalam) and for co-starring with heroine Shiela in 110 of the Malayalam ones. Hardly surprising, then, that of the 806 films made in India in 1987, 167 were in Tamil and 163 in Telugu.

Above all, Tamil films have exercised a social, political and cultural influence stronger than anywhere else. Politics stepped in quickly, in the shape of the Dravida Munnetra Kazhagam (DMK) party which stood for southern nationalism and the revival of Dravidian culture. They were anti-Hindi and anti-North and their rising sun symbol can be seen on many walls. They used films to reach the mass public, in the way Bengal had done during the Independence struggle, and they introduced crude rising sun symbolism.

The campaign was a winner. The Congress Party was destroyed and DMK came to power. Its first three Chief Ministers were all from the film world, the third being M. G. Ramachandran, elected in 1977 as the first real superstar Chief Minister. MGR (as he is known) was a matinée idol for 30 years. Later, he broke away from the DMK to form his own party.

Silk and cotton dyeing The splashes of cherry red, deep green, punk pink, lilac and seaside blue that catch the eye on rooftops, among cows and bullocks in back gardens, along alleys and on roadsides are skeins of newly dyed cotton. Somewhere nearby is the dark dyeing room. Here, cotton is boiled hard to render it good for absorbing dye. Then it is hung from poles across a large stone tank, heated by a wood fire underneath, containing the warm water in which the dye is dissolved. After rinsing and squeezing the cloth in a wooden mangle, it is put out to dry.

To dye silk is slightly more complicated. Raw silk contains 30% sorocom (silk gum) which is removed by boiling in soda ash, soap and water in big copper pans, again heated with wood fires. (Fires bypass the constant electricity cuts that plague even big cities and prevent the necessarily precise timing.) Then the silk is dyed like cotton, ending with a wash in cold, diluted acid, termed scrumping, which gives the silk its lustre and crispness and is also a fixative. Unlike cotton, silk is dried in the shade. As in most areas of India, the dyes are now chemical. Even indigo, once so vital to Indian trade, is now only grown in the Cuddapah district of Andhra Pradesh.

Cotton lunghi weaving Lunghis, worn by men in the South, are the coloured, usually check, versions of the northern white dhotis. The clue to finding weavers' houses is the loud clatter of shuttles flying to and fro as the weaver works at amazing speed on looms set up over a pit. He controls the shuttle and movement of warp threads with foot pedals. Several weavers, both men and women, may work together under a palmyra leaf awning, their ages ranging from eight to very old age.

An adept weaver turns out two 2-metre lunghis a day, his family usually sticking to one colour and check size. Quality, and thus price, is determined by the number of weft threads, the coarsest with only about 20, the finest up to 100. You can buy direct from the weavers, having looked at prices in government shops (which also give an idea of the range available). Sometimes 4-metre pieces are available, the weaver having done a two-in-one job. Some lunghi weavers also make cotton towels with pretty fish motifs on the borders.

Handloom silk sari weaving Altogether more sedate than the frantic clack-clacking of lunghi weaving, and with a tradition stretching back, possibly even to the 3rd century BC. The heavy, lustrous and richly brocaded Kanchipuram sari, developed for temple rituals under the patronage of the 4th-century Pallava kings, is every southern belle's dream, her equivalent of a Zandra Rhodes ball gown and well on a par with the weaves of Varanasi, Orissa and Gujarat.

These exquisite, dazzling silks are woven in dark, modest rooms down narrow alleys or in little white-washed houses with palmyra roofs, often near dyers. Weaving is a family affair, with plenty of variations of method. For instance, the man may sit on the floor spinning silk on to shuttles while the children sort the threads for the palo (patterned end). The mother will be weaving the main sari (5-7 metres) with an older child, worked on the reverse side before changing the warp threads for the metre of palo.

It takes two weavers working on a loom 15-20 days to complete a good silk sari, plus a week to prepare the silks and tie the threads on to the loom. The bundle of knotted threads that dangle from the loom mysteriously contain the elaborate pattern of the border and palo. The weaver can tug a knot between rows to alter the arrangement of weft threads. The shuttle is thrown from end to end, between the two weavers. The senior weaver will sit on the border side to check the pattern for mistakes and to control the valuable zari threads of gold and silver. Each row is tightened with a comb, and threads often have to be unmuddled between rows.

If there is a mistake in an important piece, such as a flashy, reversible wedding sari heavy with gold zari work, the weaver takes it to a master craftsman who, after negotiations over price, corrects the barely visible error overnight. It is painstaking craftsmanship, provided at ridiculously low prices.

Some weavers abandon the bundle of knots for revolving cards of wood, which automatically create the pattern, and use the pedals-in-pit system of throwing the shuttles, completing an inferior sari in three days. Others weave sari lengths and palo without changing warps, and add a metre on the end, to be cut off and made into the matching chola (tight-fitting bodice). Weavers of cotton saris are even speedier, tossing off one a day.

Weavers are especially easy to find in and around all southern towns – Hyderabad, Mysore, Bangalore, Madras, Madurai, Thanjavur, Trivandrum, etc. There are about 20,000 silk weavers and 10,000 cotton weavers in Kanchipuram alone. Weavers are always thrilled, and a little bit abashed, that people should be interested in their work.

To order special pieces to be woven by a master craftsman, and to see methods and designs, consult the Weavers' Service Centres in Madras and Kanchipuram or ask at the Tourist Office. Although it is nice to buy a sari direct from the weaver, it is best to buy them in big city shops, where choice is wide and the prices are reliable.

ANDHRA PRADESH AND KARNATAKA

Banjaras The colourful gypsy tribe, also known as Lambadis and Sugalis. They originally came from Rajasthan, where they traded salt and reared cattle. Now the largest tribe in India, numbering about 10 million and concentrated in Madhya Pradesh, Maharashtra, Andhra Pradesh and Karnataka. They came to the Deccan as baggage carriers for the 17th-century Mughal armies, but now follow their original occupation of cattle rearing.

They live in close-knit tandas (settlements) and speak their own language, gor boli. It is the family of a Banjara bridegroom, not the bride, that gives the marriage dowry. Banjaras celebrate any event with wild singing and dancing.

Their dress and jewellery is magnificently bold and colourful. Women wear a bright patchwork langa (full gathered skirt) of pink, mustard, emerald green and piercing blue. They also wear a chola (blouse) and an odni (shawl) edged with coins. Each has areas of beautiful embroidery which they work themselves, sewing from bottom to top to show the progress from earth to sky up the ladder of life, adding mirrors to ward off wild animals. Heavy silver jewellery – up to four kilos on a woman – adorns ears, arms, nose, neck and ankles. Ivory and bone bangles stretch up to the armpits. Tassels and ornaments are tied on to hair worn in ringlets. The most characteristic elements of a Banjara woman's appearance are the huge, jingling, chandelier-like earrings and zig-zag anklets.

They move about the country in bullock carts decorated like the caravans of European gypsies, to whom they may be distantly related. They are mostly seen in the markets, and along the roads of north Karnataka and around Hyderabad and, incongruously, working on road and construction sites. Pieces of their embroidery work and their jewellery can be found in markets.

Bidri ware A technique of decorated metalwork unique to India, developed under the Mughals and named after Bidar, in north Karnataka, where it is thought to have originated. Dishes, hookah bases, boxes, ewers and other pieces are cast from an alloy of zinc, a little copper and tin, and sometimes lead. Each piece is then decorated with very fine arabesques, flowers, geometric patterns and sometimes scripts, the designs inlaid in silver, brass and, in the past, gold. The piece is coated with a paste of mud and sal ammoniac which, when later removed, reveals the metal, now a rich, matt black, the perfect foil to the gleaming inlay. Craftsmen work in the alleys around Charminar in Hyderabad and in Bider. However, their pieces can be bought throughout India.

Pearls Adored by the Nizams, who ate them powdered, rubbed them over their bodies for good health and draped great chains of them around their necks. Hyderabad is still the pearl market of India, concentrated in a row of shops on Pertherghatty Road, near the Charminar. Here thousands of pearls arrive from Japan between December and March (the Gulf supplies have dried up), to be sorted, pierced, sorted again and either sold or re-exported.

Sorters divide this kachcha mal (raw stock) of unlustrous blobs according to size, shape and colour (white, pink, blue, brown, etc.). A decision is taken whether to pierce the pearl horizontally or vertically. It is then clamped on to wood, drilled with a sharp needle using a very basic bow-and-string-drill (pearls split easily), then cleaned in a solution of hydrogen peroxide and dried in the sunlight, inducing a chemical reaction which whitens it even more; the length of soaking and drying can vary between 15 and 50 days. The pearls are then washed, sorted, graded (according to shape, shine and colour) and strung on silk.

The sorting and grading is done in the shops, where women from all over India come to buy this year's pearls, and prospective mothers-in-law bring their son's bride-to-be on a serious shopping spree. Prices are a fifth of British prices and the pearls are bought by weight (the shop-owner will calculate how many are needed for a 3-, 4- or 5-string necklace and matching earrings, bracelets and rings) as the best stringing and clasps are found in Bombay (see p. 151). Natural pearls are a better buy than cultured as they do not taint. Old pearls can be traded for new.

Sericulture 70% of Indian silk is grown in Karnataka, with Bangalore the centre of the sericulture market for India and for export. In 1981, 3,200 tons were produced here from an area of

304,088 acres of mulberry bushes. Special farms for breeding and rearing the silkworms are fascinating to see and open to visitors.

Japanese male moths are mated with local Mysore females for the best strains. (Tops of cocoons are merrily snipped off to demonstrate the aristocratic orange pupa.) After mating, the female is put on squared paper, covered with a conical hat (she is too shy to lay eggs in the light) and left for 24-30 hours, by which time she will have laid 400-600 eggs. She is then crushed, examined under a microscope and, if diseased, the eggs are destroyed. If not, they hatch after 10 days and are sold to the mulberry bush owner for 30 paise. He rears them to the cocoon stage, then sells them to the reeler, the person who twists the yarn and winds it on to reels.

Rearing is merely a question of satisfying the insatiable appetite of the worms for their 26-28 days of solid eating, during which time they moult four times and become 10-15cm long. They live entirely on freshly picked leaves from mulberry bushes which produce six crops a year, just about keeping pace with their hunger. Then the worms turn from white to yellow and furiously spin their cocoons for the next three or four days. In fact, they are discharging a viscous solution which dries to form fine fibres, each cocoon unravelling to 1,200 metres or so of silk yarn. The cycle is then complete. Of the several farms along the Bangalore-Mysore road, Tippu Silk Farm, founded 1912, is the oldest in Karnataka. It both breeds and rears and is open to visitors at all times of the day.

Reelers often live and work in the dyeing and weaving area of Bangalore. A taxi driver can always find one (several of his brothers and cousins will inevitably work in silk). The reeler's workers reel, double and twist the silk on thundering machinery in a boiling hot room – the heat increases the crispness of the silk. The reeler also prepares the warp threads for saris on a huge wooden wheel frame. Then the silk thread is steamed in a hot dustbin to prevent it untwisting. Reelers sell through the Government of Karnataka silk auctions. The weavers buy the silk and take it to their favourite dyers. As well as at the independent firms, all the processes can be seen at the Government of Karnataka Department of Sericulture in Bangalore.

THE NILGIRI HILLS

Spices A masala (blend of spices and herbs) is essential to every Indian dish and gives it the basic flavour. The meat and vegetables are added later, then the liquid. And India's spices, which have improved food world-wide for centuries, were traded like gold with Greeks, Romans, Arabs and Chinese, then Portuguese, Dutch, French and British. It was the stranglehold on spices by the Arabs and the Venetian

middlemen that inspired Vasco da Gama's discovery of the sea route around the Cape of Good Hope (1498), Christopher Columbus's attempt the other way – when he bumped into America – and Magellan's maiden circumnavigation of the world. And it was trading that brought the Europeans to India.

The spices come from the South, mostly between the Kerala coast and the Nilgiris. Indeed, the word curry is derived from kari, Tamil for a thin, spicy sauce which enlivens the bland diet of rice. Pepper was, and is, the king of spices. And Kerala produces 95% of India's pepper crop – see it growing on Kerala homesteads and then being offered to the goddess of Kodungallur Temple with bawdy songs and a big harvest feast.

Cardamom, of which 60% is Kerala grown, is a member of the ginger family and grows in big, broad-leafed bushes in evergreen mountain forest. The seeds sprout from the base and are picked by women, dried and often used as aphrodisiacs. South India also supplies roughly 70% of the world's ginger and haldi (turmeric) requirement, the ginger grown mostly in Kerala, the turmeric in Andhra Pradesh. Both rhizomes are used medicinally, too; ginger as a digestive, haldi as an antiseptic and by women to soften the skin. With those properties, 98% of the 320,000 tons of haldi produced in India annually is consumed by the home market. Cinnamon looks like cassia (found in the north) and is the inner bark of the lateral shoots of pruned trees, sold in tightly curled quills.

Nutmeg and mace come from one tree, for the mace is the soft outer membrane of the nut whose kernel is the nutmeg. A pinch of nutmeg in a teaspoon of honey should cure an upset stomach. The best cashewnuts are grown in the Nilgiris and along the west coast, right up to Goa, with Kerala again producing the most.

Chillies, grown in Andhra Pradesh, and some other states, come in all sizes. The big ones are eaten as vegetables and called capsicums (probably introduced into India by the Portuguese). Mild paprika is crushed red capsicum. Red pepper is stronger. Chilli powder is next up in strength and whole chillies have the most fire. Most of these can be seen growing in Kerala and on the Cardamom and Nilgiri slopes. All can be bought fresh in the bazaars.

Coffee Traditionally believed to have been introduced from Moka, the Arabian coffee centre, to Mysore by an Arab Muslim saint, Haji Budan Baba, to keep sufi mystics awake during all-night whirling sessions. It was certainly here and in Kerala by the 1720s. Both climate and terrain proved perfect for growing coffee and ports such as Cochin and Alleppey were already trading with Arabian and Red Sea ports.

There are two main species of coffee bush,

arabica and robusta. Each has many different varieties of bean such as Billigiris, Bababudans, Shevaroys, Pulneys, Nilgiris, Malabar-Wynaad and Naidubattam. The beans grow in pairs but if there is a freak single bean it is called a Peaberry and prized by connoisseurs. Although India only produces 2.3% of the world market, Indian beans are highly sought after. Most beans are grown in Karnataka, Kerala and Tamil Nadu.

The lush, green foliage of coffee bushes first produces starry white flowers in March, then berries, which are picked by women. They are then dried for seven days, either with their husk, as 'cherries', or without, as 'parchment'. Then they are cured, hand-sorted by specialists, graded, tasted and finally marketed through the Coffee Board at Bangalore. Coffee bushes can be seen on lower hillsides (700-2,000m).

South Indians grind their beans fresh and make very strong coffee, addding lots of hot milk and sugar to make a sort of rich cappuccino. Small restaurants serve good coffee, as do the string of Indian Coffee Houses in Kerala. In big hotels, you should be sure to ask for fresh Mysore coffee otherwise instant coffee, which is now, sadly, considered more fashionable, is served automatically.

Tea Grown in the Nilgiris. It is neither of the quantity nor the quality of that in Darjeeling and north-east India, but enough of the hills are covered in squat bushes to encourage curiosity and an explanatory visit to a tea estate.

Women pluck tea leaves in the morning, deliver full baskets about nine o'clock, and then go out again in the afternoon. The leaves are withered, rolled, sifted, fermented, dried, sorted and graded. The bigger the leaf, the better the flavour. Tea dust is the dregs. Visitors to a tea estate soon become tea snobs. To them, cheap teabags full of dust are dismissed as a thing of the past. Glen Morgan Tea Estate at Paikara, near Ooty, is one of the few where the owners, Mr and Mrs Vadera, still live on the estate, in an enchanting gingerbread bungalow. Tea-maker Mr Sadanand is happy to explain every process of the Indian and Japanese teas grown there. He also has some leaf liquor for visitors to taste. Open 9am-3pm, best before 10am for action.

Todas A small tribe living on the west slopes of the Nilgiris, who claim descent as the chosen people of their creator, Aanu, and whose handsome men and women wander through and around Ooty, draped in toga-like puthukulis (shawls) and silver jewellery. Their lives revolve around tending their sacred horned buffalo and maintaining a tall, conical temple that functions like a dairy. The elected temple priest, like a dairyman, puts the buffalo out to graze in the morning, brings them in at night and is responsible for the milking and for making butter and buttermilk. The tattooed Toda women are not allowed near the temple-dairy or the buffalo, yet, rarely in India, they can choose their own husbands, and even take several. While the men tend the buffalo and collect firewood, the women gossip, wash their hair in buttermilk and wind it round bamboo to make long ringlets. And they embroider their puthukulis in striking red, blue and black. The Todas live entirely on dairy products, berries and roots and they keep bees for honey. They are vegetarian but consider agriculture beneath the dignity of the chosen people, so they come into Ooty to buy grains and rice in the market.

KERALA
African Moss The enemy waterweed which is threatening to throttle beautiful Kuttanadu, the 260 sqkm area of backwaters, paddy fields and coconuts palms between Alleppey, Kottayam and Quilon. The velvety leaf and its cushion of inter-twined fibrous roots have spread at an alarming rate over the last 15 years, with a drastic effect on locals' lives. It has so polluted the water that it cannot be used for drinking or washing. By preventing the sun's rays penetrating the water, aquatic life and fish have died. It has blocked up rivulets and canals so that boats, often the only means of transport, cannot get through. And no-one has devised a means of controlling it.

Kerala temple festivals Every temple holds a festival for its deity between late December and early June, so it is possible to bump into one every day. Each is a local variation of a set form of ritual combined with a ceremonial procession, the biggest being Trichur's Pooram. The deity, symbolised by a golden shield, is paraded down the middle of a main road on the gaily caparisoned back of the biggest and tallest elephant, escorted by other suitably dressed elephants (usually four or six) and entertained with loud drums, cymbals and horns and trumpets.

Toddy Fermented liquor made from the sap of coconut palm, collected just before the palm blossoms. (It will not then produce fruits.) Toddy men can be seen shinning up the tall palms before sunrise and after sunset, knives in teeth, earthenware bowls around their necks. They slash the trunk just beneath the leaves and collect the sap. Drunk fresh, it is sweet, refreshing and very good for the stomach. After fermenting with sugar for a few hours, it is like beer. After a few more hours it is a bitter, intoxicating liquor. Toddy shops are little dens. If encouraged to taste, beware of adulterated liquor.

Chinese fishing nets Weird contraptions made up of large, delicate teak frames and nets perched above the water like giant praying spiders. They are an efficient and effective way of fishing the backwaters from Cochin right down to Quilon. They were possibly introduced by Chinese traders, like much else in Kerala – deep roofs of houses, temple architecture, conical fishermen's hats and Chinese paper and porcelain.

The structure is simple but expensive to set up and costs about Rs5,000. A combination of cords, pulleys and weights is attached to the two strong poles that soar into the air from the platform. From their tops hang four wooden talons, the netting suspended betwen their tips. It takes four men to operate the seemingly fragile gadget, working the weights and pulleys to swing the net down into the water. Perhaps 15 minutes afterwards, they haul up the catch – sardines, mullet, crab, lobster and freshwater fish. Like everything else in Kerala, the fishermen have their own union to protect themselves from the net owners or, as they put it, the 'stranglehold clutches of exploitation'.

Kathakali Literally, story-play. The most important of the classical dance-drama styles, derived from a form of yoga and revived from almost extinction about 40 years ago. Dancers with weird, elaborate and brightly coloured make-up and costumes perform a religious pantomime dance to recount stories from the great epics. Originally the ritual lasted throughout the night. A dancer (always a man) trains for about 20 years, starting in early childhood. He is kept in peak condition with special aryavaidya massages.

The performance is worship which begins with a good four hours of preparation. The make-up to assume the stylised character is in the strictly traditional colours, head-dress and costume. All make-up and costume is prepared especially for the dancer, using minerals, vegetables and woods. It is all highly symbolic and applied in a fixed order. A green face denotes the pacha character, the hero king or a god such as Krishna, who wears a crown and a white frill from ear to ear. Thadi (beard) is a demon character, whose face is black, with a red beard, and who wears an outsized crown, false nose and a big frill. He is also a comic character.

The actor is dressed by assistants in a gathered skirt like a tutu, a jacket, jewellery and head-dress. He slips a seed from the cunlappuvu plant inside the lower lid of each eye to turn the white a flaming red.

The actual dance, lit by a brass lamp and accompanied by musicians, is as formal as the preparation, yet highly dramatic. It takes years to learn and demands extraordinary muscle control to contort the face and eyes into exaggerated, caricature expressions and to perform sudden leaps, spins and freeze-balances.

Leading exponents to look out for include Guru Gopinath and Chatunni Paniker. The easiest place to see a kathakali performance, including the make-up, is Cochin, where there are daily shows, with explanation and narration, at Art Kerala, Menon & Krishnan Annexe, in a lane off Chittor Road (tel: 39471); performances 6pm make-up; 7pm dance, and at Kathakali Theatre, Cochin Cultural Centre, Durbar Hall Ground (6.30pm).

Krishnayattam, a precursor of Kathakali, is performed at Guruvayur temple, outside Trichur, every clear night from October to April, starting around 10pm. Mohiniattam, meaning dance of the enchantress, is suitably graceful, fluid and seductive. It is found in programmes of Kathakali and Bharata Natyam (see below).

TAMIL NADU

Ayyanars Huge, brightly painted, heraldic terracotta figures of equestrian deities with their horses and elephants, found on village outskirts throughout Tamil Nadu, always with a tiny shrine. They protect the villages from all calamities such as plagues, hauntings and hurricanes. They make barren land fertile, cure illness and act as village watchmen at night – hence the horse, elephant or dog for the deity. A priest looks after each group, performing puja at noon and accepting offerings on behalf of the deities: milk, coconuts, fabric, silver, even prized cattle. Extra money is offered for special requests, followed by thanks when they are granted: either a celebration at the shrine, penitent fire-walking, even more penitent swinging on a hook driven through the shoulder muscles (neither ordeal seems to leave scars) or the offering of another horse. Especially prolific between Madras and Madurai.

The most sensational ayyanar sanctuary is near Pudukatai, outside Tiruchchirappalli, at Namuna Samdran: hundreds of horses, often three deep, form a half-km avenue through a deserted wood. Some are old and rotting, others are newer. They are increased each year when the nearby villagers make a new horse, paint it pink, green, yellow and blue, and offer it to the earth.

Stone-carving Practised on the local granite throughout the state but especially at Thanjavur (Tanjore) and Mahabalipuram. The government is funding the revival of the craft, setting up centres which now attract top carvers who make sculptures for Hindu temples worldwide. All the laborious processes are done in one compound, from chipping smooth the granite block and drawing the design in red chalk, to cutting, chipping, rubbing and polishing the shape – just polishing a capital with emery takes two to three weeks. There is even a resident blacksmith to sharpen tools.

Bharata Natyam Probably the oldest classical Indian dance form, performed for centuries by devadasis (girls dedicated to south Indian temples), following religious texts. It suffered considerably after the British passed the Devadas Act outlawing the devadasi practice. However, the dance was revived early this century.

It is performed solo, by a woman, who begins with alarippu, a dance symbolising the body unfolding as an offering to the gods. She then combines nritta, pure dance, with nritya, emotions described with bold face and hand expressions, to describe the many moods of a young girl's live, as recounted in the poems. The poems are sung by the nattuvanar (conductor) and accompanied by musicians.

The dancer's face may be by turn hurt, laughing, pensive, perturbed or solemn; her hands tell of the moon, anticipation of a love letter, lotus flowers or a bee collecting pollen. Strong rhythms are crucial, heightened by the dancer jingling her ankle bells in fast and strong, often stamping, footsteps, to wittily answer the nattuvanar or musicians.

The centre of Bharata Natyam is Madras. Leading dancers include Leela Samson, Sonal Mansing, Bharati Shivaji, Alarmel Valli, S. Kanaka, Yamini Krishnamurti, Shanta Rao, Indranai Rehman, Vyjayantimala and Kamla and Padma Subramanyam. Balasaraswati, the last of the great devadasi exponents (see Thanjavur), died in 1984.

There are daily performances at the Kalakshetra centre, Museum Theatre, Music Academy, Raja Annamalai Hall and elsewhere (the Tourist Office advises on which dancer to see). There are also regular performances in Bombay (Kala Mandir) and Delhi (Triveni Kala Sangam). Related to Bharata Natyam are the Tamil Nadu Bhagavata Mela dance-drama and Kuravanji dance-opera. So is the Kuchipudi of Andhra Pradesh, recently popularised by dancers Raja and Radha Reddy. Now about 40 years old, they were married as young children, trained together, and their devotion to dance has won them India's highest award, the Padma Shri.

The cities

Southern cities are quite different from northern ones. The pace is slower, and the fewer monuments are usually well balanced with delightful markets, minimal hawkers and plenty of everyday life to watch quietly as the mind and body relaxes. The pace is only slightly faster in Madras and Bangalore, the fourth and fifth largest cities in India, which have most of the action and most of the luxury hotels offering the sort of pampering common in the North. Life out of the cities is altogether simpler; and the magic of the more remote or less visited places easily compensates for an overnight stay in a modest hotel. The key to the South is Out and About, not Where to Stay.

The Deccan: Andhra Pradesh

HYDERABAD

Former capital of the Croesus-rich Nizams who maintained their isolated, Muslim, extravagant court life right up until the 1950s (officially stopping in 1947). They ruled a land bigger than France, whose population was (and is) mainly Hindu and very poor. Today, Hyderabad is the sprawling, crowded and decaying sixth largest city in India and twin capital (with ugly expanding Secunderabad) of Andhra Pradesh, a huge state that takes in most of the Nizam's land plus the Telugu-speaking part of Madras state to the east. The artist Andrew Logan likened it to a great city which has been flattened. Historically, power in Andhra Pradesh moved from Buddhist Ashok's to the Hindu Chaulukyas and Cholas before the Muslims arrived in the 14th century.

Hyderabad was laid out on the banks of the Musi River in 1591 by Mohammed Quli (ruled 1580-1612), when the water supply of Golconda city-fort became inadequate. It was a strict grid plan of two broad intersecting streets with a big arch at the crossing (the Charminar), some 14,000 shops, schools, mosques, baths and caravanserais lining the streets. In 1652, the traveller Tavernier compared it to Orleans, 'well built and opened out', and by 1672 Abbé Carré found it 'the centre of all trade in the East'. Mohammed Quli was fourth of the Qutb Shahi dynasty (1512-1687) which finally lost Golconda to Mughal emperor Aurangzeb in 1687, the year after he won Bijapur.

After Aurangzeb's death in 1707, the Mughal empire weakened and in 1713 the Mughal-appointed viceroy of Hyderabad, Mir Kamurddin Khan, given the title Nizam-ul-Mulk (Regulator of the Land), declared independence and initiated the Asaf Jahn dynasty. Their riches, from land and gifts, made them some of the wealthiest individuals in the world. Gold bricks were piled in stacks and chests overflowed with diamonds and pearls.

Stories, some apocryphal, abounded. When the tenth and last Nizam, who ruled 1911-1950, was offered an egg-sized diamond by a jeweller, he pondered for a moment on how to use it, then asked for six more, to make a set of buttons. A 280-carat diamond was used as a paperweight. He was rumoured to be a miserly host yet he presented the Royal Air Force with a complete squadron of Hurricane fighters on the outbreak of the Second World War. The nobility lived in eccentric style: a Minister of Justice was reputed to rise at 4.30am, exercise with dumbbells, swallow two huge pills of opium, go riding, then return for a hearty tumbler of chicken soup.

As the main Muslim court of India after the collapse of the Mughal Empire, Muslim nobles and merchants from the North as well as Muslim immigrants came south to cocoon themselves in their traditions, cuisine, dress and culture – an introverted Muslim refuge in the Hindu South. Old Hyderabad still has a 19th-century, courtly air about it. But it may not exist much longer: the Andhra Pradesh Government want to put a bulldozer through the lot to 'modernise' the only part of their capital left with any character.

THE HARD FACTS Airport 7km from Hyderabad centre. Four hotels for different tastes: flashy new, reliable oldish concrete, and two characterful old.

Krishna Oberoi, Banjara Hills (tel: 222121; telex:0425 6931); the Oberoi Group's first hotel in South India is an unashamedly flashy, up-market marble machine, with matching prices. 274 rooms, all mod. cons of the highest quality, good food and beautifully landscaped gardens. For more intimate and friendly good service, the *Gateway Hotel* on Banjara Hill, Road No.1, Banjara Hills (tel: 222222; telex: 0425-6947); known as the Banjara; concrete, lakeside building, newly refurbished. Part of the Taj Group's Gateway hotels. 124 rooms, some overlooking the lake where there is also a wide restaurant terrace for watching Hyderabad's Sunday kite-flying. All mod. cons include a good pool, excellent food (especially Hyderabadi Mughlai).

For character, the *Ritz Hotel*, Hillfort Palace (tel: 233571; telex: 0425-6215); an ex-palace built in Scottish baronial style for Princess Niloufar, daughter-in-law of the Nizam and now a genteel hotel for over 30 years. 40 rooms, some with controllable air-conditioning. Adequate facilities; grounds nice for tea and drinks; reports of disappointing food. Rooms vary from poky to extremely spacious.

The *Rock Castle Hotel*, Road No. 6, Banjara Hills (tel: 335412/3), modest hotel, former favourite with the Raj and still has a loyal clientele and strong character, but is rather far from the city centre. 22 rooms, extensive gardens.

Stop press: the new deluxe *Bhaskar Palace Hotel*, Banjara Hills (tel: 223676), part of the Ashok ITDC group, with 225 rooms, has good reports, particularly of the 'fantastically good' food in its revolving rooftop restaurant.

Tourist information is scanty. Try both the Government of India Tourist Office, 3-6-369/A/25 & 26 Sandozi Building, 2nd floor, 26 Himayat Nagar (tel:66877); they run unsatisfactory day-long tours of the city (8am-6.30pm) which give a fleeting look at Golconda Fort and

waste time at the gardens and the zoo. And try Andhra Pradesh Tourism Department, Lidcap Building, Himayat Nagar and their Tourist Information Bureau at Yatri Niwas, SP Road, Securdrabad. The best news and entertainments information is found in *The Deccan Chronicle* (performing arts are at Ravindra Bharati). There is no good guide-book. The bookshop A. A. Hussain, on Abid (also known as M G) Road, is an essential stopping-point for stocking up on information if travelling south through Karnataka.

The Banjara will arrange sailing on Husain Sagar Lake and, for the desperate, golf is available on very brown greens. Indira Park is pleasant and has rowing. There is a lot of local publicity for dreary lakes, dams and reservoirs. Quite naturally, the Indians get very excited about water; Europeans usually get quite enough back home.

Having a strongly Muslim element, Hyderabad museums and some shops close on Friday.

OUT AND ABOUT The best way to see Hyderabad's buildings is to start by going out to the earlier city of Golconda (11.5km, see below). Back in the dusty, sprawling double city of Hydrabad and Secunderabad, start with the **Charminar,** the central landmark of the old city; a carved, marble triumphant arch with upstairs mosque and minarets, built in 1591. (If you can pursuade the chaukidar to open up, there are excellent views from the top.)

Surrounding it is one of the best bazaars in India and certainly the most interesting and colourful in the South. There are old chemists with bottle of sickly sweet Muslim perfumes and wooden boxes of spices, herbs, powders and scales; walls of rainbow-coloured bangles; piles of lunghis; Banjara women jangling their goblet-sized earrings; huge coloured tassels for decorating the hair; Muslim women jostling to buy bangles, silver and thick brocades; smart ladies buying pearls; and antique shops selling off courtiers' clothes and trinkets. In the tiny alleys, craftsmen use fingers and toes to work on fine silver filigree.

Nearby is the huge Mecca Masjid (1614-87), the Nizams' tombs in a row on the left of the courtyard, and the Asar Khana (relic house), with beautiful tiles.

Few of the old city palaces in the surrounding streets can be visited, but it is interesting to wander the dusty streets of Chowk and Lad Bazar (west of Charminar) to glimpse evocative, decaying facades; also find here the old Paigarh, Chaumhalla and Deorhi Asman Jah palaces. However, to see the huge, extravagant and immaculate Falaknuma Palace, built in 1872 by a noble out beyond Jahannuma Palace (really just a garden) and after 1911 occasionally used as a guest house by the Nizam, apply to the Chief of Protocol, Secretariat, Secretariat Road (your hotel will help).

For an idea of the opulent, nawabi taste, the extraordinary **Salar Jung museum,** sited right on the Musi river, displays a tiny part of the vast collection formed by Nawab Mir Yousuf Ali Khan Salar Jung III (1889-1949) and his ancestors, whose family produced five of the Nizams' prime ministers. Originally housed in Salar Jung's palace, the Diwan Deori (the prime minister's house, still standing about a mile north of the Charminar), it was moved in 1968 (and reportedly much pillaged) to fill 38 galleries of a dull, pink, concrete box with some 40,000 objects. Salar Jung travelled in Europe and the Middle East for 40 years, box of gold in hand, to buy whatever tickled his well-trained eye, be it fine Indian jade, French ormolu furniture or high Victorian oil paintings.

Particularly impressive are the ground-floor rooms containing family heirlooms, the textiles, lacquer, sculpture, decorative arts and miniature paintings. Upstairs are rooms of jade, bidri ware and armour. And just a fraction is on view. The corridor storage cupboards are stacked from floor to ceiling. Café, reference library, good publications. Open Sat.-Thurs., 10am-5pm.

The Government Archaeological Museum in the Public Gardens has fine sculpture from local Buddhist sites and from Warangal, plus bidri ware, coins, arms and armour and textiles (open Tues.-Sun., 10.30am-5pm).

On the north bank of the Musi lies the newer town established by the British. The fine British Residency, like a vast British stately home, was built by the Nizam for James Achilles Kirkpatrick to designs by Samuel Russell in 1803, and is 'one of the finest Georgian houses in India' (Philip Davies). (It is now a college, but can be visited.) Kirkpatrick was so popular with the Nizam that he was adopted as a son and became the only person to represent the British and the Nizam simultaneously; but his marriage to a beautiful Hyderabadi aristocrat, although at first approved by the Company powers, so alarmed the later Governor General, Lord Wellesley, that he narrowly escaped a public inquiry. Sunsets are best seen from the Birla Mandir, the modern, dazzling white hilltop temple which was built by the Birla Foundation in 1966-76 of Rajasthan marble, decorated with reliefs of the Ramayana and surrounded by statue-studded, lush gardens. Several kilometres north of here lies Secunderabad.

RESTAURANTS Best Hyderabadi food is at the *Banjara* and *Krishna Oberoi*; then at two restaurants on Basheer Bagh: *Mughal Durbar* and *Nilgara*. The best biryani can be found at *Hotel Medina*, near the Charminar. Cheap and crammed with locals. Haleen (lamb cooked with wheat) is a special Hyderabadi dish. (For more on Mughlai food, see Delhi eating section). Special local sweetmeats are ashrafi (gold coin), with a Mughal stamp on each one, and badam ki jali (almond nest).

The adventurous should try one of the many Irani cafés for nihari, the sustaining traditional breakfast. Try the *Rainbow Restaurant* on Abid Road (also called M G Road) and order paya (chicken soup), ladled from a huge cauldron, shirman (bread) and pauna (rich tea made with milk), served 5-8am (see also Bombay eating). The really brave polish it off with a digestive paan from across the road.

For other cuisines, good south Indian food is found at the several branches of *Kamat*, the best one being at Ravandrapati. Locals patronise the *Blue Diamond* Chinese restaurant, but for a blow-out deluxe Chinese meal go to the *Oberoi*. Local Andhra dishes are found at *Shampuri* in Tilak Road and at the *Satkar* and *Sampurna* hotels.

SHOPPING AND CRAFTS The Charminar bazaar has everything from pearls and the special Hyderabadi bangles to bidri work and silversmithing. The pearl shops line Pathergatty, one of the Charminar's principal roads, and Mangatrai Ramkumar is one of the more helpful. Lepakshi Handicrafts Emporium at Gun Foundry (top of Abid Road, good packaging and shipping) has good bidri ware, including cuff links, dishes and boxes. There are kondapalli (sandalwood toys); Andhra Pradesh fabrics such as ikat weaves from Pochhampalli or Koyyalagudam; striped and checked silk from Dharmavaram; dark fabrics from Narayanpet; the broad double-stripe palos of Madhavream saris; and himru (cotton and silk mixtures), worn by Muslim women who are not permitted to wear pure silk.

The assistants at Lepakshi Handicrafts can put visitors in touch with the AP Weavers Cooperative Societies and the Weavers Service Centres who can advise on which weaving villages to visit; for instance, Pochhampalli is 60km; Koyyalagudam 80km. Andhra Pradesh has recently successfully revived the finest ikat weaving. And kalamkari (kalam is the bamboo stick used for painting) painting and printing tradition is alive and well, too, practised at Srikalahasti and Masulipatnam; the incredibly fine designs recount the great Hindu epics. Find a variety of all these at the big Handloom House is on Mukharam Jahi (Salar Jung) Road. There are more fabric shops on Nampali Road. Jamma Raat flea market is held early Thursday morning near the Charminar.

GOLCONDA

11.5km from Hyderabad. A magnificent, deserted fort-city of the Qutb Shahi kings, built on a steep, granite hill. In the 14th century the Hindu Kakatiya kings of Warangal gave the modest hill fort to the Muslim Bahmani kings whose capitals were Gulbarga, then Bidar (see below). The Bahmani kingdom was divided between five governors who each declared independence at the turn of the 15th century, initiating the dynasties of Bidar, Berar, Ahmadnagar, Bijapur and Golconda.

Sultan Quli Qutb Shah (1512-43), the first of seven Qutb Shahi rulers, and his two successors, the brothers Jamshed Quli (1543-50) and Ibrahim Quli (1550-80), built the fort which was lost to Emperor Aurangzeb after his long siege of 1687. It followed the pattern of Gulbarga and Bidar fortifications but was larger and more impregnable. The legendary diamond bazaars (supplied from mines at Parteal and Kolur, 130km away) lined the road up to the Fateh Darwaza (double gateway) guarded by Abyssinians. A curtain wall across the gateway made it difficult for enemy elephants to gather momentum.

Inside, enough buildings remain to reconstruct in the mind's eye the complete layout and lifestyle of the rich and wealthy state. There is a sophisticated Persian-wheel water system; hot and cold water pipes; Turkish baths; bazaars; a ministers' hall with built-in shelves for the files; massive weights for measuring out elephant food; ingenious acoustics between gateway and citadel; royal palaces with scented gardens; a swimming pool and secret hide-outs for the watchful eunuch guards of the zenana; a people's complaints room; natural air-conditioning and roof-gardens in the hilltop citadel; and even fragments of a celadon china dinner service.

Nearby are the more complete and just as impressive Persian-style, bulbous-domed tombs of the royals, silhouetted against the clear blue Deccan sky and set in a beautiful garden of blossoming trees and clouds of bougainvillea. They are based on the tombs at Bidar but are much more flamboyant and baroque, with stucco ornament, fancy pinnacles and blown-up, bulbous domes. A ruler would have his tomb built during his lifetime, often with a small mosque for the last rites beside it; then it was furnished with carpets, chandeliers, gold brocades, silver censers and manuscripts. Good little guidebook. Small museum nearby. The Fort and tombs are best visited for a long morning, taking a guide. Exposed and hot, so take a hat.

WARANGAL AND HANMKONDA

157km north-east of Hyderabad. Definitely a challenging day trip from Hyderabad for architecture buffs. It is also worthwhile if you are going on south to see the wonderful Chalukyan temples at Aihole, Badami and Pattadakal. The journey passes paddy fields, piles of perilously balanced giant boulders, old forts and every sort of people from bejewelled Banjaras to rats-tail-coiffed fakirs (religious men).

The Kakatiyas ruled from their mud-brick fort at Warangal from the 12th to the 14th centuries, until conquered by the Tughlaqs of Delhi. They took the Chalukyans' architectural style to new heights, seen in the *Hanmkonda temple*, built in 1163 by King Rudra Deva. The low-roofed, carved building has a massive, monolithic Nandi bull in front of it and a hall of elaborately carved columns, giving it the nickname 'Thousand-pillar Temple'. (South Indian temples often have a 'Thousand-pillar Temple' but few have anywhere near that number of columns.) Badrakali temple is on a hillock between Hanmkonda and Warangal. The *fort* remains at Warangal are spectacular, with massive walls and a free-standing gateway. The interior of the fort is strewn with quantities of black stone sculpture.

The really keen go on north 77km to catch a handful of 13th century Kakatiya temples; first to the elaborately carved Ramappa Temple (1213) at *Palampet*, considered one of the finest pieces of Deccan architecture with fine carvings of mythical beasts, dancing girls and musicians, a great black nandi and good lakeside picnic spots, and then 6km further to *Ghanpur* for the two temple ruins. It is best to go by car or bus. There is a good ITDC trip (excluding Palampet) in a fast, air-conditioned bus, but they need some persuasion to admit that it exists. To stay, modest accommodation at Warangal.

ANDHRA PRADESH BEACHES

If the barren countryside of Hyderabad makes you long for lush valleys and beach-lapping waves, there are two off-beat beaches on the Andhra Pradesh east coast, accessible by air, rail and road. *Vishakapatnam* (about 637km), known as Vizig, has seaside hotels, long empty beaches and some old buildings to visit (see p. 202). *Machilipatnam* (350km) known to the British as Banda, lies south-east of Hyderabad at the mouth of the great Krishna river. Probably India's least visited beach, there are British-built bungalows by the sea and some of the finest kalamkari workers to watch at work in town (see p. 220); Vayudoot flies to Vijayawada, 70km away; stay at the modest sea-shore *Circuit House* (bookable through the Collector, Krishna District, Andhra Pradesh).

The Deccan: Karnataka

BIDAR

110km north-west of Hyderabad, 40km north-east of Gulbarga. Described by historian Simon Digby as 'a sensational stone fort built on a natural bluff rising from the plain'. Bidar was the capital of the Bahmani kingdom 1428-c 1489, then of the Barid Shahis until Ibrahim Adil Shah II of Bijapur annexed it in 1619. Besieged by Aurangzeb in 1656 and under a series of Mughal governors until 1724 when it was swallowed up by the Nizams. The *tombs* on the plains outside the town are magnificent. There are eight fine Bahmani ones at Ashtur, their interiors decorated with calligraphic and floral designs in gold and bright colours. A watchman opens them and supplies a mirror to reflect the light into the tombs (open daily, 8am-5pm). The lesser Baridi tombs are west, towards Nanded.

Inside the walls, the old town of Bidar surrounds the soaring, green and yellow tiled Madrasa (University), founded in 1472 by Mohammad Gawan, merchant traveller and scholar. He equipped it with a library of 3,000 manuscripts and made it a centre for scholars from throughout the Muslim world. You can see bidri work being done in the narrow lanes.

The *Inner Fort*, mostly built by Mohammad Shah (1482-1518), is entered through a massive double gateway. Beyond lies a complete city fort. Inside the entrance, on the left, is the Rangin Mahal (Colourful Palace), whose rooms are exquisitely decorated with tiles, inlaid mother-of-pearl, carved granite and carved wooden pillars. If locked, the museum curator has a key. Good views from roof. There are also baths, a mosque, palaces, audience halls and pavilions, many with coloured tiles, paintings and carving intact. The little museum in the middle is excellent (open daily, 8am-5pm).

To stay overnight, the fort itself has modest rooms; otherwise, the State-run *Barid Shahi* (tel: 571); or *Habshi Kot Guest House* (apply to Executive Engineer, Bidar).

GULBARGA

110km from Bidar; 145km from Bijapur, along a road that descends through rolling hills of wheat fields, with rather wild-looking locals clad only in a loin-cloth. It was the Bahmani capital from 1347 until the move to Bidar in 1424. Ala-ud-din Hasan Bahman Shah, a Persian adventurer from the Delhi court, established the Bahmani dynasty after he left the service of mad Mohammad Tughlaq, the Delhi Sultan who in 1327 forced the Delhi populace to move to a new capital at Daulatabad in the northern Deccan (see p. 56). The architecture of Gulbarga, Bidar and Golconda has a distinct style, merging Persian and Delhi Sultanate elements.

There are several interesting things to see, east and west of the modern, industrial town. To the west, bullocks with incredibly long, red-painted horns loaf about in the wide, muddy moat around the *fort* which now contains only the Bala Hisar (citadel), some of the towers and the splendid Jami Masjid (1367) with its unusual domed mihrab. Because of its resemblance to Cordoba's mosque, local legend attributes its design to a Spaniard. Nearby are five big, black, domed cubes which are royal *tombs*.

East of the city lies a dazzling white *Dargah* (Shrine) of the Muslim Chishti saint, Gesunawaz (1321-1422), who migrated here from Nizamuddin in Delhi. Its plastered exterior is a foil to the riot of lace-like red, yellow and silver arabesques covering the interior walls. (Women have to peep through the doorway.) The tomb of his favourite wife, opposite, is also covered in murals. Four more royal tombs at nearby Haft Gumbad, beside the lake.

In the town, the historic *covered bazaar* and side-streets are packed with activity for the Saturday market. Peasants flock in from the surrounding plains, bringing their bullocks, carts and wares, buying supplies and having a good time. To stay overnight, or just to eat, go to *Hotel Pariwar*, Station Road (tel: 1422/1522), spotlessly clean, south Indian food only.

Gulbarga's old ruined city, *Firuzabad* (25km), lies on the road to Bijapur; probably established around 1400, with surviving walls, bastions, gateways, Jami Masjid, etc. (plus grand tomb complex 2km to the north), showing a one-off royal building project influenced by both Vijayanagar (see p. 225) and Central Asia. Good picnicking spot.

BIJAPUR

145km from Gulbarga; 120km from Badami; about 250km from Hampi, through dusty roads, past Banjara women in all their red, blue and saffron finery, limbs sparkling with ivory; past men with deep saffron or dazzling pink turbans. Bijapur is a perfect provincial city, a pre-industrial time-warp. Life here ambles along gently, in the fabulous walled Muslim city of broad streets, majestic buildings, lawns, ex-palaces, old houses with carved balconies, ruins and mosques. Transport is by bicycle rickshaw or by tongas with jingling bells, driven by children who constantly honk-honk their squeezy horns. There is hardly a car. Banjara gypsies, processions of white bullocks doused with pink water, an antique palanquin, and pipers and drummers add splashes of colour to the bustling evening bazaars.

The Chalukyans ruled Bijapur until 1198 when their kingdom was divided between the Hoysalas in the south and the Yadavas in the north. The city was annexed to Ala-ud-din Khilji's Delhi Sultanate in 1318 with his son as Governor. Then, when the Tughlaqs took over Delhi and Sultanate power in the South waned, two kingdoms rose in this area, divided by the River Krishna: Bahmani (capital Gulbarga, then Bidar) in the north and Vijayanagar (capital Vijayanagar, or Hampi) in the south. In 1489 Yusuf Adil Khan, Governor of Bijapur for the Bahmanis, declared independence, founding the Adil Shahi dynasty. The four other governors did the same sooner or later, at Bidar, Berar, Ahmadnagar and Golconda – only once joining forces to crush the mighty Vijayanagars at the Battle of Talikota in 1565. Like the Rajput rulers in the North, their unwillingness to join forces enabled Aurangzeb finally to pull each into the Mughal yoke; Bijapur was taken in 1686, a triumph the emperor celebrated with a grand entry and by having his victory inscribed on Bijapur's great gun, the Malik-i-Maidan.

The reign of Ali Adil Shah I (1557-79) marked Bijapur's rise. He expanded and consolidated the kingdom, laid Bijapur's waterworks, built the central moated *citadel* of halls, palaces, pavilions and gardens, encouraged the arts and built the *Jami Masjid* to commemorate the Talikota victory. (See the painted mihrab behind a black curtain.) Under his successor, Ibrahim Adil Shah II (1580-1626), Bijapur reached its political, cultural and territorial zenith. The kingdom stretched right to Mysore. Mark Zebrowski compares Ibrahim to Akbar and calls him 'the greatest patron of the arts the Deccan produced'. *Ibrahim Rauza*, the exquisite walled tomb and mosque of the ruler and his family, is just one of the sublime buildings he constructed. The exterior is covered with faded floral murals and carved Arabic calligraphy. Romantic silhouettes are enhanced by the bulbous Turkish domes here, as at Golconda, instead of the straight-necked Persian shapes.

Then began the decline. His son, Mohammad Adil Shah (1626-56), built the huge-domed, ponderous *Gol Gumbaz* for his mausoleum. The dome is thought to be second in size only to St Peter's, Rome. (Exceptional views from the roof outside the whispering gallery.) It is set in a pretty garden, with a gatehouse now housing the museum which has old Bijapur carpets and paintings upstairs (open Sat.-Thurs., 10am-5pm). Then came over-stretched extravagance at the end: the soaring arches of the *Bara Kaman*, Ali Adil Shah II's even bigger tomb (wonderful at sunrise), which was still unfinished when the dynasty fell to the Mughal, then Nizam, overlords.

Bijapur does not excite everyone, particularly those arriving here from Vijayanagar's splendours. Reports vary from 'mournful' to buildings 'as huge as they are ugly'.

But most visitors allow at least two days (tempting to stay longer) to see the many fine buildings, hiring as transport a rickshaw boy who will wait at each building. Most are open constantly; a few 8am-5.30pm. The vegetable and fruit market, where villagers sell their produce, is particularly large and varied here, and the shops around have busy tailors, bird-sellers and nice simple cafés. Behind the market, towards the Upil Buruj and the gun, copperworkers beat away at great dishes and plates. And an evening trip to the local cinema is great fun.

Stay at the Karnataka state-run *Hotel Adil Shahi* (tel: 934); simple, usually clean rooms (with mosquito nets, essential here) around a central garden courtyard with cascades of bougainvillea; order meals several hours in advance; the nearby *Hotel Adil Shahi Annexe* is slightly more expensive. Reports say the *Tourist Bungalow* has much improved and is now clean, with 'gets-there-in-the-end' service. *Hotel Tourist* and *Hotel Midland* are recommended for food. Helpful Tourist Office in the Adil Shahi (open Mon.-Sat., 10.30am-1.30pm; 2.15-5.30pm). As at Gulbarga and Bidar, there is no good guide book or book shop, so arrive prepared.

If heading westwards to Bombay from here, a good route is via Panhala and the Shivaji forts around Chiplun (see p. 156).

AIHOLE, PATTADAKAL AND BADAMI

The three sites are very close to one another and lie 120km from Bijapur; 100km from Hubli; 150km from Hampi. Here is to be found some of the earliest Hindu architecture and the foundation of the achievements that followed: three clusters of glorious, well-preserved *Chalukyan caves and temples*. They are all cleaned and maintained within spick and span lawns and blossoming trees. Round about are peaceful rural farms. The bullocks' horns are decorated with big pompoms and bells. And there are delightful children (who, for once, do not ask for coins or pens), itinerant musicians and the occasional overflowing cartload of villagers full of festive gaiety.

The Early Chalukya kings, sworn enemies of the Pallavas, became powerful rulers in the central Deccan from the 4th to the 8th centuries. Aihole was the first capital, replaced by Badami from the reign of Pulakesin I (543-44) (who marked his accession by a horse sacrifice) until 757 when the dynasty was overthrown by the Rashtrakutas. Pattadakal's importance was as the second capital, a religious centre and coronation city during the 7th to 9th centuries. (The Late Chalukyas ruled 10th-12th centuries at nearby Dambal, Lakkundi and Ittagi, see below.)

Aihole Aihole is 46km from Badami, 32km

from Pattadakal. Here, the earlier temples are simple and squat, with heavy, flat roofs. Yet they are decorated with pierced stone windows and columns crisp as if turned on a vast lathe only yesterday. There are sculptured images of loving couples, rosettes and friezes. Lad Khan Temple is probably the earliest; Meguti, Kontigudi and the apsidal Durga are progressively more complex until they acquire a tower over the shrine. The Durga Temple (late 7th century) has stunning reliefs on the ambulatory and a developed shikara (tower). This looks forward to the northern, Indo-Aryan Hindu architecture. More remains are strewn in and around the town. To stay overnight in this delightful, remote setting, go to the *Tourist Bungalow*; clean and simple. They will prepare meals for passing visitors. Order on arrival so that then it is ready when you have finished seeing some of the temples.

Pattadakal Badami 14km; Aihole 32km. The buildings, grouped closely together here and built for royal ceremony, are now higher and more complex; sculpture has taken off. And the architecture interestingly draws on various styles from north and south India. Most impressive are: the large Virupaksha (or Lokeshwara) Temple (c.745), covered in lively sculptures recounting the major battles of the great Mahabharata and Ramayana epics and depicting Chalukya social life; and its neighbouring Mallikarjuna (or Trailokeshwara) Temple (c. 740), whose carvings concentrate on the Bhagavata Purana, the story of Krishna; see also the gently swaying, loving couples. Both temples were built by queens of Vikramaditya II to celebrate the defeat of the Pallavas at Kanchipuram; and both temples are built in a nascent Dravidian style, which was already being developed under the Pallava dynasty (5th-8th centuries) in Tamil Nadu (known then as Dravidadesh).

Other temples follow the Indo-Aryan style of the North, such as Papanath Temple (c.680). About 1km from the temple compound, in the Badami direction, is a Jain temple with two beautiful stone elephants. There is no accommodation.

Between here and Bandami lies Mahakuta, well worth stopping at to see an Early Chalukya temple complex still in use, the two main temples (7th century) and a dozen smaller shrines grouped round a central tank.

Badami Badami is 46km from Aihole, 14km from Pattadakal. The only lively town of the three. The slap-bashing of women washing clothes in the tank (man-made lake) and their gossip and singing echo all round the sheer cliffs rising high either side. Beside the water, bullocks, orange rickshaws and children squeeze between the tightly packed, white-washed houses, which have exterior stairs leading to the roof.

The four large rock-cut cave temples (6th century) in the south-west cliff have magnificent sculptures of giant-sized gods, so vivacious they seem about to leap out for a dance. After the second cave, at the top of perilously steep steps, is a ruined fort area with incredible views. (Try to avoid the unofficial cave guides.) These are particularly interesting if you are going on to the Pallava caves at Mahabalipuram.

On the other side of the tank lie the pristine and fascinating museum and the waterside Bhutanatha Temples. There are more temples and ruins up the cliff, which is topped by Malegitti Shivalaya Temple. It is the inscriptions on these temples which testify to cultural relations with the enemy Pallavas, and explain the cross-influences here and at the later temples at Aihole, etc. What the architectural historians debate is who developed which building and decorative element first.

To stay overnight, the nicest places are the *Tourist Bungalow*, clean but only two suites, so be sure to book; or there is the state-run *Chalukya Hotel* next door, clean and friendly, with good food. Here it is important to make a fuss over being given boiled water to drink and, if you ask, they will make fresh, strong morning coffee. There is reasonable local food at *Laxmi Vilas* restaurant, next to the tonga stand. The Archaeological Department and Tourist Office are both useless, so arrive prepared.

DAMBAL, LAKKUNDI AND ITTAGI

To come this far and not continue to the astounding deserted city of great Vijayanagar at Hampi, one of India's marvels, would be a shame. Furthermore, the very rural route here takes in the three Later Chalukya cities of Ittagi, Dambal and Lakkundi (10th-12th centuries) plus other most beautiful and quite isolated sites of well-preserved Late Chalukya temples. As Christopher Tadgell says: 'the Badami-Hampi drive includes sublime buildings which are a synthesis of northern and southern schools'.

Taking food and drink supplies, start off southwards. First stop is *Gadag* for the Sarasvati Temple (9th century). Nearby, on a detour along the Bangalore road, *Dambal's* Dodda Basappa Temple (12th century) is close to the more southern Hoysala temples near Mysore. (There is a Rest House here.) Then, back on the road to Hospet, the little town of *Lakkundi* has a remarkable 17 Hindu and Jain temples (11th-12th centuries), each built of schist, precisely carved and richly decorated. Between here and Hospet, a road to the left leads first to *Kukkunur* where temples of the 9th and 10th centuries fill the development gap between early Gadag and later Dambal and Ittagi; and then to *Ittagi* itself where the fully developed Mahadeva Temple

(1112) even outdoes Gadag's finery. Every element of the porches, enclosed mandapa and towered sanctuary, has been finely lathe-turned or faceted and then given incredibly delicate decoration. And, a fascinating eccentricity, there are little models of all the known varieties of shikaras (temple towers). Ittigi is a good picnic stop.

VIJAYANAGAR (HAMPI)

150km from Badami; 350km from Bangalore. Palatial capital of the Vijayanagars, the largest empire in South India's history. At its height under Krishnadevaraya (1509-29), the city rivalled Rome in splendour and controlled almost all of India south of the Krishna and Tungabhadra Rivers. The Vijayanagars rose at the same time as the Bahmanis. While fighting in the Deccan, the Sultanate army took two local Telegu princes prisoner, brought them to Delhi, converted them to Islam and sent them back south to restore Sultanate authority.

Once that was done, the princes, Harihara and Bukka, broke loose to establish their own kingdom in 1336 – and reverted to Hinduism. In 1346 their victory over the Hoysalas made them pre-eminent in the South. Harihara planned and built the magnificent new city of Vijayanagar (City of Victory), which became the capital in 1343.

The city was vast: 33 sqkm within seven concentric lines of fortifications, sustaining a population of about half a million and alive with international bazaars that impressed European travellers and were reputed to sparkle with, literally, piles of gold. Modest-sized buildings were embellished with profuse and sumptuous carvings, described by the architectural historian, Percy Brown, as 'a range of ideals, sensations, emotions, prodigalities, abnormalities, of forms and formlessness, and even eccentricities, that only a super-imaginative mind could create . . .' He compares it to the Baroque period in Europe as the 'supremely passionate flowering of the Dravidian style'.

Wealth came in from controlling the spice trade to the south, the cotton trade to the southeast, clearing surrounding forests for agriculture, elaborate hydraulic engineering for irrigation and, of course, the levying of a land-tax. And wealth went out on imported horses for the cavalry and a mercenary army of a million (many of whom were Turks). Tragedy struck in 1565 when four of the five independent Deccan Sultans that had split up the Bahmani kingdom finally joined forces to win a crushing victory at the Battle of Talikota. (It was a short-lived victory as the Mughals already had their eye on the South.)

Today, it is a most magical place to visit. The deserted buildings of the ruined city straddle the barren hillocks piled with huge Karnataka boulders, all glowing fiery orange at sunset. Down beside the Tungabhadra River is *Hampi bazaar*, worth visiting first. In the bazaar is the bookshop, Aspiration Stores. It is run by the helpful Guthi brothers and stocks A. H. Longhurst's good guide, *Hampi Ruins*, lots of other useful books, post-cards and, usually, detailed map of the ruins. Hampi Tourist Counter, on the same side, supplies useless guides and a joke map and is to be avoided. Here also is the main temple complex.

After this, it is best to set off on foot, hired bicycle or by car, to seek out buildings in the Royal and hilly Sacred centres. Don't miss, amongst other wonders, the Ramachandra (or Hajari Rama) Temple with carvings of dancing girls and scenes from the Ramayana. The palace throne platform is coated in exuberant carving. There are majestic elephant stables, the queens' bath house and much, much more. At the Sacred centre, found up through the banana groves, the great Vitthala Temple (16th century) with its richly carved animal columns, is sublime at sunset; with its rich carving, open mandapa, carved stone chariot and three gopuras, George Michell, a Vijayanagar devotee, describes it as: 'one of the outstanding achievements of the period'.

The most pleasant place to stay is *Hampi Power Station Guest House*, 3km from Kamalapuram. Book in writing to the Superintending Engineer, HES, Tungabhadra Board, Tungabhadra Dam, Hospet (tel: 8272), ordering meals if you want them. Kamalapuram, at the south end of the ruins, is where the *PWD Inspection Bungalow* (a converted temple) is, opposite the Archaeological Office. There is other modest accommodation in and around the ruins, none to be recommended. At *Hospet* (10km), there is a very helpful Tourist Office on Patel Road, near the very good Shanbhag restaurant at the corner of College Road and Taluk Office Circle. *Malligi Tourist Home*, off Hampi Road (tel: 8377), is OK; the newish hotel on Railway Station Road is not; commute to the ruins from here by auto rickshaw. From Hampi or Badami the road west to Goa, via Belgaum, is a glorious drive up over the hills, then plunging down among the lush green palms to the sea (worth pausing at Dambal).

VIJAYANAGAR-BANGALORE

There are two routes. The direct one has a stop at *Chitradurga* (where the Hubli road joins) to stretch legs by clambering about the 17th century fort later taken by southern hero Haider Ali after which Tipu Sultan added a palace. The indirect one (with more interesting landscape) goes via *Gooty*, *Penukonda*, and *Lepakshi*. The first, 50km north of Anantapur, is the great fort

(1509-30) where Clive's Maratha ally Murari Rao lived – see the special seat from which he watched prisoners be hurled to their deaths; later taken by Haider Ali. The second, outside Anantapur, is a Vijayanagar fort where the royals came after the 1565 defeat, a massive affair with Hindu and Muslim sacred and royal buildings, well worth exploring. The third, a few km further south, is the huge Virabhadra temple complex (16th century) built by two brother governors of this area of Vijayanagar and still preserving not only its fine sculptures but also its extensive, brightly-coloured paintings in the mandapa showing stories from the Hindu epics and, most interesting, portraits of the two patrons.

BANGALORE

350km from Vijayanagar; 140km from Mysore; 185km from Hasan. An excellent and efficient base for booking up, resting up, shopping and equipping oneself before setting off north, south, east or west. This is the capital of Karnataka state and India's fastest-growing and fifth largest city. It is also the seventh fastest-growing city in the world; between 1970 and 1980, its population increased by 75%, much of it caused by the influx of science-based industries. Its epithets of being a garden city and a naturally air-conditioned city are almost entirely inappropriate today.

Countless blossoming trees have been axed. The Preservation of Trees Act, imposing a hefty fine or imprisonment for illegally felling a tree, has had little effect. Concrete mixers worked over-time. And smog has arrived. However, the more traditional occupations of coffee-trading, sericulture, stud farms, horse-racing and film-making still thrive. There are more cinema seats per capita (with heavy competition from Trivandrum) and a wider linguistic range of films than in any other Indian city. And there are big parks, wide avenues, plenty of trees with hydrangea-sized blooms. And some elegant bungalows survive – just.

It was Kempe Gowda, a feudal lord of the Vijayanagar kingdom, who built a mud fort here in 1537, enlarged and rebuilt in stone by Tipu Sultan's father, Haider Ali. After being the subject of numerous diplomatic gifts and sales, Bangalore became a British garrison town in 1809, in place of unhealthy Srirangapatnam. The British constructed wide avenues for their troops; built pretty Gothic and Classic bungalows for their families set in gardens with roses, tennis courts, croquet lawns and aviaries; and erected churches, museums and colleges. They erected a statue of the plump Queen-Empress Victoria – now just a few steps from the skinny Mahatma. They even built the little Russell Market to protect the memsahibs, following scandal when a money-lender assisted a lady to pay for an abortion and then demanded her favours himself.

In 1937, the happy Winston Churchill wrote from Bangalore that he and two chums, Reginald Barnes and Hugo Baring, had taken over a 'palatial bungalow' from a friend. The columns of its deep verandahs were 'wreathed in purple bougainvillea'. They had two acres of land, 150 roses, kept about 30 horses and devoted themselves to 'the serious purpose of life . . . polo'.

There are still those who feel equally happy about Bangalore. Bruce Palling, veteran Indian hand, praises it as 'the Versailles of the South' with its 'sense of order, of civic pride, enormous botanical gardens and wacky museums'.

THE HARD FACTS There are good air connections north and south, including direct flights to Goa, Madras, Trivandrum and Mangalore for beaches (see Sun chapter). Airport 7km from city centre. There are two special festivals in addition to the regulars: Karaga, symbolising strength of mind, when people balance tall piles of pots on their heads; and Kadaleskaye (Groundnut Fair), held at the Bull Temple to appease the great bull who might destroy the crop. Bangalore still blossoms with jacaranda, laburnum, cassia, pride of India, peacock glory and camelfoot in April-July and bougainvillea, jasmine, honeysuckle and other creepers from December onwards. It is always busy with businessmen, supplemented at week-ends by race-goers (May-July; October-February) so book well ahead. There are two excellent hotels near the golf course, each with a distinct character, and a runner-up plus an emergency if the first three are full.

West End Hotel, Race Course Road (tel: 29281; telex: 845 2337). Bangalore's oldest hotel: elegant, traditional and spacious, with great style and decorum, the verandahs and main rooms arranged on three sides of a spacious lawn. There are more immaculate gardens and annexes behind, covering 20 acres in all. There are white cane chairs, flowers and pot plants everywhere. Now run by the Taj group who have restored the old wing (worth asking if a room here is available; impossible to book in advance). David Lean's 'A Passage to India' cast enjoyed it. Definitely the place to be staying during the races.

140 rooms. All mod. cons include a good pool. Tea or candle-lit cocktails on the lawns are delightful, with Thai chef preparing Thai food in the evening.

Windsor Manor, 25 Sankey Road (tel: 28031/ 79431; telex: 0845-8209). This newish, gloriously kitsch and successful take-off of a Raj Regency hotel has every detail right, from circular marble lobby and the bell-hops' uniforms to the English wood-panelled bar, English prints, chintz curtains, and deep sofas for tea and dainty cakes. The interior was designed by Kiran Patki. It is run by the Welcomgroup.

140 rooms. Mod. cons include a large swimming pool and terraces and good business services; golf by arrangement; restaurants and poolside barbecue usually excellent.

Gateway Hotel on Residency Road, 41 Mahatma Gandhi Road (tel: 568888; telex 0845-8367); gleaming white marble lobby with tinkling fountain characteristic of Taj group style, of which this hotel is part. Built more for the businessman than the holiday-maker. 162 rooms. Mod. cons include good health club, gym and beauty centre; pool. The coffee shop emphasises south Indian food. Elsewhere the theme is Chinese or American.

The ITDC's classy-looking **Hotel Ashok,** Kumara Krupe, High Grounds (tel: 79411; telex: 0485-2433) has the slowest staff and the murkiest swimming pool water imaginable – but it does have a tennis court, large grounds and live Indian music in its restaurant.

A plethora of tourist offices. Best are the Government of India Tourist Office, KFC Building, 48 Church Street (tel:579517); Karnataka Tourist Office at F-Block, 1st floor, Cauvery Bhawan (tel: 579139); and KTDC Tourist Reception Counter, 12-12A Shrungar Shopping Centre, (tel: 572377), a circular complex at the corner of Brigade Road and M G Road. Karnataka STDC, 10/4 Kasturba Road (tel: 212901) runs a city tour which takes six hours to see the few city sights and ends at the government soap factory; but they also do good 13hr day trips to Mysore and Srirangapatnam, to the Hoysala temples, to Vijayanagar and even up to Ooty.

Now is the moment to buy books and maps, book trains, buses and planes, and to rent a reliable car and driver since some of the best things to see in the South are away from the main roads. Travel agents include Cox & Kings, High Point IV, Shop No 4111, 45/1 Palace Road (tel: 260509), particularly reliable in South India. Now is also the moment to book up for Nagarhole wildlife sanctuary, through Jungle Lodges and Resorts, 2nd fl, Shrungar Shopping Centre, M G Road (tel: 575195). They can also arrange fishing for mahseer and carp in the Cauvery river at Mekadatu (100km). *The Deccan Herald* gives good news coverage and entertainments (i.e. cinema) guide. Good bookshops are Higginbotham, Gangarams, and The Book Cellar, all on M G Road; for a good second-hand bookshop, go to the cantonment. Best guide-books are the *TTK Bangalore Guide* and Morris's *Guide to Bangalore.*

The golf course is in the town centre, between the West End and the Windsor Manor hotels. Both can arrange a game. Bangalore United Services Club has swimming, tennis, billiards, squash and badminton. Access is via a member (ask your hotel management to fix it). At Kempe Gowda Road, the Santosh Cinema is said to get the latest releases and is air-conditioned – if you haven't seen a popular Indian movie yet, this is the moment. Performances of Karnataka's strong dance and music (especially lively in March and April) tend not to be advertised so, if interested, ask at the local office of the Indian Council for Cultural Relations (ICCR), 1, 12th Main Road, Vashanth Nagar (tel:71485); the Bharatiya Vidya Bhavan, Race Course Road (tel: 27421), or the Karnataka Sangeeta Nataka Academy, Canara Financial Corporation Complex, Nrupathunga Road (tel: 72509). Bangalore takes a serious siesta 1-4pm, after which markets and shops stay open until 8pm.

OUT AND ABOUT Bangalore is not crammed with sights. In the **city centre**, public buildings surround the 300-acre central Cubbon Park (1864), stocked with benches and shady trees. Here are the Gothic public Library, High Court, the obligatory statue of Queen Victoria and three museums. The excellent Government Museum (1887) houses 18 sections, its treasures including the fine Atukar stone (*c* 950), the Hero stone (*c* 890) and finds from the great Harrapan site at Moenjodaro in Sind, excavated in 1922; some good miniature paintings and plenty of pasty, fleshy faces of the Tanjore and Mysore rulers (open Thurs.-Tues., 9am-5pm). The Venkatappa Art Gallery, housing the painters' turn-of-the-century works for the court, is in the museum building. The Technological Museum is next door (open Tues.-Sun., 10am-5pm).

The massive grey granite wedding cake on the north side of the park is Vidhana Soudha (Secretariat and State Legislature) built in flamboyant neo-Dravidian style in 1956. It is open to visitors after 5.30pm, apply to Under Secretary (Protocol), Dept. Social and Administrative Reforms, Vidhana Soudha (tel: 79401).

Kempe Gowda Fort is currently closed to the public (with no immediate prospect of re-opening), but the remains of **Tipu's palace** are open, their walls, ceilings and niches painted Pompeian red, blue and yellow with floral designs and trellices, the black columns outlined in gold (open daily, 8am-10pm). The South Indian Windsor Castle of the Mysore rulers is open for the week that includes November 1.

Lalbagh Botanical Gardens, laid out by Haider Ali in 1760, has delightful 19th-century pavilions, lamps and halls set in 240 acres of well-planted avenues and flower-beds, pleasant for an early morning or sundown stroll. (Flower shows the week of Jan. 26 and Aug. 15.) Tipu Sultan introduced many new species brought by ambassadors from Kabul, Persia, Mauritius and France. He also made an unsuccessful attempt to introduce mulberry bushes and a silk industry. Mysore only became the silk-growing centre of India after his death.

On the hill beyond is the Bull Temple, built by Kempe Gowda, its monolith Nandi bull claimed by locals to grow in size each year – but so far it has not outstripped India's largest Nandi, at Lepakshi (see p. 226). The immaculate and charming race-course should not be missed, whether the races are on or not. South of it lies cinema-lined Kempe Gowda Road and the scented city market, piled high with flowers; Karnataka grows about 70% of India's flowers, that is, about 34,000 tons on about 20,000 hectares. There are pretty Gothic bungalows with monkey windows surviving in Langford Town, their painted green, red, mustard and white houses and gardens well maintained by Bangalore's new rich. But the fine buildings of the cantonment are fast disappearing under the developers' bulldozers.

RESTAURANTS Quite a good choice. Smartest of all is the immensely plush *Prince's Restaurant*, 9 Brigade Road (tel: 578787, best to book), with the top food, clientele and service (including good steaks). Its adjacent *Knock Out Disco* is the only one available. It is free to restaurant clients Tues.-Thurs., otherwise about Rs40 per couple (who have to be one of each sex – singles not admitted). There are a few seedy places elsewhere, to be avoided. All food at the *Windsor Manor* should be good, in the Chinoiserie coffee shop, at the poolside barbecue (North-west Frontier food) or in the restaurant (South Indian chicken Chettinand recommended), but recent reports are mixed. The poolside barbecue of the *West End* is good; inside restaurant not.

Outside the hotels, the most fun place to eat is on the first floor of the *Public Utility building*, above the cinema on M G Road; not luxurious, but good food and balcony views down to the world living hard below. For spicy Andhra food eaten off a banana leaf, go to the popular *R&R Restaurant*, Church Street. *Blue Fox*, M G Road (including fish and meat), and *Chalukya* (vegetarian, near the West End), have good south Indian food. The *North Indian Tandoor* on M G Road is excellent. Chinese food is good at the *Ashok's Mandarin* and at *Chinese Hut*, 45 Palace Road. *Mavalli Tiffin Room* on Lalbagh Road has excellent south Indian breakfast. Best before 7am.

SHOPPING AND CRAFTS The best shopping in the South is here and in Madras. Fine **silk** is the best value, woven into crepe de chine, georgette, chiffon, soft silk and spun silk, all priced by weight. (There is often a 10% discount for payment in foreign currency.) Traditional Mysore silks are in deep blue, mustard yellow, turquoise, chestnut and burgundy. Georgettes are often woven with checks. Top of the range and quality is found at Vijayalakshmi, M G Road; Karnataka Silk Industries Corporation (KSIC), Gupta Market, Kempe Gowda Road; Imor, 49 Victoria Layout (selective, closed Wed.) and Janardhana Silk House, Unity Building, J C Road. KSIC also has thick rugs made of the waste silk, in plain colours, all sizes.

Other local products include the sweet-scented sandalwood and objects of rosewood and brass (in the interests of conservation, ivory should be avoided). Karnataka's emporium, Cauvery, on M G Road, has a fair range, as does Poomphuhar (Tamil Nadu's) on Brigade Road. Kairali (Kerala's) is on M G Road, while the Khadi Gramodyóg Bhavan is on Silver Jubilee Park Road.

On Commercial Street, there is quality **silver-smithing** and fair prices at C. Krishniah Chetty and Sons, whose shop sign proudly announces '1869-1984, A Glorious 115 Years'; old silver, brass, wood etc. at Asia Arts and Crafts; and, just before it, a little lane of tiny jewellers who have regular stock and will alter and copy pieces.

In Langford Town area, Artworks, in Kanara Bank Building on O'Shaughnessey Road, stocks well-made goods from all over India, the only shop of this range and quality and with reasonable prices. The reliable Natesan's Antiquarts is at 76 M G Road (smaller showrooms at the West End and Ashok). On and around Avenue Road, there are lanes of gold and silver smiths, and the back lanes sell spices and agarbathi (incense sticks).

To see all **sericulture** processes (see p. 214), ask a taxi driver, the KSIC shop manager, or go to the government Department of Sericulture or to the Weavers' Centre upstairs in the Life Insurance Building on Kempe Gowda Road. On the Bangalore-Mysore road, silk-growing farms along the roadside can be visited, or make a small detour to Chennapatna and Ramalangram villages.

The various heavily promoted picnic spots and waterfalls are not that attractive. However, Whitefield (16km) is interesting for its few old bungalows around the church and for Brindavan ashram, the headquarters of Sri Satya Sai Baba, who, as the literature puts it, 'draws thousands of visitors all the year round searching for peace and the healing touch'. Rather more down to earth, indeed right below the earth, are Kolar Gold Fields (100km), with some of the deepest shafts in the world, going down to 3,000m. To visit, apply to the Secretary, Kolar Gold Mining Undertakings (Central Administration), Oorgaum PO (tel: 77).

SRIRANGAPATNAM (SERINGAPATAM)

125km from Bangalore; 15km from Mysore. An island fortress town synonymous with Tipu Sultan, whose tiger-mania and hatred of the English are summed up in Tipu's Tiger, his musical box toy of a tiger devouring an Englishman that would growl and shriek when wound up. It is now to be seen in the Victoria and Albert Museum, London. After the fall of Vijayanagar, Mysore became independent under the Wadiyars. In 1759 Haider Ali, a self-made, illiterate but politically brilliant Muslim, deposed Chikka Krishna Raj Wadiyar and ruled until his death in 1782. His son, Tipu (1750-1799), also an outstanding leader, ruled until British sieges of his capital, Srirangapatnam, in 1792 (when he surrendered half his territories and two sons) and then 1799, led to his death. (The fifth generation of descendants lives in Calcutta.) Lord Wellesley then put a five-year-old Wadiyar on the throne and kept a watchful eye while getting on with British expansion in the South.

Tipu was highly cultivated, unlike his father, and a democratic ruler, yet he was obsessed with the destruction of kaffirs (non-Muslims). Even in his dreams he played the role of royal tiger chosen by God to devour his enemies. He surrounded himself with tigers, real and false; tiger-head canons; sitting-tiger mortars; tiger-head sword handles; and had tiger symbols on his soldiers' uniforms.

The *fort* at Srirangapatnam was mostly destroyed by the British, but it is extremely evocative to explore the dungeons, the site of Tipu's final death, etc. Daria Daulat Bagh, Tipu's beautifully painted *summer palace* (1784) stands outside the fort, set in a very lovely garden. Repainted murals surround the main rooms of the mostly teak palace, both fine decorative arabesques and pictures of Tipu's battles. Spot in the pictures the clean-shaven British, the moustachioed French (Tipu's allies), and the Nizam of Hyderabad, shown as a cow and then a boar after he double-crossed Tipu. (To keep up supplies of money for his wars, Tipu had twelve mints.) The excellent museum in the small upstairs balconied rooms includes fine drawings of Tipu's sons. (Open daily until 5pm; good guides.) Dovecotes at the garden entrance were for pigeon post. It is possible to picnic among the roses, mango trees and lawns before going to see the dazzling white *Gumbaz* (1784) at the other end of the island, with its Turkish-inspired bulbous dome coated in fussy decoration, an echo of Bijapur and Golconda tombs. Tipu laid out the gardens and planted them with trees from Kabul and Persia. Inside is the very evocative mausoleum of Haidar Ali and Tipu (1799). The rosewood doors are inlaid in ivory with delicate floral designs.

SOMNATHPUR, BELUR, HALEBID AND BELAVADI

Rural drives past paddy fields, bullock carts, tiny villages and brick kilns lead to *temples* built at the climax of the culturally precocious and dynamic Hoysala dynasty (1006-1310). With those built by the Somavamshis (Orissa), Chalukyas (north Karnataka), Solankis (Gujarat) and Chandellas (Khajuraho), these mark another peak in Hindu architecture.

The Hoysalas rose from brigand hill chieftains of the Western Ghats to rulers of the plains, where they extracted rich revenues and taxes as well as political allegiance from their conquests. But it was Vishnuvardhana (also called Bittideva), ruling from Belur (1108-42), who finally broke away from his Chalukya overlords to establish the Hoysala kingdom. He converted from Jainism, the Chalukyas' faith, to Vishnuism – hence his change of name. His grandson, Ballala II (1173-1220), extended the empire to cover the south Deccan and called himself Maharajadhiraja (King of Kings). A century later, the third attack by the Muslim army of the Delhi Sultanate crushed the Hoysalas in 1310.

With great patrons of poetry, music, painting, dance, architecture and literature for rulers, temple art reached new heights. The buildings, based on Dravidian architecture, are quite squat and usually star-shaped. Some still have their sikhara (tower) and are raised on a big platform. The material is a blue-grey soapstone that is easy to carve when newly quarried but hardens under exposure – hence its crispness today.

The sculptures covering the buildings are vibrant animals and human figures who dance, play music, make love, make war and trot along in timeless processions. The recesses and projections of the star shape offered the optimum amount of surface for decoration. As at Khajuraho, the carvings are very easy to look at. The architecture helps by highlighting some parts while throwing others into almost black shade. The layout of the carvings helps by contrasting strong horizontal bands of friezes with tall single figures. It also offsets complicated narrative scenes from the epics with a simple running floral motif. Finally, areas are divided with deep cuttings that resemble solid black lines.

While Somnathpur is a small outing from Mysore, the other sites are much further away and really deserve an overnight stay.

Somnathpur 137km from Bangalore; 45km from Mysore; 25km from Srirangapatna. The temple, built in 1268 and dedicated to Keshava, is the easiest to reach and perhaps the most sublime and perfect of all the Hoysala temples. It is set in a cloister courtyard. (Steps at the far end on to the roof.) The building is complete, finely proportioned and the sculpture is glorious, especially the six horizontal friezes running round the temple base: hamsas (geese), yalis (hippogryphs), cavalry, guardian elephants and a floral band flank stories from the epics, each story ending with a closed or half-closed door. The temple guardian should have copies of P. K. Mishra's guide, *The Hoysalas*. He certainly has the key to a very clean lavatory. No refreshments.

Hassan 185km from Bangalore; 90km from Mysore; 40km from Belur; 32km from Halebid. Worth starting very early from either big city and stopping here for a South Indian breakfast en route to Belur – *Hotel Sathyaprakash* is clean and good. To stay overnight, go to ITDC's *Ashok*, Mangalore Road (tel: 8731-7), or the more modest *Amblee Palika* in Race Course Road (tel:7145-7). Tourist Office almost opposite.

Belur 225km from Bangalore; 130km from Mysore. When Vishnuvardhana (1108-42) defeated the Cholas at Talkad in 1116, he commemorated his victory by building the Channekashava Temple in a spacious, walled complex. It is an early Hoysala masterpiece – and quite different from the almost contemporary but much simpler Lakshmidevi Temple (1113) at *Dodda Gaddavahalli*, on the Hassan-Belur road.

At Belur, the riot of carving matches the quality of the architecture. As well as countless elephants running round the base and story scenes, there are delightful figures of women putting on make-up (especially on the brackets under the eaves), playing with a pet parrot, removing a thorn from the foot. Some are signed by the sculptor. There are also wonderful guardian beasts and lots of internal decoration. This is a living temple, so a drummer and piper summon the faithful every now and then, a huge gold and red lion, elephant and horse are stored in the cloisters for festivals and the temple chariot sits outside the gateway. The two subsidiary temples are Channigariaya and Viranarayana. Good guides are available.

Halebid 32km from Hasan; 15km from Belur. Capital of the Hoysalas for three centuries and known as Darasamudra. There is a large complex and open-air museum (which sells postcards), set in a beautifully kept garden with shady, flowering trees, beside a lake (a nice picnic spot); the keen can walk the vestiges of fort ramparts. The double Hoysaleswara Temple, designed and begun by Kedaroja for the ruler Narasimhal (1141-82), was still incomplete after 86 years of chiselling. Here the riot of flamboyant carving is even more Baroque and extravagant than at Belur, particularly on the southwest side, and is considered by many to be the peak of Hoysala carving. Just beyond the complex is another, less visited temple. The whole site is run by the Archaeological Department. There are good guides.

Belavadi 12.8km north of Halebid, on the Banavar-Belur road. Worth catching this little-visited nearby temple in a tiny village. Built around 1116, its overall effect is even more horizontal than the other temples. There is less decoration, but the columns are very sharply chiselled and the deities in the three shrines are especially fine. (To see them, the villagers will call the priest, who unlocks the doors and then performs puja. Visitors should give an offering.)

Either cut across from here to *Harnahalli* or reach it from Hassan. Worth the effort to see the Lakshmi Narasimha Temple (1234), a well-preserved mature Hoysala temple comparable to Halebid's.

SHRAVANABELGOLA

52km from Hasan; 158km from Bangalore; 90km from Mysore. Jain pilgrims flock here to the 17-metre high image of *Lord Gomateshvara* (Bahubali), carved into the rock of Indragiri hill and visible from 25km. Jainism was introduced to the South by Chandra Gupta Maurya and held powerful sway until the Hoysala conversion and Jain internal disputes. Every 12-14 years the Mahamastakabhisheka ceremony is held here (next one 1993), when Jains pour in to witness the anointing of the deity. Water, ghi (clarified butter), dates, almonds, poppy seeds, coconut milk, bananas, jaggery (sugar-cane), sandalwood, flowers and even gold, silver and precious stones are poured over the head and cascade down the huge body.

MYSORE

140km from Bangalore; 90km from Hassan; 150km from Ooty. A pretty, slow-paced, palace-filled, rural town, rich in craftsmen and fortunately left in peace by busy industrialised Bangalore, probably because it has avoided having an airport. Beloved by R. K. Narayan, who uses it as the inspiration for his Malgudi novels and writes of it: 'The atmosphere is placid and poetic, and one is constantly tempted to enjoy the moment, setting aside all other thoughts.' This is true for the visitor.

The Wadiyar family were the Maharajas from the 14th century until Haider Ali's takeover in 1759, and were then restored by the British in 1799 when the five-year-old Krishnaraja was installed. Left with nothing much to do, the 19th century maharajas earned a reputation for superb hospitality and spectacle, political stability and progress. Mysore Week became the Raj's Ascot Week, its highlight the massive khedda (a round-up of wild elephants for training), when the Maharaja miraculously produced electricity, running water and an orchestra in the depths of the jungle.

Their building had the same flamboyant approach: a Scottish baronial mansion at Ooty, a South Indian Windsor Castle at Bangalore, Italianate Rajendra Vilas and then, after a fire in

1897, the new city palace. There were five palaces and 12 mansions in Mysore alone. The many peppermint green, pink and yellow buildings with turrets, pavilions and domes were mostly built by the stylish and powerful rulers, giving Mysore the feudal atmosphere found in many Rajasthan cities. The ex-Maharaja, in his thirties, lives in a corner of the gigantic, fairytale Amba Vilas city palace (floodlit on Sundays, 7-8pm) where he runs his stud farm. Two of his former palaces are now hotels.

THE HARD FACTS A pleasant and comfortable base for visiting the Hoysala temples and Srirangapatnam. Dussehra festival (September-October) is worth seeing, and the races on the delightful little local course are great fun. Nearest airport Bangalore, although Vayudoot's schedule may come here soon. For hotels, choose between a bombastic palace with unreliable standards, an excellent town centre hotel, or the soon-to-open hillside palace well out of town.

Lalitha Mahal Palace Hotel (tel: 26316, 27650; telex: 0846-217) is huge, overlooking the city. It was built in 1931 for foreign visitors, so that they could be served meat – the Maharaja was strictly vegetarian. It has a gloriously grand pale yellow and green hall with huge chandeliers, sweeping staircase and Italian marble balustrade. Original furnishings include Heath Robinson freestanding baths whose dial taps provide bath, shower or an onslaught of sprays from every side. Part of the government Ashok chain which tries hard – recent repainting of the cavernous dining-room (ex-ballroom) makes it look like 'the inside of a Wedgwood cheese dish'. 54 rooms (including pale-blue royal suite) behind cool, deep verandahs. It is essential to be in the old building and overlooking the city. Mod. cons include pool (dirty), tennis, billiards, table tennis, extensive and well maintained gardens, slow service but some charming elderly ex-royal servants. Best to go for lunch to soak up the ambiance and enjoy the local magician who, among other tricks, produces 15 nails out of his mouth. Reports vary wildly and emotionally over stays here: from 'our most enjoyable in India, service friendly, courteous and efficient' to 'the most unpleasant Indian hotel we have ever stayed in, . . . food very ordinary and very expensive'.

Rajendra Vilas Palace (tel: 20690; telex: 0846-230) is a small, Italianate villa built in 1939 on steep Chamundi Hill outside the city so that His Highness could get a spot of peace during the Dussehra festivities; HH has recently given up running his crumbling palace and the Taj group's Southern expansion will reach here, after considerable tarting up, in late 1991. Who knows how much of the original furniture and

fittings – and original royal staff – will survive? It is essential to have a car if staying here.

Hotel Metropole, 5 Jhansi Lakshmi Bai Road (tel: 20681, 20871, telex: 0846-214). Currently, the most practical and well-run place to stay, with all reports good. 18 rooms, only four air-conditioned, each in the colonial tradition of bedroom, dressing room and bathroom. Spacious lawns, excellent food cooked by a chef who has been there for 20 years and specialises in North-West Frontier dishes.

Quality Inn Southern Star, Vinobha Road (tel: 27217; telex 0846 256), good reports from this newish, well-located hotel. 108 rooms, all mod. cons include swimming pool and poolside barbecues.

State Tourist Office, 2 Jhansi Lakshmi Bai Road (tel: 23652); very helpful, run tours around and outside Mysore. News and events can be found in the *Deccan Herald* and *Mofussil Diary*; books at the well-stocked Geetha Book House, K R Circle.

To book up wildlife park visits: for Bandipur go to Project Tiger, Government House (tel: 20901) and for Nagarhole go to Assistant Conservator of Forests, Wildlife Preservation, Chamarajendra Circle, Vanivilas Road (tel: 21159). But bookings for a trip with Tiger Tops are made through Jungle Lodges in Bangalore (see above). Racing season is August-October (Sat., Sun.), when the Bangalore smart set come across. Mysore connects with Mangalore (220km) for a beach. From there, the coast road down into Kerala has been described as 'like the Côte d'Azur before it was discovered'.

OUT AND ABOUT Amber Vilas (1900), the city palace, is the unmissable attraction. Designed by an Englishman named Henry Irwin (who also designed Madras's Art Gallery), its Indo-Saracenic style permitted, as Giles Tillotson has pointed out, 'a means of being simultaneously Indian and progressive'. That is, while it looked Indian, it was unashamedly imperial. Inside, it incorporates everything that is grand, huge and fun: glorious stained glass with peacocks and flowers; avenues of carved pillars; huge inlaid doors; walls coated in gold and red arabesques; and marble floors polished to mirror-brightness. Open daily, 10.30am-5.30pm, no guide-book, guide or postcards.

There are several other things worth seeing: Devaraja market, alleys perfumed with piles of flowers, spices and everything else, full of colour and action; the town centre Zoo; Sri Chamarajendra Art Galley, Jaganmohan Palace, for Indian miniature paintings, musical instruments (open Fri.-Wed., 8am-5pm); and Sri Chamundeswari Temple, a healthy climb up Chamundi Hill (4km of steps – or 13km by car), passing the huge monolith Nandi bull (cafés at the top).

Brindavan Gardens (19km) are undoubtedly the local sunset spot and, despite the crowds, are very beautiful: gardens with cascading fountains beside the Krishnaraj Sagar, courting couples take snaps of each other and, as the sun sets, pretty illuminations are switched on to oohs and aahs. Tea or cocktails can be taken on the semi-circular hotel verandah, which is another ex-royal guest-house.

RESTAURANTS If palatial surroundings do not make up for the food, try the *Metropole, Ridge* and *Hoysala* hotels, *RRR* at Gandhi Square, *Gun House Imperial* and the *Punjabi Bombay Juice Centre*, Dhanvantri Road.

SHOPPING AND CRAFTS Shop at Kaveri Arts and Crafts Emporium, Sayaji Rao Road (closed Thurs.) for local sandalwood, rosewood, teak, inlay (wood and ivory), silks and agarbathi (incense). Sandalwood is quite expensive. If it is offered cheap, it is likely to be another wood, with added scent. For safety, buy at government-approved shops. Sri Lakshmi Fine Arts and Crafts, opposite the Zoo, has a very good range of goods; their factory of craftsmen at 2226 Sawday Road, Mandi Mohalla, Mysore is open to visitors and sells stock.

Karnataka Silk Industries Corporation factory shop, Mananthody Road, has the best range of quality handloom and machine silks, with an informative sales officer, Mr Gupta. The on-site weaving is by machine, not handloom (open Mon.-Sat., 7.30-11.30am; 12.30-4.30pm). The other KSIC silk shop is in town, Visweswaraiah Bhavan, R K R Circle.

At the Government *Sandalwood Oil Factory* (which produces 60% of the Indian production), see the basic distilling process and how incense is made, then buy goods (open Mon.-Sat., 9-11am; 2-4pm). In the back lanes find craftsmen working with bamboo, wood, inlay work and weaving. Mysore is also the centre for *incense sticks*. In many homes, adept women and children furiously turn out up to 10,000 sticks a day. They roll sandalwood putty on to slivers of bamboo, then dip them into powdered perfume before drying them in the shade.

The Nilgiri Hills

OOTACAMUND (OOTY OR UDAGAMANDALAM), TAMIL NADU

159km from Mysore; 298km from Bangalore; 86km from Coimbatore, 280km from Cochin. Altitude 2,268km. A wonderful journey, whichever way is chosen. It can be approached from Mysore through banyan avenues and wildlife sanctuaries with scampering mongoose and strolling elephant, or from the palms and pine-apples of Trichur. Or it can be reached by train. The rise is through thick forests of creeper-filled trees, scratching monkeys (road notices announce they have right of way) and spice bushes, emerging among fat cows, rolling Nilgiris (blue hills) like Cumbria in England, spongy hillside carpets of tea bushes, wild arum lilies, twittering birds and air scented with pine and eucalyptus.

Ooty is known by local Tamils as Udagamandalam. Ootacamund (meaning village of huts) is where the British came to cool off, the maharajas followed them, and a few smart Indians continue their habit. John Sullivan, Collector of Coimbatore, took a fancy to Ooty in 1819, was the first European to build a house there and had the lake built in 1823. The British, quick to sniff out anything cool in India, were hot on Sullivan's heels, followed by the maharajas.

By 1821 the mountain pass was in use. The British built Surrey-style houses, planted gardens and founded the glorious Botanical Gardens funded by public subscription in 1840. Both Raj and rajas enjoyed pukka British pastimes: riding, golf, tennis, hunting, racing and polo. There was a full social season, complete with flower shows and dog shows. Snooty Ooty it most certainly was. And, from 1869, it became the summer headquarters of the Presidency of Madras. The Duke of Buckingham built a hills edition of Government House in 1880 with a pillared portico copied from his seat at Stowe in Buckinghamshire.

Today film-stars and foreign firms maintain the houses – still a status symbol – smart honeymoon couples flock here in the winter, and the flower show, dog show and hunt, pink coat 'n' all, continue. But with a slightly hollow ring. The palaces are rarely opened, the club is kept pristine for a handful of aged members, staying on because 'it's like Devonshire with better blooming roses and three servants'. Smart Ooty is rather run-down. What thrives is an Indian hill town producing eucalyptus oil, making cinema film, building hydro-electric schemes and market gardening, set amid charming scenery and a perfect climate.

Ooty may be low on Raj nostalgia but the description by Lord Lytton, Viceroy 1876-80, still holds good: 'It far surpasses all that its most enthusiastic admirers and devoted lovers have said to us about it. . . . Imagine Hertfordshire lanes, Devonshire Downs, Westmoreland lakes, Scotch trout streams and Lusitanian views!'

THE HARD FACTS Driving up or down between Mysore and Ooty, there are two routes: via Gudalur-Naduvattam-Pykara or, steeper but even more beautiful, via Masinagudi-Kathati. Coming up from the South, the train is a must (see Getting there section at beginning of chapter). The usual options for hotels: efficiency or romantic character. Tariffs operate for high season April-June; all other months are low season, with possible reductions.

The Savoy (tel: 4142-9; telex: 0853-240) is probably the best-run and most atmospheric of all India's colonial hotels. Opened in 1841 as Dawson's Hotel by Mr H. Royal Dawson, it is now run by the Taj group to pukka high standards. The main part is built around a cottage (now Garden Cottage), using beams dragged up by elephants from Tipu's palace at Srirangapatna (other beams were used for repairing Ooty's church).

60 rooms scattered around the main building, annex and charming cottages, each with a verandah (and full room service). Good garden, wood fires and hot water bottles if needed. Good Indian and European food served in a dining room panelled with Karnataka rosewood. But it lacks public rooms. Good billiards table and cues, plus a marker who plays, too – snooker was invented down the road, at the Club. Tea and Britannia biscuits can be taken on the lawn. As Ooty is very small ('everyone knows everybody here'), staff on front desk can probably make possible whatever you want, from riding to visiting Government House or a tea garden.

Fernhill Palace, Fern Hill (tel: 2055; telex: 0853 246). HH the (ex-) Maharaja of Mysore's hilltop pad – he keeps a cottage in the grounds to stay in during May. Splendid, deep pink Scottish-baronial building (1842 and 1873) with magnificent views west across the valley and a lawn from which to watch the hour-long, flaming red sunsets. Now in the hands of the Taj, due to re-open totally revamped at the end of 1991. As with Mysore's parallel project, HH's furniture (including beautiful billiard and card tables) and the wonderful sleepy-country-house atmosphere may, or may not, survive.

The Tourist Office is useless. Higginbotham's bookshop has guides. Racing is April-June, enlivened in May by: a visit from the hunt, belonging to Conoor Staff College; the two-day flower show in the Botanical Gardens, around the 14th; the dog show and, at the end of the month, Founder's week at the smart Lawrence School at Lovedale. This is Tamil Nadu state, where total prohibition is officially in force. It is wiser not to carry drink but the bars of both hotels serve liquor without demanding permits. To visit a tea estate, see p. 216.

OUT AND ABOUT Ooty is a doing, not seeing, place. However, a stroll around town reveals some red-tiled Raj villas, the private Nilgiri Library and the *parish church of St Stephen*, de-

signed by one Captain John Underwood in 1829. It is Gothic outside, Tuscan inside, with more teak from Tipu's palace for the roof. If possible, visit the very fine *Club*, built as a villa in 1831-2 by the Hyderabad merchant Sir William Rumbold, and rented by Lord William Bentinck when Governor-General. It then became the social centre for tea planters and the military, where an English subaltern named Neville Chamberlain invented snooker in 1875. (Write to or ring The Secretary for admittance, or ask at the Savoy; members of the Royal Overseas League have reciprocal membership and can both visit and stay here by writing in advance.) See also John Sullivan's Stonehouse (1823), Ooty's first house, the library, law court and survivors of the old houses: Baroda Palace, The Cedars (the Nizam's), Aranmore (far away Jodhpur's), Woodside, Crewe Hall, Lushington Hall and Elk Hill House.

The terraced *Botanical Gardens* on Dodabetta Hill below Raj Bhavan (Government House) were laid out by the Marquis of Tweedsdale in 1847. They cover 51 acres, boast 650 plant varieties and incorporate Sullivan's lake. There are orchids, ornamental and medicinal plants, rock plants, ferns and mature trees. The knowledgeable Curator of the Nilgiri Agri-Horticultural Society is found here; and this is the venue for the May flower show and the, equally important in Ooty, South Indian Kennel Club show. Go through them to reach Government House (arrange permission through the Savoy), seemingly frozen in time but in fact used now as the summer house for the Governor of Tamil Nadu. Painted pea-green, the ballroom sat 600, the corridors are lined with foxed Daniell prints, the Belgian glass imported for Raj banquets shines in cases, crested British china plates stand in piles, and 12 gardeners keep up the herbaceous borders.

SHOPPING Silver and embroidered shawls are sold at the Toda show-room at Charing Cross. The jewellery, actually made by another tribe and sold to the Todas, can also be found at silversmiths in the old bazaar. Mrs Evan Piljain Weidemann also sells Toda shawls. At Spencer's there is local honey, and Kathleen Carter's Cheddar and Wensleydale cheeses. Also distilled eucalyptus, geranium, lemongrass and camphor oils. There is a belief that eucalyptus oil keeps mosquitoes away; it does not.

KEEPING FIT Riding is easy and cheap: horses are brought to the hotel or found at the Boat House, to be hired with or without escort. Boating is on Ooty Lake (1.5km, 8am-6pm). To fish for trout at Avalanche, a licence and hired tackle may be obtained from the Assistant Director of

Fisheries, Fishdale, Ooty. The Hon. Secretary, Nilgiri Game Association, Ooty, should be contacted for chikar (hunting). There are good walks out in the hills. Wenlock Downs (8km) are about 60 sqkm of undulating grassland and shola forest (hotels provide picnics). A car will deliver walkers and collect several hours later. Alternatively, local buses make a similar journey. Nearer the centre, the view from the top of Dodabatta ridge, which rises behind the Botanical Gardens and is the highest in Tamil Nadu, is superb on a clear day. A pathway above the gardens leads to a Toda village (see p. 216). Hotels can arrange golf.

AWAYDAYS   Several interesting places to visit, driving through the unspoilt hills. The nearest tea garden is *Glen Morgan* (see See how it's done section, above). *Kotagiri* (23km), lower down, is the Nilgiris' oldest hill station, discovered by the British before Ooty but now a quiet backwater surrounded by thick forests and a golf course; nearby are *Catherine Falls* (8km), *Elk Falls* (8km) and *Kodanad View Point* (16km, stunning view eastwards down to plains). *Coonor* (17km) is another quiet hill station with tea gardens, Sim's botanical park (an annex of Ooty's) and nice walks with views compared by Lady Charlotte Canning to that of the Mediterranean from the corniche at Monte Carlo – one view is even called Lady Canning's Seat (stay overnight at *Hampton Manor* on Church Road, run by Mr and Mrs Dass).

At *Lovedale*, the John Lawrence Memorial Asylum (Lawrence School), built by the British in the 1860s in memory of Lawrence of the Punjab, is a caricature of an English boarding school, full of pukka Indian boys: monastic Romanesque buildings in a lovely setting where every pupil dreams of escaping to the smoky city. To visit *Mudumalai Wild Life Sanctuary* (64km), contact the District Forest Officer, Nilgiris North Division, Ooty for information and accommodation.

Kerala

Most of the temples in Kerala are not open to non-Hindus; but the exterior architecture of many is beautiful enough to merit a detour.

TRICHUR

200km from Ooty, via Mettupalaiyam, Coimbatore and Palghat, 80km from Cochin. Through dazzling green paddy, coconuts, pineapples and blue cacti, studded with the odd pink cinema and toddy shop, to an attractive and prosperous town with large, sparkling, brightly painted houses. The great *Trichur Pooram* is held here, in the town centre (see Festivals, above). There is also the beautiful Vadakkunnathan

Temple (12th century), built under the Chera dynasty, a complex of steep-roofed wooden buildings, some open to non-Hindus. Guruvayur (29km west, on the coast) is where the night-time Krishnayattam temple dance is performed, but only for Hindus. To see this, it is best to stay in the *Tourist Bungalow*. Kerala Kalamandalam (Arts Academy) at Shoranur (29km north) is where Kathakali dance has undergone its renaissance, under the stimulus of the poet Vallathol, and is the principal training centre (see p. 217). Training can be seen in the early morning. Performances are at night. Stay overnight at the nearby *PWD Rest House*.

COCHIN AND ERNAKULUM

80km from Trichur; 67km from Kottayam; 63km from Alleppey; 210km from Kodaikanal; 280km from Ooty. Ernakulum is the undistinguished mainland town which has the Kathakali dance halls (see See how it's done, above) and is connected with Cochin over the narrow bridge. Cochin is its picturesque harbour with islands, backwaters, pretty buildings and a rich history. There seems to be more water than land here. Cochin is also one of India's busiest ports and has one of Kerala's two airports, but neither encroach on its beauty.

Some say the Jews arrived in Kerala over 2,000 years ago, as refugees from Jerusalem when it fell to Nebuchadnezzar in 587BC. Certainly, they have been a strong community in Cochin for the last 1,000 years, although now the lure of Israel has reduced their numbers to about 30 – not one child. The Portuguese (arrived 1500), Dutch (arrived 1602, pushed out the Portuguese 1663) and British followed, all hungry for spices, and all leaving their mark.

THE HARD FACTS   Both nice hotels are on Willingdon Island, a man-made island named after the Viceroy, Lord Willingdon, and constructed by a Mr Bristow in the 1920s and 1930s out of waste when the harbour was dug deeper. Two hotels here. *Malabar Hotel*, Willingdon Island, Cochin (tel: 6811; telex: 885 6661); built in 1934 as a hostel by the Port Trust of Cochin, now run by the Taj Group who have refurbished it to make it, as one fussy guest judged, 'one of the finest hotels in the South. The setting is heaven, the service good.' Indeed, the setting is glorious: right on the top of the island with lawns to the water's edge and a jetty, looking on to little fishing boats and catamarans laden with coir (coconut fibre) and with boatman's hut on top. Big ships pass by, too. The views look across to Mattancherry, some old British trading buildings and some Chinese fishing nets. 100 rooms, some in a new block; all mod. cons include swimming pool; centralised air-conditioning will not please everyone. The somewhat gimmicky rice-boat restaurant is in fact very good. Mohiniattam dance recitals, Kalaria-payattu martial art demonstrations, backwater picnic cruises. Very romantic to organise supper in the little waterside wooden pagoda, then take a moonlit row.

The other, more modest, hotel is the *Casino Hotel* (tel: 6821; telex: 885 6314). It makes the very best of its site, back from the water. It was built in the 1950s as a restaurant opposite the terminus of the big trains to South India – after this the line was single-track only. 71 rooms including one suite with beautiful Keralan decor. The old part is the nicest. There is a spacious garden, swimming pool, motor launch and an excellent restaurant judged by one gourmet couple as 'magnificent – undoubtedly the best restaurant we encountered in India, the skill displayed in the choosing, cooking and serving fish and shellfish exceeded the standard found in many of London's well-known restaurants. Enormous crayfish/lobster; tiger prawns, angel prawns, pomfret and white salmon all cooked to perfections'. Efficient, friendly staff; also centrally air-conditioned.

The lovely *Bolgatty Palace Hotel* on Bolgatty Island (tel: 35003) was built by the Dutch in 1744 and used as the British Residency. It is state-run (or rather, not run) and in such a sad state of dilapidation that it is only worth being rowed across (from the High Court Jetty in Ernakulum) to catch its fleeting beauty before it tumbles down. An exemplary Government of India Tourist Office is in the annex of the Malabar hotel, run by Mr V. Lakshminarayanan. There is not much literature but good advice on the whole area. The Cochin tour (Wed.-Mon., 9am and 2pm) includes Mattancherry and Gundu island to see the coir factory. There is no guide book. For shopping, local crafts are good both inside and outside the hotels, but there is probably a better range of quality goods in Bombay.

OUT AND ABOUT It is quite tricky to move about, so it is best to shop and sight-see at once. The ferry system is obscure. It is better to hire a boat and a rower. When negotiated away from the hotels, the prices reduce by 50% or more. Exploring Mattancherry and Fort Cochin is most fun by bicycle, hired from any bicycle shop. Otherwise, use a car. There is a boat tour of the harbour, not to be confused with the backwaters here (further south, see below). Those driving to Ooty from here can hire excellent cars which come complete with quadrophonic stereo thanks to Gulf money (so keep some tapes handy).

There is not a lot to see on Willingdon Island. Over the bridge to **Mattancherry** the old docks and merchants' houses lie to the right, and beyond them the Jewtown: horizontal striped warehouses, blue-shuttered houses, two good handicraft and antique shops called Athena Arts and Indian Arts and Curios, plus new shops opening each season (bargain for painted jewellery and money boxes, nut-crackers, masks, ivory bracelets and spice boxes) and a fine synagogue. It was built in 1567 and rebuilt after destruction by the Portuguese in 1662, with an upstairs gallery for women, Chinese willow-pattern floor tiles, 19th century Belgian chandeliers and beautiful interlocking benches (open daily 10am-noon:3-5pm, knowledgeable custodian).

Nearby is the so-called **Dutch Palace**, set in a walled garden backing on to mango trees, built by the Portuguese in 1557. It was then diplomatically given to the Cochin Raja, Veera Kerala Varma (1537-61) and repaired by the Dutch. Upstairs, the beautiful rooms have remarkable Hindu wall-paintings illustrating the Mahabharata (Raja's bedroom, left) and Ramayana (stair room, right), with carved teak ceilings and a vast teak Indian swing in the Rest Room (open daily, 9am-5pm).

At the tip of the isthmus is **Fort Cochin**, a parody of an English country village. Here the British coir merchants lived in fine houses and gardens surrounding the church and green, where Sunday cricketers watched from shady trees. It looks just the same today. The church, dedicated to St Francis, was the first European church to be built in India. It was built in 1546 (replacing an older wooden one) by Franciscan friars who accompanied the Portuguese admiral, Albuquerque. Vasco Da Gama established a factory here in 1502 and returned to Cochin as Portuguese Viceroy in 1510, to die here in 1524. His tombstone can be found at the east end of the church, on the right. Many other Cochin colonial notables are also buried here, including John Christie of Pierce Leslie and Co. whose handsome building can be seen from the Malabar. The church was successively Protestant Dutch, Anglican and is now Church of South India. It is packed on Sundays, when the punka is still operated. This is a manual air-conditioning system. Men pull strings to move the large fans which are suspended from the ceiling. South of St Francis's Church lies the jolly Santa Cruz Cathedral (1557), its interior painted from top to toe with provincial mock marble, tiling, arcading, garlands and the stages of the Cross on the ceiling. The whole east wall is a riot of pink, blue and yellow.

CHRISTIANITY came to India early. Today's Syrian Christians in Kerala – which with Tamil Nadu and Arunachal Pradesh account for 60% of India's 16 million Christians – claim to have been converted by St Thomas and thus to follow the earliest traditions of the Apostolic Church in India. The saint is believed to have landed at

Cranganore in 52AD and converted a few Namboodiri (Brahmini) families; their descendants are still very aware of their importance and careful about whom they marry. St Thomas then went on to Mylapore, near Madras, where he converted some locals before being martyred by Hindus in 68AD.

Later, another Christian connection was made by the see of Seleucia-Ctesiphon in Mesopotamia, from about 450. Later still, the Jesuit missionary St Francis Xavier arrived in Goa in 1542; and it was Jesuit missionaries who came to Akbar's Mughal court at Agra. Missionaries of almost every denomination followed, in particular the Protestant British, Dutch and German ones in the 18th century, much helped by the Anglican church's supremacy under British rule. It was the missionaries who brought printing to India.

In 1556 some Jesuits taking a press to Abyssinia for Christian propaganda broke their journey at Goa and did not continue; St Francis Xavier used it the next year to print *Doutrina Christa*, a catechism used to teach children at Jesuit schools and colleges. Later, William Carey (d.1834) and his followers, Joshua Marshman and William Ward, came to Serampore and started the first printing press and newspaper in Bengali. In addition to the three states with high Christian populations, Goa and Maharashtra have large numbers of Roman Catholics; tiny and mostly tribal Mizoram and Nagaland in the north-east have almost every Protestant sect. The Christian tradition has always promoted literacy (Malcolm Muggeridge taught Shakespeare and Wordsworth in 1920s Kerala). Kerala's literacy rate is India's highest at 93%, while Tamil Nadu and Maharashtra follow with 40%. Also, Keralans are as voracious readers as Bengalis and the Malayala *Manorama*, published from Kottayam, has India's highest circulation, 641,554 copies.

The Syrian Christians of Kerala have thrived down the centuries, in commerce, culture and politics, and in numbers. Today, 25% of Keralans are Christians, their churches a glorious mish-mash of Portuguese, Dutch and British church architecture. Syrian Christian events happily mix religion with pageantry and politics, staging lavish fireworks displays attended by 'big-shot' ministers from Delhi.

Up on the shore facing Vypeen Island stand the incongruous Chinese fishing nets, looking like pop-art sculptures, best seen in action from 5pm onwards (see See how it's done, above). Across the water, on tiny Gundu island, is the coir (coconut fibre) factory where doormats are made. They can be made to order, all colours and patterns, even incorporating a 'welcome home' or more personal message; then shipped home.

Ernakulum does not have much besides the fascinating Kathakali performances. Cochin Museum, opposite Indian Airlines, houses Cochin raja memorabilia. Tea, spices and cashewnuts are sold in the market. The freshly roasted cashews are sold according to size: jumbo, full, half or broken, costing about Rs70 per kilo. At Curio Palace on M G Road, there is old and new carved rosewood and walnut, masks and other kathakali props and jewellery.

For eating in Ernakulum, *Ceylon Bake House*, opposite Woodlands on M G Road, has good Kerala food, open noon until 2am; *Jancy Café* on Shanmugam Road serves good South Indian food (appam and puttu recommended); the rooftop *Chinese restaurant* of the *Sealord Hotel*, Shanmugam Road, has splendid views and a terrace; and Ernakulum ice-creams are delicious, including fig, pineapple and mango flavours.

At the north end of Shanmugan Road is High Court Jetty, for hiring a boat and rower to go to *Bolgatty Island* or to explore the backwaters. This can take a few glorious hours – or even a day.

KUTTANADU

The area stretching from Cochin to Quilon, known as the backwaters, where life is lived on, beside and often in the water (see p. 216). On the water people fish, go to school or to work, punt their narrow dug-out boats along with a tall pole, which is plunged into the water, pushed and then shipped out just before disappearing beneath the surface. Other boatmen paddle furiously, skimming along the canals. Lazy ones tag on to motor ferries. Artistic ones carve the wooden prow. Others put up sails. Boatmen of bigger dug-outs, carrying loads of coir, copra (dried coconut meat) and cashews, have small palmyra leaf huts to live in.

Beside the water, women wash clothes and pots and pans. Brightly painted houses and thatched huts are built on narrow walkways, often seeming to float on nothing. They jostle for space with tailors and fruit shops and with jackfruit trees (good wood for house-building), mauve flowering creepers, coconut palms, cows, pigs, chickens, ducks, banana palms, red and white flowering trees, pineapple palms and, of course, Chinese fishing nets. On the other side of the walkway are fields of wheat, to be harvested before the monsoon when the whole area is flooded. When Malcolm Muggeridge came here to teach in the 1920s, fresh from university, he thought it was like paradise and would often take a boat and be pushed through this beauty with the tall pole until the stars came out, then sleep on board.

The only way to see this area is on the water, hiring a boat to explore up creeks and taking ferries from town to town with the local commuters. Towns are bases for exploration and are very incidental. Ferry timetables have their own logic: the Quilon-Alleppey boat was out of service for well over a year. If you are travelling through Kerala by car, the driver will drop you at, say, Kottayam ferry, then drive furiously to meet you at Alleppey while you gently chug through the green fields of African moss, past coconuts. It is much further for him. Barring strikes, there should be ferry services between the following: Kottayam-Alleppey (journey 3 hrs; ferries depart hourly 6am-6pm); Alleppey-Quilon (journey 8 hrs; daytime service); Cochin-Alleppey (night service sometimes operates); Quilon-Guhanandapuram (service sometimes operates). Your hotel will check.

KOTTAYAM

By road, 68km from Ernakulum; 37km from Alleppey; 117km from Thekkady Wildlife Sanctuary. Driving here by road from Cochin, past whackily coloured churches, mosques, temples and flashy new homes built with Middle East money, it is worth pausing at Vaikom (large 16th century temple, Hindus can go in to admire the murals) and Ettumanur (fine Keralan wooden 16th century temple, with fine carving). It is a busy town, full of churches, the headquarters of Kerala's several newspapers and a major centre for the Kerala Syrian Christians. (For more on Christianity in Kerala, see Fort Cochin, above.) In Kottayam, it is best to stay at the *Anjali Hotel* (tel: 3661; telex: 888-212). It is clean and comfortable. The chef will, if asked in advance, prepare the local freshwater fish, karimeen, in the Keralan way.

ALLEPPEY

By road, 37km from Kottayam; 63km from Ernakulum; 85km from Quilon; but nicest by far by ferry from Kottayam. A quiet market town, trading bales of coir rope, and piles of sacking and green bananas along its canals. Split coconuts can be seen drying in the sun. The essential black umbrellas carried by every Keralan are sold at Cochin Umbrella Mart on the high street. To eat, drink or relax, go to the Indian Coffee House, opposite the Hindu temple. It has a Parisian café atmosphere, with excellent coffee and food in charming and spotless rooms. It is run by a co-operative, with 13 other branches in Kerala. Alleppey bursts into action in high summer for Onam (see p. 209). The nearby beaches are beautiful. Stay overnight at *St George's Lodge* or the *Government Rest House* or the newly built *Alleppey Prince*.

QUILON

By road, 85km from Alleppey; 71km from Trivandrum; 198km from Thekkaday Wildlife Sanctuary; or, driving from Cochin (110km) and stopping at Kaviyur for its rock-cut temple (8th century, Kerala's best-preserved earliest monument) and the very Keralan 11th and 18th centuries Mahadeva Temple; and then at Chengannur for the Narasimha Temple (mostly 18th century, glorious carving for Hindus to see). Quilon is one of the oldest ports on the Malabar Coast. Its church is one of seven believed to have been founded by St Thomas himself; and it is probably the 'Coilum' visited by Marco Polo. After the Phoenicians, Persians, Greeks, Romans and Arabs, the Chinese established a busy trading port here from the 7th to 10th centuries, even exchanging envoys under the 13th-century ruler, Kubla Khan. Later came the Portuguese (1503), Dutch (1653) and, last century, the British.

Today, it is an unimportant, rather sprawling market town, with wooden houses overhanging the winding back streets. To stay overnight, Quilon has one of the most delightful places in Kerala, the *Tourist Bungalow*, which was built as the British Residency. It is set in extensive gardens maintained by three gardeners, with a jetty on to Ashtamudi Lake, next to a park on the outskirts of the town. It is spotless and well-run by Kerala state, and has simple rooms with Kerala wood-framed chairs, all with shower, tub and hot water. Pilastered first-floor drawing room is furnished with prints of Warren Hastings' victories, card tables, flower stands and wine-coolers. It is popular, so book in writing, requesting air-conditioned room (only 3). There is boating on the lake (if no boats at hotel, hire one in town) and the sands of Thangasseri beach are 3km away. Forget the nearby overrated Portuguese, Dutch and British ruins.

Along the roads, look out for the occasional mosque. The Malabar Muslims, known as Mappillas, arrived as Arab traders in the 8th century and were given land and religious tolerance. They are nothing to do with the destructive invaders of North India and preferred trading with their clients to converting them to Islam.

TRIVANDRUM

10km from Kovalam; 71km from Quilon; 87km from Kanya Kumari (Cape Comorin); 154km from Thekkady; 307km from Madurai. Driving from Quilon, Anjengo (meaning Five Coconut Trees) makes a nice stop, to see remants of the English factory (established 1684). An attractive, hilly town whose real name is Thiru-Vananta-Puram (Abode of the Serpent), but the British could not cope with that. Raja Marthanda Varma (1729-58) transferred his capital here from Padmanabhapuram in 1750, dedicating the whole state of Travancore to Sri Padmanabha (Vishnu). Royal succession is matriarchal, through the eldest sister's eldest son. The ruler is not supposed to marry in case his love is diverted from his state to his children. The present ex-Raja continues to be very devout, crossing the town from his palace every morning, at about 7.30am, to worship at the Padmanabhaswamy Temple. But his city is now the Communist capital of Kerala, stocked with all that that implies: government buildings, information, shops, bazaars, museums and, of course, a constant parade of strikers outside the Secretariat. (The site is so popular that unions have to book up their demonstration space months in advance.) The one drawback is that it lacks any metropolitan atmosphere.

THE HARD FACTS Trivandrum has one of Kerala's two airports (3km from the centre), so it connects into the spider's web of Indian Airlines and serves the Maldives (Male) and Sri Lanka (Colombo). Difficult to recommend a hotel in town, and anyway far nicer to stay at one of the increasing number of well-run beach hotels, some family-run (see p. 276), and enjoy the extraordinarily beautiful drive from them to the airport.

There is a superb Kerala government Tourist Office at Park View (tel: 61132), conveniently opposite the gateway to the zoo, gardens and museums complex. Kerala Tourist Office, Thampanur, near Central Bus Station (tel: 2643) runs tours around the city, to Padmanabhapuram Palace and Kanya Kumari (Cape Cormorin) and to Thekkady Wildlife Sanctuary. There is a Government of India Tourist Office at the airport. On M G Road, there are bookshops, Natesan's and other antique shops, the government emporia and Tourindia travel shop run by Mr Varghese whom Alexander Frater consulted in his quest for the monsoon as he came with the recommendation that he 'knew Kerala better than anyone'. Everything of interest closes on Mondays.

To find out more about the special *Kerala martial arts* and their associate special massage techniques, visit the Kalarippayat Centre and meet C. V. Govindankutty, the master. The art is said to have been invented by the gods to protect Kerala. Even last century, every Kerala boy and girl trained and, until the British banned them, sharp prods were used which could kill if jabbed into one of the body's 108 pressure points. The British also banned *ayryavaidya massage* and medicine, based on theories some 5,000 years old and practised especially in Kerala, since they thought it 'a product of heathen, superstitious minds'. Today, the British come here to learn more about this mysterious but successful healing method based on special diet and massage using a mixture of boiled rice, powders, oils, herbs and saps of medicinal plants. Europeans are joining the many Indians who come to Kerala for ayryavaidya treatment during the monsoon. As one local put it: 'The monsoon cure is big business in Kerala these days'. As for the monsoon, Trivandrum's meteorological office is the most important in India since around June 1 each year it is the first to announce the official arrival of the much-awaited monsoon. The best place to watch it arrive is Kovalum beach.

OUT AND ABOUT At the centre of the old fort area is **Padmanabhaswamy Temple**, with nice old houses built around its tank and back streets. It is worth a peek for the goporam (pyramid gateway), the carved columns and the daily temple procession, at about 12.30pm. The two temple festivals are in March-April and October-November, each lasting 10 days, with a big procession down to the sea. Although it is closed to non-Hindus, much can be seen from the outside. Keralans use their temples in a different way from Tamils: they go there to pray, then leave, whereas Tamils make the temple the centre of social, cultural and commercial life, full of banter, music, shops and open to all and sundry.

The other interesting area is the 64-acre **Zoo and Botanical Gardens**, containing the museums (zoo and gardens open daily, museums open Tues. and Thurs.-Sun., 8am-6pm; Wed. 2-6pm). R. F. Chisholm designed the new, gaily painted, hilltop Napier Museum (1874-80) for the Governor of Madras, touring south India to study its architecture before embarking on the project. When the collection originally opened in 1857, the only other museums in India were at Madras, Calcutta and Karachi. The museum was not a success, so the gardens and zoo were laid out two years later to try to attract visitors. Inside are fine Chola bronzes, stone carvings, masks, puppets, gold jewellery, musical instruments and raja's knick-knacks (good guide book). The other museums house natural history, contemporary paintings, a gallery for Ravi Varmar, and a good collection of minature paintings (firmly locked up at the moment, but worth trying to see).

PADMANABHAPURAM PALACE, KERALA
55km from Trivandrum; 45km from Kovalam; 32km from Kanya Kumari. One of the finest buildings in Kerala. Splendid palace of the former capital (dating from 1550), built of teak with deep, overhanging roofs, elaborately carved, and furnished with rosewood, all probably Chinese-influenced as a result of trading both commodities and craftsmen. See especially the carved open hall where the king addressed his people; the richly carved ceiling of the hall behind; the upstairs council chamber with broad-seated chairs for ministers to sit on cross-legged and an ingenious air-conditioning

system; the dance hall, pool, temple, women's quarters, guard rooms and the wonderful tower whose topmost room is reserved for the god, complete with bed and murals for his comfort – the raja took the room below it.

There are good guides, but no guide-book. Open Tues.-Sun., 7am-9pm. If going by bus or train, get down at Thakkalai. On the Trivandrum-Padmanabhapuram road is *Balaramapuram*, a centre for cottage industries where almost every family dyes and weaves. Warps of 50 metres or so are prepared and combed out on rickety trestles under jackfruit trees.

KANYA KUMARI (CAPE CORMORIN), TAMIL NADU
32km from Padmanabhapuram; 87km from Trivandrum; 300km to Madurai. The Land's End of India. This is where the waters of the Arabian Sea, Indian Ocean and Bay of Bengal mingle – souvenir stalls sell packets of sand of three colours taken from three beaches washed by the three seas. The sun rises out of the sea one side, and sets down into the sea the other. It is of enormous importance to Hindus who believe that to bathe in the waters is to be fully cleansed. This is because the goddess Parvati did penance here in order to marry the god Shiva. Alexander Frater recently described it as 'a shabby little town, its only sizeable buildings a few gaunt hotels and one or two ornate temples'. Be that as it may, the faithful come here from all over India. It was here that Swami Vivekananda, who founded the Ramakrishna order (and whose missions throughout India thrive today) meditated in 1892 before leaving for America (see the memorial). The ghats are especially lively just before sunset, when pilgrims bathe in a rocky pool near a Kumari temple. They also visit *Suchindram* (6km) to do puja at the even more sacred Siva temple (17th century). Sunrise and sunset here are sensational; even more so on full moon nights when the moon rises as the sun sets. To see both, arrive for sunset and stay at the TTDC *Cape Hotel*.

Tamil Nadu

MADRAS
45km from Mahabalipuram; 62km from Kanchipuram; 145km from Vellore; 300km from Tiruchchirapalli. The seaside capital of Tamil Nadu and India's fourth largest city, Madras is a major port and a centre for the textile, leather, and motor industries and for engineering factories. The world's top fashion designers employ workers from Madras; Zandra Rhodes has the beadwork of her creations stitched here. Yet, spread over a flat 80 sq km or so, its elegant colonial centre sprinkled with gardens, palms and a broad esplanade along the shore, it actually feels airy, especially after Bombay or Calcutta. The luxury of space has resulted in relatively few tall buildings, too.

While the rest of Tamil Nadu is dominated by the monuments of the great Pallava, Chola and Pandya empires, central Madras is dominated by its British Fort, decaying classical houses plastered in white chunam and soaring Gothic public buildings. For it was here that the East India Company got its first foothold on the east coast. (It had already established a factory at Surat, north of Bombay, in 1612.)

The Company arrived in 1639, was given land by the friendly Raja of Chandragiri, built Fort St George in 1641, had between three and four hundred weavers working there and started exporting cloth back home. Twin towns developed: Fort St George for the Europeans; Madraspatnam or Black Town for the Indians, confusingly renamed Georgetown in 1911, when King George V visited Madras. In 1688 James II granted a municipal charter, the first in India. By 1740, British trade in India represented 10% of all Britain's public revenue. Madras was the chief British settlement, a position maintained until Calcutta stole the limelight in 1772. Many of the early British heroes passed through Madras before moving up the coast – Clive, Hastings, Wellesley and the man who was to found Calcutta in 1690, Job Charnock, who had the local Pallavaram granite named after him as Charnockite.

Various periods of trouble with the French followed: they occupied Madras 1746-9 but the able young Clive finally defeated them and their leader, Dupleix, at the battle of Arcot in 1751. Meanwhile, south of the Fort, the spacious garden houses of residential Madras continued to expand further and further into the countryside, making it a relaxed garden city punctuated with clubs and churches instead of a tight-knit Imperial powerhouse. On arriving there in 1780, Eliza Fay found 'its whole appearance charms you from novelty, as well as beauty. Many of the houses and public buildings are very extensive and elegant . . . I could have fancied myself transported into Italy, so magnificently are they decorated, yet with the utmost taste. . . . Asiatic splendour combined with European taste [are] exhibited around you on every side, . . . and all the pomp and circumstance of lucurious ease, and unbounded wealth.' Mrs Fay also thought the Madras surf 'terrible', the beach 'remarkable fine'.

Another flowering in the 1870s and 1880s embellished the classical city with grand Victorian Gothic public buildings designed by R. F. Chisholm and Henry Irwin – although Kipling would shortly be describing the city as a 'withered beldame brooding on ancient fame'. And an elderly leather merchant, with a twinkle in his eye, recalls life in Madras even in the 1940s as 'glorious fun, like an overgrown university, and always that cooling sea breeze'.

Today, the clubs are less amusing and many of the great studios are devoted to sound processing, not film-making. However, M. G. Ramachandran adds a touch of glamour. The former matinée idol, who played Robin Hood roles in the Errol Flynn and Douglas Fairbanks tradition, continued to make films while he was an MP, only reluctantly stopping when he became Chief Minister of Tamil Nadu.

THE HARD FACTS The air is clearest December-January, but tree and flower blooms are best in March. There is a *dance and arts festival* mid-December to early January, a marathon of performances daily from 2pm to late at night in several locations. It is well worth aiming to be in Madras to see it. Madras is a busy commercial city, so there are good flight connections within India and to Sri Lanka and the Andamans. Airport 14km from city centre. Here is a good opportunity to take an interesting train journey across the South (see beginning of chapter) but remember there are two stations: Egmore serves the south, Central the rest of India. The more adventurous can take a boat to the beaches of the Andamans (three days' journey, see Sun chapter), booking through K. P. V. Shaikh Mohammed Rowther & Co, 202 Linghi Chetty Street (tel: 25756/7/8).

Madras hotel options have improved. In town, choose between old and new styles, both Taj run; for more congenial hotel life, stay down the coast at their beach hotel (or a cheaper one, see Sun chapter), and come in to shop and see the sights and dancing. The rival Welcomgroup have two hotels here, too, one mid-town, one just outside.

Connemara Hotel, Binny Road (tel: 860123; fax: 860193; telex: 41 8197). Formerly a spacious town house of the Nawabs of Wallajah, with large rooms, fountains, courtyard gardens and stables. It was bought and converted into a hotel in the 1930s by the immensely successful Spencer & Co, the shop that started in Madras in the 1860s, then opened branches throughout British India to supply the Raj memsahibs with everything from Ovaltine and paraffin to furniture and its famous Spencer's Torpedo No.1 Cooking Range. Now run by the Taj group, fully refurbished and roundly praised by all who stay there. 150 rooms, the old ones largest, the poolside ones with french windows. All mod. cons include pool, dance and music recitals at the open-air Rain Tree restaurant serving delicious Chettinand cuisine, the Kolam regular restaurant and a poolside coffee-shop. Discerning locals use the large shopping arcade. *Taj Coromandel,* 17 Nungambakkam High Road (tel: 474849; fax: 44 474849; telex: 41-7194).

A concrete tower with rooms of singularly dreary anonymity, compensated by good views from higher floors (they go up to 7). Efficient Taj group service, exceptional food and good Indian classical dance performances. 240 rooms. All mod. cons include excellent extensive health club and beauty salon, pool and lawn. There is a poolside coffee shop, pleasant bar (rare in India), both the Chinese and Indian restaurants are excellent, and the Indian one has three good Bharat Natyam dance programmes nightly.

Welcomgroup's two hotels are the Chola Sheraton and Park Sheraton.

Welcomgroup Chola Sheraton, 10 Cathedral Road, (tel: 473347; fax: 44 478779); telex: 41-7200). 133 rooms in the group's oldest hotel, a soulless 1970s building, but all mod. cons include pool. *Welcomgroup Park Sheraton,* 132 TTK Road, PO Box 1453 (tel: 452525; fax: 44 455913); telex: 41-6868) 160 rooms and suites in sparkling new building in Adayar Park. With extensive grounds and shopping arcade, good pool, rowing, and, after a sticky start, some good reports coming through.

Like Bombay and Calcutta, Madras has the pre-and post-Independence street name problem, the most important being Anna Salai, still known as Mount Road (good for shopping), and Netaji Subhash Bose Road, still called Parry's Corner (commercial area).

For good modest accommodation right in town, the YMCA Vepery, 74 Ritherdon Road (tel: 32831) is right opposite the High Court, in a red sandstone building given by a Postmaster-General of the US; the YWCA is at 1086 Ponamalee High Road (tel:39920).

The Government of India Tourist Office, 154 Anna Salai (tel: 869695, open Mon.-Sat., 9am-5pm) is excellent, stocking the city map and leaflets including information on dance. It will advise on which is the best of the many good current dance performances. (Go clutching copy of *The Hindu*.) But, beware, dance performances tend to start early, around 6pm. It will also organise visits to film studios (such as Vauhini). It runs daily tours of the Fort and museums, 2-6pm plus day trips to Kanchipuram-Thirukkalikundram-Mahabalipuram and to Tirupati. And it stocks the free monthly booklet, *Hello Madras*. Cox & Kings (India), is at Hotel Connemara (tel: 860123; fax: 850193). Tamil Nadu Tourist Office is at 143 Anna Salai (tel 840752); Kerala Tourist Information Office, 28 Commander-in-Chief Road (tel: 478884). If Madras is the first stop in a South India, tour, now is the moment to book up (see also Information, at chapter beginning).

News and complete listings of dance and cinema can be found in *The Hindu*. The best guide-book is S. Muthiah's *Madras Discovered*.

Best bookshops are Pai & Co (found by turning left out of the Government of India Tourist Office) and Higginbotham's, both on Anna Salai, and Giggles Book Boutique in the Connemara hotel. The Archaeological Survey of South India is in the Fort, behind St Mary's Church, and provides information on temple sites right across the state.

Officially, there is currently total prohibition in Tamil Nadu: foreigners need a liquor permit (obtainable at the Tourist Office) for buying alcohol from shops, but not for drinking in the recommended hotel bars and restaurants. Shops are mostly open 9am-8pm, without a siesta. Monuments such as the good museums tend to close on Fridays. Several countries have representation here, including the UK, 24 Anderson Road (tel: 83136) and the USA, Gemini Circle, Anna Salai (tel: 83041). The British Council, extremely informative, is at Local Library Authority Building, 150A Anna Salai.

OUT AND ABOUT There are two interesting areas, the compact Fort, focus of the first substantial British settlement in India, and the buildings scattered in the former residential area, now the city centre, several of them remarkable examples of British architecture. In all, this is a feast for the keen colonial historian.
The fort and north Madras Although the bastions of the *Fort* were completed in 1642, there were several rebuildings, the last being when the French left in 1749. There are several interesting buildings inside. St Mary's Church (1678-80, rebuilt 1759), the first Anglican church in India, was originally designed by Chief Gunner William Dixon with walls 4ft thick and a roof 2ft thick to withstand attack. There are windows with pretty stained glass, elegant cane seating, walls covered in memorial tablets and a graveyard with some of the oldest British tombstones in India.

Elihu Yale was the first to be married here (1689). He arrived in Madras in 1672, aged 24, rose in 15 years from Company Writer to Governor (1687-92). He stayed in Madras to augment his fortune and gave £560 worth of books and pictures to the Collegiate School in Connecticut, where his father had emigrated, which led to the university being named after him. Charnock's three daughters were baptised here and, in 1853, Clive was married here.

Behind St Mary's is Clive House (next to the Archaeological Survey office), the dilapidated Wellesley House, and the Arsenal (1722) whose portico is crowned by two lions carrying the East India Company's coat of arms. To the north are the mightily grand Governor's House (now the Secretariat) with black pillared portico, Cornwallis Cupola and the Officers' Mess (1780-

90), now a good museum of Madras history. It has everything from prints of terrified Europeans landing through the surf on to the beach to portraits of Major Stringer Lawrence, Queen Victoria (by Sir George Hayter) and Edward VII (open Sat.-Thurs., 10am-5pm).

Just north of the Fort are the lighthouse and the *High Court*, (1888-92), the second largest judicial building in the world, after London, and considered the finest Indo-Saracenic building in India. Designed first by J. W. Brassington, then revised and completed by Henry Irwin and J. H. Stephens, it is described by Jan Morris and Simon Winchester as 'one of the most romantically exciting of the British buildings in India'; its interior 'spectacular . . . like a Piranese jail in its contrapuntal and crypt-like surprise – court after court, staircase after staircase, warrens of arcaded and vaulted corridors, half-hidden alcoves where the lawyers gossiped, huge verandahs thronged with litigants, cool galleries, . . . a palatial porte-cochere, . . . and on top of the building . . . a bulbous and eccentric tower, . . . really a lighthouse'. Certainly worth a wander; don't miss the Central Tower whose light tower and crypt are open most days (good view from the top).

North again, *Georgetown* overlooks the man-made harbour, its grid-plan the earliest piece of English town planning in India. Here are two more magnificent buildings: the Southern Headquarters of the State Bank of India and R. F. Chisholm's General Post Office (1875-84).

West of here, passing the Indo-Saracenic Central Station (1868-72) and Moore Market (c.1900, both by Irwin), lies *St Andrew's Kirk* (1818-21). Designed by Thomas Fiott de Havilland and Colonel James Caldwell and modelled (like so many colonial churches) on St Martin-in-the-Fields, London, Philip Davies enthuses that it is 'the most ambitious neo-classical church in India, a magnificent building of considerable sophistication'; see the circular interior with star-studded ceiling, the cane pews and louvred doors for ventilation. A nearby footbridge leads to Egmore Station and to the excellent *museum complex*, of the central Museum building, Connemara Library (1896, Irwin again), and the National Art Gallery, its exceptional collection (founded 1851) well laid out and displayed. If you are going on to see South Indian temples, this is a good moment to get your eye in; there are fine stone sculptures and bronzes from the Pallava, Chola, Pandya and Vijayanagar dynasties; don't worry about the lack of labelling and guide-books (both open Sat.-Thurs., 8am-5pm but bronze gallery only opens at 10am).
Central Madras Crossing the Cooum River, something much more Indian can be found: the 8th century *Parthasarathy Temple* on Triplicane

High Road and, down in Mylapore, *Kapaliswa-rar Temple* off R K Mutt Road, its gopuram painted up with Rowney colours. And, from late afternoon onwards, there is music from drums and double pipes, puja, women exchanging horoscopes and hawkers selling ribbons and jasmine. (The festival of Sixty-three Saints of Shaivism, held in March-April, is very spectacular.) But British buildings still dominate. In *Triplicane*, find the shoreside Senate House and Presidency College with, inland, Christ Church, the famous Spencer & Co (1897), Higginbotham's (1844) and the old building of the once-glorious Madras Club, founded 1831 and soon known as the 'Ace of Clubs'. In *Mylapore*, find *San Tomé Cathedral* (rebuilt 1893-6), where St Thomas's remains are believed to be kept – he is believed to have been martyred at nearby Little Mount. Here, too, are several surviving elegant white villas and a few old garden houses, surrounding pristine garden squares which are often owned by private firms who compete to produce the best blooms.

Bordering all these and more proud buildings is the hugely wide sandy **marina beach,** nearly 13km long, glorious for a walk (not glorious for swimming). Along the shore, a backdrop of mostly British buildings gasps for sea breezes. From the south upwards, the Lutyens-like University Examination Hall, Chisholm's Presidency College (1864), the domes of Mohammed Ali Wallajah's Chaepuk Palace (1768), and the Senate House. Bullocks and people share the sands, and boats bob on the water. Fishermen launch their catamarans (from the Tamil, meaning tied logs) at 4-5am, returning 2-5pm with their catch of pomfret, bekti, small sharks, lobster and prawns. Then they lay out their nets on the beach.

The headquarters of the **Theosophical Society** are just across the Adayar River, in a gloriously leafy and serenely peaceful 270-acre garden which should not be missed. The Society, whose adherents advocate the essentially spiritual nature of man, was founded in the USA in 1875 by Madame Blavatsky who came to Madras four years later. Its splendid library contains some 17,000 manuscripts (open Mon.-Sat., 8.30am-10am and 2-4pm. Garden open daily, sunrise to sunset). It is best to combine a visit to the gardens with a dance performance at the nearby Kalakshetra School of Indian classical dance.

Some of the most beautiful of the old colonial houses are scattered around **Adayar, or Guindy, area,** such as the current home of the Madras Club on Chamiers Road where mulligatawny, the Raj version of the Tamil pepper soup, was created. The Club was built as a house by Robert Moubray in 1771, and has gardens down to the river; in 1891 it opened at the

Adayar Club, the name it is still fondly known by. (Apply to the Secretary for a visit, tel: 450121.) Other good buildings to seek here include Caldwell and de Havilland's St George's Cathedral (1814-16), St Thomas's Mount and its church, pretty Madras Race Course and the atmospheric Chettinand Palace and also Ramalayam on Lattice Bridge Road, the Maharaja of Travancore's home, now a children's school. Finally, in *Guindy Deer Park and Snake Park*, the Raj Bhavan, built as the Governor's house, is open to visitors. The park is a rare treat: some 300 acres of natural forest right in the city, stocked with corkscrew-antlered black buck, chital and monkeys. Here too are a reptilium and India's first snake farm, set up by conservationist Romulus Whitaker and stocked with the many species of Indian snake, only five of them poisonous, living in pits. (Open daily, 9am-6.30pm).

SPORTS The colonial tradition provides quite a good selection of sports. At Guindy, south of the Adayar River, there is the charming racecourse (November-March). Temporary membership of the Madras Race Club is available (tel: 431171); the Madras Riders Club is at the Race Course (tel: 431231). And a rather sandy, 18-hole golf course (beware of hitting the park's deer), open to visitors by applying to the Cosmopolitan Golf Club, Mount Road (tel: 441840). The Boat Club offers instant guest membership (tel: 453190). Apply in writing to the Secretary of the Madras Gymkhana, housed in an elegant colonial house on Anna Salai, beside the river, for tennis, squash, pool, billiards, table tennis and beautiful gardens. The MCC (Madras Cricket Club) has, naturally, cricket, as well as tennis, squash and billiards.

RESTAURANTS Excellent Indian food and an idea of dance is to be found at all the deluxe hotels (a really serious dancer does not do the hotel rounds; go to a cultural hall for that). Madras is an excellent and safe place to eat fish, either tandoor cooked or as the special fish curry; there are also special Chettinand chicken dishes, and the rich Mughlai Hyderabadi dishes. For Chinese food, again the hotels. There is the only rooftop restaurant in Madras, *the Sagari* at the Chola Hotel, or there is the *Taj's Gold Dragon*. Apart from hotels, try the excellent *Buhari* on Anna Salai and the restaurant next door where clients pack out three floors with a good atmosphere, and where food is ordered by number. The more adventurous find good food in tiny places such as *Café Amin*, next to the Police Station in the Royapettah area or *Velu Military Hotel* in Eldams Road. *Amaravati* restaurant, on Cathedral Road, does a superb biryani (and sweetmeats) as does *Queen's* on

Nungambakam High Road. For south Indian food, *Woodlands* drive-in on Cathedral Road is the best of their several branches. *Desaprakesh Hotel* has a roof garden restaurant.

The Madras evening highlight is without doubt a performance of Bharata Natyam dance (see p. 218). To sample south India films, good cinemas include Sathyan, Devi and Safire. And that's it. As a couple of jet-set students at the university complained: 'After 10pm, Madras is dead'.

SHOPPING Madras is the best place to shop in Tamil Nadu, so don't rely entirely on the good hotel arcades. **Fabrics:** The South Indian cottons and silks from Madras and nearby Kanchipuram are some of India's finest. The Weavers' Service Centre is at 56 Chamiers Road (tel: 450210), for information on weaving, where to see it and where to buy master craftsmen's pieces. Co-Optrex, at Kuvalagan on N S C Bose Road, is a five-storey, air-conditioned building next to the museum, and the headquarters of the South Indian handloom goods. It stocks everything from dress to upholstery fabrics, sold by sari or metre length. Conran, Habitat and FabIndia (of Delhi) all buy here. Khadi Krafts, Kuralagam, stocks khadi silk saris. Rasi Silk Shop has quality south Indian silks and is behind Kapalishwara Temple, where lots of tiny, traditional Brahmin shops sell oils, scented powders for the bath and Indian make-up (Rasi has a second, smaller branch on M G Road.) More good silk can be found at Nalli's and Kumaran's, both at Panagal Park, Mambalam.

On **Anna Salai** there is the classic Raj department store, Spencer's, whose wonderfully period stock includes Merritt treddle sewing machines, and a good chemist. Also on Anna Salai are the state emporia of which Kaveri (for Karnataka state), Kairali (for Kerala), Poompuhar (for Tamil Nadu) and the Victoria Technical Institute (VTI) are the best.

VTI has the jazzy cotton appliqué lanterns used to decorate temple chariots for southern festivals. (See them dangling from the Valluvar Kottam, a stone chariot memorial to the poet-saint Thiruvalluvar, in the Nungambakkam area.) They also stock useful and beautiful picnic baskets at and wonderful canework laundry baskets the shape and size of baby elephants. (These are apparently worth shipping if you fill up the body with other purchases.) Poompuhar has nice lanterns, cane mats, small stone elephants and good bronzes and wood carving. Much comes from their workshop at Kallakkurchi village near Tiruneliveli, outside Madurai.

Good antique sculpture, paintings and brass can be found at the Aparna Art Gallery, near the Connemara. With all the **leather** tanning and export, Madras has hopped on the bandwagon of copying the latest European designs, and the prices are even cheaper than in Bombay and Delhi. Find up-to-the-minute leather jerkins, suede coats, luggage, bags and shoes in the Taj and Connemara arcades and the excellent emporium opposite the Taj Coromandel (open daily 9am-10pm). Italian shoe designs can be found at Vasson's, 829 Anna Salai Road, and elsewhere (Madras is a major shoe-making city). Madras bazaars are not as colourful or good as elsewhere.

Moore Market, next to Central Station, has everything from pink plastic elephants to black wigs and piles of second-hand books. Beware of pick-pockets in China Bazaar and Evening Bazaar where it is almost impossible to resist such bargain offers as 'buy your teeth here' and 'sex specialist, come and look'.

TIRUPATI AND TIRUMALA, ANDHRA PRADESH
Round trip about 340km. A fascinating trip for the hardy and curious, for this is a very sacred Hindu pilgrimage centre and one of the few where non-Hindus are permitted to enter the holy of holies and thus see, feel and understand a little more about the spirituality and strength of Hinduism. The best way to go is on an ITDC or TNTDC day trip, leaving Madras 6am, returning 9pm. (Part of the ticket price goes to the temple.) 98% of the fellow passengers will be pilgrims. The faithful make for Tirupati all the year round. The temple complex is built on the peak of Tirumala hill in the Seshachalam range, surrounded by mango, tamarind and sandal trees. With the Chola, Pandya and, most importantly, Vijayanagar rulers endowing it (their local capital was Chandragiri, 11km away), and its continuing attraction for more than 10,000 pilgrims each day, the temple is reputedly the wealthiest in India.

At *Tirupati* town, there is a technicolour cluster of painted houses and temples at the foot of the hill. There are also several temples including the central Govindaraja Temple (16th-17th centuries), built by the Vijayanagars and Nayakas, although the central shrine housing images of Vishnu and his consorts is 9th-10th century.

Worldly pilgrims now change buses for a terrifying trip up 11km of hair-pin bends (fine views) to *Tirumala*, their goal. The stunt driving demanded of the bus-driver is equally breathtaking. Ominous signs offer 'space for sick vehicles'. A serious pilgrim climbs the hill as part of the pilgrimage, the sadhus (holy men) with painted faces carrying a suitcase or bedding on their heads and black umbrellas.

At the top, the pilgrim's first job is to have his head shaved – men, women and children alike – as part of the cleansing process. The temple bazaar has a variety of goods on sale including long-eared pink plastic rabbits (pilgrims are like any other tourist) and scented offerings of marigolds, camphor, coconuts and sugar (a symbol of wealth). The milk of broken coconuts scents the air. The coachload queue-jumps past the chanting faithful who wait their turn for hours, sometimes days. Their chanting reaches fever pitch as they near the sanctum sanctorum. Inside, the incense-filled air is intoxicating and the holy atmosphere drives many into a state of spiritual ecstasy – some even collapse – followed by physical and emotional exhaustion when they emerge into the temple precinct, smiling with a deep, spiritual serenity.

KANCHIPURAM

70km from Madras; 65km from Mahabalipuram. It is an amusing drive, along palm-fringed roads busy with bullocks dragging loads of long bamboo. There are travelling salesmen with red and green plastic pails, which they sell for old clothes, not money. And workers thrash grain in the middle of the tarmac road so that passing car wheels help with the work. As usual, there are many tanks where women are washing saris and adding splashes of vibrant colour as they put them out to dry. Bathing people share the water with bullocks cooling off.

Kanchipuram (Golden City), is one of the oldest towns of India and one of its Seven Sacred Cities. It is, unusually, dedicated to both Shiva and Vishnu – the other six cities are dedicated to one or the other (see Varanasi for Hinduism). It is an exceptionally pleasant rural town of broad streets, full to the brim with exquisite temples and master weavers. And, in the January wedding season, halls are dressed up with canopies of banana leaves, tinsel and garlands of marigold and jasmine. Musicians strum outside.

The town's monuments and weaving tradition date from when it was the capital of the *Pallava* and Chola empires, the two successive political forces in Tamil Nadu after the Guptas. The later Vijayanagar occupants added buildings too, as did the Nayakas. The Pallavas were at their most powerful from the 6th to 9th centuries and often at loggerheads with the contemporary empires of the Chalukyas of Aihole and Badami in the Deccan (see p. 223) and the Pandyas of Madurai in south Tamil Nadu (see p. 250). The rulers, whose capital from the 7th to 9th centuries was Kanchipuram, believed in their divine right, tracing their ancestry straight back to Brahma, the first of the Hindu trinity.

Although this ancestry might be contested, they certainly rose from local ruling dynasty to wealthy empire, extending their influence right up to Badami and promoting agriculture to increase both produce and taxes. In addition to rice, the main crop and bartering unit, there were coconuts, mangoes, plantains and oil extracted from cotton and gingelly. Tanks, so essential for water, were built by the whole village, lined with stone or brick and strictly managed by a committee. The tax system became all-pervading, like Britain's VAT, touching toddymen, letter-carriers and even marriage parties. Only weavers to the royal court were exempted.

Political power and cultural patronage leapt forward under Mahendravarman I (600-630). He was a dramatist and poet who was converted from Jainism to Shaivism by the saint Appar, and he ended Jain influence in Tamil Nadu – hence many Pallava temples are dedicated to Shiva or Vishnu. During his reign, some of the rock-cut temples were chiselled at the Pallava port of Mahabalipuram. It was under the Pallavas that Dravidian – the Pallava name for Tamil Nadu – literature, applied arts and architecture developed a distinct and influential character that contributed substantially to Indian civilisation.

The *Dravidian* temple follows a basic format whether big or small, and is usually full of life and colour. Gopura (gate-houses with soaring, pyramid towers) pierce the high walls of the complex, which then has a number of concentric walls (containing administrative buildings and subsidiary temples ending with the central sanctuary. The tops of the walls are crammed with multi-limbed gods. The lowest caste, the Hariyans, were not permitted to enter the temples until after Independence, so they worshipped their deities outside the gopura, looking at the sculptures.

Inside, various courtyards, subsidiary temples and a tank surround the central shrine, which is entered through mandapams (hall-like porches) and surmounted by a vimana (pyramid tower). Gopura, temples, mandapams and vimana are all smothered in a riotous confusion of writhing, leaping, fighting and dancing deities. Many have recently been painted up in vivid hues using gloss, not the original matt, paints. This preserves the stonework but gives heart attacks to archaeologists.

The temple was the centre of all village or town life. It was built by the locals, for the locals; for their trading, meetings, worship and enjoyment. Here lived their gods, who loved, fought, married, had birthdays and went on holidays – and still do today. A village without a temple is likened to a man without a soul. The temple was also the background to the intense devotional cult of Tamil Hinduism which stimulated hymns, music, dance and gifts of silk. The choreography of temple dancing developed from the jigs of simple folk to the sophisticated Bharata Natyam, performed by girls living in the temples. Combined attacks by the Pandyas of Madurai and the Cholas of Thanjavur brought down Pallava power in the 9th century.

The thousand or so temples in and around Kanchipuram span a thousand years. They are found in three groups: the northern ones, dedicated to Shiva; the eastern dedicated to Vishnu; and the southern Jain ones, found over the Vegavati River. Here are one or two especially worth a look; some have restricted entry for non-Hindus.

In the northern group, *Kailasanatha Temple (c. 725)* is one of the earliest and finest in architecture, sculpture and murals; built of sandstone by the Pallava ruler Rajasimha, its only later addition being the front built by Mahendravarman III. It is simple, small-scale, with one of the first examples of a gopura and mandapam. There are beautiful sculptures of gods (Parvati in particular) and yalis (hippogryphs) and there are also vestiges of wall-paintings in the miniature wall shrines. Here too is the *Vaikuntaperumal Temple* (late 8th century) whose lion-pillar cloisters are precursors of the so-called 1,000-pillar halls of later temple complexes.

At the north of this northern group sprawls the great Dravidian complex of the large *Ekambareshwara Temple* (16th-17th centuries), the principal Shaiva sanctuary, with delicate carvings on the 1,000-pillar temple; begun by the Vijayanagar ruler Krishnadeva Raya, further embellished by the Nayakas, with many carvings of Prithvi (goddess of the earth) holding Shiva's emblem, the lingum. (It is worth asking to get on top of the buildings for a splendid view. The custodian's office is behind the 1,000-pillar temple.) Finally, *Kamakshi Temple* (16th-17th centuries) is where the principal chariot festival happens (February-March); the elaborately carved wooden chariot is stored in the high street for the rest of the year.

In the eastern, Vaishnava group, the *Varadaraja Temple* had both Chola and Vijayanagar patrons; while in the southern, Jain group, the Vardhamana Temple is really two double shrines built by the Cholas, decorated with murals in the 17th century.

The most pleasant way to visit the temples is to hire a bicycle for the day – there are no hills here. And, en route, it is good to stop off to see cotton dyeing, lunghi weaving and silk master weavers behind almost every door (see See how it's done, above). Living temples close noon-4pm. There is no tourist office but further information can be obtained from the Archaeological Survey, opposite Kailasanatha Temple (often closed). The Weavers' Service Centre, 20 Railway Station Road (tel: 2530), advises on where to see weavers. During April, the south Indian New Year, every temple gives its god a procession and there is street theatre in the evening. If necessary, stay overnight at TNTDC *Traveller's Lodge*, Kamakshi Amman, Sannathi Street, taking full food and drink supplies – but it is much nicer to stay on the coast (see Sun chapter.

VELLORE
145km from Madras, via Kanchipuram and Arcot (120km direct from Madras); 180km from Bangalore. This is the site of the 16th century *Vijayanagar fort* and, within it, the Jalakanteshwara Temple (fine carving), both in good condition. The fort, a perfect *Boy's Own* piece of military architecture with a moat, round towers and underground water supply, was probably built by Vijayanagar vassal Sinna Bommi Nayak. It then had a succession of occupants: Mortaza Ali, who claimed the Arcot throne; the Bijapur Sultans; the Marathas; Daud Khan of Delhi and finally the British, who imprisoned Tipu's family here after the fall of Srirangapatna. *Arcot* is also worth pausing at to see the ruined fort. Here Clive defeated the French under Dupleix in 1751. Clive's room is above the gate. See also the ruined palace of the Nawabs of the Carnatic and the tomb of the saint, Tipu Auliya, after whom Tipu Sultan was named.

CHOLAMANDEL
10km south of Madras. A seaside village where a genuine community of artists live and work. There is a permanent exhibition of works for sale and visitors are welcome to meet the artists. The more creative visitors can attend workshops for painting, fabric printing, sculpture, etc., and stay in the pleasant, simply furnished Artists' *Guest House* close to the beach (tel: 412892). (Apply in writing.)

TIRUVIDAVENTHAI
37km south of Madras, just beyond Covelong. It is a temple village in the perfect, unspoilt setting of a small valley.

MAHABALIPURAM (MAMALLAPURAM)
45km from Madras; 20km from Covelong; 65km from Kanchipuram. The Pallavas' second city and port for their capital, Kanchipuram, was already a famous port in the 1st century, known to Greek traders. It is now a village sitting quietly among its fabulous rock-cut temples, giant frieze and shore temples, all of them both beautiful and important to the story of the South Indian temple. (And those keen on the architectural debate of who influenced whom will need to compare these with the equally early and architecturally important monuments built by the Chalukyas at Aihole, etc, in the Deccan, see above.)

The unfinished *Five Rathas* (legend says they were named after the Pancha Pandavas, the five hero brothers of the Mahabharata) are 7th century embryos of the future Dravidian temples, each one a single block of stone carved as a temple chariot in the shape of a miniature temple, with a huge stone elephant in the middle.

Right in the village centre, the huge and glorious *frieze* is cut on to a flat granite rock-face, 28m long and 12m high. It was produced under Narasimhavarman I (*c*630-70). A mass of animals and figures probably recount the Mahabharata episode of Arjuna's penance: after Krishna persuaded him to fight, Arjuna did penance to Shiva for the guilt he felt in killing fellow humans. On the right, the Ganga River flows from Shiva's hair.

The hillside is scattered with eight *mandapams* (7th-century), wall-like temple porches cut into the rock) with bold figure sculptures inside, one with Krishna raising Mount Govardhan to protect his people from the wrath of the rain-god, Indra, another with elephants pouring water over Lakshmi. There is also a huge, balanced boulder, known as Krishna's butter (the cave above is his kitchen).

The sole surviving *shore temple* – archaeologists are hunting under the sea for the others – was built by Rajasimha (690-715) and, with the Kailasanatha Temple at Kanchipuram, is the first substantial Pallava monument. A row of Nandi bulls is on guard on the surrounding walls. The carving of a cow being sacrificed is right beside the actual sacrificial stone, serving as a perpetual sacrifice to appease the gods.

There is a nice open-air museum. Stonemasons and sculptors work in the town centre. The village is best enjoyed by simply wandering about for a few hours at sunset and sunrise. Fishermen launch their catamarans at daybreak, first offering a little prayer. Other locals fish from the shore using a short net. *Silver Sands Hotel* is good for seafood (grilled lobster delicious) and swimming. Accommodation is here at this or one of the other beach hotels (see p. 276).

From here travelling through very rural Tamil Nadu, it is important to take picnics, plenty to drink and ensure a good driver.

TIRUKALIKUNDRAM

15km from Mahabalipuram; 50km from Kanchipuram. There are two fine temples, both worth seeing, one down in the village and one on the summit of a tall hill. It is a steep climb, but a good view at the top. The keen go on to *Uttaramerur* (40km) where the Pallava ruler Dantivarman (c.796-817) built two interesting and fine temples which look forward to Chola developments: the Sundaravarda Perumal (c.805) and the Kailasanatha, restored in the 11th century.

TINDIVANAM TO PONDICHERRY

Starting from Pondicherry (60km) or coming down from the north (Madras is 132km), at Tin-divanam turn westwards to *Gingee*, the first stop. The huge fortress encompassing three hills has the usual southern history: originally Chola, rebuilt by the Vijayanagars in 1442 (whose impressive walls and bastions you see now), later taken by Bijapur, then by Shivaji and finally the British. Enter through the gate in the east side; then, through seven gateways to the citadel, find the eight-storeyed Kalyana Mahal. On to the exotic temple town of *Tiruvannamalai*, where there is seldom a white face. Here, at the Shiva temple of Arunachaleshvara (16th-17th centuries), one of the largest in South India, the four spectacularly carved outer gopuras lead through the first wall to two more, with plenty of intricate carving of yalis, riders, etc. and then through these to the sanctuary. At the annual Shiva festival (November-December), a great bonfire is lit on the nearby hilltop, and devotees prostrate themselves whenever they see it. This temple will either spur you on to Madurai and other great temples, or ensure you avoid them. Onwards, along the Pondicherry road, a return to early Pallavan building with a hilltop temple (8th century) at *Panamalai* and a cave temple (7th century) at the slight detour of *Mandagapattu*. From here, Pondicherry is 55km.

PONDICHERRY

160km from Madras; 60km from Chidambaram; 180km from Tiruchchirappalli (Trichy). If you are coming from Madras, it is worth starting very early to have time to detour inland (see above). Pondicherry was capital of the French settlements in India right up until November 1, 1954. It was founded by François Martin in 1674 and rebuilt by Jean Law 1756-77. It is now an eerie ghost town with closed colonial shutters keeping out the deserted streets of Law's tidy White Town, near where the governor's elegant house looks out to sea. Across the canal is the Black Town, with all the trappings of a perky Indian rural town.

To add to the incongruity, the headquarters of the not altogether convincing *Sri Aurobindo Ashram* and movement are here, on Marine Street. Sri Aurobindo Ghosh (1872-1950) was born in Calcutta, got a first-class classics degree at Cambridge, worked for the Maharaja of Baroda, returned to Bengal briefly for the Independence struggle, then retired here to practise the spiritual discipline of yoga.

His principal disciple was a Parisian, known as the Mother (1878-1973), who established the ashram and education centre. In 1968, she founded the nearby futuristic and optimistic town of Auroville, designed by the French architect Roger Anger, for people of all religions, politics and cultures to live together. It is still unfinished. Apparently things have not been the same since her death. (Open to visitors

8am-noon; 2-5.30pm; dining room and several guest houses; quantities of literature and nice hand-made marbled paper for sale.) To stay, enter into the spirit of decaying, forgotten seaside town and try *Hotel Pondicherry Ashok Beach Resort*, Cinnakalapet (tel: 468) or the Sri Aurobindo Society's 8-roomed *Sea Side Guest House*, 10 Goubert Avenue (tel: 6494).

CHIDAMBARAM

120km from Tiruchchirappalli; 60km from Pondicherry, along a narrow, very rural road, with water and islands of coconut palms on either side. If the temples of Thanjavur, Tiruchchirappalli and Tiruvannamalai excite you at all, then this trip is a must. But be warned: the temple closes noon-4pm and there is nothing much else here.

A Chola city from 907 to 1310, the exquisite early shrine at Chidambaram marks the holy spot of Shiva as Nataraja, the cosmic dancer. Nataraja was a favourite Chola deity, so the *Sri Nataraja Temple* here (12th-13th century) was gradually embellished with many fine buildings and became a repository of dance and literature. Two high walls surround the 55-acre temple complex, pierced by four mighty gopura. The exquisite relief panels of women on the walls of the gopura porches, each in a different pose, are a catalogue of the 108 positions for classical Bharata Natyam as laid down in the Natyashastra, the Sanskrit treatise on Indian dance and drama. There are even dancers carved on the ceilings.

Through the main gopura from the village, the main shrine is straight ahead. Every column inside is carved but see especially the corner on the right of the entrance where the Parvati Temple, roofed in copper gilt, contains both a beautiful image of Shiva Nataraja (Lord of Dance) and a tiny shrine. The oldest part of the complex is designed in the form of a temple chariot with wheels and horses. Its 56 pillars were praised by the architectural historian, J. Fergusson as 'most delicately carved, . . . ornamented with dancing figures, more graceful and more elegantly executed than any others of their class, so far as I know'.

The large temple tank is behind the main shrine, with temples to Parvati (again) and Subrahmanya. Diagonally across from the temples, huge reliefs of elephants decorate the exterior walls of another temple. To stay overnight, there is a very modest state *Tourist Lodge*.

From here, there are two routes to Thanjavur, the first with a touch of colonial remnants, the second a temple hop.

CHIDAMBARAM-THANJAVUR VIA TRANQUEBAR

40km down the coast from Chidambaram, this was a Danish settlement (1620-1845) built by the Danish East India Company, with a Dansborg Fort (1620), Zion's Church (1701), the Lutheran Mission Church (1717), several old Christian mission churches, charming Dutch colonial houses lining King and Queen Street and a fine Collector's House beside the sea. To stay, the modest *Tourist Bungalow* is in Dansborg Fort. Beyond it lies the great temple town *Tiruvarur* (50km), where the Cholas worshipped Shiva as Somaskanda with equal piety to that of the Nataraj image at Chidambaram, resulting in an almost equally impressive temple complex (13th-17th centuries), with plenty of later Nayaka additions. From here, the road southwards leads to *Point Calimere Bird Sanctuary* (see p. 253); the road westwards to Thanjavur (70km).

CHIDAMBARAM-THANJAVUR VIA GANGAKONDACHOLAPURAM

Heading off inland, Srimushnam (25km) has two temples, the Chola (10th century, good carving) and the Nayaka (Bhu Varaha Temple, 16th century, very richly carved). Next stop is *Gangakondacholapuram* (25km) which, as its name suggests, is a tongue-twister meaning 'Ganga brought by Chola king city'. Indeed, it was built by Rajendra I (1002-44) to commemorate his trip up to the sacred Ganga and the water he brought back. It is a vast building, modelled on his father's Brihadeshwara Temple in Thanjavur. There are fine sculptures, a huge tank where the Chola vassal rulers brought more Ganga water when they visited the king's court, and soaring gopura visible for miles around. The next temple is at *Tribhuvanum* (25km), the last huge Chola complex, founded by Kulottunga III (1178-1218).

Then comes *Kumbakonam* (6km), a centre for gold and silver-smithing as well as for growing the much sought after betel, used to make paan. Here are some 15 shrines, four of particular merit, all covered in fine sculpture: Nageshvara (9th century), very fine sculptures; Sarangapani (13th-17th centuries), the largest, with an 10-storey gopuram second only to Meenakshi Temple's at Madurai; Rama (16th-17th centuries), and Kumbheshvara (17th century), a large Nayaka temple housing remarkable silver vahanas (vehicles for transporting deities at festivals). Every 12 years the Ganga is believed to flow into the Mahamakham Tank; pilgrims flock to bathe and the water level rises, either with Ganga water or the extra bodies. (The next time it is due is in 1992.) About 20km south-west of here along the north bank of the Cauvery river, lies Tillaisthanum's Chola temple; while right here, just over the Arasalar river to Darasuram, Airavateshvara Temple (12th- century) is a very fine late Chola royal foundation of Rajaraja II. Finally, on the road to Thanjavur, 40km away,

Pullamangi's temple is temple addict and temple historian Christopher Tadgell's 'most wonderful, one of my favourites'.

THANJAVUR (TANJORE)

50km from Tiruchchirappalli; 158km from Madurai. Those arriving here will already have gathered Chola power and patronage was considerable; those arriving with no Chola experience soon will. For to understand the importance of Thanjavur, it is important, first, to understand the importance of the *Cholas*. If Dravidian arts and culture developed under the Pallavas, they flourished and crystallised under the Cholas. The historian, Romesh Thapar, considers 'the standards established during this period were regarded as classical and came to dominate the pattern of living in the south, and to influence and modify at certain levels the patterns existing elsewhere in the peninsula'. The huge temples in the Chola capital, Thanjavur, and its surrounding cities, can be seen from miles around and were the social, cultural and economic focus of Chola life.

The Cholas were mere chieftains in Tamil Nadu from the 1st to 8th centuries. Then one leader conquered Thanjavur, declared it a state and quickly claimed descent from the sun. Real expansion and consolidation of power came under Rajaraja I (985-1014) and his son Rajendra (1012-44) - they ruled jointly for two years. Campaigns from Kerala to Sri Lanka and from the Maldives up through Orissa to the Ganga brought most of the Indian peninsula south of Bombay and Puri under Chola control along with parts of Sri Lanka, Malaysia and Sumatra. Strong and lucrative trading links were established with South-east Asia, China, Persia and Arabia. Then, in the 12th century, the Deccan empires, especially the Hoysalas, expanded from the North, while in the South the Pandyas of Madurai saw their chance and took it, becoming the dominant power in Tamil Nadu.

The Chola kings ran lavish royal households and were great art patrons. They encouraged the god-king cult through image-worship of past rulers and by building temples as monuments to dead kings and symbols of royal grandeur, emphasised when the raja-guru (king's priest) became the king's confidant and adviser for things both temporal and spiritual. Officials, chosen for their caste (the Cholas became very caste-conscious), birth, connections and qualifications, oversaw an administration that was divided into village units, each with a committee for everything from taxes to gardens and, of course, the valuable tanks.

In this way, central government kept in close contact with the farmers, whose efficiency brought in two or three crops of paddy a year, the biggest export earner. And there were plenty of other trading goods, including textiles, spices, drugs, jewels, ivory, horn, ebony, sandalwood, perfumes and camphor. The major imports were the fabulous and expensive Arab horses which the Indians never learnt how to breed. Trade was controlled by merchants and guilds who, naturally, became rich enough to buy whole villages and donate them to a temple. Likewise, the villagers were encouraged to gain spiritual and social respect by giving most of their earnings to the temple - to a lesser degree, still true today.

Indeed, the temple was the centre of all. The main building was paid for by the king or a rich merchant, keeping to the same basic form as the Pallava temples at Kanchipuram (see above), although the gopura (gate-houses) gradually became as big as the vimana (tower over the shrine). This employed hundreds of local artisans, often for several years. And when built, it was the locals who maintained the temple, went to school in it (where their formal education was in Sanskrit) and were on the committees and assemblies held in it.

They even gave their women to it. A daughter could be dedicated to the temple at birth or when very young, to become a *devadasi* (female slave of the gods), thus averting calamity for her family. Her life was devoted to giving herself in worship to the gods, for which some underwent the tough discipline of learning Bharata Natyam dance. However, the system was abused, the priests' carnal appetites satisfied and the devadasis often became little more than caged prostitutes. The devadasi cult continues today, often unhappily. In Belgaum, young children are annually 'married' to the god, while devadasis reaching puberty are whisked off to stock Bombay brothels. In an effort to counter this, the Karnataka government is currently offering Rs3,000 to any man who will marry, and thus save, a devadasi. Surprisingly, since the girls are considered impure, several marriages have been arranged, and reported with much fuss in the press.

Brihadeshwara Temple (c.1010) at Thanjavur, the principal Chola capital, was naturally the biggest and richest of them all - 'monumental in concept, design and execution . . . the greatest architectural achievement of the Chola era' (Davies). Built by Rajaraja I (985-1014) as a temple-fort and dedicated to Shiva, its moat is now used by the giggling and chatting women as they do their laundry. A huge Nandi bull guards the gopuram. The vimana is 64m high. All the richly detailed carving is of the highest quality; the podgy white faces of frescoes around the inner courtyard walls and ceilings are still fresh and there is a portrait of Rajaraja with his guru, Karur Thevar, a picture of a royal visit to Chidambaram, and Shiva riding a chariot drawn by Brahma. There is a small but informative Archaeological Museum off the inner courtyard. In its heyday, the temple's immense annual income included 500lb of gold, 250lb of precious stones and 600lb of silver, made up from donations, contributions and revenue from its hundreds of villages. The Seppunaikam Tank is beyond the temple.

About 1km away is the *palace* of the Nayakas of Madurai, built around 1550. There are beautiful halls and a garden courtyard, one section now housing perhaps India's finest collectin of Chola bronzes and statues. The Saraswati Mahal Library has a remarkable collection, tragically suffering from worms and rot. (Palace open Thurs.-Tues., 10am-5.30pm). The Protestant missionaries headed for this area of India first, and nearby is the missionary C. F. Schwartz's church (1777), a marble by the English sculptor, Flaxman, inside.

In Thanjavur *town*, it is worth seeking out one or two of the other 70 or so temples. Craftsmen can be seen working at stone-carving, wood-carving and in brass and bronze. Copper inlaid with brass and silver is the characteristic work of the city, as is the repoussé work (tapping a design in to the relief from behind). There are silk weavers, musical instrument makers (especially of veenas and mridangams) and a pretty bazaar. To buy crafts, the state emporium, Poompuhar, on Gandhi Road stocks new goods as well as attractive bits of last year's discarded carved wooden temple chariots. To stay overnight, go to the ITDC *Traveller's Lodge*, Vallam Road (tel: 365), with gardens and a restaurant open to non-residents (exceptionally slow service). Or stay at the TNTDC *Tourist Bungalow*, Gandhiji Road (tel: 601), which also has maps of the town.

If temple addiction has taken hold, as well as all those Chola temples on the Madras-Thanjavur route (see above), there are yet more at nearby *Thirukaniyur* (10km north) and *Thiruvaiyaru* (13km, music festival in January). Each is a pleasant rural trip.

TIRUCHCHIRAPPALLI (TRICHINOPOLY)
53km from Thanjavur; 130km from Madurai; 310km from Madras; and is serviced by an airport. This tongue-twister means City of the Three-headed Demon, more commonly known by its British nickname, Trichy. The former, much fought over, citadel switched around between the Pallavas, Cholas and Pandyas. Right in the centre, visible for miles around, is the *Rock Fort Temple* (7th century, comparable to Mahaballipuram), reached by climbing up a tunnel of 437 steps to the top where there is the reward of a splendid view, especially down to the Ranganatha (or Raghunathanswami) Temple and, to the right of it, the smaller Sri Jambukeswar Temple on Srirangam island in the Cauvery river – the real reasons for coming here.

Ranganatha Temple (13th-17th centuries), dedicated to Vishnu, is vast, one of the biggest in India. It is also one of the most complete. Built over a number of centuries, its 250 hectares spread over an island in the Cauvery River, whose irrigating waters are so essential to the paddy crop and are held as sacred as the Ganga's in the north. The Cholas may have founded it; but the Pandyas, Hoysalas, Vijayanagars and Nayakas expanded it, and visitors usually see the work continuing today. Its seven concentric walls and 21 gopura contain colourful bazaars in the first layer and Brahmins' houses in the second.

The temple proper is at the centre. There are painted ceilings and remarkable carving, much of it newly painted. Two unpainted parts are especially beautiful. One is the small 10th century section on the left after passing through the last but one gopuram, with sublimely delicate female figures (a shy maiden awaiting her lover, another putting on jewellery, another standing with a parrot at her feet). The other is across the main courtyard to the right, where the sensational row of pillars on the Narayana Temple are carved into men on rearing horses spearing tigers, each pillar a monolith (probably 15th century). The 10-day Vaikunta-Ekadasi temple festival, beginning December 24, is worth attending. The central temple opens 6.15am-1pm; 3.15-8.45pm.

The smaller *Sri Jambukeswar Temple* (dedicated to Shiva – south Indian temples often come in pairs, dedicated to Vishnu and Shiva) has a mere four enclosing walls and seven gopura, which have nice carvings and painted ceilings, open 6am-1pm; 4-9.30pm.

Apart from temples, the various Christian churches include St John's (19th century) where the great Indophile Bishop Heber was buried after he died drowning in a bath in 1826. To stay overnight in Trichy, try the *Sangam Hotel*, Collector's Office Road (tel: 25202), recently refurbished. The Tourist Office is in TNTDC Tourist Bungalow (open 8.30- 10am; 5-8.30pm).

Two short rural trips out of town from Trichy lead through paddy fields and villages to north and south. Northwards, find a (relatively) small Chola temple (10th century) at *Srinivasanallur* and some vigorous, bold Pandyan sculptures in the caves (8th century) at *Namakkal*. Southwards, find *Pudukatai*, capital of Pudukatai state whose rajas benefitted from British friendship and security and left a pleasant, well-built city with a good collection of paintings in the museum. On the way back, there are *Sittannavasal*'s cave temple (8th century) and *Kodumbalur*'s temple (9th century) built by Chola feudatories. On neither trip will a European face be seen.

MADURAI

130km from Tiruchchirappalli; 158km from
Thanjavur; 307km from Trivandrum; 440km
from Madras. It is also serviced by an airport
and good trains. Madurai is a temple town
throbbing with life and teeming with pilgrims
and industries to serve them, just like all the
temples used to be. This is the one place in the
South where a temple continues to live at almost
the scale of action for which it was designed.
And it has done so for hundreds of years,
attracting pilgrims the year round but particularly during its two big festivals, celebrating the
birthday of king Tirumala Nayak and the marriage of Meenakshi to Shiva (see Festivals,
above).

The *Meenakshi Sundareshvara Temple* (17th
century) constitutes most of the city. At its heart
stand the two temples of Shiva (as Sundareshvara) and Devi (as Meenakshi). Surrounding
them, the bazaars sell everything from temple
offerings, spices and garlands of jasmine to bangles, strip-cartoon comics recounting the gods'
escapades and plastic green frogs that hop. It
has granaries, kitchens, store rooms and so on.
Every facet of Hindu ritual is practised. The
faithful cleanse themselves in its tanks, sit chatting, loll about, pray, meditate, perform puja,
visit the museum or climb to the top of a gopuram, where there is a superb view. Here, the
gopura (gateways) are tallest of all, dwarfing the
vimana (central shrine).

From dawn until late at night, its avenues of
carved deities, courtyards and temples are
seething with trumpeting musicians and drummers. Processions escort a deity on the move
(Meenakshi has plenty of companions living in
the temple), the temple elephant takes a stroll,
there are meetings, gossips, reading and the
odd snoozing body. The wealthy give substantial donations into a large safe beside the holy of
holies, and are rewarded with a sliding scale of
processions – the highest buys a golden chariot
procession which keeps the donor well in with
the deities and impresses the neighbours.

If this is your first Tamil Nadu temple, a good
dose of temple life can be found here, both by
day and evening. None other is as colourful as
this. If you have toured down from Madras,
stopping to see the Pallava and Chola temples,
this is what they were all about.

The Pandyas ruled from Madurai, with temporary Chola intervention, until the 13th
century. Muslim raids devastated all their buildings, then the Vijayanagars added Madurai to
their vast empire, with the Nayakas as vassals.
Having won independence, the Nayakas ruled
from 1559 to 1781, when the British arrived.
Although Meenakshi temple had been established for centuries, and was the centre of
Sangam (ancient conferences to promote Tamil

literature), the bulk of the buildings now standing were erected under the most powerful
Nayaka ruler, Tirumalai Nayak (1623-55).

Meenakshi, daughter of a Pandyan ruler, was
born with three breasts, one of which was to disappear when she met her Romeo, neatly fulfilled when she saw Shiva on Mount Kailas.
They met back in Madurai eight days later to
marry, Shiva doing so in the form of Sundareshvara. The temple has nine gopura with writhing
figures, and two slender, gold vimanas. Beside
the tank, just in front of a mural of Meenakshi
and Shiva's wedding, there are two monolith
sculptures, supposedly of the 12th century king
who began the temple and his Chief Minister.

The best way to see the temple is simply to
wander around. Good music is played most
nights, 6-7.30pm and 9-10pm. The south-facing
gopuram can be climbed. The whole inner temple opens 5am-12.30pm; 4-10pm. Photography
is only permitted 12.30-4pm but there are excellent large black and white photographs sold
at low prices in the bazaar and hotel.

THE HARD FACTS Two or three nights can
easily be spent at the very pleasant *Pandyan
Hotel,* Race Course Road (tel: 42470; telex: 445-
214), 57 rooms, all mod. cons, slightly in need of
some maintenance but has charming staff and a
good restaurant (especially for South Indian
food) much patronised by locals, and well nurtured garden; or the *ITDC Madurai Ashok,*
Alagarkoil Road (tel: 42531; telex 445-297), 43
rooms, all mod. cons. Neither has a pool. There
is a good Tourist Office at 180 West Veli Street
(tel: 22957).

OUT AND ABOUT Apart from the temple,
there are a few other places to see. Tirumalai
Nayaka Palace (1636), restored by Lord Napier,
is now partly a mediocre museum, with dance-
drama and concerts performed in the courtyard
(daily, 8am-5pm). Mariamman Teppakkulam
Tank (1646) has a central island for cool royal
picnics. This tank is where the great Teepam
(Float) festival is held. There is another Gandhi
Museum here, this one well laid out and housing, along with much else, the khadi dhoti the
Mahatma was assassinated in and his glasses
(open Thurs.-Tues. 10am-5.30pm). And there
are, of course, more temples scattered around
as well as dyeing, cotton lunghi weaving and
silk weaving down almost every alley.

About 10km out of town, the *Tiruparankum-
dram rock-cut temple* is very lively, although
much smaller than Meenakshi Temple. There is
a facade of huge blue and yellow dragons. Inside, there is a maze of dark rooms filled with
multi-limbed sculptures, red neon lights marking up which god is which in long strips of
Tamil, flickering oil lamps, a bazaar, the temple

elephant wandering about and people worshipping, jostling, gossiping and lounging around.

SHOPPING In the shops and bazaars of the temple there is fun, out-size costume jewellery – mostly of little value. In the emporia and neighbouring shops there are good fabrics, brass trays and figures, wood-carving, stone-carving and the brightly coloured, appliqué cotton lanterns that are used to decorate temple chariots.

RAMASWARAM

160km from Madurai. A trip for temple-addicts. Known as the Varanasi of the South but it lacks its magic and its light. The *Ramanathaswamy Temple* is huge and impressive, with seemingly endless carved corridors. But it is easiest to see en route to Sri Lanka – and even then, this is the nastiest way of getting there. As one hardened, round-the-world traveller said: 'Ramaswaram is one of the few real pits. And never take the ferry to Sri Lanka unless you are keen on character building.'

KODAIKANAL

120km from Madurai; 150km from Thekkady Wildlife Sanctuary; 210km from Cochin; 150km from Coimbatore. Apart from Thekkady Wildlife Sanctuary, this is the nearest place to get cool from Tamil Nadu or Kerala. It is a charming, peaceful backwater hill station reached from Tamil Nadu by the beautiful drive across the plains and up into the woods and waterfalls of the Palani range which branch off northeast from the Cardamom Hills. From Cochin, a perhaps even more spectacular route leads up via *Munnar* and Udumalpet, through Periyar Wildlife Sanctuary (see below). Munnar is set in a glorious valley of tea gardens, with overnight accommodation at the *High Range Club* (write to the Secretary in advance) or the *Residency Hotel*.

Unlike Ooty, Kodaikanal – or Kodai, as it is fondly called – is mercifully forgotten by most Indians, tourists, seekers of Raj nostalgia and modern industry. It has a slightly warmer climate too, free from cold spells.

The town clusters around the lake where gingerbread Raj houses nestle in well-tended gardens along the shore. There are boats to row and horses for appetising rides before a hearty breakfast. There are good rambles on the surrounding hills. The orchid museum run by the Jesuits at the Sacred Heart College may have reopened; the general museum should be open; both merit a detour. Stay at the old *Carlton Hotel*, Lake Road (tel: 252), 93 rooms, modest, period hotel with character, extensively but nicely modernised, overlooking lake; essential to book during India's holiday periods, especially Christmas; much-praised breakfasts.

Wildlife sanctuaries

The South is stocked with good National Parks, mostly concentrated in Tamil Nadu and near its borders. They are substantially easier to get to than many parks elsewhere. The distances are often short, the roads are good and the scenery en route is stunning, especially up to Thekkady from Kottayam or Madurai. Many sanctuaries lie conveniently between two interesting places and easily fit into an itinerary. And the Madras Snake Park, the Crocodile Farm and Vedanthangal Water Bird Sanctuary are right on the doorstep for visitors to Madras and the beaches south of it. To stay in these parks, be sure to book accommodation and jeeps in advance.

Bandipur, Mudumalai and Nagarhole interlink. Mudumalai lacks the range of Nagarhole, while Bandipur's new jungle huts are good but lack the Kabini setting at Nagarhole.

BANDIPUR, KARNATAKA

October-June and September-October best, although good all the year round. It lies on the Mysore-Ooty road. Fly to Bangalore, then by road 219km; train or Vayudoot plane to Mysore, then by road 80km; from Ooty 80km by road. It is all right to stay in any of the *Forest Lodges* or *Guest Houses*, the *Wooden Cottages* (3, each sleeps 12) or *Swiss Cottage Tents* (4, each sleeps two); or *Venuvihar Lodge* right up in the Gopalaswamy Hills, 20km from Bandipur (visitors carry their own provisions, book through Park Director). Book other rooms and in-park transport (essential) from the Divisional Forest Officer, Mysore or Field Director, Project Tiger, Government House Complex, Mysore (tel: 20901). Explore on the good network of roads by elephant, or observe from machans (tree-platforms) at water-holes.

There are 400 sqkm of mixed deciduous forest, the original sanctuary of the larger Venugopal National Park. Currently being expanded under Project Tiger, it is lush, well-stocked and was the first South Indian park to be included in Project Tiger. It adjoins Mudumalai sanctuary (across the River Moyar) and Wynad sanctuaries. Game moves freely between them. It is possible to see gaur (Indian bison), chital (they come near the Lodges at night), tiger, leopard, sambhar and herds of the famous Karnataka elephant (the best for war) at water pools. There is good bird life, too.

MUDUMALAI, TAMIL NADU

December-June. On the Mysore-Ooty road. Arrive as for Bandipur (see above). The distances by road are 97km from Mysore, 64km from Ooty. There is lots of accommodation, including *Mountainia Rest House* at Masinagudi Village (a collection of cottages, the deluxe ones are best, with good food plus bar) and *Sylvan Lodge* at Theppakadu Village (4 suites, good food). You can book a room and in-park transport through the District Forest Officer, Ooty; Safari Travels, Ooty; or State Wildlife Officer, Forest Department Block III, Administrative Buildings, 81 Mount Road, Madras. One nice place to stay is *Bamboo Banks*, with charming and informed Parsee owners (book through Mysore or Ooty touristoffice). Another is *Jungle Hut*, Bukkapuram, Masinagudi, Nilgiris, an 18-acre 'nature haven' just outside the park, run by Joe and Hermie Mathias (book with prepayment, current tariff Rs250 per room per day). Explore remoter areas by jeep and thick jungle by elephant.

400 sqkm of thick, mixed deciduous hill forest in the Nilgiris, adjoining Bandipur and Wynad sanctuaries. It is rich in wildlife near the villages but well worth exploring further afield. It is possible to spot leopard, giant squirrel, tiger, elephant, gaur (especially around Theppakkadu's teak forest), sambhar, chital, mouse-deer, boar and two types of monkey, the bonnet and common langur. Spring and summer are good times for visibility, with blossoming and fruiting trees and rich bird life (Great Black woodpeckers, barbets, Malabar Grey hornbill, etc.). Autumn is good for lush, tall grass, herds of gaur and elephant and exceptionally large herds of mature, antlered chital (spotted deer) around the Masinagudi-Moyar area. The park also contains an Elephant Camp where the huge beasts are trained to help with logging, acting as mobile cranes to lift huge sandal tree trunks on to lorries.

NAGARHOLE, KARNATAKA

October-May; cover too thick to see game immediately post-monsoon. Travel as for Bandipur, then 224km by road from Bangalore, 94km south-west of Mysore. Stay at the state-run beautiful new river-side *Kabini River Lodge* just outside the park, incorporating the restored Maharaja of Mysore's Hunting Lodge and Viceroy's Bungalow. 36 beds, bar and good food (open mid-September to mid-June). Book through Jungle Lodges and Resorts, see p. 227; and book early with a deposit to confirm. If no room, there are various state-run jungle lodges and cottages. Explore by jeep (booking it on arrival, since the closed bus is no good), coracle (buffalo-hide boats) and observe from machans.

284 sqkm of tropical deciduous trees, swamps and streams, densely inhabited by elephant (see them early morning and evening), tiger, leopard (this is the most likely place in India to spot one), gaur (Indian bison), several species of deer, crocodile, water fowl and rich bird life. Some fishing, especially for mahseer, a powerful fighting fish of the carp family, growing up to 150lb in weight. Some of the biggest are found in the Cauvery River, best January-March. The government Elephant Camp for training elephants can be visited.

Currently the best park in India for visitors (soon to receive competition from Corbett park), run by Anglo-Indian John Wakefield. Rave reports include 'the highlight of our trip, wonderfully knowledgeable naturalists, we saw so much from the coracles and then more than 60 varieties of bird on the walks'; 'superbly run, with a clear routine'; 'ideal even for people with no animal knowledge'; 'paddling about the lake in a coracle at dawn, watching the elephants, was like being in an evolutionary time-warp'; 'barbecues down by the lake magical'.

RANGANATHITTU WATER-BIRD SANCTUARY, KARNATAKA

June-September. As for Bandipur, then 133km by road from Bangalore, 20km north-east of Mysore, 2km from Srirangapatnam. No accommodation. A beautiful island in the Cauvery River, rich in bird life, includes a mixed heronry, red wattled lapwing, white ibis, spoonbill, open bill stork, egret, darter, cormorant and river tern. Boats for hire. Observation point.

PERIYAR, THEKKADY, KERALA

December-May. Fly to Cochin, then by road 208km; fly to Madurai, then by road 160km; 119km by road from Kottayam, 258km from Trivandrum. It is best at dawn and dusk, when there are wonderful night noises. So, it is worth spending a night or so here, rather than going for the day. Stay at the smartish and newish *Aranya Nivas Hotel* (tel: 23), overlooking the lake. It is comfortable, with mod. cons but bad food. It is also well placed for forest walks. However, there are two much nicer alternatives, with character. The first is *Hotel Lake Palace* (tel: 24), an old bungalow on an island, with pretty garden. Of the six rooms, nos 44 and 66 best for views. This is a good place for viewing game. Stipulate Indian cooking when booking to avoid dreary Raj food. The second is the charming, three-roomed *Government Rest House* in the forest. Book direct; information from the Wildlife Preservation Officer, Thekkady. Explore forest on foot, lake by boat and observe from machans.

Over 700 sqkm of hilltop sholas surrounding a vast artificial lake built by the British in 1895 for irrigation (old tree trunks stand sentry in the lake), up in the Cardamom Hills near the border of Tamil Nadu and Kerala. It is one of the largest sanctuaries in India, was established in 1934, is part of Project Tiger and is the best place to watch wild elephant. It is best to take the 7am boat up the lake between hills with the shapes and colours of the Scottish Highlands. Mist rises from the water, game stirs and elephants come to drink – they even swim in the lake sometimes. And there is gaur, boar, dhole (wild dogs), otters and freshwater tortoise. Bird life is rich: herons, kingfishers, egrets on the water; hornbills and fishowls in the dense forests of spices, blossoming trees and creepers. When it is hot, the tiger and gaur come down to the water.

Two new sanctuaries in the Cardamom Hills are the *Mundanthurai Tiger Sanctuary*, to the south of Periyar, and the *Anamalai Tiger Sanctuary*, north of it. Both are for the keen wildlife spotter, rich in animals but as yet not very organised for tourists, even by the standards of Indian wildlife sanctuaries. Further information from Tamil Nadu or Government of India Tourist Offices.

VEDANTHANGAL WATER BIRD SANCTUARY, TAMIL NADU
October-March but busiest December-January. By road, 80km south of Madras. It is nicest to stay at a seaside hotel nearby (see Sun chapter). Further information from Chief Conservator of Forests, Madras. This is a major breeding sanctuary for migrating birds and the South's equivalent to Bharatpur outside Agra (see p. 79). The best times of day are early morning, as the birds wake, and 3-6pm, when they return. Flocks can be of several thousand, including several varieties of heron, egret, stork, pelican and ibis.

POINT CALIMERE, TAMIL NADU
November-January. By road, 150km from Thanjavur to the north coast point of Palk Strait Accommodation is available at the very basic *Forest Rest House*, or in Thanjavur, which is preferable. Further information from the Chief Conservator of Forests, Madras. Although there are black buck and wild pig to see, this is really a place for ornithologists. The tidal mud flats attract thick flocks of migratory water fowl to swell the rich local water fowl population. First come teals, sandpipers, shanks, herons and thousand upon thousand of flamingoes which rise up in pink clouds. Then, in spring, see mynas and barbets, etc.

CROCODILE BANK, TAMIL NADU
Season all the year round. Between Covelong and Mahabalipuram, 42km south of Madras by road. No accommodation. Open daily, 8am-6pm.
This is a farm for breeding crocodiles which are endangered as a result of hunters. It is highly successful and is now helping to repopulate Indian wildlife sanctuaries. In a somewhat sinister way, it is a fascinating place to visit. Guides show visitors eggs, newly hatched babies and fully grown crocodiles. The different types live in seemingly overcrowded groups in disarmingly low-walled pits and the guides take delight in demonstrating feeding time to visitors, teasing enormous beasts with a dangling dead rat before hurling it among them to be fought over.

For **Madras Snake Park**, Tamil Nadu, see Madras, above.

Find out more

Lutyens, M.: *Krishnamurti: the Years of Awakening*, London, 1975
Meister, W., (ed.): *Encyclopedia of Indian Temple Architecture, South Indian Lower Dravidesa*, vols I & II, Delhi, 1983
Menon, A. S.: *Cultural Heritage of Kerala, An Introduction*, Cochin, 1978
Merklinger, E. S.: *Indian Islamic Architecture, The Deccan 1347-1686*, UK, 1981
Murphy, Dervla: *On a Shoe-string to Coorg: An Experience of South India*, London, 1976
Muthiah, S.: *Madras The Gracious City*, Madras, 1990; his other books on Madras include *Tales of Old and New Madras*, Madras, 1989
Narayan, R. K.: *Swami and Friends*, 1935, the first of many delightful novels set in fictional Malgudi, inspired by Mysore, many available in Penguin paperbacks
Panter-Downes, M.: *Ooty Preserved*, London, 1967
Ramaswami, N. S.: *Mamallapuram, An Anotated Bibliography*, Madras, 1980 (quotes the relevant passages from all books on the subject)
Sarabhai, M.: *The Sacred Dance of India*, Bombay, 1979
Sarkar, H.: *Monuments of Kerala*, Delhi, 1978
Sewell, R.: *A Forgotten Empire*, Delhi, 1982
Sloss, R.: *Lives in the Shadow with J Krishnamurti*, London, 1991
Strong, S.: *Bidri Ware, Inlaid Metalwork from India*, London, 1985
Wiles, J.: *Delhi Is Far Away, a Journey Through India*, London, 1974
Woodcock, G.: *Kerala: Portrait of the Malabar Coast*, London, 1967
Yazdani, G.: *Bidar: Its History and Monuments*, Oxford, 1947
Zebrowski, M.: *Deccani Painting*, London, 1983
Zebrowski, M.: 'Bidri: metalware from the Islamic courts of India', *Art East*, 1982, no. 1

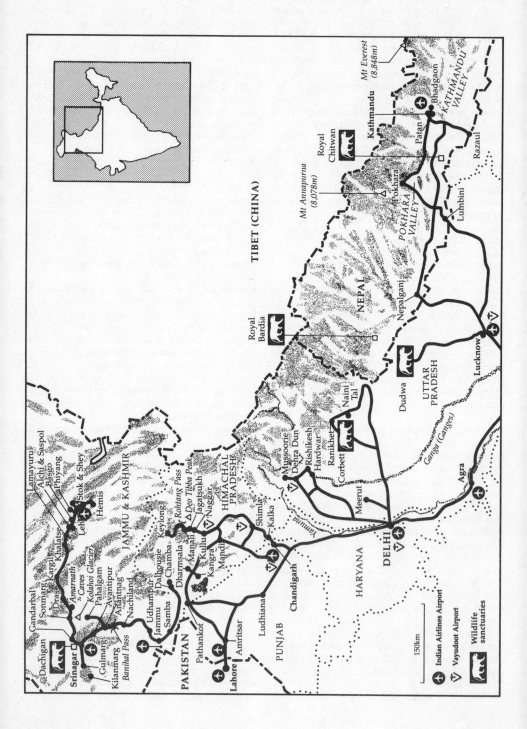

Mt Everest
(8,848m)

Bhadgaon

Kathmandu

KATHMANDU
VALLEY

Patan

Royal
Chitwan

Lumbini

Razaul

Mt Annapurna
(8,078m)

Pokhara

POKHARA
VALLEY

TIBET (CHINA)

NEPAL

Nepalganj

Royal
Bardia

Lucknow

Naini
Tal

Dudwa

UTTAR
PRADESH

Ganga (Ganges)

Mussoorie
Dehra Dun
Rishikesh
Hardwar
Ranikhet
Corbett

Agra

Meerut

Lamayuru
Alchi & Saspol
Basgo
Phiyang

Stok & Shey

Hemis

Leh

Khalatse
Kargil
Dras

Gandarbal
Sonmarg
Amarnath
Caves
Kolahoi Glacier
Pahalgam
Avantipur
Achabal
Nachiland

JAMMU & KASHMIR

Rohtang Pass
Deo Tibba Peak
Jagatsukh
Naggar

Keylong

HIMACHAL
PRADESH

Manali
Kullu
Kangra
Mandi

Shimla
Kalka

Yamuna

DELHI

HARYANA

Chambal

Dalhousie
Dharmsala

Udhampur
Jammu
Samba

Chandigarh

Ludhiana

PUNJAB

Amritsar

PAKISTAN

Lahore

Pathankot

Dachigan
Srinagar
Gulmarg
Kilanmarg
Banihal Pass

Gandarbal

Udhampur

150km

✈ Indian Airlines Airport

⟱ Vayudoot Airport

🐾 Wildlife
sanctuaries

The hills and Nepal:
Playtime paradise

Apart from playing at politics, Delhi is not hot on recreation. But the Himalayas, a plane-hop away, are one big, beautiful amusement park with an abundant choice of games between the green Shimla slopes and the snowy Nepal peaks. Despite current political unrest, most of the region is as fashionable for Indians now as it was for the British when in 1832 the Governor-General, Lord William Bentinck, initiated the British habit of abandoning Calcutta's cloying summers for Simla, as present-day Shimla was known.

From 1865 until Independence the Viceroy and his entire government decamped there from Calcutta, and later Delhi, in trainloads of trunks, papers and officials. They went all the way up in March to govern most of the sub-continent from a castle, a country mansion, mock-Tudor houses and red-roofed chalets amid the serious business of gardening, racing, polo, cricket and amateur theatricals at The Gaiety. It was an astounding act of self-confidence. Baden Powell, Kitchener and Kipling played there. Lord Lytton, while Viceroy, directed his own play in 1876. In October, they came all the way down again.

When Lutyens saw it in 1912 he wrote: 'It is inconceivable, and consequently very British! – to have a capital as Simla is entirely of tin roofs . . . if one was told the monkeys had built it all one could only say "what clever monkeys – they must be shot in case they do it again".' Today, Shimla is a rather run-down but evocative Raj time-warp amusement arcade, where ex-colonials join the smartest Indians in roast chicken and rice pudding. For more on similar lines but with varying degrees of beauty and spruceness, the cluster of hill stations north-east of Delhi, in Uttar Pradesh, contain gems such as Naini Tal and such disappointments as Mussorie.

North of Shimla is quite different. Here, still in Himachal Pradesh state, lie the perhaps more enticing, perhaps more beautiful and certainly more Indian and more flower-strewn valleys of Kullu and Kangra. Glorious walks and gentle treks pass through the prosperous villages with their well-built, traditional wood and stone houses of which Kipling would surely have approved. The wood is often the local favourite, deodar, or cedar, whose chopping down is now carefully monitored by conservationists. Between the villages, where there seem to be con-

stant festivals and celebrations, the open hills are well-cultivated with rice and lucrative fruit orchards, the woods are mature and handsome, and the springtime flowers are of astounding variety. There is nothing run-down here; the valleys seem to have achieved that rare balance of dynamic prosperity and conserved beauty.

Christina Noble, who lived in and around Manali at the head of the Kullu Valley for 19 years, pondered on current changes: 'Apple trees are being planted in the ropa (rice terraces) – easy money and less work to cultivate than rice . . . Manali is a boom town, changed almost unrecognisably from the messy single street it was when I arrived.' Her friends' lives have changed, too. 'Varma sells ice cream, Fanta and Thums Up from a fridge, and so many newspapers and even books that he doesn't need to bother with tea and puris any more.' But, immediately outside the town, the landscape is a ravishing as ever. 'Duff Dunbar itself is hidden by the lie of the land but I can see up to Lumba-dukh, to the alps below the Kali Hind Pass, and away up Solang valley.'

Further north still, out of Himachal Pradesh and into the state of Jammu and Kashmir, the joys of the legendary Kashmir Valley were discovered by the Mughals. Akbar, the romantic couple Jahangir and his Nur Jahan, and Shah Jahan were all crazy about it, cooing 'happy valley', 'paradise on earth', 'only Kashmir'. Nehru, himself a Kashmiri, wrote in 1940: 'Sometimes the sheer loveliness of it all was overpowering. How can they who have fallen under its spell release themselves from its enchantment?' (Huxley was less keen in *Jesting Pilates*, accusing the Kashmiris of having a 'genius for filthiness'.) Until the recent unrest, Srinagar was still sublimely romantic, perfect for wandering the gardens and drifting about aimlessly in a shikara on the lakes, a justifiably favourite honeymoon paradise for newly-weds worldwide. Now, officials will probably suggest visitors find other cool spots – one report reckoned there had been 19 tourists to Srinagar in 1990. However, by-passing Srinagar, the more rugged, mountainous landscape further east is well worth the effort to get there, for it forms the dramatic backdrop to the incredible monasteries of Leh.

There is more than just walking to do in the hills. The world's highest and extremely pretty golf course is at Gulmarg. There is winter snow-skiing, trekking on stocky ponies, fishing at

Pahalgam and luxurious camping beneath the cliffs of the Leh monasteries. And, for the really keen, there is big-time trekking and mountain climbing in the Nepal and Pakistan mountains. Nepal also has river-rafting, game-spotting from elephants and, the ultimate joy ride, a dawn flight over Mount Everest – the easy way to see the roof of the world that Sir Edmund Hillary and 111 others have seen the hard way (including 5 women – Miss Pal was the first Indian woman to reach the top, in May 1984). Pakistan has luscious valleys to rival India's, and the man-made feat of the Karakoram Highway slicing through the mountains to Gilgit and into China (see p. 97).

Everywhere, the air is fresh and exhilarating, the views arrestingly lovely. Roman Polanski goes there 'to get as far away as possible . . . ever higher through glorious rhododendron forests, heading for the snow line . . . the extraordinary Himalayan panorama, with its plunging valleys and soaring mountain ranges . . . I'd seldom felt happier.' John Cleese and his pals went there and found a serenity unavailable at home. And in this peaceful beauty live the hill peoples with their own distinctive customs, crafts, architecture and festival and fairs full of folk dancing and music.

So, if the heat of the Indian plains becomes unbearable, head north.

THE HARD FACTS
Note: with the current unrest in Jammu and Kashmir state, it is wise to follow the travelling advice of your local mission, checking again immediately prior to departure. In the hopes that conditions improve, there is some information below.

WHEN TO GO Each area has an optimum season (see below). While the rest of India puts up umbrellas against the June-September monsoon, Kashmir is fresh and sunny. In HP (Himachal Pradesh), weather is very localised. There will be fine views in one area and downpours and mist in another. For flowers, head for the foothills in March-April, higher up in June-July. Lotus blossoms cover the Srinagar lakes in August. Autumn colours in Kullu are blinding. Nepal is in blossom April-June, but February and October have the best weather. So check carefully, according to your taste. It is also worth coinciding with the better festivals and fairs, such as those at Leh, Kullu, Rampur, Mandi, Chamba and Renuka.

GETTING THERE: GETTING AWAY In most cases it is best to fly up to an area, often with stunning views from the plane (see Getting there section of Delhi chapter), although there are some collectors' train journeys. The drive up from Delhi is not especially pretty. Once there, you can use one place as a base for sport, relaxation and the occasional foray. Alternatively, you can walk/trek/drive for a few days, flying out from another airport. There are some exceptionally splendid drives, such as from Jammu to Srinagar, and memorable flights, such as from Srinagar up to Leh. See sections below for more.

WHERE TO STAY While a few hotels offer European facilities, the luxury tends to lie in character and in charming, caring, old-fashioned service that is sadly disappearing from Delhi hotels. A whole family attends to 2 guests on a houseboat. Fishermen have the flies put on their hooks. Trekkers may have a staff ratio of 10 to 1, with people to carry belongings, pitch the tent, cook full meals and tend to every need.

Remember the altitude when packing: summer evenings get distinctly chilly and winter brings snow. On the whole, the food is not exciting and the Raj nursery influence persists to make it difficult even to sample local food, especially in Kashmir. Nor does the night life thrive, apart from local folk dancing.

WALKING AND TREKKING Little exercise preparation is needed for those keeping below 11,000 feet. Those going above may need more. Trekking varies from a gentle amble to serious climbing. It is essential to check exactly what is involved. One London City businessman's view is that: 'Days spent in the Kullu Valley are one of the most stunning things to do in India. Serious trekking is uncomfortable, unsexy, sordid and shakes some people rigid. The food is crummy. You don't change clothes for 10 days. But there's no other experience so glorious. Nothing in the Alps to match it.'

There is no age limit for trekkers, but they should be fit, do a bit of walking to get into shape and, if in any doubt, have a medical check-up. There will not be room service and baths but, as one trekker addict put it: 'There is an extraordinariness about being in such mountains that words cannot convey. I cannot go a year without this sort of experience.' Trekking can be quite challenging, but, with a good Sherpa, no trekker is ever pushed to do more than he feels able to.

Several tour operators produce excellent booklets on trekking, covering everything from what to pack, and how to pack it, to the daily trekking routine, how to take photographs and how to have a pee at 8,000 feet. Some brief their clients in London before going out to lead the walks and treks. (For suggested British tour operators, see p. 6). Always hire a guide, porters and ponies to carry supplies and tents. Walking may sound uninviting, but the scenery, views, flora and nurse-maid service repay the small effort. Remember to pack insect repellant, suntan lotion (thin air equals scorching sun), plenty of camera film and a good drinking water bottle – as Christina Noble says, 'it is difficult to get a half-decent one in India'.

If the trip is not already planned from home, the recommended Delhi travel agencies (see Delhi chapter) should give reliable advice, make up an itinerary exactly suited to your interests and sportiness and then book the lot for you.

SHIMLA (SIMLA), HIMACHAL PRADESH

The setting for Kipling's *Plain Tales from the Hills*. A thick Raj atmosphere somehow persists against the odds in this former summer capital of British India, now capital of Himachal Pradesh, jammed with too much with traffic, too many people, a good number of tourists and often not enough water. Personal views differ dramatically, from the 'so wonderfully evocative, pine-scented air' to the 'nothing to recommend itself'. It depends how desperate is the desire to seek out the past, and how efficient the visitor's goggles are at blocking out the present.

To inspire the imaginations of those seeking out Raj atmosphere, Lady Wilson, who annually moved up there with her husband from their preferred Calcutta, left some piercing observations in her diary of 1903-4, written on her first night for a fortnight without socialising. 'One lives so constantly in public in Simla, that the solitude of unknown crowds [in Calcutta] is a pleasant change. . . . I hear nothing but rickshaws whirling past, their bells tinkling and their runners shouting "take care", all of them . . . carrying overwrought humanity to their twenty-third or possibly fortieth consecutive "tamasha", a ball, a play, a concert, or more probably the inevitable "burra khana", with which my mind is obsessed.' She then muses on the special Simla 'burra khana', or dinner party. 'How often will the word "position" with a capital "P" be exchanged? We are all so anxious in Simla to be in the right position for our position, in the right place, and talking to the right person at the right time, as befits our position, whether our hearts are heavy or our pockets are light, that I sometimes think it would be a public benefit to burn its effigy.'

THE HARD FACTS Set at 2,213m in the Shivalik hills of pine forests, the best months are April-June when irises and lilies fill the meadows; monsoon comes in July; September-October are pleasant again before snow December-March. Get there by first taking the daily 6.15am flight to Chandigarh, arriving 7.25am. It is then 110km by bus. But much more fun is to take the Himalayan Queen on the narrow gauge railway built 1903-4, leaving Kalka (a 14km taxi drive away) at 8.20am, arriving Shimla 2.35pm.

This will not suit architecture buffs. Spacious *Chandigarh*, India's first planned city, was conceived by Le Corbusier and Maxwell Fry as the capital for the Punjab state (shared with Haryana) – with a thoroughly questionable influence on post-independence Indian architecture. It is now 30 years old, with mature trees and gardens. Chandigarh's other eccentric attraction, for which people fly in specially, is the stone and broken china sculpture garden. Outside the town, Mughal followers can find a small but charming terraced Mughal garden at *Pinjore*, beyond Kalka, nice for a picnic. For a good nose around, stay overnight at the *Hotel Chandigarh Mountview*, Sector-10 (tel: 21257; telex: 0395-337), modest but adequate, with a nice garden.

In Shimla, *Oberoi Clarkes*, The Mall (tel: 6091/5; telex: 206); turn-of-the-century, centrally sited, mock-Tudor building with stunning views acquired by Mohan Singh Oberoi in 1935. He arrived in Shimla in 1922 with 25 rupees and got a job as a front desk clerk in the Cecil Hotel. 12 years later he mortgaged his assets and his wife's jewellery to buy the nearby Clarkes. Four years later he bought the Oberoi Grand in Calcutta. By the mid-1950s he had 14 hotels, often formerly run by British or Swiss families who traditionally ran hotels. Clarkes has 35 rooms and all mod. cons. Good excursion advice, picnics, and meals served inside or in the garden. The other Oberoi hotel, *The Cecil*, reopens after refurbishment in 1991.

Two other charming hotels: *Chapslee* (tel: 3242); built in the 1830s next to Aukland House and known as Secretary's Lodge until it became the hill palace of the Maharajaa of Kapurthala; one of the oldest manor houses in Shimla with extensive grounds, good views and period furniture; 5 suites, so book. *Woodville* (tel: 2722); a 1930s mansion built as a summer palace for the Commander-in-Chief and use by several before the Maharaja of Jubbal bought it; now family-run with extensive grounds (croquet) and fine views, 10 rooms and a suite.

Helpful HP Tourist Office, The Mall (tel: 3311). They run pleasant tours into the surrounding hills. Good guide-book from Maria bookshop (which stocks old and new books and prints) on The Mall.

OUT AND ABOUT The Mall is the main street on the crescent-shaped ridge covered by the town. It is the hub of Shimla and nice to stroll along. You can pause for refreshment, and to watch the world go by, in one of the many cafés and restaurants. There are a number of Indian coffee houses, including Davies with its Raj club style.

Just near Clarkes Hotel, on the corner, is the site of Mr Isaacs' shop. Kipling based Lurgan Sahib, who trained Kim to spy, on Mr Isaacs. On and near The Mall there are stylish houses built by British sahibs and called 'Strawberry Hill' and 'The Grotto'. Kennedy Cottage there is the first British house in Shimla, built 1822. Then there are some grander British buildings: the Gothic Christ Church (1857), the Municipal Buildings combining Scottish baronial with Swiss chalet, the mock-Tudor public library next door, the Scottish baronial Viceregal palace and mock-Tudor Barnes Court.

The bazaar is as mixed as the architecture. There are local tribes, stocky hill people and tall Punjabis. Himachal State Museum has Pahari miniature paintings, an unusually good collection of Pahari sculpture and other treasures (open Tues.-Sun., 10am-5pm). For the best view of Shimla, go to the top of Jakko hill – beware of monkeys at Hanuman temple; for afternoon promenades, go along the Ridge. Buy Kullu shawls.

SPORTS Best to get out of town for golf (at Naldera), trout fishing (at Hatkoti), winter skiing (at Kufri, 16km), and summer walks and picnics in the unpolluted, still pine-scented surrounding hills. *Chail* has two recommendations: the world's highest cricket ground and a lovely bird sanctuary attracting many special hill birds and dubbed by some 'the best solution to being in Shimla'. To stay, the HPTDC have turned the Maharaja of Patiala's summer palace into the *Chail Palace Hotel*, with rooms in the main building and in various cottages.

OTHER BRITISH HILL STATIONS.

While Shimla, or Simla as it then was, was being established, the British built other hill stations with furious energy, spurred on by dreams of cool comfort and recuperation for the body, and tennis parties and herbaceous borders to remind them of Home. Between 1815 and 1947 they built more than 80. Shimla was the 'Queen of hill stations', where the government did its business for six months of the year, while Ooty in the south was more select and soon known as 'snooty Ooty'. Today, it is the smaller, backwater ones which retain the most atmosphere, that is, the local building styles adapted to create a pale imitation of Home are still suffused in holiday-making nostalgia, homesickness and a slight melancholia.

The hill stations served the main cities of the presidencies, into which Indian administration was divided. So most are in the north, serving Calcutta and later Delhi. Some of the others may be on your route. Bombay's nearby hills conceal Pune and the serene Mahabaleshwar and Matheran (see Bombay chapter), while between Bombay and Delhi lies Rajasthan's only hill of any size, Mount Abu (see Rajasthan chapter). Madras and Bombay share the Nilgiri Hills where busy Ooty is surrounded by quieter stations plus, further south, Kodaikanal (preferred by many) and the wildlife park of Periyar (see p. 252). Calcutta's nearest cool air is in fact not Shimla but Darjeeling or, for those with permits, the north-east frontier states, especially Shillong (see p. 191).

Here in the foothills of the Himalayas, several stations are worth visiting in addition to Shimla, often more for their breathtaking surrounding scenery – for which the spot was originally popular – than for their now somewhat shabby town centres. Here are two routes from Delhi into Uttar Pradesh state, and a little-visited extra north of the Kangra valley.

NORTH-EAST FROM DELHI TO MUSSOORIE, UP

Head straight for Mussoorie (269km), pausing in a valley of the Siwalik Hills to see Dehra Dun. Various British-founded institutions are here, most famously Doon School, India's answer to Eton, and less famously the headquarters of the Survey of India. The Forest Research Institute's Museum on Chakrata Road and its Botanical Gardens at Subhash Park on Rajpur Road are both worth visiting. Mussoorie is 34km beyond, a scenic, twisting road up to 2,002m. Set on a spur of the lower Himalayas, with old cottages nestling quietly in the greenery, the stunning views, dramatic gorges, flowers and good fishing remain unspoilt. Not so the town, of which Zoe Yalland, returning after many years, lamented: 'I loved it so much, and went back to find a cement resort, not even the red tin roofs'. To stay, avoid the Savoy and Roselynn in favour of one of the simpler surviving hotels; the church has had its windows smashed in, but do drop in to the Municipal Gardens before going off to explore the still sublime hills.

The return trip can detour to Rishikesh and Hardwar. A beautiful road leads to *Rishikesh* (76km), a Hindu meditation centre and springboard for Hindu pilgrimages to Bandrinath, then to the holy city of *Hardwar* (25km) where pilgrims bathe in this especially sacred spot of the Ganga almost comparable to Allahabad and Varanasi.

EAST FROM DELHI TO NAINI TAL, UP

The Delhi-Naini Tal drive is about 320km, so it is wise to take food and drink in case a good roadside café does not coincide with hunger pangs. If you go to Meerut, it is better to stay there overnight, rather than traipse back into Delhi or drive by night to Naini Tal.

Soon after leaving Delhi, colonial historians will want to detour to the prosperous town of

Meerut (72km), where the 1857 Rebellion broke out (known by the British as the Mutiny) (see p. 87).

The large cantonment has a grand, tree-lined avenue for its Mall, plus club, interesting cemetery and beautiful church; elsewhere, plenty of Muslim monuments include Nur Jahan's tomb for the fakir Shah Pir (1628). To stay, various modest hotels.

For a real collector's item, about 12km north-west of here is Sirdhana where the infamous but tiny Begum Sumroo is buried in the church near her palace; converted to Roman Catholicism after her husband's death, she ruled as a widow for 40 years, growing increasingly benign in old age.

Naini Tal benefits from being less fashionable than Mussoorie. With honesty it can still be described as picturesque, and devotees still compare it to England's Lake District. Founded in 1841 in the Kumaon Hills at a height of 1,934m, its buildings are dotted round a sacred lake where visitors now take boat rides lounging on a squashy sofa-seat and gazing at the surrounding hills, the nearest thing to currently out-of-bounds Kashmir. And the views from the hills are breath-taking: to China, Deopatha and Ayarpatha peaks. Don't miss the Gothic St John-in-the-Wilderness church (1846) or F. W. Stevens's Government House (1846). It is possible to imagine how devastating the 1880 landslide must have been to this little community, when the hotel, assembly rooms, library and more, plus 150 people, were buried beneath mud.

To stay, *Shervani Hilltop Inn*, Shervani Lodge, Mallital (tel: 2128) is just outside the town (complimentary transport to and from it), and has very cheap off-season rates (July-mid-September, November-April); *Grand Hotel*, The Mall (tel: 2406) is mid-town, period but not very grand. *Ranikhet* (74km) is worth an outing on a clear day purely for the spectacular view of the Himalayas including the twin peaks of Nada Devi about 100km away; and the trek from here to *Pindari Glacier* is equally memorable. *Corbett Wildlife Park* (see p. 99) is nearby.

DALHOUSIE, HIMACHAL PRADESH
Best to combine a visit here with Jammu or with the Kangra and Kullu valleys (see below). A very picturesque, narrow gauge railway chugs up from Jammu to Dalhousie, set at 2,035m on the summits of three Himalayan peaks near the Ravi river. Lord Napier selected the site in 1851, Captain Fagan plotted it out, and the Earl of Dalhousie (Governor-General 1848-56) gave his name to it. Its peak of popularity was during the 1920s and 30s, as a cheap backwater Shimla for those who could not afford the real thing. Its mock-Tudor, Surrey-style houses are still fur-

nished with commodes and dotted with beautiful fireplaces. *Aroma-n-Claire* (tel: 99) is one of many slightly run-down but charming Raj hotels. Beyond Dalhousie, through a beautiful mountain forest, the 56km-long road descends to *Chamba* (926m), a pretty hilltop town and a centre for the Gaddis, the local shepherds who spend winters in Kangra and migrate to higher summer pastures. Don't miss the very finely carved temples and three museums: Bhuri Singh Museum (local arts), the Temple of Deviri-Kothi (old Chamba school paintings) and the 18th century Rang Mahal Palace, where the Raja of Chamba's women lived until 1947 (large collection of good 19th century paintings). To stay, the *Old Residency* is a state guest house; or *Hotel Akhandchandi*, College Road (tel: 2371). From here, the 120km railway trip down to the thriving trading town of *Pathankot* is spectacular.

THE KULLU VALLEY, HIMACHAL PRADESH
Between 200 and 4,000m. Kullu town is at 1,200m. The narrow valley runs north from Mandi, past Kullu and Manali to the Rohtang Pass. The Beas River flows through this fertile, terraced valley, the most accessible one in the area. Excellent for long walks and treks in flower-covered valleys and up through pine and cedar forest. The agrarian peoples are hardworking, honest, deeply religious – there are about 6,000 temples – and love a party. This mixture results in a prosperous, still mainly agricultural land, particularly at the northern end where, thanks to the lucrative apple and tourist industries, the people are well-fed and clothed and their houses are well built and maintained.

THE HARD FACTS Go April-May for blossoming trees and flowers, September-October for dazzling autumn colours, local fruits (especially apples), clear air and light. There are dancing and fairs at any excuse. Every village has its own god who is taken to visit related gods, given a bath, even has a birthday – all with much merriment, dressing up, processions and plenty of the local chang (rice or barley-based liquor).

The whole of Mandi is decorated for *Shivarati* fair (February-March), when deities are brought on palanquins and chariots. There is folk dance, drama and music played on the hill instruments such as karnal, dhol, narsinghas and drum. But best of all is *Dussehra* in Kullu (September-October), 10 days of solid celebration beginning on Vijaya Dashmi, the day it ends in the rest of India. It commemorates not so much Rama's victory over Ravana as an idol of Ragunathji in Kullu, to which some 200 gods from the surrounding villages are brought to pay homage, followed by nightly folk dance competitions.

Flights go to nearby Bhuntar airport (weather

permitting). Otherwise, fly to Chandigarh (see Shimla, above), then 8 hours by road 270km to Kullu, 310km to Simla, or take the overnight bus from Delhi (6pm to 9am). Approaching from the north, the mountain railway built in 1928 from Pathankot to Jogindarnagar (about 40km from Kullu) is a train-buff's delight.

In Kullu, stay at *Kullu Valley Resort*, arranged in cottages, restaurant with superb views; the HPTDC's *Hotel Sarvari*, or the HPTDC's more expensive 6-roomed *Silver Moon*. In Manali, there are more than a hundred hotels to choose from in this booming tourist town. As Christina Noble is quick to qualify: 'Do not be appalled by this. Just use it as a base for a comfort hotel and for good shopping'. Comfortable hotels include *Negu's Mayflower*, family run, of the 'cream cara-mel and trout' variety, old with style, unosten-tatious; *John Banan*'s, the less well-run old favourite, again with style, and the *Honeymoon Inn*, cheaper and, despite its name, less romantic than the others. Both Kullu and Manali have good Ashok *Travellers Lodges* (tel: Kullu 79; Manali 31), and Manali's has big rooms with fine views. Tourist Office by the maidan in Kullu (tel: 7), in the main street of Manali (tel: 25), both with advice on walks. The Himalayan Mountaineering Institute is for more ambitious climbs, has equipment for hire and Sherpas to guide; the most exciting climb is up Hanuman Tibba, 5,929m (2 days). The impressive Rohtang Pass trek, which begins at Kothi, is easier (4,000m).

Beware: both Kullu and Kangra valleys are quite low and get very hot in summer.

OUT AND ABOUT The valleys are strewn with perfect little surviving bazaar towns, each built around wonderful carved wooden tem-ples. They are quiet and friendly to wander, and the affluence of the people is surprising after Nepal and Kashmir. Many locals are land-owners. Crops are maize, rice, wheat, barley, potatoes, pulses and, of course, apples.

Peep inside houses – almost every one has a loom for weaving tartan or striped tweeds and the very fine pashmina wool, made from the undercoat that a high altitude goat grows. The goats are kept by the nomadic Gaddis.

Fabrics, shawls and Tibetan and Ladakhi jewellery (lots of refugees here) can be bought in Manali, as well as new tankas (paintings on cloth) and carpets with a cut pile. Buy local woollen shawls at Bodh and other weavers near the temple. Manali honey is delicious. Prices are absolutely fixed here and no credit cards taken.

Do not miss *Old Manali Village* (2km) nor the old wooden *Hadimba Devi Temple* (c 14th-16th centuries) among the cedars (3km). There are also two former Kullu capitals: *Naggar* (25km) with fort and castle-turned-hotel, 'a spectacu-

larly nice place to stay', with fine position, deep varandah and charming surrounding village; and *Jagatsukh*, the earlier capital, with old tem-ples. And Kullu itself is loved by Indian hills buff Zoe Yalland as 'the most beautiful of all hill towns'.

At *Mandi*, Triloknath Temple and Rewalsar both merit a look. There is trout fishing on the Beas at Raison, Katrain and Kasel, March-October, licences through the Tourist Office from the Director of Fisheries, Dehra Gopipur. There are also treks up the Malana, Parbati, Solang and Seraj Valleys and up Deo Tibba (6,000m).

THE KANGRA VALLEY, HP

Containing the impressive Kangra fort, this whole valley is delightful, full of cornfields, orchards and acres of red pepper plants, and flowers everywhere. It starts near Mandi (see above) and is lower than Kullu and subse-quently hotter, with a short July-August mon-soon. At *Palampur*, where the hills are coated in tea gardens, pines and deodar (cedars), the best place to stay is in fact on an old tea garden: *Palace Motel*, Taragarh, District Palampur (10km from Palampur, towards Baijnath), is run by distant Kashmiri ex-royals. With the tea-gar-dens of Assam and Darjeeling thoroughly private, this is probably the only commercial way of spending a night in a tea manager's home in the magical peace of a tea garden. The alternative is the adequate but modest *T-Bud*, at Palampur. Palampur is a good base for visiting *Baijnath* (Shiva Temple), *Tashijong* (Tibetan monastery), and *Chamunda* which is on the way to Dharamshala (40km).

At the top of the valley lies the hill station of *Dharamshala* (founded 1855), now more famous for its Tibetan refugees. For above it, at McCleodganj, lives the Dalai Lama, exiled in 1950. Surrounding him are some of his Tibetan refugees, various temples and monasteries and a good Tibetan Handicrafts Centre. Stay here at *Bhagsu* HPTCD, perched on a promontory, or down at the *Dharladhau Hotel* in Dharamshala. In addition to the Raj buildings of McCleodganj and Forsythganj in the upper part of the station, do not miss *St John-in-the-Wilderness* church (1860) found in a forest grove between them; the splendid stained-glass windows are a memorial to Lord Elgin (Viceroy 1862-3) who loved this area for its similarity to his Scottish homeland and who died here.

JAMMU, JAMMU AND KASHMIR

At 305m. Thriving, bustling capital of Jammu and Kashmir with some of its old character. It was the Maharaja of Kashmir who bought a Rolls Royce, signed the usual agreement that the car could only be driven and repaired by a

Rolls Royce-trained chauffeur and then remembered his position. He was a maharaja; they were merely tradesmen. So, he sacked the chauffeur. Rolls Royce took him to court, won and sold the car second-hand in Bombay.

Jammu was formerly the cultural centre for the fine miniature paintings produced at the courts of the hill states during the 18th and 19th centuries. Worth pausing here to see two excellent collections of paintings, both open the year round.

THE HARD FACTS   Flights connect Jammu with Delhi, Chandigarh, Srinagar and Amritsar. Stay at either Hotel *Jammu Ashok* (tel: 43127; telex: 0377-227) right opposite the Amar Mahal Museum; or the *Asia Jammu-Tawi*, (tel: 49430; telex: 0377-224), with better facilities including pool. J & K tourist Office, Vir Marg (tel: 5324). Fishing the Tawi river for the plentiful mahseer, seeng and mali only possible with a permit from the Tourist Office in Srinagar and own fishing equipment.

OUT AND ABOUT   First stop is *Dogra Art Gallery*, Gandhi Bhavan, facing the New Secretariat. It was set up in 1954. There are some 600 paintings as well as terracottas, arms, sculptures, manuscripts and murals. They include the outstanding illustrations to the Rasmanajari (Posies of Delight), a 14th century Hindu text by the poet Bhanu Datta, describing the behaviour and feeling of lovers. They were painted for Raja Sangram Pal and his half-brother Hindal Pal (1660-70) by the finest Basohli court artists who use bold designs and flat areas of vivid colour, further enriched with green beetle wing. Only some paintings on view; try asking to see more. (Open Tues.-Sun., 7.30am-1pm in summer; 11am-5pm in winter.)

Amar Mahal Museum is also worth visiting. Dr Karan Singh's collection is exhibited in a French-designed palace complete with furnishings, built on a bluff overlooking the Tawi River in 1907 by Dr Singh's grandfather, Raja Amar Singh; hall hung with 47 illustrations to the Nala-Damayanti (part of the epic Mahabharata) recounting Nala and Damayanti's marriage, followed by Nala gambling his kingdom away, then recovering it; painted at Kangra, 1800-1810, with soft tones, in a lyrical detailed style striving for realism. (Open Tues.-Sat., 5-7pm; Sun., 8am-noon, closed holidays.) Honey, dried fruits and pretty wicker baskets with yellow and red painted decoration are the things to buy. Around Jammu are good hill forts (Samba, Bahr), temples (Purmandal, Basohli). There is a good trip to Dalhousie hill station and Chamba (see above).

SRINAGAR, JAMMU AND KASHMIR
At 1,768m. Mughal-designed gardens; British-designed holiday houseboat cottages; Kashmir's hills; lakes bordered by tall chinar (oriental plane trees); flowers and pampering. A perfect combination for romantic relaxation. And, if you stay on a houseboat, it is as near to privacy as is possible in India. Days slip away deliciously on the houseboats on Nagin or Dal lake. Deep 1930s sofas invite a good read or a snooze. From the sun-trap boat roof or the carved porch there is the gentle life of the lake to watch. An electric blue kingfisher dives for its dinner. The wily Kashmiris glide past on laden boats, crying out their wares: 'floot, minalal water, fledge' (fruit, mineral water, fudge).

Afternoons are for outings taken lounging on the canopied, floral double bed of a shikara boat (with names like 'Queen of Sheba'), being paddled to Mughal gardens or through the backwaters of Srinagar. Tea of scones, lotus-blossom honey and fresh macaroons at 4pm prompt, whether on a boat or shikara. Mr Bulbul, the flowerman, appears out of the sky-drenching, hour-long sunset to present gladioli picked from his floating florist shop of zinnias, marigolds and carnations. A moonlit paddle. Candlelit dinner.

It all seems a dream. And until Kashmir finds political stability, it will remain only a dream for tourists. But just in case things settle, here is the minimal information

THE HARD FACTS   Go April-September. Spring for almond, walnut, pear and apple blossom and flowers; August for big lotus flowers which grow on sturdy stalks above their huge pancake leaves, covering the lakes. It gets chilly towards the end of September. When regular flights return to operation, they should be daily up from Delhi and Jammu. 18km into town. From Jammu the 8-hour drive through the beautiful Kashmir Valley is best. Choose between staying on a houseboat or at the lakeside Oberoi Palace. J & K Government Tourist Reception Centre, off Sherwani Road (tel: 72449/77303/73648/77305) (also at airport). Here are also the director of Fisheries (tel: 72862) for fishing permits and hiring rod and tackle. Beware: whether booking a houseboat or shikara ride, buying a carpet or a piece of lacquer, check on quality and every detail and bargain very hard. Many Kashmiris are smiling rogues making a tidy fortune from tourists, their principal source of income for the last century. Their hard-luck stories are rot.

Houseboats When the British finally discovered Kashmir, the Maharaja of Kashmir forbade European building on his land. So the ever resourceful island race 'improved' the lakes and took to boats. The first charming, carved houseboat was built around 1875. Now they stand cheek by jowl along the shore of Nagin Lake and on parts of the much nicer Dal Lake. For optimum peace, beauty and a cleaner lake, go for the east bank of Nagin Lake (boats therefore face west). The east-facing bank of Dal Lake, behind Nehru Park, is good (see sunsets from the roof). Avoid the hugger-mugger crush at the south-east corner of Dal Lake (known as Boulevard) and the west side of Nagin Lake which is in shadow for the afternoon and misses the ritual sunset. Beware: happiness is advance booking. If not, houseboat owners operate a cartel, and the tourist office is not that helpful. One recommendation: Gulam Butt and family's Clermont Houseboats at the quiet, upper end of Dal Lake (book by letter or cable: Nasim Bagh, Hazratbal, Srinagar).

OUT AND ABOUT Do as much as possible by boat. Go up the *backwaters* of Srinagar, founded in the 6th century by Raja Pravarasen II. Locals nip about in narrow dugga boats, shopping at tiny stores like packing cases on stilts. Life is lived mostly on the water. Vegetables are grown on the floating gardens (called rads and dheems), built on heel, a water weed, and willow saplings. The mass of lotuses between them are merely fillers. If you get up early (about 5am), you can catch the magic early light and boat down to the vegetable market which seethes with activity, the haggling often progressing to fisticuffs.

The famous terraced *Mughal gardens* are both lakeside and perched on the hillsides. Shalimar Bagh (Garden of Love) is the most sophisticated, with fountains and cascade, built by Jahangir for Nur Jahan in 1616, the top terrace for courtesans only (ITDC son et lumière in English, 9pm, quite picturesque). Nishat Bagh (Garden of Bliss, 1633), is infinitely more romantic, less 'preserved' and was laid out by Nur Jahan's brother, Asaf Khan. The oldest garden, Nasim Bagh (Garden of the Morning Breeze), was laid out by Akbar in 1586. Chasma Shahi (the Royal Spring) is the smallest garden, begun by Jahangir, completed by Shah Jahan in 1632, now restored.

Boat trips A delightful shikara day trip goes through the bird sanctuary on the north-west side of Nagin Lake, then through Anchar Lake to Candarbal. Joanna Lumley described it as 'the most blissful scenery, rather non-Indian except for the mountain backdrop. There are acres and acres of lotuses. A glorious, peaceful day.' (5-6hrs there, shore-side picnic, 3hrs back). A longer but utterly blissful two-and-a-half day shikara trip goes up to Manabel Lake (bookable through Srinagar Tourist Office).

In town, apart from seeing the wooden Jami Masjid and wandering the lanes behind the

canals, there is the good *Sri Pratap Singh Museum*, housed in an old palace: everything from 4th-12th century stone sculpture to a 17th century tapestry map of Srinagar (open Thurs.-Tues., 10am-5pm, closed holidays).

For some sport, a clamber up Sharika Hill to the 18th century Hari Parbat Fort, surrounded by almond orchards and Akbar's wall; or up Takh-i-Sulaiman (Throne of Solomon, now Shankaracharya Hill) brings rewards of good views. There is also sailing, swimming, water-skiing on Nagin Lake, golf and fishing (rainbow trout, April-September, mahseer August-September). Pleasant exercise is to hire a bicycle (from Boulevard shops) and go around the north ends of Dal and Nagin lakes.

Food can be dull, especially on the houseboats. But real Kashmiri cuisine is good. It is still heavily Persian influenced and rich. The Oberoi hotel and some houseboat cooks can be persuaded to prepare some of the 17 meat courses that make up a wazwan (royal dinner) feast. Dishes might include gushtaba (meatballs cooked in yoghurt and spices), tobakmaz (shin of mutton cooked with cashewnuts, poppy-seeds and onions), kebabs and biryanis. Restaurants in Srinagar include *Lhasa's*, off Boulevard, where Tibetan refugees cook excellent Chinese food. Try Kashmiri tea, kahwa, very sweet, flavoured with saffron, cardamom and almonds. It is possible to find classical Sufiana Kalam music in town. Some houseboat owners can advise, including Abdul Razac who is to be found on Aristotle Houseboat, Dal Lake (opposite Boulevard).

SHOPPING AND CRAFTS Note: provided the carpets, papier mâché, crewel work and shawls continue to be made, then top quality products can be bought in Delhi.

A **carpet factory** has areas devoted to each process of carpet-making. In one a man is laboriously drawing designs on graph paper which are then translated into book form; after that, women duplicate them by hand. In the weaving room whole families, excluding the women, sit at the looms, their fingers speedily twitching the wool and silk into tight knots – the nimble fingers of the young boys are released for half-day schooling. After the grand tour, it is sale-room time: hundreds of carpets of every size and colour are thrown down before the boggling eyes of the client who is oiled with cold drinks or tea. If buying, keep to the big factories and bargain hard; carpets can be shipped home (see Shopping section of Delhi chapter).

In **papier mâché** factories a hotch-potch of discarded paper is soaked, dried in a mould, then painted by men and boys who fortunately still avoid chemical colours. They grind coral for red, lapis for blue, quartz for white, charcoal for black, cardamom for yellow and gold leaf mixed with salt for gold. There are grades of papier mâché: the top one is rarely exported and uses real gold. In all grades many of the patterns are more delicate than those exported. The varnished boxes, eggs and paper-holders are easy to carry; bigger trays and lamps are best bought at the last city before flying out of India. Kashmiri walnut bowls, with the knarled knots, are a very good buy. So, too, are the walnuts and walnut oil.

The Kashmiri **crewel-work fabric** with bold, meandering tree-of-life. The Muslim men sit together in their dark houses, dressed in kaftan-like wool pherons, slipping kangris (willow wicker baskets of hot charcoals) underneath them during the winter. As they gossip, they chainstitch over designs drawn out in ink on coarsely woven cloth. The piece is usually 50m long, about 130cm wide and, unless it is a special commission, no two bales are identical in colour or design. So here is a chance to buy unique, hand-embroidered furnishing fabric relatively cheaply – about Rs80-120 per metre which, even after shipping, is half London prices. Of course, it can also be bought made up as cushion covers and bedspreads.

Then there are the **Kashmir shawls**. The craft was possibly introduced to Kashmir from Persia ('shal' is Persian for woven fabric) by Sultan Zain-ul-Abdin (1423-74), together with paper-making, sericulture (silk growing) and fruit trees. After a period of decline, the emperors revived the art and stocked their wardrobes with shawls, since when they have remained expensive and much sought after. Shahtus shawls were the finest of all, and today's lower-grade version is still pricy. They are woven from pashmina (known in the West as cashmere, from the country of its origin), the inner, soft fleece grown by mountain goats in the winter and shed in spring. An even finer wool from the throat of the ibex was used to make the legendary shawls that can be passed through a ring, very rare today.

Originally, a dozen or so specialists worked on a shawl. Up to 300 colours were prepared and a shawl took several months to complete. Weaving, hereditary and restricted to men, was the most skilled operation, yet the designer got the highest salary and the shawl-broker, who acted as middle-man between the ustad (master weaver) and foreign merchant, made the serious profit.

The floral designs of the 17th century tightened up in the 18th century into stylised butas (floral motifs) and by the 19th century into the familiar stylised kairi (mango) known as Paisley, even by Indians. By around 1800, those who could not afford the woven shawls could buy embroidered ones which expertly imitated the woven effect.

Akbar initiated the practice of stitching two together so that there was no 'wrong' side showing. He also gave shawls to foreign dignitaries, a tradition that persists. Shawls had enough value to be part of the East India Company's bribing equipment. Then, as 19th century trade with Europe increased, standards went down to satisfy first British, then French demand. Napoleon's gift of a shawl to Josephine set off a shawl rage amongst the Empire aristocracy – Josephine had 300-400.

Wild prices were paid but the weavers could not keep up, so Norwich and Paisley manufacturers stepped in. When Lion & Paisley's imitation wool and silk shawls costing next to nothing flooded the market around 1835 – hence the term Paisley – the Kashmiri market was severely reduced. Now the weaving is being revived, and shawls of all qualities are made.

It is best not to buy crafts from the boatmen. And beware of small Srinagar shops, too. Either be sure of what you are buying and barter hard, or go to a fixed price government emporium of which there are many. Kashmir Government Art Emporium, Residency Road, and Government Central Market, Exhibition Ground, are both good. Bigger spending should be done at these. Their shipping should be reliable too.

The **tailors** in Kashmir are excellent. To have a Kashmiri suit of pyjamas (baggy trousers, from the Hindi) and straight shirt made, choose one of the many tailors who all sit cross-legged working at Singer hand sewing machines. He will say how much material to buy and where, measure obscure distances all over the body very quickly without writing anything down, and produce a perfectly fitting suit the following day. Ideal for hot travelling down on the plains.

GULMARG, JAMMU AND KASHMIR
Note: Like Srinagar, access is subject to current political conditions.

38km from Srinagar, at 2,730m. Spring in this valley of the Pir Panjal range is almost unrivalled (only Yusmarg, south-east of here, is supposed to beat it). Jahangir, whose albums are full of flower illustration, once collected 21 different varieties here. Apart from glorious walks, treks and riding, there is the highest natural golf course in the world (2,650m) and, in winter, the best skiing in India (but do not expect Gstaad or St Moritz standards).

THE HARD FACTS Season mid-May to mid-October (May-June for best flowers); mid-December to mid-March for decent skiing. Fly to Srinagar, then bus or taxi, doing the last stretch through the pines from Tangmarg by pony.

Three nice places to stay, all with good atmosphere, character, pretty settings and breath-taking views. Best is *Highlands Park*, a fine building with good gardens; then there is *Nedou's* or *Woodlands*. The charming, well-equipped Government Tourist Huts are bookable through Srinagar Tourist Office or travel agents. For ski instruction, mountaineering and trekking, contact the Indian Institute of Skiing and Mountaineering, Gulmarg.

OUT AND ABOUT   Good walks, treks and rides include the Outer Circular Walk (11km) encircling Gulmarg, with stunning views right down to Srinagar and up to Nanga Parbat (8,137m), the fifth highest mountain in the world, especially good at sunset. Also to Khilanmarg, Alpatha Lake, Tosha Maidan and in spring, Yusmarg. Gulmarg's 18-hole Golf Course, with small wooden club house (temporary membership immediate, Rs2 per day, clubs for hire), is up to international standards (tournaments held here and at Srinagar) but its hazards include streams, air so thin the ball flies further and kites swooping down to pinch the ball. Skiing will seem rather quaint to Europeans, but is the smartest and best in India. There are a few ski-lifts, runs up to 10km and nursery slopes; ski equipment and toboggans can be hired. Also, an ice-skating rink, with skates for hire.

PAHALGAM, JAMMU AND KASHMIR
Note: Like Srinagar, access is subject to political conditions.

98km from Srinagar, at 2,130m. Excellent treks and fishing in the Liddar Valley. The town, originally a shepherds' village, lies at the junction of the fast-flowing Lidder and Shashnag Rivers below blossoming alpine meadows full of sheep and mountains thick with pines and firs, populated by berry-eating brown bears.

THE HARD FACTS   Go mid-April to mid-November, climate cooler than Srinagar, warmer than Gulmarg. Fly to Srinagar, then a day's drive. See *Pampore* for saffron production, *Sangram* for cricket bats, and *Avantipur* for 9th-century Hindu temples; after Rnuntnag a detour leads to beautiful, atmospheric *Achabal Mughal* garden before going up to Pahalgam.

The hearty stay in tents, complete with electricity, equipment hired from one of the dozen agencies here (or booked at Srinagar Tourist Office). Others go for comfort at the two rather expensive hotels, both overlooking the river: *Pahalgam* in the bazaar area, rooms with river views, picnics provided, log stoves at night; or *Woodstock*, nearer the river. Fishermen need to pay for permit, beat and gillie at Srinagar Tourist Office; rod and tackle for hire locally.

OUT AND ABOUT   Good walks and treks in every direction range from gentle strolls to 5-day treks. They include Mamaleswara, Tulian Lake (16km, views), and *Amarnath Cave* (47km, at 3,962m), believed to be Shiva's home – an ice Shiva lingum is fed through the limestone roof, and pilgrims flock there for Yatra festival on full moon of July-August, all vividly described by V. S. Naipal in *An Area of Darkness*. More ambitious trips are to *Kolahoi Glacier* (36km) and to *Sonmarg* (74km), a good base for further treks. Fishermen can hook plenty of trout June-September and mahseer August-September (Spring water is too cold). For June trout fly-fishing, drive up beside the Lidder for about 3 hours. The golf course has more stunning views (temporary membership immediate).

LEH, LADAKH, JAMMU AND KASHMIR
Note: Like Srinagar, access if subject to political conditions.

434km from Srinagar, at 3,505m. This tiny, barren, remote town high in the pink granite Karakoram range of mountains in the Indus Valley is the capital of Ladakh. It has only been open to foreigners for a decade. Its past importance was as a junction on the silk route (where roads met from Sinkiang, the Indian plains and the Middle East) and as a centre of Tibetan Tantric Buddhism, although Buddhism was possibly first brought to Ladakh by emissaries of Ashoka in the 3rd century BC.

The friendly Ladakhis ingeniously irrigate fields to grow barley and preserve their Tibetan culture and religion which is now hard to find in Tibet. Buddhism still thrives: there are over 50,000 lamas residing in the lamaserais of Ladakh. The perilous, cliff-top gompas (Buddhist monasteries), newly restored with profits from tourism, are the sights to see, glorious in the thin, bright sunlight under a dark blue sky. They pay good dividends for the adventurous, determined people who get to them.

THE HARD FACTS   A trip to Leh is governed by the weather. In theory the road from Srinagar is open mid-May to mid-November, but snow may shorten the period considerably. Worth coinciding with Hemis festival in June-July, three days of constant celebrations plus masked dances. Either fly up from Delhi (Mon. and Thurs.) or Srinagar (Wed., Fri. and Sun.), sensational views of the Himalayas; or go 434km by road from Srinagar (reasonably exhausting but stunning scenery). Best is to go up one way, down the other. As the weather is capricious, flights are often cancelled, and there are often two planeloads fighting for one set of seats. So make friends in very high places and allow an extra day to get back, just in case.

The journey up by road, slightly hair-raising

at moments, crosses Zoji La (3,529m), Namika La (3,718m) and Fatu La (4,094m) Passes and takes two days of 10-hour drives, overnight at Kargil. Six-seat jeep is better than Class A bus as it gives freedom to stop and peek at mosques, monasteries and views, most especially at Lamayuru Gompa, the first of many and formerly very grand, with 400 monks.

On finally reaching Leh, there are various rum hotels, of which the best bets are: *Kang-Lha-Cheu* and *Lha Lha-Ri-Mo*, both central. Far better and more peaceful (Leh attracts a surprising number of European bus-loads) is to stay at Mountain Travel's *Ladakh Serai* (11km), a camp of beautiful, comfortable tents (far removed from Girl Guide days), adapted from the yurts used by Central Asian nomads, pitched amid willow trees, near the village of Stock. Ideal base for visits to the monasteries, short treks and for river rafting. Bookable through ExplorAsia (see p. 7).

Tourist Office in the Dak Bungalow, for information on monasteries, map and advice on trekking and the current half and whole day rates for jeep-taxis to see the scattered gompas. Indian Airlines is next door.

OUT AND ABOUT Navigate steep lanes in and around Leh to see outsides and insides of gompas at very odd times. In town, climb up to the 16th century Leh Khar Palace, fine view of the Zanskar mountains across the Indus River (open 6-9am; after 5pm); then go on up to Leh Gompa (Red Gompa), more views, built 1430 and find good Buddha inside (open 7-9am; 5-7pm). Then to Shanka Gompa to see gold statues (2km).

It takes a few days to see the important gompas out of town using a jeep-taxi, but each journey is different, with good walks and scenery (take picnics). They include *Spituk Gompa*, with a good collection of masks, the seat of the head lama (10km). There is *Phiyang Gompa* (red sect of Buddhists) and village (20km), *Thiksey Gompa*, 12th century, 12-storey hilltop gompa with 10 temples, all full of statues, tankas (paintings on cloth), wall-paintings and a huge engraved pillar, views down into green Indus Valley (17km). *Hemis Gompa* is the largest and most important, with wall-paintings, statues and a superb collection of tankas including possibly the biggest one in existence, exhibited every 11 years (next time 1991) (49km).

Stok Palace (16km), where the royal family live now, and the 15th-century ruined *Shey palace* (15km), where they used to live, reached through flower-strewn Choglamsar, are also worth visiting. For a longer trip, well worth the effort, go to *Basgo*, *Saspol* and *Alchi*, the most important early Buddhist monastery in Leh.

Tibetan food is not very good, mostly noodles. Give shopping a miss: what little is sold here can be found cheaper elsewhere. But do see if there is a game of local polo. It is played at Leh on probably the highest, and certainly the most spectacular, polo ground in the world.

Nepal

Out of India and up into the highest kingdom of all, ruled by King Birendra Bir Bikram Shah Dev. Following recent events, the king now has constitutional rather than absolute powers and his people enjoy a greater democratic freedom. In the May 1991 elections, the two main political parties, the Communists and Congress, ran a close race. The democratic Nepal Congress Party won 110 seats, the Communist Party 69. And, in the first free elections for three decades, G. P. Koirala became the third son of one family to be democratically elected Prime Minister (his elder brothers held the post in the 1950s).

Arriving at the capital, Kathmandu, is like walking into a Brueghel painting, with wooden houses, flags and flowers, men and women quietly preparing food. In India, there are no casinos, so Kathmandu is the nearest place where the Indian rich can nip out for a quick night's gambling. Looking out from the city, the drama begins. 25% of Nepal is above 3,000m. The greatest Himalayan peaks of Everest, Kunchenjunga, Lohotse, Makalu, Cho Oyu, Dhaulagiri, Manaslu and Annapurna touch the sky at well over 8,000m. This is a land of soaring mountains, rivers rushing through deep gorges, tiger-inhabited lowland jungles and whole valleys of rhododendrons, peopled by tribes with a rich variety of customs and languages.

Buddha was born here, at Lumbini. But now Nepal is officially 90% Hindu and the only Hindu kingdom in the world. However, in practice, religion mixes both – many Nepalese profess Buddhism and Hinduism at once, with fervour. The country is thick with beautiful temples and wayside shrines, proportionately more than any other country. And there are possibly even more festivals than in India.

As well as wandering in the colourful villages and market, there is game-spotting, river-rafting and, of course, trekking. Nepal is the home of the courageous, stocky Gurkhas and the mountaineering Sherpas. It is not obligatory to scale Everest (8,848m), affectionately known as Chomolungma (Goddess Mother of the World) by the Sherpas of Khumba, but it is certainly true that the most interesting scenery and peoples of Nepal can only be reached by trekking. But do not fear. Nepal is one of the safest places for a trek. It can be tailored to extreme gentleness and resemble a pleasant walk, free from all cares, with frequent stops, thoughtful

Sherpas, cooks and porters.

To see game, the Royal Chitwan and newer Royal Badia parks are two of the finest wildlife sanctuaries in Asia. Chitwan, one of the world's flashier holiday spots, stages the World Elephant Polo Championships, Nepal's answer to Ascot. In season there is usually a spattering of the world's royals mingling with showbiz royals like Goldie Hawn, Robert Redford and Michael York and sporty royal Bjorn Borg. A week of trekking, game-parking or valley-hopping in Nepal easily slips into a trip to north India.

THE HARD FACTS If Nepal is on the itinerary before leaving home, buy and read the weighty, newly revised *Insight Guide to Nepal*. Season is October-April; October-November for harvest festivals, clear air and trekking; February-March for high altitude flower spotting; April-May for trekking, river-rafting and spotting game in Chitwan NP; July-September is monsoon. Best blooms, including double jasmine and orchids, are April-June, sadly hidden sometimes in the heat mist. Worth aiming for the concentration of festivals after the rich harvest (August-October), Dasain with plenty of animal sacrifice (October), Nepal's version of Durga Puja), Tihar in honour of Lakshmi (October), the King's birthday with processions and fireworks (December 28), Baisakha Purnima celebrating Buddha's birthday (April-May) and many more.

Fly up to **Kathmandu**: good connections by Indian Airlines from Delhi and Varanasi, Calcutta and Patna; and other airlines, including Royal Nepal Airlines and Thai International. All fares are expensive compared to internal Indian flights and package trips do not reduce them much, so it is better to spend several nights in Nepal, if possible. Going by train or bus is hard work, although there is the stunning mountain highway drive along Tribuvan Rajpath to Kathmandu after the Calcutta train ends (after several changes) at Razaul, and a bus connection from Darjeeling (special permit needed).

Busy time at the new airport, described as 'cleaner, but the same system'; its benefit is an upstairs restaurant for passing time when flights are delayed. On the ground floor, find the tourist information desk, hotel counter, foreign exchange counter (for Nepal Rupees, which, like the Indian version, may not be imported or exported). The 7-day visa can be bought here, current cost £20. This can be extended at the Central Immigration Office in Kathmandu. Special permits needed for trekking outside Kathmandu Valley are obtained from the Immigration Department at Thamel in Kathmandu, or in Pokhara.

For up-market accommodation, it is essential to book a hotel and check its taxes; they can in-crease a bill by 22%; there are always plenty of modest rooms.

Everest (tel: 220567/220288; telex: 2260); 157 rooms, many with grand views; every facility includes excellent pool and restaurants (some rooftop). Very warm atmosphere, efficient service and near the town centre.

Soaltee Oberoi (tel: 211106; telex: 2203); 300 rooms (including 18 suites), ensure one with the panoramic views; every facility including pool, tennis, mini-golf, casino, 4 good restaurants including Himalchuli serving Nepalese dishes. Located on the fringes of town, and somewhat formal in atmosphere. With SITA travel agency, the hotel sometimes runs a package deal from India which includes '3 nights of luxury and excitement and Rs1200 in free casino coupons'.

Other, less flashy hotels, include the following:

Hotel de l'Annapurna; 140 rooms, pool, garden and located on the very central Durbar Marg. A Taj Group hotel, so bookable at any of their Indian hotels or through central reservations (see p. 12).

Hotel Yak and Yeti; 110 rooms, tennis, pool, good food in much older restaurant, central.

Hotel Malla; 75 rooms (including 8 suites), tennis, garden, new but built with local character, quite central, friendly.

Hotel Shangrilah; reasonably central, with lovely garden, pool and good food and service.

Hotel Himalaya; well positioned, on the rising road to Patan so very good views, plus pool, food OK.

Then two cheaper hotels, both clean:

Shankar; 135 rooms, stylish former palace of the Rana set in large gardens on town edge.

Kathmandu; up the road from the Shangrilah, with adequate accommodation, no pool and minimal garden.

In Kathmandu, the Government Tourist Office is on Ganga Path (tel: 11203), for brochures, maps and even film shows; Indian Airlines, Durbar Marg (tel: 11196). Best of many travel agencies for tours and individual arrangements are: Everest Travel, Basantapur Square (tel: 11121); Kathmandu Tours and Travel, Dharma Path (tel: 14446); Yeti Travels, (Tel: 12329/11234) and Gorkha Travels (tel: 14895), both on Durbar Marg.

For rewarding trekking and mountaineering, book well in advance. In addition to these, the best, safest and most reliable international agent is Adventure Travel, Durbar Marg, near Annapurna hotel (tel: 223328; fax: 9771 221379; telex: 2216 TIGTOP NP); this is the booking office for Mountain Travel, Himalayan River Explorations, Tiger Tops and Adventure Travel Nepal, as well as regular booking agency for large or small travel needs. Mountain Travels was founded in 1964 by Colonel Jimmy Roberts,

British explorer and mountaineer, employing 170 Sherpas and responsible for assisting Chris Bonnington to be first up the south-west face of Everest and helping Habeler to be first to the top without oxygen (see p. 7 for its ExplorAsia London address). For river-rafting, you will get a good time with Himalayan River Exploration. Tiger Tops is the company which runs accommodation at Chitwan and Bardia NPs.

Transport within Nepal is by Royal Nepal Airlines, New Road (tel: 14511), taxi or bicycle – excellent for the Kathmandu Valley, find newish ones with working brakes in the bazaar. Saturday is considered dangerous by locals, so everything is closed. Sunday goes like a fair. Alcohol is very expensive, so take rations.

OUT AND ABOUT This is a country with immense variety. The travel agents listed above can cater to every taste. Books listed in the bibliography should also help. But, on a first visit, wrench yourself out of bed to see the sunrise over Everest and also to take the morning Mountain Flight. Also, see something of Kathmandu Valley and its three cities: Kathmandu, Patan (Lalitpur) and Bhadgaon (Bhaktapur). Before unification in the late 18th century, each was an independent kingdom of great culture and affluence, fed by the trade route traffic.

The two early rises The dawn trip to Nagarkot Hill (45mins, leave 5am wearing several jumpers) to see sunrise over the Himalayas is unforgettable (or see it as a mini-trek, sleeping out overnight); then warming breakfast (including delicious local curd) in nearby Bhadgaon (see below) at the chalet-like café next to the tallest temple. The fine 5th-12th century art of Changunarayan temple is a pleasant 2-hour walk from here and Thimi, where the big, brightly painted, papier mâché dance masks are made, is on the road back to Kathmandu.

The early morning Mountain View flight is well worth the cost (book on Royal Nepal Airlines through a reputable and therefore influential travel agent; go for the first flight as this one is rarely cancelled; and check visibility). In the thin, fresh sunlight at 6,000m, the plane flies along the mountain range, past the 10 highest peaks in the world and back again. Passengers are given a check-list plan of the peaks before and a certificate of their momentous, breathtaking journey after.

In **Kathmandu**, in the old market place and around Durbar Square there are exquisitely carved buildings and both the Old Royal Palace and Kumari Devi (House of the Living Goddess). The Kumari is carefully and ruthlessly selected at about five years of age and remains goddess until puberty, when she loses deity status and another is chosen.

Across the Bagmati river lies *Patan*, the most

Buddhist of the three towns. It is the place to see beautiful temples and 17th century buildings in and around its Durbar Square and to buy high quality bronze and carved wood. *Bhadgaon*, at the other end of the valley, is the most unspoilt and medieval. The tiny cobbled streets are lined with beautifully carved old black and white houses and temples. There are no cars, the pace is slow, farmers and millers amble about and potters throw beautiful pots on huge turning stones.

In the valley around Kathmandu, see the hilltop *Swayambhunath Temple*, with its watchful eyes of Buddha; *Pashpatinath Temple* and Bodnath stupa beyond it; and *Kirtipur*, a medieval town busy with dyeing and weaving. Go north to see one of the largest sculptures of sleeping Vishnu at *Budhanilkantha*. For rewarding day walks in the valley to see the rural villages, hire a Sherpa who directs the taxi where to drop him and his wards and where to collect them at the end of the day.

Further afield, the stunningly beautiful *Pokhara Valley*, with its backdrop of the Annapurna range, is worth seeing. In the jungle, try three days and two nights of white-water rafting on Sun Kosi, Trisuli or Gandaki Rivers: some paddling, some splashes and lots of fun (fastest flowing in October and spring). You can also do the classic trek to Everest Base Camp, encircle Annapurna Massif, or go into the heart of Nepal to Langtang Valley. You can also combine rafting and trekking, or go to the Royal Chitwan National Park by raft. In the spring, there are treks devoted to seeing the blossoms, not only hillsides of rhododendrons (whose blooms get stronger the lower they are) but orchids, gentians, azaleas, daphne and viburnum.

FOOD, ENTERTAINMENT AND SHOPPING
The food in Kathmandu is better than anywhere else in the hills. As well as the inevitable Tibetan and Nepalese, tourists can sit in the highest kingdom and go on a disorientating world tour of flavours, picking up bortsch and brownies, chateaubriand and chow mein. Sample the meat pies from Pie Street (full of hippies and known locally as Freak Street).

In town, the local favourite is *Banchagaar* (meaning Nepalese kitchen), found not far from the clock tower. At the *Everest Cultural Society* or the *Oberoi's Himachuli* (both with Nepalese dancing), there is good Nepalese food: soups (alu tama, thukpa gundruk), then rice, vegetables, millet bread and sikhani (yoghurt pudding) washed down with either raksi, a rice-based liquor, or chang, the local beer made with rice, millet or barley. The *Yak and Yeti Chimney Room* offers food and atmosphere (large open fire in old palace hall). *Boris's*, on the outskirts, has Russian food, ambience and Boris, formerly a Russian ballet dancer but since the 1950s an excellent hotelier and restaurateur. There is good Indian food amid Pahari paintings and Indian musicians and ghazel singers at *Gahr-e-Kebab*, near Hotel de L'Annapurna.

Nepalese dance and music can be found at the National Theatre, Everest Cultural Society (7pm, nightly) and, for a good setting, at the Sweta Machendranath temple near Indrachowk. Night life does exist – just. Either win or lose a fortune at the Oberoi Casino where play is in Indian Rupees or US dollars and there is no restriction on taking winnings out of the country (free buses there from other hotels; free drinks to encourage players).

Shopping is good but now very tourist-orientated, as in Kashmir, so bargain very hard or go to fixed price Government emporia. Good buys are the jolly masks from Thimi; brass from Patan (cast by the rare lost wax method, as in Orissa); khukris (the short, lethal, Nepalese daggers); jewellery and wood carving and some of the fine pieces of dhaka woven cloth from the Kosi hills.

Wildlife sanctuaries

ROYAL CHITWAN NATIONAL PARK, NEPAL
Season mid-September to mid-June; best Feb-May for seeing game when the grass is short. Fly to Kathmandu, then 130km south by road or another flight to Megauli, near the park; lodge collects guests by elephant during the cool season. But the most exciting way to arrive is by a three-day river trip starting from near Kathmandu.

There are various places to stay: Tiger Tops' *Jungle Lodge*, the *Tented Camp* and *Tharu Village*. All are bookable through Adventure Travel in Kathmandu (see above) or through a good travel agency in Delhi or London. The treetop Jungle Lodge is built of the local hardwood, sal; 20 rooms, attached bath (hot water), log fires, quite social, very comfortable. Tharu Village is a longhouse with central communal area, adapted from the local Tharu people's villages and built and decorated by them; 12 rooms with modern plumbing, local food and dance and visits to Tharu villages.

The Tented Camp is now in the Surung Valley, the large safari tents (20 beds, hot water and showers) pitched around the campfire, good jungle atmosphere and peace and quiet. Each is efficiently run by one management, so guests can spend a few nights at one and then move on (package tours available).

Each has a kitchen and bar and expert guides day and night who also give evening talks; the team is trained by naturalist and tiger expert Dr Charles McDougal and naturalist, K. K. Gurung. Safaris conducted on elephant.

Lying in the Rapti Valley of floodplain jungle and elephant grass only 150m above sea level, this fine park was established in 1962 as a rhinoceros preserve. The 932 sqkm of forest and rivers can be explored by elephant or Land Rover to see one of the 350 great Indian one-horned rhinos. There are now fewer than 1,500 in the wild and the largest numbers are here and at Kasiranga National Park in Assam (see Calcutta chapter). There are also leopard, wild boar, sloth bear, deer and monkeys. And visitors have a serious possiblity of seeing one of the about 100 Bengal tigers from a specially built blind. The rivers contain freshwater dolphin and the gharial crocodile (now being saved from threatened extinction).

For sports, there is canoeing, swimming, bird-watching (some 400 species) and nature walks. The gharial crocodile conservation farm can also be visited. The crocodiles are reared in captivity and then released into the wild. In all this is one of Asia's leading wildlife parks.

ROYAL BADIA NATIONAL PARK, FAR WESTERN NEPAL
Season Nov-May; best Feb-April. Fly from Kathmandu to Nepalgunj, then by new road 2-4 hrs to Karnali camp beside the Great Karnali River. Stay at *Tiger Tops Karnali Camp*, tents pitched in a stunning jungle setting, or an hour's drive away at *Tiger Tops Karnali Lodge*, a wooden building on the edge of the park; both run by Tiger Tops (bookable as for Chitwan, above); opened 1985, accommodation in double safari tents; wildlife watching by raft, Land Rover and on foot; mountain trekking and fishing. Best to stay at least 5 nights.

Nearly 1,000 sqkm, this reserve is drier than Chitwan Park, so good for walking to see wildlife and the local Tharu culture. It also has better visibility and fewer humans, so more sightings. Spot several kinds of deer, blue bull, wild boar, sloth bear, tiger, leopard and wilddog; also some swamp deer, black buck, rich birdlife and, in the river, dolphin, crocodile and otter.

DACHIGAM, KASHMIR
Note: Like Shrinagar, access is subject to political conditions.

Season June-July. Fly to Srinagar, then by road 22km, then trek on foot or pony. Camp or stay in Srinagar (see above). Information and permits from the Game Warden, Srinagar Tourist Office. Former royal game reserve of sub-Himalayan forest, notable for the hangul (Kashmir stag, related to the Scottish red deer) and the Himalayan black bear and brown bear. Down in the Lower Dachigam there is an excellent heronry along the river.

Find out more

Ali, Salim: *The Book of Indian Birds*, Bombay, 1979

Akbar, M. J.: *Kashmir: Behind the Vale*, Delhi, 1991

Anderson, J. G., (ed.): *Nepal, Insight Guide*, APA Productions, London 1983

Archer, W. G.: *Indian Paintings from the Punjab Hills*, vols 1 & 2, London, New York and Delhi, 1973

Armington, S.: *Trekking in the Himalayas*, Lonely Planet Guide, South Yarra, Australia, 1979

Bezruchka, S.: *A Guide to Trekking in Nepal*, London, 1981

Cleare, J.: *Collins Guide to Mountains and Mountaineering*, London 1979

Crowe, S. et al.: *The Gardens of Mughal India*, London, 1972

Fleming, R. and R. and Bangdel, L. S.: *Birds of Nepal*, Kathmandu, 1979

Fleming, R. and R. and Bangdel, L. S.: *Kathmandu Valley*, Kathmandu, 1978

Gurung, K. K.: *Heart of the Jungle*, London, 1984

Keenan, B.: *Travels in Kashmir*, Oxford, 1989

McDougal, C.: *The Face of the Tiger*, London, 1977

Mierow, D. and Shrestha, T. B.: *Himalayan Flowers and Trees*, Kathmandu, 1973

Raj, P.: *Kathmandu and the Kingdom of Nepal*, Lonely Planet Guide, South Yarra, Australia, 1982

Schettler, R., and M.: *Kashmir, Ladakh and Zanskar*, Lonely Planet Guide, South Yarra, Australia, 1981

Woodcock, M.: *Collins Handguide to the Birds of the Indian Sub-Continent*, London, 1980

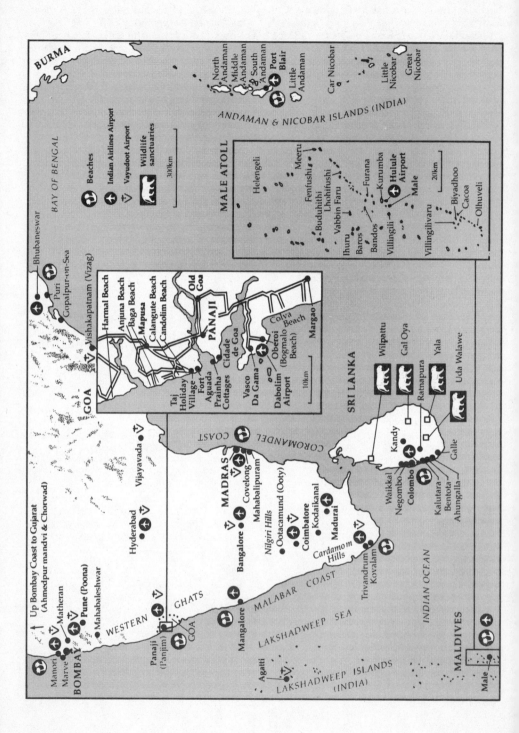

Sun, sand and switch off

However glorious the Mughal monuments and the Tamil temples, the palaces and forts, the hills and exotic wildlife, however fascinating the Indian peoples and their traditions and crafts, it is always good to spend a few days simply flopping. Swimming, sunbathing, sleeping and eating are a magical combination for unwinding from the worries of work at home on arrival in India, before setting off to do sight-seeing. And it is just as good at the end of a tour to soak up the sun for a while before returning to a cold climate.

India has 6,000km of coastline. It should be a paradise of beaches with good facilities. But, although hotels are mushrooming, it is not yet. This is mainly because there is no seaside holiday tradition among Indians. The rich usually head for the cool hills; the less rich might visit family or go on a pilgrimage; the poor do not have holidays. Few Indians swim and none is in search of a suntan. Quite the opposite. The rule in India is: the paler the skin, the better. The pale skin of a young girl is a major commodity and increases her value to would-be suitors and it is included in the match-making advertisements of each Sunday's *Times of India*. An occasional gaggle of Indian girls may go wave-jumping, in full saris, amid yelps and screams of delight, but most Indians think the Western habit of toasting the body and dancing in the waves is quite mad.

The horse-shoe of almost continuous silver, palm-fringed coast encasing the Indian peninsula is therefore hardly developed. Where beach hotels exist, only a few satisfy the demands of the sophisticated Western beach-hopper. The only two serious resort areas are Goa, south of Bombay on the west, and the coast south of Madras on the east, with the Kerala coast beginning to come alive. It is all very well forgoing some creature comforts to see and experience a few of India's great attractions, but when it comes to looking for pure relaxation, the demands for a quality environment, good facilities and efficiency are usually stepped up – although those seeking off-beat beaches will find some stunners in India.

Without question, Goa supplies the best of everything, making it tops for pure beach enjoyment. There are good hotels, good food, good beaches and good water and sports. But, for someone who gets itchy feet after a few hours lolling in the sun, the Portuguese sights

of Goa do not compare with the Hindu glories on the east coast of Tamil Nadu. Here, the Coromandel coast just south of Madras has much less of a resort atmosphere, but a quality hotel and fascinating nearby sights.

Across on the west coast, in Kerala, the very beautiful Malabar coast is just beginning to be exploited for tourists, although hippies have been there for some years. The award-winning architecture of the Kovalam Beach Resort is stunning and the facilities are good, even if the service is unreliable; and there are now a range of more modest, family-run hotels nearby.

For many visitors, the quieter beaches are more fun; and certainly some perpetuate the spirit of Indian adventure to even reach them, while others are so rural that a white face is rare. It is reasonably easy to escape from most big cities and find seaside peace. The quick escape routes from Calcutta are to nip down to Puri or serene Gopalpur-on-Sea or, further south, Vishakapatnam. From Bombay, there are nearby Marve and Manori if there is no time to get to Goa or go further up the coast to traditional Bombay beach hotels described by one beach hopper as 'Bombay Butlins but fun'; beyond are the beaches of Gujarat with their splendid 1930s palaces-turned-hotels. From Mysore and Bangalore in southern Karnataka, the quiet sands of Mangalore are an alternative to Goa. And from Hyderabad, Vishakapatnam is trumped for adventure by Machilipatnam.

Apart from these mainland spots, sun seekers must hop across to the islands. Most obvious and best equipped is Sri Lanka (Ceylon), off the southern tip, in the Indian Ocean. The large island is becoming increasingly like one big, up-market holiday resort for Westerners escaping from their depressing winter climates. Its hotels, beaches and facilities are extremely good. Quite the opposite is found on the newly accessible Andaman and Nicobar Islands in the Andaman Sea, across the Bay of Bengal, where life is extremely simple.

For pure paradise and total escape, the tiny islands of the Maldives are worth visiting for a minimum of a week. There is sun, sand, wonderful marine life, very simple living and nothing much else. You may even have an island entirely to yourself.

If switching off for you means also cooling off, then it is best to head for the fresh air of the Himalayas, stretching from Gulmarg and Srinagar in the west right across Nepal to Darjeeling. Here are autumn colours, snowy winters and spring and summer flowers. In Rajasthan, the nearest relief from the desert heat is Mount Abu. Near Bombay, there are Matheran, Mahabeleshwar, and Pune hill stations. In the South, the Nilgiris and Cardamom Hills offer cool, refreshing peace at the Ooty and unspoilt Kodaikanal hill stations and in the richly forested wildlife parks.

THE HARD FACTS Hotels should be booked well in advance for the peak season, November-February, and especially at Christmas.

Beware of the sun: it is very powerful. Pack the full quota of full-strength suntan lotions, after-sun lotions and sun-burn lotions. Even Goa fails to overcome import problems to have good brands on sale. Indian beaches are usually very clean (with the exception of hippy ones at Goa and Kovalam and the beach at Puri), but take some antiseptic to put on any cuts. One or two hotels have in-house doctors who supply soothing camomile lotion for sunburn and prickly heat, although it is worth packing some of that, too.

A Sony Walkman and a few tapes are good for relaxing music and a little radio can pick up All-India Radio, the BBC World Service or blasts of the latest local Indian film music. Remember to pack plenty of batteries for both. You will have to take a supply of reading matter, so stock up in the big cities. Beach hotel bookshops, where they exist, are not good.

Newspapers, weeklies and glossy magazines are luxuries and eyed greedily on your arrival. Eventually a fellow guest will ask to borrow them. Even Goa, an hour's plane-hop from international Bombay, can easily get many days behind with the *International Herald Tribune*.

Despite the miles and miles of glistening white sands on the Coromandel and Malabar coasts, it is wiser by far to stick to the hotel area for scantily clad sun bathing, to avoid offending locals. It is not considered polite to scamper across Madras sea front or Bombay's Chowpatty beach in a bikini. And it is best to be sensitive to local approval or disapproval on the quieter, but irresistible, stretches of sand. Beware of the under-current in some places, which can be quite strong, so check with the hotel or local fishermen before taking a dip.

Goa

THE HARD FACTS It is possible to go all the year round as Goa is very beautiful during the monsoon (June-September), but certainly best November-February. The pre-Advent Carnival at Panaji (February-March) is a pale shadow of the former colourful and exotic spectacle, and locals do not hold out hope for its improvement, whatever the tourist literature might say.

Getting to and from Goa is easy. Flights go from Bombay and Bangalore to Dabolim, Goa's airport. The steamer trip between Panaji in Goa and Bombay may be revived, but if so the accommodation will be bad and the route is likely to remain well out to sea and not to stop at ports, making it a boring journey. Car drives are especially beautiful across the Western Ghats from Hampi or, harder work, along the unspoilt coast down from Bombay (see p. 155) or up from Mangalore. (Beware: taxi fares Bombay-Goa and Goa-Bombay can be exorbitant; it is best to shop around outside the hotel and ensure the price includes all permits and border taxes.) Train journeys from Bangalore and Bombay take over 20 hours (to Delhi about 46 hours), but they are cheap and the scenery is beautiful; and the train from Hubli winds its way over the hills to create a journey of 'spectacular views, waterfalls, gorges, cliffs, tunnels and viaducts'. Those staying at the three Taj hotels should hop off their train at Goa-Margaon, rather than going on to Gao-Vasco da Gama.

Tourist Information is found in Panaji. The Government of India Tourist Office is at Communicada Building, Church Square (tel: 3412), and is very good. Goa Tourist Office, in the Tourist Home, Pato (tel: 5583) and next to the Kadamba Bus Stand (tel: 4132), is less good. Goa Tours and MGM International Travels (tel: 2150) are both reliable, and Dempo Travel Agent on the waterfront by the Customs House is good, too, with helpful driver-guides. Good bookshops are Singbal Book Depot, Sarmalker Book Depot and those in hotels recommended below. Well worth buying Myriam Kaye's *An Illustrated Guide to Bombay and Goa* (Delhi and London, 1990).

THE BEACHES Over 100km of some of the most beautiful, palm-fringed beaches in the world. Certainly the longest quality stretch of silver sands in India. So there is no need to stick to the hotel's patch. If it is at all possible to grade these glimpses of Paradise into beautiful and more beautiful, then the 40km of Colva come tops: sparkling sand, coconut palms, calm clean sea and hardly a soul. Baga, north of Calangute, also rates very high; and Candolim, south of Calangute, is a new favourite with good hotels. At the moment, the smiling hippy population centres on Anjuna, Chapora and Calangute villages, attracting good little markets and restaurants, but their presence definitely discounts them from the Paradise stakes. The nicest way to move beaches is by boat and hotels with motor boats will zoom you a few km up the coast and collect you by boat or car later. Alternatively, use bicycles or taxis, but bargain hard.

WHERE TO STAY

There are dozens of hotels in Goa, not all of them good. The following is a selection of those which have consistently happy guests. As elsewhere in this book, the deluxe hotels are followed by a range of more modest, often family-run, ones.

Note: almost all hotels have a range of rates, the highest being for January-February, the lowest being June-September.

DELUXE HOTELS

Fort Aguada Beach Resort, Sinquerim, Bardez
Telephone: 87501-7; telex: 0194-291
Airport: 45km; Panaji port: 10km; railway station 55km (free transport to and from airport).
130 rooms, including 32 cottages, attached bath; all sea-facing. Single: Rs550-1,350; double Rs650-1,350 according to season.

All first-class facilities include pool, extensive and mature gardens with hammocks, bookshop, chemist, beauty salon, masseur, babysitter, doctor, fishing (salmon and mackerel), clay-pigeon shooting, scuba-diving, Beach Buggy and bicycles available, indoor restaurant, poolside barbecue and bar, beach café. Room service 7am-11pm only.

Sports and Fitness Complex: water skiing, sailing, para sailing, wind surfing (9am-6pm); 2 tennis courts (one floodlit), badminton, squash, volleyball, basket ball, full gymnasium, hydrotherapy (steam and sauna rooms, whirlpool), beauty parlour (men and women), billiards.

The best beach hotel complex in India, built and run by the Taj Group. Guests here and at the neighbouring Aguada Hermitage and Taj Holiday Village (see below) can use all the above facilities. Each hotel has a different mood, so you can stay a few days at each, mixing luxury (here), utter luxury (Hermitage) and a simpler lifestyle (Village). Fort Aguada has beautiful, low-lying architecture that sprawls up the hillside from seemingly endless Calangute Beach, incorporating the beachside ruins of the 17th century Portuguese fort (sensational sunset views). Opened 1974, enlarged 1983. Local Goan furniture throughout; good food; dolphins frolic in the sea at sunrise; hammocks for afternoon siestas. Recent complaints of poolside barbecues being marred by loud piped Western music.

The Taj Holiday Village, Sinquerim, Bardez
Telephone: 87514-7; telex and access as for Fort Aguada.
144 rooms (some air-conditioned) arranged in cottages of 1-3 bedrooms, all with bath and balcony. Rates per person Rs350-1,500, according to season and whether a-c or not. Goan-style cottages are clustered amid the palms, right by the

beach and next to Fort Aguada, with their own giant swimming pool and informal bar and restaurant (Goan and Portuguese food). Room service limited to hampers for breakfast, tea and cocktails. Very relaxed, perfect for a romantic escape to simple peace and privacy with excellent facilities nearby (guests have the use of Fort Aguada). Beware: walls are thin, so ensure a shared cottage has a fellow guest with similar ideas of quiet and loud hours of the day and night; also, chipmunks and sparrows invite themselves into the rooms. Furthermore, in high season this village becomes more of a true resort, and one recent visitor described her stay as 'little more like an up-market Butlins with more coach parties than we had been led to believe'.

Aguada Hermitage (for booking, communications, access and facilities, see Fort Aguada)
40 air-conditioned suites in deluxe Villas, each with living room, bedroom, bathroom, balcony/verandah and private garden. Price per villa Rs1,150-5,000 according to season and villa type.

One suite per villa, except for 3 which have 2 suites each. So utter luxury and utter privacy on the slopes above Fort Aguada. Room service stops at 11pm. Contact with the outside world is by telephone or in chauffeur-driven courtesy cars down to Fort Aguada.

Hotel Oberoi Bogmalo Beach, Bogmalo, Dabolim
Telephone: 2191 3311-5; telex: 0191-297
Airport 2km; Panaji port 30km; railway station 7km
118 rooms on 8 floors, all with sea view, small balconies and attached bath; currently enlarging for conference facilities. Single Rs650-1,400; double Rs775-1,400, according to season; some week-end package deals.

Tip-top facilities include baby-sitter, beauty salon, video room, large pool with children section, fully equipped gymnasium and health club (sauna, Turkish bath, aryavaidya oil massage), tennis, volley-ball, 9-hole golf course, wind-surfing, para-sailing, water-skiing, scuba-diving, water polo, yoga classes; arrangements for speed-boat and river cruises, fishing, bicycles, treks to nearby villages; good Goan dishes and local sea-food served at indoor restaurant; poolside and beach barbecues, snacks and bar (daily live music); full 24-hour room service.

It is built right on a secluded beach near a tiny Goan fishing village, about 10 minutes from the airport. The beach is good but small by Goan standards; the pool area quite small and lacks lawns. However, beach sports and water sports are excellent here. Health fanatics rave over the gymnasium's exercise machines and the health club's massages. And Colva Beach, one of the most sensational in all Goa, is very near.

Cidade de Goa, Vainguinim Beach, Dona Paula
Telephone: 3301-8; telex: 0194-257
Airport 26km; Panaji port 7km; railway station 45km
101 rooms including 4 suites, all sea-facing, with balcony and bath. Single Rs600-1,350; double Rs700-1,400, according to season. Excellent facilities include all mod. cons plus beauty salon, health club (sauna, massage), yoga club, two swimming pools (freshwater and salt-water), video films and games, tennis, table tennis, indoor games, wind-surfing, water polo, fishing, motor launch excursions; bicycles, motor bikes and cars for hire; arrangements for hiking, trekking, shooting and frog-catching (a Goan rainy season pastime); restaurant serves very good Goan, Portuguese and Mughlai dishes, coffee shop extends on to poolside terrace, bar (local musicians), poolside buffet.

Another piece of Charles Correa architecture (see Kovalam, below), this time with clear, crisp lines, rooms opening on to courtyards and terraces down to the sea, described by Correa as 'Moorish casbah concept' but approved by guests as 'very beautiful, like a Portuguese fishing village; lovely landscaping'.

Rooms are designed in three styles using local furniture: Gujarati, Portuguese and the Goan Damao; restaurant decoration by the Indian cartoonist, Mario, a Goan whose drawings are found in almost every Indian glossy magazine.

STOP PRESS ON DELUXE HOTELS
Stop press: the following two five-star deluxe hotels opened recently but, according to reports, each 'instantly works'. Each is part of an up-market international hotel chain which has provided 'every facility you can think of' and installed its own top management to create dream holiday beach resorts – competition for the Indian chains. Both are set on magnificent beaches, 50 minutes' drive south from Panaji airport, Margao is the local railway station. They are four miles apart, just about walkable for a change of deluxe scenery and a taste of a different restaurant, then a taxi back.
The Leela Beach, Mobor Beach
Telephone: 23873/4, 23038; fax: 834 221203; telex: 196 258
160 rooms and villas overlooking an artificial lagoon. Rooms US$50-195, according to season. Part of the Leela Kempinski Group.

On a 65-acre site the peach-painted Portuguese villas are set amid plenty of space for privacy and trees for rest; ideal for a family holiday; all run smoothly by the Dutch manager.
The Ramada Renaissance Resort, Colva Beach
Telephone 23611; fax bookings to Bombay headquarters no. 445225.
118 rooms all with sea views and balcony. Singles US$43-81, doubles US$50-90; suites US$66-110. Part of the Ramada Group.

Low-rise buildings on a compact site, oozing German comfort and efficiency. Mr Meisslein currently rules as king, with a rod of iron. If service is central to happiness, this is your resort, although some might crave a little holiday liveliness.

MIDDLE RANGE HOTELS
Dona Sylvia Resort, Cavelossim, near Colva
Airport 40km; Panaji port 45km; railway station 15km.
Rooms Rs 400-795, according to season
All facilities and mod. cons.

Set in 25 acres south of Colva Beach on 'one of the most beautiful white beaches in the world', the rooms are low-lying villas blending Mediterranean and Goan styles. Perfect for privacy and beach relaxation. New, should mature well.
Majorda Beach Resort, Majorda, Salcette
Telephone: 207512/0203; telex: 0196-234
Airport 18km; railway station 8km
108 rooms, attached bath; central air-conditioning. Singles Rs605-1,185, doubles Rs715-1,185, according to season.

All mod. cons plus swimming pool, health club, gymnasium, squash, table tennis, Fun Centre with indoor swimming pool.
Like Dona Sylvia, located well south of Panaji, but near the pretty town of Margao.

MODEST HOTELS
The following, more modest hotels, have rates at roughly singles Rs300-450, doubles Rs400-600. Lack of deluxe facilities is well compensated by the peace and gentle atmosphere of a smaller hotel run by a helpful Goan family.
Prainha Cottages, Dona Paula; information and booking address: Palmar Beach Resorts, 1st Floor, Glendela, Rua de Ormuz, Panaji
Telephone: 4004
13 cottages linked together, each with attached shower and verandah. No air-conditioning, communal dining-room, car/motorbike/bicycle rental. This is perfect for a quiet time, away from the jet set. These simple, newly renovated cottages are patronised by discerning diplomats and other old India hands. They are set on a very secluded beach (black sand) on a rocky part of the coast, well run, spotlessly clean; run by Aires Dias, whose brother runs the excellent O Pescador restaurant about 50m away. A bicycle or car gets you to endless golden beach in minutes.
Hotel Fidalgo, 18th June Road, Panaji
Telephone:6291-9; telex: 0191-213
123 rooms, attached bath and central air-conditioning, with plenty of facilities such as pool, health club and a choice of restaurants. This and the following Ronil Beach Resort are for the sociable holiday-maker on a modest budget.
Ronil Beach Resort, Baga Beach

Telephone: 2268

82 rooms with attached bath, arranged in eight buildings around the central pool and lawns; ideal for a jolly, sociable holiday at a modest price.

The following guest houses are all well run, clean, with cosy atmosphere and located on Candolim Beach, between Calangute and Aguada: *Surfside Guest House, Conqueiral Holiday Home* (beautiful Goan architecture), *Schubet's Manor* and the d'Souza family's *Holiday Beach Resort* right on the sands.

OUT AND ABOUT Goa is very un-Indian. Its history stretches back to the Mauryan Empire of the 3rd century BC. Then followed a string of distant rulers such as the Chalukyas, Vijayanagars, Bahmanis and the Adil Shahis of Bijapur. But its character today was determined by the Portuguese rule from 1510 to 1961. There is a strong Portuguese flavour about everything, from the Konkan language to the pretty floral dresses worn by locals. And the interesting sights are Portuguese too, including some fine churches.

Be warned: moving around Goa needs much patience since the Nehru Bridge has collapsed, its successor collapsed before completion and the ancient ferries brought into use operate at a lazy, on-holiday speed with frequent delays.

Panaji has pretty narrow streets, attractive buildings and cafés. Old Goa has Se Cathedral, the Basilica of Bom Jesus and the Convent and Church of St Francis of Assisi, which has beautiful murals and an excellent museum round the back (selling S. Rajagopalan's good booklet, *Old Goa*). Slightly separate from this group is the Baroque Church of St Cajetan, built by 18th century Italian friars in the Greek cross style. The nicest way of getting from Panaji to Old Goa is by ferry: breakfast in a Panaji café, lunch on board, Old Goa sights early evening before taxi back to the hotel or on to a restaurant. Most of the other ferry rides are equally pretty. It does not really matter where they go: there is always a nice walk, a nearby beach or a village taverna the other end.

Margao town, in the south, still smells strongly of the Portuguese, and the surnames of the big families are Alvares, Rebello, Silva, Figueiredo and Miranda. They own some of the most beautiful of the large, old Portuguese houses here and at nearby Loutolim, now lived in by the descendants of those who built them 400 years ago, their very fine interiors a mixture of Portuguese, Indian and Chinese skills. The exceedingly hospitable owners patronise the hotels for dinner, and often invite foreign tourists back to these wonders. Quite a different sort of sight-seeing is to go north from Panaji to Mapusa for the colourful weekly market, where Indian and Portuguese products are laid out side by side.

One of the most exciting things to do is to go out with the fishermen. Your hotel room boy normally has at least one relative who is a fisherman and he will fix it up. The long day starts early, but you are usually given some of the catch at the end.

RESTAURANTS It is tempting to stick to an exotic diet of superbly cooked seafood – lobster, giant prawns, oysters, crabs, mussels, shrimps, etc. Local Indianised Portuguese dishes are also delicious, such as chourisso (Goan sausage), sarpotel (pig's liver) and suckling pig. All the hotels mentioned above have good indoor and outdoor restaurants. They will also cook anything bought – or caught – oneself. In the hotels, an evening at the rustic *Taj Village* is especially nice, with between-course strolls along the sands; the *Bogmalo* is especially good for Goan dishes. Across the bridge from Panaji, the *O Coqueiro* at Porvorim is the best of all for unusual Goan dishes.

The current best seafood restaurants in towns are *La Paz* and *Zuari Hotel*, both at Vasco, *Hotel Madnovi's* on D B Bandodkar Road, Panaji, and *Longuinhos Bar & Restaurant* at Margao. On the beaches, there is *O Pescador* at Dona Paula (see Prainha Cottages hotel, above), the *Dolphin Restaurant* and *Matol Baiai do Sol* are the best of several on Colva; *St Anthony's Bar & Restaurant* on Calangute, *Martin's Beach Corner* at Caranzalem, and the *O Coqueiro* at Bardez.

Local Goan wines are much cheaper than the Indian Golconda and Bosca, but local **feni** is the thing to try. There used to be whole villages devoted to making it, such as Bogmalo village, where every house had a distillery. Feni is made from either the cashew apple or the coconut palm and usually sold after the first distillation. But in the Bogmala tavernas, double distilled feni is served, the second distillation flavoured with cumin, ginger, etc., and producing a smooth liqueur. Try asking for cumin seed palm feni or sasaparilla palm feni, made from a medicinal root.

SHOPPING The traditional Portuguese work in malachite with gold filigree is cheap and pretty, often sold in sets of necklace, earrings and rings. Platinum beads set in gold are typical Goan Christian jewellery and the fisherwomen still buy chains of it as a form of security, to prevent their men getting at the savings. Another Christian tradition is to make roses out of coral. Find all these, of good quality, at Sirsat Jewellers, Panaji. For shopping and colour, the Friday market at Mapusa is excellent: every sort of fish, spice, sausage, flower and vegetable for sale, as well as delicious fresh cashew nuts and quantities of appliqué work including Banjara tribal work, and Gujarati wedding hangings.

Coromandel Coast

THE HARD FACTS These sparkling beaches, where the fishermen launch their catamarans at dawn, are on the east coast of Tamil Nadu state, south of Madras, at Covelong and Mahabalipuram. Their beauty rivals Goa's, exceeding it for some visitors. Both recommended hotels have huge, empty beaches one side and the good coastal road behind them, providing the perfect combination of relaxing on the beach with sightseeing to some of the real wonders of India. No other Indian resort has this combination.

Best season is November-February, when fair skin still turns lobster red in less than an hour. After then, the really sizzling heat begins and there are liable to be water shortages. Beware of the east coast undertow of the Bay of Bengal and always check before swimming. As a result of this danger, a hotel swimming pool is an important asset but, if possible, check near the time of arrival that it is filled – there have been cases of empty seaside pools in November. Very easy access to the main three resort hotels: fly or train to Madras, then drive south for about an hour. Madras is the base for information, entertainment (Bharata Natyam dance) and shopping (See p. 239).

WHERE TO STAY
The Fisherman's Cove, Covelong Beach, Chingleput District, Tamil Nadu
Telephone: 6268; telex: 41-7194
Airport 36km; railway station 35km; central Madras 30km
100 rooms and cottages, all with attached bath. Single Rs750-1,000; double Rs850-1,100, according to season.

All mod. cons plus swimming pool, spacious lawns, new tennis court, table tennis, chess, children's playground, fishing, boating, rowing, horse riding, daily video films; restaurants in hotel and on beach. Live bands at weekends.

Three-storey hotel built in 1974 by the Taj Group, well decorated with local cane chairs and roll-up blinds, all providing local and restful atmosphere. The circular cottages are right on the beach, at the bottom of the hotel lawns, their verandahs looking directly on to dazzling white sand and sea; described as 'heaven' by several guests. The pool, set amid a mature garden, is a major advantage when it is dangerous to swim (occasionally emptied); check at any Taj office on arrival in India. Glorious walks along the totally empty beach; starlit cocktails on the lawns; tandoori prawns and 'the largest lobsters I've ever seen' at beach café. One recent visitor reported: 'We're not beach people, but this is the most beautiful beach we have ever seen, far more so than any at Goa'. Management still unreliable, but efforts afoot to improve.

VGP Golden Beach Resort, Injambakkam Village, Madras
Telephone: 412893/414701/414791; telex: 41-444
Airport 25km; railway station 20km; central Madras 10km
58 rooms, including 3 suites, bath attached. Tariff on application; some rooms do not have air-conditioning and are about 40% cheaper.

Facilities include car rental, travel agent, beauty salon, camel and horse fun rides; restaurant and coffee shop.

Very well placed for nipping into Madras and sited on another very quiet stretch of beautiful beach, some rooms arranged as cottages on stilts. Again, a hotel enjoyed by the Madrasis for its food. Reports say that it is great fun, like Hollywood gone mad, a mixture of Butlin's and a Bombay talkie. Madrasi families come on hols, out to enjoy themselves: magicians entertain the children, sareed women dance in the waves and they all picnic in the large gardens amid huge models of outsize animals.

OUT AND ABOUT A huge quantity of fascinating things to see on the doorstep (see pp. 239-47).

Malabar Coast

THE HARD FACTS There are just two isolated beach resorts in the 1,000km of western coastline between Goa and Kanya Kumari. Kovalam is on the Malabar Coast near the tip of India, just outside Trivandrum in lush Kerala. Mangalore, the other, is less developed but an interesting town at the southern corner of dry Karnataka state, not far from the sensational Hoysala temples. The Malabar climate is softer than the Coromandel's. Its season stretches September-April; monsoon and humidity last from May to August. Access is easy: for Kovalam, a plane or train to Trivandrum (see South chapter) or the goal of a drive through Kerala or Tamil Nadu; for Mangalore, a plane or the goal of a drive from Bangalore or Mysore, or along the coast.

KOVALAM, KERALA

WHERE TO STAY
Kovalam Ashok Beach Resort, Kovalam, Trivandrum, tel: 68010/65323; telex: 0435-216. Airport 19km; railway station 14km; central Trivandrum 13km. 125 rooms, including 2 suites, plus *Halcyon Castle*, 40 cottages, and 16 detached units, all with bathroom attached. Hotel: single Rs950, double Rs1,100, suite Rs2,200; Halcyon Castle deluxe suite Rs900; cottage or unit: single Rs825, double Rs975.

Good facilities and all mod. cons plus large

pool, tennis courts, table tennis, chess, excellent and extensive yoga and massage centre, water sports (water-skiing, motor boats, paddle boats, etc.). Disadvantages: the centralised air-conditioning tends to be fridge-cold; the double rooms have a bath tub, singles have just a shower; Halcyon Castle has no room service; poolside barbecue Sat. evenings only.

The showpiece for the government-run Ashok Group has a glorious site and a fine building, and service is reportedly improving. Charles Correa's beautiful design won him an award from the Royal Institute of British Architects. The lobby and public rooms, including the swimming pool and a large terrace which faces out west over the sheer cliff, are at the top of the hillside site. The view is remarkable at all times, especially sunset. The rooms drop down the hillside to the beach, each room with its own very large balcony (which cannot be overlooked), good views and local coir and cane furnishings. Halcyon Castle, above the hotel, lacks room service and doubles with the business meeting rooms. But good reports of Kovalam Grove, the cluster of self-contained cottages right down on the beach, each with terrace, refrigerator (room service for breakfast and tea only), surrounding another swimming pool and snack bar.

Fishermen launch their catamarans on the long beach at 7am, returning 4-5pm and others fish from the shore using huge nets. The beach area near the hotel is cordoned off from hawkers and furnished with life guards (take advice from them on sea current; they can also fix up trips with fishermen – the hotel will cook any lobster and crabs caught), changing huts and bar for drinks and Indian snacks. Past bad service and bad food are improving, slowly; but room furnishings need maintenance.

If the advantages do not outweigh the disadvantages, there is a cluster of simple, atmospheric, friendly, family-run hotels in the bay south of Kovalam. Try the *Moonlight Guest House* on Kovalam Beach's back bay; *Rockholm Seaside Hotel* set on the rocks by the lighthouse between two good beaches, with an excellent restaurant; *Hotel Palmanova* suitably palm-surrounded, right on the beach; and the unfortunately named *Hotel Seaweed*, five minutes' walk from the beach but friendly and with good food.

OUT AND ABOUT For the sights of Trivandrum, Padmanabhapuram and Kanya Kumari, see pp. 237-9. The nearby hippy beaches have lots of cheap and cheerful café-restaurants serving delicious fresh crab.

MANGALORE, KARNATAKA
THE HARD FACTS The Konkal coast of Karnataka is still almost entirely free of tourists. Best season September-May. Certainly, the nicest way to arrive is along the beautiful coast road from Goa (about 370km) or Cochin (about 450km), which was compared to the Cote d'Azur before it was exploited. And the drive across from the glorious Hoysala temples (about 150km), Mysore (220km) or Bangalore (320km) is pretty too. Alternatively, there are direct flights to Mangalore from Bombay and Bangalore.

WHERE TO STAY
Summer Sands Beach Resort, Chotamangalore, Ullal, Mangalore; tel: 6253/6284. Airport 30km; railway station 12km; central Mangalore 10km. 128 rooms, including 64 suites, arranged in 42 cottages, bungalows and family houses, all with bath attached. Single Rs110; double Rs155; suite Rs190. Only 29 units have air-conditioning; rates cheaper without. Off-season discount.

Facilities include all mod. cons plus good swimming pool, deep sea fishing, sailing by arrangement, mini golf, tennis court, health club (massage, hydraulic bath); poolside and beach restaurants.

The cottages, bungalows and houses are built in the local architectural style amid coconut groves, overlooking the Arabian Sea; larger units have sitting room and terrace. Good pool and excellent, empty beach (patrolled to preserve privacy). Restaurant lit by lanterns serves well-prepared local Konkan dishes including seafood (fish, prawns, sometimes lobster), and the toddy and feni liquors.

An alternative is Welcomgroup's *Manjaran*, Bunder Road, Old Port, Mangalore (tel: 31791; telex: 832-316). Airport 8km. 100 rooms (many with view), all mod. cons, pool, restaurants include poolside barbecue. Although it overlooks the sea and the harbour, this is not a beach hotel and fellow guests are likely to be businessmen rather than holidaymakers.

OUT AND ABOUT Apart from the empty beaches up and down the coast, the old part of Mangalore is fascinating. Its strong Christian influence goes back to St Thomas and his disciples colonised St Mary's Isles, where Vasco da Gama arrived 14 centuries later. French, Italian and German Christians have left their mark, too. So seek out the old city centre of Milagres, Rosario Cathedral close to the old port, and the 19th-century St Aloysius Chapel inspired by Rome's Sistine Chapel. Also, you can ask the hotel to arrange a visit to the palatial colonial Chateau de Lou (open by request), described by architect Charles Correa as 'the pièce de résistance of colonial architecture'; and also ask to hear the choir of Balmatta Musical Association.

Further afield, the Hoysala glories of Belur

and Halebid are not far, nor are the Jain statues at Karkala and Venus (53km). For a boat trip, the local fishermen of Ullal will take hotels guests out for the day. Your hotel will advise on finding the local Bayalata-Yakshagana (local song and dance), Korikatta (cock-fighting) and Thalim (martial arts using daggers and firebrands). Mangalore has its own special food, including suckling pig, special pork 'leitao', a hot pork and mutton dish cooked in green spices called sorpatel, and, of course, plenty of dishes using the cashewnuts grown nearby. In Mangalore, shopping is best at Hampankatta for local crafts using coir, jute, banana and pineapple, as well as feni and fresh cashewnuts and coffee.

OFF-BEAT BEACHES Since these are unlikely to be the sole destination of a visitor but rather a night or two between some adventurous sightseeing, they are included in the main text, above. Hotel buildings are often glorious, if unsophisticated in services; and beaches are likely to be empty of all but the old local fisherman or early stroller. It is essential to pack all sun-soaking equipment, and to check currents carefully before swimming.

See Introduction to this chapter and pp. 152, 166, 198-202 and 221.

Sri Lanka (Ceylon)

Apart from Goa, the most sophisticated and best equipped beach resort hotels for India holiday-makers are here. Sri Lanka means Resplendent Land. It is highly accessible. Despite current political unrest in the north of the island, planeloads of sunseekers arrive from all over the world to escape winter and pep up their tans on the south-west beaches. A few days of flopping on a Sri Lankan beach can easily be tagged on to the front or back of an Indian holiday. Sri Lanka's beaches are magnificent but there is much more – a people, language, history and culture that are all outside the orbit of this book.

THE HARD FACTS There are no formalities or visas required for holders of Commonwealth, European or United States passports for stays less than 30 days. To avoid the monsoon, head for the south-west coast December-March and the north-east coast April-September. Access is easy: direct to Colombo on international flights; direct connections with India between Colombo and Madras, Bombay, Tiruchchirapalli and Trivandrum. The airport has a good tourist desk, car rental, hotel reservations desk and bank for buying Sri Lankan rupees (Indian rupees should be left in India).

To find out more, the best guide book is Tony Wheeler's *Sri Lanka, a travel survival kit* (Lonely Planet, 1982 and later editions). For full information, contact the Sri Lanka Tourist Board at 13 Hyde Park Gardens, London W2 (tel: 262 5009).

For all its social sophistication, some basics still cannot be bought in Sri Lanka, so pack as for Goa (see above), adding anti-mosquito preparations (absolutely essential, sticks better than aerosol, Autan is a good brand) and a jumper for going up into the hills. Suntan lotion is imported, but not on sale everywhere.

WHERE TO STAY
The coast of Sri Lanka is bursting with hotels. They come in all sizes, characters and qualities. As in Goa, off-season prices plummet from May to October, and tariffs even in high season can be negotiated. Those listed below are at the top of the market and recommended on their merits as beach hotels alone: good beach, swimming, facilities, food and service. When making reservations, it is best to confirm that the hotel will arrange collection from the airport. All are on the south-west coast and thus good December-March. The first three lie south of Colombo, the next two north of it, and the last one right by the capital. When the north-east coast becomes accessible again, it is, if anything, even more beautiful but less developed.

Triton Hotel, Ahungalla
Telephone: 97.228/218; telex: 21142
125 rooms, including suites, bath attached.

Facilities include all mod. cons plus health club, exceptionally good pool, tennis, badminton, billiards, indoor games; several restaurants and bars indoors and outdoors, barbecues.

Sri Lanka's current top hotel, a bold design by Geoffrey Bawa who was also architect for the new parliament complex in Colombo. Buildings open direct on to the long beach, with no buildings either side.

Tangerine Beach Hotel, Kalutara
Telephone: 42.2640/2295; telex: 211889
167 rooms, including 7 suites, bath attached.

Facilities include all mod. cons plus large pool, 2 tennis courts, water gardens; plentiful restaurants and bars.

Well-designed hotel with particularly nice rooms and pool area, set amid the palms of a 12-acre, landscaped coconut property. Faces on to a wide, clean, 500m-long beach protected from the quite rough sea of the south-west coast by a coral reef.

Bentota Beach Hotel, Bentota
Telephone: 48.5176/5266; telex: 21104
135 rooms, attached bath.

Facilities include all mod. cons plus gymnasium, health club, pool, water-skiing, boating, river cruises up the lagoon, mini-golf, tennis; good restaurants.

A slightly older hotel built on the site of a Portuguese fort, with beautiful views over the lagoon on one side and the sea on the other. Just near the hotel is Brief, the home of the elderly landscape artist, Bevis Bawa, open to the public. His house is a museum of antique furniture and contemporary works of art, set in a most lovely garden.

The Dolphin On The Beach, Waikkal
Telephone: 031.3129; telex: 21601
76 rooms, all with balcony or patio and bathroom.

Facilities include all mod. cons plus enormous pool, sailing, boating, wind-surfing, water-scooters, water-skiing, deep-sea fishing, 8-hole golf course, 2 tennis courts, billiards, squash, table tennis; indoor and outdoor restaurants and bars include Sri Lankan cuisine.

New hotel conveniently near the airport for a short stay, the buildings arranged in four clusters amid 8 acres of landscaped gardens reaching down to the private beach. Boasts one of the biggest pools in Asia: five linked pools along the facade, the central one with water jets, making a total of 25,000 sqft.

Brown's Beach Hotel, 175 Lewis Place, Negombo
Telephone: 31.2031-2; telex: 21552
132 rooms, bath attached.

Facilities include all mod. cons plus pool and good food.

One of the older beach hotels, with a gentle atmosphere and a pretty beach garden. Negombo is particularly interesting, having retained its strong Dutch character (it was their vital cinnamon port) in the fort, lagoon rest house and in the many canals and churches; the British influence seems to be restricted to weekend cricket matches on the green beside the fort, watched from the shade of the great banyan tree. Still a flourishing port, the fishermen bring in boatloads of lobster, crabs and prawns, to be auctioned on the beach and sold at the fishmarket.

Taj Samudra Hotel, Galle Face Centre Road, Colombo
Telephone: 546622l telex: 21279
400 rooms, including 28 suites, bath attached. Part of the Taj Group, so bookable in India or London (see p. 12).

Facilities include all mod. cons plus health club with gymnasium and sauna, attractive pool, tennis and squash; also a well-equipped business centre; restaurants and bars include a coffee shop and barbecue.

Located on the beach on the magnificent 11 acre site of the old Colombo Club, it is within easy reach of the city centre.

OUT AND ABOUT A car plus driver is even cheaper than in India, but it is important to establish the price and the overnight and meals rates before leaving base. Colombo has everything a capital should have and is worth a visit:

fort, harbour, bazaars, National Museum, churches, new parliament buildings, good shopping and old hotels to take sustenance in, such as the *Galle Face* (built 1856) and the *Taprobane* (at the port, good views from fourth floor restaurant). Good restaurants in Colombo include *Cosmopolite, Alfred House Gardens, Colombo 5*, run by a French-Vietnamese couple; *Renuka* in Galle Road and *Galle Face Hotel* (both for curry).

There is plenty to buy, above all the gems from Ratnapura. The cheaper moonstones, quartz (all colours, lemon, smoky, rose, brown), garnets and the more pricy sapphires, star rubies, cat's eyes and aquamarines are all best bought at the hotel shops, not in the back streets. The State Gem Corporation at 24 York Street, Colombo, is reliable and has several branches including one at Bentota Beach Resort. All their gems are guaranteed and they will also inspect gems you may be wishing to buy from other shops, to confirm they are what they purport to be.

Pretty sarongs for the beach are very cheap, as are local masks, batik work, basketry and clutch bags woven in all colours, all found in Laksala, the Sri Lanka government emporium. Tailors are very cheap and good and will copy clothes, but the Indian fabric is better than the rather coarse Sinhalese cotton. Barbara Sansoni's excellent Barefoot shop in Galle Road, Colombo (another branch in the Intercontinental Hotel, Colombo) can arrange a tailor if it proves tricky to find one.

North from Colombo lies *Negombo* fishing village, past a Dutch canal, Portuguese churches and palms (see Brown's Beach Hotel, above). South is *Galle*, with a big Dutch fort, the charming *New Oriental Hotel* (tel: 1684) for refreshment and, inland, the Sinharaja, the last primeval rainforest left in Sri Lanka. Southeast is the gem-mining capital, *Ratnapura*, with three gem museums and the gateway to the pilgrimage up the 2,243m Adam's Peak. Up into the hills, *Kandy* is a very pretty provincial town and former capital with a most beautiful nature reserve and glorious botanical gardens, very well maintained and considered one of the most important in the world. Stay at the colonial *Queen's, Swisse* or *Citadel* hotels.

For wildlife, there are four *national parks*: Yala, Walawe, Wilpattu and Gal Oya, each with a better chance of seeing animals if you stay overnight.

Republic of Maldives

A paradise of more than twelve hundred tiny coral islands off the south-west tip of India. Most islands are uninhabited but where there are natives they are mostly Muslim, proud and friendly. The islands that are open to tourists are all similar. Their size varies from small, about 3 sqkm, to tiny, about 700m by 120m. Each has simple cottage accommodation, swaying palm trees, the finest white coral sand and is surrounded by crystal clear water, ideal for skin diving and snorkelling.

Visitors find the marine life superior even to Thailand's and the Maldive government intend to keep it that way, strictly prohibiting hunting fish and collecting shells. Above the water activities are wind-surfing, some sailing and waterskiing, exploring uninhabited islands by boat and some fishing excursions. There is no night life, little jolly camaraderie and the simple food consists of a large dose of fish. People come here for total peace and privacy. The smaller the island, the greater the isolated paradise quietude and the simplicity of life. A recent report suggested the islands will be submerged beneath the rising ocean in a few decades' time; so go while they still exist.

THE HARD FACTS There are no formalities or visas required to visit the Maldives. Season November-April; showers but not heavy monsoon May-September. Access is by air to Hulule Airport at Male from Trivandrum and Colombo; then boat to the island you are staying on (2-7hrs) – so it is better to go for a week, or more. (Before catching the boat, it is worth looking at the recently restored coral temple in Male.)

There are now more than fifty resort islands, all of them offering something slightly different. Some have reefs close to the shore which are ideal for snorkelling; others have long stretches of shallow water over a sandy bottom, ideal for children but snorkellers have to take a boat out to the reef. Some islands are simple, others very luxurious – more so than the two Taj Group resorts. The easiest and most reliable way to book a hotel is through a tour operator who can obtain the latest, constantly changing information, and who will also coordinate the plane and boat connections. Alternatively, book up with the Taj hotel group, the only big chain operating in the Maldives so far, for one of their two island resorts. It is definitely better to book than just to turn up.

Pack a complete supply of reading, music, drawing, painting, games (chess, cards, etc.) and other pastimes, plus pre- and post-sun lotions and beach towels. A mask, snorkel and flippers are much cheaper at home than to buy or hire on site – although the water is so clear it is hardly necessary. And pack a bathing costume – nudity is frowned upon. And an airbed is ideal for floating on the still waters of the lagoons (again, expensive to hire on site). The best things to buy there are sarongs, flip-flop sandals and the very special black coral. There is a spirit licence for tourist islands but the rest of the Mal-

dives are dry; non-alcoholic drinks, even water, are extremely expensive – a recent visitor was paying the equivalent of $2 for a bottle of water, $1.50 for a can of Coke. The most useful currency is US dollars, although a local Maldive rupee currency exists. To find out more, Tony Wheeler's Sri Lanka guide (see above) has a supplement on the Maldives.

WHERE TO STAY
All the accommodation is arranged as cottage-bungalows strung along the beaches. The choice of island depends upon how remote you want to be from Male and how often you want to bump into fellow humans. Here is a short selection to choose from. Rooms range from US$70 to $200 and always include full board.
Villi Varu Island Resort, Vilingilivaru
and *Bi Ya Doo Island Resort, Biyadhoo*
The two Taj group resorts, both on South Male Atoll, are both bookable c/o Prabhalaji Enterprises Ltd, H Maagala, 2 Amir Ahmed Magu, Male; or through Taj Central Reservations (see p. 12). Tel: 960.343598 (Villi Varu) and 960.343516 (Bi Ya Doo); fax: 960.343742; telex: 77003. Airport 32km.

Villi Varu has 60 rooms, 36 of them with airconditioning; Bi Ya Doo has 96 rooms and full air-conditioning. Rooms US$70-125 according to season. Each room at both has hot and cold water and a refrigerator. Each resort has a swimming pool, diving base, wind-surfing, snorkelling and boat excursions; each has an air-conditioned restaurant and bar. The Bi Ya Doo is the plusher of the two. Elsewhere, with a few exceptions, the facilities tend to be very minimal – but that might be just what you are looking for. It is even possible to camp on uninhabited islands.
Other islands The following are some of the islands open to tourists, together with their distance from Male:

Bandos (15km); Baros (20km); Buduhithi Coral Islands (40km); Cacoa (22km); Forykolhufushi (5km), peace disturbed by the Male Club Mediterranée; Furana (10km); Helengeli (60km); Ihuru (22km); Kuramathi (45km), particularly rich in coral and fish life, Barakuda of Hamburg run the island's diving school; Kurumba (5km); Lhohifushi (35km); Meeru and Fenfushi (45km); Olhuveli (45km); Vabbin Faru (20km); Villingili (5km).

Andaman and Nicobar Islands (India)

A string of more than 300 almost virgin islands lie quietly in the Andaman Sea, east of the Bay of Bengal, hardly touched by modern civilisation. These are for the traveller who wants to play explorer between swims and snorkels, the under-water fanatic who thought the Maldives were good but wants to be more impressed, and the travel snob who enjoyed the beauties of Goa and the other resorts before the rest of the world knew where they were on the map. James Cameron called the archipelago 'about the most tranquil and beguiling place I ever visited. Golden, warm and empty beaches between un-polluted turquoise bays. There are very few re-maining places both wholly lovely and wholly unspoilt. And this is one of them.' This remains true.

The northern islands are the Andamans, with Port Blair as capital and a mixed population of aborigines, Burmese and Indians. The southern islands are the less accessible Nicobars, almost entirely inhabited by tribes. Thickly forested hills of teak, mahogany and rosewood stretch right down to the soft white sand that twinkles with finely shredded shells. Under the indigo blue and crystal clear sea, the coral and marine life are stunning.

As in the Maldives, the islands inhabited by the protected tribes are out of bounds to tourists. In the Andamans and Nicobars, this leaves only a dozen or so that are regularly open to visitors, plus others by arrangement. It is worth arriving with the special permits needed to visit these. On her trip there, Josceline Dim-bleby found the Andamans 'much more beauti-ful than Goa but very backward and not ready for tourists. There was a strange and wonderful atmosphere, as if we were eighteenth century explorers.'

THE HARD FACTS In theory, formalities for visitors have been considerably relaxed and it is possible, but difficult, to collect a permit on arrival at Port Blair airport or port. In practice, to avoid any possible delays, apply for a permit from your Indian Embassy or Consulate before leaving home. The permit is limited to two weeks. The completed forms, including re-quests to visit restricted areas, take only 48 hours to process if delivered personally and about two weeks by post. If an Andamans trip is decided upon in India, apply to the Foreigners' Registration Office in Bombay, Calcutta, New Delhi or Madras for a regular two-week permit, but to the Ministry of home Affairs, New Delhi for restricted areas.

Season is December-April, with monsoon May-October. A soft breeze cools the tropical climate slightly. Access is by air or sea. Flights connect Port Blair with Madras and Calcutta. The sea trip from Madras or Calcutta takes three days but it is not very picturesque, the boat is very hot and the water is often choppy. In addi-tion, there is no fixed timetable. However, to find out the next sailings and to book, contact The Shipping Corporation of India, 13 Strand Road, Calcutta or their Madras agents, K. P. V. Sheikh Mohammed Rowther & Co., 202 Linghi Chetty Street, Madras. The SCI also have an office in Bombay, at 229-232 Madame Cama Road.

The easiest way of going is with TCI, a most reliable Indian travel agent, who set up indivi-dual tours to the Andamans, using the Anda-man Beach Resort (see below) where they also have their Andamans office (tel: 2599/2781; cable: TRAVEL-AIDS). TCI's other offices are in all major cities. As with the Maldives, it is wiser to pack everything – German and Italian visitors are known to bring even their cooking utensils and a small Calorgas stove so that they can cook their fishing catch on the beach. Collecting coral is strictly forbidden.

WHERE TO STAY
Andaman Beach Resort, Corbyn's Cove, Port Blair
Telephone: 231881; telex: 2366. Rooms Rs500-675.
32 rooms, all with balcony and bathroom. Facil-ities include all mod. cons plus library, wind-surfing, water-skiing, sailing, scuba-diving, snorkelling, fishing, tennis court, croquet, vol-ley ball, table tennis, restaurant and bar.

A newish hotel, likened by one visitor to a government high school building. Views through a row of palms on to the crescent-shaped beach of Corbyn's Cove.
Bay Island, Marine Hill, Port Blair
Telephone: 2881. Rooms Rs500-900.
48 rooms, some air-conditioned, attached bath.

Facilities include transport counter, beauty salon, health club, doctor on call, sea-water pool, fishing, snorkelling, scuba diving, indoor games, video, restaurant.

Lavish new building, using local architectural traditions and furnishings, with pretty views overlooking Phoenix Bay. Restaurant serves good local fish dishes as well as Indian and Bur-mese food. The disadvantage: no beach by the hotel.

OUT AND ABOUT The archipelago has been called 'Paradise plus'. The plus stands for the flora and birds in the rich jungle. The Maldives are simply 'Paradise'. Early mornings are magical, as the mist lifts off the water and the islands come into focus while dolphins play in the water. In *Port Blair* there are interesting Anthropological and Marine museums, a bazaar and the Cottage Industries Emporium (shells, wood-carving). Hiring a boat can be tricky as there are not enough to supply the few tourists' needs. The harbour tour is not worth the effort; the British built, atmospheric Cellular Jail is. To eat in town, locals meet at the simple but clean *Dhanalakshmi Hotel* in *Aberdeen Bazaar*.

To avoid the problems of finding a boat and getting permission to visit other islands, the Andaman Beach Resort runs a variety of excursions, by road and boat, and the TCI desk will try to arrange any others. They include one to Chiriya Tapu at the southern tip of *South Andamans* where there is good fishing in the creeks, interesting bird life, mango groves and lovely beaches. Another trip goes to *Wandoor Beach*, where the sea is exceptionally rich for snorkellers and divers.

Boat trips include a day spent on uninhabited forest islands of Grub, Snob, Red Skin and Jolly Boy, all surrounded by beaches and excellent snorkelling and scuba-diving to see coral, tropical fish, shells and turtles in the clear waters. And fishermen can have their catch grilled on the beach. Another trip is to *Cinque*

Island, actually a group of islands, where you can camp overnight. Again, exceptionally clear water and rich marine life make ideal diving; the lush forested islands are rich in bird life and flora; and the fishing is good.

There are now just a few tribal groups left and, despite protection, the Indian government's current encouragement to immigrant farmers may mean they have little peace to look forward to. The gentle Onghies with naked, painted bodies live on Little Andaman. The more savage Jarwas live on the west coast of South Andaman, the Nicobaris on Car Nicobar and the Shompens on Great Nicobar. All these areas are worth trying to get permits for, as is Ross Island in Port Blair harbour, where the beautiful Raj buildings are being throttled by rampant vegetation and trees.

Calendar of Indian festivals

Thousands of festivals are held in India every year. The religious and national ones are celebrated with great gaiety. The cultural ones attract some of the many great Indian performers. Hardly a day passes in India without a festival taking place somewhere near where you are. They range from small, one-day village or temple celebrations to a fortnight of high quality arts performances or religious ritual. However, only a few have fixed dates. Hindu festivals follow the lunar calendar and their dates are only decided upon during the previous year. Some festivals are local to one area or one town. Even the national ones are best seen in certain cities, as indicated below. Most cultural festivals are held during the winter months.

By October of each year, your nearest Government of India Tourist Office will have available a list of the major festivals together with their dates for the following year.

Below are listed a few of the more colourful and interesting festivals, with their approximate dates, and the best places to witness them; refer to the Festivals sections of those cities or to the index to find more information. See Pakistan sections for their festivals.

January
Feast of the Three Kings January 6. Goa
International Film Festival Delhi on odd years (1987, etc.); another major city on even years (see Delhi)
Park Circus arts festival Calcutta
Tyagaraja music festival Thiruvaiyaru, near Thanjavur
Pongal (Sankranti): begins January 14 or 15. South India, especially Tamil Nadu (Madurai and Tiruchchirapalli)
Delhi Rose Show Safdar Jang's Tomb, Delhi
Kite Festival January 14. North India, especially Gujarat (Ahmedabad) and Rajasthan
Makara Sankranti 3-day festival of dolls in Hyderabad
Lori mid-January. Punjabi festival celebrating the height of winter
Rimpa music festival Varanasi
Republic Day January 26. Across India in state capitals; best in Delhi
Folk Dance Festival January 27-28. Delhi
Beating Retreat January 28/29. Delhi

January-February
Teepam (Floating Festival): Madurai
Desert Festival Jaisalmer

The livestock fair Nigaur, near Jodhpur
Vasant Panchami Across India but especially in the North (where it marks the first day of spring) and in Bengal (where it honours the goddess of learning, Saraswati)
Ulsavom 8-day festival includes elephant procession, dance and music. Shiva Temple, Ernakulam
Temple Car Festival Srirangapatnam, near Mysore

February
Feast of Our Lady of Candelaria Pomburpa February 2. Goa
Carnival Goa
Tansen music festival February in Delhi; December in Gwalior
Lucknow arts festival Lucknow
Dhrupad music festival Delhi
Maharaj Kalka Bindadi Kathak dance festival Delhi
Dhrupad music festival last week of month. Varanasi
Delhi Flower Show Purana Qila, Delhi
Desert Festival Created in 1979, a festival of Rajasthan culture held at Jaisalmer

February-March
Shankar Lal music festival Delhi
Shivarati February-March. Shaivites throughout India spend the whole night worshipping Shiva. Best at Mandi, Chidambaram, Khajuraho and Varanasi
Holi Across northern India but best in Rajasthan and especially in Mathura and surrounding villages
Nattiyanjali Festival Chidambaram
Mahashivaratri Shiva festival with car procession at Ramaswaram
Chariot Festival kanchipuram

March
Khajuraho dance festival Early March. Khajuraho
Jamshed Navroz New Year's Day for Parsees following the Falsi calendar, best witnessed in Maharashtra and Gujarat
Float Festival Teppakulam, in Tiruchchiapalli

March-April
Gangaur (Gauri Tritiya) Rajasthan, especially Udaipur and Jaipur, Bengal and Orissa (where it is called Doljatra)
Mahavir Jayanti A Jain festival dedicated to

Mahavira, 24th Tirthandara, best seen at Jain religious centres in Gujarat
Ramanavami Celebrations of the god Rama's birthday are held in temples throughout India
Lent Procession, all the saints of the Franciscan Third Order (the only other besides Rome), at Valhi in Goa
Ashokashtami 4-day Shiva festival at Bhubaneswar
Chandana Yatra, spring Vaisakla festival at Simhchalam
Elephant Festival Jaipur, coinciding with Holi
Ugadi New Year's Day, celebrated across India with local distinctions
Brahmotsavam 10-day festival at Ramaswaram
Shaivite Festival Madras

April-May
Pooram Trichur
Chitrai Festival, or Meenakshi Kalyanam Madurai
Spring Festival Celebrations in the orchards of almond blossom at Srinagar in Kashmir.
Baisakhi Across northern India and in Tamil Nadu, celebrating the Hindu solar New Year. Best seen in the Mughal gardens of Srinagar and in the Punjab where Sikhs celebrate Guru Gobind Singh's formation of Sikhs into the Khalso (the pure one) in 1689

May-June
Buddha Purnima On full moon night, Buddha's birth, enlightenment and his attainment of nirvana are celebrated at all Buddhist centres, such as Sarnath

June-July
Rath Yatra Puri
Car Festival Serempore
Hemis Festival Leh

July-August
Minjar Chamba
Teej Rajasthan, especially Jaipur
Nag Panchami Jodhpur
Amarnath Yatra On full moon, Amarnath, near Pahalgam
Jhapan Vishnupur, near Calcutta
Raksha Bandhan Across northern and western India, where girls tie rakhi (tinsel and silk amulets) around the wrists of men in memory of the god Indra's triumph in battle after his consort gave him a rakhi

August
Vishnu Digambar music festival Delhi
Independence Day August 15. Across India but best in Delhi

August-September
Janmashtami (Krishna's birthday) Celebrated across India; best seen in Mathura, Dwarka, Agra, Delhi and Bombay
Onam Throughout Kerala but best at Kottayam

Avani Moolam, the Meenakshi Temple, Madurai
Festival of Our Lady of Health Velankanni in Thanjavur
Kailash Fair Kailash, near Agra

September
Ganapati (Ganesh Chaturthi) Bombay
Bhatkande music festival Lucknow

September-October
Navrati Ahmedabad
Dussehra One of the most colourful of all festivals, celebrated across India. Best in Varanasi and Delhi (called Ram Lila in both), in Calcutta (called Durga Puja) in Mysore (called Dassehra) and in the Kullu Valley (where it begins the day it ends in the rest of India

October
Sadarang music festival Calcutta
Gandhi Jayanti (Mahatma Gandhi's Birthday) October 2. Across India
Karwa Chauth In Delhi, after a day of fasting, Hindu women dress up in wedding saris and make offerings to their mothers-in-law
Birth anniversary of Raja Raja Chola Thanjavur

October-November
Diwali Across India but best in Delhi and the North
Bali Yatra Festival and fair at Cuttack, Orissa, celebrating the ancient traders who sailed to Bali

November
Govardhana Puja Hindus throughout India worship the cows, their sacred animals
Sonepur fair The largest cattle fair in the world, lasting a month, is held at Sonepur in Bihar, on the banks of the Ganga
Shiva Festival Tiruvannamalai
Sangeet Sammelan music festival Delhi
Sir-Singar music festival Bombay
Lavi fair second week of November. Rampur
Nanak Jayanti The birthday of Guru Nayak, founder of the Sikh religion, is celebrated by Sikhs; best seen at Amritsar and Patna
Children's Day November 14, Jawaharlal Nehru's birthday, is celebrated by children throughout India
Desert Festival Bikaner's more modest answer to Jaisalmer's February festival

November-December
Pushkar cattle fair November-December. Pushkar
Ulsavom 8-day festival includes a daily elephant procession. Tripunithura Temple, Cochin

December
Lalit Sangit Parishad music festival Varanasi
Feast of St Francis Xavier December 3. Goa

Feast of Our Lady of Immaculate Conception December 8. Goa (Panaji and Margao)
Tansen music festival Gwalior
Paus Mela arts festival Santiniketan, Bengal
Christmas Day December 25. Across India but best in Delhi, Bombay, Goa and Calcutta
Shanmukhananda arts festival Bombay

December-January
Madras dance and arts festival mid December-early January. Madras
Kumbh Mela is the huge religious and commercial fair held every three years consecutively in one of four places: Allahabad (Uttar Pradesh), Nasik (Maharashtra), Ujjain (Madhya Pradesh), and Hardwar (Uttar Pradesh). Hindu pilgrims and every variety of Hindu holy man gather from all over India to cleanse themselves in holy water. The huge fair provides endless food, markets and entertainers. The next Kumbh Mela is at Nasik in 1992, then Ujjain in 1995
Chrysanthemum Show and Fete Delhi
Mohini Alankaram, Vaikunta Ekadasi and the *Car Festival* all at Sri Ranganathaswamy Temple, Srirangam
Margazhi Festival Srivilliputhur in Madurai

Muslim festival dates move right around the year, following the lunar calendar. The best places to witness them are the old Muslim centres of Lucknow, Old Delhi, Hyderabad and Ahmedabad. The principal ones are:
Ramadan (30 days of fasting)
Id-ul-Fitr (also called Ramzan-Id, celebrating the end of Ramadan)
Id-ul-Zuhar (also called Bakr-Id, commemorating Abraham's attempted sacrifice of Ishmael)
Muharram (10 days long, commemorating the martyrdom of Mohammed's grandson, Imam Hussain)

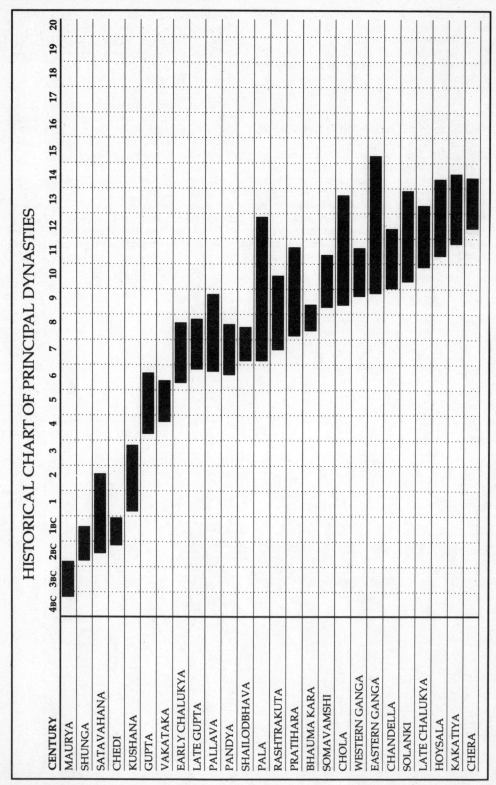

HISTORICAL CHART OF PRINCIPAL DYNASTIES

CENTURY	4BC	3BC	2BC	1BC	1	2	3	4	5	6	7	8	9	10	11	12	13	14	15	16	17	18	19	20
MAURYA
SHUNGA
SATAVAHANA
CHEDI
KUSHANA
GUPTA
VAKATAKA
EARLY CHALUKYA
LATE GUPTA
PALLAVA
PANDYA
SHAILODBHAVA
PALA
RASHTRAKUTA
PRATIHARA
BHAUMA KARA
SOMAVAMSHI
CHOLA
WESTERN GANGA
EASTERN GANGA
CHANDELLA
SOLANKI
LATE CHALUKYA
HOYSALA
KAKATIYA
CHERA

1947

© Copyright Louise Nicholson

Century	4BC	3BC	2BC	1BC	1	2	3	4	5	6	7	8	9	10	11	12	13	14	15	16	17	18	19	20

DELHI SULTANATE
BENGAL SULTANATE
VIJAYANAGARA
RAJPUT RULERS
JAUNPUR SULTANATE
GUJARAT SULTANATE
MALWA SULTANATE
BAHMANI SULTANATE
BARID SHAHI SULTANATE
ADIL SHAHI SULTANATE
QUTB SHAHI SULTANATE
MUGHAL
SURI SULTANATE
NAYAKA
PAHARI
TRAVANCORE RAJAS
MARATHA
SIKH
MALLA
WADIYAR
SETHUPATI
NAWABS OF ARCOT
NAWABS OF BENGAL
NAWABS OF OUDH
NIZAMS OF HYDERABAD
BRITISH INDIA UNDER
CROWN RULE

287

Key dates in India's history

BC
c324	Rise of Maurya dynasty
c273-236	Reign of Emperor Ashoka

AD
4th-6th C	Gupta dynasty
6th-8th C	Early Chalukya dynasty at its height (Deccan)
6th-9th and 12th-13th C	Pallava dynasty of South India at its height (capital Kanchipuram)
9th-13th C	Chola dynasty of South India at its height (capital Thanjavur); Rajaraja I rules 985-1014, Rajendra rules 1012-44
10th-12th C	Chandella dynasty at its height (temples at Khajuraho); Danga rules 950- 1002
10th-13th C	Solanki dynasty at its height (Gujarat)
10th-13th C	Late Chalukya dynasty at its height (Deccan)
1006-1310	Hoysala dynasty of South India at its height (capitals at Belur and Halebid)
1206-1526	Sultanate period (capitals Delhi and Agra)
1206-1290	Slave dynasty (capital Delhi)
1290-1320	Khilji dynasty (capital Delhi)
1320-1413	Tughlaq dynasty (capitals Delhi and Daulatabad)
1414-1451	Sayyid dynasty (capital Delhi)
1451-1526	Lodi dynasty (capital Delhi)
1336-1565	Vijayanagar empire in South India at its height (capital Vijayanagar)
14th-20th C	Rajput rulers
1347-c1489	Bahmani kingdom of the Deccan (capital Gulbarga, then Bidar)
1489-1686	Adil Shahi dynasty (capital Bijapur)
1502-1648	Lodi dynasty, then Mughal capital is at Agra
1512-1687	Qutb Shahi dynasty (capital Golconda, then Hyderabad)
1526	Battle of Panipat: Babur defeats Ibrahim Lodi, initiating the Mughal Empire
1527	Battle of Khanua: Babur defeats the Rajput confederacy
1526-1707	Great Mughal period (capitals Agra, Delhi and Lahore)
1526-1530	Reign of Mughal emperor Babur (lived 1483-1530)
1530-40 & 1555-6	Reign of Mughal emperor Humayun (lived 1508-1556)
1540-55	Reigns of Sher Shar Sur (died 1545) and his son, Islam Shar (capital Delhi)
1556-1605	Reign of Mughal emperor Akbar (lived 1542-1605)
1565	Battle of Talikota: The Deccan sultans ally to defeat the Vijayanagars
1568	Maharana Udai Singh moves the capital of Mewar to Udaipur after the third sack of Chitorgarh
1600	East India Company receives its trading Charter from Elizabeth I
1605-1627	Reign of Mughal emperor Jahangir (lived 1569-1627)
1612	British establish their first factory in India, at Surat
1627-1658	Reign of Mughal emperor Shah Jahan (lived 1592-1666)
1648	Triumphal entry of Shah Jahan into newly built Shahjahanabad (Old Delhi)
1632-1653	Shah Jahan builds the Taj Mahal at Agra
1639	East India Company establish a trading post at Madras
1661	Mumbadevi, the largest Bombay island, is part of Catherine of Braganza's dowry when she marries Charles II
1658-1707	Reign of Mughal emperor Aurangzeb (lived 1618-1707)
1690	Job Charnock founds British Calcutta
1699-1744	Reign of Maharaja Jai Singh II of Jaipur (laid out Jaipur in 1727)
1719-1748	Reign of Mughal emperor Mohammad Shah
1751	Battle of Arcot: The British, under Clive, defeat the French, under Dupleix
1757	Battle of Plassey: The British, under Clive, recapture Calcutta from the Nawab of Murshidabad

KEY DATES IN INDIA'S HISTORY

1759	Hyder Ali (died 1782) deposes Chikka Krishna Raj Wadiyar of Mysore
1774-85	Warren Hastings is the first Governor-General of Fort William in Bengal
1775-1797	Reign of Asaf-ud-Daula, Nawab of Lucknow
1782-1799	Tipu Sultan rules Mysore kingdom until the second British siege when he is killed
1798-1814	Reign of Sa'adat Ali Khan, Nawab of Lucknow
1834-5	Lord William Bentinck the first Governor-General of India
1837-1858	Reign of the last Mughal emperor Bahadur Shah II, deposed by the British
1857	The 1857 Rebellion, known by the British as The Mutiny
1858	November 1. British India placed under direct government of the Crown. Viscount Canning the first Viceroy and Governor-General of India
1862-67	Sir Bartle Frere is Governor of Bombay
1869	Suez Canal opens
1875	Prince of Wales (later Edward VII) visits India
1876	Disraeli proclaims Queen Victoria Empress of India with effect from January 1, 1877
1885	Indian National Congress Party founded
1889	Second visit of the Prince of Wales
1899-1905	Baron Curzon of Kedleston is Viceroy and Governor-General of India. Holds 1903 Delhi Durbar to ensure the Princes' loyalty
1906	All India Muslim League founded
1911	December 12. George V, King and Emperor, announces at Delhi the transfer of the capital from Calcutta to Delhi
1920	The Non-Co-operation Movement begins
1921	Prince of Wales (later Edward VIII) visits India
1930	Mahatma Gandhi leads Dandi march from Ahmedabad, protesting against the British monopoly on salt production and its tax
1931	February 9. Inauguration of New Delhi
1935	New Government of India Act passed, giving 14% of Indians the vote
1947	August 15. India Independence Act. Jawarharlal Nehru is India's first prime minister, until May 1964
1948	January 30. Assassination of Mahatma Gandhi in Delhi
1949	November 26. Constitution adopted and signed
1950	January 26. Constitution of India comes into force
1965	Hindi proclaimed the national language
1966-77	Indira Gandhi is Prime Minister of India
1973	Project Tiger launched by the World Wildlife Fund
1975	June 25. The President declares a State of Emergency, which lasts until March 1977 when there is a general election, Morarji Desai (Janata Party) becomes Prime Minister and the State of Emergency is revoked.
1980	January. Indira Gandhi returns as Prime Minister. She is assassinated on October 31, 1984, at no.1 Safdarjang Road, New Delhi. President Zail Singh swears in her son, Rajiv, as Prime Minister.
1984	December.General election: Rajiv Gandhi wins an overwhelming majority
1989	November. General election: V.P.Singh becomes Prime Minister.
1990	November. V.P.Singh resigns; Chandra Shekhar takes over and calls a general election for May 1991.
1991	Population census. India's official population is 844 million, with a diminished growth rate. The largest cities are Bombay (12.57m), Calcutta (10.86m), Delhi (9.37m), Madras (4.3m) and Bangalore (4.1m). May 21. During the elections, Rajiv Gandhi is assassinated at Sriperumbudur, near Madras. Narasimha Rao is elected Congress (I) president and, on completion of the elections, forms a government as Prime Minister.

Glossary

Although English is the connecting language of India and you do not need a Hindi phrase book, there are some words in Hindi and other Indian languages that it might be useful to know. In addition, some English words carry an unfamiliar meaning in India. Amid the vast plethora of Hindu gods, the ones you will encounter most often are also included.

a-c: air-conditioning; a room may be 'a-c' or 'non a-c'

ahimsa: non-violence, reverence for life

atcha: OK

afion: opium

air-cooled: system of cooling a room by fans or an electric machine fitted into the window

agarbathi: incense

apsaras: beautiful nymphs who seduce men and are consorts to gods

ashram: spiritual retreat; centre for practising yoga and meditation

attar: perfume

avatar: incarnation of a god

ayah: nanny/nurse for children

ayyanar: large, painted terracotta figures of deities

baba: religious master; also used in a broader context to denote respect

bagh: garden

baksheesh: gift in the form of a bribe to get service, a tip to reward service or a direct gift to a beggar

Balarama: brother of the god **Krishna** (q.v.)

bandhana: tie-dye method of printing fabric

baoli: step-well, often elaborately decorated

bash: party

bazar: market, market-place

bearer: similar to a butler

beedi: small, hand-rolled cigar

Bhagavata Purana: epic chronicle of the god Vishnu (q.v.) and his incarnations; books 10 and 11, about **Krishna** (q.v.), are especially popular

Bhagvad Gita: Song of the Lord, a glory of Sanskrit literature and part of the epic **Mahabharata** (q.v.); **Krishna**, as Arjuna's charioteer, reveals himself as god incarnate and expounds on the human struggle for love, light and redemption

bhang: hashish (north India)

Bharata Natyam: classical dance of Tamil Nadu

bhavan: big building, big house

bhisti: water carrier

bhopa: folk balladiers of Rajasthan

biryani: Mughlai dish of meat and rice

Bodhisattva: near **Buddha,** that is, a follower of Buddha capable of attaining **nirvana** (q.v.) who postpones it to show others the way

Brahma: Creator of the universe; head of the Hindu Trinity of Brahma, **Vishnu** (The Preserver) and **Shiva** (The Destroyer), collectively known as Trimurti; sometimes **Saraswati** (q.v.) is his daughter or consort; his vehicle is Hamsa, the goose

Brahmin: highest of the four Hindu castes (q.v.)

Buddha: The Enlightened One, from the word buddhi, meaning intellect; The Buddha was a prince, Gotama Siddhartha, who lived in the 6th to 5th centuries BC

cantonment: military and administrative area of a town, built and used by the British during the **Raj** (q.v.)

caste: station of life into which a Hindu is born. There are four: Brahmins (priests and religious teachers); Kshatriyas (kings, warriors, aristocrats); Vaisyas (traders, merchants, professionals) and Shudras (cultivators, servants, etc., formerly called Untouchables). See also **Hariyan**

chai: tea

chajja: deep eaves, especially on Mughal buildings

chappals: sandals

chappati: fried, unleavened bread

chat: snack

chaukidar: doorman, watchman

chauri: fly whisk

chhatri (or chattri): mausoleum, tomb, cenotaph; in architecture, a domed octagonal kiosk

chikar: hunt (sporting)

choli: tight-fitting blouse worn under a sari

chowk: market place

chunam: polished lime plaster

Congress (I): a division of the political Congress

Party formed in 1969 by Indira Gandhi – hence (I)

crore: ten million, written 1,00,00,000

curd: yoghurt; also known as **dahl**

dacoit: armed robber, bandit

dargah: shrine of a Muslim saint

devi: a goddess; **Devi** (or Mahadevi) is another name for **Parvati** (q.v.)

dhal: pulses (lentil, split pea, etc)

dharma: Buddhist teachings

dhobi: clothes washer

dhoti: white cloth worn by men

dhurrie: flat-weave rug

Diwan-i-Am: public audience hall

Diwan-i-Khas: private audience hall

dosa: paper-thin rice pancake

durbar: court audience or government meeting

Durga: a malevolent aspect of the goddess **Parvati**

Dravidian: South Indian architectural style, derived from Dravidadesh (country of the Dravidians), the old name for the area covered by Tamil Nadu state

emporium: shop, often large and selling local crafts

fakir: Muslim holy man who has taken the vow of poverty; also applied to Hindu ascetics

feni: cashew or coconut-based spirit drink made in Goa

Ganesh: elephant-headed god of learning and good fortune, son of **Shiva** (q.v.) and **Parvati** (q.v.); also known as Ganapati

Ganga: goddess or personification of the Ganges, the sacred river of the Hindus; name by which the river is referred to by Hindus

ganja: hashish (eastern India)

Garuda: eagle or mythical sunbird, vehicle of the god **Vishnu**

ghat: steps down to a river, lake or tank; can also mean mountain

ghazel: light Urdu songs

ghi: clarified butter

gompa: Tibetan-Buddhist monastery

gopi: cowgirl, milkmaid; especially befriended by the god Krishna

gopuram: temple gate-house with soaring, pyramid tower (South India)

gulli/galli/gali: alley, lane

guru: spiritual teacher, holy man; his pupils/ followers are called **chelas**

gymkhana: social club, usually run on traditional colonial lines, with pleasant club house, spacious grounds and good sports facilities

ha: yes

handloom cloth: mill-spun yarn that is woven by hand

Hanuman: the monkey god, Rama's ally in the **Ramayana** (q.v.)

Harijan: Children of God, the name coined by Mahatma Gandhi to describe the Shudra caste (Untouchables)

haveli: courtyard town mansion

hookah: hubble-bubble pipe in which the tobacco smoke is cooled by passing through water

howdah: elaborate seat on top of an elephant

idli: rice cakes

imam: Muslim leader

Indra: god of rain and thunder

ITDC: India Tourism Development Corporation: if the first initial is replaced by another, it usually refers to the state-run equivalent, such as K for Kerala

Jalebi: a sweet of rings of deep fried batter soaked in warm syrup

jali: carved stone or marble balcony

jharokah: projecting balcony

ji: suffix used as mark of respect, as in Gandhiji, daddyji

johar: mass suicide by fire, committed by women to save themselves from a conqueror

Kali: The Black, the fearsome goddess of death and destruction who is one aspect of the goddess **Parvati** (q.v.); also known as Chamunda

Kaliya: serpent demon whom **Krishna** subdued

kama: desire, physical love, worldly pleasure, one of the four goals of life in Hindu philosophy; Kama is the god of love

karma: the idea that deeds in previous existences dictate the favourable, or less favourable, form of man's present and future incarnations

Kartikeya: god of war, son of **Shiva** (q.v.); also known as Subrahmanya

kathak: classical dance of northern India, from katha (story)

kathakali: story play; also used to describe the classical dance-drama of Kerala

kathputli: puppeteering

kebab: marinated meat, fish or vegetables

cooked on a skewer

khadi: cloth that is spun, dyed, woven and printed by hand

Krishna: blue-skinned god of human form, considered by some to be the 8th incarnation of the god **Vishnu** (q.v.) but worshipped by many in his own right; protagonist of the **Bhagavad Gita** (q.v.); the gopi, Radha, is his lover and consort

kulfi: traditional Indian ice-cream, flavoured with pistachios and cardamoms

lakh: a hundred thousand, written 1,00,000

Lakshmi: goddess of wealth and good fortune, consort of **Vishnu** (q.v.); also known as Shri

lassi: thin yoghurt drink

lingum: phallic emblem of the god **Shiva** (q.v.), representing energy

liquor: spirits/alcohol, thus liquor store, liquor permit

Lok Sabha: House of the People; this and the **Rajya Sabha** (Council of States) are the Lower and Upper Houses of the Indian Parliament

lunghi: coloured version of a **dhoti** (q.v.), worn in the South

machan: watchtower in a wildlife park

Mahabharata: epic poem recounting the civil war between the Pandavas (of whom Arjuna was one) and Kurus over the right of succession, whose hero is Arjuna, with countless subsidiary stories. About 90,000 couplets long, passed on by oral tradition and probably first written down 4th to 2nd century BC

mahal: palace, queen

maharaja: great ruler, thus king

Mahatma: great soul, thus Mahatma Gandhi

mahout: elephant keeper/rider

maidan: open grass space in a city/town

mali: gardener

mandapam: hall-like porch of a temple

mandir: temple

marg: road, as in M G Marg; meadow, as in gulmarg (meadow of flowers)

masala: mixture of spices and herbs used in cooking; also used broadly to describe any mixture, such as the commercial Hindi films

masjid: mosque, thus Jami Masjid (Friday Mosque), the principal mosque of a town

meenakari: enamelling

mela: fair

memsahib: Western married woman; used broadly as a term of respect to all women, as 'madame' is used in French

mendhi: myrtle leaves whose orange dye is

principally used to decorate the hands and feet of women

mihrab: prayer niche of a mosque, containing the *qibla* (indicator) for the direction of Mecca

mithuna: amorous couple, as found in temple sculpture

mojadi: leather slippers

moksha: enlightenment, release from worldly existence; one of the goals in life in Hindu philosophy

monsoon: rainy season, the period varies in length but usually falls sometime between June and October

muezzin: Muslim who calls the faithful to prayer, usually from a minaret of the mosque

Mughals: Muslim dynasty ruling large tracts of northern and central India from the 16th to 18th centuries

Mughlai: cuisine of the Mughals, Persian in origin

mullah: Muslim priest

murg: chicken

nahin: no

namaste: a word of respectful greeting when people meet or depart, accompanied by the gesture of putting hands together, fingers pointing upwards

nan: baked leavened bread

Nandi: bull; vehicle of the god **Shiva** (q.v.)

nawab: local ruler

nimbu paani: refreshing drink of fresh lime juice and soda water; also called nimbu soda or fresh lime soda

nirvana: in Buddhist philosophy, the state of release from the cycle of rebirth and thus the achievement of total peace; the term is also used by Hindus

nivas: house, accommodation

paan: betel nut mixed with condiments, chewed as a digestive

pakora: a meat or vegetable snack fried in gram-flour batter

pallia: commemorative stone, seen along the roadside, often carved

palo: decorated end of a sari

paratha: a bread layered with butter, sometimes stuffed with meat or vegetables

Parvati: Daughter of the Mountains, goddess of peace and beauty; the female energy of the gods, also known as **Devi,** who also has a destructive power manifest in various forms such as **Kali** (q.v.) and **Durga;** consort of **Shiva**

pichwai: painting on cloth

pietra dura: stone (often marble) inlaid with coloured stones or gems to form patterns

pol: gate

poppadum: thin, crisp lentil pancake, often eaten as an appetiser

pukka: correct, in the colonial sense; genuine

puja: worship, prayer, religious offering

pundit: teacher, professor (of scriptures, music, etc.)

Puranas: 18 collections of traditional Hindi myths and legends

purdah: curtain behind which Muslim women live, screened from men and strangers; the practice of women living in purdah spread to Hindus

pyjama: baggy trousers, usually worn with a kurta (long shirt)

qawwali: mystical poems set to music, sung in chorus

qila: citadel, fort

Raj: rule, usually referring to the British rule in India

raja: ruler, prince

Rajput: Hindu rulers of Rajasthan and the Punjab

Rama: 7th avatar of the god **Vishnu** (q.v.), the human hero of the epic **Ramayana** (q.v.), brother of Bharata and Lakshmana; his wife is Sita

Ramayana: epic poem recounting the story of good king **Rama** (q.v.) who, aided by monkey and bear allies, rescues his wife Sita from abduction by Ravana, the multi-headed demon king of Lanka (Sri Lanka); about 24,000 couplets, with an oral tradition until it was written down around 4th to 2nd century BC

raga: the musical mode providing the framework for improvisation by the musician; there are ragas for all times of day and all moods; they inspired the development of a complex iconography in Indian miniature painting

rath: temple chariot or car, often of carved wood, on which temple deities are paraded at festivals; monolithic Pallava shrine

rickshaw: mode of transport: a bicycle rickshaw is a small, two-wheeled cart pulled by a bicycle; an auto-rickshaw is a covered, three-wheeled vehicle powered by a motorbike; in Calcutta, some rickshaws are still pulled by men or boys

sadhu: a Hindu ascetic

sagar: ocean, large lake

sahib: lord, master; broadly used as a term of respect, as 'sir' is used in English

sampsa: a meat or vegetable snack wrapped in short-crust pastry and deep-fried

Saraswati: goddess of knowledge, music and the arts; sometimes daughter or consort of Brahma

sari: long length of fabric worn by women

sati: a widow's honourable self-immolation, often on her husband's funeral pyre; outlawed by the British under the Regulation XVII Act of 1829 but continued for many years after this

Seven Sacred Cities: Varanasi, Hardwar, Ujjain, Mathura, Ajodhya, Dwarka and Kanchipuram are sacred pilgrimage centres for Hindus. Each city is dedicated to **Shiva** (q.v.) or **Vishnu** (q.v.) except Kanchipuram which is dedicated to both

Shaivite: worshipper or **Shiva** (q.v.)

shakti: life force, spiritual energy

Sherpa: a Nepalese people renowned as high-altitude porters and mountain guides

Shesha: the serpent on whom **Vishnu** (q.v.) reclines on the Cosmic Ocean

shikara: in boating, a luxurious gondola-like boat on which people are paddled around the lakes of Srinagar; in architecture, a beehive-shaped tower on a temple (also written as sikhara)

Shiva (or Siva): The Auspicious, third member of the Hindu Trinity; symbol of destructive and creative energy manifested in many forms such as **Nataraja** (Lord of the Dance); his consort is **Parvati** (q.v.); his sons are **Ganesh** (q.v.) and **Kartikeya** (q.v.); his vehicle is Nandi, the bull; his emblem is the **lingum** (q.v.)

Sita: wife of **Rama** (q.v.)

sitar: stringed musical instrument

sof: aniseed seeds, a digestive chewed after eating, often delivered gratis in restaurants

stupa: Buddhist relic mound

supper-club: restaurant, usually with live Western music and dance floor and not restricted to members

Surya: god of the sun; Aruna, symbol of dawn, is his charioteer

tabla: small drum

tandoor: clay oven

tank: water reservoir, artificial lake

tatti: grass matting, often soaked in water and hung across windows to cool the air during the hot season

tazias multi-coloured tinsel, silver or brass replicas of Husain's tomb paraded at the Muslim festival of Muharram

thali: circular platter on which a vegetarian meal is served in **katories** (small dishes)

thik hai: OK (eastern India), like atcha

tiffin: light lunch

tikka: dot of paste, often red, worn by Hindus (the dot worn by married Hindu women is called **shuhag**); in cooking, tikka is meat or fish marinaded and then cooked in a tandoor oven

Tirthankaras: the 24 Jain teachers

Tonga: mode of transport: a cart drawn by a pony

tri-cuisine: restaurant menu offering Indian, Chinese and Continental dishes

toddy: spirit drink made from coconut palm sap

Untouchable: see Harijan

Urs: festival on the death anniversary of a Muslim saint

utsav: festival

Vaishnavite: worshipper of **Vishnu** (q.v.)

vimana: principal temple or central shrine, including sanctuary and porches, of a Hindu temple complex; also used to refer to the tower surmounting this building

vina: the primary stringed instrument of classical Indian music

Vishnu: The Preserver, second member of the Hindu Trinity (cf.**Brahma**); symbol of the creation and preservation that maintains the balance of the forces which sustain the universe. His ten principal incarnations (avatars) include Matsya (1st, the fish), Kurma (2nd, the turtle); Varaha (3rd, the boar); Narasimha (4th, the man-lion); **Rama** (7th, hero of the **Ramayana**, q.v.); **Krishna** (q.v.) or Balarama, his brother (8th, both in human form but opinions vary as to which is an avatar). His consort is **Lakshmi** (q.v.); his vehicle is **Garuda** (q.v.)

wallah: fellow, thus rickshaw-wallah, dhobi-wallah

yali: a mythical composite animal made up of a lion, horse and elephant, often carved on temples

yoga: psycho-physical discipline involving the practice of meditation, exercise positions and breathing control to achieve spiritual peace

zari: gold or silver metal thread used in weaving brocades, now often applied to imitation thread

zenana: women's quarters of a household

Index